The ASTD Technical and Skills Training Handbook

Other McGraw-Hill Books Sponsored by the American Society for Training and Development

Piskurich
THE ASTD HANDBOOK OF INSTRUCTIONAL TECHNOLOGY

Craig
TRAINING AND DEVELOPMENT HANDBOOK

The ASTD Technical and Skills Training Handbook

Sponsored by the American Society for Training and Development

Leslie Kelly   Editor in Chief

McGraw-Hill, Inc.

New York   San Francisco   Washington, D.C.   Auckland   Bogotá
Caracas   Lisbon   London   Madrid   Mexico City   Milan
Montreal   New Delhi   San Juan   Singapore
Sydney   Tokyo   Toronto

Library of Congress Cataloging-in-Publication Data

The ASTD technical and skills training handbook / Leslie Kelly, editor
in chief ; sponsored by the American Society for Training and
Development.
    p.   cm.
    Includes bibliographical references and index.
    ISBN 0-07-033899-X
    1. Technology—Study and teaching—Handbooks, manuals, etc.
2. High technology industries—Employees—Training of—Handbooks,
manuals, etc. I. Kelly, Leslie. II. American Society for Training
and Development.
T65.A86   1994
607.1'5—dc20   94-28037
                                                  CIP

1 2 3 4 5 6 7 8 9 0 DOC/DOC 9 0 9 8 7 6 5 4

ISBN 0-07-033899-X

*The sponsoring editor for this book was Harold B. Crawford, the editing
supervisor was Virginia Carroll, and the production supervisor was Donald F.
Schmidt. This book was set in Palatino. It was composed by North Market Street
Graphics.*

Printed and bound by R. R. Donnelley & Sons Company.

This book is printed on recycled, acid-free paper containing a
minimum of 50% recycled de-inked fiber.

American Society for Training and Development Handbook Advisory Board

Contents

Preface

The information superhighway is forcing every workplace to look at the integration of technology into all aspects of work life. As a result, the need for technical training is accelerating at a dizzying pace. Most workers can't sit still and hope that their computer skills will not be needed. Corporations, in an effort to become more productive, are expecting their workers to use computers extensively and productively. Since the older workers are new to this technology, just the technical training needs in computer skills alone are overwhelming. Though college education is a plus, the knowledge and skills gained in that environment are becoming obsolete quickly. For example, experts estimate a college engineering degree is good for only three years after graduation. After that period of time, engineers need continuing education in large doses in their technical areas of expertise just to avoid becoming obsolete. Again, the demand for technical training is and will be enormous.

This Handbook and its yearly supplements will help technical trainers do their jobs well and keep them up-to-date on the latest technical training concerns.

It was created through the persistence of Harold Crawford of McGraw-Hill who saw a need for a book that provides how-to information and advice for technical trainers. Unlike the trainers tucked away in the human resource departments of most major corporations, technical trainers are the hands-on technicians who, the majority of the time, have been recruited from the technical ranks. Rather than hiring individuals who have training background, corporations recruit their resident experts and turn them into trainers. Harold heard many a cry for HELP from these people who wanted a hands-on reference that would give them A-to-Z advice on how to become good trainers so that they could share their knowledge with their colleagues. Because of the pressing need for this Handbook, it has been completed in record time with the help of an outstanding advisory board and truly expert authors.

For years I have talked about the Woodstock Effect to colleagues, using it to refer to events in my life that meant the chemistry of a group or event was outstanding. I must admit that working with everyone on this project has been a real highlight of my professional life.

The handbook advisory board is one of the best groups of professionals that I have worked with during my 16-year affiliation with the American Society for Training and Development. The advisory board is composed of some of the most respected experts in the technical and skills training field. Without their tireless and timely help this book would not exist. This was not a prestige, do-nothing group. The group functioned as author selection advisors, author chapter advisors, chapter editors (at least five chapters apiece), information sleuths, mediators, and cheerleaders. The deadlines were unreasonable at times, but always met. Their responsiveness during the entire project was deeply appreciated. Because of their help, the Handbook was turned in almost a month early, a rare phenomenon in publishing.

Special thanks go to Rod Boyes, who picked up extra work and constantly helped with chapter re-edits; Johnna Howell, who found chapter authors; James Lacy, who edited more pages than the rest of the group combined; Rick Sullivan, who made this book happen with the help of the ASTD Technical & Skills Professional Practice Area; and Vic Haburchak, who found authors and case study writers, and mediated changes. John Robinson, Bob Anderson, Gabe Pall, and Nancy Kuhn added their expertise, making chapters special.

The authors' work will speak for itself. With the help of the fax, long mail delays were nonexistent. Overseas work was a breeze. The authors met their deadlines and did their rewrites in record time. This is a very talented group of authors with an amazing breadth of knowledge, skills, and experience. The readers will be pleased with all the how-to information.

Nancy Olson, Head of Publications for ASTD, gave me the opportunity to do this Handbook and her belief in my ability to complete this massive undertaking made the work easier. She also helped me maintain a very positive perspective. I am indebted to her for all her help.

Finally, I must thank Harold Crawford at McGraw-Hill. He made working on the book easy and meeting deadlines a pleasure. This project was his idea and his enthusiasm provided the catalyst to get it done.

Leslie Kelly

The ASTD
Technical
and Skills
Training
Handbook

1

The History of Technical Training

Richard A. Swanson

Richard J. Torraco

Dr. Richard A. Swanson *is the founding editor of the* Human Resource Development Quarterly, *the research journal of ASTD. In 1993 he received a national award from ASTD for his scholarly contributions to the Human Resource Development Profession. Swanson's 1994 book titled* Analysis for Improving Performance: Tools for Diagnosing Organizations and Documenting Workplace Expertise *was published by Berrett-Koehler. His 1988 Jossey-Bass book,* Forecasting Financial Benefits of Human Resource Development, *received the outstanding book award from NSPI. Swanson has consulted with many of the largest corporations in America including AT&T, Citicorp, 3M, Honeywell, Kellogg, and Pemex.*

Richard J. Torraco *is a consultant in human resource development and a Ph.D. candidate at the University of Minnesota. His research activities include the analysis of work, theory building in human resource development, and linking human resource development with organizational performance. He has written numerous published articles on human resource development and has presented scholarly work at professional conferences both in the United States and abroad. He is currently teaching graduate courses in human resource development at the University of Minnesota in the areas of training, strategic planning, and cost-benefit analysis. Mr. Torraco has managed workplace health and safety programs and served as a training consultant to business and industry for over twenty years.*

A study of the history of learning reveals that training and education of all types, technical and nontechnical, are largely the products of social and economic conditions. Scott's (1914) early characterization of education is still meaningful: "education is the attempt of a civilization to perpetuate what it believes to be most vital in itself" (p. 73).

Over time, the concepts of training and education have been identical, overlapping, or totally discrete depending on the present social, political, and economic conditions. Even so, the following definitions from *The Training Within Industry Report* (Dooley, 1945) help capture the essence of the training and education perspectives:

Education is for rounding-out of the individual and the good of the society; it is general, provides background, increases understanding.

Training is for the good of plant production—it is a way to solve production problems through people; it is specific and helps people to acquire skill through the use of what they learned (p. 17).

1.1 Technical Training Within the Human Resource Development Profession

Technical training has a unique role in the history of the human resource development profession. As you will read in this chapter, technical skills training—in the form of parent-child, master-apprentice workplace learning models—has existed throughout all recorded history of the human race.

Furthermore, technical skills training gave birth to the training profession as we know it. The industrial revolution of the 1800s, and its pounding rate of technological change, demanded a training response. In the United States, the National Association for the Promotion of Industrial Education in 1912 (later to become the American Vocational Association) was founded on the heritage of advancing workplace industrial skills training. With a similar concern about technical workplace skills, the American Society of Training Directors (later to be named the American Society for Training and Development) was founded in 1945 *following* the dissolution of the 1940–1945 Training Within Industry Service of the United States War Manpower Commission (Dooley, 1945).

When the contemporary training profession was born in the United States in the early 1900s there was little demand for management training. The human faculties of intelligence, leadership, and industriousness were thought to be innate, not characteristics to be developed through training.

While the training profession acknowledges a number of schemes for segmenting its components, technical skills training is almost always listed. Among the three major types of training identified today are:

- *Technical-skills training.* Focused on people-system, people-thing work behavior

- *Management training.* Focused on people-idea, people-people work behavior

- *Motivational training.* Focused on people-beliefs, people-values work behavior (Swanson, 1982).

1.2 History as a Tool for Understanding the Past and Predicting the Future

The full history of training and education carries with it many general learning principles and culture-bound methods. A number of the historic technical skills training principles have since been scientifically tested and validated. Even so, some of the proven principles are put aside by persistent educational and training methods that were born in now-extinct economies and societies.

For example, Pestalozzi (1898) told us that "there are two ways of instructing, either we go from words to things or from things to words." While research supports his instructional principle of *things-to-words*, elitist stereotypes among present day practitioners still favor words over the artifacts of life. Thus, the propensity toward training lectures over hands-on training experiences.

The history of technical training helps the reader understand the following:

1. The *origins* of technical training

2. The major *developments* and events

3. The reason why the profession is as it now exists

4. Some of the forces that will likely shape its *future*

1.3 The Beginnings of Technical Training: Survival Through Labor and Learning

Human experience and the nature of human development have passed through many stages since the very beginning of the human journey. Training in its most simple form was found among our most primitive ancestors. The development of early humans was driven exclusively by the need to survive. At this time, what little could be called training and education "consisted of learning how to obtain the necessaries of life for self and family, and how to propitiate the unseen powers supposed to be active in nature" (Davidson, 1900, p. 21). Although *learning* involved the making of simple tools from wood, stone, and fibers, primitive man knew nothing about the productive use of fire and of metals. Harnessing these elements would later become critical to man's further development.

The context of primitive training and education was limited to the family or tribe, and it was an informal, and even chaotic, activity. It occurred through unconscious imitation of the head of a family or group, usually the father. Even as recently as the early twentieth century, Monroe (1907) points out: ". . . the father, then, becomes the one who trains the younger generation in the formal conduct of life—in the proper way of doing things" (p. 8). Yet despite its informality, an essential feature was apparent even in this most primitive form: "the fitting of the child to his physical and social environment through the appropriation of the experience of previous generations" (Monroe, p. 1).

1.3.1 The Use of Tools and Mutual Cooperation

Eventually humans gained the ability to control fire for the cooking of food, the smelting of metals, and the making of simple mechanical and agricultural tools. This allowed people to engage in *crafts* and undertake domestic activities that were previously impossible without basic tools. It also led to a true division of labor wherein some pursued weaving, others became carpenters, still others became stone masons, and so on.

For the first time, people began to rely on tools and on each other to meet their needs. Indeed, humanity's progress through the ages has been inextricably linked to the development of practical tools and securing the bonds of mutual cooperation necessary for survival. With the development of tools and bonds of mutual cooperation came a new form of education, one characterized by *conscious* imitation rather than *unconscious* imitation (Bennett, 1926). The transfer of skill from one person to another now became a conscious process. Learning occurred through deliberate imitation of examples provided by one who had achieved mastery of a particular skill. Yet, training followed no theory or system and had not yet become a rational process. Those seeking a skill simply copied a model over and over until it could be precisely reproduced. Despite some advancement, the training of one person by another was still a quite primitive process.

Especially during humanity's early history, we are reminded that modest intellectual development came almost exclusively through efforts to adapt to a harsh physical and social environment. As Davidson (1900) states, "human culture advances in proportion as men husband their powers by the use of implements, and by union for mutual help. Such husbandry requires higher and higher education" (p. 25). As the history written here reveals, the training and education needed for human progress was painfully slow in developing.

1.4   500 B.C.–500 A.D.: The Influence of the Greeks and Romans

The key Roman legacy has been their ingenuity in creating the institutions needed to carry out political and social agendas. Although the Romans did not have as profound an influence on education as did the Greeks, the Roman educational infrastructure and organization of schools continued to persist well after the conquest and fall of the Roman empire.

1.4.1   The Greek Disdain for Menial Work

The legacy of the Golden Age of Greece has been a philosophy of education that, unlike any culture since that of ancient Greece, is most consistent with the present notion of a *liberal* education. Indeed, the Greeks were the first to see education as providing an opportunity for individual development (Moore, 1936). The Greek's legacy has often gone unnoticed.

The Greek conception of education included many dimensions vital to individual development that are still valued today. Human inquiry into all phases of life—nature, man, the supernatural—was an important dimension of Greek education that is today often considered the pursuit of knowledge for its own sake. The moral dimension of education, which emphasized the ethical rights and responsibilities of individuals, first found expression during the Greek era. In addition, aesthetic education and education's role as an agent of culturation and citizenship were first proposed by the Greeks. Above all, the Greeks viewed education as a vehicle for individual development and personal achievement and a means for developing and diversifying their talents.

Despite this perspective, the Greeks did not hold the same generous view of training in the trades and mechanical arts (Bennett, 1926). They felt disdain toward what were seen as menial occupations in agriculture and manufacturing such as farming, cattle raising, shoemaking, smithing, and toolmaking. Socrates is credited with providing some reasons for this contempt for handwork. He wrote of these trades as ruining the bodies of those who work at them, having gloomy and distasteful working conditions, allowing little time for leisure, and providing no development of the mind or soul (Moore, 1936). With this attitude toward manual work, it is not surprising that training in manual arts had no place in the education of Greek youth of the upper classes. Yet training in manual arts was not completely shunned by the Greeks, for it was through an enduring system of *apprenticeship* among the lower classes that skills were developed in goods production, construction, agriculture, and other areas which were instrumental in the historic accomplishments of Greek civilization. *Apprenticeship training clearly had an important role in the development of ancient Greece.*

Several contributions to the development of ideas about learning by well-known Greek philosophers are noteworthy. In the following sections we review significant contributions to educational thought from three major Greek philosophers: Socrates, Plato, and Aristotle.

1.4.2 Socrates: The Socratic Method of Inquiry

The influential work of Socrates (469–399 B.C.) is known to us only through the writing of others, for, unlike other major Greek philosophers, Socrates wrote nothing. It is upon Plato's portrait of him that we chiefly rely for information about the work of Socrates. Socrates developed a dialectic method of inquiry to achieve more universal and complete knowledge than one might achieve alone. Socrates' methods of teaching, and, in particular, his use of dialogue, called into question the effectiveness of formal lecturing which was the accepted method of instruction at the time.

Socrates' method of inquiry, known as the *Socratic method,* was based on careful dialogue and adroit questioning for the purpose of discovering the underlying truth in a particular line of reasoning. Socrates would initially accept the views and line of reasoning of another person, often a student, and then through skillful questioning, he would further develop these views until the contradictions and logical inconsistencies in the original position were apparent to both Socrates and his student. Following his own instincts for logic and adhering to an open dialectic process, Socrates continually sought to develop the capacity for logical reasoning in others.

Socrates believed that all individuals should possess the capacity for logical reasoning. In fact, Socrates felt that the development of skills for reasoning and forming logical conclusions should be the general goal of Greek education. However, these views on education clearly ran counter to the dominant educational practices of the time which relied primarily on the transfer of preformed information to students through formal lecturing. Like much of the thinking on education first offered by Greek philosophers, Socrates' notion of an open dialectic process for education was quite advanced for its time, for it would not be until the twelfth century and the enlightened views of scholasticism that dialogue, open questioning, and debate would slowly come into their own as accepted methods of educational exchange.

1.4.3 Plato's *Republic*

In the *Republic* Plato (420–348 B.C.) brings together the domains of politics, education, and philosophy through the literary form of a dialogue, in which Socrates, Plato's mentor, is both the narrator and chief figure. The *Republic* is Plato's exposition of an ideal society in which he develops an elaborate system of knowledge that integrates his thinking on philosophy, the nature of knowledge, politics, justice, and educational theory. The *Republic* is a carefully developed series of ten "books" through which Plato provides his conceptions of justice, individual virtue, the characteristics of an ideal society, the role and training of those who govern, and the laws and relationships that bond individuals together as a society.

In the *Republic* Plato also develops a comprehensive theory of education and provides the first well-articulated breakdown and description of the content of elementary and higher education. Plato prescribed a curriculum for primary education that was based on instruction in reading and writing, recitation from selected literature, and training in music and gymnastics. Higher education, which Plato felt should address the development of the ideal qualities of leadership in the "philosopher-ruler," was composed of studies in mathematics, geometry, astronomy, harmonics, and philosophy. The scope and detail of Plato's thinking on the composition of an ideal education is quite remarkable when one considers that Plato integrated his thinking on education into an elaborate pattern of ideas dealing with the fundamental issues that confront human beings as citizens.

1.4.4 Aristotle: The Father of Scientific Thought

Aristotle (384–322 B.C.) was the first of the great western thinkers to attempt to systematize knowledge and develop a language through which scientific inquiry could be conducted. Aristotle realized that in order to formulate principles to guide scientific study of the natural world, he first had to develop the field of logic by carefully analyzing all the elements of reasoning. He did this through a series of treatises on logic referred to as the *Organon*. Each work examined a component of the reasoning process (i.e., the term, proposition, syllogism) from the perspective of its place in the structured search for principles by which the observable world could be scientifically studied (McLean and Aspell, 1970). Aristotle's *Organon* provided the original basis for scientific thought in a wide range of intellectual disciplines. His efforts to systematize knowledge were so fundamental that he not only provided a basis for scientific terminology, but for everyday language as well. Aristotle defined terms, such as *cause, principle, category,* and *subject matter,* in a scientific context for the first time. These and other terms defined by Aristotle have been used in the language of science and everyday life ever since.

Much of Aristotle's thinking on education is expressed in *The Politics,* a very practical treatise on the ways in which education should enrich the lives of Greek citizens. Aristotle believed that the responsibility for providing a proper education to all should be under the control of the state; it should not be left in private hands. The ideal curriculum should develop the mind and the body. According to Aristotle, such a curriculum consisted of the following:

1. Reading and writing
2. Music
3. Gymnastics
4. Drawing

Although providing intellectual education was the first priority of the state, it also must attend to practical education for good citizenship. The intent of education in civics was that adults understand their responsibilities to the state and acknowledge the necessity of service to others. Aristotle believed that the role of education also included the development of character. For Aristotle, good character was the result of intellectual and moral training, and moral behavior, like other desirable characteristics, had be nurtured and practiced if it was to become a durable trait.

Aristotle's negative view of learning the practical arts and trades reflects the Greek attitude of disdain toward any education undertaken for its practical or occupational value. Although Aristotle espoused the learning of "useful things" such as reading, writing, and drawing, he drew the line at education for the purpose of performing a wage-earning occupation and any training in mechanical skills and crafts which were only practiced by slaves in ancient Greece. All subjects dealing with trades and occupations should be excluded from the curriculum of free men, as Aristotle felt that "they absorb and degrade the mind" (Curtis and Boultwood, 1966, p. 44).

1.4.5   The Pragmatic View
of the Romans

The Romans adopted Greek ideals but went further by integrating them into Roman life through the establishment of related laws and institutions. Unlike the standards of excellence and harmony held by the Greeks, the Romans were a more practical people whose judgments were based on usefulness and effectiveness. Although their influence on education was not nearly as profound as that of the Greeks, the Romans provide an example of how laws and political infrastructure can be used to achieve long-term social, economic, and cultural change.

The great Roman achievements in public works, architecture, and the construction of roads and aqueducts is well known, and yet there is little evidence that the handwork and mechanical arts required for these accomplishments were valued by the Romans. Like the Greeks, the Romans relied on tradespeople and laborers to develop the infrastructure of their empire, despite the fact that technical and manual skills were never held in high esteem.

Romans acquired these skills through *family apprenticeship*. An important duty of Roman fathers was the development of practical skills and trades in their children.

The Roman empire, like others which reached a period of great success, eventually began to decline. Roman life became more corrupt as lethargy and materialism replaced the virility and strength of character associated with early Rome. Roman education became artificial and drained of the vitality it once had. Even before the invasion of Rome by barbarians from the north, education provided by the early Christian Church was gradually replacing Roman education in both substance and spirit. The influence of Christianity on the purposes and methods of education was to continue to grow throughout the Middle Ages.

1.5   300–1300 A.D.:
The Middle Ages

The goals and methods of training continued to be influenced by the many developments which occurred during an extended period in history known as the Middle Ages. Barlow (1967) characterizes the period spanned by the Middle Ages in the following way:

> The so-called Middle Ages account for approximately a thousand years of history between ancient and modern. Beginning in the early 300's and extending into the early 1300's, the period is divided into

two nearly equal parts. The turning point between the *early* and *later* Middle Ages is marked at 800, when Charlemagne was crowned Holy Roman Emperor (p. 18).

The influence of Christianity permeated medieval life. Although successive imperial decrees during the fourth century made Christianity the official religion of the Roman empire, for all practical purposes institutional control of the people had already passed to the Church. In the wake of the decadent Romans and barbarous Goths and Vandals, there was a great need for the structure and moral discipline that Christianity offered. The Church also embraced the lower classes which had been neglected by the pagan society of Rome and the elitist culture of Greece. Greco-Roman culture and education were methodically displaced by the training and rituals of Christianity: training in Church dogma and spiritual consciousness replaced Greek aesthetic and intellectual ideals and rigid moral training and discipline were substituted for Roman materialism. Under the dominance of Christianity, the education of that era received a completely new character.

1.5.1 Augustine: The Fusion of the Classics and Christianity

Augustine (354–430) was a Christian teacher of rhetoric and oratory who was thoroughly versed in the classical philosophy and literature of Greece and Rome. Augustine, more than any other thinker of his period, brought about the fusion of the intellectual traditions of Greece and Rome with the Christian religion (Curtis and Boultwood, 1966). He sanctioned the study of the classics at a time when a deep division was occurring between the Roman empire and the Church.

Although Christians of this time had no special antagonism toward the Roman empire, they were forced into a difficult dilemma when Roman authorities demanded that they demonstrate their loyalty to Rome through sacrificial rituals that Christians considered idolatrous. When Christians refused to pay homage to the pagan gods of Rome—more out of concern for betraying their Christian faith than for lack of loyalty to Rome—they were persecuted and imprisoned. This led to Christian cynicism toward a culture that they increasingly saw as pagan and materialistic. As the schism between Christians and the Roman authorities widened, Christians increasingly rejected all things pagan. For them, this included the philosophy and literature of Greece and Rome.

Under these conditions of antagonism between Christians and the Roman empire, Augustine's position on the value of classical literature stood in contrast to that of other senior clergy of the Church. As opposed to the uncompromising view that there should be no mingling of Christian religious beliefs and the heathen world reflected in the classics, Augustine saw value in classical thinking and literature. Although Greek and Roman ideas often reflected a materialistic, secular world, ancient learning contained valuable contributions to the intellectual development of Christians, and Augustine felt that Christians should select what was useful and moral from the classics and put it to use in the service of Christ.

Although later in his life Augustine questioned his liberal view of the classics, Augustine's acceptance of the intellectual value of the classics and his position in favor of integrating classical thought with Christian ideals is of no small historical significance. Many emerging universities were strongly aligned with the Church, and the teachings and philosophy of the Church strongly influenced the course of education throughout the centuries ahead. Without a champion for classical philosophy and literature at a time of its wholesale rejection by the Church, the influence of classical thinking on education may have been diminished.

Augustine's ideas on education appear throughout the many volumes of his works. However, one of his works, *De Magistro* (*On the Teacher*) is a treatise devoted exclusively to the true meaning of the activities of teaching and learning. Augustine believed that learning was not simply the process of receiving ideas from the teacher; true learning must be an active process, not a passive one. Therefore, rather than viewing the teacher as imparting knowledge, Augustine believed that the role of the teacher began by arranging an environment conducive to learning and introducing ideas to students. After attending to the proper educational environment, teaching should then be focused on stimulating students to think and to learn.

Augustine also played a pivotal role in shaping what would become the curriculum for secondary and higher education for the medieval period and beyond. The origin of the notion of the *liberal arts* can be traced back to Plato, who identified subjects such as grammar, rhetoric, and dialectic as essential elements of the liberal education intended for all free citizens. The idea of the liberal arts was an important part of the Greek cultural tradition inherited by Rome. The liberal arts were preserved through the period of Roman dominance by Varro, whose writing contributed to Augustine's ideas on the liberal arts. Scholars of the third and fourth centuries took on what they saw as the important task of formalizing the content of the liberal arts and establishing the number of subjects to be designated as the liberal arts.

The initial identification of subjects and the differentiation of content into what would become the liberal arts had begun before the time of Augustine. However, Augustine was keenly interested in what the content of a Christian education should be. He wrote two treatises on subjects he considered important, one on grammar and another on music. Augustine worked in conjunction with other scholars to link together grammar and music with five other subjects which eventually became known as the *seven liberal arts*. The seven liberal arts were composed of two groups of subjects: the *trivium* (grammar, rhetoric, and dialectic) and the *quadrivium* (arithmetic, geometry, music, and astronomy).

Together these seven subjects became the core curriculum around which formal education would be built for many centuries to come. As institutions of learning became more specialized, the subjects of the quadrivium became the basis for studies at the university level, and the trivium of grammar, rhetoric, and dialectic became the basis of Grammar school studies.

1.5.2 The Influence of Monastic Schools

An important element of Christian discipline and teaching is the spiritual value of one's own labor. This was exemplified by the fervor and discipline of early Christian monastic life. As the intellectual landscape became more barren in the Middle Ages, the burden of academic learning and preserving the classics fell almost completely to Christian monasteries.

The Christian value of labor and the role of the monastery as guardian of academic learning combined to provide an environment conducive to the advancement of manual labor and training in manual and mechanical arts. Monasteries operated many small-scale agricultural and goods-producing functions needed to maintain an independent existence such as gardens, mills, bakeries, and various shops for construction and maintenance. Monks and prelates skilled in these trades directed monastery operations and provided the necessary training in agriculture, practical arts and crafts, and various building and mechanical skills (Bennett, 1926). Practical and technical training such as it was at that time was a central part of monastic life.

Monasteries were also the center of intellectual life and preserver of literature and art throughout the Middle Ages. All who participated in monastic life were taught basic reading and writing skills. In addition, monks worked tirelessly at writing manuscripts, producing and preserving books, and developing their skills in the arts of painting, music, and sculpture. As the skills of writing and bookmaking were held in high esteem, academic and artistic training were also an important part of monastic life.

1.5.3 St. Thomas Aquinas

The recognition of the significance of the work of Aquinas (1225–1274) requires an appreciation for the growing political influence of the Church at a time when the rich intellectual heritage of antiquity had not yet been rediscovered. As the Church continued to grow from a small community of believers in Christ's teachings into a powerful political institution, the ideology of Church doctrine changed and its intellectual influence grew. Although the Church was beginning to acknowledge the need for a more universal and comprehensive ideology, it continued to nourish the aspirations of Christians with a growing body of official, religious dogma. The Church taught that the road to truth for all Christians began with faith, and that the scriptures provided the authority and direction for Christian beliefs. Yet, Church Fathers realized that theological doctrine alone could not sustain the Church through the growth and changes ahead. A broader intellectual base was needed.

The rich intellectual traditions of antiquity had not been entirely swept away in the turmoil of Rome's decline at the hand of outside invaders. The classics of Greece and Rome had survived the material and spiritual devastation of the early Middle Ages only through the isolated efforts of the clergy in monasteries and churches. As the Church continued to grow and acknowledged the need for a broader intellectual base, its own clergy possessed the only link to the rich legacy of Greek philosophy and learning.

But the Church was reluctant to adopt the secular philosophy of the Greeks, for it was based on logic and reasoning that could easily lead Christians away from Church beliefs based on faith. In an intellectual environment strongly influenced by the Church, philosophy was subservient to theology and logical reasoning could not contradict religious doctrine. The relentless logic of Greek philosophy directly challenged a central premise of early medieval thinking—that reason should never contradict faith. The primacy of faith in Christian thinking diminished the rigor of argumentation for, before an argument began, one presumably already knew the basis for the answer. The answer was to be found in faith, despite the direction any logic or line of reasoning might take. According to the Church, it was faith and religious beliefs supported by authoritative, ecclesiastical sources, not logic or reason, that ultimately led to "truth."

Thus, a monumental challenge had to be overcome before the Church could accept the open-ended, divergent style of Greek philosophy. Given the primacy of faith in Church ideology, how could the Church accept Aristotelian philosophy in which one never knew at the outset where an argument would lead or what the conclusion would be? Was it possible to synthesize the intellectual rigor of Aristotelian philosophy with the dogma of Christian theology?

The synthesis of Aristotelian philosophy and Church theology was achieved, and this synthesis represents the great intellectual accomplishment of this period. Although several scholars were involved in the rediscovery of Aristotle, the integration of Aristotle with Christian theology was, above all, due to the efforts of Aquinas. Aquinas had fairly reliable texts of Aristotle's work at hand when he began writing his extensive commentaries that explained the work of Aristotle and integrated it with contemporary philosophical beliefs. These attempts to unite in one body of knowledge the rigorous inquiry of Aristotelianism with the theology of the Church began the intellectual tradition known as *scholasticism*.

Aquinas studied at Naples, Cologne, and Paris, and thereafter, he became well known as a teacher of philosophy and theology. Aquinas was not only concerned about the content of Christian education—knowledge that reflected the certainty of Church dogma *and* the rigor of classical thinking, he also studied the methods through which instruction should take place. Instructional methods and resources of Aquinas' time were crude and ineffective. Even at the level of universities which began developing during the early medieval period, typical instruction consisted of a monologue delivered by the master at a pace which was often too rapid for meaningful learning. Books were both costly and rare. Poor students did not own books, and even wealthy students were fortunate if they possessed one or two books including the Bible.

Aquinas sought to improve this learning environment which he felt offered no real exchange of ideas through the use of two methods of instruction which were to became the primary teaching methods in medieval universities. Aquinas' efforts were focused on improving the work on teaching methods begun by Pierre Abelard. Also known as *scholastic methods of instruction*, these methods of instruction were called the *lectio* (the lecture) and the *disputatio* (the disputation or debate). These techniques for improving the deficient medieval learning environment represent the origins of two instructional methods that are still commonly used today.

The lectio or lecture was formally established as a teaching process which began with a literal reading of important passages from the text by the master, followed by the master's interpretation of the text to explain and emphasize key ideas. Students were expected to listen attentively and remember as much as possible, for they might be asked from day to day to recite what they knew from memory. As the pace of the master's delivery was quite rapid, eventually it became acceptable for students to make written notes during the lecture.

As a formal lecture of this kind would inevitably give rise to misunderstandings and questions, the *disputatio* or discussion emerged as a way of clarifying misunderstandings. The educational methods espoused by Aquinas promoted a learning environment where any of the master's points or conclusions could be questioned by the student. The *disputatio* could also be initiated by the master himself who would pose a central question or problem to the class. After a lengthy and elaborate discussion which usually lasted two or more days, the master would summarize the arguments made and present his solution to the problem. Both of these instructional techniques, the lecture and the debate, have obviously had a major influence on educational methods that has persisted to the present.

Outside the monasteries and other channels of Church-sponsored education, participation in skilled labor was also a principle means of learning new skills and improving one's economic position. As crafts and trades became more differentiated and specialized, apprenticeship continued to emerge as the dominant mode of transmitting practical and technical expertise from one person to another.

1.5.4   Merchant and Craft Guilds

One of the most characteristic features of medieval life in the later half of the Middle Ages was the organization of merchant and craft guilds. These associations were formed among those with common interests for mutual protection and benefit. Craftsmen and artisans organized themselves by occupation to protect themselves from substandard workmanship and low wages and selling prices. Working hours were strictly regulated and quality standards for products and workmanship were established. Some guilds even prescribed the tools and methods a guild member must use to perform their trade.

By the fourteenth century, most guilds had begun offering education to members and their children in addition to the apprenticeships by which one initially earned membership in the guild. Guild-sponsored educational activities were of two kinds: elementary education provided by the clergy for the children of guild members, and an apprenticeship indenture system for the sons of guild journeymen. These were provided both as benefits to members and to further the interests and influence of the guilds. The first craft guild for which a written record exists is the Candlemakers' Guild of Paris in 1061 (Barlow, 1967).

As guilds maintained strict standards for the skills needed to gain membership, they were forerunners of the craft unions of today which still require a prescribed level of competence for membership. Like the guilds, today's craft unions also regulate the quantity and quality of work, restrict the number of new apprentices, and closely monitor wages and prices.

As crafts and trades became more differentiated and specialized, apprenticeship continued to emerge as the dominant mode of transmitting practical and technical expertise from one person to another.

1.5.5   Apprenticeship

Apprenticeship has been a basic and persistent influence on the development of technical training, and is probably the most important nonschool institution around which technical training has grown. With roots in the very beginning of recorded history, apprenticeship training from father to son and master to apprentice has been the most enduring of all methods for transferring knowledge and skill. Bennett (1926) observes that up until the nineteenth century a great majority of people, even those from the more progressive nations, received no formal schooling, and what education they acquired was through trade and occupational training in the form of apprenticeship.

Davis (1978) characterizes apprenticeship as a system for preparing the young to become skilled workers. The three stages of apprenticeship—*apprentice, journeyman,* and *master*—varied in length and in sophistication of expertise developed. One began training as an apprentice for a period of about seven years under direction of a master, one who had achieved the highest level of expertise at a particular trade, craft, or skill. The master was expected to provide apprentices not only with occupational training, but also with the same moral, religious, and civic instruction that would be given to his own child. The master gradually would impart all of the mysteries of his craft—the generally not-so-mysterious rules, recipes, and methods of applying basic arts and sciences to the craft—to apprentices over the course of their training. As a journeyman who had achieved the basic skills and understandings of his craft, one could begin working as a day laborer, start to earn a fixed wage, and if mutually agreeable, work with other masters of the craft. After another period of several years developing skills as a journeyman, one may have mastered the competencies expected of the craft or present a masterpiece to demonstrate the skills and achieve the level of master. A master craftsman could set up his own shop, take on apprentices, and provide instruction in the craft.

Apprenticeships have not enjoyed continuing support in the United States over the years. Over the long term, this has had a significant influence on our competitiveness in the international arena.

1.6   1400–1700 A.D.: The Renaissance

By the close of the thirteenth century, a restless individualism was awakening the intellectual dormancy of the Middle Ages. The unity of medieval thought was broken by a rebellion against medieval discipline. During this period, a revival of classical learning occurred known as the *Renaissance*. Two developments facilitated the intellectual revival of the Renaissance and eventually brought education within the reach of more than just the rich: the use of the vernacular in writing and the invention of printing. Latin had long been the dominant language of learning and religion even though the great masses of people did not understand it. Even minor progress in bringing reading and writing skills to more people could not take place until this language barrier had been penetrated. In the fourteenth century, books began to appear in language more people could understand with the appearance of books such as Dante's *The Divine Comedy* and Bocaccio's *Decameron*. Shortly thereafter in about 1450, the printing of books from type was invented. Prior to this, books had to be meticulously copied by hand from manuscripts, a process that inhibited the widespread availability of books and other printed materials. Yet despite these advances, the Renaissance was a great revival of learning for the few with wealth and education. It would still be centuries before more people could begin to enjoy the benefits of education and personal development. The most common type of training at this time continued in roughly the same form it had always been—the master-apprentice system.

1.6.1 Engineering and Technical Training in the Middle Ages

During the period from the sixth to the tenth centuries (which some historians have referred to as the *Dark Ages*), engineering and architecture, which contributed so much to the rich tradition of the Roman Empire, ceased to be recognized professions. The work of engineers and architects was carried on by master masons and other experienced craftsmen. During this period of general cultural decline, construction in stone became rare. Wood and plaster were used instead, hence the familiar half-timbered homes depicted in medieval drawings and wood carvings. By the tenth and eleventh centuries, kings and popes began to rely more on the clergy for architectural and engineering projects. As churches and monasteries were repositories for classical works reflecting the culture of Greece and Rome, it is not surprising that many churches and public building projects continued to emerge during the Middle Ages in the grand Romanesque style.

Finch (1960) notes that by the fifteenth century material in books on engineering and surveying began to address problems of military engineering related to the use of military hardware. Military engineers of this period were pioneering new practices and techniques in ballistics and structural mechanics. For example, to refine the use of military cannons, engineers experimented with techniques for determining the range of a distant and inaccessible target, such as a fort or a ship at sea. Military engineers eventually succeeded in fitting tangents and circles to hypothetical trajectories for cannonballs. These studies of projectile trajectories and other studies in military structural mechanics led to the development of techniques in mathematics and military engineering that were well ahead of civilian engineering practices of the day. Indeed, a great deal of the engineering expertise refined in the military was easily transferred to civilian construction projects, and much of the technical training that supported the engineering accomplishments of this period took place in the military.

The Renaissance had heralded a new era of philosophical thinking. A continuous stream of social, political, and scientific advances began to appear as great minds struggled with the practical and philosophical problems of the day. New conceptions of the rights of individuals, the role of the state, and the laws by which men should be governed were boldly expressed by the enlightened political thinkers who emerged from this period, and as the Renaissance grew into the "age of reason," modern scientific thought was to begin and provide a foundation of basic advances upon which present scientific thinking is based.

Several figures profoundly influenced historical developments, including advancements in education and training, during and after the Renaissance. Four such influential figures were Martin Luther, John Locke, Jean-Jacques Rousseau, and Johan Pestalozzi. The influences of these men are examined in this history because each has made an important and uniquely different contribution to the development of technical training. In addition, each of these figures comes from a somewhat different time during the period of the fifteenth through eighteenth centuries. This allows us to trace a rough chronology of educational developments as they affected technical training during this period.

1.6.2 Secular Education for Girls and Boys: Martin Luther

In addition to the criticism Martin Luther (1483–1546) directed at the Roman Church that catalyzed the Protestant Reformation, he was also critical of the education given in monastic and ecclesiastical schools. Luther, an Augustinian monk and professor of theology at the University of Wittenburg, abhorred the rigid discipline and harsh restrictions of Church education to which he referred as "monkish tyranny." Consequently, he proposed that education should no longer be dominated by religion and the Church. He felt that education should embrace both religious *and* secular domains, and that educational reform should come through the power of the state, although existing institutional structures for delivering education developed through the centuries by the Church should continue to be used.

Luther's vision of education included a remarkable notion for that period—that education be given all people, not just the rich, and be available to girls as well as boys! His view of education was much broader than what could be provided by the schools of his time. Education should go beyond religious training and emphasize the Classics—mathematics, logic, music, history, and science—such as they were known at the time. Most important for the development of technical training, Luther advocated a school day of two hours to allow children to devote time for the development of trades and practical skills. As quoted in Monroe (1929), Luther wrote in his *Address to the Mayors and Councilmen of the German Cities:*

> . . . My opinion is that we must send the boys to school one or two hours a day, and have them learn a trade at home the rest of the time. It is desirable that these two occupations march side by side.

Luther publicized these views in 1524. It was not until the later part of the nineteenth century that the idea of combining trade and academic education in the schools was taken seriously.

1.6.3 Sensory Learning: John Locke

John Locke (1632–1704) possessed a broad range of intellectual interests and wrote a number of important works on the many subjects in which he had expertise. He studied philosophy at Oxford and later received a degree in medicine, which he practiced for a short time. He became a Fellow of the Royal Society of London and eventually developed a theory of education that combined practical and moral training with intellectual training. He also produced some of the most influential works on political thought ever written (Ebenstein, 1969). Yet it is his two works on the philosophy and methods of education that have had a lasting effect on the development of technical training.

In his *Essay Concerning Human Understanding*, Locke formulated his theory of knowledge which emphasized experience and the perception of the senses as important bases of knowledge. Later known as *empiricism*, this epistemology shaped Locke's ideas on what should constitute an ideal education. Locke's *Some Thoughts on Education* was written as a series of letters to a friend who requested Locke's advice on the education of his son. This important series of writings specifically laid out the purposes of education, how problems in educating the young should be overcome, and of significance to the development of technical training, what components of education should be provided. Locke firmly believed that education should address the development of logical thinking and preparation for practical life. Consequently, he wrote that an education should include the learning of one or more manual trades, as well as physical, moral, and intellectual training. In addition to learning the skill of drawing, Locke particularly approved of woodworking and gardening as ways in which the young could benefit from a broader, experiential education than could be gained from books alone. Although these were novel ideas at the time, Locke's generous view of the philosophy and substance of education can still be seen in the educational methods of western nations at the present time.

1.6.4 Experience, the Best Teacher: Jean-Jacques Rousseau

The visionary ideas about education of Jean-Jacques Rousseau (1712–1778) appear to have grown out of his own life. In his earlier years, the restless, self-indulgent Rousseau moved from one work experience to another far more than was acceptable for the time. He was an engraver's apprentice, a lackey, a musician, a seminary student, a clerk, a private tutor, a music copier, and the author of a prize-winning thesis written for the Academy of Dijon on "Whether the progress of the sciences and of letters has tended to corrupt or elevate morals." The latter experience demonstrated his brilliant, yet quite controversial ideas on the failures of contemporary social progress. His ideas on the values and moral principles which should guide the state and its obligations to the people found full expression in the *Social Contract*, Rousseau's major political treatise that was the ideological basis for the French Revolution and an important influence on our own Declaration of Independence.

Quite possibly through the circumstances of his own life, Rousseau firmly believed that experience is the best teacher and that education must be formed around the active experience of the young. Rousseau's ideas for how education should evolve from a rigid, book-bound process to a more natural, spontaneous experience are found in his delightful and eloquent *Emile*, named for the child of Rousseau's imagination whose education and development Rousseau traces from birth to marriage. In explaining Emile's adolescent development in a section of the work entitled "The Choice of a Trade," Rousseau states:

> . . . *show him the mutual dependence of men, avoid the moral aspects and direct his attention to industry and the mechanical arts which make themselves useful to each other* [italics added]. As you take him from one workshop to another, never let him see any kind of work without putting his hands to it, and never let him leave till he knows perfectly the reason for all that he has observed. With that in view, set him an example by working yourself in the different occupations. To make his a master become an apprentice. You can be sure that he will learn more by one hour of manual labor, than he will retain from a whole day's verbal instructions (Boyd, 1962, p. 86).

Rousseau clearly valued handwork and the mechanical arts as a central component of the education of the young. Yet it is significant to note that as the foregoing passage indicates, Rousseau would have Emile learn a trade not so much for its practical use as for its value in acquiring a broader and more meaningful education. Rousseau's recognition of the value of technical training in educating youth marked the beginning of a new era in education, and an important contribution to the development of technical training.

1.6.5   The Father of Manual Training: Johan Pestalozzi

With the contributions to education of Johan Heinrich Pestalozzi (1746–1827) came further movement from the old education of the simple acquisition of knowledge to the evolving notion of education as organic development. For the spirit and energy of his work, and the importance of the educational principles he proposed, Pestalozzi has been called the "father of manual training." Pestalozzi came from a Swiss family of modest means and self-admittedly was of no more than average intellectual ability. Yet his contributions not only set a new course for education and technical training in Europe, but they were among the strongest influences on the development of education and training in the emerging American colonies as well.

Pestalozzi concerned himself with the nature of education as a whole, and his ideas spanned a broad conceptual spectrum. His work included educational theory and philosophy, the institutional settings best suited to education, and the most effective techniques for teaching technical skills. According to Bennett (1926), Pestalozzi's broad conception of education and training grew naturally out of a number of factors which include:

- His intense desire to improve the conditions of the poor, and of children in his native Switzerland

- His firm belief that such improvement must come through education if it was to be permanent

- His opinion that school should be closely connected with and prepare one for life in the home, rather than leading one away from it

- His interest in the natural, experiential education of Rousseau

- His successful use of manual labor, tools, and objects as means for teaching traditional school subjects

- His belief that engaging children in manual labor for the primary purpose of their development might also be used to pay for their education

Through practices in the schools he established, Pestalozzi demonstrated that the subject matter of education should be part of the immediate environment of the learner and used to develop sense perceptions and formation of judgments. Pestalozzi's methods demanded the analysis of subject matter into its component parts and the use of inductive learning methods by proceeding from simple to complex elements as the way of achieving mastery of the whole.

In his writing, Pestalozzi (1898) states, "There are two ways of instructing, either we go from words to things or from things to words. Mine is the second method." This simple yet powerful truth is at the core of Pestalozzi's work, which has had such an important effect on the development of technical training. Pestalozzi's contributions to education and training were carried forward by other influential figures whose work reflected Pestalozzi's influence. Pestalozzi's notion of experiential learning figures prominently in the formal method of instruction developed by Johann Herbart, Philip von Fellenberg's system for school organization and administration, and Wilhelm Froebel's emphasis on "self-activity" and the value of learning through handwork (Bennett, 1926).

1.7 Apprenticeship Training: The Dominant Method in Colonial America

The Europeans who came to settle North America were people of piety and culture who had reaped the fruits of the Renaissance and Reformation, and who respected the importance of education. As apprenticeship was the dominant educational institution of the time as it had been for centuries, the early colonists in America brought apprenticeship with them in much the same form as it existed in the mother country of England. But because, as Seybolt (1917) points out, there were no guild or craft organizations in the colonies through which apprenticeships could be established, the scope of apprenticeships became broader and they were administered by municipal authorities. Although apprenticeships were eventually to be displaced by a system of schooling in the wake of the industrial revolution, early Americans expanded the role of apprenticeship as the dominant method of culturation and training of those who would build the new nation.

The English laws that provided for the apprenticeship of poor children were primarily enacted to insure the safety and physical welfare of the poor and only secondarily as a means of instruction. As early as 1641, colonial authorities broadened the scope of apprenticeship to emphasize its educational purpose. The colonists wished to make apprenticeship available to *all* children whose education might be neglected, not just the poor. This reliance of the colonists on apprenticeship was particularly important because of the strong value placed by the colonists on the merits of "one's own labor." Not only did they feel that teaching young people practical skills and trades would be profitable to the community, they also held Puritan beliefs in the virtue of industry and the "sin of idleness." The Massachusetts Bay Colony consequently enacted a comprehensive apprenticeship law for all children, which required training in skills needed for a "calling" and the development of the "ability to read and understand the principles of religion and the capital laws of the country" (Seybolt, 1917, p. 37).

Shortly thereafter, in 1647, the beginning of what was to become the American public school system first appeared. Early Americans realized that all parents and guardians were not able to teach reading and writing, despite the requirement that all children be given this elementary education. As a result, the General Court of Massachusetts ordered that every town of fifty or more homes recruit a teacher from the district and be responsible for paying the teacher's wages. Thus began the our nation's system of free public schools.

Among early American leaders who influenced the development of American education, Horace Mann (1796–1859) should be singularly distinguished. Davidson (1898) writes:

> . . . the first man who fully understood the needs of the nation, and undertook to meet them in large, practical ways, was Horace Mann, to whom American culture owes more than to any other person. He was exactly the influence needed by the nation in her hour of spiritual awakening (p. 246).

Mann recognized the needs of the poor and uneducated of the new nation and saw the important role of education in alleviating them. In addition, he possessed the vision to formulate a broad plan for a new system of education and had the persistence and energy to see it carried out. Indeed, as head of the Massachusetts Board of Education and later as a U.S. congressman, Mann worked tirelessly to establish a system of education that met the needs of the people and the nation.

His belief that education should develop one's intellectual *and* practical skills furthered the advancement of practical and technical training in the new world. He felt that

> education should be a preparation for life, domestic, economic, social, and not merely the acquisition of curious learning, elegant scholarship, or showy accomplishments. Its end should be the attainment of moral and social personality (Davidson, p. 251).

After visiting the schools of Europe in 1843, he issued his famous *Seventh Annual Report* which became the basis of school reform in Massachusetts. Later, in a report to the School Committee of Boston, Mann emphasized the development of practical skills, especially drawing, in school curricula (Bennett, 1926). Indeed, as part of his contribution to the American educational system during our early history, Horace Mann also positively influenced the integration of practical and vocational training within general education.

1.8   The Industrial Era

As America left behind its colonial beginnings and entered the nineteenth century, it slowly shifted from an agrarian to an industrial economy. Like other developed Western nations at the time, the United States underwent a traumatic, yet invigorating transition in the workplace from a period of almost total reliance on manual processes to an era of continuing industrialization. Unlike in the European nations that shaped its development, however, America's shift to an industrial economy was accompanied by a permanent decline in apprenticeship training. Apprenticeship was displaced by a number of public and private institutions for work-related training that became the basis for many of the training arrangements we use today. In this section, we examine the development of technical education and training in America as it struggled to become an industrialized nation.

1.8.1   The Decline
of Apprenticeship

Well before the onset of the industrial era in the later part of the nineteenth century, the system of apprenticeship training that had served the nation so well in earlier times, was showing signs of weakness. Even before the appearance of factories, the close interaction between master and apprentice was eroding as apprenticeship became more entrepreneurial and less pedagogical. The responsibility for training apprentices was more frequently being turned over to journeymen, and rather than the one-to-one learning relationship modeled after earlier father-son apprenticeships, the number of apprentices in a single shop could be as high as ten or more. As early apprenticeships in this country were administered by local authorities and were not under the strict regulation of craft and merchant guilds as they were in England and Germany, apprenticeships were gradually losing the developmental purpose for which they had been established and were becoming more exploitative of apprentices.

Eventually, however, the decline of apprenticeship became quite pronounced as the industrial advances of the later nineteenth century created a new demand for workers trained in a different way. As early as the middle of the eighteenth century, new machinery and other inventions of the emerging industrial era began to bring about remarkable changes in how work was performed. These changes were particularly apparent in the textile industry at that time, where processes performed manually at home were slowly moved to early "manufactories" which housed new, automated looms and other inventions for textile manufacturing. Similar innovations were occurring in other industries such as printing, agriculture, and furniture manufacturing.

The weakness of apprenticeships and lack of other systematic approaches to technical training for the non-college-bound in this country have been cited as major factors in the decline of America's industrial competitiveness (Johnston and Packer, 1987; MIT Commission of Industrial Productivity, 1989; National Center on Education and the Economy, 1990; William T. Grant Foundation Commission, 1988). While apprenticeships continue to decline in this country, they remain a strong component of workforce training in Germany, Austria, Switzerland, and other nations. In Germany, for example, a *dual system* of vocational education moves young people from schools into jobs along a route that involves a mix of company-based training and special vocational courses. The majority of German students leave school and enter apprenticeships that are offered in approximately 400 occupations. Each apprenticeship is based on a training curriculum that has been negotiated by officials from government, employers' associations, and trade unions. These curricula are regularly revised to keep pace with technological change. Similar, well-structured paths from school to work are missing in this country and this has resulted in underdeveloped human resources which has been detrimental to our nation's productivity and competitive performance. Compared with countries which have such systems, the United States is at a serious competitive disadvantage in its ability to meet the technical challenges that so strongly influence today's business performance. Other countries that rely heavily on structured training to develop general as well as specialized skills "find it easier to respond to rapid and unpredictable changes in technology and markets" (MIT Commission of Industrial Productivity, 1989, p. 84).

During America's period of industrialization, however, new ways were needed for training workers. Apprenticeship was unsuited for the more automated work in the evolving factory system. In addition, it was simply unable to keep pace with the growing demand for industrial workers. The important changes in the workplace brought by the industrial revolution required corresponding changes in the preparation of workers.

As America entered the twentieth century and the industrialization of the economy continued, innovations occurred in work design which fundamentally transformed the nature of work: *scientific management* and the introduction of *mass production methods*. Scientific management is based on work originated in the early eighteenth century by Babbage (Davis and Taylor, 1972), which was further refined and popularized by Frederick Taylor. Scientific management is based on two straightforward principles (Taylor, 1912):

- Break complex tasks down into simple rote tasks that can be performed with machinelike efficiency

- Control the large number of workers needed for production with a hierarchical management structure

This elegant concept of production efficiency was first implemented in manufacturing after the turn of the century, and was soon adopted and developed into a complete system for mass production by Henry Ford. The mass production system required a cadre of engineers, planners, schedulers, supervisors, maintenance personnel, and quality inspectors to keep operations running smoothly and to prevent costly production delays. Direct-line workers performed simple, repetitious tasks, and depended upon a large number of similarly specialized support staff to troubleshoot and control the production process. This approach to production permeated the industrial sectors of the economy and was responsible for the United States' dominance of the world market for manufactured goods during the middle part of this century.

1.8.2 Technical Training and Corporation Schools

During colonial times, free public schools for elementary education had been established. Secondary schools were established after the founding of the nation's first publicly supported high school in Boston in 1821. Yet means had not yet been devised for providing technical and industrial education for the many who were needed to work in the nation's expanding industries. Providing technical training in the schools along with general and academic courses was an obvious option, but this was not seriously pursued until the late 1800s.

Although still separate from the growing system of public education, a few private manual training schools were established throughout this period which were to have lasting effects on the development of technical training. During the eighteenth century, mechanics and tradespeople formed technical societies for the purpose of mutual assistance and economic advancement modeled after the trade associations of England. A result of these associations was the establishment of "mechanics' institutes," which provided formal training in mechanical arts, as well as instruction in reading, English, mathematics, and other subjects. A mechanics' institute was founded in New York City as early as 1820, and a few years later, the Franklin Institute in Philadelphia and Ohio Mechanics' Institute in Cincinnati were established. These facilities had libraries for apprentices, and most offered education to the children of mechanics. Although only a small number were established, mechanics' institutes were the earliest examples in the United States of institutions which formally offered both technical and general education. They served as an important example for the later development of private manual training schools, and positively influenced public perceptions of manual work and the technical training it required.

Corporation schools were the first programs of formal instruction to be sponsored by businesses for their employees and held on company premises (Beatty, 1918). This precursor of today's company-based training function was first developed in the railroad industry in 1905 as a way of improving the performance and efficiency of those who worked in railroad maintenance shops. Prior to this time, similar training for machinists was first offered in the evening at R. Hoe and Company, a New York City manufacturer of printing presses (Bennett, 1926). Apprenticeship training in the trades, on which companies had previously relied for trained workers, was inadequate for current skill and production demands. Corporation schools, or factory schools as they were also called, provided technical training in the skills and trades needed in a particular industry and included instruction in mathematics, mechanical and freehand drawing, and other practical skills needed by workers. The concept of corporation schools caught on quickly as similar schools were established by Westinghouse, Baldwin Locomotive, General Electric, International Harvester, Ford, Goodyear, and National Cash Register around the turn of the century.

1.8.3 Public Education and Technical Training

Although privately sponsored programs for providing technical training to workers had been successful, there was strong resistance to the integration of technical training within the public schools. Opposition to this had developed among conservative educators who felt that the integration of technical training would lead to lower academic standards. They felt that moral training and instruction in the basic subjects would provide the best preparation for the world beyond school. Education for work had no place in the public schools. On the other hand, criticism of the general curriculum of the public schools was growing because it was seen as failing to reflect the life for which it was supposed to be preparing youth. Much of what was learned from books in the classroom had little applicability to the world beyond. Education needed more relevance. This could be provided by offering work-related training along with general education in public schools.

The struggle over what should constitute the proper education of youth, and to what degree technical education should become the responsibility of the schools, was not limited to just this country. England, France, and Russia were also dealing with changes brought on by industrialization. All three countries had achieved some progress in improving their educational systems. After studying the Russian system for providing technical training, American proponents of offering manual training in the schools came to the basic and surprising realization that principles involved in manual skills could simply be put on the same educational plane as other school subjects (Bennett, 1937).

The School of Mechanical Arts was created at the Massachusetts Institute of Technology in 1876. The Manual Training School of St. Louis was quite successful and was quickly copied in both its administration and curriculum in Chicago. Although these schools were privately funded, they demonstrated that such schools could be successfully established. Support for this training was growing and public funding for manual training schools would soon follow.

The first high school for manual training fully supported at public expense was founded in Baltimore in 1884. In the following year, a second school supported as part of the public school system opened in Philadelphia and a third in Toledo. Although these schools were physically separate from the general high schools, the actual integration of manual training courses into general high school curricula was also beginning to occur. By 1884, manual training courses and general academic courses were being offered in the same public high schools in Cleveland, Boston, Minneapolis, and other cities (Bennett, 1937).

In 1912 the National Society for the Promotion of Industrial Education was formed. This group of educators was committed to promoting industrial education in public and private schools. The Society later changed its name and eventually merged with the Vocational Association of the Midwest to become the present American Vocational Association. In 1913, a group of industrialists organized the National Association of Corporate Schools to promote training in industry and business, and this later became the American Management Association (Dooley, 1945).

Charles R. Allen, recognized authority on industrial-vocational education in public and private schools served as one of the training leaders in the United States. Allen's famous four-step job instruction method served as a bridge among a number of parallel industrial training developments in the nation. As a staff member of the private Dunwoody Institute of Minneapolis, he and Charles Prosser, head of Dunwoody, continued to influence training theories and practices.

The years 1919 to 1940 in the United States have been characterized as the "standstill years" in terms of technical training. Allen's publications on job instruction and the documentation resulting from the Emergency Fleet Corporation from World War I kept the important early 1900s knowledge about effective and efficient technical training from being lost (Dooley, 1945). In 1937, the National Association of Industrial Technical Teacher Educators, an association of college and university industrial-technical teacher educators, was formed to helped advance the profession of technical teacher training (Evans, 1987).

1.8.4 The Role of Government in Technical Training

Early support for technical training and vocational education came from state legislatures. The success and growth of early private manual training schools permanently established these technical training schools as important sources of skilled workers. In addition, demands of manufacturers, labor leaders, and the general public for more of this instruction and more skilled workers increased. Responding to these increasingly vocal and better-organized constituencies, state legislatures funded technical training curricula within public education in schools in Massachusetts, Ohio, Pennsylvania, and in other states. Shortly after 1900, Massachusetts, long a leader in promoting practical and technical training, established independent schools for industrial and technical training, funded these schools with state money equal to half of local expenditures, and allowed administration of these schools through a commission of vocational education which was established independently of the State Board of Education.

Similar innovations supporting the advancement of technical training both within and outside of public education occurred thereafter in other states. State legislation promoting vocational and technical education became more common as interest spread from the industrial states of the East to the Midwest, and later to the South and far West. The greatest initiative for state legislation supporting the development of vocational and technical education came from the Morrill Act of 1862 signed by Abraham Lincoln. Also called the Land Grant Act of 1862, this legislation provided a comprehensive and far-reaching scheme of public endowment of higher education that was to bring higher education within the reach of the average citizen, not just the wealthy, for the first time. It established programs of training at the college level in agricultural education, industrial and trade education, and home economics education, and did much to clarify the image of this type of technical training in the eyes of the public. In keeping with the mission of land grant universities, Professor Homer Smith of the University of Minnesota helped establish the University's Department of Industrial Education in 1914. The Department prepared teachers of industrial subjects.

Another major step forward in establishing technical training as a component of public education was the enactment of the Smith-Hughes Act in 1917. It provided for a permanent, annual appropriation of $7 million for programs of industrial, agricultural, home economics, and teacher training within public education. The legislation was carefully crafted to strike balances between three sets of vested interests:

1. Management and labor—with each seeking to regulate vocational training in order to control this important source of skilled labor

2. Educators who felt there should be more integration between practical and academic education and those who felt there should not be integration

3. Among those supporting vocational education, those who felt this should occur through public institutions and those seeking to keep vocational education out of the public schools

The Smith-Hughes Act seems to have balanced these competing interests quite well, for as Bennett (1937) states: "The law passed was probably the best compromise that could have been obtained at the time" (p. 550). Since the Smith-Hughes Act, three subsequent federal laws enacted between 1929 and 1936 authorized further increases in spending on vocational education. The 1963 and 1968 vocational education acts again increased the funding for vocational and technical training, but with an increasing emphasis on addressing social problems and assisting disadvantaged groups rather than first addressing industry requirements.

1.9 Twentieth-Century Influences

Several important influences on the development of technical training emerged in the half-century surrounding America's involvement in the two world wars. These include the training demands placed on our educational system by the wars themselves and the changes that resulted, the rise of the American labor movement during this period, and the impact of the technological innovations initiated during and after war involvement. In this section, each of these important influences on the development of technical training are examined.

1.9.1 World War Influences

America's entry into the two world wars of the twentieth century added great new demands to the existing need for more workers with mechanical, technical, and scientific training. As industrial advancements continued to spread into more and more industries, technological developments outstripped the capacity for training qualified workers. America's war involvement mobilized the nation's efforts in every area, including training and education. The nation's educational system had to prepare young men of military age to contribute to the country's defense, in addition to the normal educational responsibilities. The nation found that new institutional arrangements were needed to improve education's ability to meet the intellectual needs of young people, as well as to prepare them for work, family, and other important responsibilities.

The types of trade and occupational training most urgently needed during wartime were automotive, machining, metal fabrication, forging, electrical, building, and drafting. As the need for those with technical training was great, the occupational and technical areas of both public and private educational institutions grew significantly. While it was unfortunate that the war effort stimulated the further growth of technical training, traumatic events have been perennial catalysts for training. Although we can only guardedly point to recent evidence that current emphasis on training is an enduring investment for our social and economic development (Swanson, 1992), we support the historical truth in Steinmetz's (1976) observation that "training has always grown best where emergency is the dominant thought" (pp. 1–9).

Wartime educational efforts of all types and contexts were reexamined. Several training innovations were developed in response to the tremendous demand for wartime training and they helped to shape modern training methods. As mentioned earlier, the basic and easily grasped four-step job instruction training (JIT) method developed by vocational educator, Charles L. Allen, was first used during World War I (McCord, 1976).

World War II brought about an enormous training effort in the United States under the Training Within Industry (TWI) Service of the War Manpower Commission. The incredible story of the TWI is fully documented in its 330-page final report (Dooley, 1945). It should be read by anyone seriously interested in the twentieth-century history of human resource development in American industry and business.

Training Within Industry was an emergency service to the nation's contractor and essential services. Its staff was drawn from industry to give assistance to industry, and its history covers the time from the Fall of France to the end of World War II—from the summer of 1940 to the fall of 1945. TWI's objectives were to help contractors get out better war production, faster, so that the war might be shortened, and to help industry to lower the cost of war materials.

Training Within Industry is known for the results of its programs— Job Instruction, Job Methods, Job Relations, and Program Development—which have, we believe, permanently become part of American industrial operations as accepted tools of management (Dooley, 1945, p. xi).

The TWI programs were accepted for good reasons. Besides being effective and elegantly simple, each day in the middle of the war approximately 6000 new workers were reporting for work. In addition, 400 workers were being appointed each day as supervisors who had no experience in directing the work of others. Each TWI program had a system to back it up: limited steps, key words, subpoints, documentation/work methods, and supporting training so as to obtain certification in each program.

The *Job Instruction* program (sometimes called *Job Instruction Training— JIT*) had four steps for "Getting Ready to Instruct" and four steps for "How to Instruct."

Getting ready to instruct:

1. Have a timetable.
2. Break down the job.
3. Have everything ready.
4. Have the workplace properly arranged.

How to instruct:

1. Prepare the worker.
2. Present the operation.
3. Try out performance.
4. Follow up.

While the four instruction steps are most recognizable, the process of *breaking down the job* prior to the instruction was critical to insuring performance. A job breakdown sheet required the supervisor-trainer to minimally list (1) the important steps in the operation and (2) the key points for each step.

The *Job Methods* program was a specific method of developing a critically constructive attitude among supervisors toward work. The purpose was for producing higher-quality goods in less time by making best use of the available resources. The four steps included:

1. Break down the job.
2. Question every detail.
3. Develop the new method.
4. Apply the new method.

With a need for even further improvements, the four-step *Program Development* method was created in 1942 in a joint session between TWI and General Motors Institute. The process included:

1. Spot a production Problem.
2. Develop a specific Plan.
3. Get plan into Action.
4. Check Results.

Deming's (1993) instruction to the Japanese in 1950 about the "Plan-Do-Study-Act Cycle" and the return of the improvement process lessons to American industry thirty years later may be one of the great ironies of the technical training profession.

The *Job Relations* program was built on the following foundations for good relations: (1) let each worker know how he is getting along; (2) give credit where credit is due; (3) tell people in advance about changes that will affect them; and (4) make the best use of each person's ability. The four steps of good job relations included:

1. Get the facts.
2. Weigh and decide.
3. Take action.
4. Check results.

Each of the TWI programs provided a unique contribution to workplace performance. The Job Relations program, more than the others, represented a breakthrough in improving people-people workplace behavior in American industry.

TWI was a comprehensive approach to training that could stand the test of today's tough criteria of being systemically, psychologically, and economically sound. In less than five years, these methods resulted in 1,750,650 certifications of supervisors in 16,511 plants and unions (Dooley, 1945).

Much of what was learned within the Training Within Industry effort concerning training and quality improvement tied to organizational performance was lost during World War II. The TWI programs were clear about their purpose, with the test coming from the refrain, "Did the plan help production?" TWI training started with performance at the organizational and process levels and ended with performance at the same levels. Dooley wrote in 1945, ". . . experience showed that looking for a *training* problem was the wrong approach and this was changed to a *production* problem" (p. 243).

The emergence of instructional technology in the 1960s created a new emphasis in the field of training and a major funding partner, the military (U.S. Civil Service Commission, 1969). During this time period, various innovations resulted in what is popularly known as the *Instructional Systems Development* (ISD) and its five phases: *analyze, design, develop, implement,* and *control* (Campbell, 1984). As the term denotes, ISD focuses on instruction, not on organization and process performance problems. These performance decisions were left to others. The peacetime military training pressures were not like the wartime industrial training pressures. The military conditions of highly standardized technology, highly standardized learners, and highly standardized jobs made the ISD appropriate for the military, and awkward at best for the variety of conditions and time constraints found in most of American businesses and industries. Notable exceptions were the nuclear power industry and some large accounting-financial firms.

The infusion of educators and industrial psychologists into the training profession, and their view of training as focused on the individual, resulted in disconnects of training from the organization and process performance requirements. The irony of Gagne's classic 1962 article, "Military Training and Principles of Learning," was his rediscovery of the value of work tasks in terms of training design and effectiveness. These lessons had been learned and documented in the early 1940s (Dooley, 1945). Today, training systems responsive to the performance requirements of the organization have moved beyond the ISD model (Swanson, 1994; Swanson and Sisson, 1980).

1.9.2 The American Labor Movement

Another important influence on the development of technical training during this period was the rise of the American labor movement. The early part of this century witnessed organized labor's successful struggle to become a dominant force in our economic development. Although the popularity and influence of labor unions has undergone significant change over time, organized labor has consistently supported extending the availability of education and training seen as broadening the skill base of its membership.

Up to the 1870s, American industrialists relied on craft workers, many of whom were trained through the craft unions of Europe and later emigrated to America, to run production activities in their factories. These skilled workers functioned as supervisors and upheld traditional craft norms of workmanship, the pace and allocation of work, and rates of pay. At the same time as new, labor-saving technologies became available, management attempted to achieve greater production efficiencies through greater investment in industrial equipment, much of which had labor-saving and de-skilling effects.

In the face of increasing factory automation, skilled workers attempted to retain control over their traditional shop floor prerogatives. It was management's challenge to this position of craft control that prompted workers to unite as the American Federation of Labor in 1881 (Lazonick, 1991). Management fought the union movement with every means available including violence and cooptation of the more skilled and experienced craftsmen lured into the management structure as technicians and supervisors. During the early part of the twentieth century, American managers and industrialists became even more insistent that skill and initiative not be left with those on the shop floor. For the same reason they were equally resistant to the passing on of relevant skills through craft-controlled apprenticeship training.

Two methods of improving efficiency and reducing costs appealed to management because they could also be used to thwart the growth of unions. The adoption of new industrial technology displaced the need for many of the skills of craft workers and reduced the overall need for labor. What labor was needed was often at a lower skill level and could be provided by hiring unskilled, immigrant labor. In both instances, unions were circumvented by managers who were fearful of losing further control on the factory floor. The larger struggle between management and labor over the control of relevant skills and production prerogatives on the shop floor has, in many ways, continued to the present.

From the beginning of the labor movement, the political orientation of unions evolved as one of expedience. With most government officials passively, if not actively, opposed to the union movement during its early years, the AFL sought conditions in which labor and management would settle their own disputes without government intervention. Freeman (1979) observes that AFL President Samuel Gompers encouraged early trade unions to avoid aligning with a political party and "reward their friends and punish their enemies" regardless of party affiliation.

Organized labor was understandably proud of the range and depth of skills represented by their various trade, craft, and mechanics unions and strongly resisted management efforts to devalue and displace these skills. Union people valued the skilled trades they represented and their position on any issue related to this was straightforward: movements that threatened this asset were to be opposed; movements that enhanced this asset would have labor's full support. From the beginning, organized labor has supported education and training seen as enhancing the skill base of their membership.

An early case illustrating how labor values education occurred shortly after the founding of the National Society for the Promotion of Industrial Education in 1912, which was established by a group of educators to promote industrial education in public and private schools. Once the American Federation of Labor was assured of the high standards of the schools promoted by the Society, and that these were not simply shortcuts to acquiring a trade, the AFL, by special resolution, formally recognized the formation of the National Society for the Promotion of Industrial Education. Supported by organized labor ever since, the Society is the present American Vocational Association.

Organized labor's concern for protecting its valued skill base and for having control over educational programs leading to employment in the trades were important reasons for labor's support for the Smith-Hughes Act of 1917 described previously. While unions were concerned that making vocational education more universally available through the public schools might erode their control of training for their professions, they took the broader view that the legislation represented an important gain for the working people in general, and that it would eventually expand the educational base available to union membership. Organized labor supported the legislation and actively shaped how it was implemented by promoting widespread union participation on planning and advisory councils for schools receiving federal support, and by encouraging their members to take advantage of new training programs supported by the bill.

1.9.3   Technological Innovation and the Computer

In the postwar years, the United States invested heavily in a wide range of basic and applied research for both military and civilian purposes. Commitments to research yielded a steady stream of product ideas and innovations. Basic research, undertaken for its own sake, often led directly to unintended, yet exciting, new commercial applications. Similarly, defense research generated technology which also had many important civilian applications. These positive developments contributed to the U.S. dominance of global markets and shaped current expectations of what research and technology could achieve. The United States is still unquestionably the leader in basic research (MIT Commission on Industrial Productivity, 1989).

New technology provided the basis for a wide range of innovations from consumer products to manufacturing systems. Innovations such as the transistor, assembly-line robot, and television led to further advancements in semiconductors, laser technology, and CNC-production equipment. Underlying much of the technical innovation of the last 30 years, however, has been the computer.

Among the numerous applications of the computer are its important uses in education and training. The computer provides both a new core technology through which training can be organized and administered, and the computer and computer programs are themselves the content of an increasing number of training programs. In insurance, education, and other service industries, computer-related expertise accounts for one of the largest performance needs addressed through training.

Early business applications of the computer were largely limited to data processing, as it was viewed primarily as an efficient record storage and retrieval system. Early computer training was provided exclusively by computer manufacturers, some of whom went so far as to administer aptitude tests designed to measure which customer employees demonstrated the best potential for participating in computer training (McConnell and Setaro, 1976). Organizations did little or no computer training themselves. In the early 1960s, the application of the computer's "complex" functions was largely limited to data processing and accounting. Computer training was considered quite technical and was left to the computer manufacturer.

As the speed and complexity of computer capabilities increased and its size underwent rather dramatic reductions, the application of computer technology spread from the business office to the factory floor, sales office, engineering laboratory, and warehouse. As virtually every business function and sector of our economy has been transformed through computer technology, it is difficult to overstate its present influence: it has revolutionized work methods and training methods.

Computer training, more than almost any other form of technical training, is available in a variety of forms from a variety of sources. In markets where there is very little product differentiation, technical computer training supplied by the manufacturer may be their competitive edge. Consulting firms specializing in integrating computer-based information and/or production systems sell systems design and training. Popular software programs often justify the extensive and specialized training programs that can even be targeted to specific worker groups and learning styles.

Today nearly all academic institutions, from two-year technical colleges to major research universities, offer education in computer science. As the academic community is a major partner in computer science research, it is also a major provider of computer science education, offering education in areas ranging from the use of basic software programs to courses on advanced computer languages and programming techniques. Public schools, including elementary and secondary levels, and adult education programs consistently offer basic computer skills and software skills training.

1.10   Recent Developments

In preparation for thinking about the future of technical training, it is important to highlight two fundamental developments occurring in the workplace—the transformation taking place in organizations and the changing nature of work.

1.10.1   Transformation of Contemporary Work Organizations

Organizations, large and small, public or private, in a range of industrial sectors, are the primary medium through which work is accomplished. The structure of contemporary work organizations is changing to more closely follow the flow of work resulting in more emphasis on the cross-functional processes through which work is accomplished. Organizations are becoming flatter and less hierarchical in efforts to reduce bureaucracy, manage costs, and be more responsive to their customers. Organizations are also becoming smaller and leaner as managers eliminate work inefficiencies and duplication of effort. A consequence of these emerging flatter, "downsized" organizations is the need for major shifts in the distribution of work tasks and roles among workers. In a workplace once modeled on narrow job definitions and a wide range of functional specialists, today's workplace is often characterized by increasingly sophisticated work methods and the presence of relatively fewer workers. Narrow job definitions are giving way to broader responsibilities and a greater interdependence among workers. Jobs are being eliminated, combined, and reconfigured as organizations fundamentally rethink the ways in which work should be done (Torraco, 1994).

As organizational and job structures change, training for those who operate within these structures must change. Within this atmosphere of change, task expertise is still required. In the first half of the century the adjustment was from journeyman mechanics being skilled in a broad range of tasks to skilled operators being proficient at the same level in fewer tasks. The challenge for many organizations now is to expand the range of tasks among workers without diluting their skill level in any of the tasks.

1.10.2 The Evolving Nature of Work

The nature of contemporary work is changing. Efforts underway in organizations to reduce costs, add labor-saving technology, and expedite communication with customers and suppliers not only eliminate jobs throughout the organization, they increase the sophistication of work for those who remain. Today's workers increasingly need to understand work operations as a whole, rather than what used to be their specific tasks within it. Monitoring and maintaining the work *system* or *process* is becoming in today's workplace what operating a single *machine* had been for mass production work. Today's workers have to make sense of what is happening in the workplace based on data rather than physical cues. According to Zuboff (1988), this transformation of work involves the development of *intellective* rather than *action-centered* skills. As employees acquire responsibility for monitoring and maintaining a broader range of work processes, their involvement is increasingly characterized by intervals of relative inactivity punctuated by periods of nonrepetitive problem solving. Gone are the days when problem solving meant making a telephone call to the maintenance department or to management.

In addition, flatter organizational structures require employees at the shop floor level to exercise more authority over a wider variety of tasks. They can no longer rely on management for planning and scheduling, as these duties are being integrated into production jobs themselves. Today's work requires an increasingly holistic perspective of the organization and attention to the demands of both internal and external customers. Procedural thinking has become subordinate to systems thinking for all workers, not just for managers.

Another important factor underlying the changing nature of contemporary work is a perceptible shortening of the half-life of knowledge. New knowledge drives the evolution of new work systems and technologies. *The half-life of knowledge in technology-intensive fields such as engineering and health care is now less than four years.* This means that the relevant expertise of an engineer completing training today will erode by fifty percent in just four years. The half-life of knowledge is not much longer in most of the other business, professional, and technical fields upon which organizations rely for their expertise.

The profound influence this constant turnover in knowledge has on the nature of work and the way work is accomplished is all too obvious to those who must continually update their work knowledge and skills. It is no wonder that the concept of the *learning organization* has gained so much attention along with the process of developing the values and systems to ensure it (Watkins and Marsick, 1993). Equally interesting is the unique problem of continually developing those who already are considered technical experts in the organization (Argyris, 1991).

Advanced technology, leaner organizational structures, and ever-changing demands of customers and government are powerful factors that are reshaping organizations, fundamentally changing the nature of work, and adding to the training needed for organizations to remain competitive. Employees in this environment need skills that enable them to function effectively as members of teams, since *teams* are becoming the basic unit through which work is accomplished in today's organizations. The skills needed for effective team performance include communication skills, understanding interpersonal and group dynamics, and the abilities to identify, analyze, and solve problems.

1.11 The Future of Technical Training

The foremost role of training in organizations is the development of workplace expertise. "Workplace expertise is the fuel of an organization" (Swanson, 1994, p. 211). Technical training enjoys a special position in the human resource development profession as it focuses on developing *technical expertise* in employees and end users.

As you have read in this chapter, the locus of control for workplace expertise was a struggle throughout the history of humanity. Examples from the early 1900s of management retaining workplace authority include the (1) de-skilling of jobs and (2) promoting workers with highly technical skills from the hourly ranks to salaried positions.

This struggle over expertise and authority will not likely change, but the variations, as we enter the twenty-first century, will be a challenge to workers, trainers, organizations, and nations. For example, while the United States ponders the merits of Germany's dual system of developing technical expertise, large German multinational corporations are choosing not to participate in it because of dual-system bureaucracy and its disconnect from the performance demands of their companies. Today, expertise can be developed and accessed in many ways and, since expertise is only one of the ingredients of performance, an understanding of performance is important.

Figure 1-1 illustrates some of the performance issues facing organizations and technical trainers today and in the future (Swanson, 1994).

The five levels of performance are:

- Understanding
- Operation

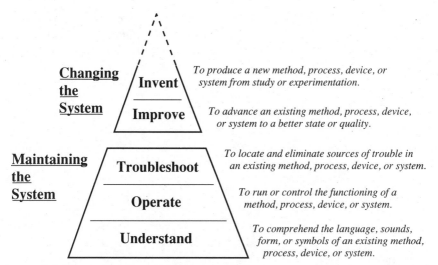

Figure 1-1. Taxonomy of Performance. (*Reprinted with permission: R. A. Swanson*, Analysis for Improving Performance: Tools for Diagnosing Organizations and Documenting Workplace Expertise, *Berrett-Koehler, San Francisco, 1994.*)

- Troubleshooting

- Improvement

- Invention

These levels portray a hierarchy that frames the expertise required of a task or process. To achieve the required performance goals, technical training must be aimed at the right technical and/or information system and at the appropriate performance level. For example, having technical training aimed at the *operation* performance level with workplace performance expectations at the *troubleshooting* performance level has been all too common and no longer tolerable.

Another example would be a corporation developing a new "System 2000." System 2000 will have some employees who need to *understand* the system in order to carry out their work while others may be required to *operate* it. In addition, some may be required to *troubleshoot* the System 2000 process as the product is being produced, while others must *troubleshoot* the system itself. The reality is that multiple levels of technical training are required to sustain any technical system (e.g., System 2000) for a company to remain competitive and that training should connect directly to required performance.

Technical jobs (and technical training) in the workplace have often been separate for those who troubleshoot from those who operate technical systems. Today we are more likely to see these performance levels combined into one job. Furthermore, the Taxonomy of Performance concisely portrays the challenge of jumping from the performance requirement of *maintaining the system* (including understanding, operating, and troubleshooting) to that of *changing the system* (including improving and inventing).

Organizations face their technical performance requirements with both the burden and enlightenment of their own history. We have watched firms refuse to invest in technical training of their hourly employees because no equivalent training had ever been provided for their top-salaried employees. When this happens, the historic struggle over expertise and power between those in power and workers requiring technical expertise comes into play. Unfortunately, this power struggle is still at work in many of today's organizations.

On the other hand, we have seen very expensive technical training systems being made available to workers on demand. These training systems, backed by sophisticated instructional technology, ensure the development of expertise and validate its attainment before the trainee is expected to perform on the job. *For a technology-based organization, these programs can be some of the most expensive and strategic business investments they make.* In this example, the economics of having or not having adequate technical expertise is what most likely elevated the value of technical training to the top of the investment list.

The good news about the future is that the best theory and research related to technical training is at work in our culture. We anticipate that this will be the case for some time. The theoretical domains that guide the technical training profession (as well as all areas of the human resource profession) are said to be: psychological, systems, and economic theories (Swanson, 1983). We will use these three domains as organizers to reflect off the history of technical training into the future.

1.11.1 Psychological Domain

The application of *psychological theory* to technical training has always been easily observed. Technical expertise has been an issue throughout recorded history along with means of developing experts. As for the future, advances in the psychological arenas of *artificial intelligence* and *problem solving* will likely have a significant impact on the future of technical training.

Artificial Intelligence. *Artificial intelligence is an outgrowth of our ability to understand, document, and replicate expertise.* This advancing body of theory and practice is creating the ability to document and pass on technical expertise in new ways. What we previously thought to be the outcome of years of work experience, can be compressed as a result of the deeper understanding derived from new analysis tools. Furthermore, what has formerly been the domain of human expertise is increasingly being built into technical systems—smart systems able to troubleshoot and repair themselves.

Problem-Solving Methods. *Problem solving has been one of the highest forms of technical work behavior and, thus, one of the ultimate outcomes of technical training.* There has been a historic struggle over the theory- versus system-specific prerequisites to technical problem solving. The theory perspective holds that having the underlying theory (e.g., mechanical or electrical) will best prepare the person to deal with complex technical problems. The second perspective argues for system-task-specific knowledge and processes needed to solve that system's problems. The range of technical systems and technical problems in the workplace begs for training and expertise that can encompass as much technical breadth as possible. This desire for general problem-solving methods, however, is in conflict with the research conclusion that system- and task-specific problem-solving methods work best.

Thus, from the psychological perspective, the future will take technical training down two tracks: (1) the use of communication technology to gain real-time access to highly specialized technical expertise via computer hook-ups, satellite transmissions to human experts and, data-based expertise and (2) the elevation of technical training content to the highest generalizable level while insuring adequate expertise to meet performance standards.

1.11.2 Systems Domain

The application of *systems theory* to technical training is experienced at both the technical content and training process levels. The general acceptance of systems theory in almost all disciplines and the shift in thinking from a *closed system* view to an *open system* view will continue to impact technical training. The history of technical training is imbedded in products, tasks, and machinery that are self-contained either in the person or the equipment. This traditional bounded-system, or closed-system, view of the world is increasingly less relevant to real-world practices. *When the technical system view is broadened beyond the machine to include the operator and the machine, the internal customer, and then the external customer, the system becomes an open system.*

Systems Thinking. Not long ago, the idea of systems thinking was primarily the purview of the technical side of the organization. Today, almost all disciplines acknowledge systems theory. And, as information systems and sociotechnical systems begin to dominate, technical training must now struggle to keep up with the reality of the workplace.

Open Systems. Systems thinking for technical training has historically been focused on hardware systems and on a closed-systems perspective. These conditions formerly placed the *designers* of production systems in a technical training leadership related role even though they had little or no training expertise. Today, that same hardware system may be viewed as only part of the production system with the operator, the customer, and the insertion of the new realities of the global economy creating a whole new systems view (Senge, 1990).

Thus, from the systems perspective, the future of technical training will take two major tracks: (1) the need to train systems thinking skills throughout the workforce and (2) open-systems thinking that demands new ways of connecting the technical training function to the core, often changing organizational processes and identifying systemic technical training content.

1.11.3   Economic Domain

The application of *economic theory* to the future of technical training is at both the strategic financial and training program investment levels. Decisions to invent, buy, and integrate new technology into the organization—including the costs to develop the workforce expertise to operate, maintain, and improve the new technology—will increasingly be critical to the success or failure of organizations.

Economic Forecasting of Technical Training Benefits. To truly become a business partner, technical training must be viewed like any other financial investment. Technical training leaders will need to become more skilled at dealing with the economic impact of technical training. To do this, technical trainers need to lead the way in determining the forecasted performance values, costs, and resulting benefits of technical training (Fitz-Enz, 1990; Swanson and Gradous, 1988; Swanson, 1992).

High-Tech/Low-Tech Technical Training Operations. From an economic perspective, a "one-size-fits-all" approach to the technical training function can no longer meet the requirements of any organization. There have been tremendous developments in high-tech training technology, including the use of simulators, interactive video, and computer-based instruction. These are important developments and, generally, costly alternatives that are not always responsive or cost effective. From an economic perspective, low-tech options, such as structured on-the-job-training (Jacobs,

1992), can be serious rivals in meeting organizational performance requirements.

From the economic perspective, the future of technical training will take two major tracks: (1) the need to strategically align technical training through the financial forecasting of the benefits technical training can add to the strategic options under consideration; and (2) the ability to select the most cost-effective technical training options (e.g., from interactive videos to on-the-job training).

1.12 Conclusion

The history of technical training teaches us that economic, political, and technological changes require concomitant changes in workplace expertise and performance. While reaction to such environmental forces will always influence technical training's content and process, it is evident that the pace and complexity of change is accelerating.

Rather than merely being responsive, technical training needs to pursue more ways to join forces with the instigators and recipients of workplace-related change. Such alliances will reduce the lag time between workplace change and workplace capability to interact with it, and increase the likelihood of wise decisions about how to develop and unleash technical expertise in the workplace.

Bibliography

Argyris, C., "Teaching Smart People How to Learn," *Harvard Business Review,* May–June, 1991, pp. 99–109.

Barlow, M. L., *History of Industrial Education in the United States,* Charles A. Bennett, Peoria, Ill., 1967.

Beatty, A. J., *Corporation Schools,* Public School Publishing, Bloomington, Ill., 1918.

Bennett, C. A., *History of Manual and Industrial Education up to 1870,* The Manual Arts Press, Peoria, Ill., 1926.

Bennett, C. A., *History of Manual and Industrial Education 1870 to 1917,* Charles A. Bennett, Peoria, Ill., 1937.

Boyd, W., *The EMILE of Jean-Jacques Rousseau,* Columbia University, Teachers College, New York, 1962.

Campbell, C. P., "Procedures for Developing and Evaluating Vocational Training Programs," *Journal of Industrial Teacher Education* 21(4):31–42 (1984).

Curtis, S. J., and M. E. A. Boultwood, *A Short History of Educational Ideas,* University Tutorial Press, London, 1966.

Davidson, T., *A History of Education,* Charles Scribner's Sons, New York, 1900.

Davis, E. G., "Education in Industry: A Historical Overview," *Education Canada,* Spring 1978, pp. 40–46.

Davis, L. E., and J. C. Taylor, (eds.), *The Design of Jobs.* Penguin, Baltimore, 1972.

Deming, W. E., *The New Economics for Industry, Government, Education,* Massachusetts Institute of Technology, Cambridge, Mass., 1993.

Dooley, C. R., *The Training Within Industry Report 1940–1945,* War Manpower Commission Bureau of Training, Training Within Industry Service, Washington: D.C., 1945.

Ebenstein, W., *Great Political Thinkers: Plato to the Present,* Dryden Press, Hinsdale, Ill., 1969.

Evans, R., *History of the National Association of Industrial and Technical Teacher Educators 1937–1987,* American Technical Publishers, Homewood, Ill., 1987.

Finch, J. K., *The Story of Engineering,* Doubleday, Garden City, N.Y., 1960.

Fitz-Enz, J., *Human Value Management,* Jossey-Bass, San Francisco, 1990.

Freeman, R. B., *Labor Economics,* 2d ed., Prentice-Hall, Englewood Cliffs, N. J., 1979.

Gagne, R. M., "Military Training and Principles of Learning," *American Psychologist* **17**:83–91 (1962).

Jacobs, R. L., "Structured On-the-Job-Training," in Stolovitch and Keeps (eds.), *Handbook of Human Performance Technology,* Jossey-Bass, San Francisco, 1992, pp. 499–512.

Johnston, W., and A. Packer, *Workforce 2000—Work and Workers in the 21st Century,* Hudson Institute, Indianapolis, Ind., 1987.

Lazonick, W., "Organizational Capabilities in American Industry: The Rise and Decline of Managerial Capitalism," in H. G. Gospel (ed.), *Industrial Training and Technological Innovation,* Routledge, London, 1991, pp. 213–234.

MIT Commission on Industrial Productivity, *Made in America: Regaining the Productive Edge,* MIT Press, Cambridge, Mass., 1989.

McLean, G. F., and P. J. Aspell, *Readings in Ancient Western Philosophy,* Appleton-Century-Crofts, New York, 1970.

McConnell, J. H., and F. J. Setaro, "Computer-Related Training," in R. L. Craig (ed.), *Training and Development Handbook,* 2d ed., 1976, pp. 28-1–28-12.

McCord, B., "Job Instruction," in R. L. Craig (ed.), *Training and Development Handbook,* 2d ed., 1976, pp. 32-3–32-24.

Monroe, P., *A Brief Course in the History of Education,* Macmillan, New York, 1929.

Moore, E. C., *The Story of Instruction: The Beginnings,* Macmillan, New York, 1936.

National Center on Education and the Economy, *America's Choice: High Skills or Low Wages,* The Report of the Commission on the Skills of the American Workforce, Rochester, N.Y., 1990.

Pestalozzi, J. H., *How Gertrude Teaches Her Children,* L. E. Holland and F. C. Tucker, trans., C. W. Bardeen, 1898.

Scott, J. F., *Historical Essays on Apprenticeship and Vocational Education,* Ann Arbor Press, Ann Arbor, Mich., 1914.

Senge, P., *The Fifth Discipline: The Art and Practice of the Learning Organization,* Doubleday, New York, 1990.

Seybolt, R. F., *Apprenticeship and Apprenticeship Education in Colonial New England and New York,* Columbia University, Teachers College, New York, 1917.

Steinmetz, C. S., "The History of Training," in R. L. Craig (ed.), *Training and Development Handbook,* 2d ed., 1976, pp. 1-3–1-14.

Swanson, R. A., *Analysis for Improving Performance: Tools for Diagnosing Organizations and Documenting Workplace Expertise*, Berrett-Koehler, San Francisco, 1994.

Swanson, R. A., "Demonstrating Financial Benefits to Clients," in H. Stolovitch and E. Keeps (eds.), *Handbook of Performance Technology*, Jossey-Bass, San Francisco, 1992, pp. 602–618.

Swanson, R. A., "Industrial Training," in H. E. Mitzel (ed.), *Encyclopedia of Educational Research*, Macmillan, New York, 1982, pp. 864–870.

Swanson, R. A., "Scientific Management Is a Sunday School Picnic Compared to Reengineering," *Human Resource Development Quarterly*, 4(3):219–221 (1993).

Swanson, R. A., and D. B. Gradous, *Forecasting Financial Benefits of Human Resource Development*, Jossey-Bass, San Francisco, 1988.

Swanson, R. A., and G. R. Sisson, "Training Technology: A Hands-on Course for Trainers," *Training and Development Journal* 34(1):66–68 (1980).

Taylor, F. W., *The Principles of Scientific Management*, Harpers, New York, 1912.

Torraco, R. J., *A Critical Examination of the Theoretical Basis of Work Analysis*, University of Minnesota, Human Resource Development Research Center, St. Paul, 1994.

U.S. Civil Service Commission, Bureau of Training, *Application of a Systems Approach to Training: A Case Study*, Training Systems and Technology Series, No. 11, Washington, D.C., 1969.

Watkins, K., and Marsick, *Sculpting the Learning Organization*, Jossey-Bass, San Francisco, 1993.

William T. Grant Foundation Commission, *The Forgotten Half: Pathways to Success for America's Youth and Young Families*, The Final Report, William T. Grant Foundation Commission on Work, Family, and Citizenship, Washington, D.C., 1988.

Zuboff, S., *In the Age of the Smart Machine*, Basic Books, New York, 1988.

2

Managing the Technical Training Function

Anthony Nathan

Dave Santi

Bill Chisholm

Anthony Nathan is President of Anthene Consulting International, located at Mississauga, Ontario, Canada. Tony's specializations include the strategic planning, start-up, management, auditing, and improvement of training, performance improvement, and organization development functions. Tony has authored numerous articles and presented at many professional conferences on training function management and other organizational effectiveness issues. He is or was a member of the National Society of Performance and Instruction, Ontario Society for Training and Development, Singapore Training and Development Association, and American Society for Training and Development.

David Santi manages the technical training department at Dofasco Steel Inc., located at Hamilton, Ontario, Canada. David has been recognized as an innovator in the development of unique apprenticeship/technician programs to meet future workforce needs in Ontario. He has also designed new multiskilling and trade assist programs that are linked to pay for competency. He has worked extensively with the Hamilton Ontario Ministry of Skills Development and Mohawk Community College. He is a member of the National Society for Performance and Instruction, Ontario Society for Training and Development,

Society for Maintenance and Reliability Professionals, and Society for Automotive Engineers.

William T. Chisholm *is the Manager of Hot Mill Operations at Dofasco Steel Inc., located at Hamilton, Ontario, Canada. Bill has used his strategic planning and change management skills in the start-up of several new departments, including the technical training department at Dofasco. He has presented at professional conferences and conducted seminars on a diverse range of topics, including statistical process control and human resource strategies. BIll has also presented material on Innovative Human Resource Strategies to the Ontario Premiers Council for Economic Renewal through Training and Education. He is a member of the American Iron and Steel Society and the Ontario Society for Training and Development.*

2.1   Introduction

The *technical training function* (TTF) is a key pillar of an exceptional technical learning system and learning organization. The TTF provides the vision, leadership, coordination, guidance, infrastructure, capabilities, support, and performance management upon which the organization depends for optimal functioning.

This chapter presents a conceptual framework of the critical elements which impact the work and effectiveness of a TTF. The chapter focuses on the following 16 macro ("big picture") or holistic elements:

1. Operating appropriately
2. Focusing on needs
3. Learning from the best
4. Developing a strategic plan
5. Developing and communicating a policy
6. Clarifying the accountabilities and roles of the TTF team
7. Understanding the roles, attributes, and selection of the TTF manager
8. Clarifying the accountabilities and roles of stakeholders and building partnerships
9. Designing an organizational structure
10. Educating and communicating continuously
11. Applying project management techniques
12. Executing the plan
13. Evaluating the TTF's effectiveness

This chapter describes models, issues, and "how to" guidelines for each element. Our intent is to provide ideas for helping the TTF's manager, team members, and key stakeholders to design, build, manage, audit, and continuously improve the training function.

Those involved with a TTF need to remember several important issues which impact their leadership responsibilities in the technical training functions:

1. The demands on the technical training community are intense. Almost every facet of corporate life feels pressure to compress cycle time, improve cost control, and improve quality—all simultaneously! For example, the technical training function must work in close relationship with the management team to focus on improving all aspects of new products and services. Their focus has to be on new product and service success and improvement of market share. However, there are other urgent needs.

2. The technical training manager must also provide technical retraining for those whose skills have atrophied. The image of the employee and his/her confidence is critical to success. Frequently, the retraining will require the cooperation of human resource management as well. This aspect is usually critical to a retraining program.

3. In many businesses the United States leads the world. In others, slowness to change is still a problem. For example, offshore competition has forced a dramatic reduction in new-product cycle time. For most U.S. firms, the days of a 3- to 4-year new-product development cycle are or have evaporated because global competition has become intense. In another example, some of the more innovative Japanese auto firms have reduced the new-car start-of-design to finished-product cycle to 30 to 36 months. Other manufacturers lag behind. The expertise of the entire technical workforce influences enormously the key success standards noted in number 1.

2.2 Operating Appropriately

The technical training function (TTF) operates appropriately when its team members are able to build a track record of meaningful results for its clients. This means the TTF is effective in resolving priority problems, realizing opportunities, and proactively supporting other changes related to improving present and future employee and organizational performance. To do so, team members must first understand and acknowledge the issues which impact their ability to operate appropriately. Some of these issues are summarized in the following.

Technical training may solve employee performance problems or take advantage of opportunities caused primarily by technical competency gaps. It identifies, develops, and reinforces the technical competencies which employees require to perform current or future jobs optimally.

Many performance problems or opportunities, however, do not require a training solution. They are usually multicausal or multifaceted, composed of many elements which impact job performance besides competencies. For example, training cannot solve problems caused by poorly designed jobs, faulty systems, or obsolete equipment. Nontraining solutions such as job design, systems engineering, or new technology interventions may be more appropriate in these cases. A holistic systems approach, as depicted in Figure 2-1, is often useful in analyzing and intervening in the performance system.

Moreover, strategic, systemic, and integrated approaches are often required to solve complex organizational problems or capitalize on opportunities (where performance elements are interrelated). The TTF needs to work on improving all the individual elements to accomplish meaningful, substantial, and long-lasting performance results.

Problems are compounded if clients arbitrarily decide to mandate training programs without consulting the TTF team. This is a dilemma for team members: do they abet training decisions which may not be in the organization's best interests? Or do they try to influence the clients to take more appropriate approaches?

To operate appropriately, the TTF team should consider the following guidelines.

- Develop clear expectations with all clients and other stakeholders that the TTF not only delivers technical training, but also is in the business of improving the performance of employees, business units, and the larger organization.

- Conduct a front-end analysis before proposing or agreeing to a training solution. It will help the client to focus on the priority performance problems or opportunities; specify the desired results; determine whether training is the only solution, part of the solution, or not the solution at all; and link solutions to business needs. The analysis should not be a time-consuming event, but it must have active participation from the business unit, with the TTF team facilitating the process.

- The TTF team should help clients consider nontraining solutions if these are more likely to yield value-added results and be cost effective.

- Strive to operate in the workplace, not just in the classroom, and have more than a "single-solution" tool kit (i.e., technical training only). Team members should evolve into performance improvement consultants who can guide, educate, and support client groups on:

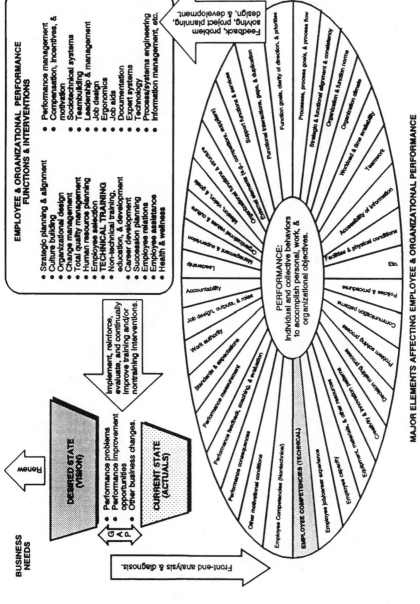

Figure 2-1. Analyzing and intervening in the employee and organizational performance system.

53

integrating technical training activities within an employee performance strategy and system

identifying and analyzing performance problems and opportunities

applying appropriate training and nontraining methods to effectively address these problems and opportunities, and support other business changes

The TTF manager should help the team develop performance consulting capabilities. For example, the manager could assess each team member's ability to handle the various performance problems and opportunities faced by clients, including those that are complex and unfamiliar, and provide the means for team members to learn and apply performance technology and consulting techniques.

2.3 Focusing on Needs

The TTF team must learn about the larger organization in which it operates. It must also work with clients to identify, focus on, and diagnose the macro needs of the larger organization and business units, link individual needs to these macro needs, and determine effective responses for addressing priority needs.

2.3.1 Understand
the Organizational Context

The TTF team must learn about the following aspects of the larger organization, as well as each business unit:

What are the organizational goals, business objectives, strategic plans, and action plans? What major changes are anticipated in the short and long term?

What products or services do the clients produce? What technologies do they use to do this?

What is the organization structure? Who are the decision makers? What are the political realities? What are the microcultures and policies of each client business unit?

How are budgets approved? What's the financial health of the larger organization?

What core competencies do employees already have? What core competencies do they need currently or in the future?

What is the history of technical training in the organization?

Who are the organization's main customers? What are the organization's marketing plans? What are competitors doing?

What industry issues or regulations affect technical training?

While this information is especially critical for a new TTF team, it is also prudent for existing teams to review these items periodically. With this information, the team can serve clients more effectively because it will be better able to

Customize technical learning outputs to each client's unique needs

Provide technical learning outputs which support the strategic directions of the business unit, link business unit needs to organizational needs, and respond to organizational changes in a timely and proactive manner

Help employees see how individual technical learning activities relate to organizational goals

Deal with culture, politics, hidden agendas, and other organizational realities

Build working relationships with clients

Some TTF teams find it difficult to learn about organizational goals, strategic plans, and needs because these are not explicitly defined and communicated. To get access to such information, the team ideally should participate in the larger organization's strategic planning sessions. However, the degree of participation by a TTF team in strategic planning varies among organizations; it may depend on the team's own abilities, as well on as the larger organization's structure and the way it manages its business. A team that is not involved in strategic planning could use the following approaches as steps to getting invited:

- Establish a technical training steering committee which reflects the different divisions, levels, and needs of the organization.

- Enroll senior managers to help develop the TTF's strategic directions.

- Be visible to senior management, e.g., by organizing meetings on training initiatives and results.

- Participate in non-training-related committees (e.g., technology, quality, or human resources).

The TTF manager can also consider additional strategies to learn about the larger organization and business units:

- Invite senior managers and business unit managers to brief the TTF team on organizational and business unit needs.

- Immerse the team in business unit operations and task forces (with the relevant manager's consent of course). Team members would benefit from interacting with line staff, observing job performance, and reviewing line documentation.

- Ensure that at least a few TTF team members have workplace experience. If the existing trainers don't have such experience, give them project work or short-term assignments in business units. Also, rotate the trainers between jobs in the TTF and business units.

- Build up a network of personal contacts and resource people throughout the organization.

2.3.2 Perform a Macro Needs Analysis

The TTF team should begin by working with senior managers and the corporate planning function to assess macro needs at the larger organizational level. The team can then work with client groups to assess their macro needs at the business-unit level and to help them link these needs to organizational needs. Both levels of macro needs will provide the basis for prioritizing the assessment of micro needs at the individual employee level and linking these micro needs to the larger context (see Figure 2-2).

The following is one method for implementing a macro needs analysis which ties training to organizational needs:

- The TTF team designs a macro needs analysis instrument similar to Table 2-1. The columns of this table can be modified to include other factors such as anticipated changes, nontraining interventions, dollar costs, opportunities, time frames, performance outputs, etc.

- The team works with each larger organizational or business unit client to complete the columns of the macro analysis table in sequence, starting with goals. Lists are made in each column for an item in the preceding column, and priorities are established.

- The process outcome is that the client has helped to define

  goals which impact business results

  objectives which translate these goals into measurable terms

  performance changes (human and/or nonhuman) required for supporting these objectives

  technical learning solutions required for enabling employee performance changes

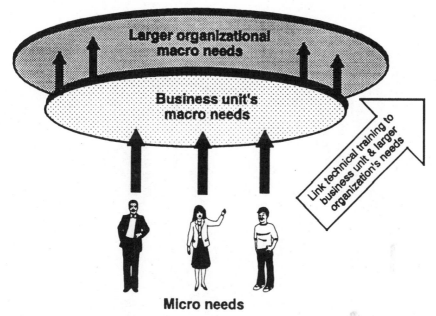

Figure 2-2. Link training to higher-level needs.

constraints to implementing the learning solutions

Thus, the clients themselves have identified the links among goals (business needs), performance changes (performance needs), and technical training (learning needs).

In performing a macro needs analysis, the TTF team should remember the following.

■ Linking technical training to organizational goals and objectives is an ongoing process. These linkages must be continually reevaluated and modified as the needs change.

■ This initial stage should be kept simple to build a comfort level and relationship with the clients. Do not overwhelm them with complicated training concepts and methodologies.

■ Once the macro analysis is completed, a project plan for analyzing any high-priority micro needs should be defined.

■ If a client chooses not to implement any of the recommended technical training solutions, alternative solutions for achieving their business objectives should be discussed.

Table 2-1. Macro Needs Analysis

A. Goals	B. Objectives	C. Performance change (human/organization)	D. Technical training	E. Constraints
Increase production output	Increase 5% per quarter	Equipment reliability will improve	Process training	Lack of experienced technical experts
			Functional training	New technology has glitches
		Employees will decrease troubleshooting time	Troubleshooting training	
Install UNIX Network	Network up by June 31	Employees will use UNIX applications	UNIX training	Lack of in-house support system
Reduce downtime	Reduce 10% by Dec. 31	Equipment reliability will improve	Reliability-Centered Maintenance (RCM) training	$3 million to design and implement RCM training
		Employees will use Total Productive Maintenance (TPM) practices	TPM training	$7 million and other resources to develop TPM intervention
Reduce defective products	Reduce 50% by Dec. 31	Employees will apply process knowledge on the job	Process training courses	$1 million to develop and implement training
		Employees will use expert system to determine source of defects	Expert systems computer training	Expert system package must be selected and knowledge engineer developed

2.4 Learning from the Best

An exceptional TTF team learns from other human resource development (HRD) functions with excellent track records by striving to learn about, measure up to, and even surpass their capabilities, standards, and practices. However, a team becomes insular if it benchmarks against HRD functions only within its industry. It should visit organizations outside its industry— even outside its country—to identify a larger pool of models. For example, the TTF team of a steel manufacturing company could study the best models of technical training in the can manufacturing, pharmaceutical, telecommunication, and/or banking sectors in the United States, Canada, Japan, Singapore, and/or Germany. This will enable team members to conceive new ideas for their own TTF's mission, vision, and practices.

As a facilitator of learning, the TTF team should be open to learning from leading-edge models, even those from almost opposite business environments. Team members should have a good understanding, before visiting other organizations, of their own organizational needs and of a method for studying the benchmark organizations. They should gather information about the technical training vision, standards, practices, operations, and capabilities in these organizations and share information willingly with their counterparts.

It's also valuable to creatively enroll key stakeholders to the study team. This provides the TTF team with opportunities for demonstrating to stakeholders just what top-notch TTFs and learning systems look like as well as for manifesting the gap between where their TTF actually is and where it could be.

Besides study visits, other ways to gather information on technical training models include networking at conferences and workshops, and reading professional journals and books.

Finally, an important issue in learning from benchmarks is this: team members must be able to quickly adapt, enhance, and apply the lessons learned to their organizations, as well as sustain and continuously improve them. Exceptional TTFs are successful through extraordinary efforts, not by ordinary efforts.

2.5 Developing a Strategic Plan

Strategic planning enables the TTF team and key stakeholders to visualize the TTF's future and develop the necessary strategies to realize that future. It is a critical first step in starting up or transforming a TTF because it can help the team control and manage its "destiny" more proactively. By clarifying the ends and means, a strategic plan guides the team members and stakeholders as they make day-to-day decisions which impact the nature and direction of the TTF. It also helps the team members and/or stakeholders to understand and focus on technical training and its new directions; develop expectations for success; become prepared, inspired, and committed to participating in these directions and providing necessary resources; and recognize and break away from past values, practices, and results that are no longer acceptable for the future.

The seven major process stages of strategic planning are outlined in Figure 2-3.

2.5.1 Stage 1:
Examine Core Values

Core values are a set of deeply held beliefs which govern, guide, and influence decisions and behaviors; the TTF's strategic directions must be based on these values. To identify core values, the TTF team members should first identify their own values, stakeholders' values, and organizational culture. Second, the team members should examine how these values affect the management of the technical learning system in the organization. Third, they should educate all stakeholders about the core values and their implications accordingly and should, where possible, obtain genuine consensus on which values support the learning system and which values impede it. Fourth, the team should set the core values down in a statement. Examples of a core value statement for a TTF team are the following.

We believe development of technical competencies is critical to performance.

We believe in partnerships with our stakeholders.

We value self-sufficiency for technical learning.

2.5.2 Stage 2:
Develop a Mission

A mission should be developed to define the TTF's purpose and what it hopes to accomplish in terms of meeting client needs and strategic objectives. The mission should be set down in a statement that is clear and achievable, and addresses three questions:

What is the main purpose or function of the TTF?

For whom does the TTF perform this function?

How does it go about performing this function?

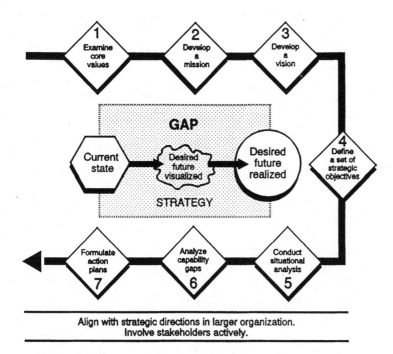

Figure 2-3. Stages of Strategic Planning.

Figure 2-4 provides two examples of mission statements which illustrate the importance of defining the TTF's purpose appropriately. In the first example, the TTF team views itself in the "training business." Its goal is to provide product-training programs only. This narrow view may prevent it from adapting to changing client needs.

In the second example, the TTF team is focused on meeting client needs related to employee competence, experience, growth, and performance. Instead of being limited to traditional training solutions, this team is flexible enough to use other options (e.g., developing job aids and supporting technological changes) to meet changing needs. This broader perspective thus allows the TTF to adapt and remain relevant to its clients.

2.5.3 Stage 3:
Develop a Vision

A vision is a clear picture of an end-state or future for the TTF that is ideal, desired, attainable, and fulfills its mission. As with the mission, a vision should be set down in a statement. Figure 2-5 shows two examples of vision

---

EXAMPLE 1:   MISSION STATEMENT THAT IS PRODUCT-ORIENTED

The mission of the technical training function is to provide timely and relevant technical training to operations and maintenance employees which ensure their readiness to meet strategic business needs and result in improved profitability, quality, and productivity.

EXAMPLE 2:   MISSION STATEMENT THAT IS CLIENT-ORIENTED

The mission of the technical training function is to guide and assist the operations and maintenance business units in improving the technical competence, experience, performance, and growth of their employees.

To accomplish this, we will work with our business unit clients to develop internal capabilities for:

- identifying, creating, developing (through planned learning processes), transferring, and reinforcing the technical competencies and experiences which employees require to perform current or future jobs and to grow on the job

- establishing an integrated system of strategies, processes, and policies to facilitate changes in employee thinking, behavior, and performance relating to technological processes.

We intend to respond to client needs, focusing on areas which will yield improved profitability, quality, and productivity. We will use cost-effective techniques to provide high-quality, timely, and relevant programs and services with measurable results.

Figure 2-4. Sample mission statements for technical training function.

statements at different levels. The TTF vision is linked to the learning systems vision, which is a higher-level vision. The TTF vision should also be aligned with the higher-level visions of the business units and organization.

The TTF team should consider the following process guidelines for developing a vision.

- Review the current state of the TTF in terms of internal clients, needs satisfied, driving forces, values, mission, activities, products, services, achievements, lost opportunities, etc.

- Visualize the future state of the TTF. First, anticipate its future clients and their needs. Second, to meet these future needs, decide what

EXCERPT FROM VISION FOR TECHNICAL TRAINING
FUNCTION (LEVEL 1)

By 1998, the technical training function team has established effective partnerships with its business unit stakeholders. Stakeholders perceive our team members as effective in supporting their business unit goals. They work closely with our training specialists, value technical learning as a competitive requirement, and participate in and provide resources for learning activities.

We provide consulting services to help each business unit establish an optimal learning environment and capabilities for continually creating, acquiring, transferring, applying, and reinforcing the technical competencies and experiences in order to support business performance and changes.

We develop a network of technical training facilitators in each business unit. We help them establish, coordinate, develop, and implement technical learning systems and initiatives in their business units. Specifically, we work with them in:

- Assessing technical learning, job performance, and change needs
- Developing a technical learning plan for addressing these needs
- Determining job profiles and performance standards
- Documenting job procedures, processes, and other standard work information
- Developing and implementing technical learning programs, and certifying employees
- Facilitating the application of the newly learned competencies on the job
- Evaluating the impact of technical learning initiatives
- Integrating technical learning initiatives with other learning and organizational development interventions

EXCERPT FROM VISION FOR LEARNING SYSTEMS (LEVEL 2)

By 1999, all employees clearly understand and continually assess their job roles, functions, tasks, performance standards, and competencies. They use their individual learning plans as a schedule for learning new competencies in a coordinated and timely manner. An effective competency-based learning system helps to identify, develop, and reinforce the key process, functional, and troubleshooting competencies which employees need to perform and grow while on the present job. Employees are certified to perform a job function or task only if they can demonstrate the required competence.

Figure 2-5. Sample vision statements.

changes are required of the TTF in terms of values, mission, activities, products, services, results, growth possibilities, etc.

- Identify the gap between the current state of the TTF and its future state. This will clarify the need for change and motivate the development of a vision statement.

- Analyze and compose the various bits of information into a vision statement which describes the TTF's desired future. The vision should:

  be aligned with the TTF's mission as well as with the corporate HRD function, business unit, and organization's strategic directions

  be centered on meeting client needs

  be challenging, yet achievable and practical

  be inspiring and motivating

  be simple, precise, and clear

Upon completion of its vision, the team can formulate the remainder of the strategic and action plans to provide the means for taking the TTF from its present state to its desired future.

2.5.4 Stage 4: Define a Set of Strategic Objectives

The TTF team must define strategic objectives which translate the vision into specific and measurable terms; the sum of these objectives should realize the vision. An example of a strategic objective is "develop at least four competent technical training facilitators in each business unit by 1998."

The team also identifies the key strategies for achieving each objective. An example is "develop and establish a Technical Trainer Development Unit by 1995."

2.5.5 Stage 5: Conduct a Situational Analysis

A situational analysis determines the TTF's ability to accomplish the vision. In this analysis, team members examine internal and external factors which may help or hinder accomplishment of their vision. The internal factors include the TTF's strengths and weaknesses. An example of a strength may be that the team is client-oriented. A weakness may be that the team does not use long-term approaches or best practices in its work.

The external factors include opportunities and threats (in the larger organization and outside) to implementing the vision. An example of an opportunity is pending legislation (e.g., transportation of dangerous goods and hazardous waste) that may create technical training needs. A threat may be the potential transfer of a key champion from an important business unit.

The team then determines specific actions for reinforcing strengths, eliminating weaknesses, seizing opportunities, and overcoming threats. An outcome of this step is that the team has proactively considered preventive actions to preclude potential problems from occurring as well as contingency actions to sustain the strategic plan if such problems do occur.

2.5.6 Stage 6:
Analyze Capability Gaps

The team compares the TTF vision (ideal future) against the results of the situational analysis (TTF's *ability* to accomplish that future). This indicates the relative ease or difficulty with which the TTF should be able to attain the vision. If the vision is not challenging enough or not attainable, it must be modified accordingly. This ensures that the vision is a realistic ideal.

2.5.7 Stage 7:
Formulate Action Plans

These action plans identify the specific actions and tactics which are required to implement each strategic objective, along with the expected results and the deadlines (within a short-term period) for achieving them. Examples include "install four computer workstations by June 30, 1995" and "implement 10 develop-the-trainer programs by the third quarter."

The TTF team then integrates the action plans into its budget, determines priorities between them, and prepares for implementation. During implementation, the team should apply project planning techniques to organize each action item in these action plans as an individual project.

2.5.8 Guidelines

The TTF team should consider the following guidelines for developing and implementing a strategic plan:

- Don't rush. This is important advice for teams which tend to be reactive and survival-oriented. It takes time to develop a good vision. And, depending on the nature of the vision, it typically takes three to five years for a TTF team to fully implement its strategic plan and realize its vision.

- Link the TTF's directions to the strategic directions and needs of the corporate HRD function, client business units, and larger organization.

Before developing its own strategic directions, the team must learn about these higher-level needs, even if they are unwritten.

- Involve the key stakeholders in the development of the TTF's strategic directions. Get approval of those who must allocate the resources necessary to implement the strategic plan. People should commit to and help implement the strategic plan if they accept the rationale for it, believe that it will benefit them, understand how it will work, and perceive a meaningful effort being made.

- Ensure that three conditions are present which increase the TTF's propensity to change: there is a clear perception of the external pressures which threaten the TTF's survival; the team and key stakeholders are very dissatisfied with the existing internal and external situation; and there are clear and compelling strategic directions as an alternative.

- Ensure that the TTF vision and strategic plan are used on an ongoing basis to drive all activities, and not merely bronze-plated for the office walls or, worse, buried in a filing cabinet. Periodically review and update these directions.

2.6 Developing and Communicating a Technical Training Policy

A technical training policy consists of general statements (relating to aims and desired actions) which clarify the larger organization's position on technical training. These statements define the parameters used to guide decisions and actions pertaining to technical training.

A clear and explicit policy can support the TTF's strategic plan and activities by

- Establishing and legitimizing the TTF's accountabilities and roles in facilitating, implementing, and coordinating the technical learning system and activities

- Defining and assigning accountabilities and roles to key stakeholders in the learning system and activities

- Clarifying the technical training plans and systems, and providing guidelines on how to accomplish, optimize, and use these

- Providing unity of purpose with consistent guidelines on identifying, planning, implementing, following up, and auditing technical training activities and practices

- Providing guidelines for reducing duplication and fragmentation

A technical training policy document usually consists of a number of components. See Figure 2-6, "Overall Technical Training Policy," for an example of a policy component. Other components of this policy document could include

- Mission, goals, scope, and importance of technical training
- Elements of an effective technical learning system
- Accountabilities and roles of

  senior management
  technical training steering committee
  technical training function
  managers and supervisors
  business unit trainers
- Strategic and action plans for technical training
- Analysis of technical learning needs
- Types and sources of technical training activities
- Selection of employees for internal and external technical training activities
- Tuition aid for external training activities
- Employee availability for technical training activities
- Application of the new learning on the job
- Measurement and evaluation of technical training activities
- Pay for competencies and performance
- Investing, costing, and budgeting for technical training
- Learning center, facilities, and equipment
- Technical training information system
- Relationship to the corporate HRD function and other business functions

In developing and implementing a technical training policy, the TTF manager should ensure that it is

- Developed by the TTF team in collaboration with business unit staff, and approved by senior managers
- Congruent with the corporate HRD policies, as well as with the larger organization's strategic directions and policies
- Consistent with the beliefs and values of key stakeholders
- Written clearly and concisely as a policy document, not confused with procedures or standards

XYZ Pharmaceuticals recognizes that technical training is a strategic investment required to provide our company with a sustainable competitive edge for the future. Technical training activities give us the ability to learn more effectively and efficiently than our competitors. Technical training is therefore a key element to expanding the performance potential of employees, our most important resource, and the company.

- The technical learning system must be derived from and remain focused on supporting our corporate, business unit, and overall HRD strategic and action plans. It should promote technical training that is results-oriented, just in time, and continuous. All training should focus on providing learning to enhance competence, job performance, and individual growth relevant to XYZ's needs.

- Employees should be offered opportunities, throughout their careers, to develop core and other relevant technical competencies and attain the highest competence requirements. This is needed to help them perform their jobs to specified standards, perform new tasks or jobs, adapt effectively to change, as well as to achieve the best possible individual effectiveness and growth. The time and effort that employees devote to approved learning activities is thus an appropriate use of their services.

- All employees have the right to receive technical training opportunities, regardless of seniority, sex, race, religion, origin, or handicap. Since self-motivation impacts training effectiveness, employees also have an obligation to take active steps to further their self-development.

- Managers and supervisors are primarily accountable for ensuring that their employees are equipped to perform jobs in the most competent, effective, and efficient manner possible. They are, therefore, responsible for the following.

  Identifying what training is needed, in collaboration with employees.

  Providing their employees with comprehensive and continuous technical learning opportunities.

  Providing employees with job experiences and feedback aimed at reinforcing their newly learned skills.

  In fulfilling these responsibilities, managers and supervisors should work cooperatively with the Technical Training Function to ensure that technical training is used optimally and appropriately throughout XYZ.

Figure 2-6. Overall technical training policy.

- Senior managers are responsible for emphasizing the importance of learning and for facilitating active participation in all training activities. They should also champion an organizational environment where employees can continually expand their competencies through training.

- The Technical Training Function team is accountable for establishing an optimal, structured, and coordinated approach to technical training at the corporate and business unit levels. It is, therefore, responsible for the following.

  Consulting and working with the business units in planning, developing, implementing, reinforcing, and auditing technical training in XYZ.

  Assisting managers, supervisors, and employees in performing their technical training responsibilities. Developing and administering core or generic technical training activities for use throughout the company.

- At XYZ, we will focus on the following aspects of the technical learning system.

  Systematically analyzing business needs and job performance to identify technical learning needs

  Designing high-quality technical training activities that emphasize measurable objectives for meeting these needs

  Applying criteria for selecting the right employees to attend the right training activities at the right time

  Implementing technical training activities using the most effective internal and/or external resources

  Ensuring that employees use the newly learned competencies on the job

  Evaluating results in terms of learning, job performance improvements, individual growth, and business outcomes

Figure 2-6. (*Continued*)

- Realistic, practical, and implementable
- Communicated to, understood, and accepted by all key stakeholders
- Accessible to end users in the workplace
- Maintained in the workplace and periodically updated

Procedures and standards should be developed next. A procedure consists of a series of specific steps that clarify *how* to implement a policy during day-to-day operations. It also describes details about what the senior managers, TTF team members, and business unit managers and employees are expected to do or not do. A standard, whether dealing with process or outcome, specifies a desired level of *quality* or results for actions pertaining to the technical learning system.

2.7 Clarifying the Accountabilities and Roles of the TTF Team

The TTF team should collaboratively define, obtain commitment for, and implement its accountabilities and roles. The TTF will be able to operate more effectively if its stakeholders clearly understand and support its responsibilities, instead of overlapping or contradicting them.

2.7.1 Accountabilities

Being accountable means the TTF team will answer for the results of its actions or inactions pertaining to its technical training responsibilities. The team needs to determine for what it is accountable. For example, the team could be accountable for planning, organizing, staffing, implementing, coordinating, reinforcing, auditing, and continually improving the technical learning systems and activities, as well as for ensuring that these are understood, optimal, and consistent throughout the organization. The team could also be accountable for helping each business unit achieve its goals and fulfill its training responsibilities.

Senior management should specify to whom or to which organizational area(s) the TTF team is accountable. The team must be delegated the authority or power to take the necessary actions to fulfill its responsibilities. It should be continually audited for achievement of its responsibilities, made to answer for these results, and given meaningful consequences as appropriate.

2.7.2 Roles

A TTF team should be able to coordinate, manage, facilitate, or perform all or a combination of the following roles.

- Provide overall leadership, guidance and assistance on technical learning, growth, and performance issues.

- Study the best models of technical training as benchmarks for its larger organization.

- Facilitate the development and implementation of a vision, strategic plans, and action plans for technical training, and link these to the corporate HRD business unit and larger organizational goals.

- Market and communicate the technical training vision, viewpoints, services, and deliverables to all stakeholders.

- Define and align the philosophies, systems, infrastructures, work environment, processes, policies, procedures, standards, and other enabling factors for facilitating and sustaining technical training.

- Develop, coordinate, and/or manage budgets and financial issues related to technical training.

- Select, acquire, allocate, manage, develop, and evaluate the internal and external resources required for implementing training plans, and facilitate team building of resources where appropriate.

- Support and learn from external consultants.

- Manage the learning center, facilities, and equipment.

- Determine learning needs at the organizational, business unit, team, job, and/or individual employee levels.

- Analyze jobs to determine task components, performance standards, and competencies.

- Develop a technical learning plan, and coordinate its implementation and follow-up.

- Design and develop technical training curricula, programs, services, job aids, and other activities.

- Instruct in and facilitate planned learning activities.

- Facilitate the transfer of learning to the job.

- Monitor, evaluate, and communicate the impact of technical training activities on employee and business unit performance, and the effectiveness of the TTF in facilitating these outcomes.

- Establish and maintain a training records and information system.

- Represent the larger organization in relations with external agencies pertaining to technical training issues.

2.8 Understanding the Roles, Attributes and Selection of the TTF Manager

The TTF manager is the organizational leader who must focus, motivate, and empower the TTF team, its stakeholders, and the organization toward realizing the technical learning vision. In doing this, he or she can steer the organization to either excellence or mediocrity in technical training. This is because the paradigms, aspirations, aptitude, competence, experience, and health of its manager often profoundly affect all other elements which impact the TTF's effectiveness. Therefore, the HRD vice president and other senior managers cannot afford to condone hiring or retaining a TTF manager who is mediocre or incapable.

The TTF manager is accountable for and performs a multifaceted job. He or she should be able to lead, manage, coach, teach, facilitate, support, and/or perform all or a combination of the TTF team's outputs or roles (see Sec. 2.7). The manager of a large TTF usually delegates most job outputs for which he or she is accountable. The manager of a small function with few or no staff may have to produce most or all outputs by him or herself.

In either situation, the TTF manager requires a very broad range of competencies and other attributes for performing the job. Examples of these competencies and other attributes are provided in the following sections; the actual combination of attributes varies according to specific organizational needs.

2.8.1 Competencies

An exceptional TTF manager may require a combination of the following competencies.

Strategic planning, project management, change management, and information systems management competencies. These are needed for planning, organizing, facilitating, following up, and evaluating technical training plans and projects.

Creative problem-solving and cost-benefit analysis competencies, as well as business experience. These are needed for analyzing problems or opportunities, selecting solutions, and developing continuous improvement plans.

Listening, communications, presentation, negotiation, proactive leadership, facilitation, team building, feedback, performance management, motivational, and staff development competencies. These are needed for building relationships, eliciting participation, acquiring resources, as well as managing and developing teams.

HRD and HPT (human performance technology) competencies. These are needed for applying the appropriate technical training and performance improvement systems, processes, and methodologies.

2.8.2 Other Attributes

An exceptional TTF manager may require a combination of the following attributes.

Visionary, conceptual, and "prudent revolutionary" attributes. These are needed for pinpointing where the client organization and TTF are and where they need to go, as well as for overcoming any status quo attitude towards training that some stakeholders may have.

Trustworthiness, a credible reputation, integrity, political savvy, diplomacy, and people-orientation attributes. These are needed for promoting training services, gaining support, building alliances, and inspiring participation.

A results focus, action bias, tolerance for uncertainty and ambiguity, adaptability, creativity, self-confidence, a sense of reality, detail orientation, resourcefulness, initiative, and perseverance attributes. These are needed for accomplishing results.

Intellectual versatility, propensity for learning, moral courage, a willingness to ask for guidance and assistance, and "walk the talk" attributes. These are needed for enabling higher levels of performance and accomplishment.

The HRD vice president or other manager should apply an effective process for selecting the TTF manager. Job performance analysis is a valuable first stage in such a process. This analysis determines the performance outputs, competencies, and other attributes for the TTF manager's job, identifies other performance elements (besides competencies and attributes) which affect the manager's job performance, and links the job performance to business performance. One deliverable of this analysis is a prioritized list of job performance outputs and attribute specifications. The HRD vice president should use the job outputs to describe the job to potential candidates as well as to key stakeholders. The attribute specifications should be used as criteria for selecting the TTF manager.

To conduct a performance analysis, the HRD vice president should apply the following steps:

1. Determine what TTF outputs are required for supporting each critical business unit or organizational goal.

2. Determine what job outputs the TTF manager must produce to support each critical TTF output.

3. Determine what tasks (in terms of performance outputs, quality requirements, and job conditions) the TTF manager must perform correctly to produce the critical job outputs.

4. Determine what competencies and other attributes the TTF manager will require for performing each essential task correctly.

5. Determine what other performance elements (besides attributes) are required for supporting the TTF manager's performance of each essential task.

Geary Rummler provides a performance analysis model (see Chapter 12, *Training and Development Handbook,* Robert L. Craig, ed.) which can be adapted for this purpose. It can be enhanced by incorporating the following models: process analysis, job analysis, task analysis, HRD competencies, and human performance technology. For example, a modified version of DACUM (Developing A Curriculum) can be used to define the TTF manager's job profile from scratch. On the other hand, ASTD's "Models for HRD Practice" provides excellent models, examples, and worksheets which can be easily adapted for identifying job outputs and competencies for the manager and other team members. Chapter 4 of this book provides further information on recruiting and selecting training staff.

The HRD Vice President generally has three options for recruiting a TTF manager: reassign an experienced business unit manager from within the organization, promote an existing staff of an HRD function, or hire a professional training manager from outside. The TTF's credibility could be enhanced if the vice president transfers or promotes a talented and reputable business unit manager to manage it. The new manager must be given appropriate opportunities to learn the training management competencies identified by the job performance analysis. If the vice president recruits externally, he or she should hire a hands-on, results-oriented, and versatile training manager who is willing to be immersed in and learn the organization's core businesses. In any case, the vice president should use the job outputs and specifications as the basis for ongoing management, improvement, and development of the TTF manager's performance.

2.9 Clarifying the Accountabilities and Roles of Stakeholders and Building Partnerships

Stakeholders are people who can impact or will be impacted by the technical learning system. They may include senior managers, business unit managers, supervisors, employees, and/or the union. Getting stakeholders to understand, accept, and perform their training responsibilities is critical to the effectiveness of the technical learning system.

The TTF team should identify the key stakeholders, clarify their accountabilities and roles in managing the technical learning system, and establish partnerships, alliances, and close relationships with them. It is essential to renew existing relationships and build new ones continually throughout the organization. As the key stakeholders change, which they will, quickly learn about and establish relationships with the new players. Do not overrely on any one key sponsor, take any alliance for granted, or assume that the TTF team's current standing within the organization will always continue.

In most organizations, there can be as many as four vital partnerships between the TTF and senior management; business unit managers, supervisors, and employees; unions; and other HRD and business functions.

2.9.1 Senior Management

Senior managers are accountable for ensuring an optimal organizational environment for technical learning and for actively sponsoring the TTF team as it develops this environment.

Solid conviction for technical training must begin at the highest levels. If senior managers lack interest, training will very quickly be deemphasized as an organizational priority. They have the hierarchical power and influence to cascade sponsorship down to their managers. Their demonstrable conviction is therefore necessary—though by itself not sufficient—for supporting the technical learning system, driving training initiatives, and legitimizing the TTF. Figure 2-7 identifies possible roles for senior managers.

The TTF team must continually build senior management conviction for technical training. The following are suggestions for doing this.

- Identify the key senior managers, e.g., decision makers and influencers. Before meeting them, try to learn about their values, thinking styles, communication styles, attitudes toward training, and criteria for evaluating the TTF.

- Meet these key senior managers to develop personal rapport and harness support. Come to each meeting with clear objectives and prepared for any concerns. Then present your ideas with logic, facts, and conviction. In doing so, think like a senior manager: position training as a business tool which can help managers solve their critical problems. Find out their priorities and seek their ideas on using training to improve business results. Explain how the TTF will respond to their concerns in a timely and effective manner.

- Promote the technical training vision, system, and activities to senior managers, highlighting the potential bottom-line impact on the organization. Familiarize them with actual technical training samples, how the process and methodologies will work, how the TTF and clients should cooperate, and what support is needed to ensure results.

- Provide specific activities for senior managers to personally participate in and support training. For example, establish a technical training steering committee or advisory council whose purpose is to support,

Senior management can perform the following roles in the technical learning system.

- Sponsor systematic technical training as a business priority.
- Ensure that senior management's conviction for technical training is clearly understood by all managers, supervisors, and employees, and that sponsorship is cascaded through all organizational levels.
- Participate in the technical training steering committee.
- Review, approve, advise, and sponsor the strategic mission, vision, objectives, plans, policies, initiatives, and priorities of the TTF team; ensure their alignment with organizational goals.
- Champion the TTF team as it coordinates the technical learning system and initiatives.
- Allocate talented people and other resources for implementing technical training plans and initiatives.
- Foster active participation from all managers, supervisors, and employees in technical training initiatives and activities, and hold them accountable for results.
- Observe and participate in technical training activities.
- Evaluate the implementation results of technical training plans, review progress toward long-term objectives, and help to resolve implementation obstacles, if needed.

Figure 2-7. Senior management roles.

advise, and oversee the leadership and management of technical training in the organization. Capitalize on leadership involvement by sensitively advertising it to the larger organization.

- Continually communicate the technical training results to senior managers and survey their satisfaction with training's contribution to their objectives.

2.9.2 Business Unit Managers, Supervisors, and Employees

Business unit staff must be accountable for technical learning results locally. The business unit stands to benefit most from improved learning; ultimately, managers and supervisors are responsible for the job performance of their employees. In addition, they are able to sponsor technical training since they have the power to legitimize and support training activities in their domain.

Supervisors and employees, in particular, directly impact the development and implementation of technical training processes, products, and services. They are well positioned to participate in many training initiatives. After a training program, this group can support the transfer of learning to the job. For example, supervisors can reinforce the newly learned competencies by providing their employees with appropriate job assignments and tracking their performance. Employees are unlikely to use their new learning if they feel their immediate bosses and peers are not committed to improving performance.

Therefore, the business units *must* be involved in technical training. Key managers, supervisors, and employees should help conceive, have ownership over, support, and actively participate in any training which affects their unit. See Figure 2-8 for a list of possible technical training roles for managers and supervisors.

2.9.3   Clarify Roles of TTF and Business Units

Problems can occur if the business units' roles (pertaining to technical training in its area) are not clear in relation to the TTF's roles. For example, a TTF may attempt to control technical training activities in the business unit or do everything independently, and involve the business unit in only

---

Business unit managers and supervisors can perform the following roles in the technical training system.

- Sponsor technical training in their area, and ensure that their employees clearly understand their commitment and participate actively in all training activities.

- Analyze problems relating to the technical performance and growth of employees, and identify their learning needs.

- Plan, support, monitor, reinforce, and evaluate the ongoing technical training of their employees.

- Allocate all resources required for implementing training plans and initiatives.

- Develop, support, and maintain competent internal trainers in their business unit.

- Support and participate in corporate technical training activities.

Figure 2-8.   Business unit manager and supervisor roles.

a secondary, perfunctory, or cosmetic manner. At the other extreme, an HRD function may be indifferent to its technical training responsibilities, relinquishing these totally to business units.

An HRD function team that operates in either way is sabotaging itself into obsolescence. The team's future is tied to its clients; it cannot operate optimally without the cooperation of business unit staff at all levels. The team does not usually have the decision-making authority or influence to implement technical training activities in the business units. The latter's managers need to prepare the groundwork for necessary alliances between the TTF team members and the business unit supervisors, employees, and union representatives.

Thus the TTF team must initiate and facilitate a collaborative effort between the TTF and business unit. This should start with helping business unit managers, supervisors, and employees define their training roles. For example, they could help to identify learning needs; analyze jobs, tasks and competencies; develop job aids and expert systems; develop and deliver training activities; and reinforce performance improvements on the job.

The team should also clarify what the TTF, as a support function, could do to help business unit staff fulfill these roles. For example, the TTF team could offer expert guidance and facilitate technical training initiatives; develop systems, processes, and methodologies; transfer training competencies; and/or support training efforts in the business units. As a next step, the TTF team should cultivate stakeholder commitment for the respective training roles of the business unit and the TTF.

The TTF team will be able to work collaboratively and effectively with business unit staff if it has nurtured close relationships and synergistic partnerships with them. The suggestions for building senior management conviction in an earlier section can be adapted for nurturing such alliances.

2.9.4   Unions

The union's involvement is vital to the implementation of technical training in a unionized organization. Unions often have a more accurate understanding of the culture, sensitivity, and politics with which the TTF team must deal. Also, unions can provide constructive and creative assistance in designing and implementing training plans. Furthermore, large-scale technical training initiatives in an adversarial labor-management climate may require more time to accomplish success. In this context, the critical issue of such efforts—creating benefits for all—may be overshadowed by parochialism, distrust, and skepticism.

In order to nurture the union's participation and ensure that it has a genuine stake in the technical learning system, the TTF team should do the following. First, arrange informal discussions to develop rapport and exchange information with union leaders. Second, handle any concerns about a technical training initiative in a sensitive manner. Seek union feedback on what it thinks would be the benefits of an effective technical learning system and what all stakeholders must do to make the system work. Third, create opportunities to work with union officials. For example, invite them to participate in the technical training steering committee and joint union-management initiatives. Also, invite union officials to be advocates for technical training. They can function as facilitators and communicators to promote training initiatives to both employees and management. They should also be able to recommend employees who can be subject matter experts or instructors.

Two trends are helping the TTF in a unionized organization today. First, employees have become more concerned about upgrading their skills; they realize that training can enhance their personal worth, capabilities, and contribution to the organization. Second, many organizations are trying to involve employees in their business, and see training as an excellent opportunity for a partnership between management and the union.

2.9.5   Other HRD and Business Functions

The larger organization may have other HRD functions such as safety training, management development, customer service training, team development, computer training, and quality management training. The TTF team cannot be isolated from or engage in turf battles with these HRD functions, as this will have a negative impact on it and may delay human resource development activities for the business units. A good rapport with the other HRD functions is crucial to avoiding duplication of effort and ensuring that client groups are not pursued by several different HRD functions at the same time. The various HRD functions need to establish a mechanism that will allow them to exchange information, share resources, and contribute jointly on training initiatives.

The TTF team also needs to develop close relationships with other human resources functions (e.g., human resource planning, career development, and selection/staffing), other organizational functions (e.g., strategic planning), and organizational initiatives [e.g., total quality management (TQM) or technological changes]. It has to work with these functions in designing and implementing integrated programs and interventions.

2.10   Designing
an Organizational Structure

How the TTF fits into the larger organizational structure may depend on several factors: the organization's philosophy on centralization or decentralization, the size and nature of the organization, the technology required to provide the training and its associated costs, the financial resources of the organization, the TTF's track record for delivering results and helping the organization accomplish its objectives, and the importance of technological learning and change in the organization. The organizational structure of the TTF itself should not be static; it may change in response to changes in the direction, needs, and dynamics of the larger organization.

Within most organizations, the structure of the TTF could be one of the following: centralized, decentralized, combination of centralized and decentralized, or externally aligned.

2.10.1   Centralized

A centralized TTF is commonly integrated within the HRD function or perhaps a human resources, technology, quality, safety, manufacturing, or other operating division. Some of the advantages of a centralized function are

- Consistent management of training vision, strategic plan, and policies
- Consistent design, development, delivery, and quality of training
- Reduced duplication of effort and overhead costs by sharing of resources and facilities
- Coordination of generic outputs for the entire organization
- One corporate information system for tracking employee training
- A higher and more visible profile of the TTF team

2.10.2   Decentralized

A decentralized TTF may operate as a self-sufficient unit that is sponsored by a specific business unit. This organizational structure is more prevalent in organizations which have diverse products and services and a variety of geographically separated divisions. The advantages of a decentralized TTF are

- Closer partnerships with the business units and external customers
- Timely response to client requests and decision making

- Closer focus on developing and delivering training which is customized to the needs of its client area
- Better access to technical experts
- More conducive for on-the-job training and evaluation, which are essential for many technical training activities

2.10.3 Combination of Centralized and Decentralized

A TTF function which is both centralized and decentralized may be able to reap the benefits of both organizational structures. Activities such as coordination, planning, policy setting, and administration can be centralized to ensure consistency of philosophy, strategic direction, methodologies, standards, quality control, and administrative controls. Decentralizing other technical training activities allows the TTF to be more responsive and closer to the client group. With a combination structure, it is important to define the accountabilities and roles clearly to avoid possible confusion or omission of training activities.

2.10.4 Externally Aligned

In this structure, the TTF is aligned or has a partnership with an external training-related organization such as a college, university, sectoral training center, consultant, or training supplier. This approach is becoming more attractive to many organizations and has the following benefits:

- Reduced overhead costs (e.g., resources and facilities)
- Ability to shop around for the best and be very selective
- Ability to contract only for the training which is needed, when it is needed
- Ability to provide a wider variety of products and services
- Increased publicity within the local community, if relevant

2.11 Educating and Communicating Continuously

No matter how good they seem to be, the TTF and technical learning system will be ineffective if their stakeholders do not understand what they can do and how to use them. Unfortunately, ineffectiveness will be the consequence if the stakeholders do not understand what they really need, are not convinced why they need training, are skeptical of training's impact on their business results, do not understand or have differing opinions about what is required for effective technical training, do not know what services or programs are available, and/or are unclear about what they are actually "buying." These issues may stem from ambiguities in the training field, since training is as much an art as it is a science. To compound matters, some stakeholders feel that they know what is good for training and do not consult the TTF team because they have conducted training as lay people.

Enlightened stakeholders, on the other hand, tend to insist on more relevant, top-quality services from the TTF. They may also be more committed to the training, since they better understand what is required to accomplish results. This leads to better training services, outputs, and outcomes, which in turn increase client satisfaction and business impact.

The message for the TTF is clear: it has to do a better job of educating its stakeholders about what exceptional technical training practices look like; what are the TTF's capabilities; how to assess, "buy," and use its services more effectively; how a training initiative will work; and what's required for results.

The TTF team must therefore develop and implement an effective communications strategy to publicize its mission, vision, goals, and activities to the larger organization. This can improve stakeholder understanding, acceptance, and commitment, ensure focus on technical training plans and activities, enhance the TTF's public relations, and even promote its services for external sales.

In implementing a communications strategy, the team must avoid the hard-sell approach; its clients will probably react negatively to the sales pitch. Instead, the team should organize a variety of ongoing communications activities targeted at the various stakeholder groups. Examples of such communications activities are listed as follows.

Meeting as many key stakeholders as possible to explain the technical learning vision, what the TTF is doing, and how it can support them. Ask for their feedback, emphasizing that the team would be flexible to satisfy stakeholder needs.

Tapping into the larger organization's informal communications network (grapevine), as this is usually an effective way of promoting the TTF's good work.

Making formal or informal presentations to stakeholders.

Writing articles and professional papers (featuring the learning vision, TTF's activities, etc.) for organizational publications, local newspapers, or industry journals.

Participating in organizational committees which provide the opportunity for the TTF team to interact with its stakeholders from other business functions.

Organizing technical training open houses, where stakeholders are invited for presentations and demonstrations of the TTF's capabilities.

Using bulletin boards, posters, newsletters, or videotapes to communicate the TTF's vision and activities and what it means to employees.

Sending articles, etc., which are supportive of the TTF's vision and activities to the key stakeholders.

Meeting with the people in the organization who do not seem to understand the TTF. Try to clarify for them what the function can and cannot do.

Developing a communications strategy for the TTF is relatively easy if it already has a proven track record of satisfying client needs. The team can highlight success stories and accomplishments built around evaluation measurements, as these are a concrete and powerful means of promoting the TTF and the benefits of technical training.

2.12 Applying Project Management Techniques

At the strategic planning stage, the TTF team would have identified the action plans necessary for implementing its strategic plan over each short-term period (see Section 2.5, "Develop a Strategic Plan"). To realize these action plans, the team has to implement the initiatives and activities of each plan as specific projects. In implementing each project, the TTF team should apply an enhanced project management process which incorporates a change management process and a consulting process, as well as conventional project management. The process model should be customized so that it is compatible to the organization and will be accepted by clients.

The TTF team uses project management to plan, organize, direct, and control temporarily assigned resources to produce a desired result, product, or service. Using this systematic and structured approach helps the

TTF team accomplish outcomes which satisfy the client, are quality-oriented, and are completed on time and within budget. Some of the other benefits of using good project management are that it:

Helps everyone see the picture of where the training initiative will take them and how it will be accomplished

Provides a strong structure for establishing people's accountabilities and responsibilities, and for encouraging better morale and productivity

Allows the TTF team to enlist staff and business unit personnel in the project team, thus integrating stakeholder groups and increasing buy-in to the training initiative

Helps estimate and acquire the necessary organizational resources and ensures that they are optimally used

Helps track and manage project progress proactively

Provides project costs and other information

Improves communications between the TTF team and clients

Figure 2-9 illustrates a four-stage model of how project management can be applied to technical training activities and projects.

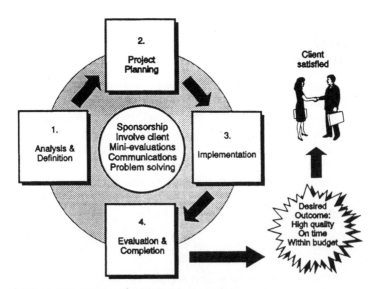

Figure 2-9. Stages of project management.

2.12.1 Stage 1:
Analysis and Definition

The TTF team must clearly identify the key clients and learn about them. They should meet with the client to understand the client's need for improvement or change; and determine whether these needs are training related, the importance of the project to them, and their commitment to its success. A variety of front-end analysis tools, including needs analysis, may be used for gathering and analyzing information at this stage. The client's people should be involved in this analysis step. Based on this analysis, the team needs to provide honest, concise, timely, and confidential feedback to the client, and involve the client in problem solving and action planning.

The TTF team and client must then jointly define the preliminary project outcomes, goals, objectives, deliverables, client's involvement, working styles, and other expectations. The TTF team also needs to orient the client to the overall process used to plan, implement, and follow up the project. The client must know what the team is doing and why, and be involved in decision making, including the selection of the project manager and initial project team. The team should initiate mini-evaluations of the project, and inform the client regularly.

2.12.2 Stage 2:
Project Planning

In this stage, the project manager and client jointly decide on a course of action, scope the work, and formulate a project plan. A project plan basically charts the actions the project team should follow during the project life cycle. Each type of project needs a different size, scope, and type of project plan to best meet its desired objectives. The project plan should

- List the clients, sponsors, and liaisons for the project.
- Describe the problem or opportunity requiring the project.
- Describe the goals and specific objectives of the project.
- Describe the deliverables the client expects to receive, including success criteria and other specifications.
- Propose the strategy for producing each deliverable.
- Break the work down into a detailed and organized structure of components, tasks, and activities (including subdeliverables and specifications) for producing deliverables.
- Identify the sequence, criticality, and links of tasks.
- Identify the project schedule showing timing and duration of tasks as well as milestones for indicating progress.

- Define the accountabilities, roles, and authority of the client and project team.
- Define the policies and procedures which provide guidelines for the project team and client.
- Identify the type, number, quality, selection, and training of human resources (including task managers).
- Identify the organizational structure required throughout the project.
- Identify other resources (e.g., money or computers) needed.
- Detail the budget, based on cost estimates for each task.
- Describe the monitoring system for evaluating progress.
- Describe the communication and reporting methods.
- Identify potential opportunities, constraints, and obstacles, and outline preventive and contingency actions for addressing them.

To prepare a project plan, the team should use project management software (e.g., Microsoft Project® or Time Line®) and tools (e.g., work breakdown structures, PERT charts, and Gantt charts). In particular, a Gantt chart can visually outline the sequence of events which has been agreed upon. This will help ensure that everyone is aware of the direction the project is taking. The type of software and tools used depends on the complexity of the project as well as the intended audience. For example, senior managers will typically want to see only the big picture, whereas task managers will need details on each step.

Before going on to the next stage, the project team members, the client, sponsors, targets, and other stakeholders must fully understand, believe in, and commit to the project plan and approaches used. This is important because it sets mutual expectations for the project. One way of doing this is for the team to present the project plan and have each key stakeholder carefully review, approve, and sign off on it. The team should deal with their suggestions, misperceptions, and concerns, and revise the plan if necessary.

The most effective way to initiate and sustain commitment for a project is to build in cascading sponsorship. To accomplish this, first, the project team must involve an executive sponsor who can legitimize the project and who has influence over the target area and resources. The executive sponsor must create the environment for the project team and its client to work together, and provide meaningful consequences to stimulate participation. Second, the team must also involve a number of local sponsors who have direct control over the target area for which the project is being implemented and can provide resources, and ensure that they help sustain the project. Without such sponsorship, the people in the target area may not support the project because they know the team lacks authority over them.

The following are some of the project elements of a major technical training project in a manufacturing company.

1. Set up the training steering committee and project team.
2. Perform an overall analysis of project needs.
3. Establish the project objectives, specifications, strategies, and tasks.
4. Estimate the project costs and budget.
5. Determine the number and responsibilities of resource persons required.
6. Schedule all project tasks.
7. Design, furnish, and equip the training center.
8. Identify and develop the internal training designers and instructors.
9. Study the new technology, equipment, and work process.
10. Implement the vendor courses to train internal resources.
11. Perform an analysis of job performance and learners.
12. Design and develop the pilot version of the training courses.
13. Print, produce, and organize all training materials.
14. Implement the pilot version of the training courses.
15. Review and revise the pilot training courses.
16. Implement the revised training courses.
17. Assist in the commissioning of new technology and equipment.
18. Facilitate the application of learned competencies and improvements on the job.
19. Evaluate the individual training courses and the overall project.
20. Conduct the close-out meeting to review and wrap up the project.

Figure 2-10. Project elements for a major technical training project.

Based on the project plan, the project manager can now go about acquiring the necessary resources, form the project team or increase its size, and assign responsibilities. (See Figure 2.10.)

2.12.3 Stage 3: Implementation

This is the "doing" stage, in which the project team must perform and complete the various tasks described in the project plan. Key success factors during the implementation stage include effective leadership, teamwork, clear communications, relentless tracking of milestones, progress reporting, performance management, consequence management, and creative problem solving.

By now, the relevant targets, sponsors, and other players should be developed in the mental models and competencies needed for implementation. During implementation, it is critical to keep these stakeholders focused on the desired end results. Project team members should use control techniques to monitor the project tasks, deliverables, work quality, delivery dates, resource use, budgets, etc. They will have to deal with tasks that are behind schedule and resolve any problems. Along the way, the project plan will probably need to be updated and revised, and resources reallocated. (Further information on implementation is provided in Section 2.13, "Executing the Plan.")

2.12.4   Stage 4:
Evaluation and Completion

In this stage, the project outcomes are evaluated against expectations and the project is wrapped up. In order for the evaluation to be effective, it is important that all team members determine and agree to the evaluation criteria up front. If mini-evaluations were conducted and the client kept informed throughout the process, there should be no surprises at this stage. While it is important to resolve problems, the TTF manager and project manager must also acknowledge and praise successes, and document lessons learned for application in other areas. This stage is concluded when the project manager presents a final report to the sponsors and disbands the project team.

The TTF team should note three final points about project management. First, know when to use and not to use it; comprehensive project management is not needed for every initiative. Second, involve the client. Clients understand their business area best and should participate in planning and implementing the project. The more a client is involved, the greater the chance of success in attainment of key resources and application of appropriate solutions. The team must therefore build collaborative partnerships and relationships with their clients, and use the latter's talents optimally in the project team. Third, prepare to deal with problems proactively. The team and client must decide up front on a process for solving the problems which inevitably occur during a project.

2.13   Executing the Plan

Many training strategic plans and action plans fail at the implementation stage, victims of poor front-end planning. During implementation, numerous factors (e.g., resistance, delays, bottlenecks, or loss of support) inevitably occur, decreasing momentum for the training and other changes. If the TTF builds up a history of poor implementation, stakeholders will become skeptical of future training projects. To avoid this, the TTF team should proactively apply the following guidelines at the planning and implementation stages.

- Determine the minimum and ideal levels of stakeholder understanding, ownership, sponsorship, and participation needed from the start. The probability of a successful implementation is directly proportional to these factors. Therefore, involve the key stakeholders early in joint planning, and ensure that they clearly understand the performance needs, technical training vision and plans, specific deliverables, and their responsibilities as sponsors.

- Think idealistically but act realistically, given the available resources, time, and stakeholder support. Do not promise what the team may not be able to deliver. Companywide efforts, for example, are usually harder to control and are more costly. It is therefore prudent to focus on a few small projects that the TTF team does well, are attainable, and are likely to yield the greatest returns. These limited efforts could familiarize people with the process and demonstrate long-term potential.

- Frame the TTF team's actions, from the beginning, within the context of client expectations and then try to overdeliver on the committed results, quality, and service. Upon delivery, have the client inspect the deliverables. Make sure the client is fully satisfied that the completed project meets their quality specifications. Since clients can choose where they obtain their training products and services, the TTF will be negatively impacted if it doesn't conform to their needs. Aim to dazzle and add value and the client will be back.

- Get it right the first time; strive to ensure that the initial activities are flawless and results-oriented. If the TTF team fails early, its credibility may be damaged. To avoid this, don't compromise on quality. A few projects done well are better than many done normally. Moreover, ensure that the client understands, commits, and conforms to the process approaches (e.g., instructional design) used in the project. This will avert a major reason underlying failed learning systems and projects, that is, the client and project team each used inconsistent, even incompatible, processes and methods.

- Be responsive and timely. An outstanding technical training program delivered six months late may have little value. If implementation takes too long, the stakeholders may become concerned about what the TTF is doing and about its value to the organization. The opportunities and momentum for change will dissipate as time passes. It is therefore important to get something immediate, practical, and visible going early in each project. This means securing early buy-in, curtailing needless talk, implementing projects in smaller chunks, being realistic and even creative with available resources, and ensuring that clients receive the deliverables on time. Of course, the TTF team should not sacrifice quality for the sake of completing a task; it should work with what it has and continue to improve where possible.

- Select a target group or business unit that is likely to result in a successful project. The target area should be important to the business and have the potential for quick, measurable results. Assess the state of readiness of the target area and its stakeholders for implementation of the proposed project. An area is likely to be ready if its stakeholders recognize the need for change, want the TTF team's help, and are relatively cooperative; if it is relatively stable; and if it has the required resources available. The team may find that some areas in the organization are ready, while others are not. If so, be prepared to adapt the project to the readiness, situational realities, and characteristics of each area.

- Initially, be prepared for less client endorsement than you believe is necessary for full implementation. Work enthusiastically on the endorsed parts, however small they may be. As the small results add up, the client will appreciate what has been accomplished, perceive that the team is reliable, and become more confident that the TTF makes a difference. Eventually the team will establish a reputation for getting things done and responding to client needs. In future, the client may be willing to involve the team in more challenging projects that focus on achieving breakthrough performance improvements.

- Be up front with all resource requirements; more resources than expected are usually required for successful implementation. Educate the client on the impact of different resource levels on project outcomes.

- Implement situationally, ensuring that the TTF team's strategy is flexible and responsive to changing needs. For example, the client may request the team to eliminate certain activities and focus instead on new initiatives that are more pressing to the business unit. Adjust the TTF's action plans to meet these needs but, unless there are sound reasons, do not dilute or dissipate the original strategic plan.

- Be a model of cost-effectiveness. Exceeding the budget may affect the team's credibility—more so if the organization is facing financial pressures. Install controls for continually reviewing the planned activities in the context of current organizational realities and opportunity costs. Cut activities which are low priority, low yield, or destined to mediocrity, and move the scarce resources to areas of greater potential.

- Be patient. Don't expect to be an overnight success, since there are many forces which could hinder implementation. For example, initially, stakeholders may require time to understand and appreciate what the TTF does and its potential value. The TTF team may also have to contend with subtle or blatant resistance from certain managers or supervisors to any changes. To complicate matters, poor organizational positioning may handicap the team's work. It may take time before things start to take shape, so persevere and keep propelling the process, dealing with any roadblocks that get in the way.

- Align the various factors and systems in the performance environment to reinforce, institutionalize, and integrate any results from the project. Develop a renewal plan for sustaining the results, planning continuous improvements, and transferring lessons learned to other areas.

- Build in a communication system to report project status, achievements, and problems to the client on a consistent and timely basis. Do not try to cover up any mistakes; use the opportunity to correct and resolve them, and learn with the client from these lessons. However, don't forget to celebrate small successes along the way, as it helps advertise progress to the organization and builds confidence. The client will be looking for information to confirm whether the project and TTF team are really needed.

- When ready, invite key stakeholders from other organizational areas to assess the outcomes and approaches used, and discuss possible application to their areas.

2.14 Evaluating the TTF's Effectiveness

It's vital for the TTF team to measure and audit the TTF's effectiveness, determine its value or worth, and demonstrate a return on investment to the business units and larger organization on a continual basis. First, evaluations provide the information and understanding that the TTF team, management, and other stakeholders need for making better decisions regarding the TTF and its activities. Specifically, it provides a measurable basis for implementing accountability and managing performance relating to the systems, processes, activities, and outcomes of the TTF. It also provides the feedback necessary for adjusting and improving these things.

Second, evaluations provide the data-based evidence to justify the TTF's contribution to the larger organization's success and strategic directions. Stakeholders tend to trust objective data about the function's efforts more than hearing about it from the TTF team. This is crucial to helping the TTF achieve visibility and credibility since today's successes can be quickly forgotten; yet the pressures to prove the TTF's value-added are greater than ever.

2.14.1 Plan the Evaluation

In planning the evaluation, the TTF team should consider building a system of mini-evaluations which monitor and provide reliable feedback on performance at various stages and areas of the TTF's functioning. This provides formative information for managing the TTF and its activities, and for prompting continual adjustments.

The team must determine the dimensions and process to evaluate the TTF. In doing so, it is important to note the words of John Zenger: "Meaningful evaluation is always in the eyes of the beholder." Since the most important beholders are the key stakeholders (e.g., business unit managers), the evaluation must be congruent with the criteria these stakeholders use to evaluate the TTF. Unfortunately, if the stakeholders have little experience working with or evaluating the TTF, they may choose unrealistic or inappropriate evaluation criteria. The TTF team must therefore understand the information that the key stakeholders need, and work with them in designing and implementing the evaluation. This includes, at the design stage, jointly selecting what areas to evaluate and defining the standards for measuring these areas:

- The evaluation areas or targets could be long-term impacts, results, problems resolved, outputs (initiatives, programs, products, or services), processes, strategic plans, staff, facilities and resources, and/or cost-effectiveness.

Table 2-2. Evaluating Capabilities of a Technical Training Function

A Capabilities (Output: Competent technical training facilitators at business units)	B Today	C 1 Year	D Gap (C-B)	E 3 Years	F Gap (E-B)
Trainer selection system	0	2	2	5	5
Job/competency analysis skills	1	2	1	4	3
Train-the-trainer competencies	3	3	0	4	1
Coaching & feedback competencies	0	2	2	5	5
Master trainers	1	2	1	5	4
Job aids for trainers	0	2	2	5	5
Resource center	5	5	0	5	0
Etc.					

Rating Scale: 0 (does not exist); 1 (unacceptable); 2 (average); 3 (above average); 4 (excellent); 5 (exceptional).

- The evaluation standards are the criteria for indicating whether performance in each evaluation area is acceptable.

In evaluating these areas, the TTF team should consider its effectiveness and efficiency. First, is the TTF functioning effectively, that is, doing the right things? This involves assessing the activities conducted to determine impact on the TTF's key results areas, such as contribution to organizational objectives. Second, is the TTF functioning efficiently, that is, doing things right? This involves assessing the activities conducted in relation to the process, resources, and effort used. The team's ultimate goal should be to "do the right things right"—that is, effectiveness and efficiency. Team members must continually ask this question: "What can we do to make the TTF more relevant to our clients and the larger organization?"

Next, the TTF team and its clients should determine the types of information required, as well as methods for information gathering.

2.14.2 Implement the Evaluation and Communicate Results

Feedback for evaluation can be obtained from external expert audits, surveys, questionnaires, interviews, focus groups, observation, product evaluation, records, performance checklists, or even informal elevator conversations. The key is for the TTF team to get as much reliable feedback (positive and negative) as possible. The team should be receptive to constructive criticism. Not only will it help fine-tune the TTF, but people will note that the team is willing to listen to their ideas.

The TTF team then sorts, analyzes, and collates the information into a user-friendly format. It must communicate such evaluation results to the key stakeholders in an ongoing and systematic manner. One of the most powerful communication mechanisms is for the business unit clients to give impartial, word-of-mouth feedback and referrals to the key stakeholders.

The team must ensure that the stakeholders have a clear picture of what's happening, address their suggestions and concerns, and help them use the information for decision making on continuously improving the TTF and its activities.

2.15 Parting Words

As a facilitator of change, the TTF manager must be prepared to embark on an aggressive, systematic, and comprehensive effort aimed at building, revitalizing, renewing, or reinventing the TTF. However, with 16 elements impacting the TTF, where do you start? The important thing is this: *begin.* Do it today. Here's how. First, select three to five elements which most impact your TTF's ability to satisfy the key clients and larger organization's needs. Second, audit your TTF in each critical element. Third, identify the problems and opportunities underlying each element, and determine actions to resolve or capitalize on them, respectively. Fourth, identify specific guidelines from this chapter which you can apply to develop or improve the critical elements in a reasonable time and practical manner. Fifth, gather in-depth information about improving the critical elements, e.g., by reading a selection of the resource books listed at the end of this chapter and visiting benchmarked HRD functions. It would also be invaluable to learn about TQM principles and apply them as an approach for improving the TTF. Sixth, formulate an action plan of specific tactics for improving each critical element, with success criteria and time lines built in. Seven, resolve to make sure these tactics work, correct them, improve them, and learn from the experience. If something still doesn't work, reject it and replace it with a better alternative.

Relentlessly apply these seven steps in a planned, proactive, and incremental manner; your TTF will not only have an increased probability of becoming exceptional, it could become better than the best HRD functions anywhere. Your stakeholders will find the TTF reliable in delivering results, and will believe, trust, and have confidence in you and your team. They will treat the TTF as a critical resource and give it more support.

Bibliography

American Society for Training and Development, *The Best Of: Managing the HRD Function,* American Society for Training and Development, Alexandria, Va. 1992.

Beer, Michael, Russell A. Eisenstat, and Bert Spector, *The Critical Path to Corporate Renewal,* Harvard Business School Press, Boston, 1990.

Block, Peter, *Stewardship,* Berrett Koehler Publishers, San Francisco, 1993.

Carnevale, Anthony P., Leila J. Gainer, and Eric Schulz, *Training the Technical Work Force,* Jossey-Bass, San Francisco, 1990.

Chalofsky, Neal E., and Carlene Reinhart, *Effective Human Resource Development: How to Build a Strong and Responsive HRD Function,* Jossey-Bass, San Francisco, 1988.

Conner, Daryl R., *Managing at the Speed of Change: How Resilient Managers Succeed and Prosper where Others Fail,* Villard Books, New York, 1992.

Conners, Roger, Tom Smith, and Craig Hickman, *The Oz Principle: Getting Results Through Individual and Organizational Accountability,* Prentice-Hall, Englewood Cliffs, N.J., 1994.

Craig, Robert L. (ed.), *Training and Development Handbook: A Guide to Human Resource Development,* 3d ed., McGraw-Hill, New York, 1987.

Darling, Philip, *Training for Profit: A Guide to the Integration of Training in an Organization's Success,* McGraw-Hill, Europe, Berkshire, 1993.

Dixon, Nancy M., *Evaluation: A Tool for Improving HRD Quality,* University Associates, San Diego, 1990.

Gilley, Jerry W., and Steven A. Eggland, *Marketing Human Resource Development Within Organizations: Enhancing the Visibility, Effectiveness, and Credibility of Programs,* Jossey-Bass, San Francisco, 1992.

Goodstein, Leonard D., Timothy M. Nolan, and J. William Pfeiffer, *Applied Strategic Planning: A Comprehensive Guide,* Pfeiffer & Company, San Diego, 1992.

Kanter, Rosabeth Moss, Barry A. Stein, and Todd D. Jick, *The Challenge of Organization Change: How Companies Experience It and Leaders Guide It,* The Free Press, New York, 1992.

McLagan, Patricia A., *Models for HRD Practice,* American Society for Training and Development, Alexandria, Va., 1989.

Nadler, Leonard, and Zeace Nadler, *Developing Human Resources,* 3d ed., Jossey-Bass, San Francisco, 1989.

Nadler, Leonard, and Zeace Nadler, *The Handbook of Human Resource Development,* 2d ed., John Wiley & Sons, New York, 1990.

Nadler, Leonard, and Garland D. Wiggs, *Managing Human Resource Development: A Practical Guide,* Jossey-Bass, San Francisco, 1986.

Nathan, Anthony, "The Art of Exceptional Technical Training Management," *Proceedings of ASTD's 48th International Conference and Exposition,* American Society for Training and Development, New Orleans, 1992.

Nathan, Anthony, "The Art of Managing Training," *ASTD Technical and Skills Training,* July 1991.

Nathan, Anthony, "How to Start a Training Department from Scratch, Revisited," *Singapore Training and Development Association Journal,* June 1987.

Nathan, Anthony, "A Primer on Developing Technical Training Systems: A Three-Part Series," *The Ontario Society for Training and Development Magazine,* March, May, and July 1990.

Nathan, Anthony, and Michael Stanleigh, "Is Your Department Credible?" *ASTD Training and Development Journal,* January 1991.

Nathan, Anthony, and Michael Stanleigh, "Riding the Elusive Wave: Building Training Department Credibility: A Two-Part Series," *The Ontario Society for Training and Development Magazine,* May and July 1990.

Quah, Jon, "Human Resource Development in Four Asian Countries: Some Lessons for the Commonwealth Countries," in Commonwealth Working Group on Human Resource Development Strategies, *Foundation For The Future: Human Resource Development,* Commonwealth Secretariat, London, 1993.

Robinson, Dana Gaines, and James C. Robinson, *Training for Impact: How to Link Training to Business Needs and Measure the Results,* Jossey-Bass, San Francisco, 1989.

Rummler, Geary A., and Alan P. Brache, *Improving Performance: How to Manage the White Space on the Organization Chart,* Jossey-Bass, San Francisco, 1990.

Stolovitch, Harold D., and Erica J. Keeps (eds.), *Handbook of Human Performance Technology: A Comprehensive Guide for Analyzing and Solving Performance Problems in Organizations,* Jossey-Bass, San Francisco, 1992.

Thomas, Brian, *Total Quality Training: The Quality Culture and Quality Trainer,* McGraw-Hill, Europe, Berkshire, 1992.

Tregoe, Benjamin B., John W. Zimmerman, Ronald A. Smith, and Peter M. Toba, *Vision in Action: How to Integrate Your Company's Strategic Goals into Day-to-Day Management Decisions,* Simon & Schuster, New York, 1989.

Warrick, Don D., "What Executives, Managers, and Human Resource Professionals Need to Know About Managing Change," in Wendell French, Cecil H. Bell, and Robert A. Zawacki (eds.), *Organization Development and Transformation: Managing Effective Change,* Homewood, Ill., 1993.

Zenger, John H., *Training for Organizational Excellence,* Zenger Miller, Inc., San Jose, 1983.

3

The Technical Training Function: Growth of Technical Training Professionalism

Patricia Chance

Livermore Laboratories

Patricia F. Chance, *an Education Specialist, manages distance learning programs at the Lawrence Livermore National Laboratory. Pat's responsibilities include program research as well as oversight of the televised degree programs offered by California State Univeristy-Chico, National Technological University, the Stanford Instructional Television Network, and the University of California-Davis. She also administers satellite-delivered short course programming from universities and vendors. Pat chairs the Stanford Company Coordinators Steering Committee and serves on the Laboratory's Continuing Education Committee. She is a certified facilitator for the Covey "7 Habits of Highly Effective People" course, which is offered on-site at the Laboratory. Pat is active in the American Society for Training and Development (ASTD). She is also an active member of the American Society for Engineering Education (ASEE).*

This chapter is targeted to meet the needs of both trainers new to the field of technical training and managers who have perhaps acquired leadership of a training function and are seeking resources. The information is not all-inclusive, but rather it is a sampling of what's available. Contact with any of the organizations or educational institutions referenced can lead to more resources and so the training network, and professionalism, can continue to grow.

The sections that follow include information to help develop or maintain professionalism in the technical training field. A section on professional organizations includes organization descriptions, activities, and publications. The Educational Opportunities section deals both with what can be learned and what can be contributed to others. A look at technical training accreditation, both academic-based and that developed by an organization, is included with sample program descriptions. Finally, a resource guide citing phone numbers and addresses of professional organizations, including those listed in the chapter, is included for easy reference.

3.1 Introduction

The growth of technical training professionalism reflects the strategic importance of training in today's organizations. Technical trainers who want to play a part in achieving their organization's goals are expected to have a thorough knowledge of the subject matter, possess excellent platform skills, and have knowledge of today's important issues. No longer is it enough to simply have the ability to train in one skill. Today's technical trainer must be up-to-date on the latest technology for delivering training. The trainer must understand the global role of the training and the organization. Trainers today must understand Total Quality Management (TQM) principles and how they relate to the design and delivery of training. Trainers must be sensitive to cultural diversity and must be able to structure training to meet a variety of needs. *Today's technical trainer must be a professional.*

However, this is not to say that corporate America is standing by, ready, willing, and able to meet the technical trainer's needs. Often, training managers become caught up in meeting the immediate customer needs. Trainers must take individual responsibility for identifying resources to promote their career growth. Professional organizations and educational institutions increasingly provide the resources needed to prepare technical trainers to train the nation's workforce to compete in the global market.

Through professional organizations, it is possible to learn what others are doing—what works, what doesn't—thereby enabling the trainer to become more effective. Not only that, technical trainers can learn the training role's importance, how it can grow, and how it can be positioned strategically to help an organization.

Industry and academe can jointly address workforce training issues by collaborating. Schools can teach basic skills to the future workforce, making it easier for industry to concentrate on more technical topics. With basic skills addressed, the technical trainer can focus on areas of expertise and develop specialty courses. Trainers, too, can benefit from university instruction to become more expert in their craft. Technical trainers can share their expertise with educational institutions, thereby strengthening the partnership and creating a win-win situation.

The effectiveness of technical training programs and trainers can be validated by accreditation. Accreditation can be either academic-based or developed by the organization. Trainers who have the opportunity to participate in such programs will strengthen their professional standing.

3.2 Professional and Other Organizations

Trainers today have the opportunity to be involved in many professional organizations. The problem for the new technical trainer is to choose which professional organizations to join and in which ones to become active. Included in the pages which follow is information on a variety of organizations, their membership, mission, conferences, and publications. The depth of each description is designed to create awareness of just how valuable professional organizations can be. For those new to technical training, this section will provide resources for the selection process. A more complete listing with addresses and phone numbers appears at the end of the chapter.

3.2.1 Training Organizations

American Society for Training and Development (ASTD). According to ASTD's *Membership Guide*, in 1942, with the beginning of World War II, the nation's workforce needed training to support the war effort. Since there was no national training society, 15 people created the American Society for Training Directors. In 1945, the first issue of the society's journal, *Industrial Training News* (today's *Training & Development* magazine), was published. In 1951, membership surpassed the 1000 mark, and a one-person staff office was opened in Madison, Wisconsin. And, in 1964, the name was changed to the American Society for Training and Development. Today, ASTD has over 55,000 members worldwide and more than 120 staff at headquarters in Alexandria, Virginia.

ASTD's mission is to provide leadership to individuals, organizations, and society to achieve work-related competence, performance, and fulfillment. ASTD's Vision 2000 is to be a worldwide leader in workplace learning and performance through leadership, applied research, information, networks, coalitions, partnerships, and development. ASTD resources include:

- Useful, current information
- Professional growth and learning
- A stronger and more influential training field

ASTD is organized by seven product areas: Conferences, Networking, Publications, Information Services, Representation, Research, and Participation. ASTD has more than 150 local chapters which offer regular meetings, newsletters, conferences and workshops, position referral services, community outreach programs, social activities, and more. Chapter membership augments national membership, providing essential products and services at the local level.

Conferences. ASTD holds two annual conferences. One is the ASTD National Conference & Exposition, which is held in the spring and features over 300 concurrent sessions presented by industry experts, all-day, in-depth preconference workshops, the latest human resources development products at the EXPO, and daily networking opportunities. This conference helps trainers find out how today's training issues will affect them, make vital connections with colleagues, and develop new skills and refine existing ones.

The second Conference is the ASTD National Technical & Skills Training Conference. It is a three-day conference, held in the fall, and features over 125 concurrent sessions and the world's largest technical training marketplace. This conference keeps technical trainers on top of the key issues and changes in the profession. The results-oriented program focuses on topics such as:

- On-the-job training
- Skilled trades training
- Expert systems
- Cost-benefit analysis

Publications. Published monthly since 1946, *Training & Development* magazine helps readers to make a difference to the bottom line by linking training to their organization's goals.

Published six times per year, *National Report on Human Resources* is the Society newspaper which covers national policy issues, the economy, ASTD news, and other happenings in the training and development field.

Published eight times per year, *Technical & Skills Training* magazine includes feature articles, interviews, company profiles, rotating special-interest columns, and a regular "You Ask—Trainers Answer" column.

Published monthly, *INFO-LINE* provides how-to information on one training topic, task, or issue, such as games and icebreakers, instructional technology, benchmarking, workplace diversity, and performance technology.

Other ASTD publications include *Human Resource Development Quarterly*, a national forum for human resources development theory, research, and communication by leading practitioners and scholars and *The Training & Development Literature Index*, a quarterly publication with references and indexes of the best new books, articles, reports, and tapes in training and development. ASTD Press publishes hundreds of books, audio cassettes, and videos, including: *Trainer's Toolkit*, which provides actual documents used by trainers in a variety of industries, and *Models for HRD Practice*, a set of four practical guidebooks to evaluate current skills and to plan professional development.

National Association of Government Training and Development Directors (NAGTADD). NAGTADD was formed in 1979 to provide leadership in public sector training and development and to facilitate partnerships among training directors to share information and resources. NAGTADD now has over 122 members, and the organization focuses on the unique needs of public-sector training and development directors. NAGTADD's goals are

- To promote professional development and help members develop human resources

- To encourage experts to share products and expertise

- To create information networks on public-sector training and development, and make them available to policy makers at all levels of government

- To provide research and technical assistance in support of public-sector training and development

- To enhance public appreciation of the public service role

NAGTADD provides information on government training and development programs nationwide within 48 hours. It also puts members in touch with colleagues who have solved similar problems. If a member wants to implement a particular program such as assessment centers, TQM, diversity, management development, or ADA, NAGTADD can assist.

NAGTADD is recognized internationally and members have implemented training programs and consulted in the Virgin Islands and Armenia, are scheduled to go to the Ukraine, and have been requested to go to Mexico.

Membership includes training and development directors from states, counties, cities, state-supported universities and colleges, and the federal government.

Conferences. NAGTADD's annual conference in the fall allows members to interact with others in the field and share program ideas. Members have the opportunity to become up-to-date on human resource and training issues around the country. Recent conferences have addressed issues such as video distance learning, Total Quality Management, downsizing, and organizational consulting.

Publications. NAGTADD keeps members on top of the latest news in human resources development through its quarterly publication, *Government Training and Development Quarterly*, which is read by NAGTADD members, personnel directors, governors, and government executives.

National Society for Performance and Instruction (NSPI). NSPI is the leading association dedicated to increasing productivity in the workplace through the application of performance and instructional technologies. Founded in 1962, its 5000 members are located throughout the United States, Canada, and 30 other countries.

NSPI is an organization whose members are valuable to each other in terms of professional development and colleagueship. The Society is a source of challenge and friendship, and provides opportunities in both the field and the organization for growth and recognition. NSPI is concerned with the whole field of performance improvement, including

- Performance systems
- Objective-based organizational development
- Job analysis and design
- Training

Members include performance technologists, training directors, human resource managers, instructional technologists, change agents, human factors practitioners, and organizational development consultants.

NSPI has an international network of local and regional chapters. These chapters provide members with dialogue and activities on a monthly basis.

NSPI supports chapters through an annual workshop for chapter leaders, newsletters, and regular support and communication with the Society headquarters. NSPI chapters offer opportunities for professional involvement year-round, and NSPI members receive information about chapters in their area. In addition, two unique chapters, Armed Forces, and the Distance Education and Training Network, serve the needs of these special groups.

Conferences. NSPI's Annual Conference & Expo is held in the winter and draws the largest gathering of performance and instructional technologists in the country. Conference participants can select from over 150 different sessions touching almost every aspect of improving human performance.

Publications. Published 10 times a year, the *Performance & Instruction* journal is filled with useful information, approaches, and methodologies that can improve skills and effectiveness. Articles address improving human performance through a wide range of techniques, including incentives and feedback, effective management, performance aids, organizational development, job design, and instruction.

Performance Improvement Quarterly represents the cutting edge in research and theory in performance technology, with articles written by some of the most important people in the business. Each article treats professional issues with depth and clarity.

News & Notes provides the latest information on NSPI events in 10 issues of the newsletter. Each issue contains the latest on activities, job openings, and resources to make trainers more effective in their work.

3.2.2   Training and Education Organizations

American Society for Engineering Education (ASEE).   The American Society for Engineering Education is dedicated to promoting excellence in engineering and engineering technology education. ASEE, which celebrated its centennial in 1993, plays a pivotal role in developing programs and policies which will enable engineering education and allied branches of science and technology to meet the challenges of global competition.

ASEE's membership represents all disciplines of engineering and engineering technology. ASEE's 10,000 members include deans, department heads, faculty, graduate students, and corporate and government representatives. Participation in this organization can lead the technical trainer to a host of educational opportunities to meet technical training goals.

ASEE offers more than 40 divisions, spanning a wide variety of interests. Members are eligible to affiliate with up to six groups.

Conferences. ASEE sponsors an annual summer conference which draws 2500 to 3000 attendees from North America and many foreign countries. The 300 technical sessions sponsored by ASEE's 43 professional interest divisions allow members to present papers and research to their colleagues. A proceedings publishes all peer-reviewed papers presented at the conference each year and is available to conference participants.

A winter annual College Industry Education Conference is sponsored by four ASEE divisions: Cooperative Education, College Industry Partnerships, Continuing Professional Development, and Engineering Technology Division. This conference is a forum for industry, government, and academe to explore partnerships in the education and training fields.

Publications. *ASEE PRISM* is a monthly magazine which features timely articles, letters to the editor, commentaries, industry and federal agency highlights, ASEE news, profiles of educators, and a classified employment section.

In addition, many divisions publish quarterly newsletters with up-to-date information on activities and industry and academe news.

National Association for Industry-Education Cooperation (NAIEC). The National Association for Industry-Education Cooperation is the nation's principal advocate for fostering industry-education collaboration in school improvement, career education, and human resource/economic development. Established in 1964, NAIEC is the national clearinghouse for information on industry involvement in education.

The Association believes that industry has a central role in helping education reshape its total academic and vocational program in a coherent, systematic manner so that it is more responsive to the needs of both students (youths and adults) and employers.

As a national voluntary, nonprofit organization, it represents a broad base of membership from corporations, trade associations, school systems, colleges and universities, an affiliated network of industry-education councils, state education departments, government agencies, labor organizations, and professional groups in the United States and Canada.

NAIEC's vision for 1991 through 1995 is, in its national leadership role in industry-education cooperation:

- To continue to broaden its base of support among businesses, education, labor, government, and professional decision makers in adopting the NAIEC model for improving industry-education collaboration at the local and state levels

- To further the professional development of education and employer representatives in organizing, planning, implementing, financing, and evaluating an industry-education collaborative system as a major vehicle for fostering school improvement and reform and, in turn, the school-to-work process

- To promote the development of a dynamic and responsive public/private/postsecondary educational system and competitive workforce through a comprehensive systemwide industry-education alliance focusing on cooperative planning, curriculum revision, staff development of school personnel, upgrading instructional materials and equipment, and improving the efficiency and effectiveness of educational management.

Conferences. NAIEC hosts a variety of national and regional conferences and training programs designed to meet the needs of industry-education practitioners involved in academic and vocational education.

Publications. Professional publications including handbooks, guides, special newsletters, and audiovisual materials on topics such as industry-education councils, community resources workshops, career/special/vocational education, school-based job placement, industry-sponsored educational materials, educational management, and economic development.

National Association of Industrial Technology (NAIT). NAIT was formed in 1968 to foster improvement in the field of industrial technology within colleges, universities, business, and industry. Membership is open to organizations, professionals, students, retirees, professional and student groups, and related associations. NAIT has the following objectives:

- Provide a certification process for recognition of the attainment of appropriate standards for industrial technology professionals

- Provide an accreditation process for recognition of the attainment of appropriate standards for industrial technology programs in colleges and universities

- Promote curricula and program standards for industrial technology within colleges and universities

- Promote personnel classifications within business and industry for graduates of industrial technology programs

- Provide opportunities for discussion of questions, issues, and problems related to the field of industrial technology

- Promote the objectives and the interests of the Association by cooperating with other national, regional, and local special-interest organizations

NAIT also features accreditation and certification programs. Membership includes educators, students, graduates, industrial representatives, and others interested in industrial technology.

NAIT has four divisions: The Industry Division is open to individuals employed in industry and to industrial organizations. Activities in this division focus on the continuing professional development of technical management personnel. Division members are active in association accreditation and certification activities and share emerging technological information through workshops, publications, and programs at the annual convention. The three other divisions are the University, the Community College and Technical Institute, and the Student Divisions.

Conferences. NAIT hosts an annual convention each fall for its members.

Publications. The *Journal of Industrial Technology* is a quarterly publication featuring articles on technology, research, and industrial careers, as well as editorials from the organization's University and Industry Divisions. NAIT also publishes program directories, monographs, newsletters, and news releases.

National Speakers Association (NSA). The National Speakers Association is dedicated to:

- Ensuring the standard of excellence in the speaking profession
- Expanding the use of professional speakers

The world of today's speaker encompasses many environments—keynotes, luncheon, and banquet presentations; seminars and workshops; training courses; and all types of continuing education. The growth and diversity in the speaking profession is reflected in NSA's continued increase in membership.

From a handful of professional speakers who wished to unit to strengthen and develop the profession in 1973, NSA has grown to encompass more than 3300 members in the United States and other countries. There are nearly 40 local chapters throughout the United States and Canada.

NSA features Professional Emphasis Groups (PEGs): PEGs have been established to provide a place where speakers with common areas of interest can share ideas and experiences related specifically to the art and business of their specialty and to thereby raise the level of professionalism of active practitioners. Benefits include special meetings at NSA conventions and workshops, quality newsletters, and meeting badge identification to assist in networking opportunities. Groups established to date are these: Bureaus, Consultants, Educators, Health and Wellness, Humorists, International, Motivational, Sales Trainers, Seminar/Workshop Leaders, Writers/Publishers.

Conferences. Members gather to build networks essential to serious professionals and to hear NSA's "best speakers" share their secrets of success at the summer national convention.

NSA also holds educational workshops in both the east and the west. These workshops are packed with state-of-the-art ideas to keep members, as well as their staff, motivated and directed between conventions.

Publications. Published 10 times per year, *Professional Speaker* is the official voice of NSA. Members are kept informed about what is happening in the speaking profession and meetings industry, and obtain new ideas from top professionals.

The *Voices of Experience* cassette program is designed to bring members information on every facet of the speaking business. Top achievers share their skills and vital information members can use. These cassettes are issued eight times per year.

Society for Technical Communication (STC). STC is the largest professional association serving the technical communication profession. It has more than 16,000 members and 140 chapters worldwide. STC offers high-caliber programs that keep both entry-level and veteran communicators aware of the latest trends and technology in technical communications. It offers innovative services for the educational and professional development of its members.

STC members represent all facets of technical communication including writers and editors, graphic artists and technical illustrators, translators, managers and supervisors, educators and students, independent consultants and contractors, and photographers and audiovisual specialists.

Conferences. STC's Annual Conference in the summer is its premier educational activity and draws about 2000 professional communicators from around the world. Attendees choose from a wide selection of educational programs, seminars, and workshops conducted by experts in the field.

Publications. *Technical Communication* is STC's highly acclaimed quarterly journal which publishes thought-provoking articles on subjects of interest to all technical communicators.

Intercom, the Society newsletter, is published 10 times a year. It keeps members up to date on the latest professional news and Society activities.

3.2.3 Other Organizations

Lakewood Publications, Inc., a Maclean Hunter Company. This company provides trainers with publications, conferences, and workshops to foster professionalism.

Conferences

- *The Best of America Conference and Expo.* This winter conference highlights best practices from the human side of business. The conference includes top speakers, nearly 70 learning sessions, important professional connections in structured networking events, valuable resource materials and ideas, gains on key issues in intensive workshops, and suppliers and products.

- *Training Directors' Forum Conference.* This spring conference enables training managers to develop a plan to maximize the effectiveness of the training and development function. Conference participants learn the lessons of top training/HRD executives, network with peers and benchmark in and out of different industries, and take home valuable reference materials.

- *Total Trainer Program.* Lakewood's summer Train-the-Trainer Conference—The Total Trainer Program is a one-of-a-kind professional development experience for working training professionals. Sample sessions include "Developing and Delivering Effective Technical Training" and "Taking the Technical Out of Technical Training." Participants experience the networking and variety of a conference, the intensive focus of a single-subject workshop, and the opportunity to tailor the program to special needs. Extensive handouts, which support the seminars attended, are provided as well as handouts from the concurrent sessions unattended. The Total Trainer Program Course Notebooks, including more than 300 pages of these handouts, are provided to enable participants to put into practice what was learned in the program. The conference also includes a self-customized professional development program including up to five competency-building sessions:

Creative Training Techniques Conference/Total Trainer Institute

Measuring and Managing for Service Quality

Conferencia Pan-Americana Para La Excelencia En Calidad Y Servicios (Pan American Service and Quality Forum)

International Service and Quality Forum

The Positive Employee Practices Institute (PEPI) Seminar Series—educational programs that emphasize participation in problem solving to quickly focus the whole team on the same objectives.

"Best People Practices in America's Most Successful Organizations" Conference

Publications. *Training* magazine is published monthly. It includes in-depth articles of interest to training professionals. It features a calendar of conferences and seminars to help trainers in planning their schedules.

Newsletters include *The Service Edge, Total Quality, Creative Training Techniques,* and the *Training Directors' Forum Newsletter.* Other resources include books, videos, and tapes.

3.3 Educational Opportunities

A variety of educational opportunities exist for today's technical trainer as both a consumer and provider. These opportunities may take the form of industry or academe collaborations, academic and nonacademic instruction for trainers, or training modules for industry provided by universities and vendors. Universities can work with trainers to provide the basics to today's potential workforce so that when the students become employees, they are ready to be trained in more highly technical arenas. Further, technical trainers also have the opportunity to both share their expertise and hone their craft through classroom teaching at community colleges and universities.

It's important for technical trainers to be aware of these educational opportunities when making decisions on career development or planning an organization's training program. Too often, resources which are readily available are overlooked. The purpose of this section is to heighten awareness of educational opportunities through description and the citing of a few case studies.

3.3.1 The Technical Trainer as Consumer

Academic Opportunities.   A master's degree can prepare one to be a technical trainer. University-quality technical education combined with platform and interpersonal communication skills can well equip the technical trainer. However, obtaining a degree is a lengthy and expensive process; it is not the only option.

A certificate program is another avenue open to technical trainers. Many universities have standardized programs, while others are willing to work with industry to develop a customized program.

In the article "Professional Trainers Go to School,"[1] the cooperative effort between a South Florida ASTD chapter and a university business school resulted in an excellent certificate program and a good model for business and academe collaboration:

> Hundreds of trainers who wanted to upgrade their skills had looked to the Center for Management Development at Florida International University (FIU) for help. At Miami Chapter ASTD meetings, many trainers had been asking about academic train-the-trainer programs. Each time, they turned away disappointed when they heard the reply, "Someday . . ." But someday has to begin sometime.

By cooperating, FIU and the local ASTD chapter developed a core curriculum that emphasized the following competencies:

> Adult-learning understanding; counseling skills; audiovisual skills; objective preparation skills; organization-behavior understanding; presentation skills; questioning skills; understanding of the training and development field; understanding of training and development techniques; and writing skills.
>
> The core curriculum was broken down into five separate courses, each course lasting from three to five weeks. The courses were: Needs analysis; Adult Education Theory; Course Development and design methodology; presentation skills; and evaluation. Two electives, The Use of Computers in Training, and Organization Development, were also offered.

Seventeen men and women, ranging in age from their early twenties to early fifties, eagerly awaited the first class. Perhaps the most interesting demographic was that their educational attainment ranged from a high-school diploma to a PhD.

The graduates' proof of professionalism was the certificate, conferred on each participant by the dean of the College of Business Administration. The new credentials signified that the graduate had met the standards of training professionalism. Already recognized in the community, the certificate now is cited in ads for trainers as a prerequisite for employment.

South Florida now has a crop of newly trained trainers, young and old, who can meet the needs of the business community. The program that FIU and ASTD created runs smoothly and represents what the training community can do when it puts its mind to it. The main result of the program, of course, is that trainers can now show businesses that they have competence and expertise—they have certificates to prove it.

"Partnerships Net Big Wins,"[2] according to Terry Crist, Leo Presley, and John Zenger. They note that many businesses are looking to postsecondary schools, companies, and training suppliers to work in tandem to meet the corporate training needs:

> One arrangement, the Minnesota Technical College System, with 34 technical-college campuses, is representative of a growing network of statewide educational systems that have formed partnerships with large training suppliers. MTCS offers technical training, interpersonal skills and leadership training—including executive development courses—as well as customized materials to address specific requirements of the state's business and industry.

Colleges form partnerships with training consultants and local employers, including both small businesses and divisions of large companies. Training managers can look at colleges to manage their training function. Rather than develop a full in-house training program, they can access existing programs at the community college level. And the college is an ongoing resource.

According to Crist, Presley, and Zenger:

> Any successful business/education partnerships take these recommendations to heart: Make everyone a winner; offer expanded support from the training supplier; use a consultative sales approach to sell programs; use training suppliers with a good reputation; keep your eye on the bottom line; don't wait for business to come to you; customize each partnership; assess how the partnerships are working.

Nonacademic Opportunities.   A variety of skills training is available from nonacademic resources. A look in any training magazine will reveal a host of companies ready to deliver just what is needed. There are train-the-trainer programs, professional development programs, seminars, workshops, and conferences. To make appropriate selections, trainers should rely on their professional networks for guidance. Examples of nonacademic resources include

- *NTL Institute*—Founded in 1947, it has a Training the Trainer Certificate Program and Trainer Apprentice Practicum. NTL offers a variety of professional development workshops.
- *Mentoring* is an excellent way to acquire needed skills. By selecting a respected colleague, a trainer can follow the mentor's example and suggestions.
- *Self-study* through videotapes, audiotapes, books, and magazines, which are all valid resources for educational opportunities.
- *On-the-job training* can also be a solution.
- *Individual Learning Centers* (ILCs)—According to Joyce W. Tuck's article, "Professional Development through Learning Centers,"[3] individualized learning centers offer a self-directed approach to education and training that taps into the preferred style of the learner, using various technologies and adult learning theory, including

Books and periodicals
Audio-based education
Video-based education
16-mm film collection
Computer-assisted instruction
Programmed instruction
Information services
Living Library

As Tuck's article explains:

> What does ILC mean for the training professional? Some trainers believe that the concept and its services may eliminate their positions. This simply is not true. An ILC provides enhanced learning options and opportunities, tools, and support to make trainers more productive, and a time and place to develop themselves professionally.

3.3.2 The Technical Trainer as Provider

Technical trainers may go to the university to participate in educating students. These trainers have a wealth of knowledge from their industry experience and can provide real-world applications for students.

In the article "Back to School for College Training Opportunities,"[4] trainers learn how "returning to school to teach" can be an option for their professional development. It is suggested as a means of supplementing income, providing a place to gain experience in training, or even serving as a consultant looking for part-time training opportunities in between jobs.

3.4 Accreditation Opportunities

The importance of "measuring success" in today's business climate cannot be overemphasized. Whether or not a program continues is based on its "success." Accreditation is one form of measurement being implemented on an increasing basis. Sometimes industry requests that their courses be accredited by universities and receive academic credit. Some organizations form their own accreditation bodies. Accredited programs are often perceived to be better due to the performance measures they include. Also, in the case of university accreditation, there is a prestige factor associated with such a program.

Accreditation is established for the regulation of instructional programs. It is voluntary and is generally administered by an association or agency. It is used to insure a specific outcome or level of education and training. It is ongoing and must be renewed to assure that all standards continue to be met. It's a form of quality assurance.

3.4.1 Accreditation Example

One example of an accreditation program is the Department of Energy's (DOE) Training Accreditation Program.[5] It is designed to assist in achieving excellence in the development and implementation of performance-based nuclear facility training programs. The Training Accreditation Program establishes the objectives and criteria against which DOE nuclear facility training is evaluated for accreditation. The Training Accreditation Program Staff provides assistance to contractors, develops training guidelines, and evaluates the quality and effectiveness of facility training.

DOE believes that the cornerstone of safe operation is personnel performing the day-to-day functions which accomplish the facility mission. Therefore, training programs and trainers must meet the high standards of accreditation. In this situation, accreditation is functioning as a quality-assurance measure.

3.4.2   Accreditation Obstacles

A 1987 Department of Education paper[6] cites a study examining the American experience of accrediting employer-provided training. Interviews were conducted with representatives of accrediting agencies, employers with accreditation programs, and people with expertise in a related field.

It was found that employer-provided training could be evaluated for academic equivalence. However, a sizable percentage of the employer-provided training focused primarily on job competencies and other corporate objectives. This rendered many courses unsuitable for assessments. Many felt that recommendation for college credit was a successful way to improve access to academic institutions, motivating employees by enabling them to acquire academic qualifications in the absence of professional recognition, and enhancing morale and quality of some corporate training departments. Increases in number of programs accredited were expected, but not in great numbers.

The literature suggests that accreditation opportunities will vary depending on individual universities, industries, and governments. Technical trainers must look to their own organizations for opportunities to participate in accredited programs.

3.5   Conclusion

It is clear that technical training professionalism has grown over the years. Today's trainer has a myriad of professional opportunities to enhance career growth. There is even the case being made for a *chief training officer* (CTO). And well it should be. Training is a strategic function within an organization and must be given serious consideration. Employee training is linked to the survival of companies competing in today's global market.

"The developments in training technologies are revolutionary," says Jack E. Bowsher, a former director of education and training for International Business Machines Corporation (IBM).[7] "The companies which make use of advanced training systems have an advantage in terms of quality and costs," Bowsher adds, noting that he believes decisions about training technologies should be managed at the highest levels of an organization.

And, for training organizations to survive within an enterprise, they must market themselves. According to L. Paul Ouellette's article "Marketing Your Training Organization Internally":[8]

> To survive during the recession, training professionals need to develop a clients-first philosophy and market their organizations effectively.

Ten Marketing Techniques:

- Brochures—to provide answers to questions asked most frequently.
- Newsletters—publicize the effectiveness of training available.
- Management Reports—annual or semi-annual report with state-of-the-department message.
- 5/15 reports—brief, monthly updates that take 5 minutes to read and 15 to write.
- Publications—magazine or feature article on training organization.
- Walk-in Center—place to view training function. Staff with service-oriented, knowledgeable, professional people.
- Presentations—Trainers can give other departments an overview.
- Brown Bag Seminars—give overviews to employees at lunch time.
- House Calls—one-on-one dialogues with other departments about the training function.
- Client Coordinators—Training Manager can appoint staff members to service specific areas of the corporation.

Technical trainers must take responsibility for themselves and their organizations to succeed in today's global economy. Continued growth of technical training professionalism is essential.

Professional Organizations Listing

American Management Association
135 W. 50th St.
New York, NY 10020
(212)903-8216

American Society for Engineering Education
1818 N St., N.W., Suite 600
Washington, D.C. 20036-2479
(202)331-3500

American Society for Healthcare Education & Training
840 N. Lake Shore Drive
Chicago, IL 60611
(312)280-6113

American Society for Quality Control
P.O. Box 3005
Milwaukee, WI 53201-3005
(414)272-8575

American Society for Training & Development
1640 King St., Box 1443
Alexandria, VA 22313
(703)683-9592

Association for Educational Communications & Technology
1025 Vermont Ave., N.W., Ste. 820
Washington, D.C. 20005
(202)347-7834

Association for Multi-Image International
10008 N. Dale Mabry, St. 113
Tampa, FL 33618
(813)960-1692

Association for Quality & Participation
801-B W. Eighth St., Ste. 501
Cincinnati, OH 45203-1607
(513)381-1959

Council of Hotel and Restaurant Trainers
9025 Coldwater, Ste. 100
Ft. Wayne, IN 46825
(219)997-6823

Human Resource Planning Society
41 E. 42nd St., Ste. 1509
New York, NY 10017
(212)490-6387

International Association for Continuing Education & Training
1101 Connecticut Ave., N.W.
Washington D.C. 20036
(202)857-1122

International Association for Continuing Engineering Education
c/o Helsinki University of Technology
TKK Innopoli
FIN-02150 Espoo
Finland
358-0-451-4024

International Federation of Training & Development Organizations
Southwell, Ampney Crucis,
Cirencester
Gloucestershire, GL7 5RY, U.K.
(44)285-851398

International TV Association
6311 N. O'Connor Road, LB51
Irving, TX 75039
(214)869-1112

Lakewood Conferences
50 S. Ninth St.
Minneapolis, MN 55402
(800)328-4329

Meeting Planners International
1950 Stemmons Frwy. Ste. 5018
Dallas, TX 75207-3109
(214)712-7751

National Association of Government Training and Development
Iron Works Pike
P.O. Box 11910
Lexington, KY 40578-1910
(606)231-1948

National Association for Industry-Education Cooperation
235 Hendricks Boulevard
Buffalo, NY 14226
(716)834-7047

National Association of Industrial Technology
3157 Packard Road, Suite A
Ann Arbor, MI 48108-1900
(313)677-0720

National Society for Performance & Instruction
1300 L St., N.W., Ste. 1250
Washington, D.C. 20005
(202)408-7969

National Speakers Association
1500 South Priest
Tempe, AZ 85281
(602)968-2552

National Staff Development Council
P.O. Box 240
Oxford, OH 45056
(513)523-6029

Organizational Development Network
P.O. Box 69329
Portland, OR 97201
(503)246-0148

Society for Applied Learning Technology
50 Culpeper St.
Warrentown, VA 22186
(703)347-0055

Society for Human Resource Management
606 N. Washington St.
Alexandria, VA 22314
(703)548-3440

Society for Technical Communication
901 N. Stuart St., Ste. 904
Arlington, VA 22203
(703)522-4114

Training Resources & Data
 Exchange
U.S. Department of Energy
Oak Ridge Institute for Science and
 Education
P.O. Box 117
Oak Ridge, TN 37831-2207
(615)576-3316

References

1. Betsy Castner and Willabeth Jordan, "Professional Trainers Go to School," *Training & Development,* July 1989, p. 77.

2. Terry Crist, Leo Presley, and John Zenger, "Partnerships Net Big Wins," *Training & Development,* September 1992, p. 37.

3. Joyce W. Tuck, "Professional Development through Learning Centers," *Training & Development,* September 1988, p. 76.

4. Wendell Anderson, "Back to School for College Training Opportunities," *Training & Development,* August 1992, p. 42.

5. U.S. Department of Energy, "Training Accreditation Program," *Training Program Manual,* March 1, 1989.

6. Tom Chaplin and Keith Drake, "American Experience of Accreditation of Employer-Provided Training—Paper No. 4," *Department of Education and Science,* June 1987.

7. George F. Kimmerling, "A Place at the Top for Trainers," *Training & Development,* March 1993, p. 47.

8. L. Paul Ouellette, "Marketing Your Training Organization Internally," *Technical and Skills Training,"* April 1993, p. 28.

4

Selecting and Supporting the Technical Trainer

Linda J. Segall
Senior Editor, The Dartnell Corporation

Linda J. Segall *is a senior editor with the Dartnell Corporation, a business information and training publisher. She edits* Successful Supervisor *and* Foremanship, *biweekly training bulletins designed to assist supervisors in effectively carrying out their supervisory roles. Segall joined Dartnell after having spent more than 18 years in human resources development and management in manufacturing, sales/distribution, and corporate environments. Her resume includes working for several Fortune 500 companies, including ALCOA, Ball Corporation, and divisions of Miller Brewing Company and Tenneco Automotive, Inc. Throughout her human resources career, she complemented her work experience by periodically writing for a number of training publications, including* Supervisory Management, Training, *and* Training and Development Journal, *and the* National Business and Employment Weekly.

4.1 Introduction

Several years ago, a 300-employee plastics manufacturer experienced a dramatic drop in demand for its product. It curtailed some operations, laid off employees, and displaced its least senior supervisor. Although the company didn't know how long the slow-down would endure, it was confident

117

that business would rebound. And so, it made what seemed to be a far-sighted decision to use the slow time to upgrade the job skills of its remaining employees. And, it put the surplus supervisor in charge of the training.

The training effort failed. A number of reasons contributed to the failure:

- Although the company inherently understood that its employees needed training, management had not articulated why the training was necessary nor had it linked the training directly to the company's goals.

- The plant manager viewed training as an interim activity to occupy the displaced supervisor until business picked up.

- Biased by his viewpoint, the plant manager threw the supervisor into the training arena without ascertaining if she had the necessary skills to do the job.

Contrast that training situation to what occurred at Ball-Incon Glass Packaging Corp., a glass container manufacturer that today has 14 manufacturing plants and approximately 6000 employees, and captures a significant share of the glass container market in the United States.[1]

Ball-Incon was formed in 1987 as a joint venture between a division of Ball Corporation and Incon, each a successful glass manufacturer. Prior to the merger, technical training in each of the companies was historically done on a hit-or-miss (mostly miss) basis. But shortly after the merger, the new company's management decided that if Ball-Incon were to survive in a maturing industry, it had to continue to deliver quality products to its customers at competitive prices. And to do this, it had to take full advantage of all resources available to it, including technological advances. But none of that could happen unless it had a qualified workforce.

Ball-Incon's acceptance of its position in its industry and market, and where it wanted to go, spawned the creation of a centralized technical training department, which today has a manager, an instructional designer, and eight full-time trainers stationed in its plants throughout the United States.

By any measure, the company's training has been successful: 12 months after they successfully complete a training program, employees on average retain *90 percent* of what they learned. The training manager attributes this remarkable accomplishment to a number of factors:

- Ball-Incon management has continued to support training, even during times of reduced operating budgets.

- Training is performance-based and supports the company's short- and long-term goals.

- Training is planned, measured, and reinforced.

- Ball-Incon trainers are *well qualified* to do their jobs.

4.1.1 How Does This Apply to You?

The success of your training efforts will depend directly on the quality of your decision(s) concerning who will do your training. You may decide to select an employee to be your trainer, or to let vendors, consultants, or even community colleges or vocational schools do your training for you—because these external sources are all legitimate options available to you. But you still have to select the *right* trainer (even from external sources) who has the *right* qualifications for the job you need done.

Fortunately, selecting a trainer approximates a regular hiring decision. But a primary difference is that you probably don't hire as many trainers as you do assemblers, welders, engineers, or quality-assurance technicians. So, you may not be fully aware of the potential breadth of a training position. You may be surprised to learn that a trainer may work in any—and most like several—of 15 different roles.[2] And the competencies required for each role differ significantly. Picking the right trainer is not simply a matter of looking in the Yellow Pages for a consultant or assigning training to your most likable or knowledgeable worker.

This chapter breaks down the selection process into a series of easy-to-follow steps. It also provides you with some tools to guide you in making a decision about selecting a qualified trainer.

The several steps in the selection process are:

- *Understanding the job: building a job description.* A job description allows you to determine the trainer's role in your organization.

- *Determining qualifications.* The trainer must have the right qualifications to perform to your expectations.

- *Weighing the advantages of both "external" or "internal" trainers.* Should you hire someone from outside your company to do the training? Or should you opt to use an employee? Each has advantages and disadvantages.

- *Evaluating credentials and selecting the trainer.* Once you decide to go "external" or "internal," how do you know if the trainer has the qualifications he or she purports?

- *Backing up your choice.* Regardless of where you find your trainer, the individual you select needs support and resources to do the job.

This section guides you in how to lend yourself to the support effort. You will also find that, at several points, this chapter references the Ball-Incon experience. What one midsized company has done, you can do too.

4.2 Understanding the Job: Building a Basic Job Description

Job descriptions aren't just for employees. The job description sets out in specific terms *why* the job exists. And it describes *what you expect* the incumbent to be responsible for doing. From the job description, you determine the skills, knowledge, and abilities required to achieve those expectations.

Remember that jobs can be performed by individuals other than employees. So whether you decide to use an employee as a trainer or to use a consultant, a vendor, or an instructor from an institution (such as a community college or vocational school), you need a basic job description to establish a mutual line of communication between you and the individual who will do the training.

4.2.1 Using a Training Committee

In some organizations, one or two persons arbitrarily decide the purpose of the trainer's position and trainer's roles. Other companies find that a 5- to 10-member training committee, composed of a cross-function of management and/or employees, takes the burden of selection away from one or two individuals and helps get better employee, supervisory, and cross-departmental buy-in for training.

A training committee may serve the organization in a number of different ways. In the context of selecting a trainer, however, a training committee examines and determines the purpose of the trainer's job (Why a trainer?), and then decides, by consensus, which roles the trainer will be accountable to perform. (See Figure 4-1, "Composition of the Training Committee.")

4.2.2 Why a Trainer?

Why a trainer? This is the first critical question you need to ask before you can develop the trainer's job description. The answer can range from concrete reasons (such as "to help us comply with OSHA regulations") to more strategic reasons (such as "to equip our employees with skills and knowledge required to take advantage of future technologies").

You and your boss may tacitly comprehend the reasons for having a trainer in your plant. But that purpose needs to be documented on paper. The person you eventually select to conduct the training may perceive your training needs completely differently from you, because this person

Who should be on your training committee? The committee's composition depends on several factors: your plant's union status, the scope of the training you plan (departmentwide vs. plantwide), and the impact of the training on other departments.

If yours is a union plant, work with the union for agreement on training and the use of hourly employees on a training committee, according to the provisions of the union contract. And, in a nonunion plant, be sure to check with your attorney concerning using nonmanagement employees on an employee involvement committee. (Although such employee participation is desirable from an employee relations point of view, using hourly employees in a decision-making capacity may jeopardize a plant's nonunion status, according to rulings of the National Labor Relations Board.*)

Ideally, a training committee is composed of insightful representatives from each group affected by the training. To determine who should be on your training committee, go down this list of groups of employees and check off any group affected by the training. Consider including a representative from each group to help you determine the purpose and roles of the trainer.

Group	Affected by Training?
Supervisors	[ ]
Team (group) leaders	[ ]
Production workers	[ ]
Maintenance	[ ]
Engineering	[ ]
Quality	[ ]
Union	[ ]
Human resources	[ ]
Accounting	[ ]
Safety	[ ]
Other	[ ]

* "Electromation and the International Brotherhood of Teamsters Local Union No. 1049, AFL-CIO, and Action Committees," 309 NLRB No. 163; "E.I. du Pont de Nemours & Company and Chemical Workers Association," 311 NLRB No. 88.

Figure 4-1. Composition of your training committee.

will be looking at your training requirements influenced by his or her own needs, experiences, and abilities. Unless you document the purpose of training, you risk miscommunication and failure of your training program.

Figure 4-2, "Why a Trainer?," suggests a number of legitimate reasons for having a trainer. Check off all those that apply to your situation.

4.2.3 Identifying the Trainer's Several Roles

The next step in clarifying the trainer's job is to decide how you want your trainer to function and support the training effort. To do this, you need to identify the primary roles (or functions) your trainer will be accountable to perform.

You may find it helpful to choose the trainer functions from the 15 functions (roles) listed in Figure 4-3, "Trainer Roles."

Check off all of the reasons why your organization needs a trainer.

[ ] To help the plant comply with the law (such as is required by OSHA)

[ ] To provide basic skills and knowledge required to do all types of work in the plant

[ ] To teach new employees how to perform existing jobs

[ ] To teach workers how to operate new equipment or machinery or to perform new work processes

[ ] To increase the flexibility of workers on the job and accommodate the demands of just-in-time manufacturing

[ ] To increase the skill level and knowledge of employees so that they will be ready to take advantage of new technologies on the horizon

[ ] To design, deliver, and implement technical training programs required for new technologies

[ ] To improve the problem-identification and problem-solving capabilities of workers for cost and process improvements and a keener competitive edge

[ ] Other _____

Figure 4-2. Why a trainer?

[ ] *Evaluator:* Measures if training has accomplished what it was designed to do. Prepares and administers pretests and posttests, analyzes test data, and reports the effectiveness of the training.

[ ] *Group facilitator:* Leads discussion groups on a variety of subjects, including group problem solving. Manages conflict within a group, assures total and balanced participation, focuses group on subject. May prepare meeting agendas and attend to other group meeting needs.

[ ] *Individual development counselor:* Helps individuals determine their strengths and areas requiring improvement. Works with individuals one-on-one to assess skills, knowledge, and abilities. May assess developmental needs against identified competencies required by the organization, or may help the individual assess developmental needs against the individual's long-term personal goals.

[ ] *Instructional writer:* Writes training materials. Draws upon knowledge of the job, work process, the organization, and the individual(s) to be trained; develops and writes training programs designed to transfer skills and knowledge to the trainee. Using knowledge of adult learning, selects instructional medium most appropriate for the transfer of skill and knowledge. May prepare job and training aids in addition to instructional program.

[ ] *Instructor:* Performs stand-up training. Using knowledge of adult learning, presents prepared training programs to groups of employees.

[ ] *Manager:* Manages the total training function. Prepares budgets, hires trainers and/or consultants, and purchases equipment, programs, and training materials. Assumes responsibility for needs identification, program development and delivery, and measurement of training effectiveness.

[ ] *Marketer:* Sells training programs.

* Adapted from Patricia A. McLagan and Richard C. McCullough, *Models for Excellence: The Conclusions and Recommendations of the ASTD Training and Development Competency Study,* American Society for Training and Development, 1983.

Figure 4-3. Trainer roles.*

[ ] *Media specialist:*   Uses audiovisual equipment to produce training aids or training programs.

[ ] *Needs analyst:*   Identifies areas in which training is needed to achieve targeted levels of performance. Measures current levels of performance against ideal or desired levels of performance.

[ ] *Program administrator:*   Makes sure that people, equipment, materials, and instructors are in place when needed. Coordinates resources, administers training budget, and purchases equipment and material.

[ ] *Program designer:*   Develops the content of training programs. Analyzes needs of the organization and the targeted training audience and designs training programs to meet those needs, selecting methods to facilitate adult learning and retention.

[ ] *Strategist:*   Works with management to develop long-term plans for training within the organization. Analyzes demographics, availability of human resources, and long-term business needs to help plan training to meet long-term business objectives.

[ ] *Task analyst:*   Identifies and describes tasks and their components used to perform work flow. Studies work flow and job tasks. Documents work processes. Identifies skills, knowledge, and abilities required to perform tasks. May recommend work process redesign.

[ ] *Theoretician:*   Tests learning theories.

[ ] *Transfer agent (coach):*   Helps individuals apply training to the job. Observes work as it is performed. Coaches employees in the application of new skills.

Figure 4-3. *(Continued)*

These 15 roles were studied and articulated in a 1983 American Society for Training and Development report on trainer competencies. It would be rare (if not impossible) for a trainer to function in all of these roles at one time. But it is not unusual for a trainer to assume and perform several of these roles as primary functions of the training position, and to fluctuate among several roles very rapidly.

For example, a trainer who is making a classroom presentation may function primarily as an instructor who presents information. But if the group begins to argue an issue, the instructor may have to put on a group facilitator "hat" to mediate the conflict and lead the group back to a learning point. Just as rapidly, the instructor may need to slip into a needs analyst role to "take the temperature" of the group to assure that learning is occurring. Each of these roles is important to achieving a transfer of skills and information.

Each role that you select needs to support the purpose of the training position. To see how this works, let's examine some of the elements of the technical trainer job description for Ball-Incon:

The company focuses its centralized training function on providing the company with a capable and qualified workforce. This is the overall purpose of the company's training program. Technical trainers, officed in plants throughout the country, *present technical training and direct a structured learning experience for employees*—the purpose of the trainer position. The job description calls for each technical trainer (called an *employee development specialist*) to *implement training programs* (instructor role), *facilitate total quality management (TQM) meetings* (group facilitator), *keep records* (administrator role), *evaluate training* (evaluator role), and *follow up training* (coaching role). Each of these roles directly supports the purpose of the trainer's job, and is the reason that systematic training was initiated within the company.

Whether you will decide these trainer roles with only the input of your boss or by using a training committee, develop consensus concerning which roles are most important to your organization. Ranking is an easy method of prioritization. (See Figure 4-4, "How to Rank.")

Which training roles will you hold your trainer accountable to perform? Ranking is an easy method to prioritize the importance of the 15 roles to your organization. Here is how to rank and develop consensus among a ranking committee:

1. List all of the roles.

2. Discuss each of the roles to make sure that everyone who is involved in the ranking process understands each role.

3. Ask each ranker to assign "1" to the *most* important role for your organization, and then to continue ranking each role in order of importance until all 15 are numbered. (Remember that "15" is *least important*.)

4. Add each person's rankings to arrive at a score for each role.

5. Sort the roles according to ranking by total scores. Remember that the lowest score has the highest priority.

Figure 4-4. How to rank.

The several roles that cluster together with the lowest rankings should be included as the primary trainer roles. For example, assume that the five members of your training committee rank *Instructor* 1, 3, 2, 4, and 6. These rankings added together equal a score of 16. If 16 is the lowest score of all the roles, it is the most important training function for the trainer to perform in your organization.

4.3 Determining Qualifications: Proof That a Trainer *Can* Train

Once you have prioritized and decided on the primary roles your trainer will play in your organization, you are ready to go on to the next step in the selection process: determining the trainer's qualifications—proof that a trainer *can* train. Qualifications (or *credentials,* as they are sometimes called) are typically cited as the *skills, knowledge, and abilities* required to get the job done.

The terms "skills," "knowledge," and "abilities" are often erroneously interchanged as synonyms. Skills result from a marriage of abilities and knowledge. Another way to think about skills, knowledge, and abilities is to remember that skills are attained and demonstrable proficiencies that are generally observable.[3] Knowledge is an understanding, acquired either formally (through schooling or training) or informally (through exposure and experience). (Knowledge cannot usually be observed firsthand.) And abilities are natural aptitudes or talents that can be honed into skills by acquiring training and knowledge.

As you analyze each of the roles in which you expect the trainer to function, you will see that the roles require different sets and levels of competencies. *Your analysis should differentiate between skills, knowledge, and abilities, because a successful selection of trainer will depend upon a good match of these credentials.*

Some skills, knowledge, and abilities will, of course, overlap into more than one role, but the most certain way to determine the qualifications your trainer requires is to analyze and list the skills, knowledge, and abilities *for each distinct role.* (And make sure you list them as skills, knowledge, or abilities.) Figure 4-5, "Example of an Analysis of Qualifications," illustrates how this is done.

A pitfall to watch for: inexperienced job description writers often tend to jump to listing qualifications in terms of arbitrary educational standards, such as "must have high school diploma," or "must have bachelor's degree in engineering." Although certain skills or knowledge may generally result from a specific level of education, write down the require-

For each role, write down a description of what you expect the trainer to do when performing the role. Then list the skills, knowledge, and abilities required to perform the role in your organization.

Example

Trainer role: Needs analyst.

Description: Identifies areas in which training is needed to achieve targeted levels of performance: working with operations personnel, identifies and specifies the ideal or targeted level of performance, generally described in behavioral terms. Designs and administers assessment tools to measure current levels of performance against ideal or desired levels of performance.

Skills/knowledge/abilities required:

- Knowledge of the organization, its goals, and its mission
- Knowledge of the job(s) performed and work process(es)
- Skill in identifying training needs
- Skill in distinguishing performance-based training needs from non-performance-related needs
- Skill in using assessment methods and ability to design assessment tools
- Interpersonal communication skills
- Group process skills
- Written communication skills
- Problem-solving skills

Figure 4-5. Example of an analysis of qualifications.

ments in terms of proficiencies and make sure that all requirements are *bona fide occupational qualifications.* When qualifications are stated as performance proficiencies, you minimize the possibility of allegations of discrimination.

When you have finished listing all qualifications for each trainer role, analyze the list you have compiled. You may see a repetition of several of the qualifications. Summarize and list all of the qualifications, in a manner similar to the example given in Figure 4-6, "Summarizing Qualifications," for a plant trainer.

Listing and summarizing qualifications like this is more than a paper-and-pencil exercise. It helps you to quantify the credentials your trainer

Analyze the qualifications you have determined that your trainer should have to perform the several trainer roles in your plant, then compile a list of all of the qualifications, similar to the example shown below:

Example: Plant trainer

Qualification	How often listed
Knowledge of the company, its mission, and goals	5
Knowledge of the job and work	5
Knowledge of adult learning	4
Problem-solving skills	4
Interpersonal communication skills	4
Written communication skills	3
Needs identification skills	3
Training evaluation skills	3

Figure 4-6. Summarizing qualifications.

needs to do the job you anticipate. It allows you to determine these credentials in an objective manner. And it leads you to the next step in the selection process.

4.4 Weighing the Advantages of Both External and Internal Trainers

Armed with a good understanding of why you need training and what you need to look for in a trainer, it is now time to think about *where* to look for the trainer. What are your choices? You may search:

- Externally, to seek a consultant, vendor, or instructor from an educational institution, who may be able to solve your training problems.

- Internally, to find a manager, supervisor, or employee who has most of the qualifications you have identified and whom you can bring up to speed easily and reasonably.

Here are advantages and disadvantages of each of these sources.

4.4.1 Vendors as Trainers

Today, with financial resources for training limited but demand for training high, it is not unusual for companies to write training into a purchase or lease agreement with a vendor. Consequently, vendors provide a considerable amount of technical training in the workplace. And perhaps rightly so—who can better train others to use original equipment than the manufacturer of the equipment?

Vendor training has merit, but it also has drawbacks. Here are both.

Advantages of Using Vendors as Trainers

- The vendor is proficient in using and knowing the new equipment or machines.

- Training can be negotiated into the purchase or lease price. This imposes no additional strain on the training budget.

- The vendor can usually offer continuing support, in some form, although that may not include training programs when you require them.

Disadvantages of Using Vendors as Trainers

- Training may be a "one-shot" deal, given only when the equipment or machinery is installed.

- The amount of training (either in hours or numbers of individuals to be trained, or both) may be limited by contract.

- Vendor training may not be available to new hires or employees assigned to run the equipment after the initial training has been given.

- You may not have control over the choice of trainers; the vendor may select and assign a trainer. Therefore, the trainer may be technically competent, but may not be literate in adult learning, and may not use training methods most appropriate for your employees.

4.4.2 Consultants as Trainers

Just as most companies occasionally use vendors for training, they also occasionally hire consultants to do some of their training for them. Some companies, in fact, rely heavily on consultants, because:

- Some companies feel that consultants can provide a level of expertise not found in their organizations.

- Others, reeling from the pressures of increased operating efficiencies, choose not to increase their labor budgets for an employee-trainer.

- Smaller companies or plants with fewer than 300 employees may not be able to afford a full-time trainer and may find difficulty in dealing logistically with a part-time position.

- Still others do not have the in-house expertise to support a nonprofessional employee-trainer.

Hiring a consultant to do your training is a good option when you need a high concentration of training to be done quickly, and the likelihood of needing that training repeated is small. It can also be a wise choice if a consultant helps introduce changes in technology, or if the subject matter of your training requires targeted expertise not available in-house.

Advantages of Using Consultants as Trainers

- The consultant's expertise can complement your in-house expertise.

- You don't increase your labor budget with an additional head count.

- The consultant may be able to facilitate changes in technology more easily than an in-house individual.

- If training is required on a one-shot basis, hiring a consultant may be more economical than using an in-house person.

- A consultant may be able to initiate a comprehensive and systematic training function that can later be turned over to an employee-trainer.

Disadvantages of Using Consultants as Trainers

- The consultant may require the use of a full-time subject-matter expert to supplement his or her credentials.

- The consultant may not understand your plant and its culture.

- If a consultant is used long-term, cost becomes a major consideration.

- If you select a consultant for his/her subject-matter expertise instead of training ability and experience, the training may be overloaded with "nice-to-know" details, and delivery may not meet the adult learning needs of the trainees.

- Anyone can call him/herself a consultant—regardless of credentials. You may not get what you think you are paying for, unless you check and select carefully.

- Some consultants will try the "one-size-fits-all" approach to solving your training problems.[4] They may try to foist a training solution on your organization, even if it isn't the best solution for your problems.

4.4.3 Educational Instructors as Trainers

A third external choice is to use instructors from educational institutions, such as vocational or community colleges. Long tapped as a source of training for apprenticeship programs, vocational and community colleges are becoming more involved in forming partnerships with industry, to meet various training needs.

A number of companies, like Ball-Incon, are beginning to look to community colleges to provide basic and remedial skills training for employees. If employees cannot read, write, or perform simple mathematical computations, companies cannot take advantage of new technologies on the horizon, many of which are computer-based. This is a real problem, validated by a National Association of Manufacturers survey. It found that 40 percent of the survey respondents could not upgrade their technologies because of basic skills deficiencies in the workforce.[5]

Most community colleges are eager to work with local businesses.[6] A 1988 survey by the American Association of Community and Junior Colleges found that 75 percent offer customized training for private-sector employers. Chapter 20 in this handbook deals extensively with how to work with community and vocational colleges as a training resource. But here are a few of the benefits and drawbacks of this training solution.

Advantages of Using Educational Institutions in Training

- Community colleges are generally willing to work with business establishments.
- Cost may be reasonable.
- Instructors have a high level of expertise in their fields.
- Instructors may be willing to conduct courses on-site.
- Employees may be able to earn college credit for courses taken.

Drawbacks of Using Educational Institutions for Training

- Education is not training. And educators sometimes have difficulty understanding the difference between "nice to know" and "need to know." (Nice-to-know details tend to overwhelm workers, who expect to learn pragmatic job-related skills or knowledge.)
- Employees who need remedial education may be "put off" at attending "college" courses.

- Instructors may not have a good understanding of plant environment work.
- Course material may be highly theoretical and employees may not see its relevance to their work.

4.4.4 Employee-Trainers

If you decide to "go internal" to meet your training needs, you may look at managers, supervisors, and employees—in other words, any person who is on (or will be added to) your payroll. There are both advantages and disadvantages to using employees as trainers.

Advantages of Using Employee-Trainers

- Employees are often subject-matter experts, with technical knowledge or knowledge of jobs, the work process, and the organization.
- Employees generally relate well to other employees.
- Employees understand the politics and norms of the organization.
- If the organization is small and cannot afford a full-time trainer, yet has recurrent training needs, an employee can job-share in a trainer role.
- Employee-trainers can accommodate themselves more easily to production and shift schedules than outsiders. And they are available to do modular training on a just-in-time basis, whereas external trainers may have a more limited availability.
- It is more economical to use in-house trainers for recurrent training needs than to hire outsiders.

Disadvantages of Using Employee-Trainers

- Trainers recruited from the ranks of employees may not have knowledge of, or skill in, adult learning techniques.
- New-hire trainers will not have job/work/organization knowledge.
- If employee-trainers lack a background in adult learning, they may have difficulty in distinguishing between "nice to know" and "need to know." (Subject-matter experts often get tangled up in the intricacies of their expertise.)
- They may not have the aptitudes for effective adult learning applications that meet the needs of the trainees. (For example, if you have a young workforce, classroom presentations should meet the needs and expectations of the MTV generation[7]—use of high-tech training aids, short training periods, and a lot of interaction by the trainees.)
- Using an employee as a trainer removes the employee from another role and increases headcount in the labor budget.

It's your call: There is nothing magic about either internal or external trainers. The solution is to choose the source that best meets your needs at the time you need to have training done. Each source has advantages and disadvantages. Weigh them all against:

- Urgency of the training
- Availability of the trainer and trainees
- Your ability to support the trainer
- Budgets

4.5 Evaluating Credentials and Making a Selection

To this point in the selection process, you have:

- Developed a job description that focuses the trainer's role in the organization
- Determined the kinds of qualifications a trainer should ideally have
- Examined the advantages and disadvantages of both external and internal sources of trainers

Now you are ready to look at and evaluate the qualifications of individual candidates for your trainer slot. To do this, resurrect the job description and your list of qualifications, and follow these steps:

1. Develop a list of questions that will reveal the level of expertise the candidate(s) has for each qualification and interview the candidates.
2. Measure the level of expertise the candidate(s) has against the desired level.
3. Ascertain your ability to support the trainer you select.
4. Make a selection.

4.5.1 Interviewing the Candidates

Regardless of whether you decide to use a vendor, consultant, or employee-trainer, you have the right and the obligation to fully assess each candidate's credentials. A number of interviewing guides are available, including one entitled *How to Interview and Hire Productive People.*[8] This book is particularly helpful in leading you through the process of finding employees who fit into the culture of your organization.

As helpful as interviewing guides are, however, they are written for generic consumption and do not give you specific questions to ask that can unveil the qualifications of a trainer candidate. Use the questions in Figure 4-7, "Sample Interview Questions," as guidelines.

Any number of books on employment interviewing techniques can provide you with pattern questions to ask in an interview. Because you may not be as familiar with training as you are with engineering, assembly, or quality assurance, however, you may feel at a loss concerning specific questions that test the trainer's experience and skills. Here are a number of questions centered on several of the more common roles your trainer might assume in your organization:

Evaluator: What is a pre-test? A post-assessment? When is it appropriate to use a paper-and-pencil assessment? Describe how you analyze the data and what you do with it. Describe your experience in developing assessments.

Group facilitator: Describe your experiences in setting up and facilitating groups. What is the difference between a group leader and the facilitator? Tell me about a situation in which there was significant conflict in the group, and describe to me how you handled it.

Instructor: What kinds of training techniques are more effective with younger employees? Why do you find them effective? What do you find to be the optimal length of time for a training module to last? Why? How do you handle disruptive employees in a training session? (Ask each candidate to demonstrate his/her presentation skills for you and several others in a mock training session.)

Needs analyst: Describe to me several different ways to conduct a needs analysis. Which has been more effective for you? Tell me about situations in which you have conducted such an analysis. What did your results determine?

Program designer: What kinds of programs have you designed? Were these adaptations, or did you do them from scratch? Where was your beginning point? What were their objectives? How effective were they? How did you measure results? What kinds of methods did you use in the design?

Transfer agent (coach):   Describe to me how to conduct on-the-job training. If you observe that an employee is not doing a task correctly, what should you do? What is your experience in coaching?

Figure 4-7. Sample interview questions.

4.5.2 Measuring Expertise Levels

A perfect world would have perfect trainers. And these trainers would be equally proficient in their subject-matter expertise as they were in adult learning theories. But the world isn't perfect, nor are its trainers.

Look at each of the qualifications you have set out, and determine if the trainer-candidate has each credential, and to what level he or she has it. Does the candidate have a high degree of expertise in the qualification area? a medium degree? or a low degree of expertise? (See Figure 4-8, "Evaluating a Candidate's Qualifications.")

4.5.3 Your Ability to Support the Trainer

Finally, before you select a trainer, you should make an introspective assessment of you and/or your organization's ability to support a trainer

---

List each of the qualifications your trainer needs. Using the information you solicit from the interview, the resume, references, and other sources, determine the candidate's level of expertise for each qualification (high, medium, low). Finally, in the last column, determine your own ability to support the candidate: Can you provide support easily and reasonably (yes or no)?

Qualification	Level of Expertise (Hi, Med, Low)	Able to Support (Yes or No)
_____	_____	____
_____	_____	____
_____	_____	____
_____	_____	____
_____	_____	____
_____	_____	____
_____	_____	____
_____	_____	____
_____	_____	____
_____	_____	____
_____	_____	____

Figure 4-8. Evaluating a candidate's qualifications.

regardless of whether you select an employee, an outside vendor, consultant, or educational instructor. Any of these may require some type of support, ranging from formal or informal on-the-job training to use of a subject-matter expert.

Go back to Figure 4-8 and fill in the last column. Indicate Y (yes) or N (no) if you can *easily* and *reasonably* bring the trainer-candidate up to your expectations through formal or informal on-the-job training or formal schooling. Remember that *easily* and *reasonably* are subjective terms. They depend upon:

- Your own expertise and expectations
- The availability of subject-matter experts
- The availability of train-the-trainer resources
- Your time requirements
- Your budget

Now compare this introspection with the reality of your candidate's qualifications. If you can easily and reasonably support the trainer in the areas in which he or she is deficient, you have a match.

Another way to do this evaluation is to compare your overall level of expertise with the candidate's qualifications. Figure 4-9, "Subject Matter Expertise vs. Training Expertise," depicts subject matter (including technical knowledge and/or job and work knowledge) matched against training (adult learning) expertise.

Ascertain where the candidate falls on this chart. The most desirable combinations are High/High (subject matter and training expertise). And obviously, the least desirable mix is Low/Low.

SUBJECT MATTER EXPERTISE	TRAINING EXPERTISE
High	High
Medium	High
Low	High
High	Medium
Medium	Medium
Low	Medium
High	Low
Medium	Low
Low	Low

Figure 4-9. Subject matter expertise vs. training expertise.

Again, because this is not an ideal world, your trainer may not have a High/High combination in all qualifications. Are you and your organization strong where the candidate is weak? If you aren't, you probably want to keep looking. But if you can support the area(s) in which the trainer is deficient, you may have found a good match.

4.6 Backing Up
Your Choice

Selecting a trainer is no simple matter. But don't think that once you have made the selection, your job is over—it's only beginning. Your selection initiates a relationship that will extend until the training program ends or until either you or the trainer dissolves the alliance.

Your continuing role in the relationship is to give the trainer support. And, as you might suspect, the amount of support you have to give depends upon the trainer's qualifications and your expectations.

4.7 Supporting
an External Trainer

Here are some of the ways you might support an external trainer, depending upon individual circumstances:

- Discuss the plant, its organization, and its culture with the trainer. Explain norms of the trainees and idiosyncrasies of supervisors the trainer will deal with.

- Provide the trainer with a profile of the training program participants; include job titles, length of service, educational level, and demographic background material (sex, age, race), plus any pertinent personal characteristics that could help the trainer relate to program participants.

- Give the trainer work-flow charts, job descriptions, and/or job task analyses to familiarize him or her with worker accountabilities and interrelationships.

- Review the objectives and desired outcomes of the training program with the trainer. Query the training methods to be used, and insist that methods are appropriate for the content of the program. (If the content is information-oriented, classroom training may be appropriate. But if trainees are to learn how to set up, operate, troubleshoot, or maintain machinery, they need hands-on psychomotor practice.) Clarify how the trainer will measure that learning has occurred, and find out how your organization and the trainer should be following-up with trainees.

- Work with the trainer to make sure that supervisors are included in the development and implementation of any training program affecting their employees.

- Assign a subject-matter expert to the trainer, if materials are to be developed specific to your operations.

- Schedule adequate time for effective training to transpire.

- Set expectations with supervisors and employees concerning their attendance at the training and the transfer of training to the job.

4.8   Supporting an Internal Trainer

When you select an employee to be your trainer (or hire a full-time trainer as an addition to your staff), your support includes essentially all of the things you would do for the external trainer. But the internal trainer has an additional set of needs which preclude your "throwing him (or her) to the wolves." This individual needs a train-the-trainer program to remove the deficiencies in his/her qualifications (unless you have unearthed the "perfect" trainer!).

The Ball-Incon experience illustrates how to develop a train-the-trainer program suitable for your employee-trainer. At Ball-Incon, the training manager seeks technical trainers who have the competencies and qualities outlined in the job description. She then performs a training-needs analysis on the developmental needs of the new trainer.

She analyzes the individual's strengths (competencies), weighs them against the ideal qualifications, and designs a training program around the individual. The new trainer successfully completes the training program when he or she performs to the level of desired competencies.

In general, the new-hire training program at Ball-Incon includes:

- Working for four months in a number of different glass manufacturing plants. The actual work experience familiarizes the trainer with the various jobs, work processes, the organization, and other trainers.

- Attending "real-time" training programs conducted by other plant technical trainers. The new trainer experiences first-hand the training programs he or she will later be conducting.

- Participating in train-the-trainer programs for each of the training programs to be conducted. The purpose of this exercise is to ensure that the new trainer is fully familiar with the content and delivery of the programs prior to presenting them him/herself.

- Attending training programs in adult learning theories and practices, such as how to facilitate meetings, how to ask questions, and how to reinforce training. This facet of the train-the-trainer program gives the new trainer important knowledge and skill in making effective training presentations that meet the needs of the participants.

As Ball-Incon's trainers achieve the desired levels of competency in each of the qualification areas, the training manager works with them to set developmental goals and gain additional training competencies. One developmental goal is to expand the scope of the trainer by developing additional competencies. Ideally, each trainer would eventually become proficient in all 15 training roles. In the future, Ball-Incon's Employee Development Specialists will be equipped to help lead the company in its continuing training efforts, regardless of how needs evolve.

You can use the Ball-Incon experience to model your train-the-trainer program. Figure 4-10, "A Sample Train-the-Trainer Program," provides a general guideline.

4.9 Summary

This chapter has described a systematic way to select and support a trainer for your organization. If you follow these recommendations, you'll put in a lot of up-front effort. The question you may be asking yourself is: "Is it worth all of that work?" That's a good question, and it deserves a good answer.

Would it be worth the effort if new-hires were able to perform as well as seasoned employees within two weeks following training—compared to an historical learning curve of about three months without training? Or if workers retained almost 90 percent of what they were taught—a year after the training occurred? Or would the work be worthwhile if your training programs had an effect on reducing the cost of quality in your plant? Or if your training resulted in an increase in customer satisfaction, as measured by a decrease in complaints?

These are results that Ball-Incon has enjoyed. These are results that a careful, deliberate selection and support of your trainer can bring to you.

Life has no guarantees, and neither does your training program. But you increase the odds of having your training succeed when you do the right things. The first "right thing" to do is to understand *why* you need a trainer and *what* that trainer will do for your organization. If you scrimp on this critical step of developing a job description, you risk wasting your company's time and money.

Non-human-resources personnel are turned off by the term *job description*. They think of a job description as administrative gobbledygook that

If you select an employee from within your company or add a trainer to your staff, you will need to provide support through a train-the-trainer program:

1. Review the trainer's job description. Describe each of the roles in behavioral terms—that is, what do you expect the trainer to do as an instructor? as an evaluator? as a needs analyst?

2. Measure your trainer's current level of expertise against the desired level: where are the deficiencies?

3. Outline a training program that spells out the expected level of proficiency for each developmental area. List specific work experiences, training programs, or educational experiences that will lead to the desired level of proficiency. Don't rush this phase of the training program.

   Arrange for the trainer to spend time working with and talking to subject-matter expert(s). Develop, with the trainer, an outline of questions to be asked of subject-matter expert(s).

   Identify specific adult-learning training experiences for a trainer who needs these. Include training in areas such as group process skills, needs assessment methods (such as the nominal group technique and the delphi method), active listening skills, feedback skills, negotiation skills, and presentation skills, all based on the skill requirements for the trainer position within your plant.

4. Certify training competencies by asking the trainer to demonstrate them to you prior to conducting any training program.

Figure 4-10. A sample train-the-trainer program.

takes a long time to prepare and doesn't help them after it's done. If that's your conception of a job description, eliminate the term from your consciousness and think about that first crucial step in terms of *clarifying your expectations.* It doesn't matter what label you decide to hang onto the task. Just don't shortchange it.

Once you know your expectations, the rest becomes relatively easy. You can determine the qualifications that support the job. You set these qualifications up as the measuring stick for each candidate's credentials. And you use your expectations for performance as a building block to base your support program, whether you are supporting an external trainer or an in-house selection.

References

1. Information about Ball-Incon is based on interviews with Charlene Giles, Manager of Human Resources and Development, Ball-Incon Glass Packaging Corp., Muncie, Indiana.

2. Patricia A. McLagan and Richard C. McCullough, *Models for Excellence: The Conclusions and Recommendations of the ASTD Training and Development Competency Study,* American Society for Training and Development, 1983.

3. Barbara Darraugh, "Course Construction," *Training & Development,* May 1991, p. 67.

4. Thomas D. Conkright, "Choosing the Right Training Solution," *Training,* August 1993, p. 42.

5. Robert N. Steck, "The Skills Gap," *D&B Reports,* January/February 1992, p. 35.

6. John Barnshow III, "Educational Resources in Your Own Backyard," *Training and Development Journal,* May 1992, p. 54.

7. Myrna Marofsky, "Training the MTV Generation," *Training and Development Journal,* June 1990.

8. Jack, Peter, and Andrew McQuaig, *How to Interview and Hire Productive People,* Fall, 1981.

Bibliography

The following sources were used in addition to those references directly cited in Chapter 4:

Amerault, Thomas, "Job Training: Who Gets It and Where They Get It," *Occupational Outlook Quarterly,* Winter 1992/1993.

"Business and Colleges Work Together on Area Job Training," *Houston Business Journal,* June 28, 1993.

Carnevale, Anthony P., Leila J. Gainer, and Eric Schulz, *Training the Technical Work Force,* Jossey-Bass, 1990.

Carnevale, Anthony P., Leila J. Gainer, and Janice Villet, *Training in America: The Organization and Strategic Role of Training,* Jossey-Bass, 1990.

Crawford, Frederick W., and Simon Webley, *Continuing Education and Training of the Workforce,* British-North American Committee, November 1992.

Darraugh, Barbara, "Course Construction," *Training & Development,* May 1991.

Denis, Joe, and Bruce Austin, "A Base(ic) Course on Job Analysis," *Training & Development,* July 1992.

Dumas, Marie A., and David E. Wile, "The Accidental Trainer: Helping Design Instruction," *Personnel Journal,* June 1992.

Garvin, David A., "Building a Learning Organization," *Harvard Business Review,* July-August 1993.

Laird, Dugan, *Approaches to Training and Development*, Addison-Wesley Publishing Co., Inc., 1984.

"Manager's File #9: Choosing an Outside Training Firm," *PC World*, January 1992.

Miller, William H., "Skill Standards on the Way," *Industry Week*, April 5, 1993.

Segall, Linda J., "KISS Appraisal Woes Goodbye," *Supervisory Management*, December 1990.

Stuart, Peggy, "Workers Upgrade Skills at Training Center," *Personnel Journal*, March 1993.

"Work-based Training," *Training*, April 1993.

5

Financing the Technical Training Function

Donald E. Treinen

Charles D. Douglas

Donald E. Treinen *has been with the Communications Workers of America since 1966. He has held numerous leadership positions in the union, locally and nationally. He served as union bargaining cochair in 1983 and 1986, and was CWA's chair of all participative programs with AT&T, 1983 to 1986. Mr. Treinen is a founding executive director of The Alliance and a founding president of Alliance Plus. He is a member of Jobs For The Future's Advisory Board, and a member of the Carnegie-Mellon Labor Management Forum. He frequently speaks and presents at labor-management conferences, and consults with a number of firms, unions, and national government bodies, here and abroad.*

Charles D. Douglas *has many years of telecommunications and labor relations experience with AT&T. He chaired the 1992 AT&T Operations Bargaining Committee in negotiations with the Communications Workers of America. Mr. Douglas is past president of the New Brunswick, New Jersey Chapter, Industrial Relations Research Association, and is a member of the Board of Advisors for Cornell University's New York State School of Industrial and Labor Relations Extension Division.*

The purpose of this chapter is to not only provide information about financing training, but to get you and your organization more involved in the ongoing discussions about workforce skills development through high-quality training. The goal of these discussions is to move toward certification of skills at a world-class level. The chapter also highlights the *school-to-work* system which prepares our future workers for the world of work, both in social and technical terms. Doing so will save a great deal of money long term by ensuring that competent workers are available.

The five major areas of the chapter are:

- Internal Financing (Section 5.1)
- Government Funding Options (Section 5.2)
- Partnerships and Coalitions (Section 5.3)
- Offering Programs to Other Companies (Section 5.4)
- Labor-Management Cooperation (Section 5.5)

5.1   Internal Financing

Employer funding of employee training in the United States is substantial. In a recent presentation[1] before the National Center on the Educational Quality of the Workforce (EQW), a figure of *$30 billion* per year was given as an estimate for such training. However, researchers commonly estimate that almost all of this amount is spent by only about *10 percent of America's firms.*

In considering this data, the presenter recommended certain essential steps needed to make sure training dollars are well spent:

- Pretraining needs analysis
- Using the best delivery methods for the population to be trained, to have the best chance to satisfy training needs
- After-training analysis to determine if change took place, if it was related to the training, if the change related to achieving organizational goals, and whether similar changes can be expected from training future participants in the program

For greater training effectiveness, the study also recommended *behavior modeling,* making sure that what is learned is transferable to the job, and showing the value of training and its application through *positive reinforcement with trainees* themselves. The following examples of how training is funded can all be evaluated using the foregoing suggestions.

5.1.1 Training Department Budgets

The first option is to fund training by *departmental budget*. Organizational policy often requires that the cost of internal training be charged to the department using the training. Managers establishing and managing departmental training budgets must make sure that costs are identified up-front to the extent possible. This is important to make sure training is done in a rational and consistent manner. Managers find themselves constantly trying to balance between their department's budget objectives and the costs of meeting those objectives. As every manager knows, the cost of training is only one of many factors to be considered.

Many companies calculate the cost per person per hour and factor it into the training budget costs. Because costs are being charged back to departments, managers' choices are helping to select training providers.

Traditionally, elaborate systems of rules, checks, and balances required the training user organization to use only the internal training provider, regardless of cost and quality. As demand for greater training quality and flexibility has grown, managers want to be able to satisfy their training needs on a competitive basis. This means looking *both inside and outside* to obtain best quality, price, and delivery flexibility.

To ensure that training is purchased on a competitive basis, many organizations are encouraging their managers to look outside, even when they have an internal training capability. When both internal and external sources are asked to bid on training, some companies use their purchasing departments to decide whose bid should be accepted. This process has helped many internal training organizations learn how to be cost competitive, and in some cases they have even become *profit centers* for the corporation.

When training organizations become profit centers, they often make their training available both internally and externally. Florida Power and Light, General Motors Corporation, Disney, and many others are now selling their workshops to the general public. Interestingly, this is one way firms can, in effect, share their knowledge about training content, curriculum development, cost, and delivery alternatives.

An example comes from AT&T. AT&T has an elaborate process to manage training costs and has given managers the flexibility to operate within this process. Any manager who has his or her own budget is allowed to pay for various support services (which includes training) through a negotiation process divided into two categories:

- *Designated supplier.* Training, development, and delivery activities are to be provided by a central supplier who serves the entire organization. The central supplier can be either internal or external.

- *Full choice.* Training, development, and delivery activities for which a central supplier has not been designated. Managers can choose their own supplier (internal or external) or do the training themselves, if they have that capability.

In both situations, a process of negotiation is expected to be used in which the manager determines the quantity and quality of service to be provided based on need. By having relatively few training services covered by the designated supplier category, AT&T has introduced *free-market competition* into its business units and departments. Even though AT&T has several of its own training organizations, this has allowed AT&T managers to drive toward cost-competitive, high-quality, responsive training. As a result, much of AT&T's training has become cost effective and of very high quality, and a number of its training organizations have become profit centers in their own right. In fact, many of these training organizations are attaining best-in-class status when compared to other firms.

These training organizations, operating in a full-choice environment, are expected to develop a portfolio of products and services (Figure 5-1), a process for pricing and billing (Figure 5-2), and a responsibility to negotiate training contracts. These training contracts were historically with internal customers. More and more, AT&T's internal training organizations are reaching out to external customers as well.

A word about pricing within this structure is appropriate.

Pricing methods can vary widely, and often do. They include *bundled pricing*, in which a dedicated training facility is established and costs include real estate and associated expenses, training developers/consultants, teaching staff, training materials, and marketing functions. AT&T and the various Bell companies still have a number of these facilities, but far fewer than existed in the Bell System prior to the breakup in 1984.

Another way training is priced is on a *usage-sensitive* basis. Usage pricing might be by class, by individual student, by training day, and so forth. Regardless of what pricing scheme is used, managers need to consider all the factors used to determine training costs. Often, a profit margin is included before a final training price is quoted.

A third way to price training is to provide a *minimum guarantee arrangement*. This requires that a contract be developed which provides a set level of training services over a set period of time, for a set price. Typically, if demand exceeds the minimum guarantee, the parties involved revert to some form of usage-sensitive pricing to take care of additional training needs.

There are still quite a few organizations in which decisions on training are made on behalf of managers, rather than by managers. In such cases, decisions are made at a very high level and often include how much training is provided, who receives it, when, and under what circumstances. Training is usually funded out of corporate-level budgets, and costs are

Entry-level training

- Repair operator curriculum
- Basic soldering
- On-the-job training (OJT)

Upper-grade-level training

- Technical specialist curriculum
- Repair technician curriculum
- Senior technical specialist curriculum

Equipment and materials required

- Oscilloscope
  Tektronix 465
  Tektronix 465B
- Digital Voltmeter
  Fluke 8600A
- AC Voltmeter
  HP 400EL
- DC Power Supply
  Power Design 5015
- Oscillator
  HP 204C
- Attenuator
  Daven T693
- Volt-ohmmeter
  KS14510

Figure 5-1. A portfolio of products and services.

normally charged to the departments where the training is used and where costs can be tracked.

Formula funding arrangements are also in use. These can be found where long-standing relationships exist between training users and training providers. Typically in this case, the formula requires the ability to *forecast training needs* based on product/service start-up, employee turnover, skill

Technical Training Curriculum
Entry Level
Upper Grade Level

Based on twenty (20) students per class
Bundled Pricing Arrangement

Allocated real estate and associated costs   _____
Allocated training developers/consultants   _____
Allocated training staff costs   _____
Profit margin (allocated to project)   _____

Total Cost Per Class

Based on twenty (20) students per class
Usage Pricing Arrangement

Option One: Cost per student   _____
Option Two: Cost per class day   _____
Profit margin (allocated to project)   _____

Option One total cost   _____
Option Two total cost   _____

Based on fifteen (15) students per class
Minimum Guarantee Arrangement

Basic price for 15 students   _____
Cost per additional student (up to 25)   _____
Profit margin (allocated to project)   _____

Basic total cost (15)   _____
Total cost (incl. cost of any additional students beyond 15)   _____

Figure 5-2. A process for pricing and billing.

progression, and so forth. Such forecasts are then used to develop a training cost formula which results in a training budget.

Finally, a word about the increasing use of *off-hours training*. Traditionally, most job-specific training was done during work hours, and often at a dedicated company training facility. The training provider did not have to be concerned about costs associated with wages, travel, lodging, and meals because these were charged directly to the student's work site.

Sometimes training can be done off-hours, or in small time intervals on the job at the work site, instead of in large blocks of time at a distant training facility. Be alert that there are some legal issues with off-hours training. Chapter 6 deals with this issue. This allows the manager using the training to substantially reduce overall training costs. Because there is always an incentive to reduce costs, training providers find that their cost structures can change significantly.

1. They now have to consider the cost of travel, lodging, and meals for their trainers, or the cost of contracting with trainers found locally.

2. They can no longer include training facility operations in their cost structures. In the long run, this could mean closing training facilities— or it could mean greater efforts to find other users of those facilities.

Regardless, shifting to localized training and/or doing training off hours has a great effect on traditional training organizations.

5.1.2 Supplier Discounting Arrangements

Price discounting arrangements can be made with equipment suppliers. The most common way to do this is through manufacturers of products and equipment where use requires training. Actually, this is not discounting as we usually think of it. Rather, providing training as part of selling a sophisticated line of equipment is a good sales strategy. An example would be a high-technology robotics operation which cannot be sold unless the purchaser is able to have employees trained quickly, thus making the employees productive and the purchase worthwhile. To meet the buyer's need, the seller provides the training as part of the purchase price.

Often, sellers and buyers of sophisticated high-technology equipment are dealing in millions of dollars. Thus, a seller needs to write off costs of production through sales, and the buyer needs to make the new equipment productive as soon as possible. Usually the buyer does not have current skills in the workforce necessary to operate and repair the equipment. (In fact, maintenance is often under contract with the supplier.) Therefore, there exists an obvious and immediate need for training.

Such training is commonly provided in at least two ways. One is to have a *technical* trainer come to the buyer's location, and orient and train the workforce during equipment installation and test. This helps the buyer because the workforce learns about the new equipment and how to operate it as it gets installed. It helps the seller because the training is paced out so enough time is available to assure that learning takes place. *The training cost can be built into the purchase contract as part of the equipment sale.*

Another way to do this training is at the seller's manufacturing location. In this case, the buyer sends a small, select staff to the site to learn how to operate the equipment. In turn, this staff will train others back home once the equipment is installed. The advantage to the seller is being able to train right at its own facility, without having to send trainers, technical manuals, equipment, and materials to a remote location. The advantage to the buyer is that operations can continue with the existing workforce, rather than having the distraction of a major training initiative while production must continue. As in the earlier case, training costs are often built into the equipment sales contract.

Beyond the cases mentioned here, however, there are many other ways to get training through suppliers. A typical example involves the purchase of hardware and software for a computer installation. The buyer should negotiate, before the purchase is made, just what the training arrangements will be. Often a company can get training as part of a purchase at a fraction of the cost otherwise incurred. In this case, a company will have one or a few employees from their data services or MIS department receive extensive training. This often includes a *train-the-trainer* course, as well as technical training. By doing this, the company can bring its training and technical expertise in-house.

These concepts can also apply to a wide range of other situations. The key is to *make sure training agreements are negotiated as part of the purchase contract*, not separately or after the purchase. Another key, regardless of how training is done, is to *make sure the supplier has demonstrated training competencies*. While one can never be sure how effective training is until the training takes place and learning is applied, certain information should be requested up front. Ask about how the seller has developed the training staff, how much experience they have, what is their level of training and education, whether they have been trained and are experienced in teaching techniques, and some detail about their ability and experience in training adults.

5.1.3 Tuition Assistance Programs

Many companies, including smaller and medium-sized ones, have tuition assistance programs. Such programs usually provide financial assistance for certificate and/or college degree courses in areas directly related to the job. In most cases, the costs of such programs are charged back to the users' departments, or are allocated back to the department in some other way. When allocation is used, it can take several forms:

1. By percent of employees within the department
2. By a department's percent of total company revenue
3. By a department's percent of total company budget

Regardless of the way tuition costs are allocated, managers need to be sensitive to how much money is used. Without tracking and budgeting, limited training funds can be used up early in a budget period. This can leave employees without financial support when they need it.

Some typical rules and guidelines associated with tuition programs include:

- An annual funding maximum per employee is preset.

- A requirement is made that the training provider is regionally accredited.

- Only certain programs and courses are fundable. Training must be related to the job.

- Employees must be employed for a certain period of time (such as at least one year of employment).

- Employees must be on active employment status when courses actually begin.

- Many courses must be taken outside of work hours. (There may be a legal problem with this. See Chapter 6.)

- Approvals for reimbursement are based on proof of satisfactory completion.

- Proof is provided that tuition was paid before reimbursement is made.

A more recent trend is prepayment of tuition, once courses are approved. Evidence exists that prepayment does not measurably reduce completion rates, and more employees tend to use tuition when prepayment is granted. Of course, companies with limited tuition budgets may have to consider if higher tuition usage will help or hurt the users' ability to complete programs (such as college degrees and technical training programs) within a reasonable period of time. Where there are limited budgets and heavy usage, individuals often have to reduce the number of courses they take in a given year or other class cycle.

Usually, tuition programs are used to help fund training or education which is only generally related to the job, thus the training is most often done outside work hours. For job-specific training, other funding methods are used and most often, the training is done during the work day.

In closing out this discussion on internal financing, a few comments about training costs and whether those costs make a difference on an organization's bottom line are pertinent.

Both buyers and sellers of training have long tried to figure out this relationship. There is only limited information on this topic, and there is not a widely accepted and proven formula. Also it would be wise to remain skeptical of defining the value of education and training only on the basis of return on investment. Much of the value of training and education is based on an individual's change in positive self-image and personal growth. Such change can have an effect on productivity, regardless of the kind of training involved.

All this notwithstanding, sometimes training is directly related to increased productivity. Often, such increases do relate directly to improvements in output, quality of product or service, and profitability. The earlier example of major equipment purchases used to change how a company produces goods and services is one. This is especially true at a *greenfield site* where a totally new operation is coming on-line. (A greenfield site, as used here, is one where a new factory or facility is built with new equipment and a new workforce.)

In 1989, a study was done on about 1700 surplused AT&T employees. The Alliance (see Section 5.5 for details on the Alliance) provided job placement test training at a cost of about $3.2 million. As a result, all 1700 were placed in AT&T jobs. Based on an average cost of layoff per employee of $24,500 (AT&T Human Resources data), AT&T actually saved about $38.5 million. While this case does not relate directly to productivity, it was substantial, and measurable. This training happened during the Alliance's 1983–86 funding cycle, when total funding was $19 million.

Another recent example showed that a branch office of AT&T's Global Business Communications Services (GBCS) unit benefited in a number of ways from a locally run training program, targeting technical, marketing, and clerical employees. According to the study,[2] managers and union representatives said the following:

- Over 70 percent of all employees took training.
- The branch was among the top profit branches in the U.S.
- 1994 training budget went from 2 percent to 9 percent of total revenue.
- Per-course training costs were significantly reduced, thus more training was made available for all employees.
- Almost a half million dollars of government funds were made available and matched with AT&T and Alliance funds.

Training organizations must figure out reliable ways to measure the value of training. Doing so can become a strong part of any marketing strategy, and a strong part of the survival and growth of the training organization. Chapter 14 on Evaluation will give some good reference points.

Next, we provide a discussion of funding options from governmental sources.

5.2 Government Funding Options

While almost all training dollars spent by organizations are their own, other funding sources are substantial. Among them are funds available for programs in partnership with state and local units of government. These include the Employment Service, Dislocated Worker Units, grants from economic development commissions, and, in some states, funds set up just for training new hires where firms are new to, or expanding in, a community. In many states, funds are also available from the state vocational-technical education agency. Still other funding comes from the federal government, most commonly from the Departments of Labor and Education. Federal programs usually serve laid-off employees, or employees who need improvement in workplace skills, often called *workplace literacy skills*. A word of caution: a traditional definition of literacy will exclude many worthwhile programs that can be funded by such grants.

When considering funds from governmental sources, keep in mind that *matching funds* or *in-kind contributions* are often required. In-kind contributions are things such as classrooms, office space, personnel, office equipment, etc. Still, using funds set aside as a matter of public policy can represent a major source of support for training. When such public funds are used to support employees being outplaced, more company funds are available for other training directly related to the organization's technical training needs.

Some typical examples of government funding to train workers for new jobs or to raise skill levels for employees in their current jobs are included, as well as a unique partnership between locals from a wide range of unions, employers, a network of public schools, and government funding at both the state and federal levels.

5.2.1 Federal Funding: Training for Laid-off Workers

Consortium for Worker Education. The Consortium is a unique project which includes a number of union locals from different international unions, a network of schools within New York City, and a number of public and private sector employers. The outcomes of the project are impressive, and funding comes from a range of public and private sources.

The Consortium for Worker Education was founded in New York City in 1985, with a mission to

> shape the growth and development of the primary resource of both its member unions and New York City: Workers and their families[3]

It provides instruction ranging from second-language training to specific skill-related credential and certificate programs.

Consortium membership is made up of union training programs from Hotel Workers; Teamsters; Garment Workers; Building Trades (six internationals); Health Care Workers; Auto Workers; State, County, and

Municipal Workers; Communications Workers; Office and Professional Employees; Transport Workers; and the unions of Metro North Railway.

The Consortium also involves employers from the firms and public agencies with whom these unions have labor agreements. Finally, the Consortium is linked with the City University of New York system of colleges.

A number of educational institutes have been created by the Consortium, including health care professions, professions in education, labor education, and apprentice programs.

The Consortium conducts research with union locals and firms in curriculum development, teaching practices, and effective union-management relations. It also maintains a resource library on curriculum and teaching materials for education and students alike. Finally, it develops *specialized curriculum projects* for specific industry and workplace-based needs.

The Consortium is funded from various sources, including grants from the U.S. Department of Education Workplace Literacy Project, supporting an Education and Careers project and careers in daycare services. The Consortium has gotten a grant from the Federal Mediation and Conciliation Service to create a labor-management–led project on team-based production systems in three area factories. Its goal is to create high-performance workplaces in the private, for-profit sector.

Consortium accomplishments include over 15,000 individuals in training and education; almost 700,000 enrollments; over half of all courses teaching specific skills (including technical training); 86 percent minority students; and over 2000 dislocated workers placed in jobs. This project is an excellent example of how the relationship between unions and employers can be of value to both.

The Alliance began its first major program delivery in early 1987. Most programs in those days were for laid-off AT&T employees. Services included:

- Information about program options and sessions on eligibility, the application process, and services available locally from the Employment Service

- Career planning

- Handling personal and family stress

- Dealing with changes in family and personal finances job interview skills

- Writing employment resumes

- Techniques for job search

- Job clubs and office services and equipment

- Training for job-specific skills

In looking at what services were needed by employees—those available through the Alliance and those available from local, state, and federal programs—many of the services were the same. Such duplication was in both program content and in funding. And the largest fund allocations were being made for high-skill and technical training. As a result, an assessment was done on how Alliance programs were funded and whether more effective funding could be done through a partnership with government programs.

Beginning in 1987, local labor-management committees were taught how to get services and funds often available through local dislocated worker units, Employment Service, and unemployment offices. The goal was to make sure services provided by these organizations would also be used. At the very least, forming partnerships wherever possible using all funding sources was the goal.

Forming partnerships between local committees and representatives of governmental agencies seemed like a logical first step. Alliance staff identified representatives from governmental units, and arranged meetings between them and Alliance committees. The result benefited both the committees and local representatives of government. For Alliance committees, this partnership provided a wide range of services sponsored by the committees and funded by the government. The partnership connected the government with many clients, without a lot of recruiting work on the government's part.

Those early efforts were not coordinated beyond each local situation and were not very effective at handling layoffs as a result of nationwide changes in technology and company reorganization. Then in 1988 AT&T decided to bring up a new technology in operator services, which presented an opportunity to build a more strategic partnership with local units of government. The idea was to bring all those who ran government dislocated worker programs together with all Alliance committees involved in programs for AT&T employees affected by the new technology. In order to make this work, talks commenced with the Department of Labor in Washington, D.C. These talks resulted in an agreement to cohost four regional conferences.

Attendees at these regional conferences, held in 1989, included cochairs of all Alliance committees. Also included were representatives of government dislocated worker units in all states within each region. Also invited were representatives of the Alliance, AT&T, and the unions.

The conferences resulted in coordination of services funded by government and services funded by the Alliance. In general, government-funded services included job search and job placement. Alliance-funded services included career planning and skills training for other work. By having government funds pick up the cost of job search and placement, Alliance funds were more widely available for skills training.

Over the past few years, the funded services have been tracked:

1991 — $953,000

1992 — $536,800

1993 — $984,000

When considering such partnerships, keep in mind that most public funds are governed by rules and regulations developed to support a particular legislative goal. Thus, be sure a request for a grant is within the rules governing grant applications or Requests for Proposals (RFP). General rules are usually published in the *Federal Register* by any agency calling for applicants to run government-funded programs. Specific rules will always be included in the grant application or RFP itself. Of course, use of funds specifically set aside for dislocated worker programs is currently not possible unless actual layoffs occur.

Finally, keep in mind that when using public funds administered directly by your company or organization, there will likely be audit requirements. Be sure these requirements are thoroughly understood prior to submitting a funding request.

5.2.2   Federal Funding:
Workplace Literacy

Over the past several years, changes in technology, markets, and workplaces changed how people worked. The skills needed also changed. This was true for most employers and their employees.

AT&T was no exception. Beginning in the early 1990s, the Alliance began to look closely at the relationship between such changes and what people had to know to be successful at work.

Technical skills were changing, as were other skills involving how people work with each other and with customers. This resulted in new ways to develop these new workplace literacy skills in the AT&T workforce.

Early in 1993, one of the Alliance's premier local labor-management committees, based in Minneapolis but serving a multistate area in the central United States, applied for a Department of Education workplace literacy grant. The idea was to bring together a number of union locals, AT&T business units, and two or three small telephone interconnect companies to run a project to do the following:

- Evaluate how changes at work require new skills and decide what new skills were required

- Decide how those skills help workers be successful in their jobs

- Decide how those skills help the company be successful in the marketplace

- Decide how to best deliver those skills

- Decide the best training to teach those skills measuring the relationship between training outcomes and better workplace results (company and individual)

The target group of workers for the project was primarily the technician forces of AT&T and the interconnects, but also included some clericals and account and sales representatives. Traditionally, the technicians were expected to be highly skilled in technical terms, but interpersonal and customer relationship skills were considered secondary. Because customers today require all employees (technicians, clericals, and account and sales representatives) to be quickly able to deal with broader telecommunication needs, a new range of skills was needed. These are commonly called workplace literacy skills by the government.

To respond to this need, Alliance staff worked with the local committee to build a partnership among AT&T, several union locals, and three interconnect companies. With the support of this partnership, the committee applied for and obtained a Department of Education grant valued at over $450,000. The grant, in this case, was awarded to the Alliance's service delivery partner, the Minnesota Teamsters Service Bureau.

The project first completed an *evaluation of training needs*. This evaluation was done with managers, union representatives, and involved employees. A range of skills were identified, including:

- Customer contact skills

- Self-management skills

- Time management skills

- The ability to prioritize work tasks

- Interpersonal relationships skills

- Teamwork skills

- Computer skills

- Quality principles

- Understanding of the customer's business

- Knowledge about competition in the marketplace

The next step was to develop *modularized training courses* for delivery to the target population. A number of these courses are now being delivered, and results are already being assessed.

While these skills are not all considered technical in nature, employers find many of them to be the very skills making the difference between getting and keeping customers or losing customers to the competition. *These skills are equally important whether in for-profit or not-for-profit organizations, public or private.*

5.2.3   Other Funding Sources

Organizations interested in the availability of public funds should consider help from their affiliated trade or business associations. While there are perhaps hundreds of these, certainly the larger and more well-known include the Chamber of Commerce, the National Association of Manufacturers, and the National Alliance of Business. They can be helpful to you if you are a member. For unions, the AFL-CIO in Washington, D.C., at the state level, and even at the local level, can be a source of information about what services are available and whether grants exist to support training for your members.

Large associations and federations will have research and political/legislative departments tracking legislative activities, including those that make public funds available for training purposes. Often, these funds are available through collaborative labor and management programs. This trend is likely to continue into the future.

5.2.4   State Funding

State-level funding for firms that are expanding or beginning operations within a state's borders varies. As an example, for a number of years, California has made funds available to firms to encourage business expansion or location within the state. Many firms have taken advantage of these funds. Typically, a firm can get state assistance when matching its own funds for training prospective employees (i.e., a company that sets aside $10,000 for training can get a matching grant from the state). Firms can also get funds to train current employees, if associated with expanding business operations requiring new job skills. A unique feature of this program, known as the California Training Panel, is that unionized firms need union involvement and support prior to getting these funds. This requirement ensures that current workers are not replaced, and encourages cooperation between labor and management.

Organizations should not overlook *economic development commissions* at state and local levels when considering business expansion or development. In many cases, these commissions do make funds available. In addition, firms might contact their elected officials, the Secretary of State or

Commerce, and the Department of Labor to find out more about possible funding. Many states have developed their own versions of the California model, and continually pursue business expansion within their borders.

5.3 Partnerships and Coalitions

The move toward passing laws that promote a more highly skilled American workforce should support proposals intended to bring skills to world-class standards and to support young people as they prepare for the world of work. Many partnerships and coalitions support these efforts.

Highlighted are partnerships between organizations providing training in a cost-effective manner. Companies and unions have built such training partnerships together, and with other organizations as well. These include educational networks; governmental units at local, state, and federal levels; and consortiums of firms working with each other.

In the past few years, concern about our nation's ability to compete globally has grabbed the headlines. Research shows the United States has fallen behind perhaps a dozen other nations in high-skill, high-tech, high-wage work. This has caused many firms to compete poorly in foreign countries—and even within our own borders when foreign firms establish a presence here. The loss of world-class skills affects both workers and business leaders.

Responding to this growing problem, recent administrations have introduced legislation to once again raise the skill level of our workforce to the quality standards required in today's world. These initiatives have taken two broad tracks, one for the current workforce and the other for the future workforce.

For the current workforce, legislation is addressing the need to create *standards and certifications*, and to do so by forming partnerships among major stakeholders. These include government, business, labor, research organizations, and the academic community.

These stakeholders now realize that legislative efforts to create a high-skill workforce need to address constant churn in the labor market. The types of jobs available are changing. We are moving from a manufacturing to a service base, from assembly lines to computer lines. Both are very technical, but very different in skills required. Technology is changing at a dizzying pace. Skill sets are becoming obsolete in shorter and shorter periods. How work is done and how people work with each other is constantly changing.

Entire industries are dying as others are emerging. Left to themselves, individuals are powerless to change these forces. It can be argued that most firms are also powerless to change many of these forces. Thus, the push is for laws in support of firms and working people moving to new markets and new work, rather than leaving behind whole communities and entire generations of workers unemployed and not immediately employable due to skill deficiencies.

Examples of such legislation include military conversion, economic development, bridging legislation funding worker retraining due to the North American Free Trade Agreement (NAFTA), the Trade Readjustment Act, and the Job Training Partnership Act. Even earlier legislation recognized the need to move workers from low or obsolete skills to the high skills needed in the labor market. The Manpower Development and Training Act was passed in 1962, and the Comprehensive Employment and Training Act in 1973. These are just a sample of such laws, usually aimed at specific groups suffering economic disadvantages relative to the public at large.

To be passed, every piece of legislation just mentioned needed *coalitions of supporters,* but business and labor almost always had very different points of view. What is clearly different now is that new proposals target the working population as a whole, rather than just the fringes. In addition, there is broad understanding and acceptance that American workers and their employers need strong, national support. They cannot do it alone.

Such broad understanding has resulted in major coalition-building. The Alliance, like many other firms, is involved. It provides data, conducts research, gives testimony, and works with others to develop laws and regulations to support training.

The Alliance is involved in school-to-work, skills standards, skills certification, research on training for high-technology manufacturing jobs, and testimony before various commissions and committees, as well as providing input on current legislation through a number of corporate and labor union coalitions.

Other organizations involved in these coalitions include the following:

- Chamber of Commerce
- National Alliance of Business
- National Association of Manufacturers
- Committee for Economic Development
- AFL-CIO (and the majority of its member unions)
- The Center for Learning and Competitiveness
- The German Marshall Fund
- Educational Testing Service
- The Council on Competitiveness

- National Planning Association
- American Society for Training and Development Industrial Relations Research Association

There are simply too many organizations involved to mention them all. These are only a sample. The main point to emphasize is the wide range of organizations, the diverse nature of representation, and the high level of commitment that they have in common.

The second of these two major tracks of recent legislation includes the Youth Opportunities Act of 1993. A few comments follow.

Over the past several years, the organization known as Jobs For The Future (JFF) has conducted field work and research on youth apprenticeship. JFF has developed a number of recommendations on effective ways to bring school-to-work programs up to scale on a national basis. This organization and others have become partners with business, labor, education, and government to raise the level of our nation's needs in this regard. What JFF has been able to accomplish is worth discussing.

Sixty-five percent of JFF's work is in school-to-work. They have a 10-year record of partnerships with companies, unions, schools, universities, and several states. In their 1993 publication, *Jobs For The Future, 1983–1993 The First Ten Years,* JFF lists a number of lessons learned regarding school-to-work. Those lessons include cost factors for employers who are, or will be, participating in school-to-work programs. For successful programs, lessons learned include:

- Active participation of employers is required.
- Academic and vocational education must be integrated.
- Work-based and school-based learning must be integrated.

A structured linkage between secondary and postsecondary educational institutions (from 9th- to 14th-grade-level education) must exist. Certification of mastery must be broadly recognized.

JFF also raised a number of specific questions for policy makers to consider:

- Will employers be willing to invest resources in developing linkages with high schools?
- Are there incentives (which can be built into public law) to encourage employer participation, while avoiding an unfair shift of costs from the private to the public sector?
- Will schools themselves be flexible and willing to undertake significant schedule and curriculum changes, to do training staff development, and to invest additional resources?

- How can the stigma of vocational education tracking be overcome?
- How can we move from a series of local programs and experiments to a national system brought to scale?

Guided by these lessons and questions, JFF is working with a number of states and the Department of Labor to support field research through actual school-to-work projects. States include Connecticut, Arkansas, Mississippi, Colorado, Indiana, Missouri, and Wisconsin. In addition, specific school-to-work projects have been piloted in New York, Michigan, Massachusetts, Oklahoma, California, Florida, Maryland, Ohio, Pennsylvania, South Carolina, and Oregon. In all these cases, employers and local school districts work together to operate these programs. In some cases, the firms are unionized, in others not. When there is a union, the unions are part of the discussions on how the projects are operated.

JFF also formed a State Youth Apprenticeship Consortium including Arkansas, California, Georgia, Illinois, Indiana, Iowa, Maine, Michigan, Minnesota, Oregon, Pennsylvania, Texas, Vermont, and Wisconsin. State policy makers and political leaders coordinate their activities and learn from each other. This strategy supports building a national system of school-to-work programs needed to prepare America's future workers for the real world of work. It is equally important for employers to have a ready source of skills, thus keeping their workforces current in the years ahead. This helps companies plan for how much training they may or may not need to do with new workers.

The Siemens Corporation of America has shared data on its Adult Apprenticeship, Technical Preparatory, and Upgrade Adult Apprentice programs, the first of which was launched in 1962 at its Lake Mary, Florida, facility. More recent Siemens projects have been started in Kentucky and North Carolina. These programs range from 2.5 years (Adult Apprenticeship) to four years (Technical Preparatory). The Upgrade Adult Apprentice Program in North Carolina was set up in a local high school, in a partnership between the local school district and Siemens.

To understand the level of financial commitment made by Siemens, consider that these programs are work-based for up to 50 percent of all time spent in the apprenticeship. According to Siemens, skill-building is directly related to being competitive in the United States.

Another project, in the fast food industry, is that of the McDonald's Corporation. McDonald's Youth Apprenticeship Program provides four years of training in business management with a specialization in food service management. It begins in the tenth or eleventh year of high school, and is completed after one or two years of postsecondary school. The program is skill- and certification-based, and uses performance standards measurements to establish career paths in the jobs of Crew Member, Crew

Leader, Swing Manager, Assistant Manager, and Manager. Each job classification has a specific number of skills to be mastered before moving on to the next level. This program is McDonald's-based, but is in partnership with Northern Illinois University and has facilities in Indianapolis, Chicago, and Detroit. Funding is from McDonald's, from charitable foundations, and from federal and state government grants.

Both Siemens and McDonald's are among those who are widely recognized for their innovation in school-to-work, and both recognize it is necessary to prepare the future workforce, and to do it today.

For readers interested in these kinds of programs, contact Siemens and McDonald's directly, through the nearest outlet of either firm. Both have been most helpful and willing to share what they have learned. A willingness to share learning will contribute greatly to the nation's ability to broaden the base of other workforce training programs. Firms, labor unions, academic institutions, research organizations, and governmental units at all levels need to become actively engaged in these programs or to start programs of their own.

5.3.1 Internal Training Strategies

A number of major corporations also have many training organizations within their various divisions and business units. Generally, these training organizations grew up around the training needs of their specific unit. As a result, redundancies in training and funding emerged over time.

Many companies function like AT&T does. Prior to divestiture of the Bell System, each Bell company, Bell Labs, the manufacturing units, and AT&T's long distance division had its own training organization. The type of training, and even the tests administered for job placement were identical. Perhaps in a monopoly such redundancies were not a concern. They may have even supported higher profits because the cost of training was taken into account when the FCC and the various state-level regulatory bodies approved rate requests and profit margins.

After divestiture, the Bell Companies and AT&T were in a competitive environment and one becoming more global each year. It was now necessary to lower all costs, including the cost of training. Still, many of the redundancies from before divestiture continued afterwards, but now among divisions and units of the same company.

Early cost-lowering efforts included closing training facilities and bringing training and professional trainers directly to the job site. This practice, sometimes called *suitcasing,* was possible because of changes in training delivery and in training technology itself. (Suitcasing is the practice of shipping training materials to a site, then having the trainers go temporarily to the site to conduct the training. They would temporarily "live out of a suitcase" away from home.) Still, some divisions of AT&T continued to do the same training as was being done in other divisions.

The most recent effort to identify and eliminate such redundancies began in the early 1990s.

The AT&T Education and Training Leaders group involves about eight to ten major internal training organizations with annual budgets of several million dollars. After discussions and a formal survey process, this group has started to identify the following to determine how redundancies could be eliminated and efficiencies attained:

- Information on training expertise

- Organizational mission

- Customer base (internal and external)

- Global experience and capability

- Curricula and professional competence

- Courses and training programs that can be shared

- Competencies needed in each training organization

- Types of delivery systems and use

Out of this effort emerged a picture of the entire AT&T education and training community. Next came the development of a *common bond statement* for all the organizations to follow, to prevent duplication of training needs. Common bond principles inside AT&T guide how the corporation and its people deal with one another, and with its internal and external customers.

That corporations and others are taking these steps, and that they are being led by the training community itself, is a clear example of how training organizations can and do form coalitions to increase their influence on an organization's bottom line. *It also shows a growing recognition that training organizations have to become a part of strategic planning, and part of a firm's marketplace success strategy.* These same principles can also be applied in public-sector organizations. Again, refer to the workplace literacy project sponsored by an Alliance Local Committee in Minnesota. This project is an example of training that can help very small employers in raising the level of employee skills—something they simply could not afford to do on their own.

Two of the Minnesota project firms are Dell-Corem and Tie Systems. They employ about 50 and 15 employees, respectively. Their employees are all technicians, doing interconnect and installation work, mainly on industrial projects. Both firms are quite new, and relied on the skills already held by their employees at time of hire. Seeing constant change in the skill sets needed on the job motivated both companies to become a part of the workplace literacy grant. Because they both had labor agreements with the Communications Workers of America, they were able to arrange participation. This resulted in giving their employees the full range of skill assessments and training that were available to AT&T's employees. There is no doubt that, without this opportunity, neither company would have been able to get the training needed to stay competitive in the interconnect market.

5.3.2 Training Through Technology

United Technologies (UTC) and its subsidiaries are using *interactive video technology* to provide degree-related courses to their employees.[4] UTC has a need to keep its professional workforce educationally up to date, and to provide professional development and graduate degree opportunities. By linking with video networks, UTC found an effective way to reduce costs and to increase learning opportunities.

This strategy for expanding training capabilities among companies was recently covered in *The Technological Horizons in Education Journal,* November 1993 edition. An article titled "Virtual University Targets Engineering" reported the work of the Collaboration for Interactive Visual Distance Learning (CIVDL). CIVDL created and operated what it calls a *virtual university,* linking engineers with world-class engineering programs by means of videoconferencing technology. As of today, CIVDL includes AT&T, Boston University, Columbia University, MIT, Penn State, Picturetel Corp., Rensselaer Polytechnic, Stanford, 3M, and United Technologies. It is an example of how firms have linked with top academic and research universities to bring world-class training and education to employees of different firms.

5.4 Offering Programs to Other Companies

Many larger companies operate training organizations that provide some training and education to outside users. Those mentioned earlier in Section 5.1 are examples of how firms provide training, and why they do. More and more, companies now expect their training organizations to think of themselves as profit centers. This shift is causing many training organizations to rethink their customer bases. They have to think about the quality of training for wider user groups, and about how to handle the cost of training and delivery. Inside AT&T, for instance, a number of major training organizations see themselves as marketing arms and even profit centers for the business units and groups they support. *They realize that internal and external customers both require high-quality, high-technology, low-cost, anytime-anywhere training.* This has caused a major shift away from traditional training done in physical facilities set up just for training, with a full-time training staff. Now trainers are using video, high-technology, suitcased courses, and traveling trainers are the norm.

5.4.1   Training Partnerships

A move toward *globalization* of training among firms is occurring. Most corporations who operate globally use, to some degree, partnerships with other firms within their industry to expand their base of operations. A firm's training arm is often in the best position to provide their foreign business partners training on everything from cultural awareness to technical know-how.

On a more localized level, many smaller companies cannot afford their own training organizations. Thus, they are often left only with skills available in the labor market as a source of trained personnel. Of course, the labor market does not always provide those skills, and it cannot provide updating of skills at the pace required. This has created an opportunity for coalition-building, as covered in Section 5.3. Such coalitions can be a place to find opportunities to buy training services at a reduced cost for the companies involved. At the same time, such training coalitions can provide a reasonable profit margin for the training provider.

The Alliance's experience with the Minnesota Workplace Literacy Project is an example. As stated earlier, the small firms who partnered with AT&T were able to receive training through a grant arrangement led by other organizations and firms. In this case, the effort was started by the Alliance, AT&T, and the CWA union locals in partnership with the Minnesota Teamsters Service Bureau.

Another way to share programs among companies is through *informal arrangements between companies.* Each company can fill a limited number of seats in a training class, thereby reducing per-student training costs while more broadly expanding training opportunities. There is one such informal partnership in the Richmond, Virginia area. It involves firms from the tobacco industry, the telecommunications industry, and various high-technology companies. In this case, classes could not be filled during off-shifts unless several companies worked together. When such informal arrangements are made, of course, *the training must fit the skills need of all companies involved.*

The training marketplace is one with a large number of players. They range from small consulting firms to large universities, and include many private, for-profit technical and trade schools.

For technical firms who are thinking about extending their training to the outside marketplace, *don't overlook the value of your own culture and experience when seeking other customers.* As an example, there is a common culture and high level of shared understanding within telecommunications. Alliance Plus (see Section 5.5) can effectively talk to potential customers in this industry because its employees have long worked with this industry. *Therefore, when seeking customers in other industries, a firm should learn as much as possible about not only the target firm(s), but about their industry in general.*

In the last two years, Alliance Plus has provided services to firms in the aerospace industry, the food industry, the electrical and electronics industry, labor unions, telecommunications, and governmental units here and abroad. Where no prior experience existed, it was necessary to become educated about these clients and their cultures. No doubt in some cases, business opportunities were lost because others were better equipped with knowledge of the potential client.

5.4.2 Support Through Public Policy

The United States Departments of Commerce, Education, and Labor see great value in partnerships to provide the training needed to create and sustain a high-skill, high-wage, high-technology American workforce. For any firm, union, or other organization seriously thinking about getting the most and best training for the smallest investment, pursuing opportunities available as a matter of public policy is also recommended. Business and trade associations and labor federations are good sources of information about what is available.

5.5 Labor-Management Cooperation

While examples of cooperation between unions and companies date back many years, such relationships targeted specifically to training of a firm's employees are more recent. For example, the building trades apprentice programs have existed for half a century or more. These programs are typically run by the union, are formal in nature, have physical facilities established only for training, and *require actual on-the-job work experience over a period of years to earn skill certification.* Once certified, workers with such skills are recognized and accepted by contractors nationwide.

Funding for apprentice programs is usually the result of bargaining between contractor associations and unions. Such funding is part of the contractor's cost of doing business, and is an effective way to train new workers for construction work. The unions also commit considerable funding to their training programs in areas such as training research and development, facilities, and staff. Thus, these programs are joint, and are the result of cooperation between contractors and unions.

A more recent trend is to develop labor-management cooperation in the industrial and information sectors. Now, many unions and employers are working together on various types of worker training programs. Among those unions are the United Auto Workers, the Teamsters, the International Brotherhood of Electrical Workers, the Service Employees Union, the Steelworkers, the Communications Workers, the Rubber Workers, the Machinists, the Garment Workers unions, a number of unions representing government workers, and the AFL-CIO's Human Resources Development Institute. These are but a few of the unions.

Labor-management cooperation in support of employee training includes all the major domestic automobile manufacturers, most of the major telecommunications companies, firms in the apparel industry, the major tire and rubber product manufacturers, most of the major steel producers, a wide range of companies in services, and many state and federal government agencies. Besides these, there are hundreds of smaller firms and organizations engaged in worker training with unions representing their employees. That these programs rarely gain widespread attention is not important here; that they work, and work well, is what is important.

One of the early programs between organized labor and employers is the UAW-Ford program, first negotiated in 1982. Similar programs in General Motors and Chrysler followed shortly. All these programs grew out of dramatic and lasting changes in the automobile industry. Foreign and domestic competition, changes in consumer demand, changes in marketing strategies, and shifts in the U.S. economy resulted in large-scale layoffs.

Layoffs in the late 1970s and early 1980s were not short-term or model-change-related events. They were layoffs without a chance for recall. As a result, the United Auto Workers and the major automobile companies agreed through contract bargaining to create programs which provide training for other jobs. These programs all have common elements. Funds are based on a formula of "cents per hour worked" and are turned over to professionals whose job is to provide training and retraining programs. Such training targets labor-market skills where growth in employment is occurring or expected. The worker selects the training, not the employer or the union. Within eligibility rules, funds and support services are available to both active and laid-off workers.

Joint labor-management training programs in the automobile industry were among the first major efforts to empower workers to prepare for their own futures. *Since the early 1980s, many other programs have evolved, and today, a growing labor-management programs industry is evolving.*

A more recent example is the Career Development Institute of the United Steelworkers of America (and over half a dozen of the major steel producers). The Institute is run by the Steelworkers, and funded through the various collective bargaining agreements. It is unique because it involves a single union with a common training, retraining, and educational program for employees in a number of companies—companies who are often in direct competition with one another. It is an excellent example of how a number of employers and a single union have negotiated funds for worker training within a single industry.

All the major telecommunications firms have programs of one type or another. One such program is the AT&T, Communications Workers of America (CWA), and the International Brotherhood of Electrical Workers (IBEW) program. Known as the Alliance for Employee Growth & Development, Inc. (referred to hereafter as the Alliance), this program was created in 1986.

As with the automobile industry earlier, by 1985 ATT began major layoffs (less than two years after the breakup of the Bell system). Also in 1985 (a year prior to normal contract expiration), AT&T and the unions tried bargaining a new agreement. These talks included the idea of an operationally independent training and retraining program, but funded by AT&T, CWA, and IBEW through bargaining, and run by full-time staff they would appoint. Although the 1985 bargaining effort fell short, the idea of a training/retraining program was carried forward, and in 1986 the Alliance emerged as the centerpiece of the national labor agreement between AT&T, CWA, and IBEW.

Funding for Alliance training and retraining programs (currently over half of all Alliance training involves specific skill and technical training) is done on a dollars-per-employee-per-month basis. This formula provided about $19 million for the 1986 to 1989 period; $54 million for 1989 to 1992; and is currently at about $67 million for 1992 to 1995. Beginning with the 1992 round of bargaining, AT&T, CWA, and IBEW also created a special fund for laid-off workers worth up to $2500 per individual. These funds are administered by the Alliance and the Employee Training Opportunities Program (for IBEW-represented AT&T factory workers). Both programs take care to coordinate these funds with their own funds.

Besides formula funding, the Alliance also runs programs funded by government grants. These are mainly for laid-off workers but more recently include active worker programs in workplace literacy. These grants are valued at about $1 million per year and are usually received by local training programs with whom the Alliance partners. More is covered about these funds and how they are used in Section 5.2.

Other significant sources of funds and in-kind services in support of Alliance programs come from AT&T, CWA, and IBEW. They include office space, classrooms, office equipment, and the cost of utilities and security. There is no accurate way of knowing the dollar value of such services. Other kinds of funding have been valued, however. Alliance-sponsored programs which directly support AT&T job skills are often funded by AT&T's tuition assistance program, and by direct funding from the various business units. In 1992 alone, the value of training so funded was almost $600,000.

Finally, the Alliance has created its own subsidiary, Alliance Plus, in response to the growing number of requests for technical assistance in developing other joint-venture training programs. Alliance Plus is a for-profit company, with profits flowing back into the Alliance for use in worker training. Alliance Plus is still quite new as of this writing. Even so, nearly $50,000 in profits has already been earned for use by the Alliance. Considering the high level of interest in labor-management participative programs, it is likely that Alliance Plus will become a major source of Alliance revenue in the future.

Because many companies are planning on similar programs, the contract language has been included. This might be particularly useful to a consortia of companies pooling their resources.

All the labor contracts creating participative programs have statements of principles, values, and mission which say why these programs were created. Following is an example:

> The Company and the Union mutually acknowledge their pride in the talents, abilities, creativity and commitment of the Company's workforce. The parties share a vision of the work environment in which all employees are encouraged to develop their skills, abilities and talents to the fullest extent possible and are furnished every opportunity to take the initiative to do so. Such an environment will not only offer the maximum opportunity to employees to attain their employment goals, but will also lead to increased commitment by employees to devote their maximum energies to improving the Company's productivity and competitiveness. It is anticipated that this level of employee commitment will contribute significantly to marketplace success for the Company and to the increased employment security for employees associated with such success.*

---

* This quote is taken from the 1986 National Memorandum of Agreements between AT&T, CWA, and IBEW.

In their research on the UAW/Saturn relationship, Saul Rubinstein, Michael Bennett, and Thomas Kochan[5] addressed the kind of worker training provided:

> New Saturn members receive from 350 to 700 hours of training before they are allowed to build a car. The workforce is trained to work in work team organization, problem solving, decision making, conflict resolution, and labor history.
>
> Further, they develop skills in areas traditionally reserved for management including budgeting, business planning and scheduling, cost analysis, manufacturing methods, ergonomics, industrial engineering, job design, accounting, recordkeeping, statistical process control, design of experiments and data analysis.

Funding for all this training is provided by the Saturn Corporation as part of its collective bargaining agreement with the United Auto Workers union.

A typical example follows of contract language on mission, and the structure for how the programs operate and what kinds of training is provided. It is also drawn from the 1986 agreements between AT&T, CWA, and IBEW.

> To help achieve this vision, a separate and distinct jointly administered entity will be established. The mission will be to make available learning experiences to employees which will enhance their occupational and work group skills; provide opportunities for personal and career development; stimulate and sustain their contributions to the Company's success through improved communication skills, motivation, improved work habits and enhanced interpersonal skills; familiarize them with state-of-the-art technology, based on the present or anticipated needs of the business; and increase the probability that if they face displacement or dislocation, they will find alternative employment, either inside the Company or in the outside job market.

All programs have well-defined structures, which can vary widely. They all have joint governance of one form or another, and joint operation on a day-to-day basis. They often use experts from the employment and training professions, and train through existing schools, colleges, and other training institutions. They usually have a joint structure at the worksite level, although the kind of structure is based on the cultures of the parent organizations and the structure of the work environment itself. The following is an example of one such structure, again drawn from the AT&T, CWA, and IBEW agreements.

> General direction and guidance, along with policy formulation, will be provided by a six-member Board of Trustees. Three will be salaried employees of the Company and will be appointed by the Company, and three will be appointed by the Union.

The Board of Trustees shall have the responsibility of appointing two Executive Directors and one Director. . . . One Executive Director will be a representative of the Company, while the other will be a representative of the Union. The Director shall be from the ranks of experienced administrators of education and/or training.

The Executive Directors shall be responsible for managing Alliance funds and ensuring appropriate staffing levels. The Director will oversee the day-to-day operations. Compensation for Alliance staff employees shall be approved by the Board of Trustees.

In identifying areas on which activities should focus, consultation will take place with Company and Union officials, as well as with professionals in such fields as higher education, industrial psychology and vocational training.

It is envisioned that the organization will generally arrange and/or underwrite these curricula (listed earlier in another section of the agreement) by contracting with accredited outside parties for delivery. In some cases, it may provide the curricula directly.

In addition, the organization will confer with, advise and offer professional and financial assistance to local training/retraining committees . . .

Many joint programs provide training to both active and laid-off employees. In all programs, specific rules of employee eligibility are spelled out, and are usually set by the representatives of the company(ies) and the union(s), rather than by training program administrators. The following example is taken from the AT&T, CWA, and IBEW agreements.

Regular full and part time employees will be eligible to participate in all activities. In addition, employees who have been displaced or who are on layoff will be eligible to participate provided they commence such participation within six months of layoff and, prior to layoff, have elected to receive any termination allowance in the form of periodic income continuation installments. . . . such employees may continue participation for a period extending one year beyond the expiration of their periodic payments, or until they find alternative employment, whichever occurs first.

The various collective bargaining agreements establishing these training programs often provide language on the work responsibilities expected of program staff. The following is an example. Again, it is taken from the AT&T, CWA, and IBEW agreements.

- Identifying educational, training and retraining needs, as well as the resources available to meet those needs
- Developing programs designed to meet identified employee needs
- Publicizing and encouraging employee participation in program activities

- Undertaking to review, evaluate, and make recommendations on proposals for the use of funds by the local training/retraining committees
- Coordinating forums, seminars, and workshops for the exchange of ideas and concepts among the local committees
- Commissioning research into, and evaluation of, alternative approaches to training, retraining, and job placement
- Contacting appropriate governmental agencies—federal, state and local—to obtain other types of governmental assistance that may be available for program activities

All these programs will have wording on how funding is done. In the 1986 AT&T, CWA, and IBEW agreements the following language was included. It was carried forward in 1989 and 1992 bargaining, but with higher funding amounts.

> For the period June 1, 1986 through May 31, 1989, inclusive, the Company will make available funds for the program which shall be calculated by multiplying the total number of regular full and part time union-represented employees on the Company payroll at the end of each calendar month during the above three-year period by $3.75. The Company shall credit these funds to an account designated for the program and its activities within fifteen days of the end of each such month.
>
> A separate and distinct checking account will be established in the name of the program. The Board of Trustees (or designated representatives) may authorize and approve expenditures and receive the necessary funds to be billed to this account.

Finally, these programs usually have specific language on required activity reports and financial accountability. The following is again taken from AT&T, CWA, and IBEW.

> The program will publish an Annual Report, detailing the training that was made available to employees, the number of participants who received such training, the funds expended and the manner in which funds were utilized.

5.6 Concluding Comments

In the future, companies will need to provide continuous learning, high-quality training and education, the best delivery methods, and raise the level of knowledge about both public and private sources for doing so. Multiple resources will be needed for companies so they can get started.

References

1. Taken from an EQW presentation in Washington, D.C., November 10, 1993. Wayne Cascio, Graduate School of Business, University of Colorado at Denver.

2. From research project of the Institute for Education and Employment, Education Development Center, Inc. 1994 report titled *From Job Security to Employment Security: The Alliance for Employee Growth & Development.*

3. From material on the Consortium for Worker Education, available from the Consortium at 275 7th Avenue, 18th Floor, New York, NY 10001, Attention: Angela Rojas.

4. From material provided by Steve Bieglecki of United Technologies.

5. Rubinstein, Saul, Michael Bennett, and Thomas Kochan, "The Saturn Partnership: Co-Management and the Reinvention of the Local Union," in Bruce Kaufman and Morris Kleiner (eds.), *Employee Representation Alternatives and Future Directions*, Chap. 10, Cornel ILR Press, IRRA Madison, Wisc., 1993.

6

Liability and the Technical Trainer: An Overview of Issues and Prevention Strategies

John Sample, Ph.D.

Sample & Associates

6.1 Introduction

The "Working Life" column of the May 1991 issue of *Training & Development* cited the following actual court settlement. It is reproduced here as a backdrop for appreciating liability and the technical trainer.

> A man who threatened to sue himself for workplace negligence received a cash settlement of $122,500—tax-free. The part-owner of a California manufacturing business was working in a factory one day when a maverick bolt snagged his sweater and yanked him into churning machinery. As an employee, the injured man hired a lawyer to sue himself as owner. As the owner, he then hired a lawyer to defend himself.

The two attorneys (they're separate people) agreed that the "owner" had been negligent in allowing the bolt to stick out and that he should pay the "employee" compensation. As allowed by federal law, the "employee" got the money tax-free and the "owner" deducted the amount as a business expense.

Makes you want to shoot yourself in the foot, doesn't it? (*Training & Development*, 1991, p. 93.)

This lighthearted view of our legal system may give way to a chuckle here and there, followed by a series of bad attorney jokes. The fact is, we live in a society that reveres our personal freedoms, and therefore we must have a judicial system for righting wrongs.

Technical trainers, along with their human resource development counterparts, are experiencing change in the practice of their vocation. Environmental threats require continual adaptation to cultural, economic, regulatory, and, more recently, the legal system (Feuer, 1985; Sample, 1994). No segment of our society is immune from the potential for litigation.

Even more harrowing, in the fast-paced world of computers where technology races faster than the law's ability to keep up with it, you could get yourself in trouble simply because the law is unclear. (Goldsborough, 1994, p. 18.)

In more pristine times, the primary reason for providing effective training was to increase the probability of correct and consistent performance on the job. Managers of technical training programs are now becoming concerned for a secondary reason. This reason involves preventing or reducing a company's legal liability. In this sense, training becomes a defense to an allegation of failure to adequately train employees and their managers. *If the primary reason were attended to by employers more consistently and effectively, the existence of the secondary reason would be significantly diminished.*

Table 6-1 outlines types of training participants who may recover damages, and Table 6-2 outlines who may be liable (Sample, 1993). Both tables represent only a partial listing of potential liability.

6.2 Purpose and Scope

The purpose of this chapter is to inform technical trainers and their managers about specific areas of potential liability as it relates to their areas of responsibilities. More specifically, the reader will be introduced to the following:

- Occupational Safety & Health Act (OSHA) work safety requirements
- Employer negligence as it relates to failure to train in the workplace

Table 6-1. Training Participants Who May Recover Damages

■ *EEOC/ADA Violations* Privacy and freedom-of-religion issues (nontraditional and New Age training) Discrimination in selection of trainees for advanced and specialized training Training that results in a disparate effect on a federally protected class of employees Testing that unfairly discriminates against employees who are non-English-speaking or culturally diverse Failure to provide assistive devices or to reasonably accommodate trainees with disabilities ■ *Injuries to Trainees* Training facility Unsafe simulation/laboratory equipment Unsafe workplace (OJT) ■ *OSHA Regulatory Requirements* General duty to train to standard Warning of workplace hazards and toxins	■ *Recovering Damages* State Government: Workplace health hazards Safety violations Criminal negligence Federal Government: OSHA violations Industry regulations (Nuclear Regulatory Commission, etc.) Environmental Resources Act ■ *Loss of Benefits* Anti Drug Abuse Act of 1988 Workers Compensation Third Parties ■ *Personal Injuries* Training facility Workplace Off-site location ■ *Property Damages* Real or personal property in the vicinity

Used with permission from J. Sample, *INFO-LINE Legal Liability and HRD: Implications for Trainers*, American Society for Training & Development, Washington, D.C., 1993.

- Equal Employment Opportunity (EEO) and Americans with Disability Act (ADA)

- Nontraditional experiential and adventure-based training

- Intellectual property, trade secrets, and copyright infringement

- Liability and the independent consultant

The chapter will conclude with a discussion of instructional approaches useful for preventing or reducing employer liability. Not addressed in this chapter will be treatments of the law that are adequately covered in the current literature. For example, questions about contract law and federal taxation of training are covered adequately in Mansfield (1991).

Table 6-2. Who May Be Liable

Trainers
- Negligent design of program, delivery of program, vendor selection, trainer selection, and/or facility supervision

Owner/Employer
- Negligent program design, supervision of training and facility, instructor selection, implementation of mandated training, and/or vendor selection
- Course content that is discriminatory.
- Vicarious liability
- Invasion of privacy

Employer
- Negligent program design, selection of instructors/vendors, supervision of training activities
- Failure to implement training mandated by statute
- Discriminatory course content
- Discriminatory selection of trainees
- Vicarious liability—intentional acts of supervisors or trainers
- Invasion of privacy

Outside Contractors/Vendors
- Negligent program design, supervision of training facility
- Misrepresentation of a safety record, credentials, experience, or other requirements, such as bond or insurance
- Contractual agreement—failure to meet specifications or breach of an indemnification agreement

Used with permission from J. Sample, *INFO-LINE Legal Liability and HRD: Implications for Trainers*, American Society for Training & Development, Washington, D.C., 1993.

6.3 OSHA and Workplace Safety

During the 1960s, sufficient concern was raised about safety in the workplace, and in 1970 Congress passed the Occupational Safety and Health Act (OSHA). One author asserts that the act has two specific functions: "to provide an incentive not to hurt people and to provide funds to compensate victims" (McWhirter, 1989, p. 235). Under this act, an employer has a general duty

> to furnish to each of his employees employment and a place of employment which are free from recognized hazards that are causing or are likely to cause death or serious physical harm to his employees . . . (OSHA, 1970).

Because the general duty requirement was so vague, Congress intended that the Secretary of Labor promulgate specific safety standards for each industry so that employers know what was expected of them.

There are several implications for technical trainers and their managers. According to a 1977 U.S. Appeals Court decision, the general duty clause of OSHA "includes training of employees as to the dangers and supervision of the work site" (*General Dynamics v. OSHARC*, 1977).

According to one expert witness specializing in OSHA training, there are several areas of potential liability for technical trainers and their managers (Sage, 1990, p. 10):

- The training results in personal harm or injury to a trainee

- Harm or injury was caused by "failing to perform a training responsibility on which the trainee depends"

- Someone else under the control of the trainer causes harm or injury to a trainee

One must keep in mind the importance of supervisors as first-line trainers in any organization. This point is important because supervisors can be held liable for failure to supervise and to train to standard. Sage (1990) and Mager & Pipe (1984) continuously advocate the importance of supervisors in changing workplace behaviors and attitudes. Sage (1990) states that the standard of care owed by trainers and supervisors to their adult learners is the duty of supervision.

> If there is a failure to exercise reasonable care in performing this duty, either in the commission or omission of an instructional act or training activity, and that failure results in an injured trainee, the trainer or . . . [supervisor] is assumed liable. (Sage 1990, p. 10.)

6.4 Employer Negligence— Failure to Train to Standard

Negligence is generally defined as "unintentional conduct that falls below the standard of care that is necessary to protect others against exposure to an unreasonable risk of foreseeable injury (Blackburn and Sage, 1991, p. 3). Negligence cases are initiated and resolved in civil courts, both at the state and federal levels.

From a training and development perspective, the elements of a negligence action are described by Henzey et al. (1991) as follows:

> *A Legal Duty or Standard of Care*—may be specified in a statute or part of the "common law" from judicial precedents
>
> *Breach of Duty*—the duty of a reasonable trainer in the industry

Proximate Cause—the breach of the duty was the legal cause of damage or injury

Injuries/Damages—injuries resulted directly from the training or lack of training

For example, in *Stacy v. Truman Medical Center* (1992), the center had a legal duty to instruct its nurses in the correct performance of their work. Although the center had a policy on fire evacuation procedures, the nurse in this instance was not trained on the policy. The breach of the duty was failing to remove the patient from a room on fire. A proximate causal link between the death of the patient (injury/damage) and the legal duty to adequately train the nurse about fire evacuation policy was argued successfully before the court. The medical center was held liable. It is generally prescribed by statute in most states that employers are protected from lawsuits by employees for negligence in the workplace by Workers Compensation laws (McWhirter, 1989).

As indicated by the preceding, negligence involves unintentional conduct. Are there legal remedies when an employer intentionally harms an employee? Under certain circumstances, employees may sue their employer for an intentional tort. From a training and development perspective, the employer must have intentionally injured the employee by failing to train the employee (Blackburn and Sage, 1991).

An employer may be sued by an employee alleging several wrongful acts that caused an injury. For example, it is not unusual to allege failure to train and to supervise to standard. In *Granite Construction Co. v. Mendoza* (1991), the employer was sued for gross negligence. The court determined that the employer knew about the peril, but its acts or omissions demonstrated that it did not care. In the Granite case, the employer had policies and procedures and training programs on safety in general, including monthly safety meetings and "tailgate" instruction prior to work assignments. Contrary to policy and training, the employee was not issued a safety vest while working on a roadway, and was struck and killed by an automobile. Although training had occurred, the employer was still liable for the gross negligence of lack of supervision at the roadway work site.

There are instances in which an employer may be criminally responsible for failure to adequately train their employees. In these types of cases, higher levels of proof and state and federal constitutional guarantees for prosecuting and defending criminal cases apply. For example, in *State v. Shoreline Support Corp* (1989), a Wisconsin employer was found guilty of reckless homicide of one of its bulldozer operators. The appeals court noted that a jury could have reasonably found that the lack of training and supervision of the employee were causally related to his death and that the employer acted recklessly in its failure to train and supervise.

In the Shoreline case, uncontested testimony established that the work site was inherently dangerous and was no place for an inexperienced bulldozer operator to be working and unsupervised. The operator was required to maneuver an 8- by 20-foot bulldozer along a strip of land which measured between 16 and 75 feet in width. The operator scooped rubble in the bulldozer shovel, made a 180-degree turn, and dumped the rubble over the edge of a cliff. At the time of the fatal accident, the operator had approximately 49 hours of experience with the bulldozer. Since the accident was not witnessed, it was reasonable to assume that the operator was not being supervised at the time of the accident. Testimony established that bulldozer operators are normally provided 1500 hours of training and supervision before working under the conditions described.

6.4.1 Failure to Train to Standard in the Public Sector

Technical trainers in the public sector have an additional source of litigation for which they must be concerned. Law enforcement and corrections are currently the most vulnerable occupational areas (Barrineau, 1987; Cardani, 1986; Whitt, 1990), although publicly operated hospitals, social services, and public utilities are ripe for potential liability (Steinglass, 1988). Examples of high-liability tasks in law enforcement include use of firearms, driving, first responder, and defensive tactics (Gallagher, 1990a; Callahan, March, 1989; Schofield, October, 1988). Corollary high-liability tasks in other public-sector settings include the handling and disposal of toxic wastes, proper care of children in foster care, residential treatment for the mentally and emotionally disturbed, emergency room practices in hospitals, the stringing of electrical wires, and the safe operation of machinery, such as forklifts in a municipal warehouse.

Consider the facts in the following case (*City of Canton v. Harris,* 1989). A mother was arrested on a speeding violation which occurred while driving her daughter to school. Upon arriving at the station, she was found sitting on the floor of the patrol wagon, and when asked if she required medical attention, she responded with an incoherent remark. She was brought inside for processing, and during this time, she slumped to the floor on two occasions. Finally the police officers in charge left her lying on the floor to prevent her from falling again. No medical attention was ever summoned for her. She was released within an hour from custody, and was taken by a family-procured ambulance to a hospital. She was diagnosed as suffering from several emotional ailments and was hospitalized for one week. She required outpatient treatment for an additional year.

The police department had a policy requiring that "jailers" at the station shall, when a prisoner is found to be unconscious or semi-conscious, or when he or she is unable to explain his or her condition, or who complains of being ill, have such person taken to a hospital for medical treatment, with permission of his supervisor, before admitting the person to City Jail.

The question before the U.S. Supreme Court was the extent to which the civil rights of the victim under the due process clause of the 14th Amendment to receive medical attention while in police custody was violated. Testimony during the lower court trial determined that shift commanders in the police department were not provided with any special training (beyond first-aid training) to determine when to summon medical care for an injured person in custody.

The Supreme Court held in the City of Canton case that the inadequacy of police training may serve as the basis for liability only where the failure to train in a relevant respect amounts to *deliberate indifference* to the constitutional rights of persons with whom the police come into contact. Further, the Supreme Court determined that focus must be on whether the training program is *adequate to the task* the particular employees must perform. Lastly, the identified deficiency in the training program must be closely related to the ultimate injury—that is, the deficiency in training actually caused the indifference to the rights of a citizen.

6.5   Equal Employment Opportunity Act (EEO) and the Americans with Disability Act (ADA) Requirements

6.5.1   Overview of EEO Guidelines

Title VII of the Civil Rights Act of 1964 prohibits employment discrimination based upon an individual's race, color, religion, sex, or national origin. Any employer who employs 15 or more employees for 20 or more calendar weeks in the current or preceding calendar year is subjected to the provisions of Title VII. This act is enforced by the Equal Employment Opportunity Commission. The Commission has the power to:

- Investigate complaints on behalf of employees and informally settle

- Dismiss a charge by issuing a right-to-sue letter, which allows the employee to file a suit in Federal District Court

- File a lawsuit in Federal District Court on behalf of the employee

The Civil Rights Act of 1991 is significant to employers for the following reasons:

- Several recent Supreme Court cases which had made it more difficult for employees to sue their employers were overturned.

- Employees have a right to a trial by jury for discrimination claims (juries are usually more sympathetic to employee claims than a judge).

- It gives employees the right to recover compensatory and punitive damages.

- It makes it easier for an employee to prove discrimination.

Program designers and evaluators are well advised to become generally familiar with certain documents. The *EEOC Guidelines on Employee Selection Procedures* (29 CFR, 1607) have been interpreted by the U. S. Supreme Court as having the force and effect of law in defining fair employment practices (*Griggs v. Duke Power*, 1971; *Albemarle v. Moody*, 1975). Another indispensable document is the *Principles for Validation And Use of Personnel Selection Procedures.* Since judges and jurors are not trained in evaluation and measurement theory, they must rely heavily on professionally developed guidelines and expert testimony for their deliberations and findings.

The reader may be wondering at this point what do guidelines for employee selection have to do with technical training? A general guideline to remember is that any significant personnel decision, including training, should conform to requirements for fairness and due process (Cascio, 1991; Ledvinka and Scarpello, 1991). More specifically, Title VII of the 1964 Civil Rights Act regulates testing of personnel, and the EEOC Guidelines define a test

> . . . as any paper-and-pencil of performance measure used as a basis for any employment decision. The guidelines in this part apply, for example, to ability tests which are designed to measure eligibility for hire, transfer, promotion, membership, *training,* referral, or retention. (29 CFR, 1607.2; emphasis added.)

One may reason from this that the following are within the purview of the preceding stated requirement:

1. Requirements for training prior to entry into a job

2. Selecting employees to attend training and development, including their retention in a program

3. The use of measures in training as measures of performance

4. The making of job assignments based upon performance in a training program

A potential legal problem for technical trainers and their organization occurs whenever any measure used for a major employment decision is discriminatory, that is if it

> adversely affects hiring, promotion, transfer or membership opportunity of classes protected by Title VII ... unless the test has been validated and evidences a high degree of utility (29 CFR, 1607.3).

Such requirements for validity have been stringently applied in selection decisions for over 20 years. In the landmark U. S. Supreme Court case of *Griggs v. Duke Power* (1971), it was held that an educational requirement of a high school degree was not job-related, and, therefore, the effect of the educational requirement adversely impacted minorities.

If training and development programs are to be held to the rationale of the Griggs case, it would be necessary to demonstrate a relationship between training and actual job performance as defined by relevant criterion measures. The Uniform Guidelines requires that:

> Where a measure of success in a training program is used as a selection procedure and the content of a training program is justified on the basis of content validity, the use should be justified on the relationship between the content of the training program and the content of the job (29 CFR, 1701.14).

According to Bartlett (1978, p. 181):

> Unless training could be demonstrated empirically to make a difference in job performance, training requirements if showing adverse impact can be ruled discriminatory. Thus, training measures would be required to have a demonstrated relationship to later job performance before they could be used for any employment decisions.

This interpretation holds as true today as it did in the midseventies (Cascio, 1991).

Technical trainers may have an occasion to use training as a criterion to validate their selection of trainees. The question to be addressed is to what extent should preemployment tests for entrance to training programs be based upon successful completion of the program, or should some other criterion, such as job performance, be required by test developers.

For example, in *Washington v. Davis* (1976), the courts addressed the use of a verbal abilities test to determine whether applicants possessed the minimum skills necessary to understand and succeed in the academic portion of police officer training. And in a case involving the teaching profession, the courts examined the validity of using national teacher certification examinations against academic teacher training programs, rather than against job performance (*National Education Association v. South Carolina,*

1978). In both Washington and NEA, the U.S. Supreme Court held that successful completion of a training program was itself the proper criterion for validating a selection device to determine entrance to a training program.

Two subsequent cases modified the court's earlier position in Washington and NEA. In *Craig v. County of Los Angeles* (1980, p. 663) the court reasoned that

> If employers were permitted to validate selection devices without reference to job performance, then non-job related selection devices could always be validated through the same expedient of employing them at both the pre-training and training stage.

A similar conclusion was reached in *Ensley v. Seibels* (1980) where the court addressed the use of a 120-item test developed by the International Personnel Management Association that was used to establish eligibility lists for police and fire personnel.

Russell (1984) cites several conclusions regarding training as a criterion measure. The first has to do with strategies for selecting applicants for technical training by employers. One strategy is to validate training performance with job performance if training is a criterion for validation of the selection device. The second strategy would be to validate the selection device with job performance. A third strategy is to use tests which establish that candidates have minimum skills necessary to complete the training program. According to Russell (1982, p. 266), the *superior strategy is to validate training with job performance if training is used as a criterion for validating a selection device.* This position by Russell still stands today as good advice for technical trainers (Cascio, 1991; Muchinsky, 1992).

For example, an employer in a technical environment could correlate actual job requirements (i.e., job performance appraisals, work samples, etc.) with performance measures from the training program (i.e., post-tests, simulated task performance, etc.) if training is to be used as a predictor for an employee selection device. An excellent review of performance assessment methods for training can be found in Priestley (1982).

6.5.2 The ADA and Technical Skills Training

The most recent federal legislation to impact employers is the Americans with Disabilities Act (ADA) of 1990. This act prohibits discrimination against persons with disabilities in employment, public services, transportation, public accommodations, and telecommunications services. The ADA became effective July 26, 1992 for employers with 25 or more employees. Employers with 15 or more workers must comply beginning July 26, 1994.

All aspects of employment are covered, including the application process and hiring, on-the-job-training, advancement in wages, benefits, and employer-sponsored social activities. In essence, the ADA protects qualified disabled persons from job discrimination (Snyder, 1991). To be considered a qualified disabled person, a job applicant or employee must be able to perform the essential functions of the job. Employers must accommodate the employee's known mental or physical disabilities unless that would impose an "undue hardship."

A qualified individual with a disability is a person who has a physical or mental impairment substantially limiting a major life activity, has a record of such impairment, or is regarded as having an impairment. A disability can include a physiological disorder or condition, cosmetic disfigurement, anatomical loss, or emotional disorder or condition.

It is important to note that the ADA does not guarantee an individual with a disability the right to the job for which they are applying. The employer remains free to make decisions based on the particular skills or knowledge necessary for the job. The decision made by the employer regarding whom to hire must be based on reasons unrelated to the existence of a covered disability. Nor is the employer required to give preference to an applicant with a disability over another applicant without a disability (Meisinger, 1991). The first step an employer should take is to determine the essential functions of a job. Technical trainers may be required to perform a job-task analysis that would meet ADA requirements for "essential functions" analysis. Secondly, employers must provide disabled employees with reasonable accommodations that are required to perform the essential functions of the job. Examples of accommodations are modifying work schedules, reassigning job duties, removing architectural barriers, and offering auxiliary aids, interpreters, or taped text. According to one source, nearly 60 percent of employers surveyed spent less than $100 for each instance of an accommodation, and another 25 percent resulted in spending from $100 to $500 for each accommodation (*News & Trends*, 1994).

There are several implications for training and development in organizations impacted by the ADA:

- *Interviewer training.* Many interviewers and recruiters will require "disability etiquette" training in order to feel comfortable interviewing applicants with disabilities. Illegal questions, such as, "Do you have any medical condition that would preclude you from performing your job?" or "Have you ever had workers compensation?" are prohibited. Instead, ask "Are you able to perform all of the tasks listed on job description?"

- *Recruiting and selecting disabled trainers.* Although affirmative action is not required by the ADA, managers of technical training programs and centers are encouraged to address the *recruitment and selection of disabled trainers*. This is important from a role modeling perspective (Navran, 1992).

- *Supervisory training.* Several aspects of the supervisor's job must be updated with training:

  1. Current employees returning to work from disability leave may require a reasonable accommodation. Special issues arise where the return to work involves workers compensation.

  2. Fear of managing the qualified disabled worker must be addressed in supervisory training. All employees, including the disabled employee, are expected to perform the essential job functions to standard. Reasonable accommodation does not mean special (unfair) consideration at performance appraisal or for promotional opportunities.

  3. Supervisors should understand the implications of alcohol and drug use on job performance. The Act specifically provides that an individual currently using illegal drugs is not a "qualified individual with a disability." The ADA does protect alcoholics and past drug users who have successfully completed treatment. Employers may hold legal drug users and alcoholics to the same performance standards as other employees, even if poor performance or other unsatisfactory behavior is due to drug or alcohol use.

- Prepare to make reasonable accommodations for the disabled learner. Many accommodations are relatively inexpensive. Examples include magnifying glasses to aid reading, taped text for those who are visually impaired, and instructional materials with large lettering (Hendricks et al., 1992). Training seminars, off-site conferences, and meetings must also be accessible.

6.6 Nontraditional Experiential and Adventure-based Approaches to Training

One of the most creative approaches for unleashing human potential of managers and executives is known variously as nontraditional experiential or New Age training, and adventure-based or outdoor experiential training. These approaches run the gamut from traditional classroom settings using highly experiential value-based exercise and activities to wilderness treks and offshore sailing jaunts. Such experiences are presumably designed to instill self-confidence and promote team-building.

There are two primary forms of this type of training:

- Adventure-based training involves a group of employees who participate in a number of physically and emotionally demanding exercises,
  which in some cases are accomplished in rural or wilderness settings.

- New Age training may employ motivational sermons, hypnosis, tran-
  scendental meditation, encounter groups, and other techniques to instill
  a new value system and/or beliefs that will enhance a person's job performance. Several areas of potential liability are possible (Vogel, 1991;
  Mitchell, 1990).

There are several areas of concern with these types of training:

- Personal injuries could occur, leaving the corporation and its insurance
  company liable for damages due to negligence and for workers compensation claims.

- Stress-related illness may result in claims for workers compensation or
  civil suits for "emotional distress" or "intentional infliction of distress."

- Constitutional issues of right to privacy and religious freedom may be
  infringed upon when participants are forced to discuss personal values
  and religious convictions. Pressure to adopt values inconsistent with
  personal values and religious convictions may place an organization
  legally at risk.

- Liability for false imprisonment or detention of a participant.

- Termination of employment for failure to participate in organizationally
  mandated programs could result in wrongful termination suits.

- Federally protected rights could be abridged if participants were not
  selected because of a handicap, or for reasons based on race, nationality,
  sex, age, etc.

6.6.1   Adventure-based Training

For some participants, adventure-based training will be physically taxing
and stressful. Participants will be away from normal comfort zones and
family routines. Under these conditions, a participant might suffer from
intentional infliction of emotional distress. Such a situation could arise out
of the participant's being humiliated or embarrassed or unable to perform
a training activity as directed.

By way of understanding the nature of adventure-based training, consider the following fictitious case scenario. XYZ Company has selected a
private vendor to conduct a series of mandatory executive development

workshops for midlevel and senior managers. The primary delivery vehicle for the program was a series of weekend "Adventure Opportunities" down a well-known regional river. Participants and training staff were in several rafts that floated down the river. Part of the adventure consisted of negotiating light rapids and carrying the rafts through shallow waters.

The trip down the river on Saturday was relatively uneventful—all the food, supplies, and passengers escaped capsizing on several occasions! Wet and tired, the group of managers and the instructional staff set up camp on a picturesque point in the river. Food was prepared, and preparations were made for the first group encounter.

The facilitator used several imaging and visualization techniques. One of the participants commented that she did not know what this technique had to do with managing the administrative services division of the company. Another person remarked that he reserved activities such as this for his church life, and he refused to participate any further. As the group experience continued, participants were pushed to reveal very privately held values. The session ended with everyone contorted in a series of yoga-like exercises. Several people commented that they felt exposed, vulnerable, and out-of-control. A combination of sighs of relief and grumbling greeted the reminder of an early start in the morning from the facilitator.

The next day brought a five-mile hike in the woods and low mountains to the west of the river. Those who forgot their hiking footwear were well blistered by the first mile of the trek. Designer sneakers and stylish aerobic outfits were no match for century old rock, gravel, and barbed thickets. Complicating the march was 90-degree heat and sunshine coupled with 80 percent humidity. To make matters worse, two of the lower-level female managers began to outpace their upper-level male counterparts. The day's hike ended back at the campsite, and after a hearty meal of trail mix, corn muffins, and beans, preparations were made for the evening group session.

Participants were pushed to exhaustion by the end of Sunday. The facilitator began the session with a comment that "tired people reveal their feelings more honestly." During the session, one of the participants became heavy-lidded and dozed off to sleep. He was awakened by the facilitator who berated him for "not supporting the team." The final blow came for several participants when the facilitator insisted that certain values and beliefs be adopted by the participants for the remainder of the weekend. Several people complained that their religious freedoms were being trampled upon. They wanted to end the program immediately! The request was refused by the highest of the senior managers in the group. The group was picked up at a predetermined point downriver the next day.

Upon returning to work a few days later, three of the participants insisted that they would not mandate attendance of their managers at the next "Adventure Opportunity" sponsored by the company. They were summoned to the vice president's office, and subsequently fired. A wrongful termination suit was brought against the company and the vendor "Adventure Unlimited."

Although the preceding case facts are fictitious, two civil court cases involving "New Age" experiential approaches have been reported. One of these cases is the Dekalb Farmer's Market, Inc. (1988) case, which was settled out of court, thereby precluding a determination on the facts by a state civil court. It was alleged that an outdoor adventure experience required of managers infringed on their rights to privacy and religion. Since this case was settled out of court, we do not know how the litigants would have fared in a court of law! Even though this case was settled out of court, businesses should be on the alert for internally produced or contracted programs that may infringe on individual rights (Sample, 1994).

6.6.2 New Age
Experiential Training

In *Hiatt v. Walker Chevrolet Company* (1987), the plaintiff alleged wrongful discharge for refusing to participate in a New Age training program. Hiatt attended a New Age training course in February 1984. At first, Hiatt thought the New Age motivational program was great. By the fourth day, however, his view had changed. At that point, he became convinced that the program was anti-Christian, and conflicted with his Christian beliefs. Hiatt left the program.

He was scheduled to attend a business meeting in California following the New Age training course. He continued on to that meeting without notifying his employer that he had left the training session on the fourth of a five-day program. When he arrived in California, he called his employer and explained that he had terminated his participation in the New Age course because the program was anti-Christian, and he could not participate in it.

Shortly after Hiatt returned from California, he was fired by his employer, Walker Chevrolet. Hiatt, in turn, filed suit against his former employer, alleging discrimination in violation of both state law and the Federal Civil Rights Act (*Hiatt v. Walker Chevrolet Co.*, 822 P.2d 1235). The employer denied the allegation, and countered by saying that Hiatt's attitude, inability to communicate with management and his peers, his failure to implement his sales plan, and excessive absenteeism were the basis for his dismissal.

The federal law applicable in this case is Title VIII of the Civil Rights Act of 1964. This Act makes it an unfair practice for an employer to fail or to otherwise refuse to hire or to discharge any individual or otherwise discriminate against an individual with respect to his or her compensation, terms, conditions, or privileges of employment because of such individual's race, color, religion, sex, or national origin. An employer may demonstrate that it is unable to reasonably accommodate an employee's religious observance or practices without undue hardship on the conduct of the employer's business. Additionally, federal law also makes it illegal for an employer to discharge, refuse to hire, or otherwise discriminate against an employee on the basis of religion.

In this case, Hiatt had to prove that:

1. He had a bona fide religious belief that conflicted with an employment practice

2. He had informed the employer of that conflict

3. He was fired because he refused to comply with the employment requirement

Hiatt was not able to meet all of the court's requirements, and was not able to meet the required burden of proof. In fact, the court found that Hiatt had volunteered to attend the training course, and that his request to terminate the program was immediately granted by Walker Chevrolet. The state court ruled summarily in favor of Walker Chevrolet, and Hiatt has appealed the court's ruling.

A second example of an extreme approach to experiential training concerned the Federal Aviation Administration's use of New Age training in its management development program (Fair Employment Practices Guidelines, March 10, 1994). The CNN *Moneyline* show obtained a copy of a secretly videotaped class session with a psychologist who advocated tying people together for long periods of time and having them take showers tied together. In one excerpt of the video, the psychologist was observed to say, "I want it to get so uncomfortable for all of you that when you hear one of your people in this room speaking like a snake, speaking indirectly, speaking like a victim, accusing, miscommunicating their personal truth or universal truth, I want it to grate like fingernails on a chalkboard. I want 23 voices in unison to go, 'Aaah, don't do that.' " (Navran, "Nontraditional Training," 1994, p. 5.)

The third example highlights the potential legal pitfalls of diversity training. A California grocery chain recently paid $90 million in damages from a class action suit filed by women employees. Part of the evidence admitted during the trial were records from a diversity workshop attended by men and women managers. One of the exercises involved participants voicing stereotypes of women and members of other minority groups. Some of the recorded stereotypes mentioned women generally, and black women in particular. According to the source reporting this case, "The direct evidence of bias on the part of managers derived from their statements in the workshops contributed to the finding of widespread sex discrimination. (Cascio, "Diversity Training Entails Legal Pitfalls," 1993, p. 1; see also Grace, 1994.)

As a general guideline, the more outrageous and extreme from actual job duties an activity or exercise an employee is asked to perform, the greater the chance that the employee will be successful in alleging violation of civil rights damages for such an activity.

Trainers who practice their discipline in a technical arena are in a better position to comply with the legal requirement of job relatedness, than are trainers who are working the "soft-skills" arena. A well-designed job analysis will determine knowledge, skills, and attitudes. Designers of technical training should be able to translate job tasks into learning goals and performance objectives rather effectively.

There is a trend of increasing involvement by technical trainers in the "soft skills" arena (Carnevale, 1993). Since the purpose of such training may be change- and/or future-oriented, it may be difficult to link such training to specific job and work tasks. Experiential programs can certainly aid in this regard. The question becomes one of balancing corporate mission and goals with employee rights. The position taken in this chapter is that avoiding potential legal difficulties may be increased with a focused analysis and design capability.

A macro analysis of the organization's future intentions will assist the training manager in the analysis phase. Senior and line managers must communicate the direction and intensity of change to technical training managers. Robinson and Robinson (1991) say it best when they admonish technical trainers to help line managers meet their business objectives (Robinson and Robinson, 1991). Experiential programs that are directly linked to the organization's business objectives will probably survive legal scrutiny so long as personal freedoms such as privacy and religion are not infringed upon.

The development of experiential exercises may become problematic at this juncture. How does the technical trainer who designs and develops experiential programs balance employee rights with organizational goals? Individual and small group exercises that focus on such human conditions as anger, affection, trust, and conflict have the potential for clashing with individual customs. Freely expressing anger may be a family trait with ethnic and religious overtones for one employee, whereas, for someone else, the expression of anger is forbidden by the person's religion.

This dilemma is often resolved by senior management in an arbitrary manner. One has no choice but to participate if expecting to get ahead! Another approach is to let the participants decide for themselves by opting out of participation. But this is not really an option since certain developmental experiences may have long-term consequences for upward mobility, and there may be no alternative routes for the employees' development.

An approach to overcoming this problem is to determine specific change requirements in an organization, and to then design specifically to those requirements. If the analysis phase determines that trust and conflict are problems worth addressing, then the design team has a *business-related requirement* for specific experiential exercises that address trust and conflict.

This approach will impact internal HRD programs and external providers who have a "standardized package" to sell. It is incumbent upon the HRD provider (internal and external) to make sure their design efforts are work- and organization-related. Failure to do so may place both the vendor and the organization legally at risk.

Eyres (1990) and Tarullo (1992) suggest that not all nontraditional training programs should be scrapped. The following suggestions may help avoid litigation:

- Review the organization's mission, strategic plan, corporate values, principles of service, operational goals, and objectives for sources of job-related training, both at the macro and micro levels.

- Complete a job-task analysis and performance criteria for knowledge, skill, and attitudes at the micro level for training requirements. Review macro-level functional area goals and objectives (customer service, quality improvement, sales, manufacturing, new product design, etc.) for job-related training requirements.

- If necessary, use systems and process documentation, survey questionnaires, interviews, or observations to document training requirements at the macro level. This is especially important for moderate to long-range change requirements (i.e., corporate restructuring, downsizing, etc.).

- Use a logically structured analysis, design, development, implementation, and evaluation approach. Link instructional methods and media to job-related requirements at both micro and macro levels within the organization.

- Make participation in extensive experiential or adventure-based training voluntary. Require a written consent that discloses the contents of the program. Any other type of consent may not be interpreted as "informed" and will therefore be unenforceable.

- Provide nonpunishing alternatives for employees who do not wish to participate in experiential activities that may intrude on constitutionally guaranteed rights, such as privacy, religion, or accommodation of disability. Design alternative developmental approaches that result in the same learning and performance outcomes.

- Never force an unwilling employee to continue an experiential activity or exercise, and make every effort to avoid embarrassing an employee, both during training and back on the job.

- Do not punish those who do not volunteer for such programs when their performance appraisals are due or when promotions are being considered.

- Choose your private vendors or contractors carefully. Check their references, program content, and, if possible, observe one of their programs in progress for safety and emergency precautions. Reduce to writing how you expect the vendor to handle instructional content and conflict. Based upon job-related data, expect the vendor to modify the design and development of media and content of their curriculum to meet the work-related requirements of the organization. Consider requiring performance bonds for vendors and contractors.

- Educate senior management and corporate legal counsel on the potential legal pitfalls of experiential approaches that are not linked to micro or macro job requirements.

6.7   Intellectual Property, Trade Secrets, and Copyright

Intellectual property consists of protected intangible property interests owned by individuals or employers. Included in this area of the law are patents, trademarks, copyright, and trade secrets (Hautman & Sullivan, 1989). Our concern for technical trainers in this chapter are with trade secrets and copyright.

6.7.1   Trade Secrets

Technical trainers must be careful in the analysis, design, development, and delivery of instructional materials to maintain security over trade secrets. Trade secrets include, for example, customer information, pricing data, marketing methods, and manufacturing processes. Under the law, a trade secret is only useful in its undisclosed state, but once made public, anyone can use the "secret." The only recourse the owner of a trade secret has is to sue the person who improperly took it or made public the secret. All others get to use the fruits of the trade secret (Lieberman & Siedel, 1988).

The more typical problem occurs when a technical trainer, who is hired by a competitor, supposedly takes trade secrets along to the new position.

Employers may require employees to sign confidentiality agreements not to disclose particular trade secrets learned on the job.

Another principle of law may be used to protect employers who wish to secure their trade secrets. The law of principal and agent may be enforced by an employer. An agent is someone who acts in the name of his or her principal. For our purposes, technical trainers are agents of their employer, the principal. The relationship between principal and agent is one of agency.

> Sections 395 and 396 of the *Restatement (Second) of Agency* suggests that it is an actionable breach of a duty not to disclose to third persons information given confidentially during the course of the agency. However, every person is held to have a right to earn a living. If the rule were strictly applied, a highly skilled [technical trainer] who went to another company might be barred from using his knowledge and skills they developed on the job. The courts do not prohibit people from using elsewhere the general knowledge and skills developed on the job. Only specific trade secrets are protected. (Lieberman and Siedel 1988, p. 723.)

6.7.2 Copyright

The copyright law protects the expression of ideas (but not the idea itself) in some tangible form (a book or magazine, video or film, microfilm, cassette tape, computer disk, etc.). Although the exact words in a book may be copyrighted, the ideas in the book are not. The following cannot be copyrighted: ideas, processes, procedures, methods of operation, concepts, principles, or discovery. However, a tangible description, explanation, or illustration of these may be copyrighted (ASTD Copyright Information Kit, 1993).

A copyright is secured immediately and automatically when the work is created, and a work is created when it is fixed in some form of a tangible expression (computer disk, print copy, etc.). Registering the work with the U.S. Copyright Office provides legal protection and redress in state and federal courts.

A copyright holder has five exclusive rights:

- To *reproduce* the copyrighted work
- To prepare *derivative works* (adaption) based upon the copyrighted work
- To *distribute* copies of the copyrighted work to the public by sale or other transfer of ownership, or by rental, lease, or lending
- To *perform* the copyrighted work publicly, in the case of motion pictures and other audiovisual works
- To *display* the copyrighted work publicly, in the case of audiovisual work

These exclusive rights are qualified by the "Fair Use" privilege (see Table 6-3). This privilege allows others than the owner of a copyright to use copyrighted material in a reasonable manner without consent. Although legal guidelines exist, "fair use" is a tricky legal concept to understand. Informational or factual content may be more freely published than creative or literary works. Portions of copyrighted works can be used for purposes of illustration or comment, as in a book or article review. Copying anything consumable to avoid buying it is a clear infringement. Nonprofit educational institutions have a limited fair-use exemption based upon classroom teaching. Most corporate and public-sector employee training and development environments will not qualify as "nonprofit educational" organizations.

6.7.3 Software Piracy and Copyrighted Art Work

Designers and developers of technical training who rely heavily on computers must be concerned about software piracy and copyrighted art

Table 6-3. Copyright and Fair Use Exemptions

Title 17 U.S.C.A. Sec. 107

Sec. 107 Limitations on exclusive rights: Fair Use

. . . the fair use of a copyrighted work, including such use by reproduction in copies or phonorecords or by any other means specified by that section, for purposes such as criticism, comment, news reporting, teaching (including multiple copies for classroom use), scholarship, or research, is not an infringement of copyright. In determining whether the use made of a work in any particular case is a fair use the factors to be considered shall include—

(1) the purpose and character of the use, including whether such use is of a commercial nature or is for nonprofit educational purposes;

(2) the nature of the copyrighted work;

(3) the amount and substantiality of the portion used in relation to the copyrighted work as a whole; and

(4) the effect of the use upon the potential market for or value of the copyrighted work.

The fact that a work is unpublished shall not bar a finding of fair use if such finding is made upon consideration of all the above factors. (As amended 1990)

Title 17 USA Sec. 201

(b) Works Made For Hire—In the case of a work made for hire, the employer or other person for whom the work was prepared is considered the author for [purposes of Title 17] unless the parties have agreed expressly otherwise in a written instrument signed by them, owns all of the rights comprised in the copyright. (As amended 1976).

work. According to one source, businesses in 1993 paid $3.6 million in fines and penalties from software piracy (Goldsborough, 1994). Table 6-4 lists an eight-point strategy businesses can take to prevent litigation and fines due to this problem.

A related problem concerns the use of copyrighted art work—in this instance, clip art. Some software companies license the owner to use its clip art for most purposes—except resale or wide distribution. In these instances, printed material or products may require permission from some software companies for the use of clip art. Other software companies freely allow unlimited reproduction and distribution of their clip art. *Buyer beware. Read and heed the software licensing agreement!*

Digital manipulation of clip art or scanned photographs does not remove the possibility of infringement, as some technical trainers may believe. According to Goldsborough (1994, p. 21), "These works are known as 'derivative works,' . . . and they're protected by copyright law in the same way as original works."

6.7.4 Suggestions for Preventing Infringement Litigation

- If technical trainers are privy to trade secrets, have them sign agreements not to compete when they are employed somewhere else. Such agreements should be specific to the trade secrets, and limited in scope and duration. Overly broad agreements are usually not enforceable. Employers should make trade secrets confidential before the law of principal and agent will come into effect (Lieberman and Siedel, 1988).

- Consider copyrighting corporate training materials. Registration provides a public record in the event that an infringement occurs. Contact the Library of Congress Copyright Office, Washington, D.C. 20559. The Public Information Office telephone number is (202) 707-3000, and the Forms Headline number is (202) 707-9100.

Table 6-4. Strategies for Reducing Software Piracy

1. Appoint a software manager to implement all aspects of company software policy.
2. Implement a software code of ethics.
3. Establish a procedure for acquiring and registering software.
4. Establish and maintain a software log.
5. Conduct periodic audits.
6. Establish a program to educate employees.
7. Maintain a library of software licenses.
8. Enjoy the benefits of complying with software license agreements.

Used with permission from Software Publishers Association, Washington, D.C.

- Do not use material that you developed for your employer. Technical trainers who decide to open their own consulting and training business may be tempted to borrow materials from their former employer. Since the employer owns the right to material developed by its employees, those wishing to use materials must secure an agreement from their current or former employer.

- Contact the Copyright Clearance Center, 27 Congress St., Salem, MA 01970, telephone (508) 744-3350 for assistance. Obtaining permission quickly from the copyright holder for copies used in meetings, presentations, with clients and colleagues, and for workshops and classroom uses takes valuable time. For an annual fee, service from the center allows your organization to make immediate authorized copies without having to obtain permission directly from the holder of the copyright.

- Seek permission to photocopy directly from the author or publisher. Some journals and trade magazines will provide authorization at no cost, as long as credit is noted on the distributed copies. Others will require a royalty payment and the credit notice. Use a clipping service that will monitor certain publications for your organization. The service will provide copies.

6.8   The Special Case for Training Supervisors and Managers

The EEO and ADA requirements summarized earlier in the chapter are representative of only a small portion of the laws and regulations impacting corporations and their management. In this section of the chapter, a special case is made for training supervisors to comply with these requirements for the following reasons:

- Supervisors are the first line of prevention and defense of a legal problem for any organization

- Most all jurisdictions will hold employers and their supervisors liable for what they know, and sometimes for what they don't know

Take, for example, harassment, which we all know comes in many forms—sex, age, race, religion, national origin, disability, etc. If a supervisor knew of a situation involving sexual harassment that was contrary to law and company policy, and he or she failed to intervene properly, then a court could likely hold the harasser, supervisor, and the employer liable to some degree (*Meritor Savings Bank v. Vinson*, 1986; Carbonell, Higginbotham, and Sample, 1990; Ballew and Adams-Ragan, 1993). But what if the supervisor did not know of the harassment, you say?

Some jurisdictions will hold supervisors accountable for what they did not know! If a supervisor "should have known, but did not know" of harassment (or other areas of liability for that matter), he or she could be held liable in certain jurisdictions. The rationale for this tough position is that supervisors will not be allowed to look the other way in the performing the scope of their duties.

Training supervisors and managers in technical environments have a responsibility to train supervisors on applicable laws and regulations impacting the scope of work of the company and it's managers, supervisors, and employees. In some industries, a general overview of employment law would be sufficient, whereas a different technology base or business context might require training in several areas of the law. Since *ignorance of the law is no defense* for the employer, reasonable training efforts should be incorporated into the supervisor and management development curriculum.

The following are examples of varied legal requirements impacting many jurisdictions for which managers may have a "need to know":

- *Negligent hiring and retention, and failure to supervise to standard.* Not only must supervisors be aware of EEO and ADA requirements for selection, they must also know that selecting employees without adequate background checks could result in negligent hiring. For example, if a newly hired employee were to become violent in the workplace, resulting in injury or death of others, and if a reasonable background check would have revealed such violent patterns in previous employment, then *negligent hiring* could be alleged. If the employer were to continue the employment of someone with consistently violent behavior at work, then *negligent retention* could be alleged. Finally, if *failure to supervise an employee to standard* results in injury or death to the employee, or to others, then negligence could be alleged.

- *Smoking in the workplace.* Although there is presently no federal law regulating smoking in the workplace, some states have enacted such legislation. In Florida, the Department of Health and Rehabilitation enforces the state's Clean Air Act. Employers and their supervisors who allow smoking in smoke-free designated areas could put their company at risk of a fine.

- *AIDS in the workplace.* Many states have enacted comprehensive laws encompassing a wide range of AIDS and health-related topics. Florida's AIDS Act includes informed consent for HIV testing, confidentiality of test results, and a prohibition of discrimination against those infected with the AIDS virus. An employer may not require an individual to take an HIV-related test as a condition of hiring or continued employment unless the absence of the HIV virus is a bona fide occupational qualification for the job in question. The ADA recognizes AIDS as a qualified disability. OSHA has extensive regulations on the AIDS virus and other bloodborne viruses. The Handicap-Rehabilitation Act of 1973 prohibits federal agencies and employers doing business with the federal government from discriminating against the handicapped. Individuals with AIDS, AIDS-related complex, or HIV-positive status are protected as handicapped persons under this Act.

- *Pay for overtime for training, travel, or homework.* The question of overtime turns on the status of an employee. The U.S. Department of Labor enforces the Fair Labor Standards Act which requires that nonexempt employees must be compensated for work that exceeds 40 hours per week with overtime pay of 1½ regular pay. Exempt employees in the private sector (managers and professionals) are not subject to this requirement. Nonexempt employees required to attend training and/or to complete homework that exceeds their normal 40-hour work week must be compensated. Travel to off-site training that cuts across a nonexempt employee's work hour is compensable.

- *Manager's personal liability.* Managers are agents of their employers, and when acting within the scope of their job responsibilities, they are generally immune from personal liability. Acting outside the scope of their job responsibilities could result in personal liability, including a payment of a percentage of awarded damages. For example, a manager who intentionally discriminates against an applicant or employee who comes under the Age Discrimination in Employment Act (ADEA) could be personally held liable for damages.

6.9 Liability and the Independent Consultant

Independent consultants and consulting firms are going to be increasingly susceptible to threats from the legal arena. The "deep pocket" theory of damages will apply more to the larger firm that has acquired financial assets that can be liquidated than to the smaller firm or independent consultant. For example, multinational accounting firms that provide consulting and training services have a greater probability of litigation than do independent consultants. Not only are the stakes higher in terms of complex systems for which expensive consulting and training is contracted, but the pockets of these megafirms are much deeper, and therefore more attractive for plaintiffs attorneys. This is not to say that independent consultants are immune from litigation. They could still lose their business assets, and possibly personal assets, if successful litigation favors the plaintiff! Incorporation under Subchapter S or C corporation status lessens some of the legal exposure.

Several issues impacting independent consultants have already been mentioned in this chapter (e.g., copyright, intellectual property, adventure-based training). The following additional issues may impact the practice of an independent consultant:

- *Insurance requirements.* Employers of consultants may require various forms of insurance—workers compensation, malpractice insurance, or performance bonds. Failure to obtain, or lying about terms or limits of required insurance, may negate a contract. Most governmental agencies and larger private-sector employers will expect consultants to make records available for an audit, and the audit might occur long after the contract was completed. Cost will vary depending on the type of insurance required, type of consulting performed, and number of people insured.

- *Negotiating consultant contracts.* Independent consultants should seek the advice of a competent attorney prior to signing a contract for professional services. Taking for granted contractual language may be problematic once the contract has been agreed upon and signed. Contract clauses that require noncompetition with similar industries should be studied closely. Also, make sure of your legal standing if the contract is ever litigated. Finally, do not hesitate to negotiate with employers contractual requirements that put the consultant at a nonreciprocal disadvantage (i.e., the employer can terminate the contract, but the consultant cannot).

6.9.1 Malpractice of Independent Consultants

Case law relative to malpractice of independent consultants is in a state of evolution. While no specific cases have been located as of publication, it is expected that attorneys for plaintiffs will be pressing for case law in the future. It is probable that statutes and case law governing malpractice litigation of professionals, such as accountants, engineers, attorneys, doctors, and other professionals, will become the model for litigating consultants.

The term "professional" is important in this context. Accountants and engineers, for example, have rigorous educational, examination, and licensure requirements, and in many states, both are defined by statutes as "professionals." For these reasons, "professional" accountants and engineers are held to a higher standard of conduct than are mere mortal citizens.

The question for independent consultants (and possibly legislatures and the courts) to consider is to what extent are they "professionals"? Anyone can be an independent consultant! Although degree programs exist for consultants, professional licensure is usually not a requirement. Licensed psychologists, for example, may consult in a variety of organizational settings.

Although their degrees and license may be for individual and group counseling, their consulting work in organizations may be outside the parameters of their training and license. Should licensed psychologists (or for that matter, any "licensed professional") who acts as an independent organization consultant be held to a higher standard than consultants without degree or license?

The answer may be that trained and licensed professionals of any type who act as independent consultants will be held to a higher standard. Another alternative could be that professional status is not the legal issue. Maybe the issue is one of opinion from experts' knowledge, skill, or experience. Holding consultants accountable for their opinions based on expert knowledge or skills may be more logical. Being a professional may assume some level of expertness, but the same is not true in the reverse. Experts may exist independently of professional training and licensing requirements.

Employers who rely on opinions derived from the expert knowledge or skill of independent consultants may have a reasonable claim against those who fail to perform as agreed (breach of contract), or who perform carelessly (negligence), or who misrepresent their knowledge, skill, or experience as a consultant (fraud) (Lieberman & Siedel, 1988).

6.9.2 Suggestions for Preventing or Reducing Litigation

The following suggestions may be useful for independent consultants who are concerned about liability:

- Reduce mutual expectations to written agreements that are reviewed by an attorney for both parties. Be specific about expectations, critical processes, and results. Resist the temptation of time and stress pressures to forgo formal agreements.

- Consider providing clients with options instead of advice. Require the client to consider options; be careful about pressuring for a particular option. Advice from individuals holding themselves out as experts may take on a higher standard of care.

- For example, consultants who provide strategic planning or organization development interventions may advise a client to change the mission, market base, or the restructuring of personnel. The failure of a business based on such advice from an expert could lead to liability.

- Consider a peer review process modeled on those practiced by attorneys, accountants, long-term care facilities, and the medical profession (Donabedian, 1989).

6.10   Using Instructional Technology to Prevent or Reduce Liability

Technical training has an additional usefulness beyond improving performance in the workplace. Documented existence of training becomes a legitimate defense to an allegation of failure to train to standard. In other words, not only do we train with the expectation of increasing the probability of correct performance on the job, we also train personnel so that the organization and its personnel can defend against an allegation of failure to train to standard (Sample, 1989, 1990).

Several sources exist that discuss practical measures that training and development programs can take to prevent or reduce liability for failure to train to standard (Eyres, 1990; Blackburn and Sage, 1992; Sage, 1990; Sample, 1989). An excellent reference text for instructional designers, trainers, and program evaluators is Ward's (1988) reference text, *High Risk Training: Managing Training Programs For High Risk Occupations.*

One of the more straightforward strategies for preventing and reducing training liability is recommended by Gallagher (1990b). His "six-layered" liability protection system for police is composed of the following components: (1) the development of policies and procedures, (2) adequate training to the task, (3) competent supervision, (4) progressive discipline when necessary, (5) policy and training review and revision on a regular basis, and (6) legal support and services. Gallagher contends that each component must be well developed, and that all six components must be tightly integrated for this approach to work effectively. Organizations other than police agencies are encouraged to adopt a similar approach where necessary and appropriate.

The following recommendations are distilled from the sources indicated previously:

1. *Develop comprehensive operational policies and procedures for identifying high-liability tasks* (Gallagher, 1990; Ward, 1988).   Continually scan your organization's environment for legal and regulatory threats and opportunities. For example, does your organization have adequate written policies and procedures that are consistent with the training requirements for the Americans with Disability Act (ADA)? It is important to remember that courts will hold organizations accountable for oral policies, as well as written policies. Also, it is one thing not to have viable policies, but it is worse when your organization has a policy, yet fails to follow its own dictates!

2. *Conduct a legally defensible job-task analysis that identifies essential function and high-liability tasks.*   Prioritize tasks suitable for training,

beginning with high-risk tasks. Consult industry and craft standards for assistance in identifying high-risk tasks (Carlisle, 1986).

3. *Develop measurable standards of acceptable performance for each task, beginning with high-risk tasks.* Tasks are generally regarded as *what* is to be accomplished, and performance standards (job performance measures) deal with *how well* a task is to be accomplished.

4. *Consider selection over training whenever possible.* Training is one of the most cost- and time-intensive modes for changing behaviors and attitudes used in organizations today. Effective selection of personnel who already possess necessary knowledge, skills, and attitudes is more cost effective than training (Cascio, 1991).

5. *Utilize a standard instructional systems design model* (Dick and Carey, 1985; Gagne, et al., 1988). A rigorous and systematic approach to designing and developing instruction ensures that the correct tasks are selected for instruction, and that a tightly coupled linkage from one stage to the next exists for purposes of documentation. Develop job-related simulations and other tests of performance appropriate for the classroom and the work site (Priestly, 1982; Westgaard, 1993). Reasons of safety and ethics often preclude the assessment of performance under actual work conditions. This is especially true of high-liability tasks. Waiting until someone has a heart attack is a poor time for assessing the extent to which an employee can perform CPR!

7. *The technical training unit should certify individual competence on each high-liability task using preestablished job performance measures.* Additional training should be required when task mastery is not to standard. Require line supervisors responsible for employees who perform high-liability tasks to qualify their employees after training, and at regular intervals. To be qualified means that the employee has been observed in a work setting by a supervisor, and that the behavior on high-liability tasks is at mastery given a job performance measure. Certification by training and qualification by management must be documented (Sample, 1989).

8. Many courts will rule that the absence of documentation equates to a finding of no training, even if the employee was trained (Barrineau, 1987). *Document the instructional process (e.g., attendance, learning objectives, pre-post-test scores, observation of a task practiced to standard) and supervision (e.g., critical incidents, disciplinary action, on-the-job remediation, referral for additional training).* Such documentation will also help prevent additional areas of litigation, such as negligent retention and failure to supervise to standard.

9. *Communicate in writing to your supervisor, and if necessary to your agency or general counsel, any concerns that you have about high-liability tasks.*

Part of your responsibility is to educate your agency personnel. Failure to do so may put the technical trainer at risk legally if a suit is brought at a later date.

10. Purchase individual liability insurance through a professional association, such as the National Society For Performance and Instruction, or through a reputable insurance agency. This type of insurance varies in cost and provides reasonable security.

6.11 Conclusion

The intent of this chapter has been to educate the reader so that he or she is prepared to make informed decisions about the practice of their craft when potential areas of legal liability are involved. The probability of a company or a technical trainer becoming involved in a lengthy litigation suit is slight; however, if the occasion were to arise, defending one's professional competence and integrity will be costly, embarrassing, and time consuming—even if found not liable!

Technical trainers and their managers must learn to consider the potential for liability in their quest for improving individual and group performance. Although several general reference texts exist for the lay person, the best resource for advice on potential and real legal problems remains competent legal counsel. Most businesses and government agencies that have technical training responsibilities also have attorneys on staff or under contract. Do not hesitate to use their expertise whenever necessary.

Unfortunately, attorneys at your disposal may not be familiar with the legal concerns of the technical trainer. Being ever the educator, technical trainers may find themselves in a position to frame issues and problems of a legal nature for their attorneys. Costly legal fees and judgments will be reduced or prevented when members of both disciplines work together to understand legal threats to their companies assets, and to resolve them in a timely manner with due process.

There is a caveat to what has been stated in this chapter! Employers will expect their technical trainers to perform to the best of their capabilities. Meeting the vision and mission of a dynamic enterprise requires a certain amount of risk taking. *Employees must not be frightened into nonperformance of their jobs because of the potential for litigation. Remember that the courts do not expect perfection in people who inhabit our institutions and businesses.* Reasonable and prudent behavior may result in mistakes of an intentional or nonintentional nature. For this reason, our country has a criminal, civil, and administrative court system to right wrongs, and a risk management system to indemnify those who are covered with insurance.

Endnote

1. This chapter is designed to provide descriptive and illustrative material on general legal concepts as they may apply to technical training programs in public and private sector organizations. While the information in this article is accurate and timely, it does not constitute legal advice to the reader. *Consult competent legal counsel for specific advice on legal situations involving technical training.*

2. The author gratefully appreciates permission to use previously published material from ASTD's *INFO-LINE 9309 Legal Liability & HRD: Implications for Trainers.*

Bibliography

American Psychological Association, Division of Industrial-Organizational Psychology, "Principles for Validation and Use of Personnel Selection Procedures, Washington, D.C.

————, Copyright information kit, American Society For Training & Development, Alexandria, Va., 1993.

Ballew, A. C., and P. Adams-Ragans, "Sexual Differences in the Workplace: The Need for Training, in J. W. Pfeiffer (ed.), *The 1993 Annual: Developing Human Resources*, Pfeiffer & Company, San Diego, Ca., 1993, pp. 247–262.

Barrineau, H. E., *Civil Liability in Criminal Justice*, Anderson, Cincinnati, Oh., 1987.

Bartlett, C. J., "Equal Employment Opportunity Issues in Training," *Human Factors* **20**(2):179–188, 1978.

Blackburn, J. D., and J. E. Sage, "Safety Training and Employer Liability," *Training & Skills Development* **3**(5):29–33 (1992).

Blackburn, J. D., and J. E. Sage, "Where Is Training and the Law Heading During the 1990's?," *1991 Technical & Skill Conference*, American Society For Training and Development, Cincinnati, Oh., 1991.

Callahan, M., "Municipal Liability for Inadequate Training and Supervision," *FBI Law Enforcement Bulletin*, March 1989, pp. 24–30.

Carbonell, J. L., J. Higginbotham, and J. A. Sample, "Sexual Harassment of Women in the Workplace: Managerial Strategies for Understanding, Preventing, and Limiting Liability," in J. W. Pfeiffer (ed.), *The 1990 Annual: Developing Human Resources*, University Associates, San Diego, Calif., 1990, pp. 225–240.

Cardani, C. L., Municipality Liability after *City of Oklahoma City v. Tuttle*: A Single Incident of Police Misconduct May Establish Municipal Liability under 42 U. S. C. Sec. 1983 When Based on Inadequate Training or Supervision, *Suffolk University Law Review* **20**:551–578 (1986).

Carlisle, K. E., *Analyzing Jobs and Tasks*, Educational Technology, Englewood Cliffs, N.J., 1986.

Carnavale, A., "Outlook: Job Skills and Technical Training," *Training & Development* **47**(2):24–30 (1993).

Cascio, W. F., *Applied Psychology in Personnel Management*, Reston Publishers, Reston, Va., 1991.

——, "Diversity Training Entails Legal Pitfalls," *Legal Insights For Managers*, Bureau of Business Practice, Number 612, Waterford, Conn., December 1993, pp. 1–2.

Dick, W., and L. Carey, *The Systematic Design of Instruction*, Scott, Foresman, Glenview, Ill., 1985.

Donabedian, A., Peer Review of Consultant Services in Long Term Care Facilities, *The University of Toledo Law Review* **20**:393–410 (1989).

Eyres, P. S., "Keeping the Training Department out of Court," *Training*, September 1990, pp. 59–67.

Feuer, D., "Protecting the Public: How Much Training Is Enough?," *Training* **22**(11):22–28 (1985).

Gagne, R. M., L. J. Briggs, and W. W. Wager, *Principles of Instructional Design*, Holt, Rinehart & Winston, Chicago: 1988.

Gallagher, G. P., "Risk Management for Police Administrators," *The Police Chief*, 1990a, pp. 18–28.

Gallagher, G. P., "The Six-layered Liability Protection System for Police," *The Police Chief*, 1990b, pp. 40–43.

Goldsborough, R., "Computers and the Law," *PC Today* **8**(5):18–24 (1994).

Grace, P., "Danger—Diversity Training Ahead: Addressing the Myths of Diversity Training and Offering Alternatives," in J. W. Pfeiffer (ed.), *The 1994 Annual: Developing Human Resources*, Pfeiffer & Company, San Diego, Calif., 1994, pp. 189–200.

Henszey, B. N., B. L., Myers, R., Phalan, J. Bagby, and J. Sharp, *Introduction to Basic Legal Principles*, Kendall/Hunt, Dubuque, Iowa, 1991.

Ledvinka, J., and V. Scarpello, *Federal Regulation of Personnel and Human Resource Management*, 2d ed., Kent Publishing Co., Boston, 1991.

Lieberman, J. K. and G. J. Siedel, "Business Law and the Legal Environment," Harcourt Brace Jovanovich, San Diego, Calif., 1988.

McWhirter, D. A., *Your Rights at Work*, John Wiley & Sons, New York, 1989.

Mager, R. F., and P. Pipe, *Analyzing Performance Problems*, Lake Publishing Company, Belmont, Calif., 1984.

Mansfield, R. H., "Training and the Law," in R. L. Craig (eds.), *Training and Development Handbook*, 3d ed., McGraw-Hill, New York, 1991.

Meisinger, S. R., "The Americans with Disabilities Act: Begin Preparing Now," *Legal Report*, Society For Human Resources Management, Alexandria, Va., 1991.

Mitchell, C. E., "New Age Training Programs: In Violation of Religious Discrimination Laws," *Labor Law Journal*, July 1990, pp. 410–416.

Muchinsky, P. M., *Psychology Applied to Work*, 4th ed., Brooks/Cole, Pacific Grove, Calif., 1992.

——, "Most Spend Less than $100 for ADA, *Technical Skills & Training*, April 1994, p. 3.

Navran, F., "Hiring Trainers with Disabilities," *Training* **29**(7):24–26,31 (1992).

——, "Nontraditional Training," *Fair Employment Practices Guidelines*, Bureau of Business Practice, Number 355, Waterford, Conn., March 1994, pp. 3–6.

Priestly, M., *Performance Assessment in Education and Training: Alternative Techniques*, Educational Technology Publications, Englewood Cliffs, N.J., 1982.

Reid, R. L., "On Target: Tools to Train People with Disabilities, *Technical & Skills Training* **3**(5):18–20, 31 (1992).

Robinson, D. G., and J. C. Robinson, *Training for Impact*, Jossey-Bass, San Francisco, 1991.

Russell, J. S., "A Review of Fair Employment Cases in the Field of Training," *Personnel Psychology* **37**:261–275 (1984).

Sage, J. E., "Safe Attitudes Minimize Trainer Liability," *Technical & Skills Training* **1**(4):9–13 (1990).

Sample, J. A., "Civil Liability for Failure to Train to Standard," *Educational Technology* **29**(6):32–26 (1989).

Sample, J. A., "How Experimental Training Can Land You in Court!," *Training Today*, Chicagoland Chapter of the American Society for Training and Development, Chicago, 1994.

Sample, J. A., *INFO-LINE Legal Liability & HRD: Implications for Trainers*, American Society For Training and Development, Washington, D.C., 1993.

Sample, J. A., "May Governmental Agencies Be Liable for Failure to Train Their Employees to Standard?," *Performance & Instruction*, 1990, pp. 29–31.

Schofield, D. L., "Legal Issues in Pursuit Driving," *FBI Law Enforcement Bulletin*, October 1988, pp. 21–30.

Snyder, K. E., "Know Your Rights," *Careers and the Disabled* **7**(1):33–36 (1991).

Steinglass, S. H., *Section 1983 Litigation in State Courts*, Clark Boardman, New York, 1988.

Tarullo, G. M., "Making Outdoor Experiential Training Work," *Training* **29**(8):47–49, 50 (1992).

Vogel, J., "Manufacturing Solidarity: Adventure Training for Managers," *Hofstra Law Review* **19**:657–724 (1991).

Ward, G., *High-risk Training: Managing Training Programs for High Risk Occupations*, Nichols, New York, 1988.

Westgaard, O., *Good Fair Tests*, HRD Press, Amherst, Mass., 1993.

Whitt, S., "Note—City of Canton v. Harris: Municipality Liability Under 42 U.S.C. Section 1983 for Inadequate Police Training," *George Mason University Law Review* **12**:757–724 (1990).

Statute and Court Case Citations

Albemade Paper Co. v. Moody, 422 U.S. 405 (1975)—Selecting employees for training.

Americans with Disabilities Act, Public Law 101-336 (1990)—Selection, supervision and training of disabled employees.

City of Canton v. Harris, 109 S. Ct. 1197 (1989)—Failure to train to standard in the public sector.

Craig v. County of Los Angeles, 626 F.2d 659 (1980)—Selection of employees for training.

Dong Shik Kim, et al., v. The Dekalb Farmers Market, Inc., Civil Action No. 1-88CV2767HTW (D. Northern District of Georgia, filed December 7, 1988)—Wrongful termination and adventure-based training.

Ensley Branch of N.A.A.C.P. v. Seibels, 616 F2d. 812 (1980)—Selecting employees for training.

Equal Employment Opportunity Commission, Guidelines on Employee Selection Procedures, 29 CFR 1607 1993—Selecting employees for training.

General Dynamics v. OSHARC, 599 F 2d 453 (1977)—Workplace safety and training.

Granite Construction Co. v. Mendoza, 816 S. W. 2d 756 (1991)—Negligence and training.

Griggs v. Duke Power Company, 401 U.S. 436 (1971)—Selecting employees for training.

Hiatt v. Walker Chevrolet Co., 822 P. 2d 1235 (1987)—Nontraditional experiential training and wrongful termination.

Meritor Savings Bank v. Vinson, 477 U.S. 57 (1986)—Sexual harassment and training.

National Educational Association v. South Carolina, 434 U.S. 1026 (1978)—Selecting employees for training.

Occupational Safety and Health Act, 29 U.S.C.A. 654 (1970)—Workplace safety and training.

Stacy v. Truman Medical Center (Unpublished Supreme Court of Missouri, July 21, 1992; 1992 Mo. LEXIS 113)—Negligence and training.

State v. Shoreline Support Corporation (Unpublished Supreme Court of Wisconsin, April 11, 1989; 443 N. W.2d 310; 1989 Wisc. LEXIS 358)—Negligence and training.

Washington v. Davis, 426 U.S. 229 (1976)—Selecting employees for training.

Glossary of Legal Terms

Appellant: One who appeals the decision of a trial court to a higher court for review.

Case Law: Decisions from the courts that interpret statutes, regulations, and constitutional provisions.

Cause of Action: A legal claim that is the basis for a lawsuit.

Circuit Court: In the federal system, an appellate court between the district trial court and the U.S. Supreme Court. In some state judicial systems, a higher-level trial court.

Class Action: A lawsuit brought on behalf of many people who are all asserting a common legal claim against a defendant.

Common Law: The basic system of law developed by the courts in the absence of case decisions from the courts or a statute.

Complaint: Legal papers filed by a plaintiff for actual injuries done to him or her by the defendant.

Copyright: Legal protection provided to the authors of "original works of authorship" that are fixed in a tangible form of expression, including literary, dramatic, musical, artistic, and certain other intellectual works.

Defendant: The person, institution, or organization being sued by a plaintiff(s).

Deposition: The verbal questioning of a witness prior to trial to discover evidence.

Discovery: The pretrial process of uncovering the evidence (see **deposition** and **interrogatories**).

Due Process: A constitutional requirement that state and federal governments conduct themselves fairly under the law and that they avoid arbitrary behavior.

Indictment: Formal charge of the grand jury resulting in a criminal defendant standing trial.

Interrogatories: A series of pretrial questions drawn up for the purpose of determining from witnesses or parties to the case who may have information about the case.

Jurisdiction: The authority of a court to act, either over a particular person or with regard to a particular cause of action.

Negligence: Nonintenional or careless behavior that leads to an injury.

Plaintiff: One who files a lawsuit against a defendant in court.

Proximate Cause: The direct or immediate cause, without which an injury would not have occurred, and sufficient to support an action of negligence.

Stare Decisis: A principle of law that cases already decided must serve as precedents to govern later cases.

Statutory Law: Body of law created by acts of state and federal legislatures.

Tort: A civil wrong, such as negligence, that may be brought by a plaintiff against a defendant for damages or injunctive relief.

Vicarious Liability: The liability of one person for the actions of another.

7

The Adult Learner in the Technical Environment

Malcolm S. Knowles

David E. Hartl

Malcolm S. Knowles, Ph.D. *is Professor Emeritus of Adult and Community College Education at North Carolina State University. Previously, he was Professor of Education at Boston University, Executive Director of Adult Education Association of the U.S.A., and Director of Adult Education for the YMCAs of Boston, Detroit, and Chicago. Since his retirement in 1979, he has been actively engaged in consulting and conducting workshops with business and industry, government agencies, educational institutions, religious institutions, voluntary agencies, and ASTD chapters and conferences in North America, Europe, South America, Australia, Japan, Singapore, Thailand, and Korea. He is the author of 17 books, the most recent being* The Adult Learner: A Neglected Species, Andragogy in Action, *and* The Making of an Adult Educator, *and more than 230 articles.*

David E. Hartl *is President of General Learning Climates, Inc. (GLC Associates), a consulting education, training, and research firm located in Tustin, California. He consults and conducts workshops with Fortune 500 corporations, businesses, government agencies, schools and educational institutions, community organizations, and other client systems throughout the United States and in the Middle East and Far East. He is the author of more than 50 papers, articles, and monographs in the fields of adult education, executive*

*and management leadership, total quality, team building, organiza-
tional change, and stress management. He has taught in the graduate program of public administration at the University of Southern
California since 1976 where he served as chair of the organizational
behavior department. Formerly, he taught in the graduate programs
of adult education at Boston University and The Johns Hopkins University.*

7.1   Wherefore Pedagogy?

All formal educational institutions in modern society were initially established exclusively for the education of children and youth. At the time
they were established there was only one model of assumptions about
learners and learning—the pedagogical model (derived from the Greek
words *paid,* meaning "child," and *agogus,* meaning "leader"; so *pedagogy*
means literally "the art and science of teaching children").

This model assigned full responsibility to the teacher for making all
decisions about what should be learned, how it should be learned, when
it should be learned, and if it had been learned. Students were given the
role of being submissive recipients of the directions and transmitted content of the teacher. It assumed that they were dependent personalities, that
they had little experience that could serve as a resource for learning, that
they became ready to learn what they were told they had to learn (to get
promoted to the next level), that they were subject-centered in their orientation to learning, and that they were motivated by extrinsic pressures of
rewards. The backbone methodology of pedagogy is transmission techniques.

As educational psychologists started researching educational phenomena around the turn of the century, they were governed largely by these
assumptions, too. But they were not really looking at learning; they were
investigating reactions to teaching. And the more they found out about
how teachers could control learners' reactions, the more controlling teaching became. Pedagogy was king.

When adult education began to be organized systematically in the first
quarter of this century, pedagogy was the only model teachers of adults
had to go on, with the result that, until recently, adults were taught as if
they were children. This fact accounts for many of the troubles adult educators encountered, such as a high drop-out rate (where attendance was
voluntary), low motivation, and poor performance. When training began
emerging as a specialty within the general adult education movement
almost half a century later, this was the only model available to trainers,
as well.

7.2 Then Came Andragogy

The first inkling that the pedagogical model may not be appropriate for adults appeared in a book by Eduard C. Lindeman, *The Meaning of Adult Education,* in 1926.[1] Based on his experience as both an adult learner and a teacher of adults, Lindeman proposed that adults were not just grown-up children, that they learned best when they were actively involved in determining what, how, and when they learned. But it was not until the 1950s, when we began getting empirical research on adults as learners, that the notion that there are differences between youth and adults as learners began to be taken seriously.

A seminal study by Houle[2] spawned a crescendo of studies (Tough,[3,4] Peters,[5] Penland,[6] and others) of how adults learn naturally (e.g., when they are not being taught). These studies document the fact that adults do indeed engage in more intentional learning outside of formal instruction than in organized programs and that they are in fact highly self-directed learners. Meantime, knowledge about adult learners was coming from other disciplines. Clinical psychologists were providing information on the conditions and strategies that promoted behavioral change (which is what education should be about, too). Developmental psychologists were illuminating the development stages that adults experience throughout the life span, which are a main stimulus of readiness to learn. Sociologists were exposing the effects that many institutional policies and practices have in inhibiting or facilitating learning (especially the inhibiting effects of rules and regulations, requirements, registration procedures, time schedules, and the like). Social psychologists were revealing the influences of forces in the larger environment, such as social attitudes and customs, reward systems, and socioeconomic and ethnic stratification.

Early in the 1960s, European adult educators were feeling a need for a label for this growing body of knowledge about adult learners that would enable them to talk about it in parallel with the pedagogical model, and they coined the term (or actually rediscovered the term that had been coined by a German adult educator in 1833) *andragogy.** It is derived from the Greek word *aner,* meaning "adult" (literally, "man," not "boy"). It was initially used to mean "the art and science of helping adults learn," but, as will be shown later, the term has taken on a broader meaning. It is a term that is now widely used around the world as an alternative to pedagogy.

---

* Another spelling that might apply here is *andro* from the original Greek word for man. However, since the "andragogy" spelling has been coined by Knowles for use in this country and elsewhere for more than 20 years and has appeared that way in hundreds of publications as a way to describe adult-oriented learning, its use is retained here.

7.3 What Do We Know About Adults as Learners?

The research cited here leads to several important assumptions about adults as learners, on which the andragogical model is based:

7.3.1 Adults Have a Need to Know Why They Should Learn Something

Tough[4] found that adults would expend considerable time and energy exploring what the benefits would be of their learning something and what the costs would be of their not learning it before they would be willing to invest time and energy in learning it. We therefore now have a dictum in adult education that one of the first tasks of the adult educator is to develop a *need to know* in the learners—to make a case for the value *in their life performance* of their learning what we have to offer. This idea of the learner determining the value of the lesson is much the same as the customer determining the value of the service or product that a business has to offer. In this sense, the value or quality of any learning will be decided by the learner, not the teacher. The andragogical principle of having the learner experience a need to know is the training field's version of one of the central ideas in the total quality field—the principle of *customer-focus.* (Likewise, the adult education concept of lifelong learning is similar to the quality movement's other central idea of *continuous improvement.*) To fully implement a commitment to quality in learning and training, trainers need to deeply understand the simple yet profound truth that the learner is always in control of what is learned. If a training program or an on-the-job learning experience is to be fully effective, the learners need to see clearly how what is being taught will benefit them and fulfill a "felt need" in them. Even when trainers are certain of the relevance and benefit of what they are training, their task is to enable the learner to see it as well. Whether it takes only a moment or a lengthy period, the time invested in creating an awareness in the learners of *why they need to learn* what is offered is among the most important investments that can be made.

In the technical environment, the experience of a felt need for learning is often complicated. New technology typically presents an opportunity for heightened performance at the cost of at least temporary frustration. For example, how many of us went through the frustratingly steep learning curve of shifting from handwriting or a typewriter keyboard to a computer keyboard? Often, the only familiar thing about the learning process was the keyboard itself, and, for some people, even the keyboard was more than just strange—it was something that women, not men, used. (As you can see, some definitely nontechnical factors like self-perception, status needs, etc., occasionally enter the "felt need" equation.) There were new "commands" to learn that made the computer do things with what you just typed. Whole new technical capacities, that were called by strange names like "electronic spread sheets," "word processing," and "computer graphics," were magically locked up inside that two-tone gray box with funny little slots in the front and were presented to us, not on paper, but on a shrunken television-like screen. It was up to us to learn and *precisely* use the keys that released all this new power and potential. With much pain and suffering, we learned that computers don't do what you *want* them to do, they do what you *tell* them to do. Why did we tolerate the frustration of having to learn our way from competent typing or handwriting, through a period of incompetent computing, eventually leading to a continuous state of evolving mastery of increasingly higher forms of technical wizardry? We tolerated the pain and learned because, for whatever reasons, we felt the need to. We saw or believed that the benefits outweighed the cost. We were willing to work harder at learning so we could work less at working, and be more productive as well. If we didn't see it this way, or feel enough of a need to learn, we probably didn't learn to work a computer. In fact, there are thousands of highly educated executives in organizations all around the world, in spite of the ubiquitousness of computers, who have not and may never learn to use a computer. They just don't feel the need for it. Other executives, cognizant of both changing technology and the leadership effect of their learning behavior on others, do feel the need to learn and have demonstrated their commitment to lifelong continuous pursuit of computer competence.

Once learners are committed, out of their own choice, to learning what needs to be learned, the learning process can proceed with little interference from internal resistance in the learner. Imagine the reverse situation: a trainer simply proceeds without engaging the learner's need to know and the learner isn't convinced of the need. To totally subvert the learning process, all the learners have to do is just sit there passively while the trainer does all the work and gets no result. This situation exists because learning is totally controlled by the learner. Even if rewards are offered or punishments are provided for behaving or not behaving in certain ways, the learner can engage in the behavior while learning to hate doing it or avoid behaving in certain ways but maintain values and attitudes that are counter to the intention of the training. Maybe just getting or avoiding certain behavior is all that is important, as might be the case with discriminatory practices based on age, race, sex, etc. If so, instituting rewards and punishment systems might suffice. But if you want learners to show initiative based on genuine learning of new values and attitudes, the training process will have to engage them in a process of discovering why it is important for them to change their views and understand the benefits they will derive from learning new ways of appreciating others. Applied to a more technical situation, if learners come to appreciate the full contribution that a new technology can make to performance and productivity, then they can learn not only the right behavior to use with the technology (e.g., pressing the right keys at the right time) but also the possibilities that can be realized if they use their initiative and become creative with the full potential of a computer program's capacity.

7.3.2 Adults Have a Deep Need to Be Self-Directing

In fact, the psychological definition of "adult" is one who has achieved a self-concept of being in charge of his or her own life, of being responsible for making his or her own decisions and living with the consequences. At the point at which we arrive at this self-concept we develop a deep psychological need to be seen and treated by others as being capable of taking responsibility for ourselves. This fact creates a special problem for us in adult education and training in that although adults may be completely self-directing in most aspects of their lives (as full-time workers, spouses, parents, and young citizens), when they enter a program labeled "education" or "training," they hark back to their conditioning in school and college and put on their hats of dependency, fold their arms, sit back, and say, "teach me." The problem arises if we assume that this is really where they are coming from and start teaching them as if they were children. We then put them into an inner conflict between this intellectual map—learner equals dependent—and their deeper psychological need to be self-directing. And the way most people deal with psychological conflict is to seek to withdraw from the situation causing it. To resolve this problem, adult educators have been developing strategies for helping adults to make a quick transition from seeing themselves as being dependent learners to becoming self-directed learners. Knowles' little paperback book, *Self-Directed Learning: A Guide for Learners and Teachers*[7] describes some of these strategies.

There is an additional spin-off benefit for helping people learn how to learn in more self-directing ways—it helps to develop their ability to act with initiative, and personal responsibility for their learning naturally transfers to other aspects of their lives, including their working lives. This natural transfer is easily illustrated in the experience of many people who have felt frustration when their organization's training programs have helped them to learn to be more self-directing and then they go back to work situations in which they are only told what to do by their supervisors or managers and not permitted to use their initiative in applying what they learned in the training. A healthy adult's need to be self-directing is a powerful force in learning regardless of whether that learning is going on in the training room or on the job.

In the technical environment, there is a strong relationship between achieving technical mastery and being self-directed. To use an analogy from music, once a pianist has achieved a certain level of competence concerning the technical aspects of the instrument (keyboard awareness, proper fingering, accurate mechanics for producing tone dynamics, etc.), there comes a point at which the learner ceases to be at the service of learning technique; the technique begins to serve the learner. From this point on, the technology of the piano permits the learner's self-directed expression. An example of musical self-directedness in the extreme would be jazz great Oscar Peterson. His technical mastery is at a level where he thinks only about the music, not even the notes. His mind and heart produce musical ideas and his technique permits instantaneous execution. It is as though the piano had become hard-wired into his brain. This kind of relationship between a person and instrument or tool is the end goal of technical training—mastery which produces maximum self-directed expression.

An implication of this reflection on self-directedness is that the concept of discipline changes from the *external* discipline provided by the teacher (e.g., the Marine Corps drill instructor) to the *internal* discipline provided by the learner (e.g., the well-practiced jazz pianist). Technical training may start out with the need for external (pedagogical) discipline by a teacher who is expert in the technical area and end up with mastery resulting from the practice of internal discipline by the learner and permits ultimate (andragogical) technical self-directedness for the learner.

7.3.3 Adults Have a Greater Volume and Different Quality of Experience than Youth

Except in certain pathological circumstances, the longer we live the more experience and more varied experience we accumulate. The greater reservoir of experience affects learning in several ways:

- Adults bring into a learning situation a background of experience that is itself a rich resource for many kinds of learning for themselves and for others. Hence, in adult education, the greater emphasis on the use of experiential learning—techniques, such as problem analysis, discussion methods, and experimentation exercises, that tap into the accumulated knowledge and skills of the learners, or techniques, such as simulation exercises and field experiences, that provide learners with experiences from which they can learn by analyzing them. For more than two decades, organizations have been deriving great benefit from this adult aspect of their workforce by sponsoring quality circles or other quality-centered techniques and asking workers to review their work processes, measure and discuss the outcomes they are getting, and suggest better ways of doing things that will save resources while improving results.

- Adults have a broader base of experience to which to attach new ideas and skills and give them richer meaning. The more explicit these relationships (between the old and the new) are made—through discussion and reflection—the deeper and more permanent the learning will be (see Boud et al., 1985). This aspect of adult experience is especially valuable in providing "building-block" types of skill training such as accounting practices or computer use, where fundamental procedures are used as the foundation for more sophisticated and complex procedures later. Adult learners will feel more valued and learn faster if the experience they already have is used as a foundation from which to start rather than to repeat things they already know. New technology-based improvements in the ways work gets done often build upon practices already familiar to workers. For instance, once someone has learned one computer word-processing program, transferring their word-processing skills to new and more powerful programs takes much less time than learning the first one. Moreover, they can more easily extend their familiarity with word-processing to incorporate desktop publishing techniques to produce, for example, new marketing materials. Learners naturally build on and apply their previous experience to new technical situations.

- It is predictable that a group of adults, especially if there is an age mix, will have a wider range of differences in background, interests, abilities, and learning styles than is true of any group of youth. Adult groups are heterogeneous groups. Accordingly, increasing emphasis is being placed in adult education on individualized learning and instruction, through contract learning, self-paced multimedia modules, learning resource centers, and other means. For example, in a large service organization where role diffusion has accelerated over the past several years due to downsizing, a wide-ranging self-development program has been instituted in which workers can select videotape-and-manual modules of instruction from a "vending cabinet" near the cafeteria. It typically takes them about three weeks to complete a module using a combination of work downtime and their own time. Competency areas include verbal and written communication, running better meetings, reading P&L statements, analyzing market areas, and about 20 others. Those who complete these self-directed modules and pass a competency assessment receive a certificate, have their achievement noted in the personnel file, and benefit from their effort at their next performance review.

- There is a potentially negative consequence of this fact of greater experience—it tends to cause people to develop habits of thought and biases, to make presuppositions, to be less open to new ideas. (How often have you heard somebody react to a new proposal, "It won't work. We tried it five years ago and it didn't work"?) Some techniques for countering this tendency might include creativity exercises, mind-opening techniques, and others. This is an especially bothersome aspect of adult experience in that it often accounts for a great deal of resistance to learning and change that is important for organizational adaptation to changing technologies, products, services, marketplaces, and customers. Methods for dealing with this resistance are often based on the first principle mentioned previously, helping the learners experience a need to know based on their own appraisal of the situation. Beyond that, however, there are some other steps that have been effective in getting people to try new ideas or skills for the first time: assuring them that they won't be punished for not being immediately proficient when trying something new; providing them with the tools and time to master the new technique.

It is sometimes helpful to use this comment in training sessions: "You don't have to believe or take anything that I say or that we discuss in this session if you don't want it. All I ask is that you suspend your prejudgments and hold your mind open while we talk and imagine that we are just putting all our ideas onto a big pile in the middle of the room. At the end of the day you can take anything you want from the pile and leave the rest, and you can have back everything you came in here with at no extra charge." It is important to say this to let them know that no one is going to try to change their minds about anything. But here's the trick: by telling them their learning is totally up to them, and that the trainer absolutely respects the truth of that situation, it means they don't have to resist the learning and therefore it becomes possible for them to be positively influenced if they find the influence to their benefit. In short, you can't change anyone until you give up trying to change them! They then can change themselves. Their experience will prevent you from changing them *and* their experience will help change to happen in themselves. Interesting paradox, don't you think? It's one that is central to the adult learning process. It's much easier to describe it, though, than it is to live it as a trainer or manager, especially if you are under a deadline to get certain training delivered or changes accomplished. Applying it under those conditions requires a real commitment to respecting adults as learners and patience in letting natural learning processes unfold. Pushing too hard will make it take longer. What helps the learning and change to go faster is to keep the learners relaxed, cheerful, unthreatened, experimental, rewarded for trying, and rewarded for succeeding with no punishment for taking risks that don't work out. Things that don't work out are only to be used as sources for learning; never as causes for punishment.

The difference in the quality of experience adults bring with them is also significant. Few youth have had the experience of being full-time workers, spouses, parents, voting citizens, organizational leaders, and of performing other adult roles. Most adults have. Accordingly, adults have a different perspective on experience: it is their chief source of self-identity. To youth, experience is something that happens to them. But adults define themselves in terms of their unique experiences. An adult's experience *is* who he or she is. So if adult experience is not respected and valued, is not made use of as a resource for learning, they experience this omission, not as a rejection of their experience, but as a rejection of themselves as persons. This phenomenon may be especially true of undereducated adults whose inability to compete successfully in a market demanding advanced education makes them particularly vulnerable to low self-esteem and defensive about the life experience they do have.

7.3.4 Adults Become Ready to Learn When They Experience in Their Life Situation a Need to Know or Be Able to Do in Order to Perform More Effectively and Satisfyingly

The pedagogical model makes the opposite assumption—that people become ready to learn what they are told by some authority figure (teacher, trainer, boss), that they have to learn because it's good for them or the authority figure demands it. Adults sometimes experience "being told" as infringing on their adultness—their need to be self-directing—and may choose to react with resentment, defensiveness, and resistance. *Adults tend to learn best when they choose voluntarily to make an internal commitment to learn.*

This principle is sometimes difficult to apply in business and industry, since, rightly or wrongly, employer-provided training tends to be perceived as employer-required training. Indeed, attendance is often compulsory. Whenever a trainer senses resistance among learners for this reason, it may help to do two things to try to reduce the resistance. First, make it public that there may be some people in the room who aren't there because they want to be. Acknowledge that this tends to get in the way of learning. Explain that there is nothing anyone can do to change the situation at this time and encourage them to see if they can have a pleasant and profitable time together anyway. More importantly, try to involve them in discovering for themselves—through participating in simulation exercises, self-diagnosing their learning needs through competency-based rating scales, or observing role models of superior performance—the value for their own lives of learning what the program has to offer. It is also important to explain the relationship between the goals of the training activity and the goals of the sponsoring organization so the participants can understand why they are expected to attend the session and apply what is being offered to their work situation. It can be a mistake to assume that employees have had the reasons for their required attendance explained to them prior to coming to the session. Therefore, it will probably help for the trainer to learn exactly what the larger purposes of the training are, from the company's point of view, and include that information in the session itself.

One of the richest sources of readiness to learn is the transitions people make in moving from one development stage to another. As Havighurst[8] points out, as we confront having to perform the development tasks of the next stage of development, we become ready to learn those tasks; the peak of our desire to learn them he calls the *teachable moment*. A typical sequence of developmental tasks in work life would be (1) to begin a process of career planning, (2) to acquire the competencies required for a first job, (3) to get a first job, (4) to become oriented to the first job, (5) to master the competencies required to perform excellently in the first job, (6) to plan and prepare for a next-step-up job, and so on through a cycle of career development. The final developmental task would be to prepare for retirement from a career. A main implication of this concept is the importance of timing our educational offerings to coincide with the worker's developmental tasks. Some examples would be to provide training in the use of a new technology (e.g., new computer software or advanced telephone system) immediately prior to or concurrent with its installation; provide supervisory training just before or immediately after promoting someone to the supervisor position; provide training concurrently with new job assignments that typically accompany organizational restructuring. In one client corporation, the training staff developed a preretirement planning program that dealt with finances, real estate options, travel, leisure time use, stress reduction, and transition management. It proved to be a hit with a large number of people because there was such a strong readiness for the program. In addition to its value to participants on a personal level, the business-case for the program was fulfilled by enabling senior members of the organization to exercise their options for early retirement packages that had heretofore gone unclaimed.

7.3.5   Adults Enter into a Learning Experience with a Task-Centered (or Problem-Centered or Life-Centered) Orientation to Learning

Children and youth have been conditioned by their school experience to have a subject-centered orientation to learning; they see learning as a process of acquiring the subject matter necessary to pass tests. Once that is done, their mission is accomplished. This difference in orientation calls for different ways of organizing the content to be learned. In traditional education, the content is organized into subject-matter courses, such as Composition I, in which the rules of grammar are memorized; Composition II, in which sentence and paragraph structures are memorized; and Composition III, in which rules of outlining, syntax, and the like are memorized. In adult education, the content is organized around life tasks: Composition I becomes "Writing Better Business Letters," Composition II becomes "Writing for Pleasure and Profit," and Composition III becomes "Improving Your Professional Communications."

This principle is commonly violated in orientation programs, in which the sequence of topics might be (1) The History and Philosophy of XYZ Co., (2) The Market and Products of XYZ Co., (3) The Personnel Policies of XYZ Co., and so on, instead of starting with a census of problems and concerns, along with problems and concerns of the organization and trainer. New hires, for example, are likely to have an immediate need to know how the company operates, who their supervisor and coworkers are, what their exact job duties will be, how their performance will be appraised, what they should read to get the background they need to do their job, how to use the telephone system and other work tools, where the rest rooms are located near their work area, and what the best way is for getting a good lunch. Next they will need to know about the personnel policies, but only those that affect their coming on staff, such as payroll forms and procedures, benefit packages, etc. If they should ever have a grievance, or if the time should come to move on to another organization, or when they approach retirement, that is when they will need to know other parts of the personnel policy document. Depending on the specific job, it will become relevant for the new hire to fill in the background on the XYZ Company's history, philosophy, market, and products at a later time after the more immediate needs are met. Depending on the situation, there may be other ways to structure an orientation program for new hires and other training programs.

The implications of this principle for technical and skills training are powerful. The utilization of a new technology or the acquisition of a new skill are nearly always motivated in adult learners by the desire to deal with a new problem or deal with an old problem in a better way. Therefore, when providing technical training for adults, it is crucial to help them make a tight connection between what they are learning and the improvements in problem solving that will result from applying their new skills in an appropriate way.

Whatever the situation, trainers will do well to consider the readiness needs of the learners and review their entire programs accordingly so they can restructure their training units around tasks, problems, or life situations. The participants will see the program as much more relevant to their lives and they will learn the content with the intention of *using* it.

7.3.6 Adults Are Motivated to Learn by Both Extrinsic and Intrinsic Motivators

One of the most significant findings of the research into adult learning is that adults are motivated to learn. Allen Tough,[4] the researcher who has to date accumulated the largest volume of information about how adults learn in normal life, has yet to find a subject in his research who had not engaged in at least one major learning project (a minimum of seven hours of intentional learning) in the preceding year, and the average number of learning projects was over seven. The problem (and our challenge) is that they may not be motivated to learn what we want to teach them; hence, the importance of following through on the first assumption mentioned—developing a need to know.

The pedagogical model makes the assumption that children and youth are motivated primarily, if not exclusively, by *extrinsic* motivators—pressures from parents and teachers, competition for grades, diplomas, and so on. Adult learners also respond to extrinsic motivators—wages, raises, promotions, better working conditions, and the like—but only up to the point that they are reasonably well satisfied. But the more potent and persistent motivators are such *intrinsic* motivators as the need for self-esteem, broadened responsibilities, power, achievement, etc. (Wlodkowski[9]). Different people, of course, are motivated to learn different things, in different ways, for different reasons. Trainers in the United States encounter people in training sessions with a wide variety of backgrounds, experiences, personal styles, and even languages. Cultural differences and family experiences often strongly influence what motivates people. Training sessions offered internationally must take into account the factors in the host environment that exert powerful influences on the participants (more powerful than the trainer's) and can determine the success or failure of the learning experience. Trainers applying andragogical principles will invest the time it takes to discover the different attributes of their audiences and shape their learning experiences to fit the differences found among the participants.

In the technical environment, there is a tendency for intrinsic motivation to provide a more natural impetus for learning because of the close relationship between the acquisition of a new skill and the immediate ability to perform in a new way that is immediately satisfying. A friend and colleague who writes computer programs is constantly learning new technical methods for solving problems. He frequently reports his deep sense of satisfaction that finally comes from having a program work exactly the way he wants it to. Another example is when a new diagnostic machine was introduced into a nearby client hospital. The staff couldn't wait to learn how to use it to its maximum potential because it would give them a whole new way to get crucial, perhaps life-saving information in a cheaper and less invasive manner than ever before. The intrinsic motivation that naturally comes from the satisfaction of learning a new technical skill is a powerful influence on adult learners.

7.4   The Technical and Skills Training Environment

The essential focus in the technical and skills training environment is on *learning*, not *teaching*. In the final analysis, it doesn't matter how the trainer performs. It only matters how the learner performs. Technical performance requires that some hard questions be asked. For example, can the learner practice the new skills with mastery? Does the new technique, as applied by the learner, produce the desired result? This technical and skills training focus is different from a traditional nontechnical training focus in which the performance of the trainer is often more carefully measured than is the performance of the learner.

There are three attributes of the technical environment that are important for technical and skills-oriented trainers to appreciate:

1. Technical training frequently requires learners to deal with precision in (*a*) learning exact skills, (*b*) following certain procedures, (*c*) performing accurately. In the face of having to be precise in their new performance, learners sometimes feel confused, incompetent, and inadequate.

2. Technical training usually requires trainers to be (*a*) proficient at the relevant technical skills themselves, (*b*) able to transfer their expertise to the learners, (*c*) able to deal with the feelings of learners in a constructive and confidence-building manner.

3. Technical training covers a wide range of learning needs from beginning to quite advanced, including (*a*) basic reading, speaking, and computational skills, sometimes involving languages and mathematics techniques not previously learned; (*b*) work- and life-management skills; (*c*) concentration and critical thinking skills; (*d*) job performance skills, especially involving the effective use of machines and equipment; (*e*) technical and organizational advancement skills; (*f*) skills for continuous improvement as a technical professional.

There are also some nontechnical aspects in the technical environment that must be mastered to support technical training in modern organizations. These include (*a*) a positive mental attitude, (*b*) clear presentation and demonstration skills, (*c*) effective interpersonal communication skills, (*d*) team development skills, and (*e*) appropriate problem analysis and solution implementation skills. Regardless of the nature of the technical environment, these are basic human skills that contribute to effective individual and organizational performance.

7.5 Implications for Andragogical Practice

The assumptions of pedagogy and andragogy have a number of implications for what we do as human resource developers and technical skills trainers. One basic implication is the importance of making a clear distinction between a *content plan* and *process design.*

When planning an educational activity, the pedagog thinks in terms of drafting a content plan, and he has to answer only four questions to come up with a plan: (1) What content needs to be covered (the assumption being that they will only learn what is transmitted, and therefore it must *all* be covered in the classroom)? So the pedagog draws up a long list of content items. (2) How can this content be organized into manageable units (1-hour, 3-hour, etc., units)? So the pedagog clusters the content items into manageable units. (3) How can these content units be transmitted in a logical sequence (rather than the sequence in which the learners are ready to learn it)? So the pedagog arranges the units in a sequence according to chronology (history, literature, political science) or from simple to complex (science, math). (4) What would be the most effective methods for transmitting this content? If unit 1 is heavily loaded with information, the method of choice will probably be lecture and assigned reading; if unit 2 involves skill performance, the method of choice will probably be demonstration by the pedagog and repeated practice by the learners. By answering these four questions, the pedagog ends up with a content-transmission plan. None of these steps is bad, just insufficient. They don't consider dynamics brought to the learning setting by the learners, which were described earlier.

The andragog, on the other hand, when undertaking to plan an educational activity, sees the task as being twofold: first, and primarily, to design and manage a process for facilitating the acquisition of content and skills by the learners; and only secondarily to serve as a resource for content and skills (the andragog prefers that there are many resources in addition to his or her own—peers, supervisors, specialists, and a variety of materials and guides in the learner's environment, and that an important part of the teaching responsibility is to keep up to date as to what these content and skills resources are and to link learners with them). Notice that it is not a matter of the pedagog's being concerned with content and the andragog's not being concerned with it; rather, the pedagog is concerned with *transmitting* the content and the andragog is concerned with *facilitating* the acquisition of the content by the learners. In this sense, andragogy is more concerned with the participants actually acquiring the knowledge and skills they must have to be effective than it is with simply transmitting what is required on a typical lesson plan.

In what is perhaps a dangerous example of an overly strict reliance on pedagogy, the training staff of an atomic energy generating installation asked for help in applying principles of andragogy to their training programs. All of the participants, every one a highly skilled trainer, immediately saw the value of emphasizing acquisition of learning over transmission of content. They felt, given their environment, that it didn't matter whether or not you could bureaucratically prove that the trainer transmitted an important point; it only mattered that the learner received and understood it and could apply it in actual practice. Nonetheless, they said andragogy couldn't be used there; not because it wasn't relevant, but because the training policies of the regulating agencies assumed that transmission equaled learning and, therefore, all of their mandatory (and bureaucratic) training directives and regulations left absolutely no time for learner involvement and the acquisition of learning, only the transmission of required content. In their efforts to assure safety through highly regulated and tightly timed training programs (strictly prescribed numbers of hours in the training classroom were required for each of several topics), the bureaucrats sabotaged the effectiveness of their own training staff.

The professional trainer, using andragogy to assure involvement and the actual acquisition of knowledge and skills by the learners, has to answer a very different set of questions to come up with a process design. The questions raised by the andragog have to do with implementing the following elements of an andragogical process design:

7.5.1 Establishing and Maintaining a Climate Conducive to Learning and Change

A prerequisite for effective learning to take place is the establishment of a climate that is conducive to learning. Two broad aspects of climate must be considered: *organizational climate* and the climate of the *training situation.*

Among the questions that might be raised regarding organizational climate are:

- Do the policy statements of the organization convey a deep commitment to the value of human resources development in the accomplishment of the mission of the organization?

- Does the leadership of the organization lead the continuous learning process by their own example?

- Does the budget of the organization provide adequate resources for the support of significant human resources development (HRD) efforts?

- Is the HRD staff involved in the decision-making process as regards personnel policies and programs?

- Are adequate physical facilities for HRD activities provided?

- Does the reward system of the organization give credit for the achievement of personal growth on the part of individuals and their supervisors?

To set a climate in a training situation, the following are conditions that characterize a climate that is conducive to learning, and the questions that might be asked in creating a process design to achieve those conditions:

A Climate of Mutual Respect.   People are more open to learning if they feel respected as worthwhile human beings. In technical training situations, where people may not know anything about the technical information or skill they are about to learn, they can still be held in high regard by the trainers as respected individuals. The trainer's attitude is key to communicating this respect. It must be sincere and supported by concrete actions. Some examples of actions that can communicate mutual respect include these: greet every individual personally, if the group is under 50, or together when larger than that; provide name tags or name tents and wear one yourself; call people by name right from the outset of the program; provide time (even if it's only a few minutes) for people to get acquainted with each other as individuals (even if it's only with some of the other participants) before launching into the rest of the program; put the training session into context so everyone understands what is going on and why; give them an opportunity to ask their own questions about the training and to indicate what they hope to get for themselves out of the training program; provide an opportunity for participants to practice what they are learning—without putting them on the spot in front of a large audience—by having them work in pairs or small groups; etc. Physical facilities also signal the nature of the training climate. Chairs and tables set in "school-room style" sends one kind of signal (*teacher* is important here). Chairs at round tables or set so people can see each other as easily as the front of the room sends another signal (*everyone* is important here). Ample lighting, good acoustics, adequate ventilation, access to refreshments, and frequent breaks also set an adult-like climate that makes it easy for people to learn.

A Climate of Cooperation Rather than Competition. Helping participants to get acquainted and actively involved in the session causes them to start seeing themselves as mutual helpers rather than rivals. Different previous experiences may qualify some more than others to achieve early mastery in certain technical areas. By cooperating rather than competing, differences in experience become valued resources for sharing and increased learning by everyone rather than unfair advantages possessed by a few in the competitive environment. In another ironic paradox, it is through cooperation in the learning environment that business organizations can become more competitive in the world of performance. Having organizational members help each other to perform well in technical areas can be critical to an organization's competitive advantage in the marketplace. They will learn to cooperate for greater competitive performance most effectively in the more andragogical learning setting.

Some techniques for inducing a cooperative atmosphere in a technical training situation include these:

- Divide people into subgroups during the training to work together
- Acknowledge effort as well as achievement
- Emphasize rewards for effective behavior rather than punishment for ineffective behavior
- Never, never, never punish or ridicule a learner for taking a risk that didn't work (if you do, neither that person nor anyone watching will ever again try anything new in your presence)
- Avoid using "win-lose" contests and exercises, etc.

An example that illustrates this aspect of a cooperative training climate applied to a technical training situation occurred in a mortgage banking situation where sales representatives are normally highly competitive. After explaining the new technical procedures and regulations that were to be used in processing clients' refinancing applications, the sales reps were divided into "helping pairs." First, one acted in the role of the processor and the other in the role of the client. Later the roles were reversed with a different set of mock application materials. The challenge for the sales rep was to apply all the steps correctly in spite of several things that were set up in the mock exercise forms to go wrong. The role of the client was to "act as you have found customers to sometimes act" when applying for a "refi." Of course, they really got into the "act." The results were numerous. They not only learned exactly how to apply the new procedures and regulations, they also learned how to overcome difficulties when things go wrong (alas, Murphy's Law applies everywhere), and they learned how the customer feels when going through the complicated administrative process. An after-effect of helping participants learn from each other as well as from the training staff was their continuing cooperation on behalf of clients. This turned out to enhance their overall business. It is often the case that the richest experiences, knowledge, and skills reside within the participants, so it is important to make access to each other's resources easy and productive.

A Supportive Rather than Judgmental Climate. Remember the old cliché, "Correct the behavior, don't judge the child." The child in all of us still hates to be judged. When judged, we learn to avoid being judged and withdraw. This stops the learning process. When people are learning a new skill or technique, they are bound to perform imperfectly. Imperfect behavior is sometimes met with comments like, "You just don't get it, do you?" or "I don't understand how you could have screwed it up so badly." (Believe it or not, these are real quotes overheard in real organizational settings.) When such comments are made in the training setting, the learning process stops and self-protection processes are invoked. The reason is because the comments tend to be directed at the person and not just at the behavior. Here are a couple of alternative examples: "Rather than doing it that way, try this and see what happens." or "When you leave out the second step, the result doesn't come out right. Try it again with all the steps done correctly." Focus on the technique or the behavior, or the specific skill that is being learned and avoid commenting in a way that could be interpreted as a judgment of the person. In performance appraisal sessions, a trainer or supervisor can use these phrases: "Here is the standard that has been established for your performance and that you agreed to. The behavior I see you doing (or the product I see you producing) is not up to the standard. What can you do to close the gap between the standard and your performance? I have confidence you can do it and I would like to know what I can do to help you be successful." This approach is very tough-minded about performance and, at the same time, regards the person with personal respect. Some other useful phrases are "I didn't like that" (*description of a personal preference*) rather than "That was awful" (*a categorical judgment*). "That was done just right" (*focused on the action*) instead of "You are brilliant" (*focused on the person*). Ironically, even positive judgments leave the unspoken implication of the possibility of negative ones later. Avoiding judgmental language altogether seems to work best. It's also important for trainers to "give permission" for people to try out new skills and behavior if learning is to be rapid and effective. An important part of "permission" is the idea that people will not be personally judged if they make mistakes.

A Climate of Mutual Trust.   Many people have learned from previous experience to react to authority figures, even teachers and trainers, with mistrust. For adults to learn at the highest and most effective rate, their feeling of mistrust must be replaced with feelings of personal confidence and credibility. Among the most powerful methods for developing mutual trust that can be employed by skilled andragogical trainers is the art of active listening—really giving your full attention to what others are saying and meaning. Getting on a first-name basis with people, as rapidly as possible, goes a long way to establishing a trust-based relationship. In training settings where participants are from varied cultural backgrounds, it may take a special effort to establish trust. The American culture has its democratic institutions and tradition of authority being derived from the people. Other cultures have strong traditions of authoritarian leadership and centralized control as the norm. If the organization in which you are working as a trainer is more authority-centered, you will need to work hard to establish a climate of mutual trust in the training setting. For example, health care facilities (e.g., hospitals, medical clinics, nursing homes, etc.) traditionally have a clearly defined authority structure which can inhibit high levels of mutual confidence. People learn on the job to be quiet, don't ask questions, and defer to authority even when they think something isn't quite right and needs correcting. Getting them to change their response to authority in the training session to a more mutually trusting one can be very challenging, yet it is exactly this which must be achieved if their personal learning and individual initiative is to be stimulated to the maximum degree.

A Climate of Fun.   Learning is one of the most satisfying and enjoyable things we do. When it is not this way, something needs to change in the learning situation. Having fun and learning go together naturally. There is a story of a university physicist named Richard Feynman who, in his first appointment as a faculty member, found he was being very serious about making a success of himself as an academic researcher and teacher. By holding such a serious attitude, he found he wasn't learning very much and wasn't having any fun. He adopted a new attitude and vowed to stop taking himself so seriously and, instead, be intentional about having more fun playing with ideas and paying more attention to the things he saw around him in his natural environment. One day in the cafeteria he saw a guy fooling around throwing a plate in the air. Feynman watched how the plate wobbled and how the university medallion on the plate rotated twice as fast as the plate's wobble rate. His mind started to play with the observation and he speculated on various explanations for the phenomenon. The mathematical formuli that he used to work out the equations of wobbles in the plate he was playing with stimulated him to reexamine and further explore some of his earlier work in electrodynamics. He was eventually awarded the Nobel Prize in physics for his creative work. As a person, it must also be noted, Feynman laughed a lot in the classes he taught and in the life he led. Having fun is critical to both maximum learning and effective teaching, it seems.

The creation and maintenance of a climate conducive to learning and change may be the most important single thing you can do to facilitate the participants' learning. It encourages them to relax, have an open mind, and stimulates trust which permits the adult learner to take risks and try new things, grow, and change. Reducing the learner's internal resistance to learning and increasing the learner's level of risk-taking are among the most important contributions to an accelerated learning process.

The first question an andragog asks in constructing a process design, therefore, is *"What procedures would I use with this particular group to bring into being the climatic conditions of mutual respect, cooperation rather than competition, supportiveness rather than judgmentalness, mutual trust, and having fun while learning?"*

7.5.2 Creating and Maintaining
Mechanisms for Mutual Planning

A basic law of human nature is at work here: people tend to feel committed to a decision or activity to the extent that they have participated in making the decision or planning the activity. The reverse is even more true: people tend to feel uncommitted to the extent they feel that the decision or activity is being imposed on them without their having a chance to influence it.

In planning a total program—all the courses, workshops, seminars—of an organization, the usual mechanism is a planning committee, council, or task force. To be effective, it is critical that it be representative of all the constituencies the program is designed to serve. (See Houle[10] for helpful guidelines.)

For a particular program, such as a course or workshop, a variety of mechanisms can be used depending upon the size of the group. If the group is small enough (under 20 people, say), it may be possible to engage all of them in the planning process. For larger groups, or groups that are to be meeting at different times, a mutual planning process might require the use of several subgroups, each of which takes responsibility for a segment of the program. For planning that takes place in advance of the program itself, it is often wise to involve all of the stakeholders in the process. Stakeholders would include some representative participants, the training faculty, suppliers, operators of the training facilities, organization leaders who have expectations regarding the program's results, and others who have an interest in the program's objectives. It is also a widespread practice to conduct a pilot session of a training program to test its assumptions, curriculum, design and pacing, resource materials, equipment, facilities, and desired learning outcomes. In technical and skills training, there sometimes is one "right way" to use a piece of equipment, complete a procedure, or solve a technical problem. The planning process needs to provide assurance that the "pilot" learners have learned and can apply the right solution at the right time in the right way before the program audience is expanded to everyone else.

The fullest individual participation in planning is achieved through the use of learning contracts, in which case the learners develop their own learning plans (see Knowles[7,11,12]). More and more organizations are using project groups of one kind or another to transfer their learning from the training setting into the work setting. These groups are expected to come up with their own organizational improvement project and actually implement it as part of the training process. In one large sales and service organization, a Fortune 500 company, the learning contract approach was adapted to provide a procedure for individual participants to plan and implement their own "Real Change Project." Using printed "Guidelines for Real Change Projects," which were sent out to participants one month before the training, participants were encouraged to enlist the support of their supervisor prior to attending the training session for the Real Change Project they wanted to work on when they returned from training. At the training session they were provided with detailed explanations of self-directed learning and real change projects and were helped to understand and develop strategies for managing organizational change. They were supported through contacts with their "change partner," who was another participant with whom they had developed a relationship in the workshop session. Long-term follow-up evaluation of the program showed that, in the overwhelming number of cases, the individual Real Change Projects were completed successfully and, in most cases, led to the implementation of other improvement projects that the participants came up with on their own.

The second question that the andragog asks in developing a process model, therefore, is *What procedures will I use to involve the learners continuously in planning?*"

The first two processes just described concerning establishing and maintaining a climate conducive to learning and change and of creating and maintaining mechanisms for mutual planning are *continuous*—they never cease throughout the training cycle. The next four processes steps are followed in *sequential order.*

7.5.3 Diagnosing the Participant's Learning Needs

The HRD literature is rich in techniques trainers can use for assessing training needs as perceived by individuals, organizations, and communities (Boone;[13] Brown and Wedel;[14] Davis and McCallon;[15] Knowles;[16] McKenzie and McKinley;[17] Mager and Pipe[18]). These needs are the appropriate source of goals for a total program (Knowles,[16] pp. 120–126). But in a particular training event involving particular individuals, a learning need is not a need unless so perceived by the learner. One of the highest arts in training is creating the conditions and providing the tools that will enable learners to become aware of their training needs and therefore translate them into learning needs. A new body of technology is being developed for facilitating this process, with emphasis on such self-diagnostic procedures as simulations exercises, assessment centers, competency-based rating scales, and videotape feedback (Knowles,[16] Wlodkowski[9]).

In the technical environment, diagnosing learning needs tends to be straightforward—help the individual establish whether or not he or she can perform the requisite skill or technique. What is the nature of the gap between the performance standard and the level of performance the individual can perform? Appropriate technical training can be provided until the required level of mastery has been achieved. However, if the individual *can* perform the skill, but doesn't or won't, it would be a mistake to think that providing training will improve performance. The problem has to do with incentive or context rather than with learning. Something else must be done to get the performance to occur. Exactly what else may require further diagnosis, but not learning diagnosis.

So the third question the andragog asks in constructing a process design is *"What procedures will I use in helping the participants diagnose their own learning needs?"*

7.5.4 Translating Learning Needs into Training Objectives

Having diagnosed their learning needs, participants now face the task of translating them into training objectives—positive statements of directions for growth. Some kinds of learning (such as machine operation) lend themselves to objectives stated as terminal behaviors that can be observed and measured (Mager[19]). Others (such as decision-making ability) are so complex that they are better stated in terms of direction of improvement (Knowles,[11] pp. 128–130).

So the fourth question the andragog asks is *"What procedures can I use for helping participants translate their learning needs into learning objectives?"* (For suggested procedures, see Knowles,[7] pp. 25–28.)

7.5.5 Designing and Managing a Pattern of Learning Experiences

Having formulated the learning objectives, the next task of the trainer and the participants is to design a plan for achieving them. This plan will include identifying the resources most relevant to each objective and the most effective strategies for utilizing these resources. Such a plan is likely to include a mix of total group experiences (including input by the trainer), subgroup (learning-teaching team) experiences, and individual learning projects. A key criterion for assessing the excellence of such a design is, how deeply involved are the participants in the mutual process of designing and managing a pattern of learning experiences?

Technical and skills training situations offer particular challenges for effective training design. There are four key considerations that will help assure technical training effectiveness:

1. Appropriate preparation of the training facilities and required equipment

2. Appropriate timing of the training (when it occurs relative to the required performance)

3. Appropriate sequencing of the training (the order in which steps for mastering the skills are learned)

4. Appropriate feedback indicating performance problems and progress

So the fifth question the andragog asks is *"What procedures can I use for involving the learners with me in designing and managing a pattern of learning experiences?"* (For suggested procedures, see Knowles,[16] pp. 235–247.)

7.5.6 Evaluating the Extent to Which the Objectives Have Been Achieved

In many situations, institutional policies require some sort of "objective" (quantitative) measure of learning outcomes (Kirkpatrick,[20] Scriven,[21] Stufflebeam[22]). But the recent trend in evaluation research has been to place increasing emphasis on "subjective" (qualitative) evaluation—finding out what is really happening inside the participants and *how differently they are performing in life* (Cronback,[23] Guba and Lincoln,[24] Patton[25,26,27,28]). In any case, the andragogical model requires that the learners be actively involved in the process of evaluating their learning outcomes (Knowles[12]).

The sixth question, therefore, that the andragog asks is *"What procedures can I use to involve the learners responsibly in evaluating the accomplishment of their learning objectives?"*

By answering these six questions, the learning facilitator emerges with a process design—a set of procedures for facilitating the acquisition of content by the learners. A graphic summary of these six questions and an illustration of the andragogical program development process are shown in Figure 7-1.

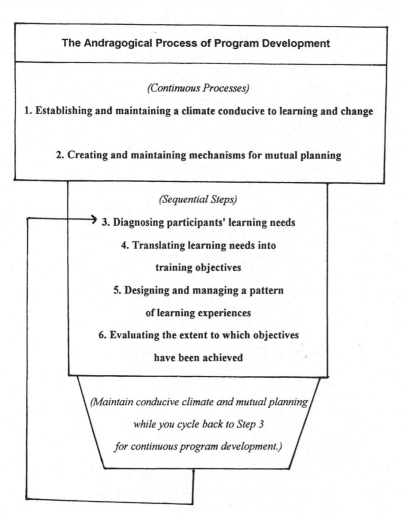

The Andragogical Process of Program Development

(Continuous Processes)

1. Establishing and maintaining a climate conducive to learning and change

2. Creating and maintaining mechanisms for mutual planning

(Sequential Steps)

3. Diagnosing participants' learning needs

4. Translating learning needs into

training objectives

5. Designing and managing a pattern

of learning experiences

6. Evaluating the extent to which objectives

have been achieved

(Maintain conducive climate and mutual planning

while you cycle back to Step 3

for continuous program development.)

Figure 7-1. The andragogical process of program development.

7.6 But Not Andragogy *versus* Pedagogy

When the andragogical model was first conceptualized in the book *The Modern Practice of Adult Education*,[16] it was sharply contrasted against the pedagogical model with pedagogy almost antithetical to andragogy. In fact, the subtitle of the book was shown as "Andragogy versus Pedagogy." During the next few years, reports came from elementary and secondary school teachers saying that they had been experimenting with applying the andragogical model in their practice and finding that children and youth also learn better in many situations when they are involved in sharing responsibility. And reports also came from teachers of adults that they had found situations in which they had to use the pedagogical model. So when the book was revised in 1980 it was given the subtitle, *From Pedagogy to Andragogy*.

Here is how it can be viewed now: whereas for 13 centuries we had only one model of assumptions and strategies regarding education, the pedagogical model, now we have two models. So we have the responsibility now of checking out which set of assumptions is realistic in which situation, and using the strategies of whichever model is appropriate for that situation. In general, the pedagogical assumptions are likely to be realistic in those situations in which the content is totally strange to the learners and in which precise psychomotor skills are involved, as in machine operation and other technical and skill areas. But even in these situations, elements of the andragogical model, such as climate setting, might enhance the learning. So, the stance that seems to work best now is not either-or, but both, as appropriate to the situation. Give instruction to show how *and* involve learners to improve practice. Transmit with enthusiasm and interest to enable the listener to hear easily what you have to teach *and* help them learn from one another through discussion and cooperative learning activities. *Artistically blend methods and approaches to make learning both effective and fun.*

7.7 Preparing for the Future

In the third quarter of this century we accumulated more research-based knowledge about adults as learners than was known in all of previous history. In the past decade, that body of knowledge has at least doubled. It seems certain that the present body of knowledge will at least double in the next decade. Professionals in the biological sciences are giving assurances that their disciplines will contribute some of the major breakthroughs, especially as regards the physiological, chemical, and neurological processes involved in learning. The technology of making resources for learning available is already in a state of revolution, especially with the development of computers and communications satellites. It seems certain that by the end of this century most educational services will be delivered electronically to learners at their convenience in terms of time, place, and pace.

What a challenge we in human resources development face if we are to avoid the obsolescence of our work force. It is clear that this challenge requires that we reconceptualize a corporation (or any social system) as a system of learning resources as well as a production and service-delivering system and redefine the role of HRD away from that of managing the logistics of conducting training activities to that of managing a system of learning resources. We would then ask a very different set of questions from those we have traditionally asked in training and development. The first question would be, *"What are all of the resources available in this system for the growth and development of people?"* Then we would have to ask, *"How well are these resources being utilized now, and how might they be more effectively utilized?"* We might come up with a chart that looks something like Table 7-1.

If nothing more is done than what has been described so far, the quality of human resource development in a corporation would probably be improved. But learning would still be episodic, fragmented, and disconnected. It can be more systematic, incremental, and continuous through the use of learning contracts, development plans, and real change projects (Knowles;[12] Hartl[29]).

A contract simply specifies what an individual's objectives are for a given learning project, what resources will be used in fulfilling the objectives, what evidence will be collected to demonstrate that the objectives have been fulfilled, and how that evidence will be validated. In one corporation, the contract is negotiated between the individual and the HRD staff, in another, it is between the individual and his or her supervisor, a representative of the HRD department, and a peer. Progress toward fulfilling the contract is monitored, and the evidence is validated by these same parties. Several corporations that are investing in total quality management processes have incorporated the contracting process into the quality improvement process.

Several things happen when a systems approach is adopted. A heavier responsibility is placed on the line supervisors and managers for the development of their personnel than traditionally has been the case. This integrates the HRD function more closely with the operating function, and line supervisors and managers derive added self-esteem and job satisfaction from their developmental role once they have become adept at it. Employees find that their personal and professional development are more integrated with their work life. A much wider range of resources for learning are available to them, and employees are more directly involved in planning and achieving their own development—adding to their self-esteem and satisfaction.

Table 7-1. Managing a System of Learning Resources

Resources	Strategies for enhancing their utilization
Scheduled training activities (courses, workshops, seminars)	■ Revise time schedule so as to make them more accessible to employees ■ Revise programs so as to make them more congruent with adult learning principles ■ Train presenters in adult education methods
Line supervisors and managers (the most ubiquitous resources for day-in-day-out employee development)	■ Build responsibility for people development into their job descriptions ■ Build into supervisory and management training programs session on principles of adult learning and skills in facilitating learning ■ Give credit in personnel appraisals for performance as people developers
Libraries, media centers (printed materials, audiovisual and multimedia programs)	■ Arrange to be open during hours accessible to all employees ■ Make information about resources available to all employees ■ Provide help in using them
Individual employees, specialists, and technicians (many people in organizations have knowledge and skills others would like to learn)	■ Store this information in a data bank and make it available to employees through an educational brokering center
Community resources (courses, workshops, specialists, etc., in colleges and universities, community organizations, professional associations, commercial providers, etc.)	■ Include in the above data bank

In one client corporation, a major American company, the old approach to managing the education and training function (employed as recently as a few years ago) was to use it as a temporary place to put managers who were on their way out of the company's leadership group and no longer considered important. In more recent years, the education and training manager position has been filled with seasoned and innovative managers who are expected to stay a while and make a difference in the total organization's culture as an insider in organizational decision making. This trend can be seen in organizations all around the United States, in many parts of Europe, and in the Far East. HRD is moving from the periphery of United States organizational leadership and bringing the continuous learning perspective as a critical consideration for organizational performance. An important role shift for HRD professionals has accompanied this move to the centers of organizational power. They have to focus less on simply planning, scheduling, and conducting training sessions and more on managing a complex system of resources to support the continuous learning requirements of the total organization. They must serve as internal consultants and advisers to help position issues and decisions that will assure continued organizational effectiveness.

The emerging relationship of HRD functions to the organizational "bottom line" is becoming increasingly direct and obvious to both those in human resources and to executive leaders. For product manufacturing organizations, continuous learning is crucial to continuous improvement, a key element in the manufacturing of quality products that can compete in the international marketplace. *In a service-based organization, where the skilled employee IS the organization's product, the training function is analogous to nothing less than the manufacturing department of a product-based company—it's the training function that produces the service organization's key resource: skilled employees.* Unfortunately, there are organizations in which human resources development is still considered by some as an expense unrelated to the bottom line which can be cut in tight times with no ill effects. Those days are gone forever. The requirement for deep involvement in continuous learning is here to stay and it will call forth the best that the HRD field has to offer. What an exciting time to be involved in one of the most important and satisfying professions in organizational life.

References

1. Eduard C. Lindeman, *The Meaning of Adult Education*, New Republic, New York, 1926.

2. Cyril O. Houle, *The Inquiring Mind*, University of Wisconsin Press, Madison, Wis., 1961.

3. Allen Tough, *Learning without a Teacher*, Ontario Institute for Education, Toronto, 1967.

4. Allen Tough, *The Adult's Learning Projects*, 2d ed., Ontario Institute for Education, Toronto, 1979.

5. John M. Peters, and S. G. Gordon, *Adult Learning Projects: A Study of Adult Learning in Urban and Rural Tennessee*, University of Tennessee, Knoxville, 1974.

6. Patrick R. Penland, *Individual Self-Planned Learning in America*, Final Report of Project 475AH60058 under grant No. G0077603327, U.S. Office of Education, Office of Libraries and Learning Resources. Unpublished manuscript, Graduate School of Library and Information Sciences, University of Pittsburgh, 1977. Available as ERIC document. Also available from the University of Pittsburgh bookstore under the title *Self-Planned Learning in America*.

7. Malcolm S. Knowles, *Self-Directed Learning: A Guide for Learners and Teachers,* Cambridge Book Co., New York, 1975.

8. Robert Havighurst, *Development Tasks and Education,* 2d ed., David McKay, New York, 1970.

9. Raymond J. Wlodkowski, *Enhancing Adult Motivation to Learn,* Jossey-Bass, San Francisco, 1985.

10. Cyril O. Houle, *The Effective Board,* Association Press, New York, 1960.

11. Malcolm S. Knowles, *The Adult Learner: A Neglected Species,* 3d ed., Gulf Publishing Co., 1984.

12. Malcolm S. Knowles, *Andragogy in Action,* Jossey-Bass, San Francisco, 1984.

13. Edgar J. Boone, (ed.), *Serving Personal and Community Needs through Adult Education,* Jossey-Bass, San Francisco, 1980.

14. F. Gerald Brown, and Kenneth R. Wedel, *Assessing Training Needs,* National Training and Development Service, Washington, D.C. 1974.

15. Larry N. Davis and Earl McCallon, *Planning, Conducting, Evaluating Workshops,* Learning Concepts, Austin, Tex., 1974.

16. Malcolm S. Knowles, *The Modern Practice of Adult Education,* 2d ed., Cambridge Book Co., New York, 1980.

17. Leon McKenzie and John McKinley (ed.), "Adult Education: The Diagnostic Procedure," *Bulletin of the School of Education* **49**(5) Indiana University, Bloomington, 1973.

18. Robert Mager and Peter Pipe, *Analyzing Performance Problems,* Fearon Publishers, Gelmont, Calif., 1970.

19. Robert Mager, *Preparing Instructional Objectives,* Fearon Publishers, Belmont, Calif., 1962.

20. Donald L. Kirkpatrick, *Evaluating Training Programs,* ASTD, Washington, D.C., 1975.

21. N. Scriven (ed.), *Evaluation in Education,* McCutchan Publishing Corp., Berkeley, Calif., 1974.

22. Daniel Stufflebeam, et al., *Educational Evaluation and Decision Making,* Peacock Publishers, Itasca, Ill., 1971.

23. Lee J. Cronback, et al., *Toward Reform of Program Evaluation: Aims, Methods and Institutional Arrangements,* Jossey-Bass, San Francisco, 1980.

24. Egon G. Guba, and Yvonne S. Lincoln, *Effective Evaluation: Improving the Usefulness of Evaluation Results through Responsive and Naturalistic Approaches,* Jossey-Bass, San Francisco, 1981.

25. Michael Q. Patton, *Utilization-Focused Evaluation,* Sage Publications, Beverly Hills, Calif., 1978.

26. Michael Q. Patton, *Qualitative Evaluation Methods,* Sage Publications, Beverly Hills, Calif., 1980.

27. Michael Q. Patton, *Creative Evaluation,* Sage Publications, Beverly Hills, Calif., 1981.

28. Michael Q. Patton, *Practical Evaluation,* Sage Publications, Beverly Hills, Calif., 1982.

29. David E. Hartl, *Guidelines for Developing Independent Learning Plans and Real Change Projects,* GLC Associates, Inc., Tustin, Calif., 1990.

Further Reading

Boud, David, Rodemary Keogh, and David Walker (eds.), *Reflection: Turning Experience into Learning,* Nichols Publishing Co., New York, 1985.

Cross, K. Patricia, *Adults as Learners,* Jossey-Bass, San Francisco, 1981.

Donaldson, Les, and Edward E. Scannell, *Human Resource Development: The New Trainer's Guide,* 2d ed., Addison-Wesley Publishing Co., Reading, Mass., 1986.

Knox, Alan B., *Adult Development and Learning,* Jossey-Bass, San Francisco, 1977.

Silberman, Mel, *Active Training: A Handbook of Techniques, Designs, Case Examples, and Tips,* Lexington Books, Lexington, Mass., 1990.

8

Instructional Design Basics

Mary Gail Biebel

Mary Gail Biebel, Ph.D. *is a Pittsburgh-based consultant who provides training and consulting services to a wide variety of organizations. She was formerly Manager of Education and Training at Alcoa Laboratories. Mary Gail is a faculty member in the H. John Heinz III School of Public Policy and Management at Carnegie Mellon University, where she also teaches in the Nonprofit Management Institute, Senior Executive Program, and College Management Program. She was the 1994 recipient of the Joseph M. Biedenbach of the American Society for Engineering Distinguished Service Award for outstanding contributions to the field of continuing professional development for engineers.*

8.1 Introduction

This chapter is intended to provide you with an overview of the concepts and terminology of instructional design. It is not intended as an in-depth examination of instructional technology, nor is it intended to advocate any particular approach to instructional design. If, at the conclusion of this chapter, your interest has been piqued and you'd like to learn more about instructional design, there is a plethora of excellent resources available, some of which have been referenced at the end of this chapter.

8.1.1 Why Use Instructional Design?

Now, more than ever, it is critical to use a systematic approach when creating training programs and materials. Organizations today are being asked to do more with less, to attend more closely to the needs of both external and internal customers, and to respond to training needs in increasingly targeted and flexible ways. Organizations are being asked to examine and streamline their critical business processes, including the process of ensuring that organizational members have the skills and information they need to do their jobs. Waste can occur in the instructional design process through training that is created by trial and error, through training that is developed to teach skills and information that participants already possess or that they don't need, and through training that doesn't accomplish its intended objectives. Understanding the basics of instructional design can help both line managers and training practitioners make better decisions about the use of organizational resources.

8.1.2 What Is Instructional Design?

Instructional design is a systematic approach to creating effective instruction. It is sometimes called instructional system development, or ISD. ISD is commonly divided into phases, each with an associated series of tasks to be accomplished. For our purposes, we will divide the instructional design process into the following three phases:

Analysis

Design

Development and Implementation

This chapter will describe the phases and steps outlined in the ISD process model shown in Figure 8-1.

There is a variety of instructional design approaches in common use. These models may sequence the tasks of instructional design differently or use different terminology; they may be based on different analytical approaches; they may vary in the degree of regimentation or flexibility built into the model; but in general they agree on the major components and characteristics of instructional design.

ISD PROCESS

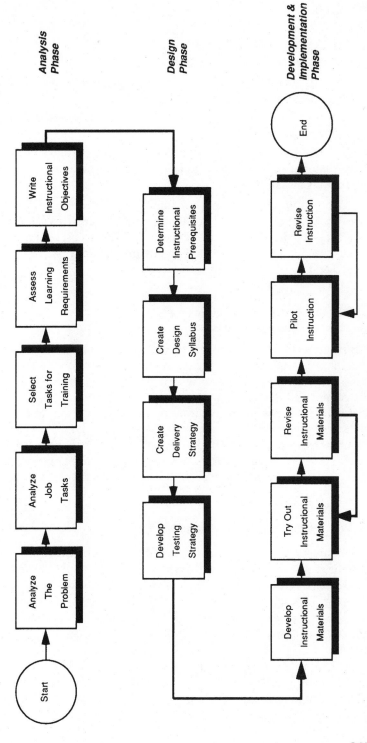

Figure 8-1. ISD process model.

8.1.3   Characteristics
of Effective Instructional Design

- Instructional design models approach the development of effective instruction in a systematic way; that is, the design, development, implementation, and continuous improvement of instruction is seen as an integrated process.

- The tasks of instructional design are interconnected; that is, each task in the sequence builds upon and uses the information generated in the previous tasks.

- No matter what model or approach is chosen, there are prescribed rules for making the associated development decisions. This is the equivalent of rule-based design in the engineering world and it provides the training practitioner with a development process that produces standardized and consistent results.

8.1.4   Using Instructional
Design in Your Organization

It is important to remember that there is no one best way to develop effective instruction and that every instructional design model has both positives and negatives associated with it. The model that you choose as your instructional design road map should work for you; it should be a tool that helps you create effective training in an efficient and orderly manner. If the tool you choose doesn't work, either modify it, or experiment with different models until you find one that is a "fit" for both you and the culture of your organization. It is more important to use a systematic process that works for you than to try to follow a process that isn't working.

8.2   The Analysis Phase

The analysis phase of the instructional design process involves the systematic study of a problem, incorporating data and opinion from a variety of sources in order to make effective decisions or recommendations about training. This phase will result in a written analysis document, which is the blueprint for the subsequent design and development of training materials. A typical sequence of tasks to be performed during the analysis phase includes:

- Analyzing the problem
- Analyzing job tasks
- Selecting tasks for training

- Assessing learning requirements
- Writing instructional objectives

8.2.1 Analyzing the Problem

Because the use of an instructional design process presupposes that a decision has been made to develop training, an analysis is often performed on the front end to ensure that the problem being examined requires a training solution. This analysis determines whether or not there is a need for instruction. All training practitioners can cite examples of managers who come to them and say, "I think I've got a training problem," and proceed to prescribe training as the solution when there may be no data to warrant it. Throwing training dollars at nontraining problems is a common example of the waste of instructional resources. Another common waste of resources is the failure to focus training on skills and business practices that are truly critical to supporting the organization's business plan, so this may also be a factor in determining the need for training.

Front-end problem analysis provides the justification for developing the needed instruction:

1. Uses tools and techniques that are similar to those used in instructional needs assessment
2. Examines the factors that affect performance
3. Determines whether or not it is a training need
4. Ends with a "go/no go" decision about developing training
5. Identifies any program goals which spell out the desired instructional outcomes; i.e., what performance gap the training is intended to address

In performing a front-end analysis, all factors that may affect performance should be considered prior to making the decision to develop instruction. Often people don't perform as desired because they don't know how to do what is expected of them on the job. Those times, of course, call for training as all or part of the solution.

At other times, people don't do what they *do* know how to do, so training might represent a waste of instructional resources. Common reasons for this situation are:

- People are unclear about the performance standards; they don't know what they are expected to do.
- People don't have the tools, information, and resources (including time) that they need to meet the performance standards.

- People don't receive adequate performance feedback; they don't know that they are not performing as expected.

- People are not given the authority to perform as desired.

- People do not perceive an incentive to perform as desired; they are punished for performing as desired.

These items listed here would be addressed by a variety of strategies such as redesigning jobs, developing job aids, and revising job selection criteria.

8.2.2 Analyzing Job Tasks and Selecting Tasks for Learning

Task analysis consists of describing and analyzing job tasks and selecting tasks for training. It is sometimes referred to as job/task analysis. A task analysis should answer the following question: *What are the most important requirements of the job?*

What does a master performer do when performing this job? The task analysis may examine the full spectrum of activities required to perform a new or existing job, or it may focus on tasks required to perform a job that is changing or being modified. In addition to describing the activities performed, the task analysis should also consider other dimensions of the job being analyzed.

What types of decisions are made in this job?

What processes are used to perform job tasks?

What steps are involved in those processes?

In what sequence are they performed?

Who provides input and what is it (i.e., data, parts, etc.)?

Who are the customers for this job?

How do customers define successful performance?

What types of tools are used?

Is this job performed alone or as part of a team?

8.2.3 Assessing Learning Requirements

Just as performance requirements vary from job to job, so, too, will the learning requirements vary. Learning to perform one job may be very different from learning to perform another. There is a variety of models for categorizing learning requirements, such as Gagne's domains of learning.

These models vary in the complexity of their categories, including, among other things, the ways of specifying cognitive processes and psychomotor skills. Learning requirements will influence the design and development of instruction, impacting the way that information is sequenced and presented, practice opportunities are structured, feedback is given, and a variety of other pedagogical choices.

8.2.4 Writing Instructional Objectives

One of the major tasks of the analysis phase is the development of written instructional objectives. These are sometimes referred to as behavioral or performance objectives as well. Instructional objectives spell out what participants will be able to do as a result of training. They should support the overall program goals identified earlier in the front-end analysis. Well-written objectives are critical to the ISD process; they shape instructional content and methodology and provide the standards against which instructional success can be measured both for the individual learner and at the programmatic level.

According to Robert Mager, whose *Preparing Instructional Objectives* is considered a classic in this area, a well-written objective should include these three components:

- *Performance*—what the learner will be able to do
- *Conditions*—the conditions under which the learner will be able to perform
- *Criteria*—the standards by which learner performance will be evaluated

8.2.5 Ways to Gather Data

Performance observation, interviewing, questionnaires, and working with subject matter experts (SMEs) are four techniques that are commonly used to gather data during the analysis phase of ISD. Each of these techniques, when used alone or in combination with other data collection tools, has both advantages and disadvantages.

Performance observation. This is a data collection technique whereby one or more persons watch master performers demonstrate a series of skills or complete specified tasks. To generate the most useful data, observation requires up-front preparation and observers who are well trained. This technique is especially useful in defining performance for jobs where much of the work is visible to an observer and less useful for jobs where the work is primarily cognitive.

Advantages of performance observation include:

- Generally creates little disturbance in work routines
- Gives the training practitioner firsthand knowledge of the job
- Process and performance variations will become clear through multiple observations
- Generates information that might not be obtained through other methods

Disadvantages of performance observation include:

- Presence of the observer may affect the results obtained
- Can be time-consuming and expensive
- Doesn't generate attitudinal or motivational information
- Observers must be skilled in area of observation

Interviewing.   This is a data collection technique used to gather analysis information either one-on-one or in groups. It can be structured, with pre-determined questions, as in a focus group, or unstructured, where the questions are more open-ended. Brainstorming and storyboarding techniques are often used when working with groups to gather performance data. Analysis groups often create process flowcharts or process maps to describe performance and outline tasks. Although brainstorming and storyboarding groups may look unstructured, they require careful planning and facilitation in order to generate the most useful and accurate data.

Advantages of interviewing include:

- Immediate responses can be obtained
- Group synergy leads to more complete information
- Helps clarify prior responses
- Creates support and buy-in for the instruction
- Generates data about multiple performance factors

Disadvantages of interviewing include:

- Requires a skilled facilitator or interviewer
- Facilitator or interviewer can significantly affect the results
- Can be time-consuming, especially with groups
- Interpretation of responses can be difficult

Questionnaires.   These are a data-collection technique used to collect written information, opinions, suggestions, and reactions from one or more groups of people. Many training needs assessments are done using this methodology. In order to generate useful and accurate information, surveys and questionnaires should be constructed by someone with expertise in this area. They should not be used to gather information that is readily available through other sources or information that is too broad to be meaningful.

Advantages of questionnaires include:

- Little disturbance to work routines
- Information can be gathered from many people at once
- Ensures confidentiality of respondents
- Generally inexpensive to administer
- Data are easily analyzed

Disadvantages of questionnaires include:

- Requires expertise in construction of surveys and questionnaires
- Rate of return can be low
- Doesn't allow for clarification of responses or follow-up unless respondents are given the option of listing their names

Subject Matter Experts.   Job analysis information is often gathered by working directly with subject matter experts, who are usually referred to as SMEs. Here are some tips that will help ensure successful working partnerships with SMEs:

- Provide an overview of the instructional design process. Clarify the role of the SMEs and the role of the instructional designer.
- Use the SMEs' time well. Develop and bring agendas to meetings and to interviews. Meet *their* needs as to the time, place, and frequency of meetings.
- SMEs are often so familiar with their subject matter that they have difficulty focusing on the basics. Ask questions in a variety of ways to compensate for this, and draw out the specifics of job requirements.
- Avoid discussions on *how* you are going to develop the training; focus SME attention on content. However, SMEs may have insights into helpful ways to illustrate or teach a given point.
- Formalize the approval process by having SMEs and/or project management sign off your summary documents.

8.2.6   The Analysis Document

The output of the analysis phase is the analysis document, which serves as the road map for the design and development of instruction. This document is the principal source of information in making the decision to purchase or develop training. A good analysis document will help the training practitioner evaluate training that is commercially available, write a good request-for-proposal (RFP), and, of course, create effective instruction inside the organization. The analysis document will include:

Instructional Goals and Objectives

- What performance gap is this training intended to address?
- What do you want participants to be able to do at the end of training?
- What do you want participants to know at the end of training?
- What attitudes do you want participants to acquire during training?

Target Audience Characteristics

- Who is the target population for this training?
- What is the size of the target population?
- Where are trainees located?
- What skills and knowledge do students already have and how much variability is there?
- What are their backgrounds and how much variability is there?
- What kinds of training have they already had? What was their experience like with this training?
- What training delivery systems are they used to?
- What primary languages do trainees speak?
- What foreign nationals will participate and what culture differences must be addressed?
- Are there special considerations related to diversity or the Americans with Disabilities Act?

Measurement Factors

- What metrics will you use to measure program success?
- What evaluation methodology will be used?
- If testing is done, how will the results be used?
- How will training results be linked to business goals?

Program Management

- In what time frame must the training be implemented?
- Who needs to know what along the way?

- What kind of participant records must be kept?
- What kind of media are being considered?
- What is the budget for this project?
- What subject matter expertise is available? Are the SMEs internal or external?
- Is the course content stable or rapidly changing?
- Are there any constraints around the delivery of training, such as requiring equipment compatibility or accommodating distance learners at multiple sites?
- What existing training and reference materials are available?
- Are there any equipment or facilities constraints?
- What information or approvals, if any, do business unit managers, training managers, administrators, publications staff, and others need to generate along the way?

8.3   The Design Phase

The design phase of the instructional design process involves taking the information contained in the analysis document and using it to develop an instructional strategy and a design syllabus or training plan for the instruction. This phase will result in a written design document, which is the blueprint for the subsequent development of training materials. A typical series of tasks to be performed during the design phase includes:

- Determining instructional prerequisites
- Creating a design syllabus
- Creating a delivery strategy
- Developing an evaluation strategy

8.3.1   Determining Instructional Prerequisites

In addition to considering what learners will be able to do as a result of instruction, the training practitioner will also want to consider what participants should be able to do as a prerequisite to instruction. What skills and knowledge are necessary for the learner to take full advantage of the instruction? Once these are determined, a strategy can be developed to ensure that participants come to training with the requisite background.

A second type of instructional prerequisite is developing a strategy to ensure that participants come to training understanding why they are there, what the instruction will teach them, and how it will be used in their job. Although this area is a perpetual concern and frustration for training professionals, it should not be overlooked.

A third type of prerequisite involves any skills or knowledge that learners might need to use the training delivery system as opposed to content knowledge that is required. For instance, participants might need a working knowledge of a certain type of computer hardware in order to enroll in a computer-based training program.

8.3.2 Creating a Design Syllabus

A design syllabus is a broad training plan for the instruction. Using the analysis document as a road map, the design syllabus should answer the following questions:

- How should objectives be sequenced?
- What content will be presented?
- How can the content be broken into learner-friendly segments?
- In what sequence should content be presented?
- How should material be "chunked"; i.e., how much material will be presented at any given point?
- What balance of activities should the design encompass? How will the training program balance and sequence instructor input, learner participation, practice opportunities, examples, questions, demonstrations, feedback, discussion, media, tests, etc.?
- How will learner reinforcement be provided?

8.3.3 Creating a Delivery Strategy

Another task of the design phase is deciding what delivery system and media to use to most effectively present the instruction. At one level, the design may include standard media choices like videos and simulations and case studies. At a broader level, the design will involve choices about the basic instructional strategy for delivering the instruction:

- Instructor-led
- Self-paced

- Structured on-the-job training
- Computer-based
- Interactive video, etc.

Chapters 9 through 11 of this handbook provide more in-depth information about these choices.

8.3.4 Developing an Evaluation Strategy

A strategy for evaluation is typically included in the design document. Guided by information from the analysis document, the design document should address these questions:

- Will prerequisite skills and knowledge be assessed?
- Will a precourse assessment be administered?
- Will a postcourse assessment be administered?
- Will assessment occur during the instruction?
- Where and how will this assessment occur?
- How will each training objective be assessed?
- What assessment outcome is required to satisfy each performance criterion?
- How will assessment results be used?

8.4 The Development and Implementation Phase

The development and implementation phase of the instructional design process involves taking the information contained in the design document and using it to develop instructional materials. A typical series of steps to be performed during the development and implementation phase includes:

- Developing instructional materials
- Trying out instructional materials
- Revising instructional materials
- Implementing the training
- Evaluating the training

8.4.1 Developing Instructional Materials

The design syllabus created during the previous phase becomes the road map for the more detailed development of instructional materials. Participant materials are created, and if the training is to be instructor-led, an instructor guide will need to be developed, too. At a minimum, learner materials will include:

- An orientation to the instruction, including what will be learned, why it's important, and how the instruction will be delivered
- The course materials that participants will use to achieve the desired instructional objectives
- A course "road map" that shows how various modules or instructional components fit together
- Evaluation materials

8.4.2 Trying Out and Revising Instructional Materials

Selected learner and instructor materials should be field-tested and revised during the development phase. The purpose of a pilot or field test is to determine if the instruction is *effective* (i.e., were the instructional goals and objectives met) and *efficient* (i.e., were they met in a way that represents an effective use of resources, including time and learner interest and enthusiasm). The amount of field-testing and revision engaged in will be determined in part by the length, complexity, and delivery strategy of the instruction. It will also depend on available funds and time constraints. Frequently, a pilot offering of training will include instructional and subject matter experts, as well as a typical group of trainees, all of whom agree to provide feedback to instructional developers.

In addition to empirical data gathered from testing, valuable information can be gained from observing the instructional process and interviewing or surveying both participants and instructors. If subject matter experts are available, their feedback on instructional content may be very helpful. The purpose of all these formative evaluation activities is to improve the instructional process and materials.

8.4.3 Implementation and Evaluation

As the training becomes part of your organization's curriculum, a summative evaluation may also be desired. Chapter 14 of this handbook provides extensive information on evaluation activities.

8.5 Working with Technical Training Vendors

The ISD process provides a useful road map to help the training practitioner develop effective instruction, and it also provides a framework for working with any external training vendors who may develop instruction for your organization.

Once a training need has been identified, the training practitioner has several ways to proceed:

1. The instruction can be developed "in-house."

2. Existing training materials or programs can be purchased and perhaps modified.

3. Learners can be sent to off-site courses.

4. An external supplier or vendor can be hired to develop instruction that meets your organization's specifications.

Vendors can be used for a specific phase of the instructional design process or to complete the overall process. The choice will depend on the capability and size of your organization's training staff, internal and external resources availability, and your organization's strategic training plan.

Even if you choose to contract out for the development of instruction, you will want to stay actively involved in the ISD process by completing the following steps:

- Preliminary analysis: What do you want?

- Request for proposal: How clear are your requirements?

- Supplier selection: How do you choose the right vendor?

- Contracting: How do you contract to ensure mutual agreement and buy-in?

- Project management: How do you manage the project effectively?

8.5.1 Preliminary Analysis

Even if you have chosen to contract out for the needs analysis phase, some preliminary analysis must be completed by the training practitioner so that a comprehensive request-for-proposal, or RFP, can be prepared. This is similar to the front-end analysis discussed earlier in the chapter. The RFP may seek services for one part of the ISD, e.g., needs assessment, or for multiple ISD process elements.

8.5.2   Request for Proposal

A well-written RFP does two things. It helps the internal training practitioner find an appropriate vendor for the project, and it helps the external training provider know when to submit a proposal for a project. The format of the RFP may vary from project to project, but it should outline the following:

- *Project background,* including project goals and objectives, project history, target population characteristics, and program management considerations

- *Project procedures,* including scope of work, major tasks involved, roles and responsibilities of the organization and the vendor, review and approval considerations, and desired start and finish dates for the project

- *Outputs and deliverables,* including the types of reports and documents desired for each ISD phase, format requirements, and review and approval considerations

- *Proposal guidelines,* including descriptions of the format and content for proposals submitted, your decision criteria, and time frame. You may also wish to provide potential vendors with a boilerplate contract for review, so that you can facilitate and expedite the contract phase which follows. Finally, you should specify how the decisions will be communicated to those who respond to your RFP, and the name and telephone number of someone on your team to answer vendor questions about the project.

8.5.3   Supplier Selection

RFPs should only be sent to potential vendors who are serious contenders for the project. Reviewing proposals is time-consuming for the training practitioner, just as preparing a well-written proposal is time-consuming for the prospective developer.

Potential vendors should be allowed at least a month to respond to your request. As part of the proposal review process, you should talk with potential vendors, either in person or by phone. No matter how well-written your RFP or their proposal, there will always be points to clarify. This interaction will also help you assess those intangible things that make up a working relationship, such as personal and work style, common understanding of instructional design, and a willingness to work together.

8.5.4   Contracting

After selecting your vendor, it is important to develop a written agreement that clearly spells out the expectations of both parties. Some issues to be covered include:

- Deadlines and deliverables
- Roles and responsibilities
- Ownership of materials
- Revision cycles
- Escape clauses (for both parties)
- Copyright and proprietary issues
- Logistical arrangements (on-site office space, etc.)
- Procedures for handling unexpected staffing changes
- Procedures for arbitrating any differences of opinion that may emerge during the project.

A well-written project with clear expectations can help ensure a smoothly run project from the beginning.

8.5.5 Project Management

Good project management is critical to the success of your project. Both the project manager from your organization and the project manager from the external vendor should be clear about their roles and responsibilities. For the internal project manager, this will include:

- Keeping the project on schedule
- Identifying SMEs
- Scheduling meetings
- Identifying and gathering internal resource materials
- Helping break through any organizational roadblocks
- Communicating regularly with the vendor
- Conducting the wrap-up meeting

8.6 Sample Request-for-Proposal (RFP)

The following RFP (Figure 8-2), which was developed by the training staff of a large aluminum company, illustrates how the ISD process was used in the development of a course on Casting Processes.

REQUEST FOR PROPOSAL

I. PROJECT BACKGROUND

A. Problem Statement

Many of our employees are unfamiliar with our company's major casting processes. A preliminary needs analysis was conducted and we would like to develop a course on our company's casting processes that would give our employees an introduction or overview to the following types of casting:

Ingot casting	*Shape casting*	*Rapid casting*
Level transfer (FDC)	Sand casting	P/M
HDC	Vacuum die casting	
DC	Permanent mold	
	(PRC)	
	(VRC)	
Joining	*Fundamental*	
Tig welding	Plasma deposition	
Mig welding	Melt spinning	
EB welding	Squeeze casting	
Brazing	Crystal growth	
	Arc melting	

B. Project Goals/Objectives

The primary goal of this project is to develop a video-based course for use in our R&D Center's Learning Resource Center. Our Learning Resource Center is equipped with 20 study carrels which are equipped with VHS Panasonic recorders.

By developing this course we hope to accomplish the following objectives:

CURRICULUM GOALS (SKILLS AND KNOWLEDGE)

Upon completion of the videotape series, the learner will be able to:

- Identify the various types of our company's casting processes
- Recognize the impact of each process on our business
- Identify applications for each of the processes
- Recall where each process fits into the chain of events (sequence)
- Identify which processes are performed at each of our company's locations

---

Figure 8-2. Sample Request for Proposal.

- Recognize the impact that each process has on the quality of our products
- Understand the implications of the various processes on materials other than metals (such as polymers and ceramics) and their impact on the future

ATTITUDINAL GOALS
The learner will:

- Become sensitive to the emphasis placed on safety procedures throughout the various processes
- Choose to seek out more information on course topics
- Believe that he/she has enough background and knowledge of solidification casting terms to communicate with peers and to do his/her job

In addition, the following questions have been identified that need to be answered in this overview course.

1. What are the characteristics for each process? Please address the following:
   A. Freezing rate
      Cell size (DCS)
      Intermetallic
      Solid solubility
      Porosity
   B. Segregation
      Macro
      Micro
   C. Grain structure
   D. Defects
      Inclusions
      Cavities
2. What are the routes for each of these processes?

   DC INGOT

      Casting>>>Scalping>>>Preheating>>>Hot Rolling>>> Continued Rolling>>>Re-roll Coil

      Roll Casting>>>Preheating>>>Re-roll Coil

      Bar Casting>>>Hot Working

3. What are the advantages/disadvantages of each process? Specifically, please address:

Figure 8-2. (*Continued*)

The technical and economic impact of the process on our business

Applications for the process

The impact of the process on the quality of our products

C. **History**
In the past, no form. l training has been offered to introduce our employees to the varic .is casting processes performed throughout the company.

D. **Target Population**
This course is intended for all new employees who have a need to become familiar with casting processes. Technicians and entry-level engineers outside the Molten Metal Processing Division and from Advanced Manufacturing, Alloy Technology, and Chemical Systems Divisions will profit most from this series. In addition, application engineers will benefit from this program. Approximately 500 learners have been identified at this time. It is assumed that they will have a basic vocabulary knowledge in this area.

E. **Constraints/Limitations**
We would like the entire course development process (analysis, design, and development and implementation phases) to be completed by November 30, 1994.

Since a preliminary analysis has been completed, we are asking that the vendor proceed from this point.

Subject matter experts have been identified. Individual or small group interviews should be conducted whenever possible.

We would prefer this to be a video-based course for the following reasons:

- The content is fairly stable and consistent.
- We want to show the flow of each process.
- The course is basically knowledge-based.

Since many of the processes are located at our plant locations, some travel will be necessary.

Video footage of some of these processes may already exist. If applicable, we would like to use these resources.

Since proprietary information will be included, a confidentiality clause will need to be included.

Figure 8-2. (*Continued*)

II. PROJECT PROCEDURE

Upon acceptance of the proposal, the vendor should begin the analysis phase of the ISD process. This phase should begin the early part of February, 1994. We will provide the vendor with a list of subject matter experts to be used on this project.

III. OUTPUTS/DELIVERABLES

A. Analysis Phase

The vendor will provide all forms necessary to complete the analysis phase. These forms may be in the form of surveys or questionnaires.

Upon completion of the analysis phase, the vendor will provide us with an analysis document that includes:

A list of instructional objectives that includes those previously identified.

A content outline that includes all the information to be discussed for each process.

At least one progress meeting will be held between our project manager and the vendor prior to completion of the analysis phase.

B. Design Phase

Upon completion of the design phase, the vendor will provide us with a design document that includes:

A detailed content outline

A learning sequence

Learning prerequisites, if any

Course design specifications

A prototype lesson

Evaluation methodology

The design document will be reviewed by our project manager and at least three subject matter experts.

C. Development and Implementation Phase

Upon completion of the development and implementation phase, the vendor will have:

Developed the videotape series

Validated the lessons

Revised and delivered the final version

Figure 8-2. (*Continued*)

IV. PROPOSAL GUIDELINES

A. Proposal Format/Content

Two copies of the proposal should be received by January 10, 1994, addressed to (—————). Proposals will be reviewed by (—————), the project manager, and one other member of our training staff. Notification of acceptance will be made no later than January 24, 1994. We request separate pricing and technical proposals.

The **pricing proposal** should include:

1. Type of contract. Provide us with both a fixed fee proposal and a time and materials proposal.
2. Description of what prices include and do not include.
3. Payment terms. We would prefer upon completion and acceptance of each phase.

The **technical proposal** should include:

1. Description of the project background. This section should include the problem, goals and objectives, target population, and constraints and limitations.
2. Procedure and schedule for getting the project done. This section should include detailed descriptions of the phases, steps, and tasks that will be completed to carry out the work associated with this particular project. Deadlines for each of these activities should also be included.
3. Outputs or deliverables. This section should include a detailed description of each of the elements you will produce. Include all relevant specifications for each deliverables.
4. Experience and qualifications. This section should answer the following questions:

   Who is the project manager who will work on this project and what is his/her background? Please include his/her resume.

   Who are the instructional technologists who will work on this project? Please include their resumes.

   What guarantees do we have that the same staff will remain on this project? In the event of a change in your staff, what input will we have into their replacement on this project?

   What project management systems do you have in place that will assure that this project will be completed according to specifications on cost, quality, and timing?

Figure 8-2. (*Continued*)

8.7 Conclusion

The ISD model presented in this chapter represents a systematic approach to creating training programs and materials. Chapter 16, "The Anatomy of a Training Program: A Start to Finish Look," exemplifies many of the points discussed in this chapter, should you seek further examples.

While following a specific design process requires both discipline and time, the effectiveness of the end product is highly dependent upon the quality of the analysis, design, and development steps used in creating the instruction. The ISD process is an invaluable tool for any organization that wants to maximize its return on investment of training dollars.

Bibliography

Bloom, B. S., et al., *A Taxonomy of Educational Objectives*, Longman, New York, 1977.

Briggs, L. J. (ed.), *Instructional Design: Principles and Applications*, Educational Technology Publications, Englewood Cliffs, N.J., 1981.

Briggs, L. J., and W. W. Wager, *Handbook of Procedures for the Design of Instruction*, 2d ed., Educational Technology Publications, Englewood Cliffs, N.J., 1977.

Carlisle, K. E., *Analyzing Jobs and Tasks*, Educational Technology Publications, Englewood Cliffs, N.J., 1986.

Dick, W., and L. Carey, *The Systematic Design of Instruction*, 2d ed., Scott Foresman, Glenview, Ill., 1985.

Gagne, R. M., *The Conditions of Learning*, 4th ed., Holt, Rinehart and Winston, New York, 1985.

Mager, R. F., *Measuring Instructional Results*, 2d ed., Lake Publishing Company, Belmont, Calif., 1984.

Mager, R. F., *Preparing Instructional Objectives*, revised 2d ed., Pitman Learning, Belmont, Calif., 1984.

Mager, R. F., *Making Instruction Work*, David S. Lake Publishers, Belmont, Calif., 1988.

Mager, R., and P. Pipe, *Analyzing Performance Problems*, 2d ed., Lake Publishing Company, Belmont, Calif., 1984.

9

Assessment of the Options

W. J. Mallory
Mallory Consulting

J. R. Steele
Ford Motor Company

W. J. Mallory *is an external instructional consultant in Grayling, Michigan. He specializes in the design and development of mediated instruction and job aids. Before starting a business, he spent 13 years at Ford Motor Company. Key assignments included instructional consulting, managing a worldwide CBT system, and designing and developing technical skills programs. He was ASTD's Technical & Skills Trainer of the Year in 1983. Before Ford, he was a Principal Scientist at Applied Science Associates, Inc. He managed the Technical Services Division, creating job aids, technical training, and conducting job-aid research and development.*

Jerry Steele *has been with Ford Motor Company for 30 years, over 10 years of which were in manufacturing and vehicle assembly plants. He presently supervises a corporate organization responsible for implementing high-technology training systems, increasing ISD utilization, and expanding the networking of company training organizations. During the 1980s, he was a Worldwide Engineering Releasing System Project Leader, Labor Consultant to Ford of Europe, and Industrial Relations Manager for five manufacturing plants in Canada.*

9.1   Introduction

The objectives of this chapter are to:

- Show the relationship of instructional needs, intended audience, etc. (prerequisites) to the design of instruction and the selection of training delivery approaches
- Separate training delivery features from delivery system technology
- Discuss and rank training delivery approaches
- Discuss and rank performance support approaches
- Provide a checklist for reviewing instructional delivery decisions
- Review cost and time rules of thumb associated with training development and delivery

Section 9.4, "Instructional Delivery Techniques and Devices," defines rating criteria and evaluates common delivery approaches. "Performance Support Delivery Techniques and Devices" (Section 9.5) discusses job aid rating criteria and scores common methods. The Instructional Delivery Decision Review Checklist (Section 9.6) has nine basic questions to help rate a program's instructional value. The final section, "Cost and Time Rules of Thumb" (section 9.7), discusses development times and decision criteria.

9.2   Prerequisites

"Let's do a 30-minute videodisc on carburetor adjustment." How many technical training programs are launched by similar management edicts? Programs based on starts like this are fraught with assumptions about need, audience, desired performance, and delivery system. Too often, we believe that more complicated or more expensive means better. The most elegant instructional solution is the one that delivers needed skills and knowledge quickly and simply, at the lowest cost. Don't choose an instructional delivery approach without the following:

- Job-related performance requirements
- Job performance certification (test)
- Program objectives (knowledge and skill)
- Criterion-referenced exercises for all objectives
- Audience characteristics critical to successful instruction

In the carburetor example just mentioned, an experienced audience could use a job aid outlining procedural steps and hands-on practice. An inexperienced audience would require background concepts, familiarization with several carburetors, and hands-on practice. In the second case, videodisk, videotape, workbooks, and several other approaches could be used for concepts, but would be unacceptable for performance activities. For a graphic example of what happens when these prerequisites are ignored, see Bovier, "How a High-Tech Training System Crashed and Burned," 1993.

9.3 Training Delivery Features vs. Delivery System Technology

9.3.1 Computer-Based

Computer-Based Training (CBT), Computer-Managed Instruction (CMI), Computer-Based Education (CBE), Interactive Videodisc, Compact Disc Interactive (CDI), Digital Video Interactive (DVI), etc., are all computer-based delivery tools. Past distinctions between computer-based delivery systems blur when one recognizes that most desirable instructional features are provided by the computer.

9.3.2 Video-Based

Video is either live (happening in real time) or recorded. Live video has certain attributes (motion, color, sound, etc.) regardless of delivery technology. Many distance-learning approaches are described by how signals are sent (satellite, cable, microwave, fiber optic, etc.) rather than with their instructional content or features.

Recorded video has the same attributes as live video, plus it is repeatable on demand. Recorded video devices differ in two major aspects: (1) how the video is stored, and (2) display device. Video is commonly stored on a variety of ½-in and ¾-in tape formats. Video is also stored on optical (laser) discs. The 11-in videodisc stores video in the current United States television standard format. CDI and DVI systems store video on 4¾-in compact discs in digital formats. A major difference is that digital forms can be displayed on computer screens.

9.3.3 Priorities

Don't pick a delivery system first, or become a delivery system technologist. Choose necessary instructional properties (motion, sound, interaction, illustrations, text, etc.) before choosing delivery systems. For additional information, see Heideman, "Selecting Media for Training," 1992.

9.4 Instructional Delivery Techniques and Devices

Training is a proper skill and knowledge intervention when the following happens:

1. Speed of performance is critical

2. Physical or environmental conditions prevent the use of job aids

3. There are psychological or social barriers to using job aids

4. All senses are used in task performance

5. Tasks are unlikely to change

The following discussions cover approaches commonly used to deliver training.

9.4.1 Rating Criteria for Instructional Delivery Techniques

These factors are used to rate instructional delivery approaches discussed here.

- *Always Available (Always Avail).* Program material availability to trainee. Materials available to suit trainee's schedule are more desirable than those requiring trainee schedule change.

- *Branching.* Pathing through instruction and remediation based on individual needs. Branching is common in programmed instruction. Branching paths through instruction are nonlinear in that different paths may be followed by each user of the instruction. Instruction in which each trainee follows the same path is linear and has no branches.

- *Competency-Based (Comp-Based).* Measurement of the trainee's mastery of instructional and performance objectives.

- *Consistent.* Program presentations give the same message to every trainee the same way. Workbooks and videotapes are consistent delivery approaches.

- *Expert Bypass (Exp Bypass).* Trainees demonstrating competence before an instructional module are allowed to skip it. This feature is often found in self-instructional programs that use pretests. It shortens training time by dropping unneeded modules.

- *Facilitated.*   A facilitator is present to solve problems, answer questions, etc. Facilitators are training delivery's Customer Support Department. They make self-instruction and group activities work.

- *Graphic.*   The ability to show visual images. Graphic adequacy is the ability to meet the resolution, color, motion, and content requirements of a program.

- *Interactive.*   A program property that requires trainees to use, apply, interpret, synthesize, problem-solve, or make other reasoned responses. Accelerated learning proponents suggest an interaction every two to five minutes during instruction.

- *Learner-Controlled (Lrnr-Cont).*   The trainee's ability to start or stop instruction and to control its content. The Expert Bypass (see preceding) is an element of learner control. Learner control permits an expert to use instruction as a memory refresher or job aid.

- *Low Development $ (Low Dev $).*   Low development cost is the cost to develop instruction. Computer-based approaches have high development costs. High development costs are affordable when the trainee population is large and the cost per trainee is low.

- *Low Equipment $ (Low Equip $).*   Low equipment cost is the cost of instructional hardware for a delivery approach. For example, computers are more expensive than videotape players, etc.

- *Performance-Based (Perf-Based).*   The instructional focus is on product, accomplishment, or the process the trainee must do on the job.

- *Pretest.*   A pretest (1) proves that trainees have program prerequisites, or (2) measures the before-instruction level of course- or module-related skill and knowledge. When used with a posttest, the second pretest use helps measure program-related learning.

- *Reusable.*   Program materials for a delivery approach are not consumed by the instructional process. Software associated with computer-based training is a reusable course material; workbooks are not.

- *Revisable.*   The ability to change materials associated with a delivery approach. Optical discs for videodisc and CD-ROM players are only recorded once and are not revisable. On the other hand, lectures and workbooks are easier to change.

- *Scored.*   The ability of a delivery approach to generate and store trainee scores for criterion-based knowledge, skill, and performance exercises.

- *Self-Instructional (Self-Inst).*   A delivery approach that does not rely on a resident instructor. Self-instructional approaches allow trainees to teach themselves and manage selection of program content as it applies to their on-the-job needs.

- *Self-Paced.* A delivery approach that allows the trainee to control rate of progress through instructional materials. In contrast, the lecturer controls the rate of instructional progress in a workshop or group approach.

- *Task-Based.* Instruction deals with tasks performed on the job. Course performance objectives are based on required job accomplishments and performance.

- *Task Practice (Task Pract).* The delivery approach provides opportunities for realistic task practice. If the task environment is critical, the approach provides or simulates the environment for task practice and competence demonstrations.

9.4.2 Rating Graphic Legend

The following section describes and ranks several delivery approaches using the preceding criteria. Rating graphics use the conventions shown in Figure 9-1.

9.4.3 Audience Response Systems (ARS)

Refer to Figure 9-2. Audience Response Systems allow lecture, seminar, meeting, and remote audience members to participate in instructional and developmental activities. Most systems give each audience member a key-

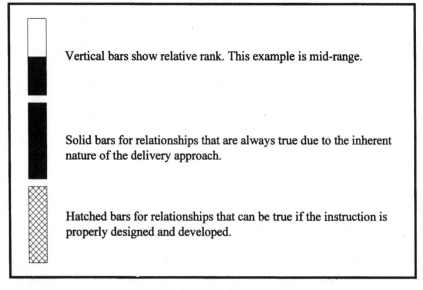

Vertical bars show relative rank. This example is mid-range.

Solid bars for relationships that are always true due to the inherent nature of the delivery approach.

Hatched bars for relationships that can be true if the instruction is properly designed and developed.

Figure 9-1. Rating graphic conventions.

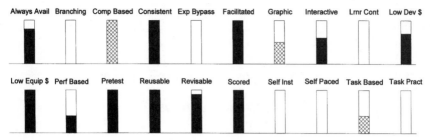

Figure 9-2. ARS ratings.

pad response device. The responders are connected to a personal computer that polls the units and stores the replies. Responses are to survey or instructional questions posed in multiple-choice format. Depending on design, the audience may or may not see a group response. In addition to television game shows, ARSs add interactivity to lectures, and speed plus privacy to group surveys.

ARSs provide a private, unobtrusive, manageable way to add interaction to local or broadcast lectures. ARSs can store and rate lectures and workshops, are useful in facilitating focus groups and collecting responses.

ARS software:

- Collects scores by trainee and exercise
- Analyzes group responses to items
- Stores scores for later analyses
- Does demographic analyses

9.4.4 Audiotape

Refer to Figure 9-3. Audiotape stores and plays back lectures in linear, talking-book style. Audio workbooks use cassette tapes and specialized workbooks. Taped lectures contain references to illustrations and criterion exercises in a companion workbook.

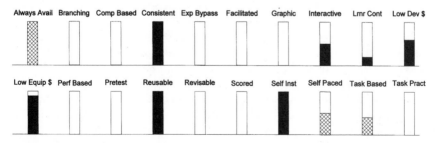

Figure 9-3. Audiotape ratings.

Cassette audio is portable. Tape players are reasonably priced. Audio-taped instruction can be used almost anywhere, from the Walkman while jogging, to the car while commuting.

Audio workbooks are an alternative to videotape in situations where motion video or animated graphics are not necessary to illustrate program concepts.

Use audiotaped lectures and criterion exercises as an inexpensive, second delivery medium when trying to accommodate a broader range of learning styles.

9.4.5   Lecture

Refer to Figure 9-4. Traditional lecture is a familiar medium. Despite the advantages of newer, more sophisticated media, lecture-based instruction is sometimes the most appropriate technique. Lectures are usually in oration or conference formats. Lecture is a one-way communication and is passive. Conference uses group techniques to communicate the message. It requires a highly-skilled trainer to keep the discussion focused.

Lectures are a good choice when development time is limited, many instructors are available, or delivery time is short.

With a large audience, use live classroom training, then complete the remainder of the training with a more cost-effective medium. If one trainer is a good instructor and a subject matter expert (SME), then live video may be the better medium.

Sometimes, the nature of training favors an on-site instructor. Group dynamics are an integral part of motivational messages. Adding new programs and policies to existing practices also requires human interactivity. Group sessions also may be highly effective.

9.4.6   Live Video

Refer to Figure 9-5. Live video training replaces the traditional instructor-led classroom with a televised program in either seminar or conference format. Live video instruction ends the need to attend training at a remote location. Live video is enhanced by allowing learners to interact with presenters. Computers and audience response systems add interactivity.

Live video instruction gives excellent results on diverse topics such as stress management, electrical engineering, and office automation. Live video training requires adaptation of presentation techniques to fit the medium. TV-type graphic and motivational techniques enhance delivery and maintain viewer interest. Competent on-site facilitators make sure the program fits local conditions. Facilitators confirm that programming reflects management interests and that learning occurs.

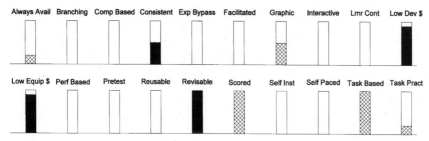

Figure 9-4. Lecture ratings.

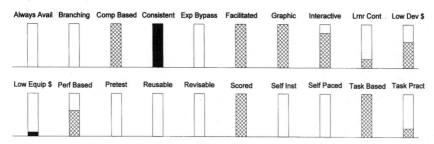

Figure 9-5. Live video ratings.

Live video seminars are long-range classrooms. Secondary media may still be required. For example, begin a program with an instructor presentation followed by viewers phoning in questions. Follow this with a panel discussion and video clips showing task performance. Finally, provide a workbook for interacting with new information.

Live video signals are sent by broadcast TV stations, microwave transmitters, cable TV networks, fiber optic networks, and satellite up- and down-links. Audience response system interactivity is added by systems that add two-way data transmission carried by radio, telephone, or with video signals. For examples, see Corrao, 1993 and Steele, 1993.

9.4.7 Multimedia Computer

Refer to Figure 9-6. Computers offer text, graphics, animation, motion video, sound, scoring, and student control of sequencing. A major advantage is a high degree of learner interactivity. Both mainframe computers and PCs are used; each has different advantages. A mainframe offers low-cost editability and distribution features. The PC offers color and graphic displays not always available on mainframe.

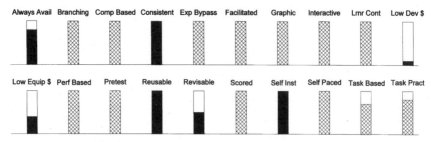

Figure 9-6. Multimedia computer ratings.

There are two reasons to use computers:

- Use computers when instructional objectives cover computer systems or software.
- Use computers to teach trainees to use a computer, to operate computer systems, solve problems, access databases, produce documents, or write programs.

For example, computers can branch to provide learners customized paths through instruction. Branching accommodates learners with varying instructional needs. Student control and pacing are critical to design. Function keys are used to move forward or backward through lessons. Menus list choices and have help options for advice on what to do next (see "Computer-Based Reference," Section 9.5.4). Overall learning time is reduced 30 to 50 percent by self-pacing and learner control.

Computer applications can also include skills training for maintenance and operating employees. They can simulate a variety of task-related processes and situations with computers. Simulations allow no-threat task practice and can provide analysis of practice sessions in real time. In addition, simulations can give diagnostic feedback to the trainee during practice.

Aviation training uses computers for flight simulation. Simulators are computerized teaching devices. They allow learners to practice operating or maintaining equipment without using the actual item.

Computer-based training (CBT) development is lengthy. Program designers need ample time to program and debug courseware. If combined with the initial equipment investment, computer-delivered training may require many students to justify costs.

The major differences in computer-based systems are the peripheral devices and controlling software. The computer's functionality is determined by several things:

1. Presentation resources (screen size and resolution, speakers, etc.)

2. Input devices (keyboard, mouse, etc.)

3. Storage devices (magnetic and optical discs, etc.)

4. Controlling software

For example, interactive videodisc uses a laser disc player for audio and video input. It uses a computer for sequencing, control, scoring, etc. A television monitor is its primary display.

Multimedia computer peripheral devices include the following.

Analog Videodisc Player. This unit uses an optical disc that is recorded (mastered) once and used only for playback. It delivers full-motion video and sound. Its large storage capacity and random access capability make it a desirable storage and playback device. Video modes and capacities are:

1. *Motion Video.* 54,000 frames for up to 27 minutes of full-motion video with two-track audio.

2. *Audio only.* Up to 72 hours of audio.

3. *Text only.* 250,000 pages. Analog video is unsuitable (low resolution) for large amounts of text, or high-resolution graphics (for example, schematics, blueprints, or maps).

Different formats can present problems if materials are intended for international use. For example, analog video formats and disc player software are different for North America and the United Kingdom.

Compact Disc-Read Only Memory (CD-ROM) Player. This unit uses a CD-ROM as an information storage device. It is similar to a computer floppy disk. Depending on format and compression technique, this small disc could store 22,000 photographic images, 150,000 text pages, or 20 hours of audio. CD-ROM can store audio, text, and still photographic information on the same disc. High-quality (digital) motion video is also available. CD-ROM applications include On-Line Manuals, Personal Computer-Based Reference or HELP Systems, and Audiovisual Databases.

The same multimedia computer has very different properties from application to application. The difference is the application or software. You must know your functional requirements before choosing controlling software. Controlling software is usually prepared by trainers using an authoring system. The authoring system contains provisions for branching, scoring, etc., to which is added desired lesson material. Course authoring is complex; after choosing an authoring system, look for system experts to help or to prepare lessons.

9.4.8 Videotape

Refer to Figure 9-7. Videotape is a linear, passive medium. However, videotape can stimulate the learner through use of graphic techniques. It delivers a dynamic presentation of sequenced events. Use of videotape is good for interpersonal skill, management development, data processing, and technical subjects. It also captures the one-time-only presentation of live video or instructor-led programs.

Videotape is an effective way to present prerecorded messages. It also can be used to record and play back performances such as "How to Improve Sales Calls." You can play roles such as the manager with a difficult employee or operator of new equipment and store the ideal performance on tape. Thus, trainees can compare videotaped practice exercises with ideal situations. Storing practice exercises requires a combination of playback and recording equipment.

Many off-the-shelf videotapes are available. Since portable recording equipment is readily available, corporations often produce their own tapes. Character generators create and store special effects, while editing consoles speed editing tasks. Making videotapes requires an expert, trained staff because today's audiences expect broadcast-quality programs.

The VHS format (½-in tape) offers trainees the option of viewing cassettes at home. In worldwide applications, remember national differences. For example, videotape formats differ between England and North America.

9.4.9 Workbooks

Refer to Figure 9-8. Print is a commonly used instructional medium. Print use is normally passive. Workbooks offer trainees an opportunity to capture and recall new skills or knowledge. Workbooks are convenient. Programs that rely heavily on other media often use workbooks as a secondary instructional medium. Workbook effectiveness depends on instructional objectives and workbook design. For example, workbooks

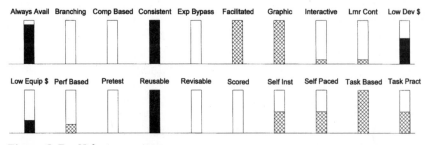

Figure 9-7. Videotape ratings.

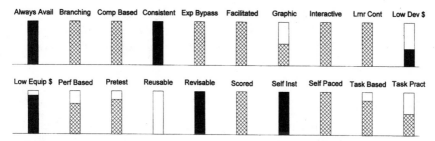

Figure 9-8. Workbook ratings.

can be used as retention pieces by letting trainees carry them away from an instructor-led or videotaped presentation. Employees may refer to workbooks at a later date. Workbooks are also valuable to employees who miss important presentations.

Studies show that trainees dislike reading from computer screens and that comprehension is lower if all text comes from the computer screen. A supplementary workbook should be used when CBT content includes heavy text use. By incorporating CBT-like branching features, the workbooks will be more effective.

Several methods are available to measure the reading level of print materials. Use computer-based tools such as Grammatik and RightWriter to check reading level and suggest possible grammatical improvements.

Structured writing principles and formatting techniques, such as Information Mapping, have been developed for effective documentation. Regular use of such principles will significantly improve instruction and job performance.

9.5 Performance Support Delivery Techniques and Devices

Job aids or performance support devices are an alternative or complement to instruction. Use job aids when:

1. tasks are infrequently performed,
2. required by regulation,
3. the cost of mistakes is too high,
4. tasks are very complex, or
5. tasks are likely to change.

Computer-based job aids have been called *Electronic Performance Support Systems* (EPSS).

The following discussions cover commonly used job aid approaches.

9.5.1 Rating Criteria for Job Aids

Be sure to read the following rating criteria definitions. Some of these criteria have the same names as criteria used to evaluate training delivery systems. Because we are now discussing job aids, these definitions are different.

- *Always Available (Always Avail).* Job aid availability to user. Job aids available to suit user's on-the-job needs.

- *Branching.* Pathing through job aid based on specific performance requirement or job situation.

- *Decision Aiding.* Decision-making information collected but not interpreted. Job aids make suggestions or recommendations, but users decide. Decision aids are not procedural.

- *Informational.* Informational aids contain some "who," "what," or "why" information. Informational aids are decision aiding, rather than procedural.

- *Low Development $ (Low Dev $).* Low development cost is the cost to develop the job aid. Computer-based approaches have high development costs. High development costs are affordable when the user population is large and the cost per user is low, or the results of incorrect performance are extreme. Examples are personal injury, potential equipment damage, or excessive operating cost associated with incorrect performance.

- *Low Equipment $ (Low Equip $).* Low equipment cost is the cost of job aid delivery hardware. For example, computers are more expensive than booklets, etc.

- *Procedural.* Job aids that list each step and the order in which it is to be performed. Procedural aids use branching to accommodate different situations arising during task performance. Procedural aids decide for the user.

- *Revisable.* The ability to change materials associated with a delivery approach. Optical discs for videodisc and CD-ROM players are only recorded once, and are not revisable. On the other hand, lectures and workbooks are easier to change. High-tech job aids that substitute for training are revised and distributed on computer networks daily.

- *Step Referent Illustrated (Step Ref Illust).* The object interacted with at the task-step level is illustrated. Exploded views and procedural aids illustrate task-step referents.

- *Task Location Illustrated (Task Loc Illust).* The general area or location of task performance is illustrated. This information shows the user where to go to perform task step(s). Procedural aids commonly contain task location illustrations.

9.5.2 Artificial Intelligence: Expert Systems

Refer to Figure 9-9. *Expert Systems* are a form of artificial intelligence. Expert systems analyze, design, diagnose, or monitor tasks within a narrow scope of human performance. These systems are computer programs that follow diagnostic and problem-solving processes of human experts. Expert systems are found on mainframe computers and PCs.

Expert systems techniques are based on:

- *Rules.* Knowledge represented as if-then rules with logical premises and conclusions.

- *Frames.* Knowledge structured for capturing regularly occurring circumstances.

- *Logic.* Logical predicates and assertions for forward and backward chaining inference.

- *Neural Network Processing.* Cognitive processes believed to be employed by the human brain.

Expert systems help in consistent decision making. They are used to create schedules, design layouts, offer expert advice, generate possible problem solutions, or monitor equipment. Expert systems can replace maintenance manuals or configure computer installations.

For maximum benefit, the expert system will explain how it reached a conclusion or why a line of inquiry was pursued. It must be dynamic, growing and changing as new information is received. Appropriate applications are critical decisions that:

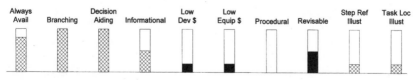

Figure 9-9. Expert system ratings.

1. Must be made quickly

2. Are made by experts

3. Involve eight or more variables

Expert system operators develop using the system without training. Apprentices using systems are productive faster. Expert systems can grow and change faster than new training can be developed.

9.5.3 Computer-Based Reference (CBR)

Refer to Figure 9-10. CBR is an on-line (look-up) reference system. It has information not given in training. It references major points or detailed information for computer system users. CBR can interface with computer-based training and computer applications software.

Computer-based reference shares the same computer technology used for job functions. It erases the distinction between training and job performance.

CBR applications include:

- On-line manuals, for business and software applications support

- Transfers from software applications to CBT and back

9.5.4 Computer Help Systems

Refer to Figure 9-11. Help systems have been called imbedded training. The name comes from the imbedding of "Help" information or instruction in applications software. Most help systems use a book metaphor and contain abbreviated versions of the user's manual. Help systems may be topically organized, providing access to application-specific information such as:

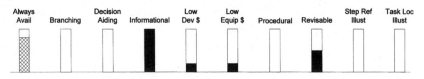

Figure 9-10.   CBR ratings.

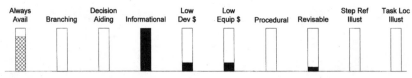

Figure 9-11.   Help system ratings.

- List of software features. Access is usually by keyword search or alphabetized list. Selecting a feature produces a description of how the feature works.

- Descriptions of keyboard commands.

Users of such systems frequently complain, "I know what I want to happen, but I don't know what they call it."

Other help systems are task-oriented and context-sensitive. In this case, when help is requested, the response is right for the task, screen, and field involved. This so-called "smart help" often tries to find the related user's manual passage.

9.5.5 Hypermedia

Refer to Figure 9-12. Hypermedia is a superset of Hypertext (see Section 9.5.7). The difference is that hypermedia information may be text, graphic, sound, or video sequences. Another difference is that a multimedia computer is required to display or reproduce hypermedia information. Other strengths and attributes of hypertext apply equally to hypermedia.

The following example illustrates how different information sources could be linked by a hypermedia application. Consider information on our thirty-fifth president, John F. Kennedy. Selecting a button labeled "The Man" causes a line-art graphic of his presidential portrait to display. Selecting a button labeled "Berliner" starts an audio track of his famous speech made at the Berlin Wall, where he said ". . . I am a Berliner. . . ." Selecting a button labeled "ask not" starts a video sequence of his famous speech where he said ". . . ask not what your country can do for you. . . ."

9.5.6 Hypertext

Refer to Figure 9-13. Hypertext is a computer-based, textual information retrieval tool. Hypertext is unlike the linear, book-style help system. It allows one to follow intuitive paths between linked pieces of information. Hypertext links are displayed as highlights or buttons in text. Selecting a link transports one down a pathway to related information. For example, while

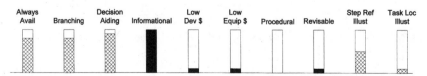

Figure 9-12. Hypermedia ratings.

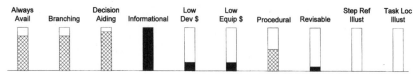

Figure 9-13. Hypertext ratings.

reviewing Hypertext information on mammals, one selects a button on the Order Chiroptera. The next information presented would be on several families of bats. Hypertext links are defined by the information preparer.

Well-designed Hypertext

1. Is organized in patterns familiar to the user

2. Shows the information organization and structure

3. Shows the current search's path through the information

Hypertext has elements of user control similar to learner control. Users are free to choose the links (and shortest paths) to necessary job-related information.

9.5.7   Printed Job Aids

Refer to Figure 9-14. Printed job aids include flow charts, decision charts, cookbooks, algorithms, and mylar-coated placards on equipment. These aids come in a variety of forms; common ones are described as follows:

- *Step-by-step lists of graphic and textual steps* to guide task performance. This format is useful for short tasks with steps that can be explained graphically. A step-by-step list is used to assemble a child's bicycle.

- *Decision charts* to guide decision making when several options are available. Use decision charts when if/then logic applies.

- *Flowcharts* guide decisions where considerable branching is involved, and clear yes/no answers are possible. This format may be confusing for long or complicated processes. Troubleshooters use flowcharts to diagnose equipment malfunctions.

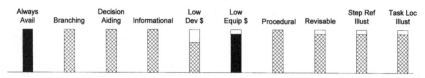

Figure 9-14.   Printed job aid ratings.

- *Checklists, worksheets, and forms* are used to document process information. They also may be used in planning tasks. These formats deal with "why," "what," and "who" information. Pilots use checklists to check aircraft systems before take-off.

9.6   Instructional Delivery Decision Review Checklist

The following questions should be asked of any technical training you consider using. These apply to off-the-shelf programs as well as ones made in your shop. A "no" answer to any of the following shows a serious defect in the instruction. Defective instruction should be discarded or improved before using.

1. *Is desired on-the-job performance the program's primary objective?*   Off-the-shelf programs rarely cover specific job-related performance. Off-the-shelf materials usually deal with common elements of skill needs. These materials can become the keystone of an effective program when combined with job specifics, task practice, certification, etc.

2. *Do the program's objectives match your skill, knowledge, and performance objectives?*   After establishing that a program has the desired results and job-related performance, do all the primary and intermediate objectives match? This is sometimes hard to do with the objectives in front of you, and almost unfair to expect from off-the-shelf courses.

3. *Do the program's criterion-referenced exercises match your criterion-referenced exercises?*   The measure of a program's intentions is criterion-level exercises. In a custom-developed program, your exercises should be included. In an off-the-shelf program, even when objectives are similar, be surprised to find matches with any of your exercises.

4. *Does the program's intended audience have the same characteristics critical to successful instruction?*   Are the program's audience performance requirements similar to those of your audience? Do your audience and the program's audience share common work and life experiences? Pay careful attention to the intended audience of off-the-shelf instruction. Programs with the correct objectives, exercises, etc. for the wrong audience may produce disastrous results.

5. *Does the program use more than one delivery approach?*   Are two or three different approaches used to make instruction more interesting and less monotonous?

6. *Is/are the program's delivery approach(es) consistent with your organization's?* Has the cost of new delivery equipment been budgeted? Can new delivery systems be reused? Will this reuse be a proper use of the medium? For example, if you buy interactive videodisc delivery systems now, are you forcing future programs to use interactive video regardless of specific program needs?

7. *Does the program use interactive delivery approaches?* Reading is not interactive! Pressing the <ENTER> key is not interactive! Interactivity comes from applying, interpreting, extrapolating, problem solving, and other forms of reasoned responses. Proponents of Accelerated Learning suggest instructional interactions every two to five minutes.

8. *Is the program consistent in its use of delivery approaches?* For example, are all knowledge tests done the same way? When program mechanics are consistent, the trainee only has to learn one set of rules. This reduces the confusion associated with using program materials.

9. *Are program activities such as knowledge tests and lectures delivered by multiple approaches?* Research found several different learning styles. Every trainee has a preferred learning style that works best for him or her. Using multiple approaches for the same instructional activity gives trainees choices and appeals to more learning styles. For example, consider using paper and pencil as well as computer-based knowledge exercises.

9.7   Cost and Time
Rules of Thumb

The following information is given with the caveat that it be used to understand proportions and significant relationships. It should not be used to bid the next job. Specifics make a big difference.

The following table gives the normal range of development times for common delivery approaches. For each delivery approach, development time is the time it takes to create one hour of delivered training. The methods can be compared directly to each other. For example, textual CBT requires between 10 (100/10) and 33⅓ (200/6) times the development hours as instructor-led for an hour of delivered instruction.

Delivery approach	Development hrs./Instructional hr.
Instructor-led	6–10
Workbook	40–50
Videotape	40–110
Textual CBT	100–200
Interactive videodisc	200–400

9.7.1 Decision/Selection Criteria

■ *Instructor-led programs* are valuable when quick reactions are required.

■ The instructional and efficiency advantages of *computer-based solutions* are possible when there is adequate development time and a large audience across which to prorate the costs.

■ *The largest part of training cost (65 to 70 percent) is trainee salary* during training. Expensive developments and delivery systems can save money when training is more efficient and shortened for many employees.

■ *The second largest part of training cost (15 to 20 percent) is travel expense* associated with off-site training. Again, with large audiences, on-site self-instruction or distance learning approaches will cut non-value-added travel time, travel fees, and save money.

■ *Job aids!* Job aids usually *cost less* than training and are developed faster. Job aids are being used in rapidly changing high-tech applications where training can't keep up. Add a step to your design process that tests the applicability of job aids to each of your program's knowledge objectives. Develop job aids when appropriate.

■ *Multimedia approaches* can be used. During design, consider major program activities (information presentation, exercises, practice, etc.) and your content needs. Choose delivery approaches best suited to each major need. This will stop bad compromises like reading books from computer screens.

Bibliography

Bovier, Connie, "How a High-Tech Training System Crashed and Burned," *Training,* August 1993.

Corrao, Phyllis M., "Customizing Off-the-Shelf Distance Learning," *Technical & Skills Training,* August/September 1993.

Heideman, Jim, "Selecting Media for Training," *Technical & Skills Training,* August/September 1992.

Steele, Jerry, "Training Technologies," *Technical & Skills Training,* October 1993.

10

Individualized Instructional Approaches

Angus Reynolds
EG&G Energy Measurements

Dr. Angus Reynolds *is an Instructional Technologist for EG&G Energy Measurements, where he leads development of advanced technology-based learning systems. Previously, he was Professor of Instructional Technology at the New York Institute of Technology. His work appears regularly in leading professional books and journals. His book* Technology Transfer: A Project Guide for International HRD *is the text for "International HRD" courses at several colleges and universities. He recently wrote* Globalization: The International HRD Consultant and Practitioner, *coauthored with Len Nadler. His* Selecting and Developing Media for Instruction, Third Edition, *coauthored with Ron Anderson, is a leading field manual and textbook on that topic. He has contributed chapters to several important works. These include* The ASTD Handbook of Instructional Technology *and both editions of* Handbook of Human Resource Development *and the* AMA Handbook of Human Resource Management and Development.

United Airlines' then-training director John Buchanan pronounced Buchanan's Law: "No amount of time and resources can teach someone what they already know." Individualized instruction offers the way to let people focus on their deficiencies while ignoring topics they have already mastered. What exactly, you may ask, is individualized instruction? The 27 experts who produced *The Trainer's Dictionary* provide us the following answer.

> An instructional technique in which the instruction is designed to be used by individual learners. The learner is taught only the material that is not already known, instead of taught everything in a specified curriculum as is true with traditional instruction. This is more than learners simply working on materials without regard to the activities of other learners in the same class. All individualized instruction is self-paced instruction. But not all self-paced instruction is individualized.

As long as we're trying to nail down just what it is, we should also determine what it isn't. Individualized instruction *may* be self-paced—learners working at their own speed to complete the learning assignment. But there are exceptions. Self-paced instruction is not necessarily individualized. Group instruction is self-paced when it operates at a speed set by learners rather than the instructor. Further, instruction may be individualized even though the pace is controlled by an instructor or facilitator.

What makes individualized instruction so great is that it is nearly always performance-based. It is usually specifically designed to provide the employee with the knowledge and skills required to perform the task on-the-job. What we know about adult learners affirms that individualized instruction matches their characteristic of wanting to learn things that are personally relevant.

In this chapter, we will explore three areas of individualized instruction: performance support, time-tested training methods, technology-based training, and then wind up with one person's ideas of what constitutes good training—one that deserves your endorsement.

10.1   Performance Support

The first step experienced instructional developers always take is to try to devise job aids. Anyone taught by Joe Harless will do an amazing job of finding a fit for job aids to solve any human performance problem. Why? They have learned that it is always cheaper, faster, and better (the only time you can get all three at once) to *help* people do their jobs than it is to train them to the same end. If used, job aids promise consistently flawless performance. This is particularly important if the results of wrong performance are critical. We can successfully generalize these circumstances to all performance support. Let's review the performance support field with a look at both traditional job aids and the latest performance support systems (PSS).

10.1.1 Traditional Job/Performance Aids

Job aids (also called *performance aids*) guide a user in taking correct on-the-job action. Take note that we call them *users*—not *learners*. Since job aids are built by trainers, some assume they provide instruction. They don't! They simply provide help. Of course good job aid designers always provide ample directions. When the job aid is complex, directions may not be enough. You must teach the user how to use it.

Inappropriate?   There are three instances when a job aid is not appropriate.

1. When there is no time to use it. For example, a police officer can't look up "drop that gun" in another language. It must be learned in advance of the need.
2. When people served by the potential job aid user want to depend on an "expert." For example, a medical doctor might benefit from use of a job aid. In our society, using one wouldn't work. Patients would see this as evidence of flawed or incomplete training.
3. A job aid will only help if used. If, for any reason, the user might ignore it, a job aid would be a poor choice.

Formats.   Job aids come in desktop, pocket, and equipment-related types. Desktop job aids are usually found in an office environment. Their format may vary, but it is most likely common 8½-x-11 or A4-size paper.

The "wallet" or pocket job aid is best for help that must be accessible whenever needed. It suits workers away from a desk who need a format or checklist. One of the best well-known examples is the "Miranda" card police officers use to accurately advise accused persons of their rights. Pocket job aids are usually a single card.

Equipment-related job aids should be physically attached to the equipment. The best-known example of a job aid is the pilot's checklist, an on-equipment aid. On simple aircraft, the list is on a plate riveted to the airplane cockpit within the pilot's view. Figure 10-1 shows an on-equipment aid.

To Rewind
Shut off water, remove nozzle leaving coupling open for release of pressure. Lay hose out flat. Place either end fitting in center slot of reel, and thread hose through roller bars. Rewind by turning knob.

Figure 10-1.   Example On-Equipment Job Aid.

Job Aid Types.   There are four basic job aid types. They are algorithm, cookbook, decision table, and worksheet. Good job aids may be combined with any or all of these.

Even if *algorithm* isn't a household word, this type of aid is very familiar. It usually has decision-making rules too complex for representation in a decision table. Algorithms have the appearance of simple flowcharts and ask questions. Often answers are simply "yes" or "no." However, we can employ other questions when they lead more directly to the outcome. Figure 10-2 shows an example of an algorithm job aid many Americans see every year.

Cookbooks guide the user through sequential activities. When the order of steps isn't critical, the cookbook can become a checklist. Cookbooks usually number sequential steps. Illustrations are often employed to help the user, and clarify difficult points. As Confucius said, "a picture is worth one thousand words."

Decision tables list rules for action. The rules may not look like computer code, but usually they follow the same sort of if- and if-then sequence. Creating useful decision tables requires great care. They must be developed exhaustively and accurately.

Worksheets (and cookbooks) are best for sequential tasks. They are different from checklists in that they collect written responses from the user. These responses come from calculations, summarize date, or gather information for further use. Worksheets come in three types to match: information collection, matrix, and computation. In a computation example, when following a procedure that includes a calculation, the user records the results before proceeding to the next step. A familiar example of this type of activity is the U.S. income tax worksheets. Figure 10-3 shows a matrix job aid.

Schedule X—Use if your filing status is Single			
If the amount on Form 1040, line 37 is: *Over—*	But not *over—*	Enter on Form 1040 line 38	of the *amount over—*
$0	$22,100	.... 15%	$0
22,100	53,500	$3,315.00 + 28%	22,100
53,500	115,000	$12,107.00 + 31%	53,500
115,000	250,000	$31,172.00 + 36%	115,000
250,000	....	$79,772.00 + 39.6%	250,000

Figure 10-2.   Example Algorithm Job Aid.

Chill Factor (Equiv. Temp on Exposed Flesh)

	30	5	−2	−11	−18
Wind	25	7	0	−7	−15
Speed	20	12	3	−4	−9
	15	16	11	1	−6
	10	21	16	9	2
		35	30	25	20
		Air Temperature (°F)			

Figure 10-3. Example Matrix Job Aid.

When to Use Job Aids. Job aids are a good choice when turnover is high or the task is simple. Research shows that, if you overestimate the knowledge of the user, the aid will likely not be useful. The simplicity of job aids also suggests them when you have only limited time or resources to devote to training. *Selecting and Developing Media for Instruction* (Reynolds and Anderson, 1992) recommends choosing job aids in these situations:

- Behavior sequences that are long and complex
- Tasks that involve readings and tolerances
- Tasks aided by the presence of illustrations
- Tasks that use reference information such as tables, graphs, flowcharts, and schematic diagrams
- Tasks with branching step structure
- Tasks that are performed rarely or the consequences of error are high

A Handbook of Job Aids (Rossett and Gautier-Downes, 1991) suggests job aids also when:

- The performance depends on a large body of information.
- The performance is dependent on knowledge, procedures, or approaches that change frequently.
- Employee performance can be improved through self-assessment and correction with new or emphasized standards in mind.

Tips for Devising Job Aids. Here is a collection of ideas that have proven worthwhile for building job aids.

- Write in short sentences and simple words.
- Wherever possible, use symbols such as arrows, underlines, and boxes to direct the user's activity and call attention to important items.

- Use algorithms for decision-making tasks.
- In algorithms, place the most frequently needed actions first.
- Use cookbooks or worksheets for sequential tasks and decision tables.
- In decision tables, sequence actions in the most likely order of use.
- In making a decision table, first make an algorithm or flowchart of the whole system. Then make the decision table to reflect the algorithm or flowchart.
- If a decision table has many conditions, convert it to an algorithm.
- In a worksheet, provide the user a copy of an already completed example.
- If the worksheet is complex, consider a cookbook to process the directions.
- Construct worksheets in small increments, written in precise terms.
- Present when-to-perform elements first, and what-to-do elements second.
- When the task combines characteristics, combine the job aid types.

Evolving Job Aids.   The use of technology to provide the job aid function is natural, although they are then not called job aids. The term *job aid* is reserved for manual, as opposed to technology-based aids. The simplest technology-based job aid is an expert system, which can incorporate all types of job aids. We usually see expert systems as one component of performance support systems. Figure 10-4 shows the evolution of performance support delivery. Remember, manual job aids won't go away. They will always be part of the performance support picture. Now let's have a look at performance support systems.

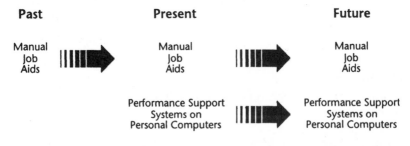

Figure 10-4. Evolution of Performance Support. (© *Copyright Angus Reynolds, 1993. All rights reserved.*)

10.1.2 Performance Support Systems (PSS)

For a long time, job aids have regularly helped people to work beyond their experience level. As computers began to be used by everyday workers to accomplish their jobs, the practicality of putting the job aid into a computer couldn't trail far behind. *Performance support systems* (PSS) are just technological job aids—really "a job aid in a box." Originally the term electronic performance support systems (EPSS) was used, but it is now less used. The "electronic" in the term is unnecessary, since all PSS must, by definition, be electronic. Let's look at the components that make them up and examples of how they are used.

Components.   Most authorities agree that performance support systems have three components. These components are:

- Expert system
- Computer-assisted instruction (CAI)
- Text retrieval

Of course, not all systems have all three components. They represent the total functionality that may be present in such systems.

In most cases, the expert system forms the backbone of the PSS because it is directly aimed at helping the employee do his or her job. The expert system provides consistent help in performing the task. The help can be based on many circumstances that vary considerably and interact in complex ways. Such advice leads to consistently accurate performance and high quality.

Sometimes the designer of the PSS determines that the employee should *understand* some aspect of the activity—not simply do it. In that case, the PSS can either offer training or simply provide it. The training will be CAI, the component of technology-based learning that teaches. This CAI is different from what we have usually seen over the past two decades. Instead of teaching the employee extensively about the topic, only the precise knowledge needed at that point in the activity is taught. This is called *granular* CAI. Granular CAI presented within a PSS is both context-specific and just-in-time.

Another support component boosted by technology is access to documents—called *text retrieval.* Employees need access to manuals, schematics, and procedures. PSS text retrieval avoids leafing through thick documents that are all too often poorly organized for quick access to needed information. Hypertext access can link text in one place or document to text in another in a flash.

When we think of combining the power and usefulness of the components, we can characterize each one by the type of help it provides. The expert system component provides advice and can be called a consultant. CAI provides instruction, so we can consider it a professor, instructor, or teacher. Text retrieval provides text access, and so functions as a librarian. Figure 10-5 shows the components of performance support systems.

Examples.   One example is a credit approval performance support system running in several banks. The PSS supports account agents in the analysis of financial statements, market data, and information about a company to approve credit lines for working capital. Without a PSS, a detailed analysis and assessment of the working capital needs for credit approval takes an experienced professional a week of work. This includes gathering data, then analyzing and writing a 6- to 10-page report. The report is submitted to a committee for approval. Using the performance support system, analysis and report generation take only 10 minutes and can be completed by any account manager.

In a manufacturing example, one plant produces a variety of waste that can be categorized, handled, and disposed of in 23 waste streams. The streams are referred to by number, such as W-17. The difference between one stream and another is often the absence or presence of one contaminant among three or four. Accidental inclusion of a particular toxic substance in waste labeled differently could result in refusal of the disposal site to accept any future waste from the factory. The waste system PSS helps workers to place waste in the correct waste stream and ultimately to assist waste processors to properly handle and process the waste for disposal.

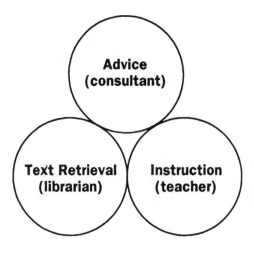

Figure 10-5.   Performance Support System Components. (*Reprinted with permission from* Building Multimedia Performed Support Systems, *McGraw-Hill, 1994. All rights reserved.*)

Performance support is a powerful tool for trainers to use. But like every other tool, PSSs are not the universal solution to all problems. There are plenty of cases where training is the best approach. In the remainder of this chapter, we will examine conventional and technology-based individualized training approaches. Next, let's consider the time-tested conventional techniques.

10.2 Time-Tested Training Methods

Many specialized technology-based training methods are available. They have a definite place—when they are the best solution to improving human performance. Cost-effectiveness is often the determining factor when choosing a conventional solution that works over a technology-based solution that solves the problem in another way. In this section, let's consider three tried and true individualized methods. They are *on-the-job training, independent study,* and *self-directed instructional packages.*

10.2.1 On-the-Job Training (OJT)

OJT is probably the most common training method in use today. In an OJT program, the worker-learner performs under the supervision of someone who is qualified to do the job. Good OJT provides observation with guided practice in a practice situation, while the learner engages in productive work. Sometimes the process is formally divided into OJT and OJE (evaluation) as two distinct phases.

Vestibule Training. A special breed of OJT is *vestibule training.* Vestibule training is instruction delivered to new employees before they start regular work. It is conducted off the factory floor or work site, using duplicate equipment and re-creating or modeling the work environment, or some aspect of it. Although the term is heard less often today, vestibule training is widely used.

Apprenticeship. Another kind of OJT is *apprenticeship.* Apprenticeship is a whole program of OJT HRD activities provided to develop a skilled tradesperson. The apprentice takes part in a formal program based on law and written agreements that may involve government and unions. In a classic program, the apprentice serves in a formal program under a master or journeyman on a one-on-one basis for one to six years. The majority of apprenticeship programs are three to five years long.

Formal or Structured OJT. OJT has a bad reputation in some quarters. It has been widely abused or given only lip service in some organizations where it has loose structure. The problem is that the employee may receive no training of any kind during the period called OJT. Sometimes any learning depends completely on the motivation of the employee to find out. At its worst, OJT transfers bad habits or attitudes to the new employee. There are cases when "they will learn it OJT" simply means turning employees loose to work at their jobs long enough to become proficient.

Because of the poor reputation of some OJT, some organizations take care to differentiate how they do it. To differentiate properly conducted OJT from the poorly done version, it is called *formal* or *structured OJT*. Formal or structured OJT is only OJT as it was always meant to be, and as it has always been conducted in some organizations. There are performance objectives, a schedule, assignment to a qualified employee, and a checklist that must be signed off as each objective is met.

10.2.2 Independent Study

Independent study could be any method of studying alone, but we have something more specific in mind. The study is often organized, structured, endorsed, and possibly supervised by some organization. Formal independent study is uncommon in organizations. To set up independent study, the learner and the organization need only agree on a goal, a method of reaching the goal through independent effort, a schedule, and a way to determine that the goal has been reached. In *The Adult Learner: A Neglected Species* (1979), Malcolm Knowles presents these activities in detail and sets out a scheme to make independent study a formalized, useful activity. There are examples to follow and it works!

In contrast, self-instruction is any learning situation in which learners take responsibility for their own learning without relying on an instructor or other leaders of learning. Although we usually think of formal independent study, this is the informal variety. The *Independent Scholar's Handbook* (Gross, 1982) comes immediately to mind. The *Handbook* is crammed with ideas for winning success in a chosen field by one's own bootstraps.

10.2.3 Self-directed Instructional Packages

Self-directed learning is an instructional design in which the learner takes the initiative to master predetermined material. The concept of individuals directing their own HRD activities is theoretically sound. George Piskurich provides complete detailed coverage in *Self-Directed Learning* (1993). We describe self-directed learning as what may be completed alone using self-instructional packages, or conducted with the help of others. The "others" can include instructors, mentors, peers, resource people, and tutors.

A self-directed learning package is a structured kit of activities that is the result of the same instructional design and development process we use to produce our best training. The learner is presented with a study plan and all the materials needed to carry it out. These are typically text. Conceptually, the package could include at least audio- and videotapes and any other learning resource that could be accessed by a person studying alone. Such packages, also called *learning resource packages,* can be very effective with the self-motivated learners that typically succeed when studying independently.

Self-directed learning has a bright future, because there is a strong trend in that direction. Figure 10-6 illustrates this trend. Expect to see commonly used learning activities that we would, in today's world, consider "highly creative." To a greater degree, the learners will be in control of their own HRD activities. The focus of their study will be the result of their personal interest and own initiative.

This completes our look at non-technology-based learning. Now let's move on to the area of learning that is growing the fastest, has changed most dramatically in the past decade, yet still offers enormous room for additional progress.

10.3 Technology-Based Training

Technology-based training is more properly called *Technology-Based Learning* (TBL). Technology-based learning resources teach, manage, and support instruction. That is important. What is more important is that they also have enormous power to make learning easier, more appropriate, or more fun. The components of TBL include computer-supported learning resources, computer-managed instruction, and computer-assisted instruction. The Technology-Based Learning Model is shown in Figure 10-7.

Past	Present	Future
Non Self-Directed	Rarely Self-Directed	Commonly Self-Directed

Figure 10-6. Future Self-Directed Learning.

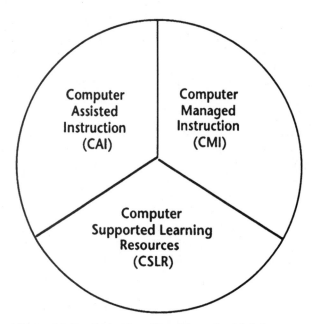

Figure 10-7. Technology-Based Learning Model.

My favorite TBL definition was given by a man called the "father of CBE." CBE (or computer-based learning) is a synonym for TBL. Donald Bitzer, of the University of Illinois, who led the pioneering PLATO project, said that CBE is "anytime a person and a computer get together . . . and one of them learns something."

10.3.1   Getting the Names Right

In *Selecting and Developing Media for Instruction,* Ron Anderson wrote that CBL has a "lexicon replete with jargon and acronyms apparently designed to baffle all but the initiated." He was right. What about CBL, CBI, CBE, and CBT? What are those terms? This part of the technology-based alphabet soup describes the umbrella term for all learning-related activities. It started in the universities, where research pioneered the use of computers for learning. The universities coined the term computer-based *education,* or "CBE." When industrial organizations began to use the CBE technology, they substituted the more comfortable term *training* to create CBT. One of the biggest users in the early days was the now-divided Bell Telephone system. Bell and other organizations chose to use the more neutral term *instruction,* resulting in CBI. Still, others who prefer thinking in learner-oriented terms preferred CBL.

Experienced users know that all the terms just mentioned are synonymous. All include the components:

- Computer-Assisted Instruction (CAI)
- Computer-Managed Instruction (CMI)
- Computer-Supported Learning Resources (CSLR)

Trends show that, in the future, CBL will not be limited to personal computers. It will reside in the technology-based tools employees use at work. The same trend in performance support systems was reflected in Figure 10-4. Since "computer" will become less appropriate as time goes on, leaders in the field are beginning to suggest *technology*-based learning (TBL), the term used in this book.

10.3.2   CBT Confusion

There is a problem. Some HRD practitioners use "CBT" as the *only* term. Often they are HRD generalists or specialists in another area. By not distinguishing CAI *lessons,* discussion of the components CAI, CMI, and CSLR becomes difficult and confusing. People using "CBT" this way seldom realize the confusion this can generate. Usually, they are completely unaware of the full range of technology-based learning!

Let's move on now to explore this range. As Maria Von Trapp sings in *The Sound of Music,* we'll "start at the very beginning . . . a very good place to start."

10.3.3   Does It Work?

I was very surprised recently to hear a question straight out of the '70s. "Does it work? Will the TBL teach the employees effectively?" People used to wonder whether computers were effective in presenting instruction. New organizations struggled with the question of whether they should use TBL. Many staged experiments to determine whether it really "worked" long after that question had really been answered. Finally, in 1980, research ended all this wasted activity. Kulik, Kulik, and Cohen's landmark study determined that TBL (then called CBE) worked as well as traditional instruction, *and is significantly faster.*

10.3.4   Computer-Managed Instruction (CMI)

CMI isn't familiar to many trainers. This surely reflects its less frequent use, not its inherent worth. Why should it be the best place to start? Here are some reasons:

- It is chronologically and logically first
- It provides the most delivery bang for the least development buck
- CAI and CSLR flow logically out of it

CMI *is* the management of instruction by computer. CMI can serve independently in support of instruction. Learning resources do not have to be technology-based. That it is not as familiar as CAI may reflect the less romantic managing of instruction compared with an "exotic" training method. The distinction is that CMI does not directly involve learning. CMI offers the power to make learning efficient, so it will receive increasing recognition as more organizations begin to use it. The modes of CMI are:

- Testing
- Prescription generation
- Record keeping

Before we discuss CMI, look over Figure 10-8. It illustrates the complete CMI concept, including the three modes. The test on the learning objectives is first. It leads to the instruction prescription of the most efficient learning resources for each case. The background represents the continuous storage of records of the learner's overall success and current progress.

As interest in individualized instruction grew, so did demands on time and effort to score grades, maintain individual records, and summarize learner and class results. CMI is a device to help instructors cope with growing clerical actions. Central system CMI evolved exceptional sophistication in the past. On the principal systems, it was the most heavily used capability. Until the current generation of personal computers, limited processing power and storage made CMI impractical. Today the needed power is there. It will soon approach the power of the best central versions.

CMI is a tool as strong as it sounds. Several years ago United Airlines proved very effective use of TBL solely through use of CMI. Remember, economy of effort is typical with CMI use. A given amount of resources, if dedicated to CMI, can offer a larger HRD reward than CAI. For example, take your entire videotape course on a given subject. You can make it even better with CMI. You relate the videotapes to objectives, and create the learning management structure. You will also reduce individual student effort. Then, when a learner fails to master one (or more) of the objectives, the CMI system suggests the proper video(s) to learn the need content. A comparable effort devoted to building CAI lessons might only replace a single videotape! Now let's briefly examine each mode of CMI.

Testing.   Testing measures the learner's knowledge of specified objectives before and after study. CAI quizzes called progress checks determine

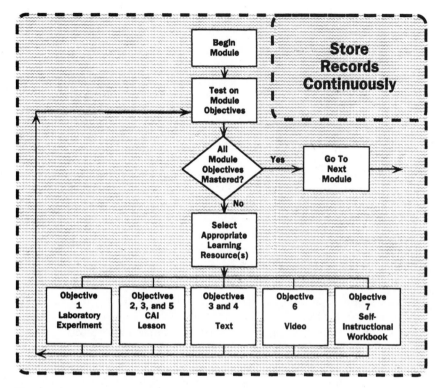

Figure 10-8. Computer-Managed Instruction Model.

the state of learning in progress in a lesson. A glance at Figure 10-8 shows that these are different from CMI events. CMI testing offers learning efficiency by verifying the learner's mastery of the objectives. This offers the possibility of graduating the learner without instruction, based solely on knowledge of the subject (remember Buchanan's Law?). How much money could organizations save if they pretested for most training? Testing is the foundation of CMI, since it accurately provides the information needed to prescribe learning activities.

Prescription Generation. The CMI system generates an instructional prescription only for each unmastered learning objective. Therefore, each learner receives an individualized prescription. As you, the learner, or I approach a new subject we bring different backgrounds and experiences. Each of us may know differing parts of the subject, but not all of it. We will each receive different prescriptions determined by the design of the CMI system. Each of us will only study those learning resources that support our individual unmastered objective(s). This shortens the time each learner must study and is the basis for instructional efficiencies associated with TBL. How much money could organizations save if they used this individualization for most training?

Record Keeping.   The CMI system generates and stores records of individual and group progress. An important feature is automatic generation of these records. There is also no need to keep a closet with shelves piled high with old records and reports. You can look only at those statistics and records you really need. The individual grade book is usually accessible to the learner.

In the practical world of learning, the use of CMI can often produce a concrete financial saving compared with traditional methods. CMI may be the best way to begin use of TBL in an organization. Now let's look at the workhorse of TBL, the computer that teaches—CAI.

10.3.5   Computer-Assisted Instruction (CAI)

CAI is both loved and hated. People love it because it has produced some remarkable, if not fantastic, success stories. Others lack faith in it because of experience with bad lessons or a dismally failed project. Most of these failures were caused by a lack of analysis and planning with resulting mismatch between instructional needs and computer system capabilities. Some were simply poor quality work. You and I want neither and we don't have to settle for less than the best.

CAI is the use of a computer in the actual *instructional* process. It is the use of a computer to interact directly with the student for presenting content. The various forms in which we can apply CAI are called modes. When you use CAI as a medium of instruction, it will be in one of these six modes:

- Tutorial
- Drill and Practice
- Instructional Game
- Modeling
- Simulation
- Problem Solving

The combination of computer and video called *interactive video* (IVD) is also simply CAI. It is not a separate mode, since it does the function of one of the existing modes. CAI may also control other media that provide the learner with necessary reference materials, performance aids, and clerical services, and simulate environmental or laboratory facilities.

CAI is a medium of instruction. Film, textbooks, and videotape are other instructional media. CBL, CMI, and CBLR (all covered in this chapter) are *not* media. Now let's briefly examine each of the modes of CAI.

Tutorial.   Because of the flexibility and capability of a computer to provide branching instruction, it can assume the role of an infinitely patient tutor. The process in a good tutorial advances as the finest tutor would personally undertake the process. Illustrations describing the method used by Socrates are often used to explain the structure of a tutorial.

A typical tutorial lesson presents some information—and then checks the learner's understanding. This process repeats throughout the lesson. Based on the learner's understanding, the learner's path continues to another point. If the learner did not understand, the tutorial presents the first point in a new way. The reinforcement process provides corrective comments to the learner. Learning *cannot* be passive. A good tutorial uses *branching*. It keeps the learner actively involved in the learning process. This structure is represented in Figure 10-9.

Poor tutorials are derisively called "page turners" and have little or no interactivity. Beware anytime you see a universally present message "Press Space Bar to Continue." It is the trademark of a page turner. Some HRD generalists are fooled into thinking that pressing the spacebar is a form of interactivity. It is simply a psychomotor act. The interactivity that counts is intellectual. Figure 10-10 shows the general linear structure.

Why, if one is better, would anyone develop or use the less effective design? The answer lies in the greater effort needed to build the branching lesson. When CAI must be created "for a price," the result is often less interactivity.

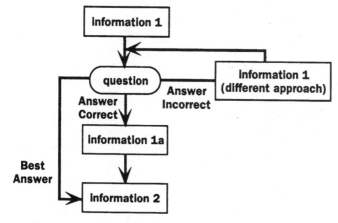

Figure 10-9.   Classic Tutorial.

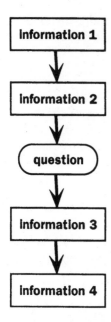

Figure 10-10. Linear CAI.

Drill and Practice.   Drill and practice is a valuable tool and also a very familiar mode of CAI. One reason we see it often is that it takes less effort to produce than the other modes. Drill and practice existed long before there was anything called a computer. It is repetitive presentation of problems to the learner. For example, "How much is two plus three?" When the learner answers, another question follows, such as "how much is three plus four?" Usually, after a given number of problems, the learner learns the total number of questions presented, number right . . . and wrong. Figure 10-11 shows the drill and practice structure.

The addition problems example typifies the drill and practice technique, but is not the only form. The drill and practice mode of CAI is successful with far more complex subject matter. Drill and practice is a good choice for learning terminology or the steps in a procedure. Sometimes, in simulations, the "simulation" cannot actually simulate anything beyond the procedure to be learned. The learner is asked to repeat the experience until the desired level of performance is reached. Another possibility is to use a real full simulator to repeatedly practice one limited procedure.

Instructional Games.   The term "game" does not mean frivolous activity. Games are the problem child of CAI. Instructional games are a completely valid and "professional" way to stimulate learning. In some organizations, powerful individuals have had difficulty believing that

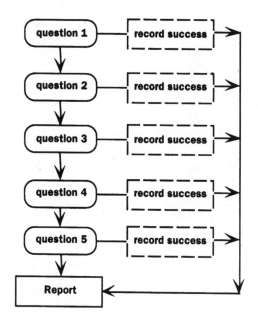

Figure 10-11. Drill and Practice Model. (© *Copyright Angus Reynolds, 1993. All rights reserved.*)

learners who enjoy the learning could be having a worthwhile experience. In fact, the use of games struck a deadly blow to some projects. Because of this prejudice, this mode of CAI is not used in all organizations. Unfortunately, the dividing line between amusement and learning is not always easily clear. It probably is unneeded anyway. The point is that learning while "playing" is, nevertheless, learning.

An instructional game has goals, scoring (usually), and an element of competition—that may be solitaire self-competition or multiple-player. There is a conflict that serves as a barrier to reaching the goal. All of this is governed by rules. In a CAI game, the computer looks up the tables, calculates, and keeps score. The learners can concentrate on the events of the game. Figure 10-12 shows the instructional game model.

Models form the basis for many instructional games. Let's move now to the models mode of CAI.

Modeling.   A model is a nonrealistic representation of the system (or representation may be unachievable). Modeling is the use of the technology-based system to represent another system or process. The learner is usually free to change values and observe the effects of the change on the model. For example, imagine a population model. We can model population accurately, but it does not lend itself to realistic representation. The

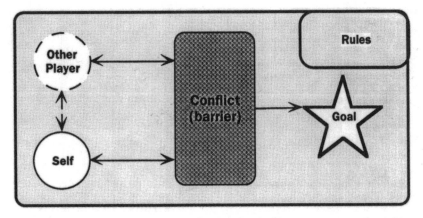

Figure 10-12. Instructional Game Model. (© *Copyright Angus Reynolds, 1993. All rights reserved.*)

learner might change demographic variables such as birth rate, infant mortality, or death rate in the model. The model would then reveal the results such new parameters would generate, if they actually took place. The display may be in a table or graph. The learner can see the effects on the population over time to learn.

Simulation.   Simulation is the representation of a situation or device, with a degree of fidelity. Somewhat like models, it allows learners to see and practice a wanted performance. Simulation provides practice that, if done in the real world, would be costly, dangerous, foolish, impossible, impractical, inconvenient, unwise, or all of these.

In this mode, the computer simulates the item of equipment, device, system, or subsystem. The simulation enables the learner to experience operating that equipment. A strength of simulation is that the learning can happen without destruction of the equipment or harm to the learner or others. Practice with a real item may tie up costly equipment and run the risk of damage in the process. Simulation techniques are extremely desirable for training in subjects where the learner must assess information and begin correct action within a short time. This is a characteristic of many high-technology occupations.

Methods of simulation include:

- Computer
- Hybrid (combined manual and computer)
- Manual

Simulation done exclusively, or nearly exclusively, by PCs and other electronic devices, is called *computer* simulation. Desktop computers communicate with mechanically built simulators through simple electronic converters to insert faults or change system line-ups at the press of a button. This combination of computer and manual simulation is *hybrid* simulation. We could mount pressure switches, gauges, a tank, and a pump on a roll-around cart to simulate the operation of a large system. This type of simulation, without computer, is considered *manual* simulation.

Simulation *fidelity* is a description of its realness or degree of accuracy. We can rank simulation fidelity as:

- low
- medium
- high

Research has shown that high fidelity is not needed for learning procedural tasks. Often, complex is *not* better, just more confusing. The appropriate fidelity level may depend upon the stage in which the learner exists in the overall training program. Low fidelity could be better for new learners, while high fidelity would be more suited for advanced learners.

The categories of simulation are either part-task or whole-task. A *whole-task* simulation is one in which training is provided for the complete task to be performed, instead of providing the learning experience in stages. The massive simulators used in nuclear power tend to be whole-task as the operator crews complete all or most of their training in this environment. The aircraft industry, on the other hand, uses smaller computer-based simulation to complement its full-scale flight simulators. These are *part-task* simulators.

The methods, category, and fidelity combine to provide 12 possible simulation types. Figure 10-13 shows the simulation model which illustrates the possible combinations.

Simulators.   We must distinguish between *simulation* and *simulators*. Simulation is a strategy. Simulators are special-purpose hardware devices that provide simulation exclusively. In many technical occupational fields, practice before using the actual equipment is both helpful and important. The classic examples of simulators are aircraft flight crew and nuclear power reactor operators. Both industries use very complex, costly, massive, special, specific, and highly realistic simulators to provide instruction in critical occupations. In both cases, the feeling is close as possible to the real thing.

The resulting learning experiences approximate the benefits of hands-on practice with the actual equipment. David C. Paquin, of Niagara Mohawk Power, says:

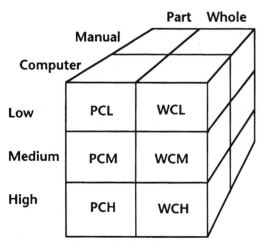

Figure 10-13. The Simulation Model. (*Reprinted with permission from* Selecting and Developing Media for Instruction, *Van Nostrand Reinhold, 1992. All rights reserved.*)

This often provides greater insight into the cause and effect relationship depicted. The special control features and feedback mechanisms can sometimes provide the student the opportunity to see and understand complex electrical, mechanical and thermal phenomena. Learners can then see [a] phenomenon not viewable in either an actual operating unit or in the normal training simulator. Only meters, indication lights, and control switches are available there for student interaction. All this combines to enhance the training experience and results in a better retention and overall knowledge of the subject material.

It is possible to combine strategy and hardware. The proper role of the computer learning station in an organization with a simulator is to supplement the specialized simulator, not replace it. The combination of simulation capability with a properly developed training program can increase the quality of training in the classroom and during full-scale simulator sessions. The airlines recognized and developed the advantage of this dual simulation-simulator method. Training on a learning station before the simulator session enables the simulator to put the trainee's knowledge to the test in a realistic way. The more costly special simulator then does not simply teach or provide experience. It tests the learner's real knowledge of the equipment. It does it in a way that other means cannot.

Problem Solving. In the past, problem solving was the least common mode of CAI in industrial HRD. That is changing as more employees use computers to do their work. In problem solving, the learner uses the computer itself as a tool to solve a work-related problem. Any software may be used depending on the skill the learner needs. Problem solving has always been a key element in math and science instruction. For an HRD example, one company's managers must learn to manage an inventory of fuel oil. Each manager uses a spreadsheet developed by the company to track inventory. The managers are presented with a month-by-month situation and asked to manage the inventory.

10.3.6 Computer-Supported Learning Resources (CSLR)

Computer-Supported Learning Resources do not teach, nor do they manage the instruction. They do make learning easier, more appropriate, or more fun. Formerly, CSLR was the least often seen component of computer-based learning. That has changed. A library is a noncomputer learning resource. We use a CSLR in the same way as a library, except a useful CSLR is always supported by a computer program. The computer program expedites the retrieval, examination, and manipulation of the information.

Let's distinguish between Computer-Supported Learning Resources (CSLR) and the learning resources which CMI prescribes. A learning resource prescribed by CMI is anything predetermined to *teach* its associated learning objective. The learning resource prescribed by CMI may be a CAI lesson, videotape, textbook, audiotape, lecture, or any other learning experience. CSLR is a completely separate part of CBL. A CSLR does not directly teach. It is, as its name suggests, a *resource* from which one may learn.

The modes of CSLR are:

- Database
- Hypermedia
- Communications
- Performance support systems

You may be comfortable with the term *database*. It is the oldest form of CSLR. It is a good exemplar of the type. A database is a pool of information, useful to a learner, but does not (itself) teach. It only provides information that we can use to learn.

Hypermedia is a newer mode of CSLR. Hypermedia is what databases have been waiting for! It provides a friendly front end to permit the user to apply the data based on individual interest. It is the opposite of CAI's structured and predetermined way. The computer program smoothes sophisticated retrieval, examination, and manipulation of the data.

Another mode of CSLR is communications. The information superhighway was made to order for CSLR. Communications as a learning resource can take many forms. We can record comments and notes in the computer for later use. Shared files can help information sharing among users with like interests. Individuals and groups can exchange notes among themselves. Instantaneous communication is possible among users of a network of any size. Learning specialists use this capability to exchange information. The learner and a (remote) subject matter expert can also communicate. Computers and communication networks also ease distance learning as video teleconferencing and computer conferencing. The shared network can be your own company's or a commercial information resource such as Compuserve.

Note that since performance support systems are not focused on learning, they are included as a mode of CSLR. They qualify as a CSLR because they are computer-based and don't teach.

CSLRs may reach their potential before the year 2000, but they await some ancillary elements to be in place. Some additional requirements are:

1. More low-cost or free public information bases are needed.

2. Better communications links such as promised by the information superhighway must facilitate connections.

3. *Development tools* (as there are for CAI and CMI) are required to make CSLR implementation easier.

4. Users (you and I) require access to even more personal computer power, bigger memory, and storage.

5. Employers need to see the clearly defined results that make them a good investment for the organization.

Some items on this list may suggest to you that CSLRs are not going to reach their potential in HRD anytime next week. That may be. But the first four items are surely going to appear. Then it will be up to you and me to make number five happen.

10.3.7 Disc-based Technologies and Interactive Multimedia (IM)

The real power of interactive multimedia is *not* the often glitzy graphics shown, but the method "behind the scenes." It is the computer program that controls the graphics. It is the result of the coming together of two major technologies. Interactive multimedia (IM) receives separate attention in the public mind because of the different talent needed to create it and marketing efforts to "sell something new." Much IM is not related to learning. When it is, it is only one more way of packaging CAI or CSLR.

Interactive Videodisc (IVD). Technical and skills trainers have exploited IVD technology quite effectively. The best IVD examples were dazzling. IVD technology places media display under computer control. It combines moving and still video images with computer text and graphics and audio in dynamic interactive learning programs not previously known. The characteristics of the basic videodisc technology are:

- The 12-in platter holds about 30 minutes of linear-play video on each side. It has synchronized dual channels of audio or 54,000 still pictures with limited audio per frame.
- Analog video and audio severely limit editing changes
- Read-only technology results from permanently recorded impressions on the disc. After the disc is mastered, change is not possible.

There are three levels of interactive video. They are:

- Level one—provides control through a manual keypad.
- Level two—uses a built-in microprocessor. It permits limited programming and resident memory.
- Level three—interfaces in real time with a PC. This greatly improves programming possibilities and adds huge quantities of memory.

IVD technology is now about 15-years-old. The stages in the life cycle of technology are shown in Figure 10-14. As a technology, IVD has reached

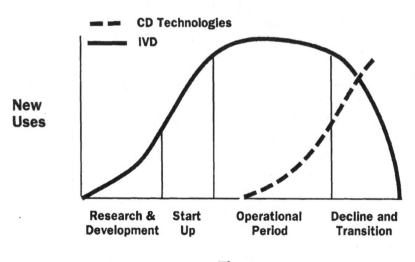

Figure 10-14. Life Cycle of Disc Media.

maturity and is well into its operational period. There are many fine pro-grams in the IVD format in use and available. Videodisc players are rugged, reliable, and will continue to be serviceable for a long time.

Instructional technologists have always known that the 12-in laser disc is an interim technology that would eventually be replaced by digital video. Today, learning stations for digital video are cheaper than for IVD. Most new training projects will be in the digital video arena. Although digital video does not strictly require a CD, it is often delivered on one. For that reason we can consider them as CD-based technologies

CD-based Technologies.   IVD and IM use optical disc video storage technologies. There are significant technical differences between 12-in IVD and a 12-cm compact disc. The digital media include compact disc (CD) data storage media. CD-ROM has 270,000 pages. In the case of an encyclopedia, 9 million words, 15,000 illustrations in black and white and color, and 60 minutes of sound were combined with 6500 dictionary entries on a single disc.

Because of its inherent advantages, these systems will eventually replace the larger and more costly 12-in videodisc. To understand the capabilities, a trainer or a manager need only think of the interactive videodisc. Like their larger counterpart, digital video technologies will deliver motion and still video, mixed with computer text, graphics, and audio under computer guidance for interactive learning materials.

Although the older IVD technology also delivered the same learning tools, in the all-digital format important new flexibility and capabilities emerge. They are:

- About 550 megabytes of digital information. It can be text, images, graphics, sound, and computer programs. All are integrated in a pack-age created by an authoring system. Then they are used under the com-mand of a computer.

- Hardware and software compression of this digital information to make gargantuan storage possible.

- Up to 72 minutes of CD-audiodisc quality sound under the control of the computer program.

- 7000 still images.

- Up to one hour of full-motion video, depending on the pixel density, display resolution, and number of colors.

- Digital still and motion images, sound, computer text, and graphics are all mixed and matched by the computer into an instructional program.

It is not possible to enjoy all of these things at the same time. That is, there cannot be 7000 stills *and* one hour of video stored on one disc.

Two digital video product lines based on this technology are in use by trainers. They are *digital video interactive* (DVI) and *compact disc interactive* (CDI). The two use quite different approaches, resulting in two *incompatible* and significantly different systems.

CD-I.   CD-I, aimed primarily at the mass consumer market, is a standard initiated by the Philips corporation. It capitalizes on that company's sponsorship of the CD-ROM and CD audio standards. CD-I is a simple-looking box (player) with built-in computer. Any TV can serve as the monitor, a plus for economy and convenience, but a minus for picture quality. The low unit cost of the player suggests that, for projects that must install large numbers of hardware, CD-I offers lower cost than other technology-based approaches.

DVI.   DVI, developed by Intel and IBM, was aimed primarily at the professional, business, and organizational market. DVI is personal-computer-based. Originally, the highest quality full-motion, full-screen video required hardware. The newest computers have the power to do the necessary processing without special hardware. DVI may be replaced by another PC-based standard modeled along similar lines.

Although the CD-I and DVI products are completely incompatible, the success of both will lead to better products and lower prices for education and training.

10.3.8 Virtual Reality

Virtual reality (VR) is a computer-generated simulated environment. The environment modeled in the VR system is called the virtual world. It is particularly useful to simulate conditions that do not actually exist, but VR may also be used to simulate actual potential conditions. For example, VR was used to allow astronauts to practice repair maneuvers for the Hubble space telescope.

There are two types of VR: *immersive* and *desktop*. Immersive VR uses special peripherals, particularly data gloves and computer graphic head-mounted displays (HMD). It gives the user the feeling of being present in a scene and able to move around in it. Desktop virtual reality is limited to standard desktop computer displays.

As you might expect VR is exciting and expensive. Although attractive in concept, at least another generation of development is required before we can expect to see many organizations using VR in training. Like all technology, it will find use first in applications where its benefits justify the expense and effort required.

10.3.9   Distance Learning

Distance learning is an increasingly useful way of supplying instruction to learners who are dispersed over a wide geographic area. It allows specialists to study advanced subjects when a reasonable-size group could not form in their own vicinity.

It also enables learners to take part in learning activities day or night, weekday or weekend. Generally, there are two distinct ways of delivering instruction. Either of them will use other media appropriately to support parts of the instruction. In this section, we will focus exclusively on the distance learning part of the instruction. Distant learners can be organized either as:

- Individuals (located in many places).

- Group(s). (The large group may include separate small groups. Usually, there is a Group at any subsite.)

Group distant learners all study simultaneously. Individual learners study in one or both of two timing varieties. They are:

- Synchronous (all simultaneously)

- Asynchronous (at different times—usually of their own choosing)

Each of these methods offers distinct advantages to the learners and to the organization delivering the instruction. In practice, organizations implement distance learning programs using one of two strategies. These strategies include the following:

- Video-teleconferencing (group synchronous)

- Computer conferencing (individual asynchronous)

The strategy selected depends on whether the learners are groups or individuals, and whether the individuals study simultaneously or at different times. Either methodology includes certain advantages, and should be selected based on the factors that best suit the instructional plan. Figure 10-15 shows the possibilities represented in the Distance Learning Model.

Computer Teleconferencing.   The model for most video teleconferencing courses is the regular classroom. The instruction is quite normal, except that at least a part of the class is in another location. Computer conferencing uses a new paradigm. Students use a computer with modem to communicate with a central computer that hosts the conferencing system's software. The instructor introduces a topic that results in student input related to the topic. Other students comment on the input of their peers. Instructors, or even students, may create side conferences to follow

Synchronous   Asynchronous

	Synchronous	Asynchronous
Group	Video Teleconferencing	Computer Conferencing
Individual	Computer Conferencing (little used)	Computer Conferencing (rare)

Figure 10-15.   Distance Learning Model.

up on a particularly interesting issue. Somewhat like multimedia, students may complete assignments using textbook, videotape, magazine article reprint, or handout. Far more preinstructional organization is necessary. Students must have all materials well before they are needed. Unlike classroom instruction, it is not satisfactory merely to sit and watch the instructor and other students. One *must* actively participate. Learners claim this key difference is a primary attraction of the method.

An excellent example of computer conferencing are the offerings of the University of Oregon. The computer conferencing courses serve a population constituted differently than video teleconferencing. Single learners study from any location. The instructor may also be anywhere. Since the premise is that classes do not meet, it does not matter that instructor and student work in widely separated cities. Realistically, computer conferencing learners often cannot meet because distances are too great. Students who rave about the advantages of distance learning by computer conferencing count the inability to meet the other students as their greatest regret.

Video Teleconferencing.   National Technology University (NTU) is an excellent representative of video teleconferencing. NTU coordinates 29 participating universities in a national delivery system that provides advanced education for engineers and scientists.

NTU broadcasts university courses over its Satellite Network. The courses emanate from the 28 universities with uplinks or broadcast stations. Direct phone lines from the receiving sites to the campus classroom provide for faculty-student interaction. Electronic mail, computer conferencing, and telephone office hours supplement this interaction. Learners report that the courses are challenging and applicable to their work environment.

NEC Corporation's corporate suburban Tokyo training center represents internal training video teleconferencing. Regular classes are conducted routinely at the Tokyo site. Corporate students "attend" who are widely dispersed in distant NEC offices in Hokkaido and Kyushu, hundreds of miles north and south of Tokyo. In this case, the linked classrooms feature live, full-motion video, telephone (FAX), and computer.

10.4 Good Training

We have examined some characteristics of sophisticated training approaches. Now let's take a look at the human side. It is important to know how well the learning we develop fits the adult learning situation. In his book *Troubleshooting the Troubleshooting Course* (1982), Bob Mager provides an excellent description of what good training ought to be.

> In short, state-of-the-art instruction derives its objectives from a real need (a job), creates instruction that is tightly related to the accomplishment of those objectives, and removes obstacles between the learners and the learning. It encourages and assists students to progress as rapidly as their growing competence will allow and makes their world a little brighter, rather than dimmer, when they demonstrate progress. It provides instruction and practice until each student can perform as desired, and then it stops.

Bibliography

Gross, R., *Independent Scholar's Handbook,* Addison Wesley, Reading, Mass., 1982.

Knowles, M., *The Adult Learner: A Neglected Species,* 2d ed., Gulf Publishing Company, Texas, 1979.

Kulik, J., C. Kulik, and P. Cohen, "Effectiveness of Computer-based College Teaching: A Meta-analysis of Findings," in *Review of Educational Research,* vol. 50, 1980, pp. 525–544.

Mager, R., *Troubleshooting the Troubleshooting Course,* Pitman Learning, Inc., Belmont, Calif., 1982, p. 136.

Piskurich, G., *Self-Directed Learning,* Josey-Bass, San Francisco, 1993.

Reynolds, A., *The Trainer's Dictionary,* HRD Press, Amherst, Mass., 1993.

Reynolds, A., and R. Anderson, *Selecting and Developing Media for Instruction* Van Nostrand Reinhold, New York, 1992.

Rossett, A., and J. Gautier-Downes, *A Handbook of Job Aids,* Pfeiffer, San Diego, 1991.

11

Group Training Methods (Detailed)

Kim E. Ruyle
Plus Delta Performance

Kim Ruyle *is president and CEO of Plus Delta Performance, Galesville, Wisconsin, an organization that develops software and technical training for industry. Kim previously managed training for a leading-edge manufacturing company and taught at two community colleges and three universities. He has extensive experience in the skilled trades as mechanic, welder, and machinist. Kim has a B.S. in industrial education, an M.S. in industrial education/industrial engineering, an M.Ed. in educational technology, and a Ph.D. in vocational education. He serves on the editorial board for ASTD's* Technical & Skills Training *magazine and the executive board of ASTD's Technical and Skills Training Professional Practice Area.*

11.1 Introduction

Effective training is a complex activity that does not happen by accident. Good trainers carefully plan and deliver structured experiences which bring about learning. During a learning experience, the trainer manipulates *variables of instruction* to facilitate the learning process. Variables of instruction are the factors which enhance (or impair) learning, including the organization of disseminated information, the rate of information delivery, the frequency of feedback and reinforcement, the instructional media used, seating arrangements, room temperature, and lighting. This is, of course, only a partial list. There are many instructional variables to attend to, and managing them effectively is one of the primary challenges for trainers.

When training is successful, the results are readily apparent—trainees are able to do something they could not do before training. They will have learned, and it is not possible to separate learning from doing. Since training does create an internal change in the learner, it is not something to be taken lightly. Trainers have a responsibility to provide learning activities that are effective and empowering, and that respect participants as individuals.

One way to categorize a learning activity is by the *source of direction* for that activity. Self-directed, media-directed, and instructor-directed activities are all common, and each has its own advantages. People engage in self-directed learning activities throughout their life. In fact, the ability to continue life-long, self-directed learning is a critical skill that should be a primary goal of public education (Adler, 1982). Presumably, self-directed learning is a personal experience for individuals, not for groups. When a technician checks a book out of the public library to learn how to read blueprints, he or she is engaging in a self-directed learning activity.

Various instructional media are often used to *support* learning activities, but text-based programmed instruction and computer-based training (CBT) are the media most often used to *direct* learning activities. Media-directed learning activities, like those that are self-directed, are typically individual, personal experiences. When a machine operator completes a CBT program to learn shop math skills, he or she is engaging in a media-directed learning activity.

Instructor-led learning activities can be delivered to one person at a time, as in a typical tutoring process, or to a group of participants, as in a typical classroom situation. This chapter discusses the most widely used methods for instructor-led, group learning activities. Each method is described with recommendations for implementation. Skills needed for effective group instruction are also discussed. Finally, some advanced, technology-based methods are presented.

11.1.1 Individual vs. Group Learning

Individualized learning experiences have some obvious advantages over instructor-directed group instruction. When learners* direct their own learning they choose their own schedule, location, and pace rather than have them dictated by the needs or desires of the instructor or other participants. Assuming learners are skilled in self-evaluation, repetition and review are potentially more focused and effective when learner-directed. Also, learner preferences for instructional media can often be more effectively accommodated when learners do the selecting.

* The terms "learner" and "trainee" are used interchangeably in this chapter.

On the other hand, group instruction has many benefits. Group training, especially when using lecture and discussion methods, can be developed and delivered quickly to a large number of people. A competent trainer generates enthusiasm for the subject matter and can effectively coach learners, especially in psychomotor skills. Group training can provide learners an opportunity to share from their life experiences and skills, a factor especially important for adult learners (Zemke and Zemke, 1988). Effective group training fosters a *synergy* from the combined inputs of the trainer and participants and frequently achieves a level of skill development and learner satisfaction that is not possible through self-directed learning.

The following factors indicate when instructor-led group training methods might be preferable to self-directed learning for a given situation:

- Information must be conveyed to large number of people

- Training must be developed and delivered quickly

- A skilled instructor is available

- Learners lack basic skills, especially reading

- Learners are not skilled in self-study and/or self-evaluation

- Subject matter is particularly difficult to grasp without intervention from an instructor

- Learners can be brought together in one place and on a set schedule for instruction

- Complex psychomotor skills must be learned and practiced

11.2 Methods

There is a variety of methods available for group training, and most of them do not require special equipment or facilities. Each does require, however, a *skilled trainer* to prepare media or teaching aids, present information, and facilitate learning activities. Effective instructors select training methods carefully because each method has attributes befitting it for particular situations. Some methods work especially well for teaching psychomotor skills—a demonstration can be an effective way to begin instructing open-root pipe welding, for instance. Other methods are well suited for dealing with affective skills and attitudes—a role play can be an effective technique for teaching supervisor skills, for example.

Consider the instructional goals and objectives, preferences of the audience, and limitations imposed by time, facilities, and equipment when selecting a training method. The information that follows provides selection and implementation guidelines for the most common group training methods.

11.2.1 Lecture

Description.   The *lecture* is simply an oral presentation of instructional material. Lectures are ubiquitous, probably the most familiar of all teaching methods. They are also probably the most abused. Since lectures are so commonplace and appear so uncomplicated to prepare and deliver, instructors are easily deceived into thinking lectures do not require as much preparation as other methods. Of course, the reality is that a poorly prepared lecture is an onus for the instructor and usually a tedious, depressing ordeal for the audience. Learners deserve better.

A good lecture is stimulating to the audience and often achieves some degree of interaction through questions and discussion. A good lecture is not read from a script. It is delivered with polished presentation skills by a credible trainer who communicates to learners enthusiastically and personably.

When to Use.   Lectures are one of the most efficient methods of presenting information. Consider using a lecture when the instructional purpose is to disseminate information quickly, especially if the audience is a large group. Lecturing is usually the most reasonable method for introducing training provided by other methods or media. For instance, a short lecture delivered prior to an instructional videotape to apprise learners of significant points might improve comprehension and retention.

Lectures provide a lot of flexibility, and skilled trainers modify the content and rate of delivery based on feedback received from the audience. If questions, facial expressions, or other body language express perplexity, the lecture can be modified while still in progress to include review material. If the group conveys understanding and impatience with the pace, the lecture can be accelerated and more content can be covered.

When it is important to stimulate interest in the subject matter, there is no better training method than a lecture skillfully delivered by an enthusiastic expert. The key is *skillful delivery.* Most college students have had professors who loved their subjects and were indeed experts, yet they succeeded in putting students to sleep. On the other hand, the most enthralling multimedia production is no match for Carl Sagan lecturing on astronomy. Good trainers understand when to lecture and are able to do it skillfully.

When to Avoid.   Instructional goals that deal with affective or psychomotor skills are rarely suited to lecture. Even high-level cognitive skills such as analysis and evaluation are difficult to teach with lecture methods exclusively. It is difficult to explain complex concepts, detailed processes, and abstractions in a lecture. In other words, unless the goal of instruction is to convey simple, straightforward facts, a lecture probably should be enhanced with media or complemented with other training methods.

Instructional media can provide visual images, illustrations, and cues to simplify complex information and enhance retention.

Recommendations. There are two prerequisites to delivering a successful lecture: (1) know your subject matter, and (2) know your audience. Armed with this knowledge, you will be able to prepare a lecture that meets your learners' needs and you will be able to focus on delivery during the lecture rather than be occupied with the content.

Prepare a comprehensive *outline* to guide the lecture after carefully considering the audience and the instructional objectives. The outline should be part of the lesson plan or trainer's guide which lists the objectives, describes materials needed, and provides a suggested schedule. An example of a lesson plan is shown in Figure 11-1. Notice how the outline is annotated enough to keep the lecturer on track, but not so much that it becomes a temptation to read. The introduction and conclusion are very important elements in a lecture and should receive extra attention during preparation.

Tailor the lecture for the audience so the vocabulary and pace of delivery is comfortable. Present the right amount of information—not so much that learners are burdened and frustrated and not so little that they are bored. When information is abstract, use plenty of concrete examples to enrich and elucidate the lecture. Specific presentation skills are covered in some detail later in this chapter.

11.2.2 Discussion

Description. A *discussion* is a managed process for sharing information between learners and the trainer. A good discussion is planned and targeted to achieve specific instructional objectives in the same way alternate training methods are planned and targeted. Discussions require learner participation, and they are often used in conjunction with lectures for that reason.

When to Use. Use the discussion method to enhance lectures and encourage learner participation in a lesson. Discussions work best with groups smaller than 20 learners (5 to 10 is best) and with content that is not rigid and restricted to facts. Instructional goals that deal with attitudes or critical thinking skills are usually well suited to the discussion method.

Adult learners with experiences related to the subject matter will be especially receptive to the discussion method because it allows them an opportunity to contribute their knowledge and express opinions. For the trainer, discussions provide feedback regarding learners' understanding and attitudes.

Lesson Plan
Arc Welding Equipment and Shielded Metal Electrodes

Objectives

After this lesson, students will be able to:

- List and describe the three major types of arc welding power sources
- Define duty cycle and explain its significance
- List the four filler classes of stick electrodes
- Describe at least two typical applications for each class of stick electrode
- Explain the AWS numbering scheme for stick electrodes
- Given an AWS electrode number (E6010, for example), state the tensile strength joint position and flux characteristics

Materials needed

- Lecture notes
- Transparencies 23, 24, 25
- Examples of stick electrodes

Estimated time: 1 hour

Lecture outline

1. Introduction (5 minutes)—Importance of selecting correct equipment—changes in process cannot be made arbitrarily—equipment must be suited to process—example of process changes at mill fabricator
2. Power sources (25 minutes)
   a. Type—Compare and contrast each and give typical applications
      (1) Motor generators
      (2) Transformer rectifiers
      (3) AC transformers
   b. Output slope—Transparency 23—Check for understanding
   c. Duty cycle—Point out significance for semiautomatic processes like MIG
   d. Polarity—Include AC *high frequency*
   e. Cables and fasteners—SAFETY ISSUES—Transparency 24—Check for understanding before continuing

---

Figure 11-1.   Example lesson plan.

3. Stick electrodes (20 minutes)—Significance of electrode selection

   a. AWS numbering system—Transparency 25

      (1) Prefix

      (2) Tensile strength

      (3) Joint position

      (4) Flux characteristics—Check for understanding of AWS number system

   b. Filler groups—For each, describe characteristics and applications

      (1) Fast freeze—E6010, E6011—Pass around examples of electrodes

      (2) Fill freeze—E6012, E6013

      (3) Fast fill—E7014, E7024

      (4) Low hydrogen—E7016, E7018

4. Review (10 minutes)

   a. Answer questions

   b. Reiterate importance of selecting correct equipment and electrodes

   c. Strong conclusion—mill fabricator example and safety considerations

Figure 11-1. (*Continued*)

When to Avoid.   Avoid the discussion method when participants have limited background with the subject and when there are strict time constraints on the instruction. Also avoid discussions when the content consists of straightforward facts (the one correct way to log on to a computer network, for instance) or does not, by its nature, allow variation (company policy for reporting a safety violation, for instance).

Recommendations.   Prepare a lesson plan similar to that shown in Figure 11-1 but that lists questions rather than a lecture outline. Use *open-ended questions* (those that require more than a one-word response) to initiate the discussion. As examples, the items that follow are questions that might be used for a lesson on customer service:

- Can you describe a situation in which the customer is *not* always right?
- How do you deal with an irate customer?
- If you were in charge of customer service, what changes would you make?

Arrange seating in a circular or U-shaped pattern to facilitate eye contact and group interaction. Do not allow any person or persons to dominate the discussion. If that is a problem, use a round-robin method of calling on people in seating order instead of allowing people to "jump in" with their comments. Remember that the discussion method is a *managed* process. The trainer is the manager and must keep the group on track. Summarizing frequently helps to keep the discussion focused and provides opportunity for the trainer to encourage participation. Refer to the information on presentation and facilitation skills later in this chapter for more information.

11.2.3 Demonstration

Description. A *demonstration* is a dramatized explanation of a product, process, or procedure. The trainer typically demonstrates expert performance of the process. Learners are often provided opportunity for guided practice following the demonstration. This training method is extremely valuable for technical trainers because it is so effective for teaching complex topics and psychomotor skills. To appreciate the value of demonstration, imagine trying to teach five-year-old children to tie their shoes if you could not show them how—if you had to communicate instructions by telephone, for instance.

When to Use. Demonstrate tasks that require manual dexterity or that are difficult for learners to understand without being shown. Logging on to a computer system might be a good candidate for a demonstration, for instance, if the process is very involved. It could be explained exclusively with words, like this:

- First, turn on the computer and the monitor.
- At the C prompt, type in the command LOGIN. You will be asked for your password. Type it in without spaces. You are now logged in.
- A START-UP MENU will come up on the screen. Select CONNECT TO NETWORK from the menu by using the down arrow to highlight the selection or by pressing F5.
- The MAIN MENU will then appear on the screen. Select the application you want from the MAIN MENU in the same way you made a selection in the previous start-up menu. You can select word processing, spreadsheet, database, electronic mail, and other functions from the MAIN MENU.
- After closing an application, as long as you are still logged in and on the network, you can return to this menu by typing MAIN at the C prompt.

The preceding explanation would be perfectly clear to the trainer, of course, and probably clear to learners familiar with computers. For the uninitiated, however, the instructions are complex and contain many subtle opportunities for errors. How is the computer turned on? What does the C prompt look like? Are you required to press the ENTER key after typing in the password? After the password is entered, what happens exactly? How long should it take for a menu to appear on the screen, and what does it look like when it does appear? These questions and others would be answered if the process was demonstrated.

When to Avoid.   An alternative to the demonstration must be used when the process is dangerous or when materials and equipment are scarce or fragile. Sometimes filmed or animated procedures will suffice for the demonstration, and simulated processes will allow learners to practice safely.

Recommendations.   Planning is at least as important for the demonstration method as for other methods. Prepare carefully and rehearse the demonstration. Take plenty of time to set up equipment and materials beforehand so learners are not kept waiting while adjustments are made or supplies are found.

Position yourself and learners so everyone can see and hear explanations. Consider differences in the visual perspective of the audience and the performer. If there are safety considerations, address them early in the lesson. Always model safe practices during a demonstration.

A common way to sequence instruction during a demonstration is to begin with an explanation, proceed to the actual demonstration, and then incorporate guided practice by having learners first explain the process and then demonstrate it to the instructor or to a peer.

As an example, consider a lesson on calibrating an instrument. The trainer might begin by explaining how the instrument is calibrated without making any adjustments. After the initial explanation, the trainer could perform the calibration while explaining once again how it is done. Following the demonstration, the instructor might ask a student to explain the calibration procedure. Misconceptions and inadequacies in the explanation would be corrected before the student demonstrates the task.

11.2.4   Case Studies

Description.   A *case study* is an event or circumstance which presents a problem to be solved or situation to be analyzed for instructional purposes. The case may be contrived, but must be realistic. Trainees are typically asked to analyze the case and suggest solutions or recommendations to address the problem presented in the case.

Case studies are useful for bridging theory and practice. They often provide an opportunity for learners to hone their communication skills and usually require high-level cognitive skills such as analysis and synthesis.

When to Use.   Textbook case studies for technical training topics are not common, and it can be difficult and time-consuming to develop good cases. When there is time for development, however, the case method is one of the best ways to develop critical thinking skills and facilitate the transfer of learning. Case studies are most often used in management and supervisory training, but there is certainly room for the method in technical training. An example of a case study used for technical training is shown in Figure 11-2.

When to Avoid.   The case study method is inappropriate for learners who do not have the necessary prerequisite skills in reading and problem solving. If case studies are not readily available from texts, it may be impractical to develop them because of the time and effort required. When problems require only recall of facts or simple calculations, full-blown case studies are superfluous; they should probably be reduced to simple story problems.

Recommendations.   Let learners know the instructional intent of the case. Devise a realistic scenario and clearly present it with the appropriate level of detail. The problem should allow learners some room for interpretation and a range of solutions. Typically there are several viable solutions for the case.

Case studies can be completed during class by individuals, by teams, or by the entire group. Solutions to case studies completed outside of the classroom provide excellent material to stimulate discussion in subsequent lessons.

11.2.5   Role Playing

Description.   A *role play* is a contrived event, situation, or circumstance acted out by trainees for instructional purposes. Two or more trainees are assigned roles which, when acted out, present a problem of some kind. The dramatization allows learners to apply knowledge of the subject matter and demonstrate human relation skills.

When to Use.   Role plays are well suited for enhancing instruction in communication and human relation skills, but good opportunities to apply the role play method in technical training are not so common. Some likely topics include management and supervision skills and customer service. Role plays are useful for providing a change of pace in the classroom and promoting learner participation. Use this method when it serves a valid instructional purpose and there is sufficient time.

When to Avoid.   The role play method is probably not appropriate unless instructional objectives are concerned in some way with interper-

---

Case Study

Purpose

This case study is to give you an opportunity to apply your knowledge of cutting tool geometry, machining processes, materials, and technical communications.

Scenario

For purposes of this case, imagine you are Jack Smith, a manufacturing engineer. Your employer, Delta Industries, manufactures machine components. This morning you received a memo in your interoffice mail from Marla Harris, an engineer responsible for product quality.

Directions

Respond to Marla by preparing a concise report and memo to answer her questions and address her concerns.

TO: Jack Smith, Manufacturing Engineering
FROM: Marla Harris, Quality Engineering
SUBJECT: Unacceptable finish on new polycarbonate spindles (Part #7788)
DATE: April 18, 1994

We are not getting an acceptable finish on the #7788 spindles since switching to polycarbonate. As you are aware, our specs indicate a surface roughness of 90 μin or better. We currently have visible galling on about 5 percent of these parts—all scrap. I have just concluded a study and found an average surface roughness of >130 μin on a random sampling of 30 parts! If we were doing more than visuals on these parts, they would *all* be scrap!

Denise Johnson, the production supervisor on first shift, tells me her instructions from manufacturing engineering are to continue to use the previous cutting tool geometry (shown in my sketch below), but to increase the cutting speed by 20 percent. The lathe operators are turning 1.5-in diameter spindles at 1000 RPM with no coolant.

Please advise:

- Is the cutting tool geometry correct?
- Is the cutting speed correct? What about feed rates?
- Should coolants or lubricants be used? If so, what are the implications for cycle time?

It's important to get this solved before the end of the month. Let me know, Jack, if you need more information from me. Thanks for your help.

Figure 11-2.   Example case study used for technical training.

sonal relations. In order for this method to be effective, learners must be persuaded to actively play their role.

Recommendations.   Role plays can be created and conducted spontaneously in the classroom, but planning will result in greater success. Inform learners of the instructional intent of the role play and, if possible, with written descriptions of their roles instead of voiced descriptions.

An example of a role play is shown in Figure 11-3. For this particular role play, trainees would be given only a description of the scenario and a description of their particular role—they would not be privy to the description of the role of their counterpart. Variations for this exercise include:

- A team of learners plays Role #1
- The instructor plays Role #2

The scene could be enacted in front of the entire group of learners and followed by guided discussion to reinforce the instructional value of the exercise.

11.2.6   Games

Description.   *Games* used in training are designed to achieve instructional objectives in a way that provides some entertainment or amusement for learners. Games have an organizational framework, rules for correct play, and a goal for players. They can be designed for individuals or for groups and often recognize a winner or winners at the conclusion, though this is not a requirement. Games prolong the time required to deliver training, but, if sensibly designed and applied, improve training effectiveness.

When to Use.   Like the role play method, instructional games provide a change of pace and stimulate learner participation. Tedious subject matter can often be spiced up with a simple game. Use a game when it meets a goal of instruction, there is sufficient time, and learners will benefit from a break from more traditional methods.

When to Avoid.   Generic games for training are readily available from commercial sources, but most require modification to fit technical training needs. Games will protract training, and it may take an inordinate amount of time to modify or develop games for specific objectives. Take these factors into account before selecting this training method.

Role Play

Purpose
This role play will help illustrate the difficulties involved in acquiring expert knowledge for instructional design or performance support system development.

Scenario
Delta Industries, a manufacturer of machine components, has just added a new product line which is fabricated using the TIG welding process. The company needs to train production welders who are skilled with MIG welding processes but are unskilled in TIG welding. The instructional designer (Role #1) has prepared an instructional analysis with assistance from the production manager. Now it is time to sit down to interview Delta's TIG welding expert (Role #2) to acquire information about the first instructional goal.

Role 1
You have worked for Delta Industries for almost a year. Previously, you spent seven years designing instruction for another manufacturer. You have a bachelor's degree in industrial psychology and a master's degree in instructional technology. Although you don't know a lot about welding, you have a good general understanding of the manufacturing processes currently used at Delta and know the target population quite well. You are about to interview a subject matter expert to find out how operators on the shop floor should set up and adjust TIG welding machines. You should initiate the interview and feel free to set some ground rules if you feel it is appropriate.

Role 2
You have worked for Delta Industries for almost 30 years. There are 20 other welders in the company, but none of them have much expertise with TIG welding. You are the TIG welding expert and proud of your ability to use the process when it has been needed in the past. Now you must be interviewed by a new employee, an "instructional designer" who probably doesn't know beans about welding. You've been told that the purpose is to contribute to the design of TIG welding training for the other production welders. From your point of view, there are several considerations:

Figure 11-3. Example of role play.

1. Your expertise has never been fully appreciated, but at least you had some special value to the company because of your knowledge. Now that knowledge is going to be shared with all the other production workers.

2. Your time is valuable, and it's a waste of time to try to teach anything technical to an office worker who has probably never had to do any real work, at least not anything that gets dirt under the fingernails. An instructional designer won't understand the technical aspects of welding anyway.

3. If the instruction is *not* successful, you might be asked to be a lead technician and troubleshooter for the new TIG welding line. That could mean a promotion.

You have decided to be polite but not too cooperative. Your plan is to answer questions but not offer any information unless specifically asked. No use giving away all the knowledge you've worked so hard for all these years. If you are really pressed, however, you plan to shower this instructional designer with details, show how much you really know about TIG welding. Sorting out the wheat from the chaff won't be your problem.

Figure 11-3. (*Continued*)

Recommendations.   Prepare learners by introducing the game, clarifying the instructional intent, and carefully explaining the rules. Manage the activity. It should be fun, but should be kept focused and constructive.

Many TV game shows can be altered slightly and infused with subject matter to create very effective instructional exercises. The instructor or a trainee can play the part of moderator. If modeled after a quiz show, an assortment of short-answer test items can provide substance. This approach is usually much simpler than attempting to modify a board game to serve an instructional purpose.

11.2.7   Peer Tutoring

Description.   *Peer tutoring* is a training method that allows trainees to formally help each other, learn from each other, and even conduct training. This is an excellent training method that has wide applicability in technical training. Peer tutoring increases learner participation, eases the trainer's workload, increases instructional effectiveness, makes it easier to pace instruction in groups with heterogeneous abilities, and increases trainees' satisfaction with instruction.

When to Use.   Incorporate peer tutoring when trainees' abilities are significantly disparate. An adage states that people never really understand a topic until they teach it. Peer tutoring provides an opportunity for tutors to affirm and cement their knowledge. For some learners, it might be easier to ask questions of fellow trainees than of the instructor.

When to Avoid.   The peer tutoring method will only work when there are trainees willing and able to tutor and others willing to be tutored. If there is unwholesome competition or mistrust among trainees, this method should be avoided until the situation is corrected.

Recommendations.   The tutoring process can vary in terms of structure. The trainer might choose to administer a very structured process and provide detailed outlines for tutors to follow. At the other end of the spectrum, peer tutoring can be a casual, unstructured give-and-take between tutor and learners. Regardless of the amount of structure provided, the trainer cannot make assumptions about the quality of tutoring. This method obliges the trainer to monitor tutoring activities to assure that learners are being well served. If there are signs of frustration on the part of tutors or learners, intervene as necessary.

11.3   Presentation Skills

The importance of *presentation skills* is obvious when the lecture method is considered. All training methods, however, require at least a modicum of verbal communication skills and stage presence. Even methods that are more learner-controlled (such as some games, case studies, and peer tutoring) require facilitation. A summary of recommendations for instructor presentation skills follows.

11.3.1   Preparation

To be unprepared is to commit the cardinal sin of training. When you are prepared, though, when you have reviewed your objectives and material and planned your presentation, the probability of making a successful presentation is overwhelmingly in your favor.

Arrive to the training session in time to set up your materials and media and, if it is the first meeting, to get to know the trainees. Introduce yourself and chat informally before the lesson begins to establish a relaxed atmosphere. Learn the names of your trainees and address them by name.

Frequently it is advisable to write the objectives and a brief outline of the lesson on the chalkboard or flipchart prior to the lesson. This communicates your preparedness and provides trainees with advanced organizers which facilitate learning. At the very least, verbally communicate the objectives and outline your presentation in an introduction. Let trainees know your intended schedule and do not stray from it.

11.3.2   Delivery

Know your trainees and speak to them in a conversational tone, clearly and loudly enough for everyone to hear. Use inflection, volume, and your body language to communicate enthusiasm and to stress important items. Make eye contact with your audience and speak to people, not to an indistinct point on the ceiling or wall.

Eschew distracting and peculiar behaviors such as jingling change in your pocket or rocking back and forth like a metronome while speaking. Also avoid inappropriate vocabulary, offensive speech, discriminatory language, and partiality.

Humor can be used effectively to enliven presentations, put learners at ease, and enhance learning. To work well, however, humor must be natural, not forced. If you have to work too hard at it, your attempts at humor might backfire.

Do not demonstrate your authority or expertise in an imperious manner. Let trainees know you are as interested in learning from them as you hope they are interested in learning from you. Plan time into your lesson for trainees to interrupt your delivery to share their experiences with the group. Encourage them to share knowledge and resources.

11.3.3   Questioning

Questioning skills are vital for trainers. Questions can be used to check for understanding, encourage participation, and guide discussions. Prepare meaningful questions to use in your delivery. Use open-ended questions (those that cannot be answered with one word) to stimulate thinking and promote discussion. For example, rather than ask a close-ended question such as "Do you think the valves might need to be adjusted?", ask an open-ended question such as "What things might be causing the engine to misfire?" Use close-ended questions to change the subject or restrain a dominating participant.

When trainees answer your questions, you have an opportunity to provide them with *feedback* and *positive reinforcement*. Feedback, in the context of group training activities, is information that lets learners know how well they are achieving the instructional objectives. Positive reinforcement is a desirable consequence that encourages the performance it follows to be repeated. Feedback and positive reinforcement are essential components of the learning process. Frequently review information and let learners know how they are doing. Use sincere praise intermittently to encourage good performance and participation.

The trainer should not be the only one asking questions. Encourage trainees to ask questions, and be open and approachable in demeanor so they feel free to do so. Never display disdain or impatience when asked questions. Answer trainees' questions clearly and check for understanding after the question is answered.

If you are asked a question that you cannot answer, it is much better to admit it than to try to fake an answer. Inform the trainee that you will investigate the question, then do it. Supply the answer for the group at the next opportunity.

You are not obligated to answer every question. When learners can find the answer on their own, encourage them to do so. Coach them to the solution if they need help.

11.3.4 Facilitation Skills

Presentation skills enable a trainer to effectively deliver the instructional message to learners. Most group training methods, however, require *learner* contributions to be effective. *Facilitation skills* are used by an instructor to enable learners to deliver a portion of the content of a lesson. Facilitation, as it applies to training then, is the *orchestration of learner participation* to achieve instructional goals. For trainers, the ability to facilitate group learning experiences is an essential competency.

Facilitation is fundamentally a management process that accomplishes several things: (1) it keeps training sessions focused on the topic and on schedule; (2) it obliges each participant to contribute to the learning experience if possible; (3) it likewise ensures that no individual participant dominates the learning experience, and, very importantly, (4) it accomplishes the instructional goals for the experience.

Facilitation skills are applicable to a wide range of business activities that are not training-related. Group problem-solving sessions and business meetings of all types are more effective when led by a skilled facilitator.

11.4 Advanced Technologies for Training

The foregoing material has presented information on common group training methods and presentation skills which have been used for many years and will continue to be important. In the future, however, technology-based methods will be increasingly important in the technical training repertoire. The following material introduces two computer-based technologies which show promise as training methods for group and individual learning situations.

11.4.1 Expert System/ Performance Support System Training Applications

Expert systems are computer programs that embody a human expert's problem-solving strategies and knowledge in a well-defined domain of information. Like a human expert, an expert system typically conducts a consultation session with a user or client to learn about a problem and then suggests a solution. Expert systems are so named because they emulate a human expert, even in the interaction with a client. One of the defining traits of experts is that they know what questions to ask, and expert systems, like human experts, do not ask "stupid" questions. They appear intelligent.

There are examples of large, commercially successful expert systems (development measured in years), but the cumulative effect of smaller programs (development measured in weeks) is probably much greater. Expert systems modules are frequently incorporated in *electronic performance support systems* (EPSSs)—computer-based job aids which contain information used by people while they perform their job. An EPSS that addresses the operation and service of a complex piece of equipment might contain operating instructions, set-up procedures, machine specifications, test procedures, repair procedures, an expert system module for troubleshooting, and even tutorials on theory of operation. These components would typically be supported by extensive graphics, even animation or video.

Electronic performance support can be far more effective than paper-based service manuals. The computer does not overwhelm the user with information because it presents just one screen—one chunk of knowledge—at a time. Navigation is easier with the computer. The user does not have to insert a thumb between pages to remember where to return. Decision-making tasks are especially easy when assisted by the computer. An EPSS can jog the user's memory, give prompts, explain and illustrate procedures, and provide just-in-time instruction.

Electronic performance support systems can enhance technical training in several ways. Activities can be designed to allow trainees to use the software, just as they will on the job, to practice tasks. Since the job aid stores knowledge needed on the job, instruction can focus on applying the EPSS instead of remembering information.

Expert system modules can be used as in-class consultants and mentors. Since many expert systems can explain the logic they used to arrive at a solution, curious trainees can probe the *heuristic* problem-solving strategies used by the system. These mental shortcuts and rules of thumb are difficult to convey in textbooks or lectures. By questioning an expert system, the learner is given insight into the knowledge and logic that human experts may have taken years to assimilate.

Activities can be designed to give trainees an opportunity to develop expert systems and performance support systems. Creators of expert systems become quasi-experts during the development process. This approach works well with teams when each team is responsible for acquiring and representing a manageable division of the knowledge base.

11.4.2 Simulation and Virtual Reality

Simulation is an exercise that substitutes or artificially devises some elements found on the job to allow trainees to practice or observe tasks. The simulation method can be used to safeguard learners when the task is dangerous or to preserve expensive materials and equipment. Some examples of simulation in technical training include simulated operation of a power plant, simulated industrial accidents for safety training, and simulated welding practice with ersatz electrodes.

Sometimes simulation is implemented as a hybrid of the case method and the role play method, and may even incorporate features of games. This hybrid variety of simulation can require many participants to play assigned roles. It is particularly useful for demonstrating and teaching high-level decision-making skills. War games used in the military are examples of this type of simulation.

Sophisticated simulations usually require a computer to develop and pose strategies to respond to participants' decisions or to control electromechanical equipment. An emerging variation of simulation called *virtual reality* (VR) uses computer-controlled devices worn by the participant to create an artificial environment.

A participant in VR typically wears a helmet, possibly gloves, even an entire suit. The articles of clothing contain sensors, actuators, and, in the case of the helmet, display devices. The VR clothing senses the participant's movement and responds in real time by providing appropriate feedback—a changing display and resistance to movement, for instance.

Virtual reality is in its infancy, and VR simulations are limited. Currently the technology is unwieldy and expensive, but that will change. Virtual reality will impact technical training significantly in the future.

To illustrate how VR might compare in the near future to present simulation technology, consider the challenges of teaching shielded metal arc cutting for underwater applications. No, this is an authentic process—not like underwater basketweaving. Construction and salvage operations frequently require metal to be cut underwater. The task is hazardous and requires diving skills as well as considerable psychomotor skills to perform the operation.

This operation could be simulated in an instructional lab facility in a tank of water. A small, specially outfitted tank could be used that allows the trainee to insert arms into special sleeves which extend into the tank. Alternately, a much larger tank could allow the trainee to fully submerge for practice. The more modest equipment would save time, space, and money, and would be safer. However, the larger, more sophisticated equipment would provide a more realistic practice.

Using VR, the training lab would look very different. Instead of a tank of water and welding equipment, there would be open floor space and a VR suit. When trainees don the suit, they enter a simulated underwater world. They feel the water pressure, they see a ship's hull to be cut through murky water, and they heft the cutting torch. When they turn their heads, they might view seaweed and fish swimming by. They can reach out and touch the sunken vessel they are working on, but nothing they sense is real. Everything is artificial (virtual reality). Students can safely cut metal in the simulated environment without consuming materials.

Technologies such as expert systems and virtual reality will mature and eventually be used to enhance technical training. Technical trainers utilizing the new technologies will need to learn a new set of skills, but the basic presentation skills and group training methods presented in this chapter will be extremely important for the foreseeable future.

Bibliography

Adler, M., *The Paideia Proposal: An Educational Manifesto*, MacMillan, New York, 1982.

Powers, B., *Instructor Excellence: Mastering the Delivery of Training*, Jossey-Bass, San Francisco, 1992.

Rothwell, W., and H. Sredl, *The ASTD Reference Guide to Professional Training Roles and Competencies*, vol 2., 2d ed, HRD Press, Amherst, Mass., 1992.

Ruyle, K. E., "Developing Intelligent Job Aids (Intelligently)," *Technical & Skills Training* 2(2):9–14 (1991).

Ruyle, K. E., "Expert Systems: They're Here Now," *Tech Trends* 34(1):41–43 (1989).

Zemke, R., and S. Zemke, "30 Things We Know for Sure about Adult Learning," *Training*, July 1988, pp. 57–61.

12

Technical Training Facilities and Equipment

Eileen West

12.1 Introduction

Among the tenets of adult learning is that adults learn better when the learning will help them address problems they encounter in their lives (Knowles, 1978). That is, adults have a need to know how they will apply the learning personally. This tenet is particularly important in technical training, because, although much of technical training is knowledge-based, to be most effective, it must hinge on practical application (Clark, 1989). Chapter 7 of this book goes into a great deal of detail about adult learning. Technical training facilities and equipment provide the context within which training participants can acquire and practice applying new skills and knowledge that will later be transferred to the job. Yet many organizations frequently fail to maximize training effectiveness because they fail to apply principles of adult learning to the training facility and its equipment. For example, facilities and equipment that create a positive learning environment not only present a nonthreatening atmosphere, but also do the following:

- Replicate the job environment to the degree necessary to achieve the training goals
- Consider the participants' physical and emotional needs
- Satisfy the participants' learning styles and preferences

- Accommodate learner interest through a variety of stimuli
- Limit distractions to the degree possible—except for distractions that simulate those encountered on the job
- Promote learning transfer to the job setting

Training that is relevant to the learner includes matching the type of application in training to the requirements on the job (Liao, 1989).

Participants often cannot achieve their training objectives because of a mismatch between the training facility or equipment and the required training outcomes. A Fortune 100 company with old plant facilities planned on doing some safety training with a joint union-management group. Without thinking through the session carefully, the company inadvertently put the participants in harm's way. On the spur of the moment, the instructor decided to demonstrate the safe use of a piece of the machinery in the room. Unbeknownst to the instructor, the machine was out of order and the sign that should have been on it had fallen off and not been replaced. When he turned on the machine, a malfunctioning gear tore off and flew into the group standing around watching the demonstration. Fortunately, no one was seriously hurt, but one participant ended up with a broken toe when the debris fell on his foot. (He had safety boots on, but the piece was large and propelled by the machine.) The instructor did need to demonstrate the safe use of some types of equipment, but not on the spur of the moment. It needed to be well planned and fit the objectives of the session.

Choice of facilities and equipment are essential. While relative costs and benefits of facility and equipment are a major part of the equation, there is much that training managers and trainers can do to assure that training facilities and equipment promote training outcomes rather than serve as distracters. This chapter will describe facilities and equipment planning within the framework of adult learning principles. The chapter is divided into three parts:

- Part I: *Equipment planning,* which includes:

  Matching primary and secondary equipment needs to the required training outcomes

  A general description of the cost-versus-benefit decisions required before selecting equipment

- Part II: *Facilities planning,* which includes:

  Planning facilities to maximize learning

  Matching the facility to the training need

  Creating an environment that is conducive to learning

- Part III: *Other facilities options* available to organizations that may be unable to support a full-time facility

12.2 Equipment Planning

For the purposes of this chapter,

Equipment refers to the machinery, tools, and materials required to achieve the required training outcomes.

Primary equipment includes all equipment used to replicate the job environment and which directly supports the required learning outcome.

Secondary equipment includes media and other equipment that supports the learning. Equipment ranges, therefore, from screwdrivers and handheld calculators to full-fidelity simulators.

The selection of equipment used in training has potential for huge cost implications. All of the major airlines have flight simulators that are used to train and upgrade the skills of their pilots. They are very, very expensive, but very necessary. In recent years the fatality rates from air crashes have plummeted significantly. Industry experts agree that the simulators are primarily responsible for curbing pilot error. Planning for such a large, but necessary, investment requires careful planning and timing, so that the most up-to-date equipment is available in a timely manner. Equipment selection, therefore, is a process that must be completed carefully using all available information about both cost and training implications. This section will address the basic considerations involved in selecting primary and secondary training equipment.

12.2.1 Identifying Primary Equipment Requirements

Primary equipment includes *all equipment used to replicate the job environment and which directly supports the required learning outcome.* For example, the airlines' goal in using the simulators is to ensure that the pilots are totally trained in normal, as well as emergency and tough flying conditions, thus ensuring that the airlines have the safest flights possible. Such things as day and night flying conditions, good and bad weather conditions, airport landing and takeoff conditions for all the airports worldwide, and every imaginable emergency condition, including all the air crash conditions for the last five years on all the airlines worldwide, are learned and practice conditions are created. Before selecting primary equipment, it is essential to analyze not only the job but the job context. Analyzing the job will provide information about the skills and knowledge required for job performance and how the job is performed. Analyzing the job context will provide information about the critical aspects of the conditions under which the job is performed and how the incumbent performs in the work environment. A few critical questions need to be asked:

- Is the job performed alone or in teams?
- What types of distracters are a normal part of the job environment?
- Does the job incumbent rely on others to produce one or more critical components in order to perform his or her job?

These types of information will provide a good basis for determining how the requisite skills and knowledge are applied and the degree of fidelity (accuracy of reproduction) that is required in training to accomplish the training outcomes.

Providing full job simulation can be very expensive, and although it may be possible to provide the exact equipment for training that is used on the job, full job simulation may not always be desirable from a learning standpoint or in terms of cost effectiveness. Full job simulation is not always necessary to achieve the desired level of learning, however. In highly complex jobs that use expensive equipment or in jobs in which safety is a major issue, it may be desirable to provide initial training on only some parts of the job or task (e.g., parts that are highly complex or highly critical to overall job performance) before training the entire job or task using the actual equipment that is used on the job. This strategy may be particularly effective as a means of allowing training participants to learn and practice critical "chunks" of information that can later be combined with other chunks and applied in the larger job context. For example, the general public can now purchase software that teaches the basics of becoming a pilot for those who are planning on taking flight instruction. Flight instructors have praised the simulation software because it has made their jobs 100 percent easier.

It may also be possible to use training devices that provide the learner with full "functional" fidelity (e.g., the exact prompts and feedback as would be provided by the equipment used on the job), combined with a lower level of "physical" fidelity (e.g., appearance). The Maritime Academy in Baltimore that keeps many of the merchant marine personnel up-to-date has a simulation lab that provides highly sophisticated simulation equipment that models various sizes of ships in various areas of the world under all types of weather conditions. Classroom work with various pieces of equipment commonly found on all ships cuts down on the time needed to practice on the full functional fidelity equipment. Someone wanting to learn to navigate the North Atlantic on a supertanker in the middle of winter can have the practical experience of doing so by using the appropriate simulator. Simulation research has shown that the initial use of part-task training devices or equipment with less than full fidelity can reduce the training time required on more expensive, full-fidelity equipment (Hays and Singer, 1989). Personnel responsible for selecting primary training equipment will need to make decisions on the degree of accuracy to the workplace that is necessary to achieve the required training outcomes. Many of these decisions can be made when the training is being designed, at which time the training content is organized and sequenced and the learning activities are planned. At this time, equipment planners should consider several factors before making decisions about equipment. These factors include the equipment's

- Overall contribution to achieving the training goals
- Cost-effectiveness for purchase and use
- Flexibility of use

When considering the overall contribution to achieving the training goals, one should determine the following:

- The degree to which the equipment supports the learning style(s) of the training participants
- The training objective or objectives it will support
- How it will support the training outcomes

Potential tradeoffs involved in using another type of equipment or equipment with lower fidelity levels should also be considered.

Elements to consider when determining the cost-effectiveness of secondary equipment include the following:

- Purchase (or lease) cost
- Anticipated useful life
- Maintenance costs over its lifetime
- Estimated amount of residual value
- User-friendliness (it costs money to train trainers and other equipment operators to use the equipment)
- Frequency of use

Overall flexibility of use includes the potential for using a single piece of equipment in several ways or for different types of training. While a single factor may be key in making the final decision on a given piece of equipment, equipment planners should consider the relative incentives and disincentives of all before making a decision. One major pharmaceutical company has a fully equipped computer training lab that receives heavy use during the day. The company now has the lab in use 24 hours a day. The employees who are in school are free to use it from 5:00 P.M. each evening to 7:00 A.M. the next morning for doing papers and assignments. In addition, those who do not have equipment on their desks, but need it to complete assignments due to the unavailability of a secretary, have top priority. It is not uncommon to have the lab full all night as people work on a variety of tasks. The lab is also open 24 hours a day on weekends. Children doing homework assignments are allowed to use it on weekends as long as a priority job is not being worked on. A side goal was the improvement of the workforces' computer skills. Their skill levels have skyrocketed because they have continuous access to the computers. The arrangement has not been abused and the equipment has been fully utilized, thus making justifying upgrades an easy task for the MIS (Management Information System) Department.

In cases where several equipment strategies are available or where some question remains as to the best approach for the training to take, it may be desirable to develop one or more prototypes to test on a segment of the training population before undergoing the cost of full-scale development and implementation. Prototyping is particularly useful and cost-effective for training that is highly complex or critical to overall operations or where there are serious safety or legal considerations involved.

It is also necessary to plan probable equipment needs into the future. Technology is changing so rapidly that equipment changes and modifications are almost a requirement for many organizations to remain competitive. Whether the equipment is a personal computer or a robot, any change in—or change in the operation of—equipment has potential training implications. Training personnel should be in regular contact with production personnel and others who make equipment decisions so that training can be planned, developed, and implemented *before* the equipment arrives.

12.2.2 Identifying Secondary Equipment Requirements

Secondary equipment includes *media and other equipment that supports the learning.* It, therefore, includes a wide range of equipment and presents an array of options for equipment planners. Equipment that is secondary for one training program may be primary for another, and many of the same selection considerations will apply to equipment in both categories. Because secondary equipment plays a supporting role in the training, equipment planners may have additional flexibility in selecting secondary equipment than they have when selecting primary equipment. The selection of secondary equipment for any given training program does have both learning and cost implications, however, and deserves careful consideration prior to acquisition.

When selecting equipment to support training media, recent technology has provided equipment planners with a virtual universe of options, assuming that there is a training need—and the budget—to support them. Two important aspects to consider when selecting media equipment are:

- Is the equipment really justified in terms of supporting the learning?

- Does the equipment have enough potential uses to justify its acquisition?

Sophisticated equipment that supports media but does *not* support learning cannot be justified at any cost. Likewise, equipment with a limited number of uses or a limited life span may just not be worth the overall cost.

Equipment that supports the learning supports the training outcome and also supports the learning styles and preferences of the training participants. When determining whether equipment is justified in terms of supporting the learning, equipment planners should consider whether the training objectives could be accomplished as efficiently with another type of equipment (or with no equipment at all). "Efficiency" is an operative term here because efficiency of training translates to cost. To determine the relative efficiency of different types of equipment, consider:

- The amount of time required to accomplish the training objectives (given the participants' learning styles and preferences) with no equipment, if that is an option, and with each equipment alternative

- How that time translates to training costs, including development costs, training preparation and delivery costs, and other costs associated with productive time lost from the job and additional travel and meal expenses.

Equipment can support the learning and still not be a good investment because it does not offer the flexibility required to justify its acquisition cost or because its effective life span is too short to justify that cost. In these cases, it may be better to consider the tradeoffs, including the possibility of reduced training efficiency and its related costs, involved in using alternative equipment. One way to make an initial determination about whether equipment has the flexibility required to justify its purchase is to:

- Review current and projected training offerings to see how many could benefit from using the equipment.

- Check the training schedule to see how often each offering is provided. If the equipment will be in storage more than it will be used, it probably isn't a good option, especially if alternative equipment is available at a lower overall cost.

It is a necessity to obtain subject matter expert (SME) input on equipment requirements early in the training design process where tradeoffs and corrections for both primary and secondary equipment are less costly.

The SMEs will help to ensure that the design and corresponding equipment decisions support the required learning outcomes. The SMEs should also be consulted throughout training development whenever there is a question about the learning strategy and to verify that the training is accurate and relevant. Remember, however, that SMEs are not necessarily also trainers and may not think in terms of training strategies and adult learning principles. Before meeting with SMEs, prepare to present your strategy in a way that they will understand and that will facilitate receiving feedback in a way that readily translates to your needs.

12.3   Facilities Planning

Think for a moment about the last training session you instructed or in which you participated. What do you remember about the training? Chances are that if the facility was good, you remember the training experience. If, however, the training took place in a poor facility, you probably remember the facility. While no facility will be perfect for all participants and instructors, *a good facility is one that facilitates, rather than impedes, the achievement of the training objectives.* A case study from the United States Post Office is included at the end of this chapter that shows the evolution of their enormous technical training facility in Norman, Oklahoma. The present facility is the result of excellent planning on their part to see that every need of their trainees is met, including on-site housing built for use during the training. The on-site housing has saved millions of dollars by allowing them to control the cost of housing, food, and transportation to and from the facility for those coming from out of town.

Facilities planning is complex and cannot be addressed exhaustively in a single chapter or even in an entire book. When planning for a new facility or for the renovation of an existing facility, it is highly desirable to hire an architect and/or a facilities design consultant. Decisions about the design of a facility should always be made by a team that consists of the facility manager, trainers, training participants, and a designer, architect, or design consultant (Leed and Leed, 1987). Each team member will bring different expectations, perspectives, and areas of expertise to the design effort. While some team members will have different levels of expertise at different points in the planning process, each point of view is equally important to planning an effective facility. This part will cover the basic factors that the planning team should consider in order to plan and develop training facilities that promote learning and minimize distractions.

Facilities planning follows the same phases as Instructional Systems Development (ISD) models: analysis, design, development, implementation, and evaluation. Just as training designers apply learning from each phase during subsequent phases to achieve the desired learning outcomes, facilities planners must use the data gathered in each phase throughout the process to ensure that the facility meets the training needs for which it was designed.

12.3.1 Facility Analysis

During facility analysis, the planning team identifies as many requirements for the facility as possible. As in training analysis, facility analysis is critical to the quality of the end product and may, in fact, save the organization money over the long term. As a minimum, it is critical that the planning team carefully analyze the following categories of information:

- The training need or needs that the facility will support
- Training participants' learning styles and preferences
- Equipment required to support the training need

Some of the questions that the planning team should attempt to answer during facility analysis are shown in Figure 12-1. Note, however, that these questions are general and that each organization will have to tailor the questions to fit the organization's specific requirements.

Planners should also determine whether the facility will have multiple uses (e.g., as meeting space). If so, training needs should take priority. Other needs should be accommodated to the degree possible without sacrificing training considerations. Too often managers worried about meeting rooms manage to get changes made in plans that leave a facility poorly designed for training.

12.3.2 Facility Design

A thorough analysis most likely will result in several design alternatives. During the design phase, the planning team will review all of the data gathered during analysis to select the most viable option and design the actual facility. Compromises are nearly always required upon review of the initial design based on space limitations, cost constraints, anticipated future training requirements, or other reasons.

To create a total learning environment, the facility design must consider a wide variety of components, including the site; the structure or structures that will house the facility; and the interior design, accompanying media requirements, and training support services needed (Leed and Leed, 1987).

INSTRUCTIONS: Answer each of the questions below. Then review your responses as a means of narrowing your organization's options for a training facility. You may need to talk with others in your organization to answer some of the questions.

General Information:

1. Approximately how many participants will be trained at the new facility?

    ____ Weekly

    ____ Monthly

    ____ Yearly

2. From what geographic locations will the participants travel for training? (Mark all that apply.)

    ____ Locally only

    ____ Eastern U.S.

    ____ Midwestern U.S.

    ____ Western U.S.

    ____ Internationally

3. What is the average length of time that a participant will attend the facility for a single offering?

    ____ 1 day

    ____ 2–3 days

    ____ 4–5 days

    ____ More than 5 days

4. Participants will be housed:

    ____ On-site

    ____ In hotels and/or motels

5. It is important that recreational facilities be located:

    ____ On-site

    ____ Off-site but in close proximity

    ____ Recreational facilities are not required

Figure 12-1.   Facility analysis worksheet.

6. List the advantages and disadvantages of collocating the training facility at an existing work facility:

               Advantages   Disadvantages

7. List the advantages and disadvantages of locating the training facility at an off-site location:

               Advantages   Disadvantages

Current Training Needs:

8. Training will take place in a (mark all that apply):
   - ____ Classroom setting
   - ____ Laboratory workshop setting
   - ____ Small group setting
   - ____ Other (list):

9. Identify the approximate number of each of the following room types required for training:
   - ____ Auditorium
   - ____ Classroom
   - ____ Laboratory/Workshop
   - ____ Break-outs
   - ____ Other (list):

10. List special equipment requirements that the training facility must accommodate (e.g., dimensions, weight, wiring, etc.):

Figure 12-1. (*Continued*)

---

11. List other specific requirements that the training facility must meet:

Anticipated Future Needs:

12. List anticipated future training requirements that will affect the facility:

Figure 12-1. (*Continued*)

12.3.3 Site Selection

The best location for a training facility depends on several factors. Before recommending a site, the planning team should investigate whether it is most advantageous for the facility to be collocated with the job site, separate from but near the job site, or at a remote location. Each option has advantages and disadvantages based on the type of training to be delivered at the facility, the number of persons receiving training at the facility, the necessity for and proximity of support facilities (e.g., food service, sleeping facilities, library and media centers), the cost implications of each option (including whether to use an existing facility or purchase or lease a new facility), the availability of recreational and other activities, and other factors. Some of the factors that the planning team should consider before recommending a training site are shown in Figure 12-2.

12.3.4 The Structure

After the site for the training facility has been selected, the planning team will need to consider and make recommendations and decisions about the design of the structure or structures that will house the training. Because the design components for the training facility itself are myriad and complex, the planning team should rely on the architect's or design consultant's expertise when determining requirements for:

Heating, ventilation, and air-conditioning (HVAC)

Electricity and telephone requirements

Site Address:	Date Visited:		

Rate the following items about the facility:

	Excellent	Fair	Poor
____ **The overall facility:**			
____ Overall ambiance	____	____	____
____ Parking availability/location	____	____	____
____ Access	____	____	____
____ Proximity to:			
▪ Public transportation	____	____	____
▪ Food services	____	____	____
▪ Hotels and motels	____	____	____
▪ Recreation facilities	____	____	____
____ **The structure:**			
____ HVAC	____	____	____
____ Electric	____	____	____
____ Telephone	____	____	____
____ Room sizes/configuration	____	____	____
____ Wall placement	____	____	____
____ Overall configuration	____	____	____
____ Storage	____	____	____
____ Restrooms	____	____	____
____ Special access for handicapped	____	____	____
____ Administrative areas	____	____	____
____ Security	____	____	____
____ **Media capabilities:**			
____ Audio	____	____	____
____ Video	____	____	____
____ Projection	____	____	____
____ Computer	____	____	____
____ Other:			
____ **How well could the facility handle the number of participants required:**			
____ During normal training periods	____	____	____
____ During peak training periods	____	____	____

Figure 12-2. Facility evaluation worksheet.

_____ **List the facility's specific strengths:**

_____ **List the facility's specific weaknesses:**

_____ **List any overriding organizational needs that make this facility particularly well suited (or poorly suited):**

_____ **Overall facility rating:**
 _____ Excellent
 _____ Fair
 _____ Poor

Figure 12-2. (_Continued_)

Placement of load-bearing walls

Placement of windows

Storage

He or she will be familiar with local building codes and can interpret equipment specifications to meet the general needs of the facility. Guidelines for evaluating the architect's design recommendations for training areas are shown in Figure 12-3.

12.3.5 Interior Design

There are many interior design components that the planning team must also consider before finalizing the facility design, and many must be evaluated concurrently with the structural design. Interior design components should be driven by the application of adult learning principles to the

Design Component	Planning Guidelines
HVAC	■ Locate away from training rooms. ■ Avoid airflow directly onto training participants. ■ Minimize fan and other equipment noise. NOTE: Fans that run constantly are preferable to those that turn on and off. ■ Require multizone or variable air volume systems with controls in every training area. ■ Verify that humidity levels will not impair equipment operation.
Electrical	■ Overestimate electrical requirements. For each training room: ■ Place 1 outlet in the floor approximately 10 ft from the front wall and centered between the side walls. ■ Place additional outlets where video monitors are likely to be placed. ■ Allow for additional outlets to accommodate equipment that the participants will use during training (e.g., computers, power tools, etc.). *Keep the outlets as close to the point of use as possible.* ■ Consider under-floor access to accommodate future wiring changes.
Telephone jacks	■ Place as required for equipment use only. *Do not place telephones in the training room unless they are required for the training.* ■ Consider under-floor access to accommodate future telephone needs.
Placement of load-bearing (structural) walls	■ Ensure that load-bearing walls do not interfere with the line of site in any training area.

Figure 12-3. Structural planning guidelines.

Window placement	■ Place as determined by the training need. NOTE: Generally, the more participatory the learning, the more acceptable windows become. Window light must be controlled for media use, however.
Storage	■ Plan for media and equipment storage close to training rooms. ■ If possible, allow enough room to store all media and equipment. ■ Plan wall storage for training materials in each training area.

Figure 12-3. (*Continued*)

overall training facility. Before making interior design decisions, therefore, it is important that the planning team review key adult learning principles as they apply to the essential training requirements for the facility. Far too many facilities are built for their aesthetic beauty and not their practical use. Training facilities will not always be as attractive as office spaces. Too many training facilities are useless because of poor lighting, insufficient space in the rooms, poorly designed media areas, and uncomfortable furniture. Trainers need to be very assertive about these and other elements when designing or remodeling a facility.

There are a multitude of interior design components of which to be aware when planning a training facility. General planning guidelines for interior design points that are key to training areas are shown in Figure 12-4. Many interior design decisions must be based on the type of training to be conducted in the facility. Listening to the trainers can be critical at this stage. For example, one company spent money remodeling an existing building into a training center. Against the wishes of the trainers, the facilities people put a brick floor in front of the elevators. One day the facilities people were using the new training rooms. All morning the rattling of cart wheels moving over the bricks interrupted the class. The impact of their decision was brought home without a word having to be said by the trainer.

12.3.6   Accompanying Media

Media decisions for training facilities should be driven by the learning objectives for the training, the training methods selected to train the objectives, and the relative costs and benefits of specific media (Clark, 1989). In fact, Finkel (1984) cautions against the use of too-complex

Design Component	Planning Guidelines
Walls	▪ If raised floors and suspended ceilings are used, require permanent walls to extend from "slab to slab," rather than from floor to ceiling. ▪ *Side walls should accept push pins, masking tape, etc., without damaging the wall surface.* ▪ Movable walls to separate training areas may be preferable to provide increased flexibility. ▪ Wall surfaces should be easily maintained. ▪ Pastel colors on wall surfaces are preferable to white, dark colors, or bright colors.
Floors	▪ Carpet where possible to reduce sound transmission. NOTE: Tile may be preferable if there is a high probability of spills or other undue wear on carpeting. ▪ If raised floors are planned, require sound-proofing in the area below movable walls. ▪ Access panels may be desirable to accommodate future wiring changes. ▪ Consider a sloped or tiered floor in rooms intended for large groups.
Ceilings	▪ Determine ceiling height based on the size of the room and media requirements. ▪ If suspended ceilings are planned, require soundproofing in the areas above movable walls.
Sound control	▪ Soundproof all areas above and below movable walls. ▪ Avoid hard, reflective surfaces on walls and floors. ▪ Carpet floors, where possible. ▪ Locate training rooms away from food services, HVAC plan, and other noisy areas. ▪ Consider "white" noise in training areas.

Figure 12-4. Interior design planning guidelines.

	▪ If raised floors and suspended ceilings are used, require permanent walls to run from "slab to slab," rather than from floor to ceiling.
	▪ Plan training rooms that are square rather than rectangular.
Lighting	▪ Provide between 80 and 150 footcandles of lighting for training areas.
	▪ Avoid shadowing. Plan for lighting that is evenly distributed.
	▪ Avoid spotlights that illuminate the front of the room.
	▪ Accommodate all special lighting requirements based on the training need.
Control switches	▪ Place all controls for each training room in a central location near the instructor.

Figure 12-4. (*Continued*)

media or too much media in the training setting. Generally, facility planners should accommodate such commonly used media as flipcharts or whiteboards, overhead projectors, and videotape in every training area and learning center. Those purchasing these media should be very careful about vendor selection and reliability of equipment. One organization built a brand new training center. When it came time to selecting the whiteboards for the classrooms and labs, they went with the low bid. The boards looked great until the first day of classes. When the technical trainer turned on the overhead projector, none of the participants near the center of the room could see the board due to the glare reflecting from the board. The whiteboards were of low quality and did not diffuse the projector glare as higher-quality boards will do. All of the boards had to be replaced. A media expert, internal or external, is the person to consult when selecting media. Mistakes are often very costly in this area. Other media (e.g., computer terminals, telecommunication, etc.), however, should be dictated by training needs and should be accommodated in interior design component planning. It is important, however, to design the facility in such a way that will allow the flexibility for future changes required by changing technology or evolving organizational needs.

12.3.7 Support Services

The provision of support services, including restrooms, food services, library and media center, housing facilities, and recreational facilities, can be critical to establishing the overall learning environment. Careful consideration should, therefore, be given to each of these areas within the context of the facility's purpose. When making decisions about support services, be sure to provide accommodations for the disabled, non-English-speaking, and those with other special needs. Some general guidelines for planning support services are shown in Figure 12-5.

12.3.8 Facility Development

During facility development, the organization will contract the work, complete the facility, and train the support staff to use the new facility and equipment. During construction, the planning team can expect many trying times and more than a few midcourse corrections. Staff training will most likely also point to several design changes. Assuming careful analysis and attention to detail during design, design changes—and, therefore, cost overruns—should be kept to a minimum. The U.S. Post Office Facility Case Study at the end of this chapter has gone through many stages of development. The result is a state-of-the-art technical training facility.

12.3.9 Facility Implementation

After the facility is complete and the staff is trained, implementation provides an opportunity to test the total facility in an actual training situation. During implementation, it is important to test all major facility components under all training conditions. The planning team should carefully solicit feedback from instructors, participants, and support staff to gain their input and suggestions on each major component of the facility. The team should maintain a list of issues affecting training and of suggestions for improving the overall quality and function of the facility so that the facility can be evaluated fairly and improvements identified and scheduled logically.

12.3.10 Facility Evaluation

Like any good training program, facility evaluation and fine-tuning should occur on an ongoing basis. *Evaluation will begin during the initial implementation and should continue throughout the life of the facility.* Special evaluation procedures should be implemented after any major changes in equipment or key design components.

Support Service	Planning Factors
Restrooms	■ Locate near training rooms, conference rooms, and lounges. ■ Do not permit plumbing to be placed in a common wall between restrooms and training rooms. ■ Allow greater capacity for women than for men.
Food service and break areas	■ Break areas should be located near the training rooms. ■ Isolate from the training area to avoid noise transmission but should be close enough that time is not lost in getting from training to the food service area.
Library and media center	■ Locate in close proximity to both training and housing areas. ■ Provide areas for individual and small group work. ■ If possible, plan for natural light for reading but artificial light (to reduce glare and improve visibility) for visual media. ■ Accommodate differing humidity requirements for paper-based materials and media.
Housing facilities	■ Provide accommodations for studying in the sleeping area, including a well-lit work space and comfortable chair. ■ Provide lounges or other common areas where participants can study in small groups. ■ Plan for refrigerators and other amenities as necessary based on proximity to other facilities.
Recreational facilities	■ Provide information about local recreational facilities to all participants as part of registration or training administrative information.

Figure 12-5. Planning factors for support services.

12.4 Facilities Options

Many organizations are unable to support full-time training facilities. There are several options available to these organizations that can enable them to support their technical training needs without incurring the long-term, continuing costs of supporting a dedicated training facility. This part will address the most common among the available options:

- Short- and long-term leased facilities
- Partnerships and/or cooperative agreements with other business entities, vocational schools, or colleges.

The selection of one or more of these options will vary widely depending on the needs of the organization and the availability of resources in the area.

12.4.1 Leased Facilities

Short- and long-term leases offer many organizations the opportunity to provide technical training without incurring many of the costs associated with owning, operating, and maintaining a full-time, in-house facility. Leases offer advantages in that they:

- Can accommodate one-time, short-term, or infrequent training requirements
- Are not accompanied by the overhead requirements of a full-time, in-house facility
- Allow for testing of different types of facilities or locations before making a long-term commitment.

Leases also present several disadvantages. They may:

- Require the organization to be responsible for a greater role in operations than it had anticipated
- Not be entirely suitable to the training need
- Not be flexible or responsive to changing organizational needs

There is a wide range of lease and rental options available, including hotels and conference centers, telecommunications centers, and office space, depending on the type and length of the training need. Organizations considering leasing space for a training facility should investigate all available options fully before entering into an agreement on any space.

12.4.2   Cooperative Agreements and Business Partnerships

Many organizations are entering into cooperative agreements with vocational schools and colleges to provide some or all of their technical training needs. Such an arrangement may be advantageous because these institutions have existing facilities, trained support staff, and—in many cases—equipment that can save the organization money. Organizations that develop cooperative agreements and business partnerships may still benefit from the arrangement, even if it becomes necessary to purchase equipment for the vocational school or college. Also, as enrollments in these institutions decline, many vocational schools and colleges are very willing to adjust their curricula or develop new curricula to meet business requirements. Organizations considering cooperative agreements with vocational schools or colleges should carefully identify and communicate their needs to several institutions to ensure that their needs can be met fully prior to entering into a long-term arrangement, however. The case study included on Lorain Community College's alliance with USS/Kobe Steel Company and Allen-Bradley Company points out how successful such relationships can be.

Business partnerships with other business entities are becoming more common, especially among primary providers and their suppliers. Business partnerships offer advantages to the business organization in that they allow the business to control the quality, timing, and cost of training. Advantages to the supplier include knowledge of the provider's exact technical specifications and quality requirements as well as the reduction or elimination of the costs associated with developing and providing training and maintaining a training facility.

12.5   Summary

Facilities and equipment planning is time-consuming and can be tedious for the planning team. It is a critical job, however, and, when carried out systematically and with careful attention to many details, one that is well worth the effort in terms of the overall effectiveness of learning, transfer of learning to the workplace, and—ultimately—return on corporate investment.

Case Study

U.S. Postal Service Technical Training Center Norman, Oklahoma

Pamela J. Osburn

Background

Training was scattered in nine leased buildings across Norman, Oklahoma, in 1987 when the U.S. Postal Service decided to build a permanent facility for training its national technical workforce. The Postal Service had established the Technical Training Center in 1969 by leasing and renovating a few floors of a University of Oklahoma dormitory. The first year, a staff of 50 offered three training programs, and postal technicians began coming to Oklahoma from across the nation.

In the late 1970s, the Postal Service began extensive efforts to automate processing of the nation's mail. Dramatic increases in technical training resulted, and by the early 1980s the center had expanded to eight more training facilities. Building renovations were frequent. Leased space included a former church, and changes were constant in the equipment and the space support each system needed. Students were bussed to and from training, and for meals.

With projections of postal automation's impact on technical training came the realization that the Postal Service was not positioned to provide required training in a timely way to large populations spread over a wide geographical area. Nancy George, currently northeast area manager of customer service and sales, and Suzanne J. Henry, currently vice president of employee relations, were then overseers of postal training and development. They led postal planners in a study of the long-term facility needs for technical training. Extensive cost analyses were performed, a proposal was developed, and in 1985 the Postal Board of Governors approved funding for a new postal-owned training facility. (The Postal Service pays for its operations from postage revenue—it has not received funding from taxes since 1982.) The facility would provide a base for centralized resident training, with designed capability to reach nonresident students in timely and cost-effective ways.

Suzanne Henry and Paul A. Crawford, the Center's manager, worked closely with architects on the facility design and function, and construction of a 290,000-sq-ft training complex began in June 1987. A phased move-in began just 15 months later, and the training facility was in full operation by January 1989.

Training Facility

The two-story training facility covers about 6.5 acres of a 55-acre site in southeast Norman. (See Figure 12-6.) It projects a sleek, high-technology appearance in the midst of a landscaped campus setting. The building is "intelligent," with automatic sensors controlling computer systems, lighting levels, room temperatures, and security systems. Its 40 classrooms and 43 labs were designed for technical training, and flexibility. A 500-ft main hallway runs the length of the facility and connects six building modules. Two administrative and services modules lie off either side of the middle, and four training wings jut from the corners. A full-service, cafeteria-kitchen accommodates up to 300. (See Figure 12-7.)

Training Wings

Each training wing contains 10 classrooms, plus training laboratories, multiuse areas, and instructor offices. A typical classroom and

Figure 12-6. U.S. Postal Service Technical Training Center in Norman, Oklahoma. (*Photo courtesy of the U.S. Postal Service.*)

laboratory has removable walls, allowing the space to be quickly modified as equipment and learning programs change. Movable heating, ventilating, and air-conditioning units are accessible through ceiling panel grids. Downsized, but fully operational, training elevators, boilers, and air-conditioning systems were included in the facility design.

Learning Technology

Planners also included the latest in learning technology. The center is equipped with complete videotape and audiovisual production studios. Sound booths and digital telephone bridges connect center instructors with students in their home offices. A full-production studio and control room uplinks live satellite training programs. The center produces its own course materials using networked computer systems, in-house graphics capability, and an on-site print shop.

Conference Center

The training facility also contains a 6950-sq-ft conference center. It will seat 450 people when opened into one large lecture hall, or can be divided into as many as six smaller meeting rooms. Each of the six meeting rooms is equipped with a ceiling-mounted projector, motorized projection screen, and its own lighting controls. The

Facility Layout / First Floor Plan

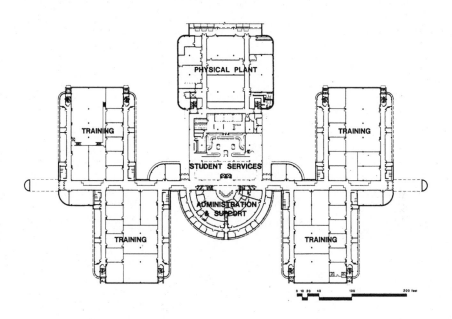

A comprehensive series of individual administrative, learning, dining, and conference areas are interconnected, making the Center completely self-contained. The two-story building is "intelligent" with automatic sensors controlling computer systems, lighting levels, temperatures for environmental systems, and building security systems. An outer parameter road connects parking areas and major access roads.

Figure 12-7.   Layout of the U.S. Postal Service Technical Training Center. (*Courtesy of the U.S. Postal Service.*)

conference center is used for staff and student meetings, as well as conferences for other postal, business, and community groups.

Housing Facility

Completion of the training facility in 1988 positioned the Postal Service to meet its long-term needs for technical training, and provided the flexibility to handle rapidly changing training needs. But student housing remained in two remote leased buildings. Some housing services were duplicated, some existed in only one location, and students still had to be bussed to and from class. Crawford led development of a second proposal for the Board of Governors, and in 1992 the Postal Service built a six-story, 1000-room dormitory adjacent to the training facility, which can support conference center users as well as technical students. (See Figure 12-8.)

Bringing housing on-site improved operations, reduced operating costs, added convenience for students, and allowed the center to meet its long-term needs for student housing. The housing facility also contains a cafeteria, plus a multipurpose gymnasium, fitness center, and game rooms for students that are in the center's care seven days a week, 24 hours a day.

Present

Today, the center's 230-member training and support staff conducts over 80 technical skills courses for postal employees from all over the United States. In-house, training is in session up to 20 hours a day. Interactive teletraining and satellite courses are broadcast from coast to coast, plus Hawaii, Alaska, and Puerto Rico. The Technical Training Center's goal is to provide employees with timely knowledge and skills to keep postal automation, facilities, and vehicles operating at peak capacity.

Curriculum

The Technical Training Center's 80-course curriculum includes technical skills and maintenance management training on computerized mail processing equipment, building systems, data communications and information systems, postage vending machines, and postal vehicles. Courses include maintenance training on an optical character reader that reads typed addresses, sprays on a bar code, and sorts 35,000 letters an hour. A person can sort about 600 letters an hour.

Training methods include attending resident courses at the center, or completing center courses offered at post offices, over teletraining, and via satellite broadcasts.

- Courses range from one-day seminars to five-week systems training.
- Average course length is 9.5 days.
- There are 850 annual course offerings.
- Number of students annually number 20,000.

Classrooms designed for learning:

- Average 800 sq ft.
- Seat 14 students at tables (can spread out technical diagrams).
- Contain video players, monitors, projection screens, whiteboards.
- Lighting adjusts for lectures, vugraphs, and video viewing.
- Connect to studio for internal video broadcasts.
- Located next door to labs.

United States Postal Service

Technical Training Center

Introduction

Today's computerized mail processing equipment can read a four-line address and sort 35,000 letters an hour. The successful delivery of the nation's mail depends more and more on such high technology processing systems, building support equipment, and postal vehicles. Keeping the equipment running is the critical task for the postal technical workforce.

The Technical Training Center, Norman, OK, is the Postal Service's national center for advanced technical training. It conducts maintenance training and motor vehicle craft training for postal employees from all over the United States.

Student Profile

TTC students are postal employees attending job-skill training. They include electronics technicians, equipment mechanics, computer specialists, and motor vehicle employees.

TTC History

In 1969, the TTC leased a few top floors of Couch Tower, a 12-story dormitory on the University of Oklahoma campus. The first year of operation, a staff of 50 conducted training for 7,000 students.

By Fiscal 1988, TTC had expanded to nine leased buildings in Norman, and was training 19,000 students a year.

Training Facility

In September 1988, the TTC moved into a 293,000 square-foot, postal-owned building designed specifically for technical training.

Some 40 classrooms and 43 labs have flexible walls and raised flooring to adjust for changes in postal equipment. Fully-operational training ele-

vators, boilers, and air conditioning systems were part of the facility design.

Student Housing

A 430,000 square-foot student dormitory was built on the TTC site in 1992. The 1,000-room dorm provides a comfortable housing environment, recreation aimed toward fitness and health, and networking and team-building opportunities for postal students.

The housing was designed to have a significant, positive impact on the technicians' learning experience.

Fitness

Fitness and recreation facilities provide safe and healthful activities that contribute to the learning environment. Facilities include a gymnasium, game room, fitness center, an outdoor swimming pool, and playing fields.

Optional fitness assessments help students choose the best activities for them, or develop personal fitness programs.

Health Care

An on-site Health Clinic provides medical aid, emergency care, and health and wellness educa-

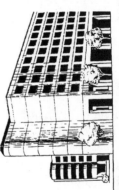

The student dormitory was completed in 1992.

tion for staff and students. It is staffed by occupational health care nurses.

More extensive health care is provided by the Norman Regional Hospital.

Automated Student Enrollment

Post offices enroll technicians for training through a nationwide computer system linking them directly to the TTC. The system also provides on-line access to course schedules, training reports and student training records.

Staffing

Over 470 postal and contract staff are employed by the Center.

◆ The training staff consists of instructors, course developers, clerical staff, media specialists, and support personnel.

◆ Contract employees also provide training and housing facility support.

Advanced Training Methods

The TTC continually explores ways to improve training, and expand training capacities beyond the Norman center.

◆ Teletraining allows TTC to deliver some courses to students in their home offices. Courses, course materials, and audiovisuals are developed by TTC instructors; and mailed to local offices. TTC instructors then conduct class over sophisticated teleconferencing equipment.

◆ The Postal Satellite Training Network takes teletraining a step further with televised instruction over a satellite broadcasting system.

◆ TTC also uses video, computer and other advanced technologies to enhance the learning process and condense student training time.

TTC — We Deliver Knowledge!

022093

Figure 12-8. The U.S. Postal Service Technical Training Center student dormitory, built in 1992. *(Courtesy of the U.S. Postal Service.)*

Labs designed for flexibility:

- Range from 1400 to 1600 sq ft.
- Raised flooring for computer, communications, and electrical hook-ups.
- Peel-up tiles and carpet squares provide access to hook-ups.
- Demountable walls between labs can be moved in a day.
- Equipment can be moved in and out through removable six-by-six-foot windows to the hallways.

Instructor offices:

- Around perimeter of training buildings.
- Near classrooms and labs.
- Window lighting supplements artificial.
- Use space-saving modular furniture.

The Technical Training Center supports the U.S. Postal Service's efforts to automate mail processing and other operations. Automation is not only necessary to handle 580 million letters a day, it is cost efficient. It costs $42 to manually sort 1000 pieces of mail, $19 per thousand using mechanized equipment, and only $3 per thousand using automation.

Case Study

Advanced Technologies Center
Lorain County Community College

Sandra Everett

Declining productivity rates in manufacturing identified nationally in the late 1970s launched an invasion of technical modernization that continues today at an accelerating pace. In an attempt to regain our market share as a global competitor, new technology was introduced into all areas of industry in this country, demanding higher skill and competency levels.

Lorain County Community College was the first Advanced Technologies Center to be built in the state of Ohio. Built in 1982 to assist industry in engineering and manufacturing technologies, it is now one of the leading technology centers in the country. Our number one challenge is to provide a facility and the equipment to meet industry's technical education and training requirements. The requirements range from basic workplace literacy to complex systems integration for automation.

International competition has generated a demand for automation, focusing on integration, or the tying of several pieces of equipment together in a systems approach, capable of communicating electronically. Workcells, flexible manufacturing systems (FMS), and computer-integrated manufacturing (CIM) are some examples of integrated systems, having the capability of producing products better, faster, and more cost-effectively. Preparing the workforce for automation requires a wide range of training and education, along with sophisticated, expensive equipment.

The Advanced Technologies Center of Lorain County Community College, along with most colleges throughout the country, has been forced to become very creative in equipment acquisition. Not only is much of the equipment cost-prohibitive, but education budgets for capital equipment have simultaneously been slashed drastically. The most successful approach to equipment acquisition for our Advanced Technologies Center over the past several years has been through a variety of partnerships. The most valuable lesson we have learned from our partnership experiences is that if partnerships are to be successful, they must be mutually beneficial, as indicated by our most recent partnership between USS/Kobe Steel Company, Allen-Bradley Company, and Lorain Community College.

Lorain Community College is engaged with USS/Kobe Steel Company in a partnership effort generating a 15-month training program in mechanical and hydraulics training (M & H), and systems repair training. This is a joint effort through the Lorain County Education and Training Consortium (LCETC) consisting of Lorain County Joint Vocational School, Lorain City Schools—Adult Education, and Lorain County Community College. One significant area of training that the college provides is programmable logic controller training (PLC). While the college has an Allen-Bradley PLC lab, USS/Kobe Steel Company requested that the training be conducted on a specific state-of-the-art Allen-Bradley PLC which the college did not have, nor had the budget to purchase. USS/Kobe Steel Company has an ongoing working relationship with Allen-Bradley, and suggested a meeting to discuss how the college might be able to acquire this very expensive equipment.

After several meetings with the three organizations, the college was able to acquire the PLCs at an affordable cost. (See Figure 12-9.) USS/Kobe Steel Company received the training they required and will continue to need over the next three years, and Allen-Bradley Company was offered resources they found to be very beneficial through the Advanced Technologies Center. This partnership is an example of a win-win situation for all three organizations involved, and we continue to find additional ways to support each other.

Bibliography

Cheng, Alex F., "Hands-On Learning at Motorola," *Training & Development Journal,* vol. 44, October 1990, pp. 34–35.

Clark, Ruth Colvin, *Developing Technical Training: A Structured Approach for the Development of Classroom and Computer-Based Instructional Materials,* Addison-Wesley, Reading, Mass., 1989.

Figure 12-9. The Allen-Bradley PLC Lab at Lorain Community College, used by the USS/Kobe Steel Company training program.

Filipczak, Bob, "Make Room For Training," *Training*, vol. 28, October 1991, pp. 76–82.

Finkel, Coleman, "Where Learning Happens," *Training & Development Journal*, vol. 38, April 1984, pp. 32–36.

Hays, R. T., and M. J. Singer, *Simulation Fidelity in Training System Design: Bridging the Gap Between Reality and Training*, Springer-Verlag, New York, 1989.

Knowles, Malcolm, *The Adult Learner: A Neglected Species*, 2d ed., Gulf Publishing, Houston, Tex., 1978.

Leed, Karen B., and James R. Leed, *Building For Adult Learning*, LDA Publishing, Cincinnati, Oh., 1987.

Liao, Thomas T., "Pre-College Technology Education and Instructional Technology," in Michael Hacker, Anthony Gordon, and Marc de Vries (eds.), *Integrating Advanced Technology Into Education*, Springer-Verlag, Berlin, Germany, 1991, pp. 127–147.

Savage, Ernest N., "Determinants of Advanced Technological Content in Technological Education Curriculum," in Michael Hacker, Anthony Gordon, and Marc DeVries (eds.), *Integrating Advanced Technology into Education*, Springer-Verlag, Berlin, Germany, 1991, pp. 21–39.

Schultheiss, Emily, "What a Well-Designed Training Room Should Have . . . ," *Office Administration And Automation*, vol. 45, July 1984, pp. 30–32, 82, 85.

Slack, Kim, "Training for the Real Thing," *Training & Development Journal*, vol. 47, May 1993, pp. 79–89.

Wagel, William H., "Building Excellence Through Training," *Personnel*, vol. 63, September 1986, pp. 5–10.

13

Technology Learning Laboratories

Aaron Agrawal
Motorola

Dr. Aaron Agrawal *is the Director of Technology Education at Motorola University. He is responsible for the development and dissemination of technology programs and learning laboratories worldwide. Prior to joining Motorola, Dr. Agrawal had 15 years of experience in management and technical positions with GCA Corp. and Gould Inc. in systems development and R&D. His technical expertise is in the areas of factory automation and computer integrated manufacturing. He is a Senior Member of SME and a Certified Manufacturing Technologist.*

13.1   Rationale/Approach

The application of new technology has, for many years, been promoted as a cure-all for companies experiencing a case of noncompetitiveness. Today, companies vying for market share in a global economy can implement a host of technologies that are available to help increase productivity and quality levels. In the factory, robotic workstations, electronic vision systems, and other automation technologies are being coupled with information technologies to create a workplace that little resembles the manual assembly production lines of a few years ago.

The factory floor is not the only place in today's businesses that is experiencing dramatic technological change. Literally everyone participating in business today, from office workers to the CEO, are also confronted with a barrage of information technologies such as computer-integrated manufacturing, networking, and databases.

What businesses discover when they begin to introduce new technologies is that their employees often don't have the skills to make full use of the technology. In many manufacturing settings, people have been working in manual assembly lines for years and are ill-equipped to work with a computer, let alone a robot. In today's office, workers accustomed to electric typewriters and interoffice mail are being asked to use sophisticated computer applications and e-mail. The training these people have received mostly consists of traditional, classroom-style courses or mentoring with no direct contact with the new technologies with which they are being confronted.

Through everyday use, people do gradually learn to use new, sophisticated technologies. That unguided learning, however, can be accidental and piecemeal. It may not keep up with the rate at which even newer technologies are introduced. The challenge before many companies, therefore, is to bring diverse, multilingual workforces, accustomed to traditional manufacturing and office technologies, into the "twenty-first century."

How does a company like Motorola integrate new technology into the way it conducts business? Who needs to get involved? Who needs to be trained and educated? How does a company get its employees to utilize the technology?

The answers to these questions can be found in a four-step process Motorola University is using that mirrors how people learn in the real world:

1. Make people *aware* of the new technology.

2. *Educate* people to promote understanding of the new technology.

3. Provide tool-based *training* to technology implementers.

4. Provide *application* assistance for implementation on the job.

The three-dimensional *Technology Training Intervention Model* (Figure 13-1) shows *learning levels* based on this four-step process. *Population* is the second dimension, broadly grouped into managers, engineers, and support personnel/users. It is necessary that appropriate training interventions be available to all populations since they all have roles in contributing to performance change. The third dimension is *technology topics* relevant to the enterprise. For Motorola, they can be grouped into three major areas: *process technologies, automation technologies,* and *information technologies.* There are many subtopic areas within each one of them.

With the model in Figure 13-1 as the framework, we need to address training implementation for the adult learner. There is a Chinese proverb which gives us a clue about adult learners:

> I hear and I forget
> I see and I remember
> I do and I understand

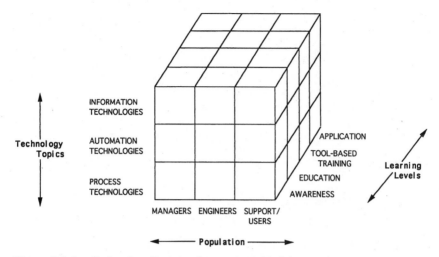

Figure 13-1. Technology Training Intervention Model.

Adult learners, as a normal aspect of the process of maturation, have different needs from young adults in high school or college. First, an environment has to be provided where the learner feels he or she is actively engaged in the material being presented. Second, adult learners need to make efficient use of the little time they have available for training. This is especially important when employees are involved in time-sensitive processes, such as the development of new products or the manufacturing of a product that is in great demand. Third, they need to be able to quickly apply what is learned to the workplace.

For all of these reasons, a purely classroom experience is not sufficient and needs to be supplemented with hands-on learning experiences. Hands-on learning is especially beneficial when:

- Simulation is needed to match the workplace environment.
- Difficult subject matter needs to be clarified.
- The skill to be learned is software-oriented.
- The interrelationships between, and integration of, new technologies need to be demonstrated.
- New technology that presently does not exist in the field is to be introduced.
- The audience is diverse in culture and language.
- Time allotted to impart training needs to be decreased.

Learning laboratories provide the means to achieve these ends. They should be specifically designed for education and training and not for technical research, development, or production.

13.2 Laboratory Types

The types of training laboratories for a given organization vary, depending upon the needs and size of the population served. Because of the complexity and costs associated with establishing learning laboratories, companies usually find it best to implement them in phases. A slow evolution is also beneficial because it is difficult to completely evaluate a company's hands-on learning needs or to gauge the impact of learning laboratories up-front.

Based on the experience at Motorola University, three types of laboratories are suggested.

13.2.1 Computer-Based Labs

These labs are essentially classrooms with computer equipment. Generally, there are three types.

Personal Computer Lab: Consisting of PCs capable of supporting DOS, OS/2, and Windows operating systems for a variety of business, engineering, and office training needs.

Macintosh Lab: Consisting of Apple Macintosh computers to support office applications training.

Engineering Lab: Consisting of engineering workstations in the UNIX environment to support complex engineering applications.

These labs should consist of 8 to 12 workstations, one for each participant. Two participants can share if learning objectives are not compromised by doing so. The instructor station should be equally equipped, and the computer monitor should be connected to an overhead projection system. A shared printer is generally needed. Other standard classroom equipment, such as an overhead projector, a whiteboard, flipcharts, etc., are also necessary.

Three different examples for room layout are shown in Figure 13-2. The first shows the workstations arranged in a traditional classroom format. The second shows the workstations in an L-shaped arrangement, which is particularly good for interaction among participants in a larger class. In the third layout, the workstations are arranged in a boardroom format. This arrangement is particularly good for small class size or for executive education programs.

Workstation equipment models are not specified here. They are dictated by the needs of the participants, available technology, and cost considerations. A general guideline, however, is to duplicate or simulate participants' work environment as much as possible. Since labs usually need to support a variety of training and education programs, the hardware plat-

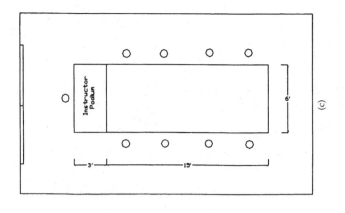

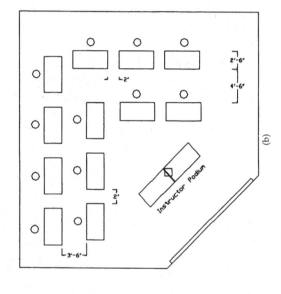

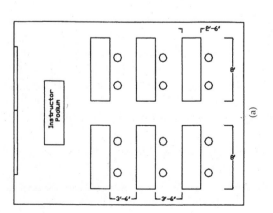

Figure 13-2. Computer-based lab layout examples.

form needs to be flexible and expandable to accommodate many application software packages.

An important requirement for computer-based learning laboratories is to connect all workstations in a room through a local area network with a file server. By connecting workstations, participants and instructors can share a networked printer, and educational software can be easily loaded from the file server. It is strongly suggested to have a control room (approximately 10 ft by 10 ft) that has separate and secure access. This room houses servers, network equipment, software media and documentation, and serves as work space for the technical support person.

13.2.2 Programmable Automation Literacy (PAL) Lab

This unique laboratory addresses the training needs of factory workforces as advanced manufacturing technologies change the landscape of the typical factory floor. The PAL lab is equipped with nine workstations arranged in a classroom that can accommodate up to 18 students as shown in Figure 13-3. (Fewer stations could be used for smaller class sizes.) The instructor station does not require a separate PAL workstation. Normal classroom equipment, such as whiteboards and a projection screen, are also shown in the figure.

Each workstation has a five-axis tabletop educational robot, a machine vision system, an electronics interface board, a sensor trainer, and a pneumatics trainer—all integrated to a personal computer shown pictorially in Figure 13-4.

The PAL workstation consists of six subsystems typical of most automated equipment, including *manipulators, machine vision systems, control electronics, sensors, pneumatics,* and *software programming.* The workstation is designed as a kit that can be disassembled, packaged, and shipped to plant locations around the world with relative ease.

Because of the variety of educational manufacturing equipment in the PAL workstation, it is used in a number of different programs. For example, a program designed for operators may use the equipment to build awareness of technology by showing, on a very basic level, what that technology can or cannot do. On another level, it is used to teach technicians how to troubleshoot automation equipment. Yet another use is to teach programming and computer integration of factory floor equipment.

13.2.3 Manufacturing Equipment Lab

This laboratory takes the tabletop educational experience of the PAL Laboratory one step further by providing a realistic, yet protected, factory environment for learners to practice job-relevant skills.

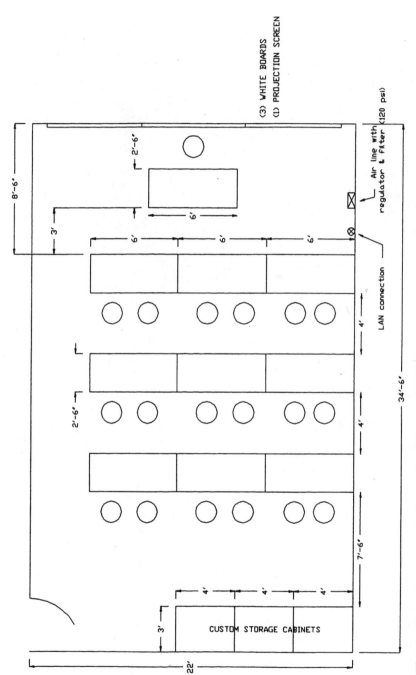

Figure 13-3. Programmable Automation Literacy (PAL) lab layout.

Figure 13-4. Example workstation in a PAL lab.

This lab is essentially a room equipped with power, air, and other utilities configured to operate the equipment found on a company's manufacturing floor. Space is provided for seating, work tables, cabinets, etc. The room can be arranged in many different ways. A sample layout of this lab is shown in Figure 13-5.

The equipment included in the manufacturing laboratory must meet the specific needs of the target population, and it need not be purchased for training use only. There are several uses for this type of learning laboratory:

- To train operators, technicians, and engineers in the use of new equipment before plant installation

- To provide flexible space for an equipment vendor who brings equipment for training

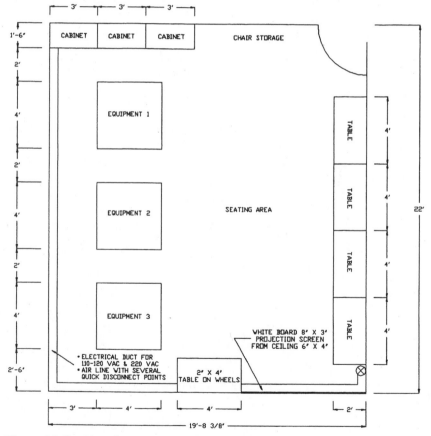

Figure 13-5. Manufacturing equipment lab layout.

- To allow advanced development groups to share equipment that is not widely available
- To make use of depreciated, yet fully operational, equipment for training purposes

13.3 Instructional Use of Laboratories

The laboratories just described can be used in a variety of ways for awareness, education, and tool-based training.

Over the years, several factors critical to the successful design, development, and implementation of laboratory-based technology education have been identified. It is recommended that a company:

- Work with a team of technical experts, instructional designers, manufacturing management, and equipment vendors.
- Perform a thorough needs analysis of the target audience.
- Ground laboratory design and course objectives in current and future job requirements, linked to business issues and corporate goals.
- Include delivery options and constraints up-front in the design of the labs and their respective courses.
- Establish rigorous requirements specifications for both labs and course materials.
- Perform rigorous development testing of all technical and instructional elements of the laboratory education system.
- Focus, at all times, on the needs and concerns of the learner.

The complete transfer of technology to a target population is a complex process. It is better handled, therefore, by providing a progressive learning experience for each instructional objective. A simple model is shown in Figure 13-6 which can be summarized as follows:

1. Classroom introduction to technology *concepts* through lecture, discussion, and team activities supported by graphics, models, videotapes, etc.
2. *Educational exercises* and experiments designed to clarify difficult subject matter with the use of educational equipment, software, and other aids.
3. Practice with real *tools and applications* in an environment that mimics the workplace, yet allows experimentation to support learning objectives.

Several laboratory-based programs are briefly described here as examples. Refer to the success factors listed earlier in this chapter when designing laboratory-based programs for your own organization.

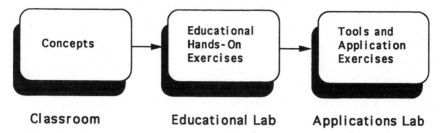

Figure 13-6. Learning progression model.

13.3.1 Motorola Awareness Programs

Technology Awareness is an eight-hour program, composed of four two-hour modules, that introduces manufacturing associates to the concepts of programmable automation. Upon completion, participants are able to:

- Be aware of business drivers for factory automation.
- Build a vocabulary of programmable automation.
- Understand process improvement through technology use.
- Develop confidence needed for additional training.

The program is balanced between the classroom and the lab. As concepts are introduced in the classroom, participants carry out simple exercises using robots, sensors, and machine vision systems in an automated factory using the PAL workstation. An important part of this program is that participants get to observe how these technologies interact with each other.

A *case study* is integrated into the "Enterprise Integration" section of Motorola Management Institute, where managers work in teams to develop a business plan for a manufacturing enterprise. The case study is based on an actual automated line used to assemble an electronic, instructional product. Teams must devise marketing and supplier strategies, develop line expansion and staffing plans, and complete a return-on-net-assets (RONA) forecast. They are given short briefings and equipment/software demonstrations. Several tools, both paper and computer-based, are provided to assist in their decision making. The completed business plan is presented to the entire class for critique.

13.3.2 Motorola Educational Programs

Machine Vision is a 16-hour training program that teaches manufacturing technicians and engineers the concepts necessary to operate and maintain a vision application. This course is a prerequisite for vendor-supplied equipment training. Upon completion, participants are able to:

- Identify hardware/software components of a vision system.
- Generate images by optimizing optics and lighting.
- Classify methods of image preprocessing and analysis.
- Operate, maintain, and calibrate a vision system.

The educational vision system of the PAL workstation makes it possible for participants to carry out a number of hands-on exercises to support these objectives.

The *Computer-Integrated Manufacturing* (CIM) overview is an eight-hour training program for employees at all job levels who need to have a basic understanding of CIM. Upon completion, participants are able to:

- Define CIM and drivers for its implementation.
- Create a map of CIM system hardware and software.
- Trace the path of a customer order through the CIM system.
- Identify further CIM training specific to the job.

This program uses an internally developed instructional software called *CIMple,* which models the entire manufacturing enterprise from customer order to shipment. This course gives participants the "big picture" they need to more fully understand their specific manufacturing system and the larger business environment.

13.3.3 Tool-Based Programs

Most tool-based programs are available from the vendors of the tool or from third-party training suppliers. They are generally equipment- and/or software-based. Some examples are:

- *Office automation tools* such as word processing, spreadsheet, database, and electronic mail applications.
- *Engineering tools* like computer-aided-design (CAD) and computer-aided-engineering (CAE) applications.
- *Software tools,* including operating systems such as DOS, Windows, and UNIX, and programming tools such as Basic, C, C+, C++, and X/Motif.
- *Manufacturing tools* such as process equipment, robot, or machine vision requiring training programs in both programming and maintenance.

By their very nature, these tools require training programs that make use of hands-on laboratories like those described in the previous section. Participants want to take part in a program that gives them the skills to quickly apply the tool back on the job. *Without adequate laboratory exercises for learning, the application of trained skills to the job is ineffective and incomplete.*

13.4 Laboratory Operations and Management

The smooth operation and management of learning laboratories are key to providing quality service and customer satisfaction. *A qualified staff of technical support is essential in creating a quality experience for customers.* To oversee the operational needs, a *systems administrator* is needed to support the computer-based laboratories and a *manufacturing technician* is needed to support manufacturing-related laboratories. They help in class setup (hardware/software), instructor support, and testing of new programs. To meet program development needs, *instructional design resources* need to be available to support design, development, and evaluation efforts.

Over time, a set of procedures and processes will evolve that suits the specific needs of the learning laboratory environment. Generally, these procedures and processes include scheduling, instructor support, quality monitoring through participant and instructor feedback, software loading and equipment setup, and financial chargebacks.

For an organization with a culturally and geographically diverse population, laboratory-based program roll-out often means more than designing and delivering a class. The lab capability needs to be available closer to the population. This can be accomplished by shipping the lab to a new location for a period of time or installing a new set of laboratories. However, complete knowledge about their use needs to go with them. It should include a *standards guide* that specifies how to establish training laboratories for sites wishing to pursue this kind of learning experience for a local population. Selected individuals at the site should receive train-the-trainer sessions on how to conduct the courses that have been designed for the laboratories.

By creating a self-sufficient environment at each location, training sessions can be conducted with the least disruption to on-site schedules and production levels. Self-sufficiency brings other benefits. On-site training groups can further develop customized, business-specific courses that address the problems and situations unique to their needs.

In summary, the success of technology learning laboratories is dependent on the following:

1. Judicious choice and implementation of hardware/software for training/education
2. Application of sound instructional design principles in training program development
3. Adequate technical support for day-to-day operation

The concepts of technology learning laboratories described here have been derived from many lessons learned in the implementation of laboratory-based training at Motorola University. These concepts, therefore, are not theoretical but have been tested and can be applied to many other businesses as well.

Acknowledgments

This multidisciplinary effort required contribution by many individuals and on-going efforts as a team. The author would like to acknowledge the following staff with Motorola University's Technology Education Center:

John Dokos and *Sanjiv Patel* for training lab development

Larry Schroth and *Kathy Burgos* for lab operational support

Art Paton, Ingrid Fernandes, and *Kelly Tanner* for training program design

In addition, contributions from the following external resources are also acknowledged:

Productivity Point International (Attn: Kent Barnett)
15 Salt Creek Lane, Hinsdale, IL 60521
Phone: (708) 920-0750
 (For Office Automation and Software Tools training)

Learning Group International (Attn: Lisa Hugus)
1805 Library Street, Reston, VA 22090
Phone: (703) 709-9119
 (For computer network training)

Questech Inc (Attn: George Emanual)
12665 Richfield Court, Livonia, MI 48150
Phone: (313) 464-9500
 (For automation-related educational equipment)

Power Technology Inc. (Attn: Arthur Peters)
36 Brandywine Road, South Barrington, IL 60010
Phone: (708) 428-5072
 (For pneumatics and sensor training systems)

Creative Training Concepts (Attn: Joanne Willard)
494 Bloomfield, Montclair, NJ 07042
Phone: (201) 509-6944
(For training program design/development)

Management & Employee Training Services (Attn: Dan Heck)
666 Central Avenue, Highland Park, IL 60035
Phone: (708) 926-9503
(For laboratory-based program instruction)

Bibliography

Agrawal, Aaron, "Accelerating Motorola's Competitive Edge," *Impact* (a Motorola Journal), December 1992, p. 4.

Carnevale, Ellen S., "Motorola Sets the Benchmark for Training," *ASTD Technical Skills & Training*, October 1990, p. 28.

Chang, Alex, "Hands-On Learning at Motorola," *ASTD Training & Development Journal*, October 1990, p. 34.

Chang, Alex, "What Automation Training Does Today's Workforce Need?," *Industrial Education*, January 1990, p. 12.

Haavind, Robert, "Motorola Workers Learn by Running a 'Table-Top-Factory,' " *Electronic Business*, October 16, 1989, p. 62.

Walsh, Susan, "Motorola Training Center Gets New Labs and Management Course," *Managing Automation*, April 1990, p. 61.

Willard, Joanne B., and Arthur E. Paton, "Laboratory Based Technology Education at Motorola," *Tech Trends*, December 1990, p. 10.

14

Using Evaluation to Improve the Quality of Technical Training

Robert O. Brinkerhoff
Western Michigan University

14.1 Overview

Like the weather, evaluation is a thing many technical training professionals talk about, but nowhere near so many do as much about it. Yet evaluation is critical to effective training. In the coming era of increasing global competition, pressure to be more and more productive with shrinking resources, and rapid change, training is more than ever a vital business function for technical enterprises. *Effective evaluation of training in this climate is an imperative.*

This chapter presents practical guidance to help training professionals use evaluation as a strategic tool for leveraging continuously improved value from training efforts.

Section 14.2	Reviews the *function of evaluation in training* and provides a discussion of some fundamental concepts
Section 14.3	Extends the discussion of the function of evaluation to explain in more detail *how evaluation specifically strengthens the business impact of technical training*

14.2   The Function of Evaluation in Training

Evaluation is a necessary and systemic part of effective training. Good training begins with an accurate assessment of training needs, proceeds through the design and development of training interventions, and ends (hopefully) with more effective job and organizational performance. Each of these phases of training raises many questions and issues:

What is the business need for the training?

What is the individual need?

What type of training is most effective to meet those needs?

How much does performance need to improve to justify the costs of training?

Is there an alternative to training?

Would program X work?

How well, once training starts, are trainees learning?

Is learning being used in more effective performance?

Has the business need been met?

Have individual needs been met?

Is more, or different, training needed?

What should be done next?

These are just a few of the many questions that must be asked and answered if training is to work. Ultimately the question that needs asked is: "Who are the customers and what are their needs?" This will determine the quality of training offered. Accurate and valid answers to these questions will lead to effective training design and delivery; inaccurate answers will almost surely lead to wasted efforts, as well as to frustrated trainees and managers. In a nutshell, the job of evaluation is to help training leaders ask the right questions (like those listed) and get accurate answers to them. The right questions come from a carefully articulated and systematic approach to training and evaluation design, and the "answers" come in the form of data (information) in and about the organization in which training leaders are working.

The literature on training evaluation contains several useful frameworks for thinking about evaluation of training. In 1976, Donald Kirkpatrick, for example, posed a simple four-part evaluation process for training:

1. Ask about trainees' reactions—whether they liked the training.

2. Ask whether trainees learned what they were supposed to.

3. Ask whether trainees are using their learning.

4. Ask whether using learning has produced any positive impact on the organization.

The Kirkpatrick model makes a lot of intuitive sense, and has been used by many practitioners to guide evaluation efforts. While it has been broadly accepted, practitioners have found it problematic to progress much beyond the first or second levels of the Kirkpatrick framework, since measurement of training usage and impact are difficult in most cases. A more profound issue with the Kirkpatrick framework is that research on training (see Tannenbaum and Yukl, 1993) demonstrates that there is little, if any, linkage among the levels. That is, liking training has little relationship to learning, learning has little relationship to using training, and so forth. A further issue, which is true of other models, is a lack of a system's view of training; we will return to this issue shortly.

Other authors have presented more comprehensive evaluation models that are also more consistent with the developmental process of training. The CIRO model developed in Great Britain (Warham, Rackham, Byrd) is typical of such approaches, posing a development sequence that begins with an assessment of the *context* in which organizational needs and issues are identified. Then, evaluation proceeds to evaluating alternative training designs (inputs), to assessing reactions, and finally assessing outputs of training, such as increased performance. Brinkerhoff (1987) elaborated on the developmental approaches with a six-stage evaluation model, that focused especially on needs analysis and evaluation of alternative training designs, before assessing training implementation and results. Similarly, the training approach promoted by Robinson and Robinson (1989) is driven by intensive front-end measurement and assessment. The value of these approaches is that they do not take training as a *given*, but, instead, focus on the rigorous assessment of the needs for training. As most training practitioners know, training often is *not* the right solution to performance problems, thus models that focus on needs analysis are especially important.

All of the literature on training evaluation clearly makes the point that evaluation of training must always be more than an afterthought. Evaluation is decidedly not simply checking—with a test, for example—to see whether some training had any results. Testing is often part of a systematic evaluation approach, but is nowhere near sufficient to address the needs of training leaders to design and deliver training that adds value to organization products and services. Effective training practice requires thinking about evaluation concurrently with the training design, and applying evaluation methods throughout the entire training cycle.

14.3 How Evaluation Strengthens Training Impact

We have noted that the function of evaluation is broader than simply checking to see whether training has achieved learning results. Evaluation is necessary to effective training practice. It promotes effectiveness and also provides the data that can be used to assess value and demonstrate impact. In this chapter, the reader will find clear direction about how to conceptualize and design practical evaluation approaches that will achieve these purposes. But to think clearly about how evaluation can be used to strengthen training and demonstrate results, we must first step back and look systematically at the training process itself.

14.3.1 How Training Adds Value: a Simple Look

The purpose of training is to add value to the products and services of organizations, through the systematic improvement of the knowledge and skills of those contributing to the products and services. Training accomplishes the value-added purpose through knowledge transfer, e.g., learning. The *logic* of training is that organizations must continuously improve performance and that one key element in improved performance is the capability—*new skills and knowledge*—of employees to perform better through changed or improved behavior. Thus, the job of training is to improve knowledge and skills through learning which, in turn, will lead to improved job performance, which will then lead to more valuable products and services. This logic is portrayed in Figure 14-1.

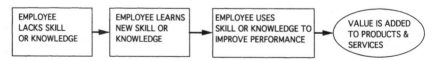

Figure 14-1. How training adds value.

The process depicted in Figure 14-1 shows that training adds value by first producing new learning, which expands employee capability for performance, which then leads to more effective and efficient performance, ultimately leading to improved products and services. Imagine, for example, that an investment company wants to increase customer satisfaction by improving the quality of the service it provides customers in an initial investment analysis meeting between the customer and an investment advisor. As part of this goal, the company has purchased a new investment analysis software program. Investment advisors need to know how to use the software so they can do an investment analysis with new customers during initial interviews with them. So, training is conducted to provide advisors with knowledge of the new skill. Then, advisors will employ their new capability in initial analysis interviews with customers; the analysis plan provided to the customer will be more accurate, complete, and useful, and, thus, customers will be more satisfied. This is the "logic" of this particular training effort.

14.3.2 Training: a Partial Solution

The intent of the training in the example is to add value by increasing customer satisfaction with the investment analysis provided in the initial interview. This logic is helpful in thinking about the purpose and focus of the training, and helps us see further how we would approach an evaluation of the training. The impact of the training, for instance, could be assessed by investigating how well the investment advisors use the new software in their work with customers.

Even though the intent of the training is to improve customer satisfaction through effective use of the new analysis software, it is very obvious that training *alone* cannot achieve the desired goal. Whether a customer is more or less satisfied at the end of the initial planning interview depends on a number of critical factors. Here are just a few:

- The marketing effort may not bring the right sort of customer into the interview, thus the analysis driven by the software will not be right for that customer.

- The software design may be too complex, thus causing advisors to abandon it in favor of their old, more comfortable, approach.

- Supervisors may feel the software is too *high tech,* and encourage their advisors to use softer, *low-tech* interactions instead.

- Advisors might hear from others that the software is not effective and enter the training with a poor attitude toward it, keeping them from learning how to use it effectively.

- The investment advisors may feel pressure to increase sales, causing them to push too hard for a sale of products beyond the initial analysis, in turn making the customer react negatively to high-pressure tactics.

- The analysis software may include examples not appropriate for the cultural diversity of some customers.

- The software training may be delivered too early, when what advisors really need is more skill in putting customers at ease and in listening more closely to their concerns.

- Some offices may not need the training, since their advisors already have achieved 100 percent customer satisfaction with an alternative initial interview method.

- Other offices may not need the training now because their problem is retaining customers in latter service stages or planning to serve emerging markets, not increasing the satisfaction of new customers with the initial interview.

Any one of these factors (or many others) could keep the training from having a positive impact on customer satisfaction. These factors exemplify a problem with which virtually all training practitioners are familiar:

> Training is *always* only a partial solution to a performance problem, and is *always* impacted by external forces. A supervisor, for example, can undo the results of even the most elaborate of training efforts with just a few, simple, negative words. Or faulty selection practices that put the wrong trainees into a training program will keep even the best training from working.

Even though training is always only a partial solution to performance problems, it is also always true that training is supposed to contribute to effective performance. That is, training is never meant to be done just for its own sake. *The goal of training is always beyond just learning; the goal is to translate learning into better performance, so that products and services will be more valuable.* So, to evaluate training from the perspective of asking only "Did learning happen?" is not enough, since learning alone does not respond to the value question. Training practitioners who cannot move beyond demonstrating just the learning impact of training cannot defend nor justify their worth to an organization. Yet, to hold training accountable for improved performance is equally wrong. To automatically *blame,* for instance, the training program in the example because customers were not more satisfied could be to miss the real cause (some other factor), and thus the organization will continue on a wrong path to fixing performance. What is needed is a more comprehensive view of training as a critical element in the larger performance improvement system and an evaluation approach that can work within this larger systemic framework.

14.3.3 A Systems View of Training Evaluation

The charge to training evaluation cannot be *to prove the training worked,* since, as we have seen, whether it works means whether customer satisfaction is positively impacted, and this is beyond the scope of training alone. The more reasonable charge for evaluation of training is to prove that the training solution fits the performance needs, and that the learning that training produces makes an effective and efficient contribution to the performance goal. To respond to these issues requires a more systemic view of training as a *process,* not as an *event.* To better frame this approach, consider an example of a data processing consulting and services company.

Assume that this data processing company has, accurately and correctly, analyzed its current position in the business and determined that it is too sales-driven—a strategy that has led to great profits, but cannot be sustained, since customer turnover and computer technician turnover is too high. Current analyses show, for example, that customer loss is related in part to service provider turnover (customers don't like frequent switching), and that service provider turnover is related in part to poorly designed service systems and misguided direction from supervising managers who push for more sales, versus more service quality. The new strategy recognizes that future competitive advantage depends on the company's ability to provide high-quality services to its customers. Thus, strategic goals are to recruit and retain the right technical consultants and operators, give them effective tools and training to meet customer service quality expectations, reduce data processing staff advisor turnover, implement a system for measuring customer satisfaction, increase customer retention (thereby lowering the cost of sales), and emerge as a more competitive and profitable company.

In this business framework, we can now see that the new systems training must fit the strategic context of stressing service quality and of reducing the push for sales alone. There are many implications for the training; here are just a few:

- Training objectives should be framed in the context of the company's new strategy.

- The training should be delivered only after certain preconditions are met, such as that the new strategic direction is clear, understood, and accepted, and that the business unit receiving training should have its customer service quality measurement procedures in place.

- The training should be scheduled so that technicians and consultants most involved in customer interactions get training first.

- Trainees should be selected to be sure that they are ready for this training, and that other training needs are not more pressing and urgent for them.

- Training examples should include reference to service quality.

- Trainers should fully understand the business needs of the business units to be trained and the new strategic direction.

- Trainee managers should correctly introduce the training to the intended trainees and make them fully aware of its importance and urgency.

- Training sessions should allow trainees to practice and become comfortable with the customer service skills in simulated interactions that accurately represent the new customer needs and concerns.

- Trainees should not leave training before they are precisely clear about and committed to how they will try out the new training.

- Managers should be able and willing to provide specific support to the trainees as they try out the new skills.

- Managers and technicians should receive accurate customer feedback as to the impact of the new interaction procedures on customer satisfaction.

Figure 14-2 represents the sorts of factors just listed, in the framework of what happens *before* the training is delivered, what happens *during* the training, and what happens *after* the training event takes place. Figure 14-2 depicts the larger training process, including critical *before* and *after* training-event factors. These factors are critically integrated with the training process and are provided by other subsystems in the organization, such as the management system, the job design system, the selection system, the equipment and tool system, and so forth. The point of this figure is to clarify the critical contribution that each of these factors makes to overall success, and to clarify the reality that these critical factors must be identified and effectively managed so that training can make the sort of contribution needed for the desired performance improvement. Obviously, if any of these sorts of critical factors is overlooked or otherwise not correctly managed, then the chances for the training to work are greatly diminished. Only when the larger training system is analyzed and managed can training be effective. *Evaluation of training, then, must be addressed to and work with this larger systemic process.*

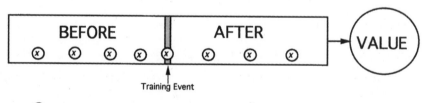

Figure 14-2. Critical before, during, and after training-event factors.

14.3.4 Whose Job Is Training?:
A Brief Diversion

Clearly, as well, many of these critical factors fall outside the purview and control of the typical technical training organization in a company. Many of these factors, it might be said, are *management's* responsibility, while the responsibility of the technical training department is to design and deliver the training event. Unfortunately, this partitioned *silo* view of training is the norm, as technical training has typically been organized as a separate department, and the job of training has been artificially segmented so that those who are responsible for the training event are distanced, often physically and always conceptually, from the remainder of the process. Where this is the case, the evaluation job becomes harder, and training leaders will have to make special efforts to implement change in their organizations (see Brinkerhoff and Gill, 1994). In any case, the truth remains that the training process is more complex and systemic than most typically envisioned, and evaluation can only proceed effectively from this systemic framework. Regardless of how they are organized and positioned, training leaders who wish to make training more effective and to demonstrate training impact with effective evaluation must operate from the systemic viewpoint.

14.4 A Systemic Approach
to Training Evaluation

This section presents readers with a comprehensive model for training evaluation (see also Brinkerhoff and Gill, 1994). The model poses the specific questions and issues that evaluation must address at each of several key stages in the training process. Following a brief presentation and discussion of the model is more detailed direction on how to collect and use measurement data to strengthen and demonstrate training impact.

14.4.1 The Systemic Model

The evaluation model is based on a four-part partitioning of the overall training process. The four parts are:

1. Formulating goals for training and establishing the linkage of these goals to strategic and business needs

2. Planning an effective training strategy that will deliver learning to key employees when and where it is needed

3. Producing and assessing learning outcomes effectively

4. Supporting the usage and refinement of learning so that it is effectively used to positively impact individual and organization performance

Figure 14-3 displays these four parts in a circular pattern, to depict the sequence of these four parts of the training process as they interact to produce added value.

The following sections explain each of the four parts of the training process, one part at a time, using an example to clarify the function of each step in the process.

Formulating Training Goals That Are Linked to Business Needs. This process step includes the explicit and implicit actions that determine whether training resources will be allocated, and the results which are expected to be achieved. In many, but certainly not all, training instances, needs analyses are conducted to help decide whether and what sorts of training the organization should provide. A needs analysis represents a typical example of a *goal formulation* activity. There are other activities that characterize goal formulation, as well.

Figure 14-3. The four-part training process.

For example, a top level management council may decide to install new technology to streamline business operations, eventually contracting with a vendor to supply and install the new equipment. A part of the discussion with the vendor will undoubtedly entail questions bearing on training—whether it will be provided, how much will be provided, and so forth. Key union stakeholders or a joint labor-management technology implementation team might also be involved. This discussion is an implicit goal formulation activity, since it results in a decision to conduct some training with some more or less explicit expectations for results.

In a similar example, though in a less obvious and formal sense, a supervisor reads a brochure about some telephone operator training, then decides to send the new receptionist to the session. This is a goal formulation activity: the supervisor's action has presumed a need and will result in the allocation of training resources, with some (perhaps only vague and implicit) expectations for how that training will benefit the supervisor's operation.

The goal formulation process includes any and all activities that shape decisions to deploy training resources. The goal formulation process cannot be omitted, though it certainly may be paid varying amounts of attention from one instance to another. When training occurs, it occurs because someone, somewhere in the organization, has either permitted it to or decided that it will occur. This process, regardless of how consciously and conscientiously it may be done, assumes or specifies a need for training, and thus shapes expectations for the value that training will add.

Planning Training Strategies. Planning and designing strategies includes all the decisions and activities that shape the nature and scope of training activities. *Designing training, writing materials, planning workshops, planning training schedules, specifying trainee selection procedures, notifying supervisors, and soliciting management involvement are all typical examples of the strategy design process.* Further decisions about whether or exactly how to do any or all of these things are part of this second process. *The training strategy design process is complete when we know who will be involved in the training design process and how; just who is to be trained; when, how, and exactly what they will learn; who will deliver or facilitate the learning and how, who will support it afterwards and how; and so forth.* The training strategy design step includes not only designing the training event itself, but planning on how to identify and manage the critical "before" and "after" factors that impinge on the success of the training process.

Producing and Assessing Learning Results. All training efforts are characterized, of course, by some sort of learning transaction. This third process step refers to the activities that produce learning, and include whatever is done (or not done) to be sure that learners learn what they are supposed to in the most effective and efficient manner possible. This process includes, obviously, the activity of teaching (or a trainee working on self-instructional modules), but also includes less obvious activities such as managing the learning environment, providing physical and psychological comfort and encouragement to learners, monitoring learning, assessing learning mastery and providing feedback, and so forth.

Supporting Learning Results So They Are Sustained and Effectively Used. Training goals are not accomplished simply with the acquisition of learning on the part of trainees. For learning to translate into added value, learning must endure, and then must result in enhanced job performance. Because technical training is intended to be applied in job performance, there are a great number of activities that must take place to support this transfer. This might include *follow-up assessments of job performance, meetings with trainees to encourage usage of training, meetings with supervisors to review trainee (and supervisor) performance, and so forth.* When training is not intended for immediate use, then activities such as refresher training, provision of job aids or written updates, and reassessment of skills represent this fourth process step.

14.4.2 How the Four Process Phases Interact to Produce High-Quality Training

The four process steps are not independent, nor are they sequential. Often, for example, training will be designed so that a series of brief learning interventions will be provided instead of a more lengthy *workshop.* Each brief learning intervention will then be followed with on-the-job application, so that trainees can build competence through practice, thus individualizing their learning while also adding value by more immediately applying their learning. *When this sort of training design is employed, there are many cycles that involve goal setting, learning interventions, and managing transfer of learning.* Usually, the design is refined and revised as the process proceeds. In any case, whether training is iterative or one shot, the four-part process must be tightly knit together.

These four process components represent the key "levers" by which training quality can be improved. The function of evaluation in this four-phase model is to identify and assess the critical quality factors in each part, then assess and provide feedback on them to training leaders so that the entire training process can be managed to produce consistently high quality results.

In many technical training settings, it is usually the case that training delivery (the learning transaction), for example, is extremely well managed, so that learning is being produced quite effectively and efficiently. It is more likely that serious quality defects will be found in the other three process phases. For instance, a very effective training module is available for training health technicians how to operate a sophisticated new piece of equipment. If trainee selection (a critical factor in the second training strategy phase) has failed to get the right trainees into this module—that is, some trainees are not ready or situated so that they operate the equipment anyway—then clearly the training will not produce effective results. Of, if after they receive training, some supervisors discourage practice with the new equipment, the training impact suffers.

14.4.3   Using the Model as an Evaluation Tool

The driving assumption behind use of the model is that each phase must be effectively executed for the entire training process to produce consistently high quality results. Effectiveness of the overall process is defined to mean that:

1. Training goals are directly and clearly linked to important business needs.
2. A training strategy is planned to effectively produce and support the use of new learning by the most efficient means possible.
3. Training interventions are effectively designed and managed to produce and verify mastery of new skills and knowledge.
4. New learning is nurtured, sustained, and managed so that it is used, when needed, to yield improved performance.

In general, a training leader would use evaluation to assess the extent to which each of the four phases is working to produce the needed level of quality. One would look, for example, to see whether the training goals are sufficiently linked to business needs and goals. Or one could use evaluation to determine whether new learning is being sufficiently supported on the job, and whether job performance is really more effective. In other words, the evaluation approach is based on using the four-process phase statements listed previously as *premises* that then must be tested in actuality to see whether and to what extent they are coming true. When evaluation inquiry reveals that there may be problems, that the premises are not coming true to the extent that is needed, then a training leader can act. Through problem solving and decision making with other key players in the performance system, the training process can be put back on a track toward consistent and high-quality results.

From a more operational perspective, the four-phase model is used to first identify the key issues and potential problems specific to each phase of a particular training effort, then to implement targeted evaluation inquiry to resolve the issue or solve the problem.

Consider the example of machine operators in a new preventive maintenance procedure. This new procedure requires operators to carefully plan production runs so that each piece of production equipment has a minimum rest period during which brief maintenance and recalibration tasks are to be performed. Assume further that an issue in the fourth subprocess (transformation of the learning to improved job behavior) of this training is whether supervisors will, under production pressure, remain committed to the new procedure, which promises more production over the long run, but which can cause brief, short-term delays. If supervisors succumb to the old pressure for production and fail to encourage and check up on whether operators are really performing the new tasks, this new maintenance procedure (and the training that was invested also) will never get off the ground. So, it would be important to do some follow-up evaluation and find out:

What are supervisors really doing by way of providing coaching and encouragement?

Are they really providing the support promised?

Or are they sending subtle, or even not-so-subtle, messages that "maintenance-be-damned, we have to get the goods out"?

If evaluation discloses that all is going well, then the evaluation data could be used to show the supervisors and operators what a good job they are doing, and to congratulate them on sticking with a tough program. If, on the other hand, the data show that supervisors really are sending old messages, then training leaders can provide this feedback to the supervisors (or their managers), who can point out the issue and begin a problem-solving attack.

14.4.4   Some Guiding Evaluation Questions

Table 14-1 lists some typical evaluation questions for each of the four process model phases that are useful in guiding evaluation planning. The questions are typical, not exhaustive. Further, they are still relatively generic. To use them, training leaders would first want to determine whether the question raises an important issue for their particular training effort. Then, assuming the issue is important, the question must be further defined to make it more specific and clearly focused on the training effort under consideration.

Table 14-1. Typical Evaluation Questions for Each Process
Model Phase

Phase 1

- Are training goals linked to business needs?
- Are learning objectives clear and specific?
- Are clear and specific job performance behaviors linked to each learning objective?
- Are business goals clearly and specifically linked to desired job performance behaviors?
- How important are the business needs to which training is linked?
- Do the business needs justify the training investment that is likely to be made?
- Can training make a substantial impact on the desired job behavior, or are learning results likely to be overcome by negative systemic factors?
- Is training really necessary? Could some other, cheaper, intervention be more effective (job aids, or incentives, for instance)?

Phase 2

- Does the training strategy adequately define necessary "before" and "after" management, supervisory and trainee preparation behaviors, and other critical factors?
- Does the training strategy aim to deliver learning as close to the workplace as possible?
- Does the training strategy provide for just-in-time, just-enough learning to optimally impact performance?
- Does the training strategy provide for the least possible disruption of production and other critical activities?
- Are trainee selection procedures likely to get the right, and only the right, people into training?
- Does the training strategy provide for sufficient job aids and other postlearning support activities?
- Is the learning design likely to produce the intended level of competence?
- Does the learning design provide for sufficient practice and feedback to assure mastery of learning objectives?
- Is there sufficient high- and midlevel commitment to the training and for providing the necessary after-learning support?

Phase 3

- Are all critical elements of the training strategy (selection, delivery of prelearning materials, etc.) taking place effectively and on time?
- Are learners clearly informed of and committed to the training they are receiving?
- Do learners understand and agree with the need to change their postlearning job performance as desired?
- Do learners understand and agree with the job objectives and business goals that are linked to the training they are receiving?
- Are learners receiving timely and accurate feedback about how well they are learning?
- How completely have learners mastered intended skills and knowledge?
- Are training leaders receiving timely and accurate feedback from learners about their issues, concerns, needs for help, and perceived strengths and weaknesses of the training?
- Are trainee supervisors and other key stakeholders being kept appropriately informed about the progress of learning activities?

Table 14-1. Typical Evaluation Questions for Each Process Model Phase (*Continued*)

Phase 4

- To what extent are trainees correctly using new learning in their jobs?
- What factors are facilitating and supporting usage?
- What factors are blocking usage?
- To what extent are supervisors providing the support and coaching needed to improve usage?
- Which trainees are making the best usage of their new learning? How? Why?
- Which trainees are making the least effective usage? What about their usage is least effective? Why?
- To what extent are the business needs that drove training being positively impacted?

Evaluation should pursue the sorts of questions listed in Table 14-1, collecting accurate data and providing the best possible answers, in the form of careful and sensitive interpretation. Answers to these questions indicate how well the current training effort is progressing toward a positive business impact, and are also useful in considering what changes and redirection are needed for future training efforts. The next section presents steps and guidance for designing evaluation studies and methods that will provide useful answers to these important questions.

14.5 Designing Evaluation of Technical Training

A question often asked by training practitioners is *"How much evaluation should we do?"* This is a good question for a variety of reasons.

First, even raising the question leads us to the very correct notion that doing evaluation of training should be a carefully planned activity; evaluation should not be a knee-jerk reaction, some sort of activity automatically bolted onto the end of each and every training intervention. Second, this is a good question because it implies the reality that there is a range of evaluation activity possible, from very little to a lot. Third, it is a good question because it begs an answer, and asking it will provoke a process to answer the question—deciding just how, and how much, to evaluate.

In one fundamental respect, however, the question is misleading. Evaluation of training is inevitable. You cannot avoid it. All training is evaluated, because people in the organization will form evaluative judgments about it. For example, trainees will react, saying to themselves and others when they have a bad experience: "That was a pretty useless training session, don't you agree?" Top managers will form opinions about the value and effectiveness of training based on what they see and hear from others, regardless of whether the training department provides them with evaluation data, and *especially* when they do not. Executive leadership will hear stories about training and will form opinions about its value and effectiveness of training as well as about the training leaders.

In this respect, training evaluation is inevitable, and the question really becomes "How much and what sorts of evaluation should we do?" This is the overarching design question. The answer to the question is simple and direct: you should do enough and the right sort of evaluation to assure that training effectively and efficiently serves the needs of the business. Evaluation design is driven by purpose, and purpose should be driven by needs for providing the best-quality training.

14.5.1 The Need for Quality versus the Need for Proof

It is a pervasive myth among training practitioners that training must be *proven*. It is very often said, for example, that evaluation of training is so difficult because, in the end, how can we ever really prove that training made a difference? One reason that the proof myth is so pervasive is that part of the previous statement is very true—that is, it *is* difficult to prove that training made a difference—extremely difficult. But the implication of the statement is that evaluation ought to try to take on the proof task, and this is, I believe, a very misguided notion.

The contribution of training to human performance and, therefore, to overall business performance, is always partial (necessary, but not sufficient), and often marginal (only a small contributor). *The factors of selection and hiring, strategic planning, job design, incentive systems, tools and equipment, and management inputs, to name a few, are also contributors to performance, and are often far more powerful contributors than training.* Consider the analogy of the engine production department in an automobile manufacturing company. The engine, in its design and quality, makes a key contribution to business performance, but by no means the only one. How well will the automobile business perform if the chassis design, or the marketing division, or the assembly plant, or the dealer network do not also perform well? The key question to evaluating the quality of a single, necessary contributor to performance is: "How well does it fit with the rest of the overall operation? Is it doing its part and doing it well?"

To set out to try to prove that training makes a difference is as ludicrous and useless as the automobile engine production department spending its precious resources on a study to try to prove how much it has caused overall business performance. First, it is virtually an impossible task to get an answer to the question; the methodology of causal analysis and statistical proof is extremely complex and fraught with tenuous assumptions. Second, it is just not a relevant question, and certainly not worth spending good money to try to find out.

A far more worthwhile aim is for training evaluation to seek to find out whether training customer needs are being met, and met well. This is precisely the approach that Cadillac and other manufacturers seek, for they know the best route to profitability and industry survival is to consistently provide quality and value to customers. This is the best path for training, as well.

Using evaluation to find out what training customers need, then designing the best product to serve their needs, then seeing how well it meets their needs and continuously improving it so that it meets more of their needs increasingly better, assures the highest-quality training. Imagine that the worst scenario comes to be: that top management is on the brink of making a decision to cut the training department. Now imagine that top management has one of two kinds of information to help them with their decision. On the one hand, they might have a detailed and sophisticated evaluation report that the training department hired a consultant to produce—one that is full of fancy tables and graphs that make an argument (inevitably flawed) that training works. On the other hand, imagine that a phalanx of the best and brightest key business unit managers come to top management and say: "Hey, if you cut training, it's over our dead bodies; they have really helped us perform!" The protesting key managers will be far more persuasive than the technical report. *The best insurance for training department support and survival is a robust and loyal base of customers; the best path to that customer base is high-quality training products and services, and these are, in turn, best assured by solid evaluation.*

14.5.2   Evaluation Design Steps

Evaluation design, like good training, is a continuing design process, since evaluation designs also must be continuously improved. And because evaluation is a learning activity (we learn how well training is meeting needs and how to make it better), the evaluation should move through iterative design-implement-redesign cycles, to redirect it as learning results indicate. Despite this iterative nature of evaluation design, it is possible to identify several discrete steps in the design process. These steps may be approached in varying sequences and feed into one another, but each step must always be attended to.

Step 1:   Identify and describe the training to be evaluated.

Step 2:   Identify and clarify the purposes for the evaluation.

Step 3:   Identify the customers of training and evaluation and clarify their needs for information.

Step 4:   Determine the key questions that the evaluation must address.

Step 5:   Determine the overall design approach that will best meet customer needs and answer the evaluation questions identified.

Step 1: Identify and Describe the Training to Be Evaluated. This step entails becoming clear about the training goals and strategy.

What are the goals and objectives of the training?

How is it supposed to impact business needs?

How is the training designed to operate?

Who is involved? How, and when?

The analysis of the training should include a detailed specification of the following:

1. Training goals and their linkage to business needs

2. Trainee selection criteria and rationale

3. Training delivery methods, steps, interim objectives, and procedures

4. Trainee learning objectives

5. Job impact objectives that specify clearly how training will be used on the job

6. Business impact objectives that specify clearly what business results will be improved as a result of improved job performance

7. The linkage among and relative importance of each of 4, 5, and 6, above

8. Trainee supervisory, managerial, and other performance support objectives and behaviors needed to make the entire training process work

Step 2: Identify and Clarify the Purposes for the Evaluation. Evaluation can serve several specific purposes. A pilot training program, for example, is designed to evaluate the feasibility of a training design, to determine how well it works, what makes it work or keeps it from working, whether it produces the desired results, and so forth. *Sometimes evaluation is used to select the best of two alternative training designs being considered.* In many instances, the author has used evaluation as a development tool. In this case, some limited and rough training is tried out with a high-need audience, then results and usage of the training are carefully evaluated to discover how successful trainees use their learning, so that training designers can leverage the results of early trials of the program into successively more powerful iterations of the training. *Sometimes evaluation is done to judge whether a longstanding training program is still needed. Other times evaluation is used to identify revision needs in an existing, but new, training effort.* Purposes for evaluation may vary, but what does *not* vary is the need to be very clear about why the evaluation is to be done.

Step 3: Identify the Customers of Training and Evaluation and Clarify Their Needs for Information. Customers for training, and the evaluation of training, vary according to the purposes of the training and the evaluation. Thus, training customer identification and training purpose identification must go hand in hand. *The primary customer of training is almost always the manager (or supervisor) of the trainees.* The manager is the person who pays for the training and the person responsible for the performance of the trainees and the unit in which they work. Thus, the training must meet the business performance requirements of this primary customer. The trainee is also, to varying degrees, a major customer. Trainees expect training to help them perform better, to teach them the right stuff, and to protect their rights to not be endangered, embarrassed, or belittled. Training leaders are also customers, for they need to know whether training is working and what they need to do to improve it. Likewise, higher levels of management are customers, for they are responsible for business performance and the efficient use of resources. External customers may also be training customers, when the people who are being trained (such as bank tellers) work directly for them. In any case, there are always multiple customers of training and of a training evaluation. They must be identified and their needs must be carefully and correctly analyzed and confirmed.

Step 4: Determine the Key Questions That the Evaluation Must Address. Those who conduct an evaluation are trying to find the answers to questions, such as

How well is the training being used on the job?

What are supervisors doing to facilitate, or to block, the application of training on the job?

How well is the role play exercise working to produce trainee skills and confidence?

Evaluation questions focus the evaluation purpose more specifically and should respond directly to the needs of customers for evaluative information.

Step 5: Determine the Overall Evaluation Design Approach That Will Best Meet Customer Needs and Answer the Evaluation Questions Identified. Evaluation advisors have a range of evaluation designs to consider and choose from. Some of the common design approaches and their useful applications include the following:

Pre/Post Measures. When the primary purpose of an evaluation is to determine whether learning has occurred or whether job performance has changed, it is often useful to take a pretraining measure of performance (such as to give a test or to track baseline job performance, such as error rates), then to compare a posttraining measure to the pretraining measure.

Some problems with this approach are that it leads one to assume causation, which is always a very tenuous issue.

Experiments. True experiments, wherein rigorous controls are used, are almost never done in training settings. But rough experiments can serve very well. It may be useful, for example, to compare the performance of some machine operators who have been trained in a new production technique against those who have only used job aids or only had a supervisor briefing, to see which approach is most powerful. The purpose of this sort of experiment, of course, is not to see whether employees are doing their jobs right; the purpose is to assess the impact of a new work process.

Case Studies. The author has used a case study approach frequently when the question is how well a new training effort is working. It is very useful, for instance, to interview a small sample of new trainees to see how their experience in using the training is going. Then this information is used to create more realistic training materials, and also to refine the training and the support needed after training.

Embedded Evaluation Design. Perhaps one of the most powerful approaches to training development and evaluation is to include the evaluation as a part of the training itself. In this approach, trainees and/or their supervisors are trained in how to assess and monitor how well the training is working or being used. (For an example of embedded design, see Brinkerhoff and Smalley, 1994.)

There are other evaluation design approaches, but these are the most frequently used. Whatever design approach is used, there are four evaluation design criteria that have been broadly applied and accepted (Joint Committee, 1986). Listed in order of priority, these evaluation design criteria specify that evaluation should be:

1. *Ethical,* not violating any individual's or group's rights
2. *Useful* for meeting training customers' needs
3. *Practical* and efficient, not squandering resources
4. *Accurate,* producing valid and reliable data

Step 6: Identify the Best Data Collection Sources and Procedures to Address the Evaluation Questions. For some evaluation questions, special instruments will need to be constructed to collect the data needed, and relevant data collection and analysis procedures will need to be designed. When, for example, an evaluation question addresses some aspect of trainee learning achievement, such as "To what extent have trainees mastered the ability to conduct a new client intake using the new AS400 system?," an appropriate measurement instrument would need to be selected or developed. Almost always, when trainees' learning or other characteristics are the focus of the evaluation question, training evaluators will need to develop (or select) specialized measurement tools, such as tests, performance checklists, or so on.

As the focus of inquiry moves closer to job behavior and business performance, using existing data (such as scrap rates, production output numbers, error rates, telephone call completion records, sales records, and so on) is advised. Existing data are preferable to training evaluators for two solid reasons:

1. Existing data are cheaper to collect

2. Businesses usually already measure the performance that matters, and training is supposed to impact what matters

As was already discussed, these job or business performance measures are not used to try to "prove" training. Training is almost never the only performance improvement intervention that is being tried out. Thus, training is always part of a larger systemic effort. The existing measures will indicate whether the system (of which training is a part) is performing as hoped. Then, if it is not, further investigation into the causes of subpar performance can indicate whether training needs to be bolstered, revised, or otherwise improved.

Step 7: Plan Reporting and Communications Actions.   Training evaluation is driven by customer needs for information, thus training evaluators need to think about how they are going to get evaluative information to those people who need it. A key principle of reporting is to "segment" the evaluation market. Training evaluators should not simply prepare an evaluation report, then give it to everyone who may have an interest. Rather, *they should plan to provide concise and targeted evaluation summaries that are specifically focused on the needs of each training and evaluation customer.* And training evaluators should not restrict themselves to providing only formal, written reports. Training evaluation reports can take the form of brief memoranda, presentations, workshops, discussions, and so forth. Usually, the more interactive the format, the better, as evaluation customers typically need and want assistance in interpreting evaluation findings and applying them to solving performance problems.

14.6   Managing
the Evaluation Process

Evaluation, like any other complex activity, must be managed effectively, or it is likely to go astray. Evaluation will always work best when it is planned and conducted in conjunction with the overall training design process, as depicted in the four-part training process model shown earlier. Because evaluation activities consume precious resources and are often fraught with implications for making decisions about resource allocations, evaluation should be carefully planned and managed.

Some guidelines for managing evaluation activities are as follows:

14.6.1 Use Project Management Tools and Principles

Evaluation tasks should be clearly specified and defined, and should be assigned to a single person or group so that responsibility is clear. Schedules of tasks and key events should be made and followed. The evaluation process should be monitored and redirected when necessary. Evaluation tasks should be budgeted so that cost projections are clear and so that actual costs can be tracked.

14.6.2 Use Professional Technical Expertise When and Where Appropriate

Not all of the skills needed for effective evaluation will be available in the organization. Measurement experts may be needed, for example, to design or select learning assessment instruments. A professional evaluator may be helpful in planning an overall evaluation strategy. Data collection and analysis experts may be needed for technical tasks within the evaluation. Whenever evaluation experts are used, it is always a good idea for internal training staff to stay closely involved, so that the organization's needs and constraints are responsively considered. It is also a good idea to include training as a part of any technical assistance effort, so that the evaluation technology can be transferred to the organization, avoiding excessive dependency on external experts.

14.6.3 Implement the Evaluation in Well-Planned Steps

Like training, evaluation works best when it is undertaken as a successive learning process. Good training cycles through several steps, as organizational needs change and as more is learned about the results and impact of learning interventions. Evaluation inquiry should be tuned to the phases of training. Some measurement data should be collected soon after training activities are implemented, then these data should be analyzed and interpreted. Following this, depending on the implications of the data, successive evaluation inquiry can be planned and implemented. In a training program in which data entry clerks were learning a new data system, for example, a few of the first trainees were interviewed on the job soon after they received training. The experiences reported by these early "pioneers" were then used to refine the next round of training, which in turn led to a more formal evaluation follow-up using a survey questionnaire. The questionnaire items were developed from responses in the preliminary interviews. The questionnaire data were then used for discussion in a series of focus group interview sessions with yet a later group of trainees. These successive data collection-training-data collection events provided rich and increasingly accurate information about how the training was being used, and pinpointed weaknesses in the training design.

14.6.4 Closely Involve and Stay in Touch with Training Customers and Other Stakeholders

Evaluation information will have the greatest impact on decision makers and other key stakeholders when these parties are kept regularly informed and involved throughout the training process. Evaluation findings are never absolutely certain and often raise many questions. For these reasons, it is not a good idea to wait until a training program is fully complete before informing interested parties about its results. More understanding and a greater ability to interpret and use the information will be created when communications are regular and ongoing. Further, because there is always a range of interests and viewpoints among training stakeholders, keeping everyone informed assures that all viewpoints can be heard and considered.

14.6.5 Implement Interactive Interpretation and Reporting Events

Written evaluation reports, like other lengthy documents and reports, are notorious for the extent to which they tend to go unread and ignored. Long evaluation reports will not receive the attention and cooperation training leaders need from key training customers and stakeholders. The author has had great success, however, when using interactive formats, such as meetings, discussion groups, and workshops, to help stakeholders understand and use the findings of training evaluations. A workshop can be designed, for example, to make a brief presentation of the key findings of an evaluation; then, workshop participants can work in small groups to discuss the implications of the findings for action about training program revisions. The workshop format helps surface and resolve concerns about uncertainty in the findings, and helps participants (such as training managers and line executives) reach agreement on action steps that must be taken to incorporate evaluation findings into further training program implementation.

14.7 Summary

Evaluation is part and parcel of effective technical training. Evaluation efforts must be carefully employed throughout the four key parts of the training process. Evaluation will help training and other key leaders assess:

1. How closely are training goals linked to and driven by critical business needs?

2. Are training plans adequately formulated to deliver a just-enough learning event at just the right time, in modes that are most likely to produce the learning needed, and least likely to disrupt important production processes?

3. How well are learning outcomes being achieved?

4. Are effective efforts being carried out to sustain, support, and build on learning on-the-job, so that individual and organizational performance improvements will add value to products and services?

Evaluation should be carefully planned and managed throughout the entire training process. A key purpose of evaluation is to assure that training customers receive the right sorts of training that best help them achieve important business results. Training leaders must work closely with training customers to understand their needs and to help them understand the key roles they must play to make training work to meet their needs. Training alone cannot meet business needs, and, thus, training evaluation cannot seek to "prove" that it did. The proper role for evaluation is to help build strong alliances between training practitioners and training customers. Evaluation does this by assessing and clarifying customer needs, assuring high-quality training interventions, and helping line managers and other training customers understand the results of training and how effective their actions are in the ongoing effort to improve business performance.

15
Skilled Trades Programs: Apprentice to Master

David C. Paquin
Agency One

Relentless increases in job specialization in the global job market make it difficult to place boundaries around the term "skilled trades." Most agree that the carpenter and the mason have skilled trades. Reynolds (1993) defines a skill as a "physical or manipulative activity that requires knowledge and has special requirements for speed and accuracy." Training programs which provide the knowledge and manual skill to perform at levels of speed and accuracy required by modern industry are skilled trades training programs.

What sets these programs apart from other training environments?

How are they properly and meaningfully implemented?

What are the challenges facing today's skilled trades programs?

Instructors and administrators must examine some critical issues to become or remain effective and competitive in their work.

15.1 Skilled Trades: Apprenticeship to Mastery

The function of a skilled trades training program is to prepare the student for work in the job market. This purpose must stand above others and cannot be lost

411

amid financial and personnel shortcomings. Nor should it take second priority to other training objectives that an instructor or educational administrator may embrace. First and foremost, the goal is to raise the skill level of an individual from beginner or apprentice to that of the master.

Apprenticeship often reminds us of American colonialism and the residential indenture system. Yet, today there are over 300,000 Americans working under formal apprenticeship training programs (Glover, 1981). These programs cover a variety of job titles; there are at least 300 apprenticeable trades in the United States, from aircraft fabricator to upholsterer (Lobb, 1978). They receive applicants at a variety of predetermined minimum entry levels and progress them to mastery status corresponding to local standards of performance.

There are two principle components of mastery in a trade:

1. Technical knowledge
2. Manual skill

These two goals are achieved usually in separate learning settings. Figure 15-1, "A Model of Skilled Trades Mastery," considers these components in identifying the corresponding required method of learning. The ability to perform an occupation which demands little technical know-how and little or no manual skill could be achieved through self-study. Extensive knowledge acquisition usually takes place in a formal classroom, with attached laboratory exercises. The development of manual skills takes practice which may occur independently alongside self-study or supervised via formal laboratory exercises or by on-the-job training (OJT). Performance of the skill is also evaluated in these settings, with each setting providing progressively more meaningful evaluation. (See Figure 15-1.)

15.2 Skilled Trades Programs

Skilled trades programs are set apart from other training efforts by their learning goals, implementation strategies, and method of evaluation (Figure 15-2). *Emphasis is placed on skill acquisition through demonstration and practice.* This takes place using real-world equipment for two important reasons. First, it ensures that the learners' practice and evaluation best prepares them for the job market. Second, learners can accept and buy in to difficult or unusual learning experiences when they can clearly see how that practice applies to the actual job. The presentation of job-related knowledge is most effective when explained to the trainee through the discussion of real-world application. Adult learners especially prefer learning activities that involve realistic problem solving (Cross, 1981).

JOB REQUIREMENTS High technical knowledge—low manual skill	JOB REQUIREMENTS High technical knowledge—some manual skill	JOB REQUIREMENTS High technical knowledge—high manual skill
LEARNING METHODS Classroom and self-practice	LEARNING METHODS Classroom and lab	LEARNING METHODS Classroom and OJT with mentor
JOB REQUIREMENTS Some technical knowledge—low manual skill	JOB REQUIREMENTS Some technical knowledge—some manual skill	JOB REQUIREMENTS Some technical knowledge—high manual skill
LEARNING METHODS Classroom or self-study and self-practice	LEARNING METHODS Classroom or self-study and lab or OJT	LEARNING METHODS Classroom or self-study and OJT with mentor
JOB REQUIREMENTS Low technical knowledge—low manual skill	JOB REQUIREMENTS Low technical knowledge—some manual skill	JOB REQUIREMENTS Low technical knowledge—high manual skill
LEARNING METHODS Self-study and self-practice	LEARNING METHODS Self-study and lab or OJT	LEARNING METHODS Self-study and OJT with mentor

Figure 15-1. A Model of Skilled Trades Mastery.

	Learning goals	Implementation strategies	Evaluation method
Skilled trades training programs	Psychomotor domain objectives dominate	Train, demonstrate, practice	Performance test
Other training programs	Cognitive domain objectives dominate	Train	Written test (if applicable)

Figure 15-2. Comparison of skilled trades and other training programs.

15.2.1 Learning Goals

The learning goals of a skilled trades training program generally focus on psychomotor or skill-based competencies. Cognitive and affective objectives, while important to the overall success of the program, are secondary to physical coordination in many trades. Technologically based jobs, such as computer technician and digital controller programmer, may require learning goals which favor the cognitive domain.

"The development of learning objectives for a skilled trades program requires a working knowledge of the psychomotor domain" (Heinich, Molenda and Russell, 1989). Also called the motor domain, it can be viewed as a progression in the coordination needed to perform a task. This classification has four stages:

1. *Imitation:*   Learners repeat what they have just seen.
2. *Manipulation:*   Learners first perform the task independently.
3. *Precision:*   Learners perform the task with an established degree of accuracy.
4. *Articulation:*   Learners perform the task efficiently and are able to coordinate multiple skills.

Learning objectives in a skilled trades program follow this progression. The trainee, or apprentice, first is required to imitate a skill following a demonstration by the instructor. As the training session goes on, expectations from the learner increase. Eventually the learner must independently perform multiple skills with accuracy.

Motor skills, while important, are not the only type of learning goals in skilled trades program. Obviously, cognitive objectives are necessary in that the student must learn certain technical information related to the skill. Also necessary are affective domain goals. Prospective workers must attain an appreciation for safety, should develop a sense of work pride, and will perform best when acting with a spirit of professionalism.

15.2.2 Implementation Strategies

Once learning objectives are determined, the actual program content is easily identified. Lesson plans, laboratory exercises, exams, and other materials are developed which deliver and test the information and skills prescribed by those objectives. The objectives and, therefore, the training materials are based on the job to be performed.

Most programs include theoretical as well as hands-on learning sessions. Some learning will occur in the classroom; some will occur in a lab or job setting. The balance between classroom theoretical knowledge and hands-on practice is determined, not only by the skill being learned (Figure 15-1), but also by entry level and learning objectives.

Skills can only be attained through practice. The student will practice the method which has been demonstrated by the trainer. These are the critical aspects of a skilled trades program. Proper demonstration followed by coached, ample practice will result in long-term skill acquisition by the learner. A five-step method for implementing effective lab exercises is provided by Paquin (1990) in *Technical and Skills Training*. These steps are:

1. Determine the task to be trained on.
2. Duplicate the task as closely as possible in the training environment.
3. Demonstrate proper lab performance to all learners.
4. Direct the performance of the lab exercise.
5. Discuss the results of the lab with all the learners.

15.2.3 Method of Evaluation

Realistic evaluation of job skills attained in a trades program is critical to that training program's credibility. *Trainees must actually demonstrate the skill to be performed.* This is done in either a lab or job setting. The job setting often provides the premium learning opportunity as students see and learn from workers with extensive experience. Often a lab setting is used due to practicality and convenience for the training group. Whether the choice is lab or OJT, measurement of trainee performance must be deliberate and consistent. Tools can be provided to the evaluator to ensure that this is accomplished.

Successful implementation of a laboratory exercise is controlled and documented using a written lab guide. An effective lab guide will contain all the information relative to the task that either the trainer or trainee would need:

- Precautions and warnings
- List of tools and equipment
- Procedure for task completion
- Standards for performance of steps
- Knowledge-based questions to further test the trainee
- Spaces for administrative information such as trainee name and number, date, instructor

A similar instrument is used to control and document task performance during OJT. This is called a *job performance measure* (JPM) and contains the same information as a lab guide. The only difference is that a JPM is administered at the job site usually by someone without a training background, while a lab guide is implemented in a training setting by an instructor. Figure 15-3 shows a JPM used to train and test technicians on calibrating a pressure transmitter.

Task Title: _____ Calibrate a Pressure Transmitter _____

JPM #: _____ 998-0004 _____

Approved by: _____

Trainee Name: _____ Date: _____

Instructions:

1. Perform each step to the criteria described. All steps must be performed successfully for the JPM to be completed satisfactorily.
2. During the *training* phase, the instructor may coach the trainee.
3. During the *performance* phase, no coaching is allowed.
4. Observe safety precautions.

Tools Required:

1. Electronic pressure transmitter
2. Test pressure source
3. Ammeter
4. Basic tools
5. Power supply

Steps: **Trainer's Initials**

1. Connect pressure source to transmitter   _____
   Criteria: No leaks, tested with leak detector
2. Connect power supply & ammeter to transmitter   _____
   Criteria: Proper connections from transmitter to
   ammeter to power supply
3. Input test pressure in 25% increments.   _____
   Criteria: Proper signals input
4. Adjust output as needed to be within ±2%   _____
   Criteria: Output within tolerance
5. Record "as left" data   _____
   Criteria: All required data recorded
6. Disconnect test equipment   _____
   Criteria: Equipment safely disconnected and
   stowed

Completion:

Trainee has successfully completed this JPM.   _____

Figure 15-3. Job performance measure.

15.3 Case Studies

A practical means to explore skilled trades training programs is to examine several case studies. The following case studies describe three actual skilled trades programs which occur in a variety of settings and which have quite different learning goals. These three settings are

1. Mechanics in a nuclear power plant
2. Inmates learning carpentry in a maximum security penitentiary
3. Electricians in the International Brotherhood of Electrical Workers (IBEW) Local 328 Apprenticeship program

Case Study #1

Nuclear Power Plant Mechanics

Dozens of nuclear training sites in the United States have programs for their mechanics similar to the one described here. Each is overseen and accredited by at least two agencies, the Nuclear Regulatory Commission (NRC) and the Institute of Nuclear Power Operations (INPO). The training programs are based upon the *Systematic Approach to Training* (*SAT*) process in which job and task analyses define training program content, setting, and evaluation methods.

An analysis of the job determines which tasks are performed by the mechanics at a particular site. A typical task would be Repair a Centrifugal Pump. Task analysis breaks this task into steps, and further into skills and knowledge-items a mechanic would need to perform this task.

The mechanical training program includes approximately 150 tasks which have been selected for training and clustered into courses. The training program is divided into *initial* and *advanced* courses. Most of the tasks are covered in the initial program which is given to all the mechanics. A sample of the tasks is represented by the following list:

1. Weld stainless steel piping.
2. Replace lakewater filter.
3. Repack a gate valve.
4. Repair an air compressor.
5. Repair a hydraulic valve operator.

About 25 additional tasks are cover in advanced courses, which may only be given to a few mechanics. A sample of the tasks is represented by the following list:

1. Inspect reactor fuel assembly.
2. Rebuild control rod drive unit.

3. Replace ion exchanger resin.

4. Remove reactor vessel head.

5. Replace feed pump seals.

For example, all mechanics are trained on the initial training task, repair a gate valve. Only a few mechanics are trained on the advanced training task, repair a diesel engine. Once mechanics have been trained on and have demonstrated successful performance of a task in the training setting, they are considered qualified to perform that task in the plant unsupervised.

Mechanics are presented with theory and general information in the classroom. Course curriculum begins with fundamental mechanical concepts such as pump theory, use of hand tools, and basic valves. Other topics are general theory including fluid dynamics, piping, and hydraulics, or are component-based including air compressors, snubbers, and steam turbine. The nuclear mechanic's training program has other subject areas which are not connected directly to work on specific equipment but which are critical to their successful performance of work. Some of these topics are self-check, safety, procedures, and emergency damage control.

The mechanical training program is performance-based, meaning the implementation and evaluation of training centers around actual job work. Instructors provide demonstrations of proper work techniques in the lab setting. Trainees are allowed to practice until they feel they can successfully perform the task under observation of an evaluator.

This same process is also performed at the work site and is referred to as OJT. *The only difference, generally, is that an instructor performs the demonstration and evaluation in the lab while a peer or supervisor performs those functions in the job setting.* Significant emphasis is placed on making the evaluation phase separate and distinct from the learning phase, such that no coaching or helping is allowed while the trainee is being evaluated.

Qualification matrices, as shown in Figure 15-4, are used to track progress through the training program. The industry considers it critical that only personnel qualified to perform certain tasks are assigned to do that work. Many programs tie task qualification progress to job and pay progression. Certain tasks are associated with job levels; completion of a designated portion of those tasks may enable that mechanic to achieve journeyman* status. There is a clearly defined progression in the job scope from apprenticeship (sometimes called helper) to mastery (often called journeyman or chief).

Qualification matrices may contain hundreds of tasks. For ease of tracking, tasks are sometimes combined into duty areas. For example,

---

* Journeyman and foreman are technical terms associated with skilled trades program and are not intended to have gender implications. They are, however, common terms to these programs and the reader should understand their meaning in this context.

	ABBOT	BROWN	DECKER	KEYES	ROBERTS	STONE	TUCKER	WINSTON	YOUNG
Repair relief valve	X		X	X	X		X	X	
Calibrate relief valve	X	X	X	X	X		X		X
Repair globe valve	X	X	X		X	X		X	X
Repair butterfly valve		X	X	X		X		X	X
Repair gate valve			X	X	X	X	X		
Align pump and motor			X	X		X		X	X
Repair air-conditioning	X	X	X		X		X		X
Clean heat exchanger	X	X	X		X	X	X	X	
Perform arc welding	X	X	X	X	X	X	X	X	X
Replace control rod drive unit	X		X				X		
Inspect hydraulic snubber	X		X	X	X		X		X

Figure 15-4. Qualification matrix used for job assignment.

the first five tasks in the matrix shown could be combined into a duty area called Repair Valves. A mechanic qualified to perform all those tasks would then be qualified in that duty area and be able to perform work on any valve. The duty area matrix can usually be captured on a single page or poster and posted in the group's work location.

Case Study #2

Inmates Learning Carpentry

A very special group of learners takes part in carpenter skills training in New York State's penitentiary system. Consider a student population with a 95 percent high school dropout rate. Consider further that each of them has been convicted of a crime serious enough to warrant long-term confinement in a maximum security facility. If that's not challenging enough, add in high trainee-trainer ratios, significant language and cultural barriers, and occasional outbursts of violence.

Yet, even though the instructors face this multitude of obstacles, there is often an impressive amount of cooperation and effort on the part of the students. The training setting is a relatively safe one in the inmate's life and provides a rare opportunity for them to demonstrate their ability to learn. In some cases, students are actually paid a small sum to attend, approximately fifty cents per half-day. The inspiring effort shown by the trainees may be because of the opportunity to demonstrate an acquisition of legitimate skills, not only to the instructor but also to themselves and their peers.

Entry-level requirements regarding reading and writing abilities must be demonstrated prior to acceptance into the carpentry program. A committee reviews individual applicants for acceptance into the program, which has two important goals: (1) it keeps the learner occupied during the day and therefore less apt to become involved in prison violence; and more importantly, (2) the program provides life skills which inmates can eventually use when they reenter society.

The carpentry program is well organized and moves the learners from simple wood cutting to advanced techniques. An employee profile, similar to a task list and illustrated in Figure 15-5, is used to monitor an individual's successful completion of each skill. This tool is important in that the skills needed in the carpentry job market have been identified and provided to the instructor and student. The skills list is broken into job areas. Each learner progresses through this standardized list. To the right of the task description are three columns. A date is entered in the first column when the trainee has received instruction on that task. A date is entered in the second column when the trainee has practiced that skill. Finally, a date is entered in the third column when the trainee has demonstrated proficiency in that task.

Typically, the instructor will provide an initial demonstration. Peer inmates, who have demonstrated proficiency and a desire to help others, often act as coaches during the practice phase. The instructor then evaluates the trainee's ability to perform each job skill. Inmates who go through this program typically perform work in these skill areas while still in the prison and often gain employment in these skill areas once released.

There are about 40 other trade skill programs available in New York State correctional facilities, including auto mechanics, cosmetology, drafting, plumbing, and welding. Most use a skill inventory tracking system similar to the one described for the carpentry program. They share many challenges unique to their environment, such as strict tool control, discipline problems, and low skill and knowledge levels for entry learners.

Case Study #3

Electricians in the International Brotherhood of Electrical Workers (IBEW)

In the early 1890s a small group of linemen and wiremen gathered together to discuss the high mortality and low pay scale associated

	1	2	3
ORIENTATION			
Write school rules and regulations			
Write shop rules and regulations			
Describe reasons for general safety and eye protection			
State use of protective apparel			
Inspect carpentry shop and equipment			
Describe course offering			
FRAMING			
Floor Framing			
Lay out, cut, and assemble built-up girder			
Install sill assembly			
Install floor joists			
Install subfloor			
Wall Framing			
Lay out exterior wall shoes and plates			
Construct corner post			
Assemble exterior stud wall			
Apply sheathing			
Cut components for interior wall			
Erect, plumb, and brace interior wall			

Figure 15-5. Employee profile—carpentry.

with their trades. They formed an organization to seek safer working conditions and a higher pay rate (three dollars per day). Over the years the group's membership and strength grew.

In 1941, the International Brotherhood of Electrical Workers (IBEW) along with a federal committee developed national standards for training and education that were published by the U.S. Department of Labor. This was done to "protect and defend" the skills of its members and meant that journeymen and technicians would become the trainers of a new generation of workers (Palladino, 1991). Today over 900,000 IBEW members benefit from the education and training from this powerful, international organization.

The IBEW implements an extensive apprenticeship program in which electricians are given classroom and on-the-job training and are methodically progressed to mastery level. The program is certified by the U.S. Department of Labor and has a history of good performance as viewed by the industry. Technical program content is determined by the National Joint Apprenticeship Training Committee (NJATC) and is constantly being reviewed and updated via new editions of course materials.

The characteristics of the IBEW training program provided here describe Local 328 in Oswego, New York, and are representative of other IBEW programs nationwide.

Entry into the apprenticeship program is competitive. Every other year, 150 to 300 applicants will apply for approximately 6 to 12 positions. They will proceed through the following series of checks before being accepted into an apprenticeship:

1. Must be high school graduate, preferably having completed a course in algebra.

2. Must take the New York State trade-specific aptitude exam (possible results are high, medium, or low).

3. Background items such as high school grades and experience are evaluated.

4. Those who scored "high" on the aptitude test undergo a rigorous panel interview. Panel members include three contractors and three union representatives.

5. Applicants receive cumulative scores based on aptitude score, background evaluation, and interview. Those with highest score are selected.

Students complete their apprenticeship program over a five-year period. Courses are provided twice a week in the evening, allowing the learners to work during the day under the guidance of a foreman. Course curriculum ranges from descriptions of the electrician's role in the construction industry to detailed studies of electrical theory. The number of hours spent on OJT to achieve journeyman level is quite high. Apprentice electricians will log 8000 hours, or four years, of on-the-job-training before they become journeymen. *Foremen must provide reports of satisfactory work in order for the student to stay in, and progress through, the program.* The Apprentice Committee will periodically review apprentice work locations and move apprentices from job to job to ensure that they receive OJT in different skill applications.

Apprentice development continues over five years through classroom and OJT. *In addition to producing positive work reports from the foremen, the apprentice must also maintain at least a 70% average in classroom work*. Successful training completion will allow them to progress through six steps, each with a corresponding pay grade. Table 15-1 summarizes this progression series.

At the completion of the five-year classroom program and 8000 hours of OJT, apprentices become journeymen. Until now a foreman has been responsible for the quality of the apprentices' work; now they are responsible for their own.

The IBEW continues to provide training opportunities once the worker has achieved journeyman level. Optional night courses are provided to sharpen skills in modern technologies and to familiarize the electrician with job-relevant safety issues. Local 328 has provided journeyman improvement courses in areas such as fiberoptics, programmable logic controllers, fire protection, hazardous materials, and motor controllers.

Of the three case studies presented here, the IBEW has the most structured progression from apprenticeship to mastery level. It incorporates the association of learner and mentor most actively, even without the formal JPM or Skills Inventory used in the other examples.

15.3.1 Summary: Case Studies

These three cases have very much in common. They each identify a set of necessary skills and systematically transfer those to the learner using a simple-to-complex approach. Similar strategies of demonstrate-practice-evaluate are present for the nuclear mechanics, the IBEW electricians, and the inmate carpenters. Emphasis is placed on hands-on training for each, although classrooms are also used as needed for knowledge-based training. Methods of evaluation within each application are held constant from one trainee to the next. Importantly, these methods all incorporate independent demonstration by the trainee of the task prior to credit being given for suc-

Table 15-1. IBEW Local 328 progression.

Apprentice level	Hours of OJT	Years of classroom	% Journeyman pay
Step 1	0–1000	0	35
Step 2	1000–2000	1	40
Step 3	2000–3500	2	50
Step 4	3500–5000	3	60
Step 5	5000–6500	4	70
Step 6	6500–8000	5	80

cessful completion of training. This is most apparent in the case of nuclear mechanics who are not qualified to perform the work until they can demonstrate proficiency to an instructor or OJT evaluator. Also common to each application, though somewhat less obvious for the inmate carpentry program, is the structured progression from apprenticeship to mastery.

15.4 Challenges to Trades Programs

Skilled trades programs in the United States share many challenges. In some cases, these challenges are opportunities to improve; in many others, they are challenges to hold onto quality and quantity standards that have already been achieved. Those training programs that are actually service branches within industrial organizations will feel the economic and human resource pain which their parent company undergoes. Other programs, independent of a particular company, will face their own economic difficulties. Certainly, time and money represent major challenges to these programs. Other challenges are continuing training for the students once they complete the initial training program and professional preparation and development of the trainers. Yet the future of technical America rests with such programs. Their survival and growth will be the difference between success and failure in the world marketplace.

15.4.1 Challenge #1: Resource Allocation

Heading the list of challenges to skilled trades programs is strategic resource allocation. Ample resources are evident when: (1) sufficient instructor and student time is available for the instructional process and (2) that process is supported with the necessary materials and equipment.

Instructors and students need ample time for preparation, study, instruction, skills practice, and on-the-job-training. Each of these five phases is critical to a successful learning experience, yet many industrial training applications seek greater program efficiency through the systematic reduction in one or more of these phases. Skilled trades training programs will not achieve their learning goals unless it is understood that mastery of a skill cannot come without practice and coaching.

A training environment is said to have a high degree of fidelity when it closely represents real-world conditions. This is especially important to skilled trades programs. Remembering that the goal is to prepare the learner for task performance in the job market, trainers will realize that the training must take place on equipment that is the same or similar to that used in the workplace.

The principal advantage of having the proper equipment is that learners can truly be evaluated on their ability to perform the work for which they have been trained. How else can one test lathe operators but to have them operate a lathe? Evaluation techniques are really the gauge by which any skilled trades program can be measured. The credibility of the graduation certificate rests almost entirely on the fidelity of the evaluation environment.

15.4.2 Challenge #2:
Adequate Continuing Training

When learners have completed their skilled trade program, they achieve a corresponding status which enables them to perform work in that field. They are often called *journeymen* at this point and are subsequently set free to perform any and all job tasks. Yet there are still many issues to be addressed:

- How do workers learn about changing state and federal codes?
- Could they benefit from hearing about safety incidents in their profession?
- How can they be expected to maintain high skill levels without periodic refresher training?

These questions are answered through the implementation of an effective *continuing training* program. Such a program uses feedback from the profession to establish a curriculum which is presented to the worker on a continuous basis. The content is far less extensive than the initial program, but contains some of the same elements. For example, electricians would be periodically refreshed on proper cable splicing techniques. Incidents of recent electrical accidents would be discussed, including cause and prevention issues.

The practical implementation of an effective continuing training program need not be intimidating. It is usually far smaller in scope than the apprenticeship training program and can be designed to have a minimum impact on resources. While the actual time required will vary depending on the job skill, generally one hour per week to one hour per month is sufficient and can be added to existing work group meetings. The instruction need not be provided by a trained instructor; often, continuing training sessions are most effectively provided by senior workers, supervisors, or outside personnel.

A good continuing training program is, however, planned and developed by knowledgeable trainers. Topics are selected based on craft-worker needs and may involve a wide range of subject matter. The technical material presented may be based on some new technology or may be intended to refresh previously learned skills. Schedules are developed far enough in advance to ensure that adequate preparation is possible. This is also helpful in scheduling routine topics which are required by one agency or another to be repeated periodically. For example, the Occupational Safety and Health Administration (OSHA) may require that certain workers receive electrical safety training on an annual basis and asbestos awareness training on a triennial basis.

15.4.3 Challenge #3: Instructor Professional Development

The trainers in skilled trades programs deserve and require continuing education for the same reasons as their students. For training programs to achieve the effectiveness and efficiency that industry and the job market will demand, instructor training programs must be properly designed, developed, and implemented. These train-the-trainer programs should have two components: (1) technical material related to the trade, and (2) instructional skills material related to the training program and audience.

Technical training for instructors is achieved in a variety of ways. Trade workshops, journals, and courses given by equipment manufacturers are just a few. For example, Foxboro electronic control systems are taught to supervisors and technicians by the Foxboro company. Valve maintenance workshops are held by electric utility users' groups. The effective acquisition and continual upgrade of technical knowledge and skill must be methodically organized and not simply a hit-and-miss result of convenient opportunities.

Too often, skilled trades instructors are drafted from the craft-worker population with little or no training provided in the area of instructional skills. They come to the classroom and lab with a wealth of technical knowledge and may even be highly motivated to teach, yet their success is limited by their inability to manage a learning environment or to communicate with their trainees. It requires much more than desire and drive to teach a trades program. Just as the electrician cannot work without a multimeter, the trainer cannot perform without having the necessary training skills and techniques.

Generally, the learners in skilled trades programs are adults. Instructors can train most effectively when they understand and implement adult learning techniques. Adults need to understand the real-world application of their training; they need to see an immediacy of application. The adult learner is a valuable resource of experience which can be drawn upon to aid the learning process. See Knowles (1984) and Cross (1981) for a complete discussion of adult learning techniques. Chapter 7 in this handbook also addresses adult learning issues.

15.4.4 Challenge #4: Training a Very Diverse Workforce

The opportunity for trainers to apply their teaching skills to a diverse learner audience expands every day. Students of a variety of backgrounds present new and interesting challenges to skilled trades training programs. Many of Knowles' (1984) adult learning principles will guide the trainer through these situations.

Individual learners, recognized for their individuality, can actually improve the overall learning experience. Certainly barriers such as language and cultural differences will challenge even the most well-prepared trainer, yet these very differences are the opportunity which must be drawn upon to take learning to higher levels for all learners. No longer can trainers and learners be content with skills applicable to local and traditional practices that were satisfactory to previous generations. The workforce and the workplace are changing; for workers and industries to survive, they must embrace those issues associated with diversity.

15.4.5 Challenge #5: Preparing Workers to Meet the Challenges of ISO 9000 and Other Certification Programs

Industries are being asked—are asking themselves—to meet tighter certification criteria as they make changes to compete successfully in their markets. Movements such as Total Quality Management and ISO 9000 place greater demands upon worker and manager alike—demands that can only be met by people who are knowledgeable in the details of these programs. As a result, skilled trades training programs must include in their curriculum descriptions of what these new requirements are as well as methods for their accomplishment.

One group that has successfully taught their workers to meet stringent certification standards is the nuclear utility industry. As mentioned in the case study for mechanics, the NRC and INPO scrutinize nuclear activities. The operation and maintenance of these plants must be within the confines of extensive rules in order for the utilities to maintain their training program accreditations and plant operating licenses. Workers are trained thoroughly on the content of these rules and on the steps necessary to ensure their implementation. Proper job analysis for any industry, nuclear or not, will formally identify certification program training needs.

15.4.6 Challenge #6: Making Sure the Workforce Is Competitive in the Global Marketplace

An issue that becomes apparent in consideration of workforce diversity and certification programs is the ability to compete globally. Once it was enough to train workers to produce products that would rival local or even national competitors' products. No longer is that strategy acceptable. The marketplace has become global. Developers and implementers of skilled trades programs must consider:

1. How is my industry affected by the marketplace globalization?

2. How does this impact on the industry affect the worker?

3. What added knowledge and skills do my workers need to support this industry in the global marketplace?

As these questions are answered for individual skilled trades programs, the changes needed in the training will become apparent. Industry, however, requires a proactive approach to preparing workers to meet worldwide competition; reactionary steps will be too late and inadequate.

15.5   Chapter Summary

Skilled trades training programs will focus on preparing their students for the job market. Greater job skill specialization and continuous application of technology to industry will require increased training. Effective training programs will respond to higher demands and provide learning environments based on current, real job skills and will evaluate trainee performance by testing their ability to perform those skills.

Skilled trades training has special characteristics regarding learning goals, implementation strategies, and evaluation methods. All aspects of the program center around the need for meaningful hands-on practice. The opportunity to practice enables the apprentice to eventually become a master. Skill mastery, applicable to today's work environment, is the ultimate goal of these training programs. It is achieved only through demonstration, coaching, and evaluation of work performed on equipment identical or similar to that in the workplace.

Today, there are countless skilled trades training programs involving millions of trainees. These programs have in common the methodical progression of apprentice to master organized in a simple-to-complex learning structure. The systematic acquisition of individual skills is usually tracked and documented as the trainee progresses through the program.

Effective training programs will maintain the most strategic use of resources, however limited those resources are or may become. Training equipment fidelity and meaningful evaluation methods will remain the gauge by which programs are measured.

Providing the best possible initial training, though, is only the foundation. A thorough continuing training program is critical to the long-term success of the worker and the workforce. This training will ensure that the journeyman is updated to newest technologies, will reinforce safety work practices, and will provide a forum upon which many current issues can be resolved.

The quality of the skilled trades training depends upon the quality of the skilled trades instructors. Train-the-trainer programs establish and maintain desired instructor skill levels. Instructors must be experts on two fronts: (1) the technical nature of their content areas, and (2) instructional techniques that correspond to the program and audience. Especially important in skilled trades programs are those instructional skills involving adult learning techniques.

Bibliography

Cross, K. P., *Adults as Learners*, Jossey-Bass, San Francisco, 1981.

Glover, R. W., "Apprenticeship Training and Vocational Education as Partners," in K. B. Greenwood (ed.), *Contemporary Challenges for Vocational Education*, American Vocatinal Association, Arlington, Va., 1981.

Heinich, Robert, Mike Molenda, and James Russell, *Instructional Media*, Macmillan, New York, 1989.

Knowles, M., *The Adult Learner: A Neglected Species*, Gulf Publishing Company, Houston, Tex., 1984.

Lobb, C., *Apprenticeship Careers*, Rosen Publishing Group, New York, 1978.

Palladino, G., *Dreams of Dignity, Workers of Vision*, International Brotherhood of Electrical Workers, Washington, D.C., 1991.

Paquin, D., "Strategies for Effective Lab Exercises," *Technical and Skills Training*, August/September 1990, pp. 14–18.

Reynolds, A., *The Trainer's Dictionary*, Human Resource Development Press, Amherst, Mass., 1993.

16

Anatomy of a Training Program: A Start-to-Finish Look

Joseph C. Mancuso, Ph.D.
Texas Instruments

16.1 Texas Instruments Learning Institute (TILI)

The Texas Instruments Learning Institute (TILI) grew out of the Texas Instruments (TI) Human Resources Development Department (HRD). TILI, located in North Dallas at TI's Park Central North site, offers TIers and external customers courses on leadership, teaming, engineering, computer hardware and software, safety, quality, diversity, and many other topics. In 1993, TILI, a four-story building with classrooms on four floors, conducted 5895 classes for 70,374 students. These courses keep TI staff current in their disciplines and in the latest corporate "cultural" advances. The TILI *Training and Education Catalog, 1994* has a complete list of the 555 courses TILI offers to TIers. Among the technical offerings are such courses as

Sheet Metal Parts Design

Thermal Design of Military Electronic Systems

Pro/ENGINEER Advanced Assembly Design

Geometric Dimensioning and Tolerancing

IMS Teleprocessing Programming

STROBE Performance Tuning

MIL-STD-2000 Wave Solder Certification

Basics of Systems Engineering

Software Requirements Process Workshop

Software Quality Assurance Concepts

TILI purchases many of its courses "off the shelf" (from external sources) like "Writing Winning Proposals," "Digital Signal Processing," and "Electromagnetic Interference"; where an off-the-shelf course will not suffice, TILI develops courses tailored to the needs of TI-specific projects. In 1993, for example, TILI developed "Configuration Management Overview" (CM100), "Managing Software for Program Managers" (SWP 330), "Mentor VHDL" (MEN 150), and others. TILI's instructional designers, instructors, subject matter experts (SMEs), and steering committee members develop approximately 50 of these courses each year through Operational Decision Package funds (government funds) and customer funding. This chapter focuses on the courses TILI develops for its technical customers.

16.2 TILI Personnel Involved in Course Development

TILI course developers are divided into four main groups:

Instructional designers

Instructors

SMEs

Steering committee members

TILI's *instructional designers* are professionals with a background in course design, needs assessment, task analysis, and evaluation. They have earned masters' or doctoral degrees in instructional systems design or instructional technology from universities such as Florida State, Syracuse, San Diego State, Indiana, and others. Instructional designers are a critical part of the course development team, leading other team members through the steps of the design process, helping to identify audience needs and wants, and ensuring the quality of the product.

Instructors augment the skills of instructional designers with their knowledge of classroom dynamics: what the audience is like (attention span, likes, dislikes), what media and format work (short lectures, mixed media), and what don't work (overlong lectures, too little instructor-student interaction). Instructors, the men and the women "in the trenches," feed information about content, students' propensities, and scheduling and pace of classes into the course development process. Most important, instructors ultimately teach the courses to students, and instructors must, therefore, be comfortable with the information they transfer.

SMEs bring their in-depth knowledge of content to course development. At TI, SMEs are often members of the technical staff, a prestigious group of electrical, mechanical, and software engineers recognized for superior work in their fields and contributions to the company. Their experience in their disciplines and in workplace situations, including proposal writing and work on projects, blends hard, scientific-technical information with colorful, TI "war stories."

The *project leader* in a course development project sometimes forms an executive steering committee and most always a steering committee, inviting members from various disciplines to participate. The executive steering committee members review all activities of the course development without participating in the actual development. The *executive steering committee* champions the course to groups and individuals within TI, gathering support for the course. The *steering committee* participates in the course development, advising the project leader, instructional designers, instructors, and SMEs on the progress of their efforts. Steering committee members also supply materials and recruit attendees for the walkthrough and pilot (later steps in the course development process).

In summary, instructional designers and instructors set the forms for the foundation of a course, and the SMEs and the steering committee members pour the information into the forms for that foundation.

16.3 The TILI Course Development Process

Presently, instructional designers, instructors, SMEs, and steering committee members follow an instructional design model contained in TILI's *Instructional Technology Design Guide*. The guide describes the model's six major areas of design and development:

Area One:	Customer focus
Area Two:	Requirements
Area Three:	Design

Area Four:	Development
Area Five:	Implementation
Area Six:	Operation and control

The six areas contain 84 potential action items for teams to complete (see Figure 16-1, "The Complete List of Action Items"). To give a flavor of the items, a discussion of eight of them follows, with at least one item taken from each of the six areas. The first number in the item corresponds to an area, and the second number designates its chronological place in that area.

Action Item 1.3 Clarify customer responsibilities. Involves determining the customer's position in the management scheme, for instance. If the customer is an upper-level manager, he or she may be concerned with fanning a course out to thousands of employees to learn certain basic principles quickly; this approach may result in lecture/briefing format as in the "Six Sigma Scorecard Overview." If the customer represents middle-level management, he or she may be interested in changing job performance in a smaller particular engineering area. Hence, the course may take the shape of a workshop like "PSpice Modeling." Course developers also identify the support that customers can offer, the customer's contacts and resources which can effect a solution to the problem.

Action Item 2.1 Establish project history file. A collection of all documents associated with the course development, from the beginning until the end. Documents include memos to customers and steering committees, surveys, questionnaires, statement of work, preliminary design review document, critical design review document, walkthrough document, pilot document.

Action Item 2.11 Conduct content analysis. Involves discussing with SMEs the data and ideas that should go into the course so that students can make appropriate decisions and learn the skills needed to perform tasks correctly.

Action Item 3.1 Review/update the project history file. Sometimes it is necessary to produce more than one iteration of a particular document. Course developers should place the latest document in the project history file.

Action Item 3.11 Select types of instruments for level 2 and level 3 evaluation. For example, using a computer-scored, multiple-choice evaluation form rather than a pencil-and-paper, essay question evaluation form. Level 2 evaluation forms gauge how much subject matter students learn in a class. Level 3 evaluations determine how well students apply what they learn in class to their jobs.

ACTION ITEM	RESPONSIBILITY

1.0 Customer Focus
1.1 Identify the customer
1.2 Clarify customer position
1.3 Clarify customer responsibilities
1.4 Clarify HRD responsibilities
1.5 Determine task feasibility
1.6 Determine goals/objectives/audience
1.7 Negotiate requirements/budget/schedule funding
1.8 Draft SOW (see SOW Checklist)
1.9 Obtain sign-off

2.0 Requirements
2.1 Establish project history file
2.2 Assemble design team
2.3 Clarify customer responsibilities
2.4 Develop project action lan
2.5 Conduct detailed needs assessment
2.6 Define customer wants
2.7 Define and analyze end user
2.8 Conduct task analysis
2.9 Relate tasks and content to needs
2.10 Relate tasks to entry-level skills
2.11 Conduct content analysis
2.12 Relate content to prerequisites knowledge
2.13 Determine evaluation criteria
2.14 Perform Pareto analysis
2.15 Determine availability of existing materials
2.16 Complete PDR boilerplate/conduct PDR
2.17 Prepare PDR agenda and materials
2.18 Obtain sign-off

3.0 Design
3.1 Review/update project history file
3.2 Update design team
3.3 Define tasks for major milestones
3.4 Identify design-phase action items
3.5 Define instructional strategies based on participant/task analysis and types of learning outcomes

Figure 16-1. Complete list of action items.

ACTION ITEM	RESPONSIBILITY

3.6   Review existing instructional products adaptable to objectives, develop list

3.7   Design instructional events to achieve objectives based on task/end-user analysis and desired learning outcomes

3.8   Sequence or storyboard instructional events

3.9   Review customer requirements or confirm viability of instructional event organization

3.10 Select media for instructional events

3.11 Select types of instruments for level 2 and level 3 evaluation

3.12 Prepare final outline of objectives, strategy, instructional events, evaluation criteria, and media selected

3.13 Present for internal review

3.14 Develop sample portion of instructional package

3.15 Complete CDR template/conduct CDR

3.16 Prepare CDR agenda and materials

3.17 Include the following in CDR document

3.18 Obtain sign-off

<u>4.0</u>   <u>Development</u>

4.1   Review/update project history file

4.2   Update design team

4.3   Define tasks for major milestones in development phase

4.4   Review function-user matrix detailed outline if all participants receive same content

4.5   Select first activity and draft

4.6   Review module

4.7   Create prototype course components for selected module

4.8   Conduct appropriate trials

4.9   Revise module based on trial results

4.10 Create templates from this module to create remaining materials

4.11 Complete steps 4 through 8 for all modules/events

4.12 Send thank you letters to participants and their supervisors

Figure 16-1. (*Continued*)

ACTION ITEM	RESPONSIBILITY

4.13 Complete rough drafts of all modules/
      events for walkthroughs
4.14 Train instructors if needed
4.15 Obtain sign-off of deliverables

5.0 <u>Implementation</u>
5.1 Update project history file
5.2 Update design team
5.3 Brief steering committee for pilot
5.4 Identify and contact participants for pilot
5.5 Brief candidate instructors for pilot
5.6 Conduct pilot
5.7 Integrate pilot feedback
5.8 Revise; repilot if necessary
5.9 Establish product baseline
5.10 Brief class administrators and begin hand
      over process
5.11 Establish plan for controlling changes to
      materials
5.12 Establish marketing plan
5.13 Obtain sign-off of project completion
5.14 Archive copies of training materials with
      project history file

6.0 <u>Operation and Control</u>
6.1 Place product under customer's change
      control plan
6.2 Identify course administrator and support
      personnel
6.3 Archive master copy of all course materials
6.4 Review delivery plan (design phase) to
      determine requirements
6.5 Implement marketing plan
6.6 Review evaluation plan (design phase)
6.7 Conduct periodic audit of evaluation
      materials based on established interval based
      on perceived stability of course
6.8 Conduct periodic course audits for cost
      reduction or enhancement opportunities
6.9 Procedures for course revision

Figure 16-1. (*Continued*)

Action Item 4.14 Train instructors if needed. Sometimes those who teach courses at TI are not experienced instructors; they are managers and others who because of their position and knowledge are asked to teach courses. To bring these managers and others up to speed as instructors, TILI offers "Train the Trainer," "Conducting Effective Business Presentations," and other skill-building courses.

Action Item 5.3 Brief steering committees for pilots. Course developers ask steering committee members to nominate one or two TIers to participate in the pilot (the "dress rehearsal" before the first official delivery of the course). Steering committee members and invited target audience members take the course as though they were students and, additionally, give feedback about course content and presentation when the pilot is completed.

Action Item 6.2 Identify course administrator and support personnel. Course administrators list the new course and its schedule of classes on TI's Training and Education Management System (TEMS), a system allowing TIers to register for classes. Course administrators also produce materials for classes, supervise classroom setup, arrange for catering, and provide other support functions.

There are 76 more action items contained in TILI's *Instructional Technology Design Guide.* However, management does not require development teams to follow the TILI model slavishly, nor do all course development projects demand implementing all action items. The model, therefore, guides development teams but does not restrict them. Each project follows its own pattern, using the model as a springboard.

Essentially, customers discuss problems with TILI instructors in various settings and seek solutions for problems which may take the form of rewritten manuals, job aids, and courses. When TILI and the customer agree that a course development will solve the problem, a development team implements some form of the model to check progress along the way.

Without completely describing the six areas and 84 action items in the model, this chapter examines the following "guts" of the steps/actions in the course development process. These are generic steps/actions in the course development process for all types of courses:

16.3.1 Step One: Customer Contact, Needs Assessment

Customers regularly contact TILI staff seeking solutions to problems. TILI staff meet with these customers and suggest the following solutions: rewritten course materials, job aids, and new courses. Staff members suggest solutions but only after dialog with the customer and a needs assessment. When TILI staff members—usually the instructional designers—conduct a needs assessment, they first survey SMEs to discover how work should be done—how a job is performed. They then question the customer to see how the customer performs the job in question. The gap between the view of the SMEs and the customer tells the course development team what the needs are.

16.3.2 Step Two: Course Requirements—The Steering Committee

Depending on the results of the needs assessment and the requirements that flow from that effort, instructional designers recommend one solution or another. If instructional designers recommend course development, TILI designates a project leader who forms a steering committee.

16.3.3 Step Three: The Preliminary Design Review (PDR)

The project leader, instructional designers, instructors, and SMEs develop a detailed outline for the course and examine it at a preliminary design review (PDR), with the steering committee present. All present evaluate the outline and add or subtract from it. When members of the steering committee approve the outline, this completes the PDR step in the instructional design process.

16.3.4 Step Four: Development—The Critical Design Review (CDR)

The project leader, instructional designers, instructors, and SMEs amplify at least one section (and preferably two or three) of the outline into a full chapter. The draft materials are presented to the steering committee, which either approves the work or suggests minor or extensive modification. This amplification of the outline into chapters constitutes the critical design review (CDR).

16.3.5 Step Five: Implementation— The Walkthrough

Following the CDR, the development team amplifies the entire outline and prepares overheads of the developed chapters. The team, in consultation with the steering committee, identifies other concerned and expert TIers and invites them to a walkthrough. Attending the walkthrough is the steering committee as well as carefully selected attendees who evaluate the chapters and overheads.

16.3.6   Step Six: The Pilot

The development team invites a group of target audience members to the first complete presentation of the course, the pilot. The target audience is composed of those TIers for whom the course was originally meant.

Depending on the evaluation of the pilot members, the course is approved for release or rejected with recommendations for improvement. Depending on how extensive the piloteers' suggested changes are, it may be necessary to conduct more than one pilot.

16.3.7   Step Seven: The Release

If the course passes muster at the pilot stage, then TILI releases the course for registration.

16.4   A TILI Course Development Case Study: The Need for a Technical Writing Course

TI released the "Technical Writing Workshop" (TWW100), TI's present technical writing course, in 1990. The course took one year to develop, and a roster of three instructors has been teaching it for the last four years. TILI offers the course 12 times a year, and students rate the course highly for design, content, applicability to workplace tasks, and instructor presentation. The course clearly meets a training need within TI.

The following steps occurred in the development of TWW100. They closely parallel the generic steps mentioned in Section 16.3.

16.4.1   Step One: Customer Problems—Ineffectively and Inefficiently Written Documents

Glen Bandy, chief engineer for TI's Business Development Entity, and a 30-year TI veteran, approached Bill Long, manager of TILI, with the results of an internal survey. The survey showed that 90 percent of TI managers experienced difficulty reading subordinates' reports. Managers also reported that TI authors took too long to write documents. Based on the results of the survey, Glen Bandy asked Bill Long to begin the process of developing a two-day technical writing course.

16.4.2   Step Two: The Need for a Technical Writing Course

Bill scheduled a meeting that included Glen, Ken Finley (instructional designer and technical writer), Ted Moody (manager of the Engineering Training Branch), and Joe Mancuso (subject matter expert in technical communication). Glen chaired the meeting and asked Bill, Ted, Ken, and Joe to develop the course. Glen offered to chair the steering committee to develop the technical writing course.

Following the meeting, the team members conducted a needs assessment to identify the problem. They began the needs assessment phase by developing a 50-question survey which was administered to 300 TI engineers. Respondents to the survey reported these opinions:

1. TI documents were not well written. Respondents noticed the weak writing skills of "other" engineers.

2. Respondents' own writing skills were adequate. (This contradiction is not unusual. The engineers recognized the problem, but saw others and not themselves as the problem.)

3. Respondents said they had received no TI training to enhance their writing skills. As far as they knew, TI offered no technical writing courses.

4. Respondents said TI did not reward engineers who were competent writers—including proposal writers—for their nonengineering skills.

5. Respondents disliked writing tasks and, instead, preferred to focus on their "productive," engineering tasks.

6. Most respondents had never taken a technical writing course in school.

Course developers, after examining responses to the survey, concluded that respondents

1. Did not recognize the difference between active voice and passive voice (grammatical constructions) sentences.

2. Could not distinguish between strong and weak verbs.

3. Did not recognize that some words were extraneous to their messages.

4. Harbored attitudes unfavorable to effective writing.

The needs assessment continued with a lengthy examination of TI proposals, manuals, journal articles, test documents, change notices, and the like in the technical library at TI's Lewisville site.

16.4.3 Step Three:
Designating a Project Leader

Because of Joe Mancuso's background in technical communication, the manager of TILI's Engineering Training Branch designated him as project leader for development of the technical writing course. Joe, a Ph.D. in English, had established and directed the technical writing program at a local university and had written two textbooks in the field.

16.4.4 Step Four: Forming
the TWW100 Steering Committee

Glen Bandy invited the following TIers to participate as steering committee members: Tom Gulledge, veteran TI technical editor; Charles Chapoton, Ph.D. in electrical engineering, radar SME, and veteran of many proposal efforts; Tom Moore, a technical writer; and four other TI engineers and technical writers. Glen decided not to form an executive steering committee, feeling that the steering committee itself was composed of a sufficient number of "connected" TIers who would champion the course throughout the company.

The steering committee met for the first time and set two major guidelines for the development of the course:

- The course must be a TI-specific course, not a generic, off-the-shelf one. That is, the course must address the problems in TI's workplace.

- Authors of the course must elucidate problems and solutions with illustrations from TI documents. Authors must also draw exercise material from TI situations and documents.

16.4.5 Step Five: Conducting
the Preliminary Design Review—
Evaluating the Outline

The 50-question survey and an examination of previously written TI technical documents convinced the development team that TI engineers employed a writing style with the following characteristics:

1. Engineers preferred the passive voice to the active voice. They used the passive voice approximately 80 percent of the time and the active voice

20 percent. Essentially, passive voice sentences contain subjects that receive action and verbs that couple a form of the verb *be* with a past participle. For instance, the sentence "The airplane was landed by the pilot safely on the runway" is a passive voice sentence. The sentence "The pilot landed the plane safely on the runway" is an active voice sentence because the subject performs the action of the sentence. Usually, passive voice sentences are longer and less clear than active voice sentences. Audiences want shorter, easy-to-understand sentences. Course developers regularly noticed sentences like the following.

Common:

"Although some platforms, such as the F-18, *will be serviced* by this equipment, it will still be too heavy and too sluggish for other platforms, such as expendable weapons and lightweight aircraft."

Better:

"This equipment *services* platforms but is too heavy to service expendable weapons and lightweight aircraft."

Common:

"The charge transfer detector *is proposed* for the MWIR band because it offers high sensitivity, better scan efficiency, good MTR, and no significant increase in overall risk."

Better:

"TI *proposes* the charge transfer detector for the MWIR band because it offers high sensitivity, better scan efficiency, good MTR, and no significant increase in overall risk."

2. Engineers often used weak verbs like forms of the verbs *be, have, do, give, make, provide, include,* rather than strong verbs like *design, develop, demonstrate, test,* which create images in the mind's eye of the reader. Course developers regularly noticed sentences like the following.

Common:

"Test operations occurring at TI and/or any team member sites *are* under the direction of the TI test verification/integration manager."

Better:

"The TI test verification/integration manager *directs* test operations at TI and/or any team member sites."

Common:

"Each team member also *has* the capability to draw on a broader base of corporate capability to support specific program needs."

Better:

> "Each team member *can draw* on a broader base of corporate capability to support specific program needs."

3. Engineers used many unnecessary words, such as

- Meaningless intensifiers (*decidedly*)
- Relative pronouns (*that*)
- Auxiliary verbs (*will*)
- Redundancies (*wide spectrum*)
- Overblown phrases (*in this modern world*)

Course developers regularly noticed sentences like the following.

Common:

> "Our organization structure ensures that *all* relevant disciplines influence the design."

Better:

> "Our organization structure ensures that relevant disciplines influence the design."

Common:

> "This plan *is evolutionary in nature and is refined continuously and updated* as the program matures."

Better:

> "This plan evolves as the program matures."

The survey and the examination of TI documents generated an outline for the PDR. See Figure 16-2, the PDR Outline.

16.4.6 Step Six: The Critical Design Review—The Steering Committee Comments on the First Module

The development team amplified the Introduction section of the PDR outline, adding third- and fourth-level headings to the existing first- and second-level headings of the PDR outline. The team then developed the third- and fourth-level headings into phrases, clauses, sentences, and paragraphs (not shown in this article). The team considered the Introduction the first module of the course. See Figure 16-3, The CDR—Module 1.0.

The Technical Writing Workshop (TWW100)

1.0 Introduction
   1.1 TWW100 Instructors
   1.2 TI Writing Problems
   1.3 Examples of Ineffective TI Writing
   1.4 TWW100 Objectives
   1.5 TWW100 Agenda
2.0 Discussion of Attitudes from Academe and the Workplace
   2.1 Use the Personal Pronoun?
   2.2 Use a Variety of Words in Technical Writing
   2.3 Do Transition Words Help?
   2.4 Write the Rough Draft as Quickly as Possible
   2.5 Correctness is the Most Important Characteristic of Effective Writing
3.0 The Technical Writing Process—Nine Stages
   3.1 Stage 1: Adhere to Customer Requirements
   3.2 Stage 2: Research the Information
   3.3 Stage 3: Brainstorm the Information
   3.4 Stage 4: Categorize the Information
   3.5 Stage 5: Sort the Information
   3.6 Stage 6: Outline the Information
   3.7 Stage 7: Design the Document
   3.8 Stage 8: Write the First Draft
   3.9 Stage 9: Edit the Draft
4.0 Recommended Writing/Editing References
   4.1 Books
   4.2 Software

Figure 16-2. PDR outline.

Following the development of Module 1.0, the steering committee met and discussed it. The committee suggested changes which the development team either accepted or challenged.

At a succeeding meeting of its own, the instructional designers, instructors, and SMEs incorporated most of the suggestions of the steering committee. At that time, the project leader assigned responsibility for amplifying the remaining parts of the outline to development team members. In three weeks, the team reassembled for a runthrough of each of their amplifications. Satisfied with a completed CDR document (in this case, an amplified outline), the team scheduled the walkthrough.

The Technical Writing Workshop (TWW100)

1.0 MODULE 1: Introduction
   1.1 TWW100 Instructors
      1.1.1 Joe Mancuso, Ph.D.
         TI experience
         Experience before coming to TI
         Publications
   1.2 TI Writing Problems
      1.2.1 Lack of clarity
      1.2.2 Verbosity
      1.2.3 Disorganized
      1.2.4 Lack of audience appeal
      1.2.5 Poor readability
   1.3 Examples of Ineffective Writing
      1.3.1 In academe and other settings
      1.3.2 In TI documents
   1.4 TWW100 Objectives
      1.4.1 Correct TI writing problems with these approaches
         Develop effective technical writing style
         Follow the steps in the technical writing process
   1.5 TWW100 Agenda
      Day 1
      Day 2
   1.6 Course Materials
      1.6.1 Participant's guide
      1.6.2 Supplementary texts
         Government Printing Office Style Manual
         Handbook of Technical Writing
         The Harbrace Handbook
         Technical Editing

Figure 16-3. The CDR—Module 1.0.

16.4.7 Step Seven:
The Walkthrough—
Do We Have a Viable Course?

The development team scheduled the TWW100 walkthrough for three weeks hence, on October 28. The project leader contacted members of the steering committee, requesting the names of invitees for the walkthrough, with the understanding that invitees be specialists in some area of document production, whether it be planning, writing, editing, or publishing documents. When the list was complete, the team leader invited 20 specialists and three backups in case one of the original invitees became involved in a proposal, had a conflict, and was unable to attend.

On October 28, the course development team presented the course overheads, stopping to approve or discuss each of them. Members of the walkthrough asked questions and commented on the general direction and specifics of the course. The group critiqued lecturettes, examples, and exercises. A scribe captured the interchange between the development team and the walkthrough attendees on a laptop computer, placing questions and comments in italics next to the relevant overhead.

The development team saved 30 minutes for a wrap-up discussion at the end of the walkthrough. At that time, the attendees underscored their most significant criticisms. They emphasized that while numerous overheads needed improvement, the course was solid. The group adjourned with the understanding that the development team would incorporate the necessary changes and then present the course one last time in a pilot before release.

16.4.8 Step Eight: The Pilot— Let the Target Audience Say That the Course Works

The steering committee again supplied a list of attendees—this time individuals representing the target audience for TWW100. The list included engineers, technical writers, and data managers (those who do research for technical writers), with limited experience in writing and editing documents.

On December 2, the instructor delivered the pilot to a group of 25 participants. He began the pilot by saying that it was a dress rehearsal for a future "opening night" when the course would be offered to TI participants for the first time. The team leader asked the piloteers to participate in the course now as both students and evaluators. He asked piloteers to engage in all course activities and note their comments and questions regarding the effectiveness of the course content and presentation in the appropriate places in the participant's guide (a hard copy of the overheads). The instructor then conducted the course as instructors would when TILI formally offered the course.

After the second day of the pilot, the team leader allowed the participants two hours to discuss the effectiveness of the course. As in the walkthrough, a scribe captured the comments of the pilot group.

16.4.9 Step Nine: The Release— TIers May Now Register for TWW100

After the pilot, the development team incorporated changes suggested by the piloteers and prepared a final draft set of overheads. This done, the steering team signed off on the course development of the "Technical Writing Workshop" (TWW100).

With TWW100 successfully piloted, the development team listed the course on TILI's Training and Education Management System which allows TIers to register electronically for courses:

> TWW100, a two-day course, runs from 8:30 AM until 5:00 PM each day. The course may run with a minimum of 8 students and a maximum of 12.

Instructors have run TWW100 with as few as 3 students and as many as 28. TILI keeps the numbers of students in each class low so that maximum interaction between instructor and student may occur. The course costs TIers an average of $300. Included in the deliverables are a participant's guide and four reference books: the *Handbook of Technical Writing* (Charles T. Brusaw, Gerald J. Alred, and Walter E. Oliu, 4th ed., St. Martins Press, 1993), *Technical Editing* (Joseph C. Mancuso, Prentice-Hall, 1992), the *Harbrace Handbook* (John C. Hodges et al., 11th ed., Harcourt Brace Jovanovich, 1983), and the *United States Government Printing Office Style Manual* (U.S. Government Printing Office, Washington, D.C., 1984).

16.4.10 The Technical Writing Workshop Course Development— A Success

At the end of each TILI class, students complete an evaluation form commenting on the design of the course, the relevance of the course to their work, and the presentation of the course by instructors. In each category over the last four years, TWW100 ranks high. Students say that the course "helps on the job" and some have even said TWW100 is "one of the best courses" they have taken.

In examining the documents students produce at the end of TWW100, instructors notice the significant changes in writing style that occur in most students. Students write clear text—even describing the most technical material—and organize large amounts of material quickly and attractively for their readers.

TILI is pleased with the course development of TWW100, as it is with so many other courses it produces. In large measure, TILI's success is due to the many talented instructors, instructional designers, and SMEs on its staff. TILI also depends on its course development model which provides invaluable guidance in achieving its many successes.

Bibliography

Brockette, Ann, and Mary Frances Gibbons (eds.), *Training and Education Catalog*, Texas Instruments Learning Institute, 1994.

Finley, Kenneth (ed.), *Instructional Technology Design Guide*, Texas Instruments Learning Institute, 1991.

Mancuso, Joseph C., *Mastering Technical Writing*, Addison-Wesley, Reading, Mass., 1990.

Mancuso, Joseph C., *Technical Editing*, Prentice-Hall, Englewood Cliffs, N.J., 1992.

17

Installation of Total Quality Management in a High-Tech Environment: The Plant 16 Experience

Michael A. Sullivan

General Motors Corporation

Michael A. Sullivan *has been an employee of General Motors for over 33 years and has had a variety of assignments that include manufacturing, maintenance, tooling, labor relations, education and training, human resources, and salaried personnel. He has a BSIE from General Motors Institute, an MBA from Ball State University, and is currently writing his dissertation for an EdD. from the University of Missouri—St. Louis. His current job assignment at Delco Remy Division, GMC, Anderson, Indiana, is plant superintendent, Plant 16, Power House, and Union/Management Analysis Team. He is also an adjunct professor for Purdue University's State-Wide Technology program in Anderson, Indiana. He and wife Sandra live in Pendleton, Indiana. They have two sons. Brad, a Purdue University and Rollins College graduate, lives and works in Denver, Colorado. Jamey is a senior at the University of Missouri in Columbia, Missouri.*

17.1 Introduction

17.1.1 Purpose

The purpose of this chapter is to provide you with information about the installation of a Total Quality Management (TQM) process in a manufacturing skilled trades environment. In addition, it is the hope of this author that the readers may gain some relative insight regarding TQM so that they might apply some of the learnings to their own particular situation. Further, it must be noted that while I have attempted to share learnings and knowledge as openly and in as unbiased a fashion as possible, the reader should be aware that while doing so, I was, and still am, a participant in the process and find it difficult to remain completely detached from the subject as I report on it. Also, it is significant for the reader to understand that the TQM process, as described in this chapter, is the result of an effort to just "do the right things," and not the result of a preplanned master strategy. While it is important to "label" the effort as TQM, it is just as important to recognize that the leadership involved did not have TQM as a goal when we began the journey.

17.1.2 Agenda

A description, history, and current situation of Plant 16 will be presented. A look at TQM from this author's perspective will follow. The actual TQM process that is ongoing in Plant 16 will then be addressed in a chronological manner, followed by my learnings, conclusions, and recommendations.

17.2 Plant 16

17.2.1 Description

Plant 16 is part of Delco Remy, a division of General Motors Corporation. The plant employs over 400 hourly employees, mostly in skilled trades, who are represented by Local 662 of the United Automobile Workers. The plant also employs approximately 25 salaried employees who are nonunion. It is located in Anderson, Indiana, a typical midwestern industrial town. The building has over 175,000 sq ft and was built in 1959. The employees produce special machines, feeder systems, control systems, material handling equipment, dies, fixtures, gauges, test equipment, injection molds, and various other tools and equipment. In addition, the employees provide tool grinding, maintenance, and janitorial services.

17.2.2 History

When the plant was built in 1959, its intended use was to house tool and maintenance service employees for the three Delco Remy manufacturing plants which were located next door. As Delco Remy's employment levels decreased in the late 1970s and early 1980s, the three manufacturing plants in Anderson, Indiana, were demolished and not replaced.

In the time span from the mid-1950s to the early 1980s, Delco Remy had developed several different organizations to satisfy Delco's needs for the products and services that Plant 16 currently provides. These organizations were staffed with skilled trades employees and their managers, and did not necessarily work together for the best interests of their parent company. In other words, their goals and objectives were not necessarily in line with each other.

During the local contract negotiations in 1985, Local 662 and Delco Remy took a bold step toward trying to improve the efforts of their skilled trades organizations. They mutually agreed to consolidate the more than 85 skilled trades classifications into 9 classifications and to relocate the various organizations to the Plant 16 building. From that reorganization effort in 1985 to late 1992, a tremendous amount of effort was made by Local 662 and the Plant 16 management to blend the various cultures into one.

Many participative managerial styles were tried without much success. As General Motors became part owner of Crosby Institute during that time frame, Plant 16 employed much of the Crosby philosophy in its efforts. It was the Crosby influence which led the union and management leaders to begin to allow employees to participate in some of the business.

From 1988 to 1991, there was much activity in this arena since there were several employee groups with the purpose of improving the workplace environment as well as the productivity of the workforce. However, by late 1991, these groups, which had at one time numbered over 30, had dwindled to less than 5, and most of the employees who had participated for a while had become discouraged and disillusioned.

To make matters worse during this time frame, Delco Remy-Anderson's employment level continued its downward spiral from a one-time high of over 16,000 to the current 1994 level of less than 5000. In addition, the union-management relationship that had appeared to be vastly improved in 1985, returned to its adversarial role, particularly in the skilled trades arena.

The General Motors Quality Network Process that was initiated in 1987 by the United Automobile Workers and General Motors management was considered by the Plant 16 management and union leadership but was given only superficial attention and effort. "Firefighting" was a way of life and no one appeared interested in changing this environment.

In late 1992, the management leadership of Plant 16 was changed. Both the plant manager and the plant superintendent were replaced. As the new leaders analyzed their new situation, they determined that the plant could not survive in what was then its environment. Plant 16 had become a cost burden on Delco Remy products and Delco Remy could not continue to "subsidize" Plant 16 by raising the costs of the division's manufacturing products. In fact, in December of 1992, General Motors announced that several of its businesses were on the market to be sold or "joint ventured." The businesses that were named put 30 to 40 percent of Plant 16's business in jeopardy.

Knowing they were at a crossroads, the manager and superintendent made the decision to approach the future from a point of view that would allow the employees and the union to become full partners in the business. The General Motors Quality Network process was selected to pursue this concept. It was, in fact, the beginnings of a Total Quality Management approach for the Plant 16 business.

There were several factors in place which led to this decision. They were as follows:

- Beliefs and values of the manager and superintendent
- Plant union leadership abilities and capabilities
- General Motors QN process was in place
- Skilled and educated workforce
- Previous participative environment
- Skilled Plant 16 hourly consultant
- Skilled Plant 16 QN hourly representative
- Sincerity and desire of manager and superintendent
- Outside environment very hostile and threatening
- Parent organization, Delco Remy and General Motors, preoccupied with survival and willing to allow innovation
- Status quo not an option
- Tough, nonparticipative approach did not work in the past
- Halfhearted, noncommitted participative approach did not work in the past

17.3 Total Quality Management

17.3.1 Overview

Jablonski, in 1992, defined TQM as

A cooperative form of doing business that relies on the talents and capabilities of both labor and management to continually improve quality and productivity using teams.

He went on to say that there are three ingredients that are necessary for TQM to work:

1. *Participative management.*   If you provide your people with the skills and support to better understand how they do business, identify opportunities for improvement, and make change happen, participative management will work.

2. *Continuous process improvement.*   The acceptance of small, incremental gains as a step in the right direction toward quality and the recognition that substantial gains can be achieved by the accumulation of seemingly minor gains over the long run—a long-term focus.

3. *Teams.*   A cross section of members who represent some part of the process under study, the individuals who work within the process, the suppliers of services and materials, the beneficiaries, and the customers. The empowerment of the people who are involved in the day-to-day operations of the organization to improve their work environment. The recognition that personal commitment toward the organization's improvement goals is achieved in exchange for individual and team rewards, recognition, and job security.

Jablonski further stated that the *six principles of TQM* are:

1. Customer focus

2. A focus on process as well as results

3. Prevention versus inspection

4. Mobilization of the expertise of workforce

5. Fact-based decision making

6. Feedback

In 1991, Darnell and Hamood defined TQM as

A system which is concerned with management approaches to improvement of all products and services, processes and systems. Further, these approaches must support the consistent management of these things after improvement has been made.

They said that for TQM to be successful, it must be seen as a long-term strategy which brings about fundamental changes in organizations, their values, cultures, structures, policies, processes, practices, and procedures. Also, the strategy for change is multidimensional, the process is incremental, and the goal is continuous improvement.

Successful processes are those that create and maintain an organizational culture which emphasizes the importance of people and promotes and practices continual improvement of quality.

As a result of studying some of the quality gurus, such as Crosby, Deming, Feigenbaum, Ishikawa, Juran, and Taguchi, to name just a few of the majors, Darnell and Hamood compiled a list of elements for success in TQM:

- The TQM process is customer-driven, goal-oriented, and creates accountability in the strategic business plan.
- Leadership and commitment to TQM is a top priority of senior management.
- Through example, management is a consistent champion of the TQM process.
- All individuals, processes, and systems—both internal and external— are involved in the quality plan.
- Teamwork and technology are balanced and continually refined.
- Communication is timely, simple, and understandable.
- An attitude of continuous improvement is directed toward all processes, products, and services.
- Measurement and information systems provide useful, uniform information for timely analysis.
- Critical measures of success encompass quality, reliability, dependability, performance, cost, delivery, safety, and customer satisfaction for the life of the product.
- Sources of waste are identified, understood, and eliminated.
- Training and education are available and effective.
- The TQM process develops people, drives out fear, and removes barriers to productivity.
- Change is anticipated and well-managed in organizational systems.
- Statistical thinking—management by facts—is evident in processes and systems.
- TQM is treated as a continuous process.
- Customer satisfaction drives and permeates the entire process.

17.3.2 UAW/GM Quality Network

In 1991, Darnell and Hamood described the UAW/GM Quality Network as follows:

The Quality Network evolved from an idea that originated in one GM operating unit for a cooperative approach for changing an organization and improving customer satisfaction. Supported by both GM and UAW leaders, it was chartered as a corporate-wide process in 1987. Today it is established throughout the Corporation and supported by salaried and represented employees and the leadership of union organizations.

The Quality Network is a joint effort by General Motors, the UAW and other Union employees, suppliers, and dealers to create a company which is more sensitive to customer's needs and more responsive to their desires. As such, it is the first truly joint process of its kind in the auto industry. The Quality Network provides the common means for achieving quality improvement and customer satisfaction. The key ingredients are

- Desired organizational behaviors (Beliefs and Values)
- Structure for appropriate involvement (Quality Councils)
- Process methodology (Quality Network Process Model)
- Minimum set of tools/techniques (Action Strategies)

The Quality Network has been built on a foundation of jointly conceived beliefs and values which outline the way the people of General Motors work together to meet customers' [sic] needs. The Beliefs and Values are

People

- Invite the people to be full partners in the business.
- Recognize people as our greatest resource.
- Demonstrate our commitment to people.
- Treat people with respect.
- Never compromise our integrity.

Teamwork

- Build through teamwork and joint action.
- Take responsibility for leadership.
- Make communications work.
- Trust one another.
- Demand consistency in the application of this value system.

Continuous Improvement

- Make continuous improvement the goal of every individual.
- Put quality in everything we do.
- Eliminate every form of waste.
- Use technology as a tool.
- Accept change as an opportunity.
- Establish a learning environment at all levels.

The Quality Network is General Motors' Total Quality Process.

17.4   Plant 16 Process

17.4.1   Chronological Events

The following provides the activities and efforts which have affected Plant 16's progress toward a TQM culture over a 17-month period of time. The information is presented in a chronological manner to allow the reader to "sense" the process as it occurred:

1992

December
- GM announces that several Delco Remy plants and product lines are for sale. The Plant 16 plant manager shares the information with the plant employees by climbing on a crane-type piece of equipment and using a bullhorn. An unprecedented type of communication in the plant and well appreciated by the employees.
- Newly appointed plant superintendent meets with all employees in small groups and shares financial, as well as personal, information.

1993

January
- *Plant 16 Quality Council begins to meet regularly,* at least once per week.
- Plant 16 management and union agree to bring work in, specifically a test inline, that had been assigned to an "outside" supplier.

February
- Realization by manager and superintendent that survival as a plant will probably depend on finding work both inside and outside Delco Remy.

March
- Superintendent's "leap-of-faith" conversation with general supervisors and plant's UAW District Committeemen. Recognition that trusting one another would play an integral part in plant's survival.
- *General Supervisors and District Committeemen, majority* of Quality Council members, attend a two-day training program on self-directed work teams.
- Same group visit other GM locations that have attempted self-direction. Visit to GM's Saturn operation in Tennessee leaves a lasting impression.

April
- Assignment of salaried employee to begin sales and marketing effort for *selling Plant 16 products outside Delco Remy.*
- Rest of Quality Council members plus several key supervisors and hourly employees attend two-day self-directed work team training.

- Quality Council beginning to handle more and more of the business functions that were traditionally split between union and management.

- Beginning awareness of Quality Council that this process must become a way of life and requires total commitment of all leaders.

- A local negotiation created by skilled trades outsourcing of work issues is conducted. *All Quality Council members participate in the traditional negotiations environment but the effort is nonadversarial and does not disrupt the activities of the QC.*

May
- Awareness of Quality Council that direction for the business in the future will require planning time.

- Quality Council meets for three days in an off-site location and pursues strategic planning for the plant.

- During the planning process, a plant vision and mission are developed (see Figures 17-1 to 17-4). *All QC members agree to buy into the vision and mission and to support them.* Each leader's commitment to the vision and mission is stressed.

Plant 16 Vision

To *Grow The Business* Through Our People, Products And Performance.

- **People**   Develop The Full Potential Of All Employees.

- **Product**   **To Be The Preferred Long Term Supplier Of Tools, Machines, Prototypes And Services.**

- **Performance** Operate As A Customer Focused, Self-Sufficient Business, Financially Responsible To Our Stakeholders

Figure 17-1.

Plant 16 People Mission

Develop The Full Potential Of All Employees

Leadership Style:
The Joint Leadership Empowers The People By Encouraging Joint Partnerships At All Levels.

Employee Development:
Provide Education And Training To Enhance The Effectiveness Of Our Employees. Therefore, Developing The Ability To Adapt To The Changing And Challenging Roles Of The Future

Job Satisfaction:
To Provide An Environment That Ensures A Sense Of Ownership In The Business.

Communications:
Implement Processes That Provides Our Employees Access To Business Information Necessary To Become Full Partners In The Business.

Performance Feedback Is Expected At All Levels Of The Organization.

Joint (U/M) Relations:
To Encourage The Process Of U/M Leadership While Ensuring The Trust, Integrity And Identity Of Each Organization.

Figure 17-2.

Plant 16 Product Mission

To Be The Preferred Long Term Supplier Of Tools, Machines, Prototypes And Services.

We Will:

- Strive To Create Partnerships With Our Customers.

- Focus On Profitable Lines Of Business.

- Create Flexibility And Maintain Versatility In Existing Lines Of Business.

- Expand And Diversify Our Products And Services.

Figure 17-3.

Plant 16 Performance Mission

Operate As A Customer Focused, Self-Sufficient Business, Financially Responsible To Our Stakeholders

We Will:

- Operate Plant 16 On A Sound Financial Basis Of Profitable Growth.

- Communicate The Financial Performance To Our Employees.

- Invest In Our People, Technology, Facilities And Equipment.

- Optimize Plant 16 Operations.

- Benchmark Our Competitiors, New Technology And Potential Markets.

- Expand And Diversify Our Customer Base.

Figure 17-4.

June	▪ The strategic plan leads to three focus councils being formed to help handle the business of the plant so as to allow the QC to become more involved in informational and approval activity. The councils were populated with QC members and other employees of the plant. This allowed for more involvement from more plant employees. The focus councils were formed as a result of the statement that the vision is to grow the business through people, product, and performance. Hence, the three focus councils were named the People, Product, and Performance Focus Councils. See Figure 17-5.
	▪ In a seemingly insignificant situation, the employees in the plant were allowed to select the color the outside of the plant would be painted. This symbolic gesture carried a powerful message.
	▪ Three hourly employees were named by the QC to work full-time with the previously named salaried employee to sell Plant 16 products to customers outside of Delco Remy.
July	▪ Other groups, called *Action Councils,* began to be formed by the Focus and Quality Councils. These groups were populated with both salary and hourly employees in the plant. (See Figure 17-6.) Some of the Action Councils are

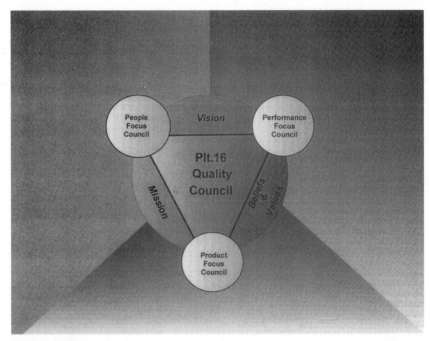

Figure 17.5.

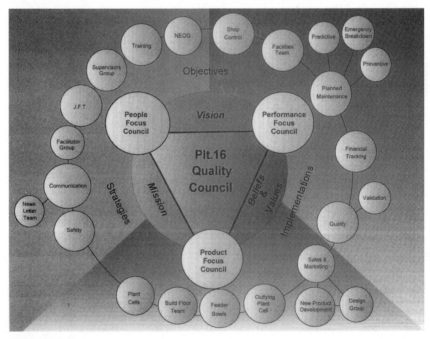

Figure 17.6.

> Planned Maintenance
>
> Safety
>
> Communication
>
> Newsletter
>
> New Employee Orientation
>
> Joint Facility Team (suggestions)
>
> Supervisors
>
> Feeder Bowls
>
> Detail Cell
>
> Training
>
> Shop Control (work order system)
>
> Facilities (rearrangement)

Some of these groups were already in existence.

- Approximately 60 plant employees, key leaders, attend the Jerry Duff Positive Leadership two-day training session. Feedback is very positive.

August
- *Full-time hourly communications coordinator is appointed by the QC.*

- Hourly employee appointed to work with two salaried employees to develop a job tracking and scheduling system that will allow the plant to become a stand-alone financial entity versus the burden center it had been in the past.

September
- Full-time salaried engineering design coordinator to handle design work coordination for outside Delco Remy customers is appointed.

- Began local contract negotiations. Most QC members involved. Some problems related in continuing to meet as a joint Quality Council while negotiating. Created strain on the TQM process.

October
- Announcement of parts of the Delco Remy businesses being sold and joint ventured. Increases continued concern for what it means to the Plant 16 business.

- National contract is negotiated and ratified. Local negotiations continue and UAW members of the Quality Council continue to avoid joint participation in the running of the business. Creates a continued problem for the salaried leadership of the plant as they try to continue to manage the business in a participative, involved manner.

- The Quality Council approves a concept called alternative work schedule (AWS) which allows each employee, hourly and salary, to have a say in which hours they are scheduled to work. The QC finds it difficult to keep consistency in this approach but "grows" from working through the issues. All employees are expected to make their scheduling decisions based on their effect on people, business, and technology.

November
■ The Jerry Duff Positive Leadership training is expanded to 20 hours and is offered to all Plant 16 employees.

December
■ *The amount of work being placed in the plant from both inside and outside Delco Remy customers has increased to the point that many hours of overtime,* approximately 56–60 hours per week, are necessary. Employees are tired but happy to see work being scheduled in front of them.

■ Learnings from feedback during the Jerry Duff training create more and more communication efforts in the plant.

■ Workload in the plant creates the need to work several employees during the week-long Christmas shutdown.

1994

January
■ Financial and delivery information beginning to show drastic improvements in the productivity of the plant.

■ Delco Remy higher management beginning to show signs of recognition that Plant 16 is more than pulling its own weight.

■ Local 662, UAW higher leadership beginning to show signs of recognition that the TQM process in Plant 16 is worthwhile and beneficial.

■ *The Plant 16 union leadership returns to the Quality Council and related meetings, signifying a return to their plant leadership responsibilities.*

■ Communication activities increased to include a video system throughout the plant as well as biweekly, one-page information-sharing newsletters from the leadership.

■ The Jerry Duff training is expanded to include 20 more hours for all willing plant employees. Training is primarily designed to teach employees how to function in teams in a participative, empowered environment. The first of the training sessions includes all Focus Council members with an additional 12 hours added for the Quality Council and Focus Council members to work on completing the business plan for the plant.

■ Four Quality Council members attend a four-day training session to learn more about ISO 9000 and its potential impact on the plant.

February
- From a desk top, the plant manager meets with all employees on the plant floor and praises the work efforts of all employees involved in finishing a particularly tough job. The job was completed on time and well below original cost estimates. The meeting was filmed to show to all shifts. As a celebration, all coffee machines in the plant were turned on for free coffee.

- Jerry Duff begins to meet with all supervisors, general supervisors, superintendent, and manager for one hour per week to facilitate learning to understand new roles and relationships in an empowered organization. Intended to lead to identification of training needs as well as personal concerns of participants. Essentially, Jerry becomes the Plant 16 organizational counselor.

- Local contract negotiations are delayed pending the outcome of joint-venture activity. *The plant union representatives are pulled out of joint activities.* However, they continue to participate in most business decisions.

March
- Local contract negotiations begin again and the plant leadership, management, and union spend most of their time pursuing a settlement, which is accomplished late in the month. Activities in the plant continue with business as usual in that the Jerry Duff classes and sessions continue and all joint meetings continue. Even though intense negotiations are underway, the plant operations proceed as usual.

- An ISO 9000 consultant spends three days in the plant performing a preassessment for ISO 9001 registration. The effort finds the plant very lacking in systems, procedures, and documentation. The Quality Council begins to debate the benefits of pursuing ISO 9000 activities.

April
- With negotiations concluded, the joint leadership begins to develop a process to continue working toward a business plan that includes the potential of the plant becoming a stand-alone business that can survive anywhere in the General Motors environment, regardless of what happens to its current GM Division owner, Delco Remy.

- The plant manager, superintendent, and general supervisors begin a process that examines each one's job tasks and responsibilities and clarifies what each should be doing and not doing. The process elevates each individual into a higher-level role and necessitates the increased empowering of all employees. The process will be continued to include the first-line supervisors so that they will be enabled to further empower their employees.

- The Quality Council, sensing the need to reaffirm its commitment to the TQM process and to develop its approach toward ISO 9000 activities, begins to plan for an off-site that will reenergize the members and establish focus for the next few months.

17.4.2 Learnings

While the process of learning never stops in an empowered environment, the following should be mentioned:

- The nonrepresented, salaried workforce resists and fears change as much, or more, as the represented, hourly workforce.
- Communication, communication, communication.
- Trust must be given to enable it to develop.
- Time becomes a precious resource since the number of people involved in the decision-making process is expanded greatly.
- Facilitation skills are a precious commodity as more and more groups are formed.
- Behavior of followers is based on behavior of the leaders.
- Meeting skills for all employees creates efficient and more productive meetings.
- Employee participation groups require constant nurturing from individuals blessed with nurturing skills.
- It takes a great amount of time for the process to provide results.
- Most people are impatient and are unwilling to allow the process to reach maturation.
- Myers-Briggs analysis of the plant employees is invaluable to determining communication methods as well as leadership action requirements.
- Voluntary leadership training utilizing situational leadership concepts enhances the change process.
- Job-specific training for employees is absolutely necessary to keep their skills current as well as to show them you care.
- The blending of internal consultants with external consultants gives credibility to the process.
- Communication, communication, communication.

17.4.3 Conclusions and Recommendations

While there is still much to be learned from the TQM process in Plant 16, here are a few thoughts that can be used in any similar situation:

- Never start the process unless the leadership is totally committed.
- Sincerity cannot be faked for very long. If you are not sincere, don't start.
- If you don't believe that people are basically good and want to do the right thing, don't start the process.
- Be prepared to spend what seems like an extraordinary amount of time. No group decision comes quickly. If it does, you'd better check your process.
- Consider problems as they occur as opportunities to establish desired behavior and show examples to others.
- Communicate, communicate, communicate.
- Be flexible relative to the union/management relationship. Recognize that there will be times when the two will differ on issues.
- Realize that you never quite "get there."
- Understand that if you are trying to implement a TQM process, you are already "there."
- There are no magic answers or activities to ensure success in a TQM endeavor. However, some definitely needed activities are as follows:

Communication
   Newsletters
   Roundtable meetings
   Employee information-sharing meetings
   Leadership walk-arounds and accessibility

Union leadership participation

Training
   Technical
   Social
   Teamwork

Employee empowerment
   Supervisors become consultants
   Employee leaders rise to the top

Financial freedom
   Internal control of finances

Management freedom
   Corporate and divisional management and union leadership allow plant level leadership to function with little or no interference

Risktaking
   Plant leadership, union, and management willing to be innovative and protect those who are

Facilitation/Consultant skills
   Develop meeting facilitators and group nurturers

As I indicated previously, this Plant 16 TQM process grew out of the desire of the plant leadership to "do the right things." Both union and management in the plant are trying to make a difference in a community that has seen employment drop significantly over the past few years. Whether the process is successful or not remains to be seen. However, as you read this, the process continues. Perhaps, you can give us a call and see for yourself how far we have come. We welcome the opportunity to share our learnings and look forward to hearing from you!

Bibliography

Darnell, G., and A. Hamood, *Highlights of Total Quality Management: Philosophies and Applications*, General Motors, Corporation, Detroit, 1991.

Duff, J. L., *The Jerry Duff Group*, Dayton, Ohio, 1993.

Jablonski, J. R., *Implementing TQM: Competing in the Nineties Through Total Quality Management*, Pfeiffer & Company, San Diego, 1992.

Quality Network Process Reference Guide, General Motors Corporation, Detroit, 1989.

18

An International Perspective of Technical and Skills Training: The Singapore Experience

John Ewing-Chow
Overseas Banking Corporation, Singapore

Annie S. W. Phoon
National University of Singapore

Law Song Seng
Institute of Technical Education, Singapore

John Ewing-Chow *is First Vice President, Training and Development Department, Overseas-Chinese Banking Corporation, Singapore. He is a founder member and certified management consultant of the Institute Of Management Consultants (IMC) (Singapore) and also a member of its Executive Council. He received his B.Sc. (Honors) from the University of Singapore in 1967 and his M. in Admin. from Monash University, Australia, in 1980. He is listed in Who's Who In The World*

(1993/94 edition). Of his 20 years in training and development, he has also served as Management Trainer and Director of the Singapore Civil Service Institute, and the Group Training Manager of the Inchcape Company. He was Chairman of the Singapore National Productivity Board's Worker Induction Program in 1991 and member of the National Trainers' Skills Standards Setting Committee in 1990. He was also Chairman of the Advisory Committee for the first HRD Asia Conference in 1992 and is again chairing the second HRD Asia Conference in 1994. His latest interests include using QFD (Quality Function Deployment) and other tools in CD-MAP (Customer Driven—Mission Achievement Process) to develop and improve products and services that satisfy and positively excite customers, right the first time.

Annie S. W. Phoon *is a teaching fellow at the National University of Singapore. She received her BA from the University of Singapore and her B.Soc.Sc. (Honors) and postgraduate Diploma in Education from the National University of Singapore. While at the National Productivity Board, she was involved in the ASEAN Human Resource Development project in Singapore, a US$40 million effort aimed at developing the Productivity Movement in Singapore. She was formerly Vice President (Human Resources) at the United Overseas Bank Group. She was a member of the National Trainers' Skills Standards Setting Committee in 1990 and the Professional Development of Trainers Task Force in 1989. She was also a member of the National Video Awards Committee in 1988 and 1989 and on the Singapore Training and Development Association Executive Committee for three terms from 1988 to 1990. She received the Singapore President's Commendation Award in recognition of her contribution to training the Scout Movement in 1991. Her interests are in learning design and development, training of trainers, and organizational development.*

Law Song Seng *is Director and Chief Executive Officer of the Institute of Technical Education, Singapore. He also served as Director and Chief Executive Officer of the former Vocational & Industrial Training Board (1981–92). He was formerly a lecturer, senior lecturer, associate professor, and head of Industries and Systems Engineering Department at the National University of Singapore (1973–83). Dr. Law was a visiting lecturer at the University of Auckland, New Zealand (1980) and a manufacturing development engineer with the Ford Motor Company in the United States (1972–73). He received a BE (1st class Hons) in Mechanical Engineering from the University of Wisconsin USA (1971 and 1972) and attended MIT Management program for Senior Executives (Fall 1989). He is a fellow of the Institute of Engineers and a registered professional engineer in Singapore. Dr. Law was past chairman of the Singapore Chapter of the Society of Manufacturing Engineers (USA) (1977/78) and a member of many committees. Dr. Law is author to more than forty papers in journals, conferences, and major reports in engineering and vocational training. He was awarded the Public Administration Medal (Gold) in the Singapore National Day Honors, 1984, in recognition of his contribution to vocational and technical training in Singapore.*

18.1 Why Singapore?

In a unique way, Singapore has achieved phenomenal economic success through what Peter Drucker called a systematic "application of knowledge to work."[1]

From an unknown and tiny British colony of only 250 square miles, approximately the size of Washington, D.C. or half the size of the Great Salt Lake in Utah, Singapore has struggled for its survival to reach world class standards in many areas, chalking up impressive firsts such as:

- The country with the least risk for investors polled annually by the Washington-based Business Environment Risk Intelligence (BERI), who also ranked its workers first in "worker attitude" and "relative productivity."

- For the fifth consecutive year, the most competitive of 14 newly industrializing economies as rated annually by the World Economic Forum and the Swiss Institute for International Management Development. Its labor force was ranked first and the most computer literate. Its education, availability of skilled people, and worker motivation were ranked second.

- The best airline, Singapore Airlines (SIA), and airport as rated by countless international travelers' magazines for many years running.

- The world's busiest port for the eighth consecutive year as well as the top bunkering and container port.

- The country with the highest percentage of citizens owning shares in the stock market.

- The highest capital adequacy ratios in the world maintained by its "big four" local banks.

- The most integrated information technology network setup anywhere in the world. It is dubbed the "Intelligent Island" and studied assiduously by gurus in IT around the world.

- The world's biggest exporter of disk drives produced by Conner Peripherals, Maxtor, Micropolis, Seagate, SyQuest, and Western Digital.

More than 3000 foreign companies have chosen to operate and invest in Singapore to manufacture products and to provide corporate and technical services. Some of the companies are 3M, Apple Computers, AT&T, BASF, Caterpillar, Du Pont, Eli Lilly, Fisher Controls, GM, General Electric, Glaxo, Hewlett-Packard, ICI, Johnson & Johnson, King Radio, Leica, Matsushita, McGraw-Hill, Motorola, NEC, Otis, Philips, Reda Pump, Shell, Sony, Toshiba, Van Leer, Westinghouse, and Yokogawa. Supporting them financially are 129 commercial banks, 116 of them being foreign banks.

Shell saw Singapore's strategic location as the shipping gateway between the West and the East as early as 1891, 72 years after the founding of Singapore, and set up its terminaling and distributing of petroleum. Participating fully in modern Singapore's first industrialization program, Shell went on in 1961 to refining. By 1990, its output of one million barrels per day made it the third largest refining center in the world, after Rotterdam and Houston. Its human resources management is a model for many, including the Singapore government. Shell staff are constantly trained and upgraded to run some of the most sophisticated refining units in the world.

In 1970, Hewlett-Packard set up a small manufacturing plant in Singapore to assemble computer memory modules. The abundance of low-cost labor, among other factors, had attracted it to this location. Its subsequent development and growth parallel Singapore's economic development. By progressively absorbing technology and know-how, HP Singapore has designed many custom-integrated circuits for its printers, calculators, keyboards, and LED/LCD displays. Its locally designed keyboards have become *the* standard for all HP PCs, terminals, and workstations worldwide. It is also the regional center for R&D for personal computer products and peripherals and for IC design and networks development. The highly automated Singapore plant now manufactures complex and sophisticated products such as optoelectronic components, wafer fabrication, network software, and others.

In 1987, Sony set up a highly automated factory in Singapore to manufacture precision key components such as optical pick-up devices and lenses for compact disc players, magnetic heads and precision cylinders for videocassette recorders and camcorders, etc., using the latest in robotics assembly technology. Due to the highly trained workers available in Singapore, Sony is able to produce these components not only competitively but at the same levels of quality as those in Japan. The skills of these employees are constantly being upgraded on-the-job in a structured manner.

These are only three of the countless success stories of multinational corporations (MNCs) from all over the world with their operations or bases in Singapore. Many of them invested in Singapore only after overcoming their initial misgivings about Singapore's small size and its (then) unknown quality of workforce. That their fears were unfounded and their positive expectations fulfilled are reflected in the steady growth of foreign investments in Singapore. From 1970 to 1989, the total cumulative foreign investments in manufacturing stood at US$18.6 billion. For 1993, investment commitments reached a new high of US$2.5 billion. Table 18-1 shows the breakdown by country investing in Singapore.

The high level of foreign investment has afforded the 2.8 million inhabitants of Singapore full employment and high living standards for most of the past two decades. Its per capita GNP rose from US$850 in 1960 to

Table 18-1. Cumulative Foreign Investments in Manufacturing by Country 1970–1989
(Gross fixed assets, S$m)

Country	1970 S$m	1975 S$m	1980 S$m	1985 S$m	1989 S$m	Growth PA 1970–89 (%)
USA	343	1118	2096	4656	7143	17.3
Japan	68	454	1187	2943	6600	27.2
Europe	423	1170	2989	4480	6582	15.5
EC	406	1111	2810	4172	6172	15.4
UK	199	481	1170	1796	2418	14.0
Netherlands	183	473	1291	1663	2583	15.0
Germany	3	105	243	245	458	30.3
France	8	22	57	190	415	23.1
Other EC	13	30	49	277	297	17.9
Sweden	3	22	41	137	166	23.5
Switzerland	12	29	111	129	145	14.0
Other European	2	9	27	43	99	22.8
Others	161	638	818	1081	1166	11.0
Cumulative foreign	995	3380	7090	13160	21490	17.6
Cumulative local	na	na	3471	7100	8023	na
Total cumulative	na	na	10561	20260	29513	na

SOURCE: Low, et al. (1993).[2]

US$15,200, which is already ahead of some developed countries such as Australia. Inflation is also among the lowest in the world. They owe this happy state to the following factors:

- Unbroken political stability which greatly bolsters investors' confidence

- A pro-business government that understands and actively participates in industry

- A well-disciplined and hardworking labor force

- A forward-looking government constantly monitoring the country's economic performance and planning ahead to overcome imminent problems and capitalize on competitive advantages

- Industrial peace created by the consolidation of unions into a powerful labor umbrella and lobby

- A tripartite system of addressing business and economic issues by labor, government, and employers

- The relentless, systematic training and education of its workers to meet the specific demands of the economy at each phase of its development

This chapter is an in-depth look at how Singapore successfully trains its workers in the technical skills required to support the economy as it transformed itself from a sleepy trading post to a low-cost manufacturing facility and subsequently to a high-technology manufacturing and financial center. *With no natural resources or hinterland, Singapore's tremendous investment in its people was a matter of national survival. Its ability to harness scarce human resources is a case study from which many lessons can be drawn.*

18.2 The Singapore Technical and Skills Training Model

In her comparison of training policies and programs to support industrial restructuring, Hilowitz[3] mentioned that countries can be ranged along a continuum, with the United States and South Korea at its two extremes. In the United States, training is mostly the domain of the enterprises, without government supervision or a centralized national training planning and administration body. By contrast, South Korea has the most centralized system, where all vocational training and education come under the control of a central administrative unit.

Singapore is somewhere between the two extremes, where the government and industry are partners. Dr. Law Song Seng, Director of the Institute of Technical Education, said:

> As much as government may wish to shoulder the responsibility for manpower development, and in particular, technical manpower, it is unlikely to succeed without the complementary role of the users (industries). By its very nature, technical and skills training is incomplete without the experience that can be acquired on the job. The partnership of private industries in supporting training should therefore be viewed as an integral part of the total system.[4]
>
> *The Singapore model is therefore one where the government actively directs and plans the macro thrust while the private sector employers play a complementary and equally crucial role in translating policies and plans into day-to-day implementation and on-job application.* To a very large extent, the success of this model is due to the frequent, deliberate consultation and dialog among the government, employers, and labor.

18.3 The Singapore Experience

The approach to technical and skills training in Singapore can be roughly divided into two historical phases:

- The first phase, from 1959, when Singapore gained its independence from Great Britain, to 1979, was the development of an integrated national training system to support the country's economic goals.

- The second and current phase began with the setting up of the Skills Development Fund in 1979 to encourage the development of an extensive, comprehensive, and permanent employer-based training infrastructure alongside the national system.

18.3.1 Phase One: Training for Survival (1959–1979)

Training for the country's economic survival began when Singapore became self-governing in 1959, the new government having inherited an education system that concerned itself only with producing English-speaking white-collar workers for its bureaucratic and administrative needs. Little effort had been made to train the general population in work skills, and education of the masses was generally left to the resources of the local community and philanthropists.

During this early period, Singapore was mainly a trading post for the region. Unemployment at 13.5 percent posed a major problem that threatened to erupt the fragile, multiracial, and fragmented young city-state. This was compounded by endemic poverty and poor health and sanitation conditions. Against this backdrop, the Singapore government invited an industrial mission from the United Nations Bureau of Technical Assistance Operations Commission to study and recommend measures for economic growth. The strategy adopted was to go for export-oriented, labor-intensive industrialization by attracting foreign investments and developing the industrial potential of the local manpower.[5]

Among the major obstacles to successful industrialization were poor education and training infrastructure, a dearth of trained manpower and a workforce that did not possess the required skills. Thus, while it was not within its scope to make detailed recommendations for training, the mission team submitted a series of specific recommendations on technical education and training programs and facilities and projected manpower requirements for the various industries.

In 1961, the government began to adapt the education system to meet the needs of an industrializing and modernizing economy:

- Emphasis was placed on the study of mathematics, science, and technical subjects.

- A technical bias was introduced into the school curriculum.

- Four new types of schools were established (vocational high schools, technical high schools, commercial high schools, and vocational institutions).

- The two polytechnics were greatly expanded and restructured to accommodate new courses to meet the new needs of the changing economy.

The switch from academic education to technical and skills training was slow. By 1967, only 6 percent of junior school graduates had received technical education. To tackle this pressing shortage of industrial skills, a ministerial-level National Industrial Training Council was formed in 1968, reflecting the extremely high priority accorded to solving this problem. As a result, a Technical Education Department (TED) was set up within the Ministry of Education to develop and implement programs in technical skills. To ensure its success, the TED drew heavily upon the United Nations, the Colombo Plan, and other technical assistance and resources.

Thus, in 1969, only one year after the TED was formed, the industrial training system was born, replacing the high school vocational education stream. Within the next three years, nine vocational institutes were established, certainly no mean feat for a fledgling department. And within the same three years, enrollment shot up dramatically from 324 to 4000—an increase of more than 1000 percent!

At the same time, the Economic Development Board (EDB) succeeded in attracting to Singapore a wide range of new industries and technical and financial assistance from foreign governments and the United Nations Development Program. By 1968, six technical training centers were established:

- The Metal Industries Limited
- The Prototype Production and Training Center
- The Electro-Mechanical Training Center
- The Electro-Chemical Engineering Center
- The Woodworking Industries Limited
- The Precision Engineering Development Center

To ensure that industrial training continued to be sustained and developed to keep pace with economic changes and objectives, the Industrial Training Board (ITB) was formed in 1973. In typical Singapore fashion, it was a tripartite body comprising representatives from employers, unions, and government. It was supported by Trade Advisory Committees from different sectors of the economy that gave input on the technical knowledge and skills required by the respective sectors. The tripartite nature of the ITB and the close interface with the Trade Advisory Committees ensured a constant direct linkage with industry so that the technical training provided was constantly reviewed and made relevant to industry.

In addition, the EDB stepped up its efforts to partner with selected MNCs. The partners created structured technical and skills training through the setting up of Joint Industry Training Centers. The following were established in direct response to industry demand:

- Joint Tata-Government Training Center (training toolmakers, precision machinists, and other skilled craftsmen in severe shortage and vitally needed by the economy)

- Joint Rollei-Government Training Center (providing training in precision mechanics, precision optics, toolmaking, and other electricians)

- Joint Philips-Government Training Center (providing two years in-center training followed by two years in-plant training in turning, metalworking, and fine sheet-metalworking)

The benefits of training programs at centers such as these are:

- They provided much needed skilled manpower in areas greatly demanded by industry.

- Expatriate trainers provided expert supervision and training.

- The centers formalized the apprenticeship system in Singapore and set the precedent for future apprenticeship schemes.

- The partner MNCs were assured of a steady supply of the skilled craftsmen they required through a bonding scheme that required all trainees to serve the partner MNCs for five years after completing their training at the training centers.

- Trainees who participated in these training programs were paid a stipend and were deferred from full-time military service a further six years after completing their four-year apprenticeship. (Military service is a compulsory two and half years military training which all able-bodied men commence after their eighteenth birthday).

Apart from the obvious benefits, the close relationship between the EDB and industry means the partners can respond extremely quickly to changing industry trends. As a result, courses for trades that were no longer in demand were quickly phased out, while those which trained workers in new and multiple skills were introduced.

18.3.2 Phase Two: Training for Higher Value-Added (1979–the Present)

In 1979, Singapore poised itself to make a major economic shift as it faced the challenges of the 80s. Having attained full employment, the nation then faced the converse problem of labor shortage and a sizable number who left school prematurely without a full high school education.

The government realized that Singapore could not compete with neighboring countries whose very much larger population and less developed economies were more attractive to investors. Investors were seeking low-cost sites for manufacturing. Singapore's government chose a two-pronged approach in response:

- First, it embarked on a high wage policy to encourage MNCs to relocate their low-cost operations to neighboring countries while giving incentives to them to bring higher value-added and high-technology operations to Singapore.

- Second, it decided to produce a workforce that is highly trained in the upper end of technical skills.

The latter is done through incentives such as giving subsidies and grants for skill training as well as through taxing employers who continued using unskilled or low-skilled workers. The mechanism for effecting this is the Skills Development Levy. Under this scheme, companies that employ workers earning below a minimum amount (currently US$630 per month) would have to pay a percentage levy (currently 1 percent of the payroll of these employees) into a Skills Development Fund. Monies in this fund were then used to give grants to employers who either upgraded their workers' skills or upgraded their operations.

The effect of this scheme is that companies which continued to use low-skilled workers or which engaged in lower value-added operations, found their cost of labor increasing prohibitively. Many finally resorted to increased automation and higher value-added technology (with the help of grants from government agencies), resulting in the need to reskill their workers. Companies which were unable to upgrade their workforces had to resite their operations in neighboring countries like Malaysia or Indonesia.

The Skills Development Fund played a pivotal role in nudging employers to actively train their staffs. This was done through the launching of various schemes such as:

- *Worker Training Plan:* Employers are given a higher grant/subsidy when they submit a "Total Training Plan" covering at least 50 percent of their workforce. For small- and medium-sized companies, this funding can be fairly substantial relative to their training budget and payroll.

- *Emerging and Critical Skills Scheme:* This encourages employers to train workers in skills that are in short supply in the economy or are needed in the immediate, foreseeable future. Employers who participate in this scheme are given double the usual training grant.

- *Training Voucher Scheme:* This scheme removes all paperwork and is especially attractive to employers who do not have the time, patience, or staff to submit bureaucratic forms or monitor grant payments. Under this scheme, employers who send their staff for preapproved courses only need submit a voucher to the training provider or vendor instead of paying cash for the training.

- *National Training Awards:* This encourages companies to step up their training efforts in order to vie for the training awards. Considered prestigious and a worthwhile goal to strive for, these awards are given on the basis of fulfilling nationally established training criteria for a particular year.

- *Training Leave Scheme:* This provides special incentives to encourage the training of workers aged 40 and above and who have not received college or university education. Subject to a stated maximum, the grant to a company is 100 percent of the allowable course fee payable to a third-party provider.

The importance of the Skills Development Fund in accelerating training efforts is reflected in the fact that from 1980 to 1993, it disbursed US$425 million to help companies train some 1.9 million employees in Singapore.

As with many issues in Singapore, the need to upgrade workers' skills and move the economy further up the technological ladder received nationwide attention. The discussion took place in various forums, and particularly in the national newspapers, whose readers offered a wide range of opinions, perspectives, and solutions. A general consensus evolved out of this public discussion, resulting in the following conclusions:

- *The school dropout:* This person must be trained for employment. An unskilled worker has no future in the world of tomorrow.

- *The worker:* A person must have an education in order to acquire modern skills or to perform effectively in the modern work environment. The worker must continuously upgrade and modernize skills and knowledge or be left behind.

- *The technical training infrastructure:* For the majority of high school graduates proceeding to higher or technical education, the technical training system must provide the preparation for transition to the world of work. Training must be relevant to the needs of the economy, and the infrastructure must provide for progression. High school graduates must have full educational and career information so they can make the right choices.

- *The employer:* Employers must invest in the training of their workers, or they cannot restructure, change to new products, or survive in a high-wage environment. Nor will they attract the best workers. Employer-based training must be systematic, effective, and on-going to achieve its effects. Companies and industries with specialized skill requirements are best positioned to establish their own training.

These conclusions formed the basis for the planning and development of Singapore's manpower resources. They also constituted the message to the population, and especially to the workers through the National Trade Union Congress, for without response from the populace, there can be no development. Probably because Singapore is so small, and also because of the government's frequent communication, there is an unusually high degree of public knowledge about questions of education and training. In many other countries, this discussion might only be a matter for specialists. Issues are frequently discussed in the newspapers with the stable and highly competent civil service constantly educating the people in the problems and needs of Singapore. This has certainly contributed much toward the receptivity to new and experimental modes of both training and production.

In terms of infrastructure, the period from 1979 until the present saw the amalgamation of the Industrial Training Board with the Adult Education Board to form the Vocational and Industrial Training Board (VITB). The new, fortified body took on the task of spearheading technical and commercial training strategies for the 1980s. The Council for Professional and Technical Education was also created and chaired by the Minister of Trade and Industry to coordinate manpower training by the universities, the polytechnics, and the technical institutions of EDB and VITB to meet new economic challenges.

The government moved quickly to motivate employers and industry to accelerate technical and professional skills upgrading by doing the following:

- Setting up of *Approved Training Centers* in companies whose training facilities and training skills met specified standards. Courses conducted in these facilities would receive VITB certification (and hence national-level recognition) while remaining tailored to each company's specific needs.

- Setting up of *Industry Training Centers* such as the
  Textile and Garment Industry Training Center
  Singapore Hotel Association Training and Education Center
  Construction Industry Development Board's Training Center
  Institute of Banking and Finance
  Singapore Retailers Association Training Center
  Jewelry Industry Training Center
  Center for Tourism Related Studies

- Setting up of collaborative technology institutes like:
  French-Singapore Institute of Technology
  German-Singapore Institute of Technology
  Japan-Singapore Technical Institute

Of special mention is the EDB's latest effort at using a *transnational* approach in facilitating transfer of technology and technical know-how from MNCs to the rest of the workforce. The successful single-partner-per-institution was developed into a transnational multiple-partnership arrangement. For example, the original Rollei-Government Training Center was transformed into the Precision Engineering Institute (PEI) in 1988. The Siemens-Nixdorf-EDB Center for Advanced Tool & Die Making and the Mitutoyo-EDB Metrology Laboratory are two of the many major cooperation projects within the PEI. Transfer of technology is through:

- Secondment of experts from MNCs on request
- Training of EDB's instructors and technical staff at the participating firms' overseas locations
- Assistance in curriculum and program development
- Donation and/or loan of equipment by the participating firm
- Commitment by the participating firm to upgrade equipment and software
- Commitment to participate for a minimum duration of three years, subject to review and subsequent extension.[2]

Table 18-2 lists the major projects established under this approach.

The Institute of Systems Science (ISS) was created with the mission of transferring state-of-the-art information technology from overseas experts to local practitioners. ISS produced postgraduate diplomas to university graduates of various disciplines to meet the urgent need for trained computer professionals who are eagerly sought after and quickly absorbed by industry. It also trained a large local pool of systems analysts, information systems managers, and specialists in both Information Technology hardware and software. Within a matter of eight to ten years, the enormous demand for trained IS professionals was mostly met by the tremendous output of ISS graduates of various specializations.

A US$308 million Japan-Singapore Institute of Software Technology was also set up in 1982 by the two governments to provide practical, hands-on training of software technicians and engineers to complement ISS's efforts.

Another government agency, the National Productivity Board (NPB), also played an important role in ensuring that the impetus for training was, and continues to be, maintained and that training is made affordable and accessible to all. Some of the programs accomplishing these goals are:

- *Fast Forward.* This program provides flexible training for workers who have family and work commitments, who work on shifts and who have little access to conventional training courses due to lack of time or formal qualifications.

Table 18-2. Transnational Projects

Project	Company
CAD/CAM	Prime-Computervision Hewlett-Packard Autodesk
IC design/CAE	Mentor-Graphics
Surface mount technology	Matsushita
Artificial intelligence	Bull
Control engineering	Siemens Telemechanique
Computer numerical Control technology	Sodick Charmille Japax Bridgeport Hamai Ikegai
Laser technology	Trumpf
Advanced metrology	Mitutoyo Carl Zeiss
Robotics/vision technology	Asea Sankyo Seiki Bosch Seiko
Manufacturing resources planning (MRP II)	Siemens-Nixdorf
Plastic technology	Battenfeld Arburg Dr. Boy

SOURCE: Low, et al. (1993).[2]

- *On-the-Job Training Program.* Developed in collaboration with Seiko Instruments of Japan, this program helps companies develop and implement on-the-job training. Three courses are offered to empower companies to conduct their own skills training.

- *Information Technology Program for Office Workers.* This 56-hour nationally driven program, known as IT Power, was developed jointly by the National Productivity Board, the Skills Development Fund, IBM, the National Computer Board, and Singapore Telecom. The training gives office workers a total perspective on IT to equip them with transferable keyboard skills for work in an increasingly computerized environment. It is the only comprehensive generic program that covers word processing, spreadsheet, and database. IT concepts, office automation, as well as IT applications in Singapore, are also covered.

- *NPB-Anderson Training Technology Center.* The Training Technology (TT) Center is the result of a strategic partnership between Anderson Consulting and the NPB. Launched in 1990, the Center's aim is to achieve training excellence through the effective use of technology. The center promotes the use of TT-based training among companies in Singapore in the areas of Computer-Based Training (CBT), Interactive Videodisc Instruction (IVI), Digital Video Instruction (DVI), and Computer-Managed Instruction (CMI). The center also assists organizations in converting existing instructor-led training programs into TT-based programs.

- *Increasing Training Opportunities (INTRO) Scheme.* This scheme encourages companies to share their in-house expertise, facilities, and training programs with other companies so as to make more training programs available publicly.

- *Training-Manager Program.* This 40-hour program was jointly developed by the Civil Service Institute, the NPB Institute for Productivity Training, the Singapore Institute of Management, the Singapore Institute of Personnel Management, the Singapore National Employers Federation, and the Singapore Training and Development Association. It is aimed at managers and supervisors who need to train their staff as part of their responsibilities. The program's competency-based training enables participants to analyze the training needs of their staff, conduct one-to-one on-the-job training as well as training for a group of staff.

As can be seen, national attention was given to increasing the technical abilities of the skilled workforce. At the same time, efforts were also stepped up to address the lower end of the workforce. Besides full-time training of school dropouts, VITB and NPB were tasked with the education and training of workers who did not complete junior or high school and who were unskilled. The result was a comprehensive system of continuing education and training, which by 1991 was already offering some 100,000 training places to about 50,000 workers a year. The programs were specifically developed to meet the needs of employers and workers in terms of training, delivery modes, and accessibility. Such programs include:

- *Basic Education for Skills Training (BEST):* For those with little or no schooling to gain basic literacy and numeracy skills.

- *Worker Improvement through Secondary Education (WISE):* For those who have successfully completed BEST to advance to high school English and mathematics.

- *Modular Skills Training (MOST):* For those who did not complete high school to upgrade or acquire new skills. A part-time program, MOST is flexible in allowing workers to complete their learning in modules without disrupting their work.

- *Training Initiative for Mature Employees (TIME):* For mature workers beyond 40 years. Courses are conducted in a few languages to provide opportunities to workers who are illiterate or poor in English to take up skills training.

- *Adult Cooperative Training Scheme (ACTS):* For young adult workers (20 to 40 years old) who have less than adequate education. Unlike TIME and MOST, ACTS adopts the apprenticeship approach comprising on-the-job and off-the-job training. ACTS' participants are fully sponsored by their employers.

The preceding programs focus on giving workers the basic foundation upon which they could later learn new skills. Without such training foundations, workers will be left far behind when the economy propels itself towards the even more advanced technologies of the 90s.

18.3.3 Training in the 90s

The challenges of the 90s are best reflected in the words of *The Next Lap,** a widely publicized book in which the government shares its broad directions for the country's long-term national development:[6]

- *Singapore's Economic Goal:* "We will become a business hub of the Asia Pacific" . . . A hub must offer first class products and services. The infrastructure must rank with the best in the world . . . "Singapore" must become a synonym for quality, reliability, and excellence . . .

- *To Reach the Goal:* "We will invest heavily in our people, to enable them to move up to (even) higher value-added and hence better paid jobs . . . Labor productivity must improve by at least 3 to 4 percent per year for the next decade. We have moved from labor-intensive to skill- and knowledge-intensive industries and services. In the next lap, skills and knowledge will become even more crucial in determining winners and losers. We need to work smarter, be better organized, and discover new work methods. We can achieve this through innovation, technology, and teamwork."

- *Older Workers:* "The younger workers have benefited from the new education system introduced in 1978. But 60,000 older workers have no

---

* This publication again illustrates how the government creates awareness and ownership of Singapore's future: a committee of Ministers of State, formed in 1989, obtained suggestions and ideas from the entire country on how various aspects of life in Singapore should be managed and what ideals were cherished by the people. *The Next Lap* is a synthesis of the hopes and plans for Singapore over the next generation.

high school education. [330,000] did not complete junior school. We will provide the means for them to upgrade their education and technical skills too, so that we can catch up with the developed countries. So far, 150,000 of them have attended BEST. 30,000 have enrolled for WISE. The government will work with the NTUC to enable more workers to attend BEST, WISE, and Fast Forward programs."

- *Postemployment Training:* "Even skilled workers need postemployment training and on-the-job training . . . The Skills Development Fund will help companies increase their investment in training from the present 1.5 percent of payroll to the 4 percent which developed countries spend."

The goal of becoming a "hub of the Asia Pacific" is already materializing. In March 1994, Sony announced a decision to turn its Singapore company into one of four global information hubs to support its worldwide operations. The US$19.6 million investment in its Singapore operations will save the company up to US$12 million a year in inventory costs alone for Sony plants in the region. Other MNCs that have made Singapore their hub of operations include 3M, BASF, Caterpillar, Matsushita, Mercedes Benz, and Toshiba.

To support the economic thrust of the 90s, forces are underway to rapidly train workers in the needed skills:

- As of 1992, every child will receive a minimum of 10 to 11 years of basic education, with emphasis on mathematics and science.

- Since 1992, the unions have become progressively more vocal in getting employers to incorporate minimum training hours per employee into their collective agreements. It is likely that employers, with some persuasion from the government, will have to accede to this request.

- Employers are also under great pressure to quickly increase their commitment to training to 4 percent of staff payroll.

- The VITB was upgraded into an Institute of Technical Education (ITE) in April 1992 to serve as a post-high-school institution. Its new focus is on full-time institutional technical training for high school graduates so that new entrants to the labor market will have more education and higher-level technical skills. Training is broad-based but rigorous with a practical bias. Having relevant and up-to-date technical skills, ITE graduates are sought after and highly valued by industries.

Besides full-time training, ITE continues to offer its wide range of continuing education and training programs for workers, programs such as MOST, BEST, WISE, TIME, and ACTS. ITE's continuing (academic) education program offers part-time and weekend classes for workers to acquire academic qualifications outside of the formal school system.

ITE also places an increasing emphasis on apprenticeship. Companies, especially the Small and Medium Enterprises (SMEs), are being encouraged to participate in ITE's apprenticeship scheme, patterned after the German dual vocational training system. Through this scheme, students who have just completed their formal schooling are attached to companies for at least two to three years. During this time, the apprentices will get to know their supervisors, the company, and its corporate culture. While they learn the necessary skills there, they also begin to develop good work discipline and positive attitudes that are important ingredients of a quality workforce. Apprentices receive an allowance but also contribute to the output of the company. The better the program, the sooner the company will benefit from having an additional productive worker. Singapore's Skills Development Fund subsidizes up to one-third the cost of training an apprentice.

A concurrent on-the-job training (OJT) drive complements the apprenticeship effort. The goal of OJT is to ensure that workers have multiple and flexible skills to accomplish different occupational tasks so that companies can cope with technological and work organization changes. To be fully competent and productive, new, as well as older, workers will need to continue learning on the job, as exemplified by the Japanese OJT practice.

To give added impetus to the promotion of OJT, the National Productivity Board launched the OJT 2000 Plan in October 1993. It aims to reach out to 700,000 workers by the end of the century. This initiative underlines the importance of the continuing education and training of workers to meet the global challenge for quality workers.

18.4   Conclusion

Though brief in its development, the Singapore experience in technical and skills training and education holds many valuable lessons for us:

1. *Economically-driven training*   Training of workers is not an end in itself, but an urgent response to needs surfacing in the economy. Instead of an idealized educational approach that tries to train people to be all things to all people, the approach of technical training in Singapore is pragmatic and focused on equipping workers with relevant broad-based skills to meet specifically targeted economic needs.

2. *Industry-government partnership.* At every stage of education and training, industry is made a direct partner of the educational process, from providing advice on content and curricula to accepting apprentices for training. This extremely close partnership has benefited both parties—industry benefits from having a ready pool of competent technical workers who can put their skills to immediate use; the institutes

benefit from having "transfer of technology" from the industry, and are confident in the knowledge that their trainees are trained in skills actually needed by the economy, thereby justifying their very existence.

3. *Tripartite planning and implementation.*   Each time the economy reaches a crossroads, action taken or contemplated always includes input from the government, labor, and employers. This tripartite formula ensures total ownership of both the problems and the solutions, thus facilitating effective implementation and execution of plans and strategies. There is no need to "sell" to each other; there is no confrontation, no "them-us" mentality, or interest groups—only joint, collaborative problem solving on issues in which all parties have a high stake.

4. *Public debate.*   The transparent nature of economic problem solving in Singapore means that issues are aired and debated, disagreements vented, and consensus achieved—all in the public eye. Such frank disclosure and discussion allows every Singaporean to become aware of the issues and actively participate in developing solutions. Solutions, when implemented, seldom meet serious public obstacles or opposition and are often highly successful because the public has understood and digested them.

5. *Constant change.*   Institutions seldom maintain the status quo for long, but are constantly given new mandates, new challenges, and new structures as the economy progresses. This dynamic state has made Singaporeans less resistant to change. This also accounts for why changes in policies and strategies are more readily accepted and why workers and unions realize that the next new thing is not a big threat to them.

In conclusion, we would like to reiterate that Singapore has no other resources it can count on than its people. Our relentless investment in people is a reflection of our lack of certainty about the future; our neverending training and education of our workers is a reflection of our belief that knowledge is essential for continued success and therefore more precious than natural resources.

BRIEF HISTORY OF SINGAPORE

1819   Singapore founded as a trading station by Sir Stamford Raffles for the British East India Co.

1959   Singapore became self-governing.

1963   Singapore gained independence from Britain by joining the Federation of Malaysia.

1965   Singapore became a fully independent and sovereign nation upon leaving Malaysia.

SUMMARY OF INFRASTRUCTURE
SUPPORTING TECHNICAL AND SKILLS TRAINING
IN SINGAPORE

Year	Institutions/Schemes
Phase One	
Up to 1960	None
1961–1967	■ Technical bias introduced into school curriculum; emphasis on mathematics, science, and technical subjects
	■ Vocational and commercial schools introduced
	■ Polytechnics expanded and restructured
1968–1972	■ Technical Education Department established
	■ Nine vocational institutions established
	■ Six technical training centers established
1973	■ Industrial Training Board formed
	■ Economic Development Board's (EDB) joint government-industry training centers established
Phase Two	
1979	■ Skills Development Levy (SDL) imposed to discourage use of low-skilled workers
	■ Skills Development Fund set up to rechannel monies collected by SDL, to train workers to meet new needs of the economy
	■ Vocational and Industrial Training Board (VITB) set up
	■ Council for Professional and Technical Education established
1980	■ VITB's Approved Training Center scheme introduced (22 such Industry Training Centers set up by 1984 with the Jewelry Industry Training Center set up in 1992)
1982–1983	■ EDB's collaborative technology institutes set up in partnership with the German, French, and Japanese governments
1983–1991	■ VITB launched programs to give basic grounding to school dropouts in the workforce:
	Basic Education for Skills Training (BEST) (1983)
	Modular Skills Training (MOST) (1986)
	Worker Improvement Through Secondary Education (WISE) (1987)
	Training Initiative for Mature Employees (TIME) (1991)
1988	■ EDB's transnational approach launched with the setting up of the Precision Engineering Institute

1987–1992	■ National Productivity Board's (NBP) schemes to spur training launched.

Increasing Training Opportunities (INTRO) (1987)

Information Technology for Office Workers (IT POWER) (1988)

Training Technology Center (1990)

Fast Forward (1990)

Training-Manager Program (1992)

1990	■ VITB introduces New Apprenticeship System based on the German dual system of vocational training
1992	■ Institute of Technical Education (ITE) established to replace VITB

References

1. Peter F. Drucker, *Post-capitalist Society,* Butterworth Heinemann, Oxford, 1993, p. 34.

2. Linda Low, Toh Mun Heng, Soon Teck Wong, Tam Kong Yam, and Helen Hughes, *Challenge and Response: Thirty Years of the Economic Development Board,* Times Academic Press, Singapore, 1993.

3. Janet Hilowitz, *Education and Training Policies and Programs to Support Industrial Restructuring in the Republic of Korea, Japan, Singapore and the United States,* Training Discussion Paper No. 18, ed. by the Training Policies Branch of International Labor Organization, Geneva, 1987.

4. Song Seng Law, *Technological Education in Singapore: A Country Report,* VITB Paper No. 3, Vocational and Industrial Training Board, Singapore, 1984.

5. Soo Ann Lee, *Industrialization in Singapore, Studies in Contemporary Southeast Asia,* Longmans, Australia, 1973.

6. The Government of Singapore, *Singapore: The Next Lap,* Times Editions, Singapore, 1991.

19

Anatomy of a Technical Training In-Service Training Day: Saudi Aramco Style

Ali M. Dialdin
General Manager, Training & Career Development

Mohammad A. Mahjoub
Supervisor, Academic Curriculum Unit

Technical trainers have bragged for years that they can go anywhere and train. If you are an employee of Saudi Aramco, you will have your mettle tested. Approximately every 18 months, Saudi Aramco holds a systemwide in-service conference in Dhahran, Saudi Arabia, where 1200 people gather to talk about training. This conference serves as a model for companies faced with multinational, multicultural, and multilingual in-service training. Managing 1200 people is an obvious challenge, but one that Saudi Aramco is handling in its own unique manner.

Saudi Aramco's Training & Career Development (T&CD) Organization serves 11,000 people a year in 14 different training locations, offering approximately 300 academic and industrial skills, college preparatory, and management/supervisory training courses. In addition, there are hundreds of technical courses specific to various line organizations within Saudi Aramco. This in-service training day has resulted in helping trainers to get to know one another better, offered a centralized location for the exchange of information, and challenged the best of organizers. However, it has also been a source of tremendous pride and sense of accomplishment for senior management, helping to guide their thinking between in-service conferences in a direction that provides continuous improvement opportunities for the staff under their supervision.

The trainers have diversified skills, educational backgrounds, and nationalities. Of the 1028 trainers in the training organization, 27 percent are Saudi, 33 percent are non-Saudi Arab or other Asian, 9 percent are American, and 31 percent are British. This diversity has helped in dealing with a working population of 57,000 employees representing 50 nationalities.

Arabic is the principal language spoken in the Middle East, so communication is facilitated by use of this language. In the field, however, the majority of Saudi Aramco employees speak English. English is taught and used as a second language in Saudi Aramco. An extensive curriculum is taught in English, with English language courses included in the course offerings each year. The English language training programs managed by Training & Career Development have enabled many employees to have equal facility with Arabic and English.

For those trainers who are hired by Saudi Aramco without Arabic language skills, opportunities are provided to learn about the language and culture of the host country. Cultural training is offered to trainers prior to working with Saudi nationals, so that common cultural mistakes are identified and misconceptions clarified.

Organizing a conference for 1200 is a major undertaking. As with most conferences, a steering committee was appointed which represented academic, job skills, and staff development areas and training management. The structure of Saudi Aramco's training organization is highlighted in Figure 19-3.

The conference was the fifth in-service training day sponsored by Training & Career Development. The aim of the in-service program was to foster the professional development of training staff through an open exchange of new ideas, methods, and technologies in the field of human resource development. The program included a wide range of subjects for *teachers, trainers, administrators, curriculum developers,* and *support staff.* Topics ranged from Microsoft access to the use of the Honeywell TDC 3000.

The *Table of Contents* of the program catalog, which was printed in English, shows the scope of the two-day in-service program. Included are the following sections (see Figure 19-1):

Contents

Figure 19-1. Program catalog table of contents.

Workshops (contd.)

Presentations

Figure 19-1. (*Continued*)

Presentations (contd.)

Panel Discussions

Index

**Visit the Safety Awareness Exhibit
and Enter Your Safety Ideas
in the Safety Contest.**
(Contest entries accepted at the Thursday Exhibit only.)

Figure 19-1. (*Continued*)

Opening Ceremony

Administrative Notes

Exhibits and Safety Contest

Keynote Addresses

Workshops

Presentations

Panel Discussions

Index: List of Presenters and Topics

Ali M. Dialdin, General Manager of Training & Career Development for Saudi Aramco, opened In-Service '94, which was held February 2 and 3, 1994. In his opening comments, he gave an overview of why this event was so important:

> We are in an era of unprecedented change in the oil and gas industry. Workplace downsizing, market globalization, and technological innovation are creating new challenges to Saudi Aramco and to all of us. Continuous investment in the skills and knowledge of our workforce is one of our best strategies for meeting these challenges successfully.

The basic organization of the in-service training day followed generally accepted conference planning techniques. A section entitled "Administrative Notes" provides some insight into how the logistics were planned. Highlights in this section included badges, agenda and map, opening ceremony and keynote addresses (in the presentation tent), exhibitions and safety contest (a big issue at Saudi Aramco), refreshments and lunch, closing ceremony, feedback forms, and coding system used. (See Figure 19-2.)

The major operating areas and training divisions of the Training & Career Development Organization are represented by an abbreviation system. (See Figure 19-3.) The scope of the organization's size becomes immediately evident. The list gives a hint of how extensive the training function is and why 1200 trainers, teachers, administrators, curriculum developers, and support staff are needed to meet the training goals of Saudi Aramco.

In addition, the "Administrative Notes" includes a listing of the session topics offered at In-Service '94. (See Figure 19-4.) The sessions are noted as *General, Computer/Typing, Teachers/Trainers, English, Math/Science,* and *Job Skills,* which assists participants in identifying sessions of interest. The list offers a real challenge in that participants were not able to attend all the sessions they perhaps wanted to.

The exhibition area was unique to Saudi Aramco's environment. Included with the exhibits were activities related to the exhibit. The

HIGHLIGHTS

➤ **Badges:** *In-Service '94 badges will be provided for presenters, session facilitators, and participants. Please wear your badge so that other participants can identify you.*

➤ **Agenda & Map:** *A detailed agenda is included with this catalog and will also be posted in different locations. A map is also included indicating the location of the workshops, presentations, panel discussions, and exhibitions.*

➤ **Opening Ceremony & Keynote Addresses:** *The official opening and the keynote addresses will be held in the Presentation Tent. Following the keynote addresses, participants will have a choice of several concurrent presentations and workshops. Locations and times for these sessions are indicated on the agenda and map.*

➤ **Exhibitions & Safety Contest:** *Refer to pages 9 to 19 for details of the exhibitions offered at In-Service '94. Note the Safety Contest being sponsored by the Academic Curriculum Unit. All contest entries must be submitted at the Safety Exhibit on Thursday, February 3, 1994.*

➤ **Refreshments & Lunch:** *Tea and coffee will be available in the Dining Tents prior to the official opening and also after the keynote addresses. During the day, tea and coffee will also be available at the other locations shown on the map. Lunch will be provided for all participants in the Dining Tents.*

➤ **Closing Ceremony:** *The Closing Ceremony will be held in the Presentation Tent.*

➤ **Feedback Forms:** *The In-Service Day Feedback Form and Feedback Forms for individual sessions are included with this catalog. Please complete these forms and turn them in as you leave the Closing Ceremony. Information from this form will be used to plan future In-Service Training Day Programs.*

➤ **Coding System Used:**

201w   = *Session 201 is offered on Wednesday only.*
202T   = *Session 202 is offered on Thursday only.*
203WT = *Session 203 is offered on Wednesday and Thursday.*

Figure 19-2. Administrative notes.

➤ Abbreviations Used:

ACU	*Academic Curriculum Unit*
ATD	*Academic Training Department*
CAATD	*Central Area Academic Training Division*
CPC	*College Preparatory Center*
CR/WRTD	*Central Region/Western Region Training Department*
DHJSTD	*Dhahran Job Skills Training Division*
ITC	*Industrial Training Center*
JSCU	*Job Skills Curriculum Unit*
JSTC	*Job Skills Training Center*
JSTD	*Job Skills Training Department*
JSTG	*Job Skills Testing Group*
JTD	*Jeddah Training Division*
KFUPM	*King Fahd University of Petroleum and Minerals*
M&PED	*Management & Professional Education Division*
MTC	*Management Training Center*
NAATD	*Northern Area Academic Training Division*
PD&ED	*Program Development & Evaluation Division*
QA&SDU	*Quality Assurance & Staff Development Unit*
RTD	*Riyadh Training Division*
RTJSTD	*Ras Tanura Job Skills Training Division*
SAATD	*Southern Area Academic Training Division*
SAJSTD	*Southern Area Job Skills Training Division*
SDG	*Staff Development Group*
T&CD	*Training & Career Development*
T&CDSU	*Training & Career Development Services Unit*
TRC	*Training Resource Center*
YTD	*Yanbu Training Division*

➤ In-Service '94 Session Topics:

	General	Computer/Typing	Teachers/Trainers	English	Math/Science	Job Skills
A Method for Teaching Controlled Writing to Advanced Students				•		
Advanced Teaching Strategies			•			
An Introduction to Claris CAD	•	•				
Analyzing the Testing Environment			•			
Applying Modern Advertising Techniques in Class Situations			•			
Business and Training in the 1990s	•					
CD ROM Materials for Information and Training	•					
Chemistry by Investigation					•	
Classroom Management Strategies			•			
Coaching to Manage Performance Problems			•			•
Computer Applications in Education			•			
Computer-Assisted Language Learning				•		
Cooperative Learning			•			
Creating Training Aids Using Microsoft PowerPoint	•	•				

Figure 19-3. Major operating areas and training divisions of the Training & Career Development organization.

In-Service '94 Session Topics	General	Computer/Typing	Teachers/Trainers	English	Math/Science	Job Skills
Creating Your Own Slide Presentation	•					
Current Trends in Language Teaching				•		
Designing Multimedia Systems for Training	•					
Discover the Digital System World						•
EFL Methodology: An Overview				•		
Electrical Grounding System						•
Enhancing Documents With Graphics in MS Word for Windows	•	•				
Enhancing Math & Science Teaching With Technology					•	
Exploring Teaching Myths				•		
Fundamentals of a Chiller System						•
Grammar and Communicative Teaching of English				•		
Guided Goal Typing		•				
Health Education Exhibit	•					
How Does Training Fit Into a Learning Organization?	•		•			
How Student Progress Is Evaluated and Reported			•			
Improve Your 35-mm Photography	•					
Improving Oral and Aural Production				•		
Innovative Techniques for Operational Amplifier Troubleshooting						•
Introduction to Aldus PageMaker on the Macintosh	•	•				
Introduction to Microsoft Word for Windows	•	•				
Investment In Excellence	•					
IRPA Model for Teaching Grammar and Writing Skills				•		
Job Skills Curriculum Exhibit & Help Desk	•					•
Job Skills Testing Exhibit & Help Desk	•					•
Job Training Standards	•					•
Keys to Successful Business Writing	•					
MAC World/SALT 1993	•	•				
Mechanical Failures and Preventive Measures						•
Microsoft Access: Databases Under GUIs	•	•				
Models in the Teaching and Learning of English				•		
NIDA Computer-Based Training Systems Exhibit						•
Operation and Control of Gas Turbines in Saudi Aramco						•
Organization and Change Through Effective Training	•					
Preparing Local Software for Math & Science					•	

Figure 19-4. Listing of session topics.

In-Service '94 Session Topics	General	Computer/Typing	Teachers/Trainers	English	Math/Science	Job Skills
Quality and Innovation in Team Building	•					
Quality Tools for Training	•		•			
Quality, Innovation, and Technology in an Information Age	•		•			
Real Time Plant Simulation for Operator Training						•
Recreational Mathematics					•	
Refresher Education	•		•			
Safety Awareness Exhibit, Contest & Help Desk	•					
Self-Help in Typing		•				
Self-Observation in Teacher Development			•			
Situational Leadership in the Classroom			•			
Speedtronic Control of a GE Gas Turbine						•
Stress and Its Management	•					
Success in Instruction: Critical Success Factors			•			
TDC 3000 Overview						•
Teacher as a Mentor	•		•			
Teacher Development				•		
Teacher Professional Development			•			
Teaching and Learning Composition Without Tears				•		
Teaching Grammar Interactively Through OHTs				•		
Teaching Reading Skills				•		
Teaching Safety	•		•			
Teaching Trainees to Think			•			
Technical Training Aids Exhibit	•					•
Techniques for Developing Oral Communication Skills				•		
Testing in English Language				•		
Training Resource Center	•		•			
Training Trends in the '90s	•		•			•
Translation Training & Certification Program	•		•			
Understanding the Trainee			•			
Using Graphing Calculators					•	
Using Microsoft Windows	•	•				
Video Production for Absolute Beginners	•					
Video Showcases 1, 2 & 3	•		•			
Writing for Critical Thinking: Information Transfer & Problem-Solving					•	

Figure 19-4. (*Continued*)

"Health Education Exhibit," for example, offered participants the opportunity to take a blood pressure screening test, body fat measurement test, lung volume test, flexibility test, and stress management test. (See Figure 19-5.)

Exhibits included "Job Skills Curriculum: Exhibit & Help Desk," "Job Skills Testing: Exhibit & Help Desk," "NIDA Computer-Based Training Systems," plus others. Of special interest was the "Safety Awareness Exhibit," which stressed the importance of traffic safety. (See Figure 19-6.)

The *keynote speakers* dealt with two broad, but crucial topics: "Business and Training in the 1990s" and "Quality, Innovation, and Technology in an Information Age." The business and training presentation covered the results of a study of global companies that have been most successful in using training to enhance their effectiveness as well as highlighting *best business practices* and *best training practices*. In addition, the role of *action learning principles* was covered. The second keynote address covered the challenges of the Information Age. The key challenge will be understanding an economy based on information versus manufacturing and its implications for training. The use of quality standards and technology in strengthening the economy were discussed.

Sessions for the participants were broken down into *workshops, presentations,* and *panel discussions.*

Workshops included a variety of topics dealing with some key subjects for technical trainers. A sample of the workshops offered is included here:

Analyzing the Testing Environment (See Figure 19-7)

Chemistry by Investigation (See Figure 19-8)

Discover the Digital System World (See Figure 19-9)

Innovative Techniques for Operational Amplifier Troubleshooting (See Figure 19-10)

Recreational Mathematics (See Figure 19-11)

Teaching Safety (See Figure 19-12)

Presentations dealt with some highly technical topics critical to the technical trainers' continuing education. Some of those topics included the following:

Job Training Standards (see Figure 19-13)

Mechanical Failures and Preventive Measures (see Figure 19-14)

Speedtronic Control of a GE Gas Turbine (see Figure 19-15)

TDC 3000 Overview (see Figure 19-16)

Panel discussions provided a format designed to foster a constructive exchange of ideas among teachers, trainers, and training management over issues of general professional concern. Of special interest was a

(Text continues on page 515.)

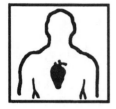

The Health Education Unit, Preventive Medicine Services Division, invites you to visit their health exhibit. Included in the exhibit will be the opportunity to test your blood pressure and fitness levels and obtain important health-related information.

- *Blood Pressure Screening Test*

- *Body Fat Measurement Test*

- *Lung Volume Test*

- *Stress Management Information*

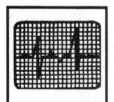

- *Flexibility Test*

- *Step Test*

- *Nutrition Information*

- *Physical Fitness Information*

Come on by & Check Your Health!

Figure 19-5. Sample catalog description of an in-service day exhibit.

Safety Awareness
Exhibit • Contest • Help Desk

Exhibit: *The Safety Awareness Program, from pilot stage to end product*
• Saudi traffic statistics • Car bumper stickers • Program handouts • Health
& Safety videos • Magnetic traffic board • and more!!!

Contest: *Contest categories: Best Safety Poster • Best Safety Slogan • Best*
Safety Awareness Program Teaching Tip • Best Company Safety Suggestion •
Prizes for best entries!!! • All contest entries must be submitted on Thursday,
February 3, 1994, at the Safety Exhibit.

Help Desk: *Curriculum writers will be on call to answer questions about*
the Safety Awareness Program or to collect feedback and suggestions.

Stay Alert – Don't Get Hurt!

Figure 19-6.   Safety Awareness Exhibit.

Analyzing the Testing Environment

Gerald W. Guswiler
NAATD

Gerald is a retired Florida educator, having served in a number of positions including High School Principal, Curriculum Director, and College Instructor. He currently teaches English at Rahimah ITC. He holds a Master's degree in Educational Administration and Supervision.

It is extremely important, from corporate, educational, and student planning perspectives, to have test results which truly reflect student performance. Dealing with test results which are not reflective of performance threatens all three categories and fails to measure the true quality of teaching.

The goal of this workshop is to learn how various aspects of the testing environment can have a positive or negative impact on student performance. It will identify and analyze the three primary components of a testing environment; namely, organizational, physical, and emotional/psychological factors.

Major organizational factors involved in a testing environment include advertising, seating arrangements, proctor roles, test security, and supplies. Physical factors include the room itself, furniture type and arrangement, temperature, lighting, equipment, and acoustics. The emotional/psychological factors revolve around being too tense or too lax. These factors will be analyzed individually and collectively to determine how they can produce either a productive or an unproductive testing situation.

The session will include an in-house produced film of a hypothetical testing situation which portrays, in both positive and negative ways, the three major components of the testing environment. Participants, working in groups, will observe and report on the different components of the testing situation.

Figure 19-7. Sample workshop: "Analyzing the Testing Environment."

Chemistry by Investigation

Ron Boodram
CAATD

Ron teaches science at the College Preparatory Center where he is also a member of the CAATD Safety Committee. He has a Bachelor's degree in Chemistry from London University.

In this workshop, science teachers will gain valuable hands-on experience in carrying out experiments using modern equipment. Six stations will be set up in a chemistry laboratory to demonstrate the following experiments:

• A *cooling curve* using a thermistor, interface, and a Macintosh. A graph will be plotted on the monitor as the experiment is being conducted.

• *The rate of a chemical reaction* using a spectrophotometer. This technique involves using colorimetric determination of concentration of colored ions which absorb (and transmit) light.

• *An investigation of pH curves* using a pH meter and various acid/base systems (such as strong acid/strong base, strong acid/weak base, weak acid/strong base, and weak acid/weak base). This experiment will involve titration which is an analytical method to determine the concentration of an unknown solution.

• *Techniques for separating substances* (such as simple distillation, paper chromatography, filtration, and re-crystallization).

• *Electrolysis and products of electrolysis of solutions.* This experiment will involve collecting products of electrolyzing various solutions. Standard electrode potential values (E°) will be used for making predictions of products.

• *Major organic synthesis reactions* using an organic preparation (such as aspirin).

Figure 19-8. Sample workshop: "Chemistry by Investigation."

306w

SESSION

Discover the Digital System World

Girguis Y. Khalil
DHJSTD

Girguis teaches digital,
electrical, and electronics
courses at Dhahran
North JSTC. He has
over 22 years of experi-
ence as a Communica-
tions Engineer in the
Armed Forces of Egypt.
He holds a Master's
degree in Military
Sciences in Electronic
Warfare.

The world of digital electronics has undergone several major changes in the last twenty years. One of the most important changes has been in the tools and techniques we use to prototype and test digital systems. In this workshop, the major differences between the analog and digital systems will be discussed.

One of the most interesting applications of the digital system is the digital clock. Girguis will simplify the operational principles of a digital clock, using transparencies that show a simple block diagram of the clock and the function of every block.

The participant will be given the opportunity to construct and test his/her own digital clock. The instruction includes how to assemble a power supply unit.

At the end of the workshop, participants will have a good working knowledge of soldering techniques and safety precautions. They will also be able to take their clocks home.

Figure 19-9. Sample workshop: "Discover the Digital System World."

311w SESSION

Innovative Techniques for Operational Amplifier Troubleshooting

Samir I. Kelada
RTJSTD

Samir is an Analog and Digital Instructor at Rahimah JSTC. He has a degree in Computer Maintenance and a certificate in Biomedical Electronic Technology. He gave a presentation on Systematic Trouble-shooting Methods in 1991 and a workshop on Troubleshooting Faulty Semiconductors in 1992.

Operational Amplifiers are widely used in Saudi Aramco's plants (Process Control Systems, UPS Systems, Analog to Digital and Digital to Analog Converters, Computer Interfaces and Computer Disk Drives). Although many books have been written about operational amplifiers, their focus has been on basic functioning concepts and mathematical descriptions. How to troubleshoot or detect a faulty operational amplifier in a complex circuit has not been adequately covered.

The lack of maintenance documentation, on various applications and circuit designs, has caused uncertainty among maintenance personnel. Therefore, after intense research, Samir detected the existence of one failure characteristic that was common to all faulty operational amplifiers. He will share some of his findings with you, including a simple and reliable test using D.V.M. that will detect any form of faulty operational amplifier in a complex or unfamiliar circuit.

Samir's innovative technique is time and cost effective, accurate, and reliable. No longer is there a need to search for the special parameters or applications of an unfamiliar circuit or to pull components out of the circuit to measure them.

This session will include a fault finding using complex boards with actual faults. You will have a unique opportunity to learn about a highly reliable technique that can save hundreds of faulty boards in Saudi Aramco plants.

Figure 19-10. Sample workshop: "Innovative Techniques for Operational Amplifier Troubleshooting."

320w
SESSION

Recreational Mathematics

KhalilA. Hammoudeh
CAATD

Khalil is Science/Busi-
ness Math/Accounting
Chairman at Dhahran
North ITC. He taught
math for ten years in
Jordan and the U.A.E.
He has a Master's degree
in Business Administra-
tion from KFUPM. He
conducted a presentation
on Recreational Math-
ematics in 1992.

Mathematical games and puzzles are more than just a fun approach to learning. They can motivate a class and generate interest. They can also stimulate logical reasoning and good thinking in learners. For example, the process of solving puzzles reinforces the trainees' knowledge in developing the basic concepts, principles and skills of geometry and algebra, and requires them to apply this knowledge at a rather complex level of understanding.

Khalil defines *puzzle* as a challenging problem for the learner. The degree of challenge depends on several factors such as age, education, and intellectual abilities. Guidelines for solving a puzzle and strategies for winning a game will be covered. These guidelines are drawn from classics of math (study the problem, organize the facts, line up a plan, verify the plan, and examine the answer). This five-step plan will be used to solve selected puzzles and other recreational activities. To this end, various methods of solving problems, such as trial and error, induction, deduction, and heuristic methods, will be implemented.

Participants, working in groups, will apply the strategies to solving problems chosen from geometry, algebra, number theory, topology, and other math topics. At the end of the session, you will be able to design puzzles and games, analyze a game and plot a plan to win it, and use mathematical concepts and skills to solve a puzzle. A handout which contains additional puzzles and games will be provided for interested participants.

Figure 19-11.   Sample workshop: "Recreational Mathematics."

Teaching Safety

326w
SESSION

John M. Lyons
CAATD

John teaches English at the Professional English Language Center and is also Chairman of CAATD's Safety Committee. He has taught English in Jordan, Lebanon, Jeddah, and the U.S. He holds a Master's degree in English from the University of St. Louis. In 1990, he participated in a panel discussion on Improving Reading Comprehension.

How can we motivate our trainees in safety awareness? How can we encourage teachers to teach safety in a way that presents a positive message? How can we help to improve our safety record in the areas of driving and sports?

In this workshop, John will model a driving safety lesson from the new Safety Awareness Program developed by the Academic Curriculum Unit. He will present one approach to this topic and show teachers how to manage time during a safety lesson.

Included in the discussion will be a safety film, with John explaining how to effectively use films in the classroom. He will demonstrate how to use the trainees' own experiences of traffic or sports-related accidents and near misses to further the safety message. Encouraging trainees to share their personal experiences enhances the effectiveness of the safety program. A list of safety-related material and resources available in Saudi Aramco will be provided to those attending the session.

Figure 19-12. Sample workshop: "Teaching Safety."

Job Training Standards

421w

SESSION

Lawrence J. Olsen
PD&ED

Lawrence joined Saudi Aramco in 1979, worked as Project Leader on various curriculum projects, and is currently Group Leader of Job Skills Curriculum Group B. He has worked in Laos, Thailand, Iran, and the United States and holds a Master's degree in Language Arts from Rutgers University. In 1990, he gave a presentation on Job Training Standards.

A Job Training Standard (JTS) describes a single functional job in a way that allows for job certification to a set standard. This is accomplished by tracking actual job performance on the job across time without interfering with normal operational requirements. This is a tall order, but can be achieved if the functional intent and purpose of the document are correctly understood.

This presentation will define what a JTS is in terms of its use in Saudi Aramco. It will discuss the importance of workable JTSs, their value and utility, their role in Saudi Aramco manpower development, and the procedures for their development.

Figure 19-13.   Sample presentation: "Job Training Standards."

Mechanical Failures & Preventive Measures   **423**w   SESSION

Hassan H. Al Rashid
RTJSTD

Hassan is a Trainer assigned to Rahimah JSTC. He came to Saudi Aramco in 1983, after working for the Saudi Navy as Senior Chief Engineer and teaching in Saudi Government schools. He has a Bachelor's degree in Marine Engineering from Pacific Western University.

This session will provide an introduction to mechanical maintenance. Factors to consider when scheduling preventive maintenance include environmental conditions, operational conditions, and machine history or data. The importance of planning and scheduling systematic preventive maintenance and inspection will be discussed as well as maintenance failures and preventive measures.

Minor maintenance failures will be examined, including measures that could have been taken to prevent the failures. Major maintenance failures will also be covered along with their preventive measures.

The operation of mechanical equipment such as air compressors will round out the discussion. The role vibration checks play in preventive maintenance will be highlighted.

Figure 19-14. Sample presentation: "Mechanical Failures and Preventive Measures."

Speedtronic Control of a GE Gas Turbine

432w

SESSION

Joseph Kurupacheril
SAJSTD

Joseph worked at the Qurayyah Seawater Treatment Plant in operations and training, then transferred to Al-Hasa JSTC where he teaches Water Injection and Basic Operator Courses. Before joining the Company in 1977, he worked in the petro-chemical industry in India.

Speedtronics is the electronic control system of a General Electric Gas Turbine. Speedtronic control provides the solid state analog and digital electronic computing components required for gas turbine control, protection, and logic sequence systems.

The control system consists of three major control loops: start-up control loop, speed control loop, and temperature control loop. The output of these control loops is connected into a minimum value gate (low voltage selector) where the loop requiring the smallest fuel input to the turbine will take control. The output of the minimum value gate is applied to the VCE voltage bus which determines the fuel flow. The VCE signal controls the fuel flow by positioning an electrohydraulic servovalve to meet the load requirement.

The protection system consists of a number of primary and secondary systems several of which operate at each normal start-up and shutdown. The primary system is electrohydraulic and the secondary systems are either mechanical or manual. The system protects the turbine from abnormal conditions such as overheating, excessive speed, excessive vibration, and flame out. The sequence logic system controls the start-up and shutdown sequences.

Figure 19-15. Sample presentation: "Speedtronic Control of a GE Gas Turbine."

TDC 3000 Overview

This session will provide an overview of the Honeywell TDC 3000 Total Distributed Control System. The TDC 3000 is a very popular system used in process industries including Saudi Aramco.

The overview will include an explanation of total distributed control and will compare this type of control with analog instrumentation.

Alfonso E. Angeles
RTJSTD

Alfonso trains senior operators in process instrumentation at Rahimah JSTC. His experience includes maintenance of instrumentation at a copper smelting plant in Zambia. He is a member of the Philippine Instrumentation & Controls Society.

Figure 19-16. Sample presentation: "TDC 3000 Overview."

Training Trends for the '90s

The purpose of this panel discussion is to investigate a critical training issue which will impact on curriculum and instruction in T&CD academic and job skills programs. The format of the discussion is designed to foster a constructive exchange of ideas between teachers, trainers and T&CD management over an issue of general professional concern.

The subject of this Directors' Panel is the teaching of *higher-order* thinking skills—preparing trainees to handle problem solving tasks that are required for expert job performance. The panel participants will review existing T&CD curricula and programs for their treatment of problem solving and critical thinking skill development, define requirements for change, and investigate alternative strategies for improvement. Questions for discussion will include:

- How can we move from rote memorization to the development of *higher-order* thinking skills?

- What types of *higher-order* thinking skills are required for expert job performance?

- How can traditional needs assessment techniques be improved?

- How can curriculum and job training aids be designed to foster *higher-order* thinking skills?

- What strategies can be used in academic and job skills training to develop trainee skills in critical thinking and problem solving?

- What applications do simulators, computers, and multimedia training technologies have in the teaching of *higher* thinking skills?

Figure 19-17. Sample panel discussion: "Training Trends for the '90s."

discussion entitled "Training Trends for the '90s," which dealt with *higher-order* thinking skills, and how Training & Career Development can prepare its students to handle problem-solving tasks that are required for expert job performance. (See Figure 19-17.)

The *Index* lists all the sessions as well as the speakers.

The majority of the sessions were done using resources found within the company. The topics were well received, with participants being given the opportunity to evaluate each aspect of the in-service program. The responses were by far very positive. The exit surveys completed at the in-service days, and subsequent telephone interviews, revealed the following:

- Over 65 percent of the respondents felt that the overall quality was *excellent* or *very good*, while only 2 percent felt dissatisfaction with the program.

- The organization and program catalog also received rave reviews, with 70 percent feeling that the organization was *excellent* or *very good*, and a remarkable 80 percent with similar feelings about the program catalog. As one participant pointed out, "It [the catalog] gave you, in a few hours, the cream of information, knowledge, and skill."

This year, for the first time, participants were asked to rate the individual workshops and presentations. Feedback was exceptional, with over 50 percent of the sessions rated *great!* This was in part because participants were able to make their choice of sessions, develop schedules to suit their own needs and interests, and, consequently, were more likely to be pleased with the sessions they attended. This positive response also shows that Training & Career Development's in-house presenters can match the high standards of professionalism expected of them by their peers.

One of the major talking points among participants at this year's in-service day was the impact made by the various exhibitions. Of particular interest were the exhibits from the Health Education Unit, the Training Resource Center, and the Academic Curriculum Unit's Safety Awareness Exhibit, all of which drew large crowds throughout the day.

Over 500 participants offered suggestions, which senior management will take into consideration when planning the next in-service day. More computer workshops and more exhibitions headed the list, with quite a number suggesting that selected sessions be made available in the outlying areas, as well as in Dhahran.

The in-service training day will continue to be a key part of Saudi Aramco's efforts to keep its training staff up to date, globally oriented, and ready to serve the technical training needs of the company. One major side benefit is the tremendous boost this professional event gives the staff. In the few days the people are together, they are able to understand their roles in the organization, know that they are valued, and see that the corporation cares a great deal about their professional and personal development.

20

Colleges, Universities, and Vocational and Technical Institutes

Robert Sheets
Northern Illinois University

Robert G. Sheets, Ph.D. *is the Director of the Human Resource Policy Program at the Center for Governmental Studies, Northern Illinois University, DeKalb, Illinois. Sheets specializes in labor market research and planning, performance management and program evaluation, and workforce preparation policy at the federal and state levels. Sheets has produced a series of policy papers on the development of market-based workforce preparation systems in the United States for the National Governors' Association, the National Commission for Employment Policy, and the Competitiveness Policy Council.*

20.1   Introduction

Colleges, universities, and vocational and technical institutes can provide critical resources to companies in planning and delivering technical training. These postsecondary educational institutions traditionally have focused on degree and certificate programs delivered through on-campus classroom instruction that was not readily accessible to most adult workers. They now provide on-campus and off-campus instruction in tradi-

517

tional degree programs as well as highly flexible courses and programs that are designed specifically for adult workers. They also provide customized training services and related training resources to companies and industry groups through education-business partnerships and contractual arrangements similar to private training vendors.

Before establishing training relationships, companies should be aware of the changing role of these institutions in technical training, the types of training services that are available, and different strategies for making the best use of these services.

This chapter provides an overview of the wide range of postsecondary educational institutions and their changing role in technical training. It also provides a summary of the training services and resources provided by most educational institutions and how businesses can contract for customized training services. This chapter concludes with a discussion of new directions in business-education partnerships for technical training.

20.2   The Changing Role of Postsecondary Educational Institutions in Technical Training

The United States has the largest system of publicly funded postsecondary education in the world. This system consists mainly of four-year colleges and universities, community and junior colleges, vocational and technical institutes, and proprietary schools. There are over 150 universities and 1800 four-year colleges in the United States. Every state has a number of public and private universities and colleges that are accessible to most companies and adult workers who meet entrance requirements. Many of these universities and colleges have branch campuses and offer programs and courses in locations throughout their service regions, their states or, in some cases, around the world.

There are currently about 1200 two-year community and junior colleges. Most adults can find at least one community college campus within thirty minutes of their homes and workplaces (Carnevale et al., 1990b). As with universities, community colleges also have multiple campuses and offer programs in many different locations throughout their districts, their states, and around the world. Many states have a diverse network for public and private vocational-technical schools and institutes that provide both high school students and adult workers with basic skills and occupational training similar to community colleges. In addition, each state also has a wide variety of proprietary schools or career colleges which operate as private, for-profit schools funded through private tuition and student grants and loans.

The historical role of these postsecondary educational institutions has been to provide general education and occupational preparation to young people before they transition from full-time schooling to full-time employment. However, over the last 20 years, this traditional role has expanded to include the upgrading and retraining of adult workers, as well as the delivery of customized training services to businesses and industry groups.

This changing role has occurred for many reasons. The first reason is the growing importance of the adult training market.

- During the 1970s and 1980s, adult workers became a significant share of the education and training market for postsecondary institutions. Recent studies estimate that about one out of two students in postsecondary institutions is now over 25 years of age and is going to school part-time while employed (Powers et al., 1991).

- The growing importance of the adult market has led to the expansion of off-campus classroom instruction to community and work-site locations and more flexible scheduling that allows adult workers to easily integrate training with work and family responsibilities. It also has encouraged the growth of computer- and video-based instruction, distance learning, and independent study courses, which allow colleges and universities to tailor their training services to individual needs.

- It has promoted the awarding of advance placement and college credits for prior work experience and training provided by employers, apprenticeship programs, and other industry or professional training programs.

A second reason for this changing role is the expanded mission of these institutions in state and local economic development and workforce training. During the 1970s and 1980s, most states and communities encouraged postsecondary educational institutions to promote job creation and retention through new education-business partnerships and customized business and training services (Northeast-Midwest Institute, 1988). Federal and state governments encouraged universities, community colleges, and vocational-technical institutes to provide a wide range of economic development services, including business planning, management training and assistance, research and development along with technology transfer, government procurement, and international trade assistance, and customized education and training services. These institutions also were encouraged to expand managerial and technical training courses and programs and related services such as career counseling and assessment to adults to improve the quality of the workforce. In addition, they were encouraged to promote stronger linkages with businesses in all training programs through work-based learning arrangements ranging from cooperative education and internships to formal apprenticeship programs (U.S.

Department of Labor, 1989). *This growing emphasis on work-based learning can now be seen in recent federal and state initiatives to establish a formal school-to-work system in the United States through business education partnerships and work-based learning arrangements that integrate schools and workplaces.*

This expanded role in economic development and workforce training will likely grow in the future as universities and two-year colleges compete for limited public funds and larger shares of the adult training market in a highly competitive training industry. There will be growing competition for adult and business customers in the face of declining enrollments of traditional college-age students, declining public funding, and increased competition from alternative public and private training providers, including employers that are establishing their own in-house training programs (Powers et al., 1988). Universities and community colleges will compete openly with public and private training vendors for training contracts and partnerships with businesses and industry groups. Given this changing environment, businesses and industry groups will find new opportunities to establish mutually beneficial business-education partnerships and other arrangements for technical training.

20.3 Training Services and Resources Provided by Postsecondary Education

Postsecondary educational institutions can provide businesses with high-quality, competitively priced training services and instructional resources. The most common training programs and services and instructional resources provided by universities and colleges are described in this section.

20.3.1 Training Programs, Courses, and Workshops

Training programs, courses, and workshops offered by postsecondary educational institutions can be classified into two major categories:

1. Noncustomized programs and services that are accessible to all qualified students through standard course schedules and locations

2. Customized training programs and services that are offered to businesses and industry groups for their employees through some type of contractual arrangement or agreement between the educational institution and the business or industry group

Noncustomized training programs and courses are the most common training services. Examples of these programs are listed in Figures 20-1

Certificates (including Apprenticeship-Related Theory)

- Automotive Services
- Electronics Technology
- Industrial Electrician Apprentice
- Machinist Apprentice
- Management and Supervision
- Manufacturing Technology
- Tool and Die Maker Apprentice
- Welding

Associates in Applied Science

- Automotive Services
- Business Computer Programming
- Electronics Technology
- Management and Supervision—Industrial
- Manufacturing Technology
- Materials Production Control
- Mechanical Design

Associates in Arts and Sciences

- Business (Accounting, Economics, Management, and Marketing)
- Engineering (Chemical, Electrical, Industrial, and Mechanical)
- Physical Science (Biology, Chemistry, Geology, and Physics)

Bachelors, Masters, and Doctorates in Arts and Sciences

- Business (Accounting, Finance, Management, Marketing, and Operations Management)
- Computer Science
- Engineering and Engineering Technology (Chemical, Electrical, Industrial, and Mechanical)
- Physical Science (Biology, Chemistry, Geology, and Physics)

Figure 20-1. Examples of common technical education and training programs at postsecondary educational institutions.

and 20-2. Customized services usually involve tailoring the scheduling, location, content, and/or instructional approach and may involve the combination of organizational development and training services (Bragg and Jacobs, 1993). Included are a few examples of customized services.

Degree and Certificate Programs.   Noncustomized degree programs range from one- and two-year associate degree programs offered by community colleges and technical institutes to bachelor's, master's, and doctorate programs offered by four-year colleges and universities. Some two-year degree programs are designed for transfer students who wish to pursue a four-year college degree. The Associate in Science (A.S.) focuses on mathematics and science. The Associate in Arts (A.A.) focuses on humanities and social science. Some two-year educational institutions award Associate of Applied Science (A.A.S.) degrees that are not as easily transferred to four-year degree programs (see Figure 20-1). Professional and technical degree programs at the associate and bachelor's levels usually consist of required coursework in a professional or technical specialty, such as electronics or accounting, and additional general education requirements that can be met through an assortment of elective courses. They are usually taught by full-time faculty or part-time faculty drawn from business and industry.

Fundamentals of Hydraulics	Blueprint Reading for Mechanical Trades
Introduction to Spreadsheets	
Machine Shop Mathematics	Technical Physics
Electronic Drafting	Database Applications
Machining Fundamentals	Basic Welding
Industrial Health and Safety	Quality Control
Automotive Brake Assemblies	Automotive Transmissions
Automotive Electrical Systems	Microbiology
Business Communications	Principles of Accounting
DOS for Microcomputers	Programmable Electronic Controllers
Electronic Instrumentation	
Computer Imaging	Advanced CNC Programming
Advanced Robotics	Computer-aided Drafting
Keyboarding	Desktop Publishing
Wordprocessing Application	Technical Report Writing
Business Communications	Effective Meetings

Figure 20-2.   Examples of common technical education and training courses at community colleges and technical institutes.

Noncustomized certificate programs are another type of training program widely offered by postsecondary educational institutions. Certificate programs usually are short-term training programs consisting of a required sequence of professional and technical training courses leading to a recognized credential. They generally range from a few weeks to two years in length and usually do not have the general education requirements found in postsecondary degree programs. As a result, they are very popular among students who want college credits and a recognized credential but do not want to take general education courses to receive an associates degree or to transfer into a four-year college degree. Common certificate programs include office machine repair, machine trades, construction trades, building maintenance, electronics, and office management.

Related Theory Instruction for Apprenticeship Programs. A special type of noncustomized certificate program offered by most community colleges, most technical institutes, and some four-year colleges is a related theory course sequence for formal apprenticeship programs. Related theory courses are usually a sequence of technical courses that are coordinated with work-site training in an apprenticeship program. These apprenticeship programs could be organized by a company, an industry association, a trade union, or a joint labor-management committee and may or may not be recognized by the Bureau of Apprenticeship and Training. The related theory courses could be taught by college faculty or experienced tradespersons hired by the school for the apprenticeship program. Students completing the related theory sequence usually receive a certificate and credits toward related certificates and associate degree programs.

Credit and Noncredit Courses and Workshops. All universities, community colleges, and technical institutes offer a vast array of "off-the-rack" or noncustomized credit and noncredit courses and workshops that are available to qualified students or the general public. These courses and workshops are taught by both full-time and part-time faculty or consultants for a general audience, not the particular needs of an employer or industry group. Some courses are offered as self-paced independent study courses that are delivered through audio- or videotapes, reading materials, and workbooks; these courses have a coordinator who evaluates the student's progress and completion of learning requirements. Credit courses are usually the same required and elective courses found in degree or certificate programs. Noncredit courses and workshops are usually designed for addressing specific topics and skills or specific technologies or products (such as a specific computer software package). Some are designed as overviews or introductory surveys, while others are designed to provide an in-depth examination of new management approaches or technologies. Most companies have seen course catalogues and brochures on these types of training services. They could address business writing, desktop publishing, blueprint reading, computer-aided drafting, supervision, and time management, among other subjects.

Adult Education and Literacy Training.   Almost all community colleges, vocational schools, technical institutes, and some colleges and universities offer noncustomized adult education and literacy training. Many of these services are supported by federal and state funding and can be offered to adults at little or no cost. These programs are designed for adults who do not have high school diplomas or who do not have basic literacy or English skills. These programs are usually offered in standard noncredit courses and workshops. Adult Basic Education (ABE) refers generally to courses providing instruction to all adults up to the eighth-grade level. Subject areas include reading, writing, math, and science, and sometimes include life skills. Adult Secondary Education (ASE) generally refers to courses that prepare students without high school diplomas to take high school equivalency tests for the General Educational Development (GED) certificate. English as a Second Language (ESL) generally refers to courses that help adults with limited English proficiency learn basic English. These courses usually address reading, writing, and oral communication within practical life situations. These adult education courses are designed to prepare adults for further education and training or entry into degree and certificate programs.

Customized Programs, Courses, and Workshops.   Most postsecondary educational institutions now compete with all public and private training vendors in providing businesses and industry groups with customized or "contract" programs, courses, and workshops. As defined earlier, customized or contract training services are any degree program, certification program, individual course, or individual workshop that has been tailored to the needs of a particular employer or industry group (by changing the scheduling, location, contents, or instructional approach). In customized training services, the client is the business or industry group who requests the training services on behalf of its employees (Powers et al., 1988). Customized training services range from merely holding off-the-rack courses in a company location for company employees to a purely customized, company-owned instructional program developed and delivered by the educational institution for a specific employer. For example, many universities, such as Northwestern University, offer their M.B.A. programs at company sites and tailor these programs to company needs. Workplace literacy programs in which employees are taught reading, math, and ESL skills tailored to company requirements and applications are another example of customized training services.

Companies have become very experienced in working with postsecondary educational institutions to customize their training programs and courses. General Motors established the Automotive Service Educational Program (ASEP) in the early 1980s to train automotive service technicians in cooperation with community colleges throughout the country (Castner-Lotto & Associates, 1988). General Motors worked with community colleges to update and customize their automotive service programs and courses, train college faculty, and coordinate these programs with in-house training provided by General Motors dealers and training centers. Intensive course work at the colleges was followed by in-house training in dealerships. ASEP graduates received college credits, certificates, and degrees as well as General Motors certification. Hewlett-Packard has established similar programs with community colleges for retraining employees to become computer operators, telemarketing operators, customer service representatives, and administrative assistants (Castner-Lotto & Associates, 1988). General Tire used Kent State University to provide customized language training to executives and managers directly involved in their international business ventures (Carnevale et al., 1988). The costs of these customized programs are usually based on standard tuition and fees plus additional customization costs (Powers et al., 1988). However, these costs can be offset by state grant and tuition subsidy programs operated by state agencies or educational institutions.

Many postsecondary educational institutions offer customized training services as part of a larger package of organizational development services. These services assist employers in implementing new management strategies and organizational systems as well as new production systems and technologies. For example, many institutions now assist employers in implementing very specific organizational systems or technologies, e.g., statistical process control (SPC) or preventive maintenance programs. They also assist employers in implementing broader organizational changes and management strategies including Total Quality Management (TQM) or implementing new organizational systems and training programs for ISO 9000 certification. Educational institutions can provide companies with consultants and training programs similar to other public and private vendors. These types of partnerships also can be financed by state customized training grant programs (Creticos, Duscha, and Sheets, 1990).

Some examples include the following: Ace Clearwater Enterprises, a small aerospace supplier in California, contracted with El Camino College to conduct TQM, SPC, and team-building training at its facilities. This training arrangement was established through the California Supplier Improvement Program (CalSIP) and was financed through California's Employment Training Panel, a state grant program (Employment Training Panel, 1994). The American Telephone and Telegraph Company (AT&T)

contracted with Longview Community College to work with in-house training staff in developing training programs to implement its new Business Resource Planning System and its Facility Management System. The college developed original training manuals and instructional materials and provided most of the direct training services through grants from the Missouri Customized Training Program (Creticos and Sheets, 1992). Northern Illinois University's Business and Industry Services assists hundreds of companies in implementing TQM and ISO 9000. This university unit also provides comprehensive employee assessments and training services including technical and literacy training. These business and training services are supported in part through state customized training grants from Illinois' Prairie State 2000 Authority and the Industrial Training Program.

20.3.2 Training Resources for Customized Training

Postsecondary educational institutions offer all the services that a private training company offers. In contracting for training services with postsecondary educational institutions, companies have the option of contracting for specific training resources that can be used with in-house training programs or training services from other public and private vendors. These resources include the following:

- Job Analysis and Training Needs Assessment
- Curriculum and Training Material Development
- Instructional Facilities and Equipment
- Instructor Training and Certification
- Personal Assessment and Counseling Services
- Organizational Development Services
- Training Research and Evaluation

Job Analysis and Training Needs Assessment.   Employers can contract with educational institutions to conduct formal training needs assessments based on job analyses or other types of needs assessment. Educational institutions can act as credible third-party vendors in identifying objective training needs based on input from both supervisors and workers.

Curriculum and Training Material Development.   Employers can contract with educational institutions to develop customized or proprietary training curricula for their in-house training programs. Most educational institutions are capable of producing curricula and related training materials for a wide variety of training approaches and multimedia applications including training books, visual aides, computer-based programs, and interactive video programs.

Instructional Facilities and Equipment. Employers also can contract with educational institutions to provide classrooms, laboratories, libraries, computers, and audiovisual equipment for company training programs that are conducted on campuses or at off-campus locations. For example, in addition to operation of the ASEP program, General Motors also contracts with community colleges for use of their facilities to conduct company training programs for dealers located far away from existing training centers. Some community colleges and universities have invested heavily in state-of-the-art corporate training facilities with advanced satellite and communications capabilities for the delivery of national and international programs and conferences. Some facilities contain college dormitories or full-service hotels for residential training programs.

Instructor Training and Certification. Many postsecondary educational institutions offer "train-the-trainer" programs for businesses and industry groups to provide industry trainers with instruction in training needs assessment, instructional design, instructional methods, instructional technologies, assessment, and testing. These programs may involve a broader introduction to training and development and lead to some type of certificate or degree.

Personal Assessment and Counseling Services. Postsecondary educational institutions can provide assessment and counseling services that range from basic skills assessment to broader aptitude assessment, interest assessment, and career counseling. Some companies have found that it is useful to have third-party organizations conduct confidential assessments of their workers and provide the companies with aggregate test scores and recommendations for establishing workplace literacy programs. Some companies contract with educational institutions to provide career counseling and outplacement assistance for workers affected by downsizing or facility closings. Educational institutions also can provide assessment and testing services for awarding college credit for prior learning in the workplace and for advanced placement in degree programs.

Organizational Development Services. Postsecondary educational institutions also provide organizational development consulting services that can be offered independently of training services. As mentioned earlier, many educational providers offer organizational development services in Total Quality Management, ISO 9000, statistical process control, material resource planning systems, and other management approaches or organizational systems.

Training Research and Evaluation. Many postsecondary educational institutions provide research and evaluation services. Employers and industry groups can initiate a partnership agreement to conduct research and development on a new training approach or program, or they can contract with educational institutions to conduct evaluations based on worker reactions, academic and occupational competencies, or work unit and business performance indicators.

20.4 Contracting for Customized Training Services and Resources

The most common business-education arrangements involve noncustomized training programs and courses in which businesses enroll their employees in standard training courses and programs. These types of arrangements are managed through the normal registration process. Program costs are based on standard tuition and fees and require no formal business-education partnership or any type of training contract.

Customized training services are usually provided to a specific employer or industry group based on a formal training agreement or contract. Companies and industry groups have entered into contracts with educational institutions to provide a wide range of customized training services and resources. The College Board and the American Council on Education found that by the early 1980s, companies and industry groups had entered into contractual agreements with almost every type of postsecondary educational institution ranging from Harvard University to small liberal arts colleges, to rural community colleges and to technical colleges. However, educational institutions still vary tremendously in their responsiveness and their capacity to deliver customized training services to different types of businesses and industry groups.

Because of the wide range of potential training arrangements and training providers, companies and industry groups should develop training arrangements with educational institutions based on a comprehensive training strategy or plan and a systematic review of potential training providers. Most customized training arrangements should be based on a formal contract or agreement that spells out the services and responsibilities of both parties.

20.4.1 Training Arrangements and Business-Education Partnerships

Companies and industry groups can develop a broad range of training strategies and arrangements based on their own training needs, their in-house capabilities, and their decisions on whether to "make or buy" training services (Carnevale et al., 1990b). These may require training arrangements with educational institutions that range from comprehensive long-term training partnerships to limited contracts for specific training resources such as the use of a training facility.

Companies and industry groups with limited training experience or limited internal expertise, but large training and education needs, may wish to develop one or more business-education partnerships in which educational institutions provide comprehensive sets of training services, including customized degree and certificate programs for employee career and educational development and customized training needs analyses and training plans. These institutions may also have the ability to customize training services. This could include responsibility for identifying and contracting with other training providers for services. In this role, the educational institutions would serve as the major planners, providers, and brokers of external training services. These training partnerships may be one component of even broader partnerships that involve joint research and development, internship programs, and faculty (or staff) sharing arrangements.

At the other extreme, companies and industry groups with substantial training experience and capabilities and companies deciding to build their own internal training units may find it more cost-effective to contract out for certain training programs or services under a competitive contracting system in which educational institutions as well as other training vendors can compete for short-term company contracts.

20.4.2 Small Employers and Training Consortia

Small companies face major problems in establishing customized training arrangements with educational institutions because they usually do not have the internal staff capacity to identify potential providers and do not have a sufficient number of employees to make customized training programs affordable. Options for small businesses include:

- Consortia with other similar businesses
- Limited partnerships for specific programs
- Training spaces made available by large companies on fee basis

- Industry/professional association training programs and courses
- Supplier training programs by large companies
- Postsecondary institution's programs for small employers

However, small companies can attain the buying power of large companies by partnering with other small companies in training consortia managed by large corporations, industry or trade associations, or educational institutions. Many state funding programs are now encouraging the formation of these interfirm training networks through "wholesaling" organizations, such as industrial, trade, and professional associations. For example, Illinois' Tooling and Manufacturing Association provides training courses for its small business members through grants from the Prairie State 2000 Authority. Many large employers, such as Caterpillar and Motorola, are working with state programs to provide training to their suppliers. Some educational institutions manage, or work with, manufacturing technology centers that link small employers in cooperative training arrangements. Small companies should explore these types of consortia available through state economic development and education agencies for developing training arrangements with educational institutions.

20.4.3 Requests and Contracts for Training Services and Resources

As previously discussed, customized training arrangements with postsecondary educational institutions, whether they be long-term training partnerships or simply the utilization of training facilities, are best developed and managed through the use of written requests for proposals (RPFs) or bids, as well as training contracts or agreements. These requests and contracts should be similar to those used by companies with any other training vendor.

Because of the growing number of postsecondary educational institutions providing customized training services and the importance of finding the most qualified provider, most companies and industry groups, especially those located in major metropolitan areas, should explore a number of educational providers and partnerships before negotiating a final training agreement.

Contacting Potential Educational Providers. Companies should begin their process of developing training arrangements by compiling a list of potential training providers and by conducting informational interviews with key staff from each provider to fully understand the nature and scope of services that educational institutions provide. Who companies should contact first at postsecondary institutions depends on the particular educational institution and the type of training arrangement that the company wants. Some postsecondary educational institutions have centralized offices that manage customized training services. These offices are usually located in continuing education colleges or corporate services offices. Other institutions have very decentralized operations, with customized services depending on the type of service originating out of a variety of offices and units. For example, departments called Manufacturing Technology, Automotive Technology, or Computer Science may operate their own contract training services. For comprehensive partnerships, companies should first contact the corporate affairs office, the president's office, or the dean of the college of continuing education. For specific training resources or services, the company should contact the college of continuing education, a business and industry services office, or the most appropriate college or department (such as the business or engineering college or industrial technology department). Companies should recognize that they may have to work with more than one unit at a particular educational institution to get the full range of training services they want.

Developing Training Requests and Contracts. After identifying potential providers, companies should develop some type of written request for proposal that details the nature and scope of the training services desired. This request could range from a short letter of inquiry to a detailed and formal Request for Proposal (RFP) depending on the type of training arrangement that is being sought. For very small and simple training projects or for very generic training programs, such as basic electronics or spreadsheet applications, a verbal request for a brief proposal or memo from the provider will probably get the process going. The training arrangement could then be finalized through a short reply letter or memo from the company.

Because of the cost and time required, the formal RFP should only be used in developing large, long-term training arrangements that are critical to the company's long-term business and training strategy (Carnevale, 1990b). The RFP should provide information on the purpose and scope of the training program, should include the number of trainees and their qualifications, and should document the major training requirements, the underlying training philosophy, and any special considerations that must be met by potential training providers. The RFP should request information on the background and capacity of educational institutions including the qualifications of key staff and the specific training services and resources that will be provided. It should also request price information with some type of cost explanation. Finally, it should request references from other businesses that have received services from the unit or training staff.

The most difficult task in crafting a formal RFP is to determine the information needed to judge the quality of the service and the degree to which the educational institution is willing to customize the standard courses and to meet the company's training needs. Although the total cost of the service is important, it is critical that companies first fully understand quality and customization differences among the proposals they receive before they consider differences in price (so they do "compare apples and oranges").

After selecting the most appropriate training provider, the company or industry group should then enter into a formal training contract or agreement. Based on examples provided by Powers et al. and the College Board, a typical training contract for a training program delivered by an educational institution minimally addresses the following questions.

Students. How many students will be enrolled and what qualifications will be required to enter training? How will the students be selected and enrolled?

Training Content and Scope. What are the major instructional units or modules involved in the training program?

What are the training objectives of these modules?

How many instructional or contact hours will be involved in each module and the total training program?

Training Schedule and Locations. What is the total duration of the training program?

How often and during what times of the day will training occur for each course or instructional unit?

At what sites and locations will the instruction take place?

Training Methods. What training methods and approaches will be used in the training program?

What will be the mixture of classroom instruction, group discussion, simulation, computer-based instruction, and on-the-job application?

Instructors. Who will teach the courses in the training program?

What qualifications will these instructors have?

Who will select these instructors?

Provider Services and Resources. What other training services and resources will be provided by the educational institution?

Will any of the following be needed: assessment, enrollment, library services, curriculum development, testing, and/or special tutoring services?

Company Services and Resources. What training services and resources will be provided by the company?

Who is responsible for facilities, equipment, and instructional materials?

Credentials and Credit Transfer. What types of credentials will students receive upon successful completion of the training program?

What types of credits will students earn toward related degree and certificate programs?

Contract Costs and Payment Schedule.   What are the total and per-unit costs for the training program and how is it to be paid.

Will a payment schedule be used?

Contract Evaluation and Performance.   How will the training program be evaluated?

What results or milestones must be achieved to receive full payment for training services?

What are the consequences for failure to meet the performance requirements of the training agreement?

Contractual agreements should be very simple agreements wherever possible. Contractual agreements for the delivery of standard credit courses in companies or the utilization of specific training resources such as training facilities can be very simple one-page memos or contracts specifying the specific resource and the total costs. However, in some cases, these agreements must be more complex and formal because of the amount of resources involved and the number of partners or vendors involved in a training program.

As mentioned earlier, the costs of noncustomized training programs and courses are usually based on standard tuition costs plus any additional training services provided to the company. The costs of customized training services are usually based on tuition costs but can vary tremendously based on the degree of customization. In negotiating the costs of customized training programs, companies should always explore all of the possible state grant programs that postsecondary educational institutions or companies can leverage in establishing training arrangements. Companies should contact state economic development and education agencies to get information on customized training grants and funding for credit and noncredit courses and programs.

20.5   The Future for Business-Education Partnerships in Technical Training

The changing role of postsecondary educational institutions in technical training, the growing involvement of companies and industry groups in training all types of employees, changing government funding priorities, and innovations in instructional approaches and technologies will provide new opportunities for business-education partnerships.

Most existing business-education partnerships consist of regularly scheduled group classes that are only loosely joined to in-house training programs, including on-the-job training. Innovations in training design and delivery and the promise of new instructional technology, such as computer-based instruction and interactive video, will allow companies and educational institutions to fully customize and integrate education and training programs and make them fully responsive to worker needs. They will allow even small companies to develop formal training programs and courses that are fully integrated into on-the-job training at the work site and can be delivered to one worker or a group of workers when they need training.

Federal and state tax policies and grant programs probably will encourage companies to invest in formal training systems and will encourage postsecondary educational institutions to help companies build these internal training systems through business-education partnerships and contractual services. Federal and state policies also will likely continue to encourage postsecondary educational institutions to establish stronger work-based learning components into their certificate and degree programs. These work-based learning components will include some type of apprenticeship, internship, or cooperative education arrangement with companies and industry groups. As now proposed in pending federal and state school-to-work legislation, both secondary and postsecondary educational institutions will be required to establish partnerships with companies to provide students with formal training and work experience as a required component of all professional and technical certificates and degree programs.

One future area for business-education partnerships is workplace literacy. Most workplace literacy programs in postsecondary educational institutions have traditionally focused on oral and written communication, English as a second language, and basic math. However, the concept of workplace literacy has changed dramatically over the last ten years to include a wide variety of skills, including problem solving and teamwork skills. This expanded concept of workplace literacy is most clearly seen in new basic skills defined by the U.S. Department of Labor's Secretary's Commission on Necessary Skills (SCANS) and the related Workplace Basics defined by the American Society of Training and Development (Carnevale et al., 1990a). Companies and postsecondary educational institutions will find it mutually beneficial to develop new partnerships to explore how to educate and train workers in these new basic skills and incorporate this training into postsecondary certificate and degree programs and company training systems.

As postsecondary educational institutions expand their organizational development and training services, they will likely become more valuable resources to companies in using training to implement company strategies and organizational and technological systems and improve performance of particular facilities or work units. Future federal and state policies will continue to encourage universities and colleges to offer special programs and services to improve the competitiveness of companies through workplace modernization and training.

Given these recent developments, the future for business-education partnerships in technical training appears very bright. These business-education partnerships will provide clear benefits to both companies and educational institutions, and will contribute to federal and state policies in both economic development and education, as well as workforce preparation.

Bibliography

American Council on Education, *Guide to Campus-Business Linkage Programs: Education and Business Prospering Together,* Macmillan Publishing Company, New York, 1986.

Bragg, Debra D., and James Jacobs, "Establishing an Operational Definition for Customized Training," *Community College Review* **21**:1(15–25) (1993).

Carnevale, Anthony P., Leila J. Gainer, and Janice Villet, *Training in America: The Organization and Strategic Role of Training,* Jossey-Bass, San Francisco, 1990a.

Carnevale, Anthony P., Leila J. Gainer, Janice Villet, and Shari L. Holland, *Training Partnerships: Linking Employers and Providers,* The American Society of Training and Development and the U.S. Department of Labor, Employment and Training Administration, 1990b.

Castner-Lotto, Jill, and Associates, *Successful Training Strategies: Twenty-Six Innovative Corporate Models,* San Francisco, Jossey-Bass, 1988.

College Board, *Training By Contract: College-Employer Profiles,* College Entrance Examinations Board, New York, 1983.

Creticos, Peter, and Robert Sheets, *Evaluating State-Financed, Workplace-based Retraining Programs: Case Studies of Retraining Projects,* Joint Study of the National Commission for Employment Policy and the National Governors' Association, Washington, D.C., 1992.

Creticos, Peter, Steven Duscha, and Robert Sheets, *State-Financed, Customized Training Programs: A Comparative State Survey,* Report Submitted to the Office of Technology Assessment, United States Congress, Washington, D.C., 1990.

Employment Training Panel, *Annual Report,* 1992–1993, Employment Training Panel, Sacramento, Calif., 1994.

Northeast-Midwest Institute, *Education Incorporated: School-Business Cooperation for Economic Growth,* Quorum Books, New York, 1988.

Powers, David R., Mary F. Powers, Frederick Betz, and Carol B. Aslanian, *Higher Education in Partnership with Industry: Opportunities and Strategies for Training, Research and Economic Development,* Jossey-Bass, San Francisco, 1988.

U.S. Department of Labor, *Work-based Learning: Training America's Workers,* U.S. Department of Labor, Employment and Training Administration, Washington, D.C., 1989.

21

Technical and Skills Training Suppliers

Tom Doyle
Ford Motor Company

Anne Mansfield
MascoTech Training & Visual Services

Darlene Van Tiem
Ameritech Publishing

21.1 Overview

Training is assuming a key role in today's technology-based business environment. Training is emerging from a last-to-be called to a first-to-be-called position. If the training department has produced good results recently, it is probably in the catbird seat. Budgets are more committed, less likely to be cut, and they are based on more objective data such as the Malcolm Baldrige or American Society for Training and Development benchmarks. Course attendance is greater. Employees are more involved in their own individual plans.

Companies are changing rapidly, and there is no slowing of the pace. Upper management may be able to envision and strategize, to merge and acquire, to engineer and finance. However, they can't get employees to adapt and acquire new skills by relying on the old techniques of on-the-job experience and reading manuals. Today's training covers interpersonal change management and the technical skills needed to keep pace.

Training departments conduct day-to-day activities through partnerships. Typically, manufacturing operations, computer, or quality departments come to the training department with new initiatives or new skill needs driven by customer requirements or anticipated market direction. The training department becomes the internal consultant, expert in knowing how to provide employees with the capabilities to operate or maintain the new equipment or assemble the new product line.

Another partnership is created between the internal training department and the external training supplier. Two training organizations work together as partners to accomplish a single goal. Partnering means that the supplier manages the project to ultimately improve the product or service of the client organization. Partnering also means that the client's training department manages the internal interfaces to support the supplier in making a fair profit.

Flexibility and responsibility are crucial to the relationship between a training supplier and a client. Internal training departments and suppliers must hone their political skills and maintain their networks so that work is accomplished effectively and sound decisions can be made quickly. Suppliers must complete projects on or before a designated date, and the client must secure approvals on proposed materials within a reasonable time.

21.2 Establishing Client Requirements

Most industrial and technology-related organizations require comprehensive technical training using a full-service approach to help define the need, scope out the situation, recommend solutions, and provide training documentation and other resources necessary to prepare employees to work with the new technology. General Motors Corporation (1993) states that "the full impact of any technology cannot be realized without integration of effective employee performance. GM is committed to improving and maintaining the technical skills and knowledge base of its workforce."

21.2.1 Early Involvement

Technical training that meets or exceeds expectations depends on adequate, accurate needs analysis; curriculum and course development that incorporates the right content into sound adult learning formats, and training delivery by someone proficient in the subject matter and in instructional techniques and learning theory. Because training development is a phased process, it is best to identify the supplier (consultant or vendor) as early as possible. The supplier should become a partner committed to the goals, approach, and time frames.

Early involvement offers suppliers an opportunity to leverage their strengths to maximize project outcomes. If suppliers are brought in at the prebid stage for discussions, they can influence the project direction based on their experience working with other clients and on the expertise and skills of their staff.

Early involvement also prevents or minimizes the need for transitions between phases. Often, one firm or individual will serve as project manager, coordinating the entire external effort and maintaining a "big picture" perspective. It is not necessary to have the supplier assigned to work on all the phases, but the supplier should agree to the work allocation plan and be kept abreast of developments. This arrangement need not cost more than a more "parceled" approach. In fact, minimizing transitions can result in lower final costs and more comprehensive outcomes.

External resources should be used for projects or assignments that the training department cannot do because they lack the skill, expertise, or the time. In today's lean organizations, training departments seldom retain skills that are needed only occasionally. In addition, training is usually responsible for routine or fundamental tasks.

One of the most critical roles of a technical training supplier is asking questions. Good questions help focus on the right business needs (Rance, 1993). Outsiders bring experiences in other work environments and an unbiased frame of reference. Organizations rely on consultants to add perspective and increase options. Consultants offer objectivity and an opportunity to break away from the mold (Girod, 1993).

21.2.2 Needs Definition

The foundation of reliable needs analysis is asking the right questions. Sharp suppliers understand the client's business sufficiently to ask perceptive questions that lead to defining root cause issues and symptoms and result in relevant training. Even minimum needs analysis requires careful planning to gather the most appropriate documents and ask the right survey questions. *Validation studies will involve the meeting with a representative group of managers and potential learners to ensure that needs are defined accurately, and that the proposed learning approach would be welcomed and beneficial.*

Sometimes, the client will have defined needs or conducted a front-end analysis before engaging a supplier. *Provision should be made, however, to allow the supplier to validate the needs analysis before embarking on the project.* In fact, if the supplier cannot validate the work of another training supplier or the internal training department, many consultants or vendors may decide not to bid on the work. The opportunity to validate is essential. *Needs definition is a formal first step,* but continues for the duration of the project. Good suppliers will make suggestions as the work progresses (Johnson, 1993). They can be viewed as "external eyes" that notice situations taken for granted by internal staff. A primary value of external suppliers is their new ideas. In fact, if they don't constantly adapt and bring in new ideas, they soon leave. Vendors also learn from the client organization. It is a two-way street (Amstadt, 1993).

As projects develop, it often becomes apparent that changes are necessary in the deliverables or project scope. For example, more departments will be involved or participants will have lower prerequisite skills than anticipated. Minor alterations should be expected as a normal advantage of custom work. Negotiations in order to accommodate these changes require trust, respect, and commitment to the mutual benefit of both organizations. The key is that *changes are to be expected and not avoided.* All too often, both sides become defensive and believe that all project specifications should be anticipated before start of work. This is not realistic or desirable. Project progress uncovers situations and circumstances that were not apparent before the effort began (Gohl, 1993).

21.2.3   Cost Targets

Cost targets are important for quality proposals and establishing trust, and necessary for reliable internal training budgets (Fry, 1993). They set parameters and define scope, enabling the supplier to focus on maximizing dollar value. For example, real estate agents always determine price ranges before showing prospective homeowners around neighborhoods. Car salespersons determine whether customers are looking for a luxury or economy model to save buyers' time. Features vary with available resources. Likewise, *if clients establish budgets, technical training suppliers will provide options that are within budget.* They may also suggest alternatives outside the cost parameters that could provide benefits that outweigh costs.

Many organizations are reluctant to give suppliers cost targets. This policy can be shortsighted, however. If the potential suppliers know what pricing ballpark they are in, they can do a better job of proposing a cost-effective solution. Some suppliers will respond with a menu of options, giving a price for a basic program and prices for options that the buyer can accept or reject.

Cost targets are best established by researching journal and magazine articles on costs and through benchmarking with other professionals (Brandenburg, 1993). Look for traditional *rules of thumb.* Records of past projects can provide reliable comparisons between cost of successful and less adequate training approaches.

21.2.4 Supplier's Relationship with Client

The key factor is the need for a partnership relationship between the client company and supplier organization to maximize the project, whether small or large. To reach the necessary level of teamwork, *the cultures of the supplier and the internal training department should match* (Amstadt, 1993). Relationship building requires time and communications to establish trust and an understanding and respect for each other's organization (Miller, 1993). The goal is a long-term relationship (Carpenter, 1993).

The presence of a technical training supplier does not mean that the internal client has no responsibilities (Britten, 1993). Work should be divided. It is not unlikely that the relationship would be approximately a 60 percent to 40 percent ratio. Typically, the consulting firm does 60 percent of the work; the client still does about 40 percent of the project.

21.2.5 Make versus Buy

The skills and capacity of the internal training department will ultimately drive the make-versus-buy decision. Corporate cost cutting has resulted in training departments staffed for routine courses such as statistical process control, instrumentation, and control or special projects such as plant launches. Training of a limited nature such as spread sheet, database, and word processing software applications or substation maintenance is usually assigned to a supplier with appropriate expertise and market reputation.

Cost comparisons are difficult but often necessary. Most internal training departments don't understand true departmental costs unless they have previously been external consultants with experience in cost analysis for proposals. This lack of understanding leads to a tendency to underestimate the time and costs incurred for internal development and delivery. *Cost comparisons, inside versus outside, should include total compensation of all associated employees plus building, equipment, and supplies.* Suppliers' prices reflect these factors; so should internal cost figures.

Training departments are seldom capable of handling all requests. It then becomes necessary to determine which projects will be completed inside and which will be bid out. Estimated usage, training development cycle time, and stability of the technology will influence decisions. As a rule of thumb, however, if the client organization has the capability and resources, the project should be done inside.

Availability of suitable suppliers and predeveloped training will help sort training requests into *make* or *buy* categories. Efficiency, content accuracy, and effectiveness are important drivers in make-versus-buy decisions (Rance, 1993). Other factors include previous experience and references, willingness to cooperate, flexibility, focus on client expectations, and fit between supplier niche and expertise and project requirements.

21.3 Types of Suppliers

Technical training is often associated with equipment and capital expenditures. Generic training, such as leadership, listening, or writing, is usually the responsibility of human resources departments. Technical training, on the other hand, is frequently contracted through purchasing departments, based on requests from operations, quality, engineering, or human resources. Because technical training suppliers are integral to technology implementation, their success is measured by the success of the entire project or initiative. Their activities may be closely linked through the bid process to an overall equipment bid. Their timetables and relationships are then part of the bigger project. As a result, there is a dependency and a trust that each external supplier and internal client interfacing on the project are working in good faith. Terminology used to define technical training supplier roles is, thus, a cross between human resources and equipment supplier concepts.

Generally, technical training suppliers fall into two categories, *vendors* and *consultants*. Considerable sensitivity exists concerning the terms vendor *and consultant*. Many client companies automatically refer to all external suppliers as vendors. Because technical training is normally associated with the formal bid process through purchasing, the client organization often will automatically refer to training suppliers as vendors. For some technical training suppliers who offer advice and provide custom instructional design, development, and delivery, the designation "vendor" is abrasive and represents already prepared solutions such as "off-the-shelf" or packaged products or some kind of hardware.

21.3.1 Vendors

For our purposes here, we have defined vendors as firms or individuals with standardized technical products or services such as seminars, packaged courses, job aids, simulations, videos, or computer-based training. Vendors of packaged or off-the-shelf products work primarily with clients needing their specific product or a variation of their product.

Purchase of the products or services is usually negotiated with a sales representative. Alterations or supplements to the training materials are scoped and priced through sales representatives rather than instructional designer-developers.

21.3.2 Consultants

·We define consultants as any organization or individual who analyzes technical performance-related situations and offers training advice, course or curriculum development, or delivery. Consultants focus on problems and opportunities and have a number of options available.

Consultant is also the preferred term used to describe a person or an organization relied upon to assume full responsibility for preparing employees relative to a project or topic. This activity will include up-front discussions, managing the entire project, conducting a needs analysis or validating a previous effort, and creating and conducting the required training. Technical training projects often incorporate a mix of media, such as graphic art, including engineering drawings and electrical diagrams, video or audio production, and computer-based instruction.

21.4 Role of the Vendor

The line is blurring between consultants and suppliers of packaged, off-the-shelf seminars and materials. Many suppliers of packaged programs will tailor or customize their materials to the specific needs of the client.

Vendors usually have a standard methodology based on experience and company philosophy. As a result, it is best to shop around by discussing alteration needs with the original vendor and other vendors with good reputations, and also to research internal capabilities. Many vendors have standard approaches to needs analysis (such as the Harless approach), formats for project management, style sheets for manual pages, or three-dimensional demonstration models, such as small-scale robots.

Vendors offer convenience and the assurance that "what you see is what you get." The concrete nature of the decision reduces risk. However, every work situation is unique and there is no "normal" environment. As a result, packaged solutions seldom provide a perfect fit with the client needs. Two common methods to address this discrepancy are tailoring and customizing.

21.4.1 Tailoring

Packaged training is most often used as published. However, because it is generic and standard, it usually does not meet the specific requirements of the workplace. Training that does not fit the work situation can be difficult to apply.

The simplest and least expensive solution is to create handouts, supplementary manuals, job aids, or problem situations extracted from real situations at existing job sites. This approach uses as-published versions of materials and supplements created by the original vendor, another supplier, or the internal training department.

Where training budgets are minimal, a tailored training package may be the best answer to a training need. For example, off-the-shelf tutorials can be purchased from local computer supply stores and supplemented with separate workbooks developed specifically for engineers. Another situation in which tailoring would be valuable is in integrating a purchased videotape into a training program so that the relevancy of the videotape is readily apparent. A generic troubleshooting strategies videotape can be incorporated into courses on hydraulics, pneumatics, or electrical maintenance fundamentals.

21.4.2 Customizing

A more expensive and cohesive approach is to incorporate the alterations into the actual packaged products. That is, through desktop publishing or media editing, current procedures and photos of actual equipment from the client's work site are added. For example, substation maintenance or heating, ventilation, and air-conditioning (HVAC) can include pictures of the actual equipment and systems, or Failure Mode Effect Analysis (FMEA) can include the actual company forms instead of hypothetical or generic worksheets. Computer-based training can include actual specifications and calculations rather than hypothetical situations for engineering training on hazardous materials transportation, simultaneous engineering modeling, or volatile organic chemical (VOC) emissions reduction.

Client organizations should request and purchase rights (if required) for ongoing alterations because technical training is job-specific and constantly changing. This situation creates a continuing need to alter off-the-shelf material. This need is recognized in the trade, and most vendors should be willing to work out an arrangement with the client. Because customizing and tailoring are seemingly easy, it is often convenient to let the vendor work independently and not establish a close interface and several approval steps (Fry, 1993). The design and development may be simplified but the need to be absolutely on target is just as critical. Underestimating importance usually leads to misunderstandings. It is critical that a design document be written that explains the approach, need for subject matter experts, and milestone and approval points. Project management and partnership are necessary.

21.5 Role of the Consultant

Most technical training consultants offer a full range of services. Either the supplier has a large cadre of generalists, specialists, and experts ready to work on any project or they have a core staff, primarily of project managers plus other critical skill areas, and a cadre of adjunct or contract employees. One configuration is not better or more effective than the other. The key is that consultants should not try to be all things to all people. *It is advantageous for technical training suppliers to have a niche* (Elliott, 1993). For example, one consulting firm may have sufficient depth of expertise to work across a variety of technical skill areas, such as ergonomics, quality, safety, and maintenance. Then, the supplier usually limits its client base to areas such as health care, or finance, or industry, or manufacturing. Another consultant may specialize in quality but have a client base that includes perhaps airlines, manufacturing, and power companies. In other words, technical training consultants usually have either specializations or market niches (Short, 1993). (See Table 21-1.)

Technical training consultants offer a variety of skill sets. It is important to match consultant skill sets to project needs. The levels of technical skills can be defined as *expert, specialist,* and *generalist* (Kooistra, 1993). Experts tend to have a narrow skill set because they have focused their energy and attention into becoming extremely knowledgeable in one area. They may offer valuable advice on complex, troubling issues. Generalists have fundamental skills in many areas and tend to see the "big picture," and they also tend to be valuable in cross-functional or multiphase projects, such as a plant launch. Specialists frequently have greater strength in one area but are usually able also to offer support in a number of skill areas at the generalist level. Any one technical project may need a variety of skill levels.

It is not unusual for generalists and specialists to be the best instructors. They have a broad enough background to be able to communicate with many people. They also have sufficient knowledge to convey the content competently. Typically, generalists provide overview and basic-level instruction. Specialists offer advanced levels of subject matter. In addition to consulting on vexing problems, experts can provide enriching learning experiences. However, because the experts' capabilities are so focused, it is often necessary to have a facilitator organize and manage the class session. Some complex, technical projects, such as expert systems development, require that all project members, including instructional designers, have, as a minimum, a generalist technical skill level (Ruyle, 1993).

Table 21-1. Technical Training Niche Classification

	Tools	Specialization	Market
Internal or adjunct	Electronics support Documentation Simulations Training design	Ergonomics Quality Fabrication Maintenance	Health care Finance Manufacturing Industrial

Maintaining an extensive internal cadre of specialist, generalists, and experts can be costly for a full-service organization. Generalists tend to be flexible and assigned to many projects. This results in little indirect labor, (nonbillable hours) and high contribution to revenue. Experts are very useful on appropriate projects but have few skills to offer on projects out of their narrower area of expertise. This limitation leads to more indirect labor costs. Consequently, experts tend to "bill out" at a higher rate to match their extra level of significance and to alleviate their indirect labor differential. *Organizations usually maintain, on a full-time basis, generalists and specialists who can be placed on a high percentage of projects and can be billed out at least 75 percent of their work time.* Full-service organizations also maintain a small cadre of experts in their niche areas. These people add depth and credibility and set direction. They are on direct labor, however, bringing in revenue only when appropriate. The matrix in Figure 21-1 illustrates hypothetical skills of a technical training consulting organization specializing in manufacturing and industry.

21.6 Choosing the *Right* Vendor and Package

In the process for selecting packaged training programs, some form of needs analysis is required; potential vendors and products must be identified; proposals must be requested and evaluated; and contracts must be awarded.

21.6.1 Identifying Potential Sources

Referrals and your own experience are the most reliable resources for creating a bid list. Professional associations such ASTD and NSPI have local chapter meetings, conferences, expositions, and seminars that provide vendors and client opportunities to meet. Both organizations also publish directories and magazines with vendor advertisements.

Some vendors offer half-day orientations in major cities that allow clients and potential clients an opportunity to learn about existing and new packaged train-

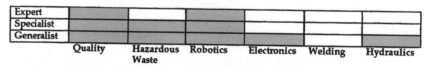

Figure 21-1. Hypothetical skills sets of a technical training consulting organization.

ing offerings and discuss successful applications of the training package. These minisessions are the most realistic and reliable way to introduce potential clients to the features and benefits of any vendor's approach.

Prepacked training also includes public or open-enrollment seminars. Many excellent courses are offered at hotels or dedicated training sites. Companies with well-developed internal curricula are now offering the courses, on a profit-making basis, to recoup costs and fund future course development or equipment purchases. Identifying seminars and determining the right one can be frustrating if internal trainers rely on catalogs and brochures. Seminar services, particularly 1st Seminar Service, maintain an extensive database of current schedules and offer cost comparisons and evaluation data from past participants.

21.6.2 Instructional Design Considerations

When purchasing packaged materials supported by customizing or tailoring services, it is easy to underestimate the complexity of the project. Although customizing or tailoring tends to minimize the extent of the effort involved, it does not decrease the number or importance of the steps in the instructional design process. In other words, since a proven training program based on extensive instructional design already exists, it is not necessary to conduct a comprehensive needs analysis or create a detailed design document. On the other hand, it is necessary to conduct a validation study to ensure that the client needs are similar to the objectives of the packaged program. A brief design document, in the form of an executive summary, should verify the approach and confirm customizing or tailoring requirements. Approval decision by the client at this point creates clearer specifications and expectations.

The chart in Figure 21-2 offers some criteria by which the packaged program and material can be judged for suitability. It also can be used to determine if any tailoring is required and, if so, what should be addressed.

21.6.3 The Bid Process

When using packaged training programs, the client should develop clear needs statements or objectives before initiating contact with vendors. Client groups affected by the training should agree as to the needs, objectives, and target audience. Selection of the vendor should follow a planned series of activities. However, the process may be formal and written or informal and oral.

The two-stage bid process seems fair and leads to better communications and smoother project progress. The process begins with capability

Insert check mark in applicable column. Total check marks for rating.
1. Not applicable
2. Inadequate
3. Total

	1	2	3
Instructor's Guide			
Content outline present			
Outcomes of instruction clearly stated			
Preparation for course delivery explained and directed			
All handouts and references identified			
Content indexed and clearly segmented for ease of use			
Time indicators for each major segment stated			
Exercises and lessons explained and proceduralized			
Detailed presentation of content and objectives given			
Participant's Guide			
Content of participant guide matched by instruction			
Clear directions for all activities given			
Content formatted for ease of use			
Applicable for use on the job			
Instructional strategy consistent throughout			
Adjunct Materials			
Appropriate for a parallel with instructional content			
Visually appealing and error free			
Graphic and illustration formats consistent			
Media			
Instructional design strategy supported			
Information accurate and consistent			
Information current			
Intended audience targeted			
Unified composition evident			
Easily readable and appropriate			
Variety of media used			
Total			

Figure 21-2. Vendor package selection criteria.

discussions focusing on the available products. Talks focus on vendor's niche, recent projects, availability, and process for customizing or tailoring. Potential vendors should be narrowed to two or three. A formal bid should be requested with sufficient detail to understand and agree upon training specifics.

Vendors realize that communications and relationships are strengthened and the project begins on a better footing if decisions are based on project definitions. Although proposals for packaged products and services are less detailed than consulting projects, vendors still cannot afford to waste time drafting proposals when the chance of winning is low. Narrowing the bid list gives each vendor approximately a 50 or 33 percent chance of winning. This approach is fair for both sides because there can be sufficient detail to arrive at a mutually satisfactory agreement.

21.6.4 Selecting the Vendor and Program

Several factors should be considered in selecting the approach and the vendor. Usually, bids within or close to budget are subjected to a series of qualitative and quantitative decisions. In this highly competitive environment, price is an essential factor. However, alignment with the needs of the business and the target population is equally important. *In fact, approximately 50 percent of training projects are awarded to vendors who were not the lowest bidder* (Britten, 1993).

Selection decisions involve two separate steps. First, bids should be evaluated on qualitative criteria, such as content validity and adequacy; instructional soundness; vendor's expertise, reputation, and past project outcomes; and business and participant needs alignment. Finalists from the qualitative considerations should be evaluated on quantitative measures such as cost and previous evaluative data. If new vendors are finalists, references should be checked before contracts and purchase orders are awarded.

Rewards and consequences of complying with client cost, quality, and delivery criteria should be spelled out before contract signing. Bonuses, as percentage of price, could be available after project completion for excellent work. Consequences could be imposed if training is delayed due to vendor performance, especially if there are financial impacts to the client business. For example, if training is delayed and consequently forces loss of production, the training supplier could share the loss. Guarantees are important so that the client will provide adequate subject matter expertise and timely approvals, and the supplier will provide drafts and final versions as agreed.

21.7 Choosing the *Right* Consultant

Selecting the right consultant is one of the most important decisions the training manager will make. Engaging a consultant means entering into a critical relationship—establishing a professional partnership. The ability of the consultant to meet training needs on time and within budget with a quality product is critical to the success of the program. The ability of the consultant team and client team to work together harmoniously and effectively is perhaps even more critical.

21.7.1 Selection Criteria

The capabilities to look for include:

- Relevant experience of the overall organization and its staff
- Financial stability
- Size of the supplying organization
- Reputation
- Trust factors—reasons to trust the consultant to deliver

Experience. The relevant experience of the consultant and its staff is a highly important decision-making factor. You want to be sure that the consultant is accustomed to designing and developing the type of program you need. If yours is a skills training project such as programming a robot or programmable controller, you want your consultant to be expert in developing skills training programs and courseware. Ask for references and samples of like work on the specific and/or related equipment and task for which you are developing training.

Financial Stability and Longevity. Especially if your program will require a staff of several designer/developers, you want to be sure your consultant is going to stay in business long enough to complete the project. The consultant may need help to support a sizable payroll over a period of time. You might negotiate payments that help support the vendor. Small businesses often need this support for large projects.

How long has the consultant been in business? If it is a relatively new organization, does it have sufficient capitalization to fulfill its commitment? This is not to say that new organizations cannot perform to your expectations. In the training community, many reputable people spin off from a parent organization to go it on their own.

Size.   Size is not necessarily a plus factor by itself. However, the larger organizations—the full-service groups who have the in-house staff to handle not only the design and development of a project but the production of the training—may well be the answer to a large, multidimensional training need.

On the other hand, independent consultants often have a network of support services. Often, they can offer the same overall capabilities that the larger organizations provide. Previous performance can be your best guide.

Reputation.   The reputation of the consultant, whether a firm or an independent consultant, is a key factor. You want your potential consultant to be known and *respected* in the training community. Sometimes a competitor's evaluation is very revealing. How reassuring it is to hear a competitor say, "It's a fine organization. They're our toughest competition." "John or Jane Jones is top notch. You won't go wrong with him or her."

Trust Factors.   Experience, financial stability, size, and reputation are all important. Often, however, the trust factor is intangible. Developing a partnership—bringing a consultant on board to be part of the internal team—is often a matter of chemistry. It is important to meet a potential consultant with whom the group has not done business. Meet not only the salesperson, but meet the key people who will be leading the project and those who will develop the courseware. Be satisfied that they will fit into your organization's culture, so that your team and their team can work together as one.

21.7.2   Identifying Potential Sources

Selecting a consultant is really a two-step process: first, developing a list of potential consultants for current—and future—programs, and, second, selecting the consultant on the basis of a response to your request for proposal. The selection process, if done conscientiously, can be a detailed procedure requiring a good deal of effort and time. Therefore, before undertaking this initiative, two activities should be accomplished. First, you, the client must have a thorough and comprehensive understanding of the scope of work being asked of the consultant. And, second, this understanding must be clearly expressed to the consultants so that they may accurately respond to your requests for proposals and for information about their capabilities.

Sometimes, the internal training department or other departments in the organization will have a list of potential consultants with whom they have worked in the past. However, not all organizations have internal training departments. *It is not unusual for marketing to be responsible for technical training, or engineering, or research and development.* Other organizations have many training departments located in various centers of expertise throughout the company. In such cases, it may be necessary to use a network to obtain names of consultants who have shown expertise in the appropriate areas. The network can be colleagues in other parts of the organization, other marketers, other engineers, or other researchers.

Journals and membership directories of societies like the American Society for Training and Development (ASTD) and the National Society for Performance and Instruction (NSPI) can be other sources. Having obtained names from these sources, be sure to verify their capabilities.

Don't be afraid, however, to look for a consultant with whom you or your company have not dealt. Sometimes, the previously unknown consultant can turn out to be a gem. For example, client companies often meet training consultants at chapter meetings and conferences of various professional associations such ASTD, NSPI, Society of Manufacturing Engineers (SME), or American Production and Inventory Control Society (APICS). In one case, the president of a training and consulting firm met the training director of a major chemical company at an ASTD conference and this meeting led to an ongoing relationship involving numerous contracts over more than 10 years.

21.7.3 Selection Process

The actual selection process will vary according to your needs, the size of your organization, whether you have an internal training department, and other considerations. Following are two approaches which you might follow. One is termed the *Basic Selection Process* and can be used for choosing a consultant when your training needs and budget are modest and infrequent. The other is the *Detailed Selection Process,* a more intensive and detailed process to be used by large organizations whose needs are complex and whose budgets can support the selection effort.

Basic Selection Process.   If your training needs are relatively modest and infrequent, following the seven-step process described as follows will most likely help you select a qualified consultant. If necessary, you can draw some additional features from the detailed process described later in this chapter. The selection process can be costly and you will not want to spend more on selection than on the project itself.

To select a consultant using the basic process, follow these steps:

1. Put together an evaluation matrix, such as that shown in Figure 21-3, for use in the initial selection of potential consultants and again, perhaps with modifications, in evaluating their proposals.

Selection criteria	Candidate 1 Score	Candidate 2 Score	Candidate 3 Score
Overall training experience			
Relevant training experience			
Quality of training materials			
Organization's financial stability			
Organizaiton's ability to meet deadline			
Reputation of organization			
Price			
Ability of organization to fit into culture			
Total scores			
Score column: Your rating of each candidate against each criterion: 1 = poor 2 = fair 3 = good 4 = very good 5 = excellent Total score: Candidate's score for all criteria			

Figure 21-3.   Consultant evaluation matrix.

2. List potential consultants. Start out with six or so and then narrow the list to three at the most. Remember that submitting proposals is an expensive process for a consultant. It is not fair to ask people to propose when you know you are unlikely to use their services.

3. Evaluate each of the consultants on the list, using the evaluation matrix.

4. If a potential consultant is an unknown quantity, arrange a fact-finding meeting to assess capabilities and see whether the all-important trust factor is there.

5. Develop specifications and a request for proposal and release them to the consultants from whom responses are desired.

6. Evaluate the proposals using the evaluation matrix.

7. Award the contract to the consultant whose proposal best meets your needs.

Detailed Selection Process

Requests for Information.   Large organizations that have substantial, continuing needs for support from outside consultants often go through a much more elaborate process to identify and qualify potential consultants. These are organizations such as major manufacturers and governmental agencies whose needs involve very large price tags—often in the six- and seven-figure range. They will issue formal requests for information (RFI), sometimes called *statements of capabilities.*

The statement of capabilities is a clear, tight, and structured request for information and can be instrumental in choosing the best consultant for the job. The statement of capabilities can contain, but need not be limited to, the following categories of information: corporate history and organization, product line and diversification, facility inventory checklist, personnel experience, quality assurance/project management plan, project experience, and sample products.

Determining the background and health of the consultant's company and identifying the company's development and growth are important. Also, you will be able to discern the success of the company's management in the training community. This corporate history and survey highlights the financial, personnel, and business strengths of the organization. The resources committed to training, courseware development, and program evaluation will be manifested to aid in determining a reliable training development resource.

The types of questions you might want to ask on such a survey vary from financial to training methodology and philosophy:

- How long has the company been providing training-related consulting services?

- What is the ownership structure of the organization?

- How many employees are actively involved in the training-related consulting/development function of the company?

- What are the annual sales of the organization's training-related function?

- What percentage of the training-related consulting function of the company is in the area of front-end analysis and needs assessment?

- What percentage of annual training-related sales is attributed to subcontracting arrangements?

- What percentage of the training-related consulting function of the company is in the area of courseware development?

- What percentage of the training-related consulting function of the company is in the area of formative and summative program evaluation?

- What percentage of the training-related consulting function of the company is in the area of Level III/IV program evaluation (long-term retention and gained efficiencies)?

As in the basic selection process, the purpose here is to determine how well the potential consultant meets the criteria of relevant experience, financial stability, size, reputation, and trustworthiness.

It should be noted that once a consultant has responded to an RFI, the statement of capabilities should be put on file and updated every few years or whenever there is a known change in the business conditions of the consultant. Obviously, the consultant should not have to submit a detailed statement of capabilities every time he/she responds to a request for proposal.

Product Line Survey. To confirm the skills that are found in the training organization, a product line survey should be made. Training requirements can be extremely diversified. Therefore, it is critical to identify and evaluate the organizational repertoire of training products and services. This inventory can help you determine whether the company is competent or expert in the training media you require for the defined project.

A possible survey may be segmented as follows and as shown in Figure 21-4:

Instructional Research and Development

- Audio-based instruction
- Compact disc-read only memory (CD-ROM)
- Computer-based instruction
- Computer-interactive videodisc instruction
- Distance learning
- Instructor-led course/workshop
- Job performance aids
- Part-task trainers (tasks related to specific part or component)
- Print media
- Real equipment (actual vs. simulators)
- Self-instructional materials
- Simulators
- Video-based instruction
- Work simulation exercises

Instructor-led Delivery

- Technical skills
- Management/business skills

Workforce Productivity Research and Development

- Human resources development studies
- Measurement systems and data collection

Rate the organizational expertise using the following scale:
 3 = superior expertise   1 = little expertise
 2 = expertise   0 = no expertise

Products and Services	3	2	1	0
Instructional Research and Development				
Audio-based instruction				
Compact disc-read only memory (CD-ROM)				
Computer-based instruction				
Computer-interactive videodisc instruction				
Distance learning				
Instructor-led course workshop				
Job performance aids				
Part-task trainers (training related to parts of tasks)				
Print media				
Real equipment (actual vs. simulations)				
Self-instructional materials				
Simulators				
Video-based instruction				
Work simulation exercises				
Instructor-led Delivery				
Technical skills				
Management business skills				
Workforce Productivity Research and Development				
Human resources development studies				
Measurement systems and data collection				
Organizational structures and procedures				
System, human factors, organizational problem solving				
Front-end Analysis				
Job analysis				
Needs assessment				

Figure 21-4. Product line survey.

Task analysis				
Performance Management Research and Development				
Content validity				
Formative evaluation				
Model performance standards				
Performance measurement manuals and guides				
Posttraining evaluation				
Summative evaluation				

Figure 21-4. (*Continued*)

- Organizational structures and procedures
- System, human factors, organizational problem solving

Front-end Analyses

- Job analysis
- Needs assessment
- Task analysis

Performance Management Research and Development

- Content validity
- Formative evaluation
- Model performance standards
- Performance measurement manuals and guides
- Posttraining evaluation
- Summative evaluation

Facilities Inventory. Another important aspect to consider when choosing the appropriate training consultant is the consultant's facilities. A successful project may hinge on the resources available to the consultant during the development phase. What is at hand and can be relied upon to complete the project in a timely and professional manner? Some items/areas you might want to consider are: audio library, audio production support, computer art support, computer programming support, copy layout capabilities, desktop publishing, line art support, mainframe computer support, PC/Macintosh computer support, photographic support, reprographics support, video production, video editing, and a videotape library.

Personnel Expertise. The consulting organization is only as good as its personnel. Identification of the company's personnel is an excellent method of determining organizational strength and expertise available to the project. Organizations that staff in a multidisciplinary fashion like to hire quality individuals who possess an excellent combination of skills. A personnel matrix serves to identify not just the key employees but all personnel resources, both internal and external.

The matrix would encompass the functions required on the development team, including project manager, instructional technologist, educational programmer, systems analyst, and any other personnel required by the project. You would rate their expertise against the items contained in the product line inventory previously discussed in this chapter. The matrix could be similar to the one shown in Figure 21-5.

Quality Assurance Plan. To assist in obtaining the best product, you should develop a quality assurance plan. Quality encompasses more than just attractive materials that are neatly formatted and error free. Quality

Use an X to denote experience in specific product or service					
Product/Service	John D.	Jane T.	Richard M.	Alice S.	Henry J.
Audio-based training					
CD-ROM					
Computer-based training					
Course evaluation					
Educational research					
Front-end analysis					
Instructor-led training					
Interactive videodisc					
Job aids					
Needs assessment					
Print/manuals/documentation					
Satellite-based training					
Self-instructional materials					
Simulation					
Video-based training					

Figure 21-5. Personnel expertise matrix.

courseware are those that work, reflect the contract specifications within the specified time line and budget. Using this plan, you can identify a consultant based upon the criteria and methodologies you designate for the design and/or delivery of quality products and services.

You might want to consider an assurance plan that covers the broad areas of project planning, product development, and final deliverable. Project planning would include the project milestone schedule, project tracking and monitoring, and project performance evaluation. Product development incorporates checks and balances, instructional system design tracking sheets, and a product review process. Also within this area the requisite personnel, physical resources, and services would be monitored.

The final deliverable provides the mechanism for validating the product and ensuring that it meets the original requirements or specifications. It is equally critical to delineate the method of deployment and distribution of the validated product or service.

Integral to the completion of a successful project for your field of business or activity is identifying the level of experience a consultant has in providing training services within your industry. There are certain subtleties in every industry, and a lack of knowledge of those subtleties can create problems for the inexperienced consultant. A consultant experience matrix will quickly assist you in recognizing those consultants who possess that extra expertise and competitive advantage in providing the most appropriate industry-specific product or service. The consultant experience matrix will serve to designate the type of project, the name of similar clients, the duration of past projects, and a list of client references.

Product Examples. The final step in choosing the right consultant is to evaluate the candidates' sample products. Through such an evaluation, it is simple to determine the extent of knowledge and expertise in any particular training medium. This effort may also assist you in specifying the appropriate media, design approach, or delivery method for your potential training effort.

Criteria you may want to consider for the sample products are:

- Clearly defined objectives
- Measurable objectives
- Appropriate media
- Sound instructional design
- Learner feedback provisions
- Attractive, error-free course materials
- Professionalism exhibited throughout product

Generally, use a five-item scale for rating, such as *excellent, good, adequate, not available,* and *not applicable.*

21.8 Obtaining and Evaluating Proposals

21.8.1 Requesting Proposals

Regardless of whether a project is to be carried out internally or externally, the client's training organization together with *the internal customer should write specifications or the request for proposal.* Some organizations encourage bids from the internal training department as well as from external consultants. Often our biggest competitors are the internal training departments (Dillon, 1993). Even if the program is to be developed *internally,* specifications should be drawn and the internal department should provide cost projections.

If the decision to use an external consultant has been made, the internal training department and internal customer together establish the criteria and process to select the consultant. Often, the purchasing department will become involved in developing the request for proposal and will want to receive the proposals and arrange for awarding the contract.

The request for proposal should clearly state what is desired in the way of outcomes, deliverables, and time frames and should also state the conditions under which the project will be carried out. Often it will state expectations of consultants' experience and expertise. Some example of these criteria could be as follows:

- *Outcome.* The program will be designed to train skilled trades people in the maintenance and troubleshooting of the electrical/electronic and mechanical systems of the ultra-high-technology X-100 Transfer Press. In addition, a train-the-trainer course is required to train plant personnel to deliver the training to the workforce. The consultant will conduct this course.

- *Deliverables.* Supporting reference and training documentation will include user reference manuals for the electrical and mechanical systems of the transfer press, blueprint manuals, instructors' guides, overhead transparencies and other training aids, and participants' workbooks.

- *Time frame.* Work on the project will commence on or about February 1. The train-the-trainer course will start on or about July 1. Pilot training will begin on or about September 1, and full-scale launch of the program is planned for early January.

- *Conditions.* The corporation will provide subject matter experts and office facilities for the consultant. The consultant is expected to maintain a full-time staff of developers on site.

- *Desired experience.* The successful bidder will furnish evidence of successful development of training programs on electrical/electronic and mechanical systems maintenance and troubleshooting, including sample outline and selected chapters or modules.

Depending on the nature of the project and corporate purchasing policies, a request for proposal can range from a verbal request to a well-known consultant to a simple letter request to a full-blown, formal request for proposal (RFP).

21.8.2 Developing Proposals

Responses to the variety of requests will also vary. However, the astute consultant will always respond in writing even to a verbal request. The consultant's response should always be "in kind." Given a letter request of a few pages, the consultant should respond in a few pages. Given a full-blown, formal RFP, the consultant should respond precisely to the specifications contained in the RFP. Not responding in kind can be grounds for eliminating the proposal from consideration. If a consultant objects to a stipulation in the RFP, the objection should be clearly stated. Suppliers wanting to take a different approach should respond to the original specifications and then submit a "Plan B" as an alternative.

The proposal is the consultant's opportunity to project the best image possible. It should address each of these issues clearly and in sufficient detail to allow the buyer to make an intelligent decision. The proposal should state operating assumptions and client and consultant responsibilities, describe the instructional approach and the qualifications of the consultant and any support staff to provide the services requested. Further, it should contain development schedules, milestone charts, payment schedules, and a discussion of how the project will be managed.

A useful technique in developing a proposal is to address the specific details of the request in the body of the proposal and attach supporting documentation such as exhibits and capabilities descriptions as appendixes. A brief but comprehensive executive summary is essential. Decision makers are busy people. A well-constructed executive summary can quickly show them whether the proposal is on target and worthy of a full reading.

Ultimately, good proposals are likely to contain about 50 percent of the final course design description. This is why it is critical to limit the number of consultants before asking for written proposals.

Both parties should avoid unnecessary verbiage and "boilerplate." Clear, succinct RFPs and proposals aimed specifically at the project at hand help assure the success of a project. Boilerplate often lacks specificity. If they are picking up boilerplate or material from other proposals, proposal writers should carefully review that standing copy to make sure it is germane to the situation to which they are responding. The same is true for the developers of the RFP.

21.8.3 Evaluating Proposals

Once you have designated potential consultants to develop your training and have sent out your RFPs, you should implement an objective proposal evaluation process. The evaluation can be divided into a number of categories such as management plan, qualification and experience, quality assurance, and cost. Most times it is advisable to separate cost from the technical aspects of the evaluation in order to give every proposal an impartial review without the cost implications looming over the process.

It is imperative that the consultant demonstrate a thorough understanding of the scope of work including the rationale and objectives stated in the RFP. Development efforts must appear focused and targeted to the goals of your specifications. Included in the RFP should be a detailed plan of action or approach to the topic at hand. A sound instructional systems design approach must be communicated and assure reliability and validity of the final product or service. There must be an apparent understanding of the rationale for this effort and the products or services to be delivered. And a milestone schedule citing the major tasks, subtasks, and completion dates must be included.

Overlaying this entire management plan should be a complete statement of the working relationship and assumptions that govern the business interface and communication between client and consultant.

The qualifications and experience of the consultant or the consulting organization's staff should be evaluated based on similar experience and/or work done within your industry. This will manifest whether there are sufficient personnel, resources, and expertise to deliver a quality product.

Finally, the consultant's proposal must be responsive to the terms, conditions, and time lines required by you or your company. Unless these items are addressed completely and satisfactorily, no contract can be entered into.

21.9 Project Management

Skillful project management is essential to the success of the project. Immediately upon award of the contract, the client project team and the supplier project team should meet for a start-of-work (SOW) meeting. Each team should have a project leader who will remain in that role throughout the project. At the SOW meeting, the supplier's project leader should review the proposal with the two teams, making sure that all roles and responsibilities are clearly defined. Especially critical are the roles of the two project leaders.

Normally, the supplier's project leader manages the project to assure that all deliverables are developed and produced to acceptable quality standards on time and on budget. The client's project manager acts as liaison with the client organization to provide subject matter experts, material reviews, and decisions necessary to continue progress.

The supplier's mechanisms for controlling the project, such as milestone schedules, tracking and monitoring methods, and status reports or project logs, should have been delineated in the proposal. They should be explained at the SOW meeting. Project management methods may range from simple milestone charts and calendars created manually to computer-generated Gantt charts and PERT (Project Evaluation Review Technique) charts incorporating critical path analysis to highly sophisticated mainframe systems used for tracking very large manufacturing projects in which training may be a part.

Depending upon the length of the project, the project team should meet periodically to review progress and solve problems. The supplier's project leader should issue status reports periodically. Depending upon the length of the project, meetings could be held and status reports issued weekly, biweekly, or monthly.

Once the project has been completed, the two teams should meet for a "lessons learned" session to evaluate what went right and what went wrong in the course of the project. This meeting can occur after courseware has been developed, but is probably more useful after the program has been validated or piloted. If the progress of the project has been adequately monitored throughout development, there should be no surprises. Such a meeting is in no way intended to be a "witch hunt" but rather a means of objectively evaluating the process and its outcomes.

Sometimes, the supplier or client may have identified additional needs or follow-on activities that can then be addressed—an opportunity the supplier will welcome. Some suppliers will also hold an internal lessons-learned session with a view to improving their performance on future projects.

When the project is finished, in addition to distributing the deliverables, the supplier will also return to the client any proprietary materials and resources used during development. In addition, *suppliers often provide electronic discs of the training materials they have created.* This is critical because technology continuously changes and training must adapt. Flexibility for making revisions requires desktop publishing formats. Manual cut-and-paste is not acceptable because it is cumbersome, slow, and subject to errors.

21.10 Confidentiality

Consultants and vendors put much effort into proposal writing, which enables clients to anticipate project outcomes. In addition, proposals contain information about project approach allowing clients to visualize the project steps. *Proposals should be respected as confidential. They should be used for evaluation purposes and not passed along to the winning vendor, in order to achieve the "best of all worlds" by incorporating others' ideas.* In addition, clients should not "steal" the proposed ideas and decide to do the project internally without compensating the supplier for their project planning.

Prepackaged programs already have copyright protection that is nonnegotiable. However, tailoring or customizing may incorporate content that is proprietary to the client organization and requires legal protection. Legal departments are an excellent resource for drafting contract language. However, the issues are complex and do not lend themselves to boilerplate wording.

Tailoring involves creating supplementary handouts or manuals but no changes to the original text. Creation of the new documents can be covered by work-for-hire statements and copyright designated to the client company.

Customizing requires alterations to the packaged materials. Frequently, changes include client-specific art work or examples for problem-solving exercises. Content changes may involve descriptions of processes, procedures, work rules, or policies that are imbedded into the existing vendor text. Shared statements for protection of ownership and confidentiality of trade secrets require specific, detailed discussions with advice from legal.

21.11 Conclusion

Training consultants are key factors in the success of almost every training department today. Few departments are staffed to handle normal training schedules and also meet the pressing demands of special situations such as plan launch or product change. As a result, it is critical to select the appropriate supplier to serve as a partner and to establish fair parameters. In addition, technology is changing rapidly and technical training must be readily adapted. Few companies can provide adequate responsiveness without the support of training suppliers. For the most part, training departments and consultants are linked by mutual need, and both parties should respect this mutual relationship and each other's contribution to the success of any training project.

Bibliography

Interviews

Amstadt, Roberta, Electronic Data Systems Corporation, Troy, Mich., 1993.
Brandenburg, Dale, Industrial Technology Institute, Ann Arbor, Mich., 1993.
Britten, Michael, Brunswick, Lincoln, Neb., 1993.
Carpenter, Carol, The High Performance Group, Southfield, Mich., 1993.
Dillon, Kelley, Triad Performance Technologies, Inc., Farmington Hills, Mich., 1993.
Elliott, Paul, RWD Technologies, Columbia, Md., 1993.
Fry, David, Chrysler Motor Corporation, Highland Park, Mich., 1993.
Gingerella, Leonard, United Training Services, Inc., Southfield, Mich., 1993.
Girod, Nancy, Livernois Engineering, Detroit, Mich., 1993.
Gohl, Judy, GPS Technologies, Troy, Mich., 1993.
Johnson, James, MascoTech Training & Visual Services (formerly Creative Universal, Inc.), Atlanta, Ga., 1993.
Kooistra, Charles, GPS Technologies, Columbia, Md., 1993.
Lebovitz, Harry, Prism Training Group, Farmington Hills, Mich., 1993.
Miller, Daniel, GPS Technologies, Troy, Mich., 1993.
Petro, Tom, Triad Performance Technologies, Inc., Farmington Hills, Mich., 1993.
Rance, Antoinette, Ameritech Advertising Services, Troy, Mich., 1993.
Ruyle, Kim, Plus Delta Performance, Galesville, Wisc., 1993.
Short, Larry G., Larry G. Short & Associates, Inc., West Bloomfield, Mich., 1993.
Spannous, Timothy, The Emdicium Group, Inc., Birmingham, Mich., 1993.
Stewart, Hardy, 1st Seminar Service, Lowell, Mass., 1993.
Strickland, Fred, Sandy Corporation, Troy, Mich., 1993.
Williams, Harry, Ameritech Advertising Services, Indianapolis, Ind., 1993.

Publications

Bader, Gloria, and Tom Stich, "Building the Consulting Relationship," *Training & Development,* June 1993.
Biebel, Mary Gail, and Nancy Kuhn, "Making the Right Match with a Consultant," *Technical & Skills Training,* April 1991.
Comcowich, William, "Looking Outside," *CBT Directions,* October 1991.
Dasher, Joan, "How Interactive Multimedia Will Meet Your Training Objectives," *ASTD National Technical and Skills Training Conference Proceedings,* American Society for Training & Development, Alexandria, Va., October 1993.
Fischer, Ron, and Mary Rabaut, "A How-To Guide: Working with a Consultant," *Management Review,* February 1992.
Kuhn, Nancy, and Mary Gail Biebel, "You Get What You Ask For!: How to Hire a Technical Training Consultant," *ASTD National Conference,* San Francisco, May 1990.

Ludeman, Kate, Douglas B. Turner, Geoff Bellman, and Jeananne Oliphant, "The Art of Choosing a Consultant," *Training & Development* January 1992.

McCullough, Richard, "Make or Buy: How to Decide," *Info-Line*, October 1988.

Reid, Robert, "On Target: Contracting with Consultants," *Technical & Skills Training*, Nov/Dec 1993.

Tracey, William, "Customizing Off-the-Shelf Training Programs," *HR Magazine*, January 1993.

Training and Manual Specifications for Equipment and Manufacturing Systems, General Motors Corporation, Worldwide Purchasing, Detroit, May 7, 1993.

22

Trends in Technical Jobs, Skills, and Training

Ellen S. Carnevale

American Society for Training and Development

Ellen S. Carnevale *is editor of Technical & Skills Training maga-*
zine, published by the American Society for Training and Develop-
ment. Prior to her role as magazine editor, she wrote and edited
several newsletters for ASTD on such topics as management develop-
ment, technical training, and the business and economic issues of
employee training. She has been a training manager with the Gradu-
ate School of the U.S. Department of Agriculture. She has also been a
community education specialist and counselor with the Alcohol Infor-
mation and Referral Center, Dane County Mental Health Center, in
Madison, Wisconsin. She has a master's degree in adult and contin-
uing education from the University of Wisconsin, Madison, and a
bachelor's degree in social work from the University of Illinois,
Urbana-Champaign.

Even though many economists devoted to surveying and analyzing the
field of worker training admit to the paucity of "good data," we should
take comfort in their continued commitment to research. And bolstered
by the current administration's agenda for education and training, researchers and trainers alike have perhaps more opportunities now than in
recent memory to flex their collective muscles, not only to keep power
brokers focused on the importance of technical training, but to continually

share the data that will strengthen this country's ability to compete and to create jobs with the support of training.

Any meaningful discussion of technical jobs and technical training must begin with a definition of terms. In 1988 research, the American Society for Training and Development defined technical workers this way:

> They utilize principles from the mathematical or natural sciences in their work. For the most part they work in industries that rely on the application of those principles to create products, services, or processes. Technical workers themselves, besides producing technical products, tend to use technology in their work. (A. Carnevale and E. Schulz, 1988.)

One argument that this research fueled is the depth of understanding that workers must have about the particular technologies they use in their jobs in order to be considered technical workers. One wonders, for example, whether a data entry operator qualifies as a technical worker in the same way as does a technician operating and servicing a computerized machine tool. The distinction is important because of the changing mix of required technical skills, and because of widespread efforts among large and small companies to implement new forms of work organization.

To answer the preceding question according to the ASTD definition, we would assume that the data entry operator would not have the depth of understanding of the computer that the technician would. The push in many technical jobs these days is to give technical workers more than a rudimentary understanding of their work-related technology. Employers are realizing the damage done when requiring workers to "check their brains at the door." Now the talk is of "higher-level" skills such as troubleshooting, problem solving, and knowledge of the science behind a piece of technology—at least enough knowledge to perform simple equipment adjustments or repairs when breakdowns occur or quality problems appear.

Jerry Wright, a 30-year veteran manager of technical education and training, and the manager of the Caterpillar Training Institute, champions the critical need for a greater degree of understanding of technology among workers on the manufacturing floor, a greater involvement of managers and engineers in the manufacturing process, and more use of teams. "Things are just too complex today for one person to do a total design, and we don't have the time," he says. New skills and knowledge include math and communication, analytical and problem-solving skills, and a higher level of technical capability (Wright, 1993).

Take the Welch Allyn Company, in Skaneateles Falls, New York. With 1400 employees, the company designs and manufactures medical diagnostic instruments, bar code scanning and decoding equipment, and industrial inspection equipment. The company's president, Bill Allyn, says that implementing Total Quality Management and introducing new technology requires a tremendous amount of training: "My only concern is that we can keep the training up." And Bill Stoffle, a senior group leader in the machining area who is responsible for setting up the new machine tools and delivering technical training, says, "the technology from being able to just run a drill press or a lathe compared to being able to figure out what you've got on a numerically controlled machine is a giant step." (E. Carnevale, July 1992.)

At Hurley Medical Center in Flint, Michigan, every technician is expected to know enough about any piece of biomedical equipment to at least conduct a preliminary fault analysis. And the hospital's six biomedical equipment technicians, responsible for maintaining and repairing such equipment, need to know how to operate the equipment as well as how to repair it. "If they don't know how to work the buttons [on medical equipment], they can't be sure if the button needs to be replaced or if it just needs to be pushed," says Lewis Moquin, supervisor, Biomedical Engineering. Mindful of the importance of focusing on the customer, Moquin says, "We have to remember that almost anything we do—there's a patient on the other end of it." (R. Reid, 1993.)

These two examples, from manufacturing and health care, are not uncommon. Jobs and skill requirements are changing, and the mandate is now here for researchers to continue unearthing what's happening, to suggest what should happen, and for employers and human resource development professionals to use all available knowledge in delivering technical training to workers.

22.1 The U.S. Technical Job Market

According to the U.S. Department of Labor's Bureau of Labor Statistics (BLS), employment in the United States is projected to rise to 147.5 million workers by 2005, compared to 121.1 million in 1992. This translates to approximately two million new jobs per year between 1992 and 2005. (BLS considers this projection to be "moderate"; the Bureau also projects "low" and "high" data sets, but the moderate data set is used here.)

The level of manufacturing employment should remain essentially unchanged, although BLS projects a loss of 517,000 manufacturing jobs between 1992 and 2005. This represents a 17.8 percent share of the non-farm wage and salaried workforce. Service employment is expected to garner 82.2 percent of the workforce in 2005, contributing 24 million new jobs. Specifically, BLS projects the following:

- Employment in health services will reflect 16 percent of the job growth.
- Technician jobs will grow 32.2 percent, with radiology and health technicians providing potentially the biggest job boosts.
- Computer analysts will enjoy a 110 percent growth rate.
- Mechanics and repairers will see a 16 percent job growth rate.

Overall, technical workers are increasing in numbers in the American workforce. While some technical occupational categories will experience job reductions, the technical workforce is increasing as a proportion of the total workforce. The mix of decline and increase among technical occupations demonstrates an increase in more skilled technical jobs (Table 22-1).

Table 22-1. Employment Changes for Selected Technical Occupations, 1992–2005

Occupation Group	Total Employment (numbers in thousands)				Percent Change 1992–2005
	1992	%	2005	%	
All employees	121,099	100	147,482	100	21.8
Technicians*	4,282	3.5	5,664	3.8	32.2
health	2,028	1.7	2,848	1.9	40.0
electrical	323	.3	396	.3	23.0
radiology	162	.1	264	.2	63.0
Mechanics/repairers	4,819	4.0	5,581	3.8	16.0
aircraft engine	131	.1	148	.1	13.0
data processing	83	.1	120	.1	45.0
Precision production	2,956	2.4	2,965	2.0	0.0
metalworking	854	.7	880	.6	3.0
tool and die	138	.1	128	.1	−7.0
machinists	352	.3	348	.2	−1.0
inspectors	625	.5	559	.4	−10.0
plant operators	308	.3	340	.2	10.0
Data processing†					
computer analysts	455	.4	956	.6	110.0
computer programmers	555	.5	723	.5	30.0
Engineers	1,354	.1	1,660	1.1	23.0
electrical	370	.3	459	.3	24.0
industrial	119	.1	138	.1	17.0
mechanical	227	.2	273	.2	20.0
Construction	3,510	.3	4,259	.3	22.0
electricians	518	.4	618	.4	19.0
structural metalworkers	66	.1	81	.1	22.0

* For the broad categories (technicians, mechanics/repairers, precision production, engineers, and construction trades), many more occupation groups are included in these categories. The groups chosen reflect those groups requiring more technical skills.
† Data processing does not exist as a broad category.

SOURCE: George T. Silvestri, "Occupational Employment: Wide Variations in Growth," U.S. Department of Labor, Bureau of Labor Statistics, *Monthly Labor Review,* November 1993, pp. 58–86.

One study shows that 40 percent of productivity improvements from the purchase of new technology could be attributed solely to the mechanics of the technology—that is, the technology did what it was supposed to do. But 60 percent of productivity improvements were the result of workers' innovation or advances in knowledge (A. Carnevale, 1992). In other words, workers improved the technology or the companion work processes that the technology affected. And more technology—from computers to computer-operated machine tools—is being embedded in production and service-delivery processes. The successful companies seem to be the ones that will purchase the needed equipment (and if they're smart, solicit workers' input before purchasing) and then allow those who know—the ones closest to the point of production—to take it from there. And when training is needed, to come up with the bucks. Fast.

A recent study by the U.S. Bureau of the Census (1993) underscores the power of technology in raising not only skill levels but wages as well. Using data from the 1988 Census of Manufacturers and the Survey of Manufacturing Technology, the study shows that wages rise with the number of advanced technologies a manufacturer uses. These advanced technologies are computer-aided design/computer-aided engineering; computer numerically controlled machines; computers used on the factory floor; local area networks; automated sensors for materials; and robotics and automatic sensors. The average wage in 1988 for a production worker in a company using no technologies is $8.63; using one to two technologies, $9.83; using three to five technologies; $10.46; and using six or more technologies, $11.84. The study also found that wages rise regardless of plant size.

22.2 Of Macro and Micro

Fast seems to be the motto for almost anything having to do with productivity improvements, regardless of whether those improvements can be delivered by humans, technology, or the reorganization of work. In fact, many companies are reorganizing work into what has come to be labeled *high-performance workplaces*. But there are many other, just-as-timely titles for the transformation of work. For instance, while some look for signs of the death of Total Quality Management, others feel that TQM is undergoing its own change from a highly visible corporate effort to an invisible, embedded system for customer satisfaction. But certain aspects of TQM, notably employee involvement, teamwork, and empowerment, are being included in what is now called high-performance work, or high-performance management.

Edward Lawler III distinguishes between a *total quality improvement effort*, where employee involvement is limited to narrow work processes, and a *high-involvement organization,* where employees know where the business is going because the business shares information (E. Lawler, 1992).

High-performance work systems seem to be a popular way to address U.S. labor market trends and initiatives: an aging workforce, a meaningful role for organized labor, cultural diversity, continued corporate downsizing, and the globalization of business. Acknowledging the force of these trends, a high-performance work system takes on the trends and successfully adapts the work systems.

In a document prepared for attendees at President Clinton's 1993 Conference on the Future of the American Workplace (the first national summit on high-performance work practices), a *high-performance work organization* was defined as a place that

> provides workers with the information, skills, incentives, and responsibility to make decisions essential for innovation, quality improvement, and rapid response to change.

Of the many strategies at work in high-involvement work, this document highlighted three (U.S. Department of Labor, 1993):

- Training
- Employee involvement in decision making
- Compensation linked to firm or worker performance

22.3 The Training-Productivity Link

While the studies linking training to productivity may not fill a bin in the Library of Congress's card catalog, there are some heartening data.

Recent studies point to productivity gains from formal training programs (Bartel, 1989; 1991). For instance, Bartel reports that businesses that were operating below expected labor productivity levels in 1983, and then started employee training programs, could document an average 17 percent larger rise in the productivity rate by 1985.

More employees are taking skill training. The data in Table 22-2 show more employees in 1991 (41 percent) said they took skill improvement training while in their current jobs than in 1983 (35 percent). Employers sponsored 16 percent of this training in 1991, compared to 11 percent in 1983. While the percentages may seem small, the increase is significant: a 45 percent increase in the amount of employer-sponsored training programs. A look at individual technical occupations shows that they received this training and, in many cases, the jump from 1983 to 1991 was substantial. Sixty-nine percent of employers underwrote the full cost of this training. BLS concludes that "employers are more likely to invest in the training of an employee who has shown the potential to use learned skills productively" (Amirault, 1992).

For all groups, occupation-specific technical training was the most common type of skill improvement training, and typically this training lasted anywhere from 13 to 25 weeks. Informal on-the-job training was common to 37 percent of workers reporting training.

Another survey, the National Longitudinal Survey of Youth (NLSY), shows that 38 percent of young adults (defined as an age range of 26 to 34) received training during the years 1986 to 1991. Nearly 24 percent of the sample received company training (the leading source of training); the company training lasted an average of 180 hours over the 1986–1991 time span.

The age range is crucial, notes economist Jonathan R. Veum (1993), because "past research indicates that most formal employer-based training is provided to workers between the ages of 25 and 34. Veum continues

> Overall, the data suggest that while employer-provided training is the most common form of training received by young adults, training received from institutions outside of the workplace plays an important role for those who are less likely to receive employer-provided training than others.

Of note to technical training are two other training providers: vocational and technical institutes and apprenticeships. According to the NLSY, 4.8 percent of young adults received training from vocational and technical institutes, with training lasting 425 hours over the 1986–1991 time span; and 1.5 percent were in apprenticeships, receiving 690 hours of training over the same time span.

International data on training are sparse. Different countries define and count training hours differently, making neat comparisons difficult. But Lynch notes that

> On the one hand, it appears that the U.S. does not spend less than other countries on training. On the other hand, when one examines the content of training by country there seem to be important differences in what firms need to provide in their training programs depending on the initial level of skills of their workers. These initial levels of skills in turn are influenced by the educational and early training systems of the countries. As a result, in some sectors for the same level of expenditures, U.S. firms do not end up with as well-qualified employees as their European or Japanese competitors. (L. Lynch, 1993.)

22.4 Delivering the Goods

A number of companies illustrate the positive impact of training. Motorola is well known for its commitment to employee training and edu-

Table 22-2. Sources of Qualifying and Skill Improvement Training for Technical and Skilled Workers (1983 and 1991 data)

| | Qualifying Training* | | | | | | | | Skill Improvement Training† | | | | | | | |
| Occupation | % with qualifying training | | % from school | | % formal employer-provided | | % informal on-the-job | | % with skill improvement training | | % from school | | % formal employer-provided | | % informal on-the-job | |
	1983	1991	1983	1991	1983	1991	1983	1991	1983	1991	1983	1991	1983	1991	1983	1991
All employees	55	57	29	33	10	12	28	27	35	41	12	13	11	16	14	15
Technicians																
health	90	90	69	68	14	14	21	21	49	59	14	13	13	22	23	20
electrical	88	90	48	63	19	20	39	31	59	65	20	24	26	35	12	27
radiology	92	98	69	66	24	10	15	15	44	52	17	13	11	17	13	17
Mechanics/repairers																
supervisors	68	71	15	26	22	34	43	41	58	58	5	15	38	35	22	18
aircraft engines	82	92	34	37	20	44	39	39	53	64	5	13	24	40	24	22
industrial machines	63	64	14	20	18	21	40	35	37	46	6	11	15	19	18	19
data processing	92	88	57	50	31	30	30	53	67	74	10	11	58	42	10	42
telephone line	74	46	6	8	37	26	33	22	67	68	10	6	57	57	16	25
telephones	57	68	8	9	35	38	27	36	73	79	5	13	55	49	28	32
electrical equipment	70	74	20	29	29	29	29	39	63	70	7	12	41	42	23	30
office machines	87	82	34	29	41	31	46	28	57	77	7	8	49	41	3	21
millwrights	60	65	13	25	23	38	37	39	47	38	11	2	18	17	24	16
Precision production																

metalworking *(partial, top row cut off — fragment legible: 70, 88)*																
tool & die	85	68	25	26	35	54	44	22	40	34	17	13	10	16	17	9
machinists	74	67	22	21	23	21	43	38	33	35	7	9	10	14	18	17
inspectors	70	58	14	25	32	17	39	32	39	52	8	14	15	21	15	23
plant operators	65	70	21	31	19	23	35	42	48	63	8	22	23	25	20	21
Data processing																
computer analysts	94	90	70	71	27	24	45	47	64	68	16	25	37	42	25	20
computer programmers	91	93	64	72	19	19	41	44	61	62	25	23	27	34	24	27
Engineers																
aerospace	100	98	79	96	18	23	31	48	73	70	36	26	37	39	20	26
chemical	95	96	92	87	13	11	19	34	59	55	23	13	37	40	19	22
electrical	92	94	71	82	18	21	32	37	65	70	24	36	35	42	21	27
industrial	85	91	54	72	15	23	41	53	51	70	21	26	23	39	18	25
mechanical	89	95	76	86	12	14	32	38	52	68	25	33	21	34	18	20
Construction																
electricians	85	80	28	29	32	39	44	40	48	49	19	13	15	21	17	16
electric power	53	66	6	18	24	42	34	29	60	67	4	10	29	33	28	35
structural metalworkers	66	81	11	6	31	67	29	14	21	33	13	5	4	9	8	25

* Qualifying training is specific training needed to obtain a job.
† Skill improvement training is training needed to improve the job skills of currently employed people.

SOURCE: *How Workers Get Their Training: A 1991 Update,* Bulletin 2407, August 1992. Washington, DC: U.S. Department of Labor, Bureau of Labor Statistics, August 1992. This bulletin was prepared by Thomas A. Amirault under the supervision of Alan Eck. Reprinted from: *Technical & Skills Training,* February/March 1993. © Copyright 1993 by the American Society for Training and Development, 1640 King St., Box 1443, Alexandria, VA 22313. Reprinted with permission.

cation. A recent report shows that the company spends roughly $200 million per year on training, and the company requires employees to spend at least 40 hours per year in training.

Motorola has a solid system for identifying training needs and delivering training. And the company has shown that its training mandate works. It is a worldwide leader in the cellular telephone and systems industry, the largest U.S.-based semiconductor supplier worldwide, the company who successfully cracked the Japanese market with cellular telephones, and an inaugural winner of the Malcolm Baldrige National Quality Award (E. Carnevale, 1990).

The Saturn Corporation, a subsidiary of General Motors Corporation, also has a training mandate. In an average year, Saturn provides 650,000 training hours to its 6000 employees. Every Saturn team member receives at least 92 hours of training each year, or roughly five percent of his or her time at work (C. Dervarics, January 1993).

Brown-Covey ranks with Saturn and Motorola, even though this industrial machine maintenance shop in Kansas City employs only eight people. Company president Leo Holder has sent all employees through a four-year apprenticeship program, at a yearly cost of $50,000. The pay-off? Brown-Covey has had no turnover in the last five years (C. Dervarics, February/March 1993).

Embedded in these examples, and in dozens more like them, is the belief that technical training needs to be job-specific and meaningful. Anecdotal evidence points to a frustration among training professionals when hearing trainees comment, "The training was good, but I don't know how it applies to my job."

Making sure training is tied to job requirements seems to be a requirement for technical trainers these days. The traditional needs analysis phase is going by other names. Joe Harless, a respected challenger of training tradition and one of the field's gurus, used to call it front-end analysis but now calls it *accomplishment-based curriculum development;* he says that the needs analysis should now begin at the level of the organization's goals, one level higher than the job (E. Carnevale, 1991).

Implicit in this new wave of needs analysis for technical training is a commitment to the learner. The learner—the one doing the technical job and the one, for whatever reason, who needs the training—becomes part of the training design process. This learner involvement pays off in real terms: Time and money are saved by designing content that's targeted and delivery methods that are efficient and effective. Trainers must not be afraid to ask whether a job aid could solve a performance problem better than a full-blown course.

For years, many technical trainers have used a different term for training: performance analysis. In simple terms, a job performance problem has many causes, and many solutions—traditional classroom-based training being just one solution. Broaden the scope of solutions, says Robert Mager, a long-time leader in the field of performance analysis. Solutions can range from individualized instruction to coaching or counseling to job redesign. Especially in technical jobs, ergonomics plays a pivotal role. For instance, what looks to be a lack of skills on the part of an employee may turn out to be a lack of adequate lighting or a machine that is positioned incorrectly (E. Carnevale, July 1992).

Other chapters in this handbook have described in detail such training options as on-the-job training, self-instruction, performance support systems, and apprenticeships. The bottom line in technical training is that all these options should be considered. In the words of Caterpillar's Jerry Wright, technical training must take place in a "truly interactive, facilitative environment, [with] infinite access to questions at the time you need the answers" (J. Wright, 1993).

One cannot underestimate the power of training technology in delivering technical training. Computers, interactive videodiscs, and simulations can cut lengthy and costly training programs into short and inexpensive learning experiences. But one can overestimate the power. Among overly enthusiastic advocates of training technology, debates abound concerning the "death of classroom training" or the "obsolescence of the trainer." Debates are always healthy; pushing for a rigid answer can prove harmful. Technical training provides perhaps one of the best "dating games" between training technology and training professionals. The training technology can simulate, for instance, a million-dollar piece of equipment that really shouldn't be at the mercy of a trainee who needs to learn how to operate it. But no training technology thus far can simulate the curiosity and creativity generated when people get together to learn. And as the statistic mentioned earlier clearly shows, 60 percent of productivity improvements are the result of workers' innovations or advances in knowledge.

Apprenticeships in particular are moving back into the spotlight, especially given the success of Germany's apprenticeship system. German companies invest around 2 percent of their payrolls in apprenticeships (J. von Brachel, 1994), and estimates show that more than 65 percent of German workers will have gone through an apprenticeship by the year 2000 (L. Lynch, 1993).

Recent data from the United States show that 75 percent of jobs require less than a bachelor's degree, and that only 25 percent of high-school graduates finish college. Given these two figures, many are concerned that no effective system exists for moving non-college-bound students from school to work.

Apprenticeships and an initiative called *tech-prep* help create such a system. In tech-prep, students begin in their junior year in high school to pursue a set course of study that alternates between classroom learning and workplace learning. The private sector plays a meaningful role by providing the workplace learning, and therefore providing a link between a community's schools and its job market.

The country's 1500 community colleges have forged those links for years. David Pierce, president of the American Association of Community Colleges, describes the community college strength this way:

> Community colleges are in tune with their communities, and the training and education that these students get will be in tune with the job market that most of the students will be going into.

He also feels that one of the community colleges' greatest assets is their ability to respond quickly:

> They are able to stay up with the industry and provide what they need on a very quick response basis, and even shift gears in midstream if they need to. (Pierce, 1993.)

Since 1989, the federal government has provided funding for Manufacturing Technology Centers across the country. Currently there are nine, and plans call for as many as 25 to 30. Their aim is to help small- to medium-sized businesses use new technology, and their services range from organization development consultation to technical training. Kevin Carr, deputy director of the extension partnership, says:

> These small- to medium-sized companies are a significant resource in our industrial infrastructure. But for the most part, they have not kept up with what they need to remain competitive in the long term. We're here to help them adopt new methods. (C. Dervarics, October 1993.)

Especially for small- and medium-sized businesses, funding training can be difficult. Many are savvy at finding alternate sources for funding, such as local, state, and federal training dollars, or consortia of other local businesses with the same training need.

22.5   The Technical Trainer's Role

Rather than initially focusing on design or delivery strategies, technical trainers need to first create a network of "customers." Success stories indicate that a trainer's customers are the trainees, their managers, their coworkers, the original manufacturers of the technology, and even the purchasers of the product or service. Then ask those customers a set of broad questions; the answers emerging in these customer focus groups will positively shape the training strategy and delivery methods.

In interviews with several technical trainers and managers, one trend emerges consistently: Their role is becoming much more that of a consultant rather than a deliverer of the training. More and more, the people who deliver the training are the subject matter experts; the people who assess the need, design the intervention, and evaluate the outcomes are the full-time trainers. By no means does this trend describe every workplace and training department. But especially in technical training, subject matter experts have powerful knowledge and experience to lend. Who better to teach others than someone who has firsthand experience? The trainer then is responsible for identifying the subject matter experts and providing the training skills that will make them effective presenters. And if the subject matter experts need to be brought in from outside the company, then the trainer might be responsible for managing the contract.

Knowledge of the business is also emerging as a requirement. William Wiggenhorn, president of Motorola University, has said this about the importance of knowing the business of the business:

> In the early 80s, we'd ask for business plans from our divisions but we couldn't get them. By the mid 80s, we could have them if we wanted. Today, however, we're told to read them. (E. Carnevale, 1990.)

He admits that often they were unable to help implement a business plan because they couldn't deliver the trained workforce.

Arguably the most common suggestion is for trainers to stop thinking of formal, classroom-based training as the only solution to a job performance problem. Along with a familiarity of other solutions to performance problems comes a familiarity with the kinds of training technologies that can best solve these problems.

Many will also counsel their colleagues to stop waiting for the phone to ring if they have been somewhat passive. Make the calls and create the meetings that will give you a voice in the business decisions.

Bibliography

Amirault, Thomas A., *How Workers Get Their Training: A 1991 Update*, U.S. Department of Labor, Bureau of Labor Statistics, Bulletin 2407, August 1992.

Bartel, Ann, *Formal Employee Training Programs*, National Bureau of Economic Research, Inc., Working Paper Series, No. 3026, July 1989.

Bartel, Ann, *Productivity Gains from the Implementation of Employee Training Programs*, National Bureau of Economic Research, Inc., Working Paper Series, No. 3893, November 1991.

Carnevale, Anthony P., "Learning: The Critical Technology," *Training & Development*, February 1992.

Carnevale, Anthony P., and Eric R. Schultz, "Technical Training in America: How Much and Who Gets It?," *Training & Development*, November 1988, pp. 18–32.

Carnevale, Ellen S., "Eyeing the Future, Intensifying Training," *Technical & Skills Training*, July 1992, pp. 24–27.

Carnevale, Ellen S., "Motorola Sets the Benchmark for Training," *Technical & Skills Training*, October 1990, pp. 28–34.

Carey, Max, *How Workers Get Their Training*, U.S. Department of Labor, Bureau of Labor Statistics, Bulletin 2226, February 1985.

Congress of the United States, Office of Technology Assessment. *Worker Training: Competing in the New International Economy*, September 1990.

Dervarics, Charles, "Manufacturing Technology Centers and Small Businesses," *Technical & Skills Training*, October 1993, pp. 22–27.

Dervarics, Charles, "Outlook: Jobs, Skills, and Technical Training," *Technical & Skills Training*, February/March 1993, pp. 24–30.

Dervarics, Charles, "T3: Training the Trainer at Saturn," *Technical & Skills Training*, January 1993, pp. 20–24.

Ferman, Louis A., Michele Hoyman, Joel Cutcher-Gershenfeld, and Ernest J. Savoie (eds.), *New Developments in Worker Training: A Legacy for the 1990s*, Industrial Relations Research Association Series, 1990.

Lawler III, Edward, *The Ultimate Advantage*, Jossey-Bass, San Francisco, 1992.

Lynch, Lisa M., *Strategies for Workplace Training: Lessons from Abroad*, Economic Policy Institute, Washington, D.C., 1993.

Pierce, David, interview conducted by author, December 3, 1993.

Reid, Robert L., "Intense Training Prescribed for Hospital Technicians," *Technical & Skills Training*, May/June 1993, pp. 14–17.

Silvestri, George T., "Occupational Employment: Wide Variations in Growth," U.S. Department of Labor, Bureau of Labor Statistics, *Monthly Labor Review*, November 1993, pp. 58–86.

U.S. Department of Commerce, "Higher Wages Accompany Advanced Technology," Statistical Brief, August 1993.

U.S. Department of Labor, *High Performance Work Practices and Firm Performance*, August 1993.

Veum, Jonathan, "Training Among Young Adults: Who, What kind, and For How Long?," *Monthly Labor Review*, August 1993, pp. 27–32.

von Brachel, John, "What Price Apprenticeships," *Across the Board*, January 1994, pp. 32–38.

Wright, Jerry, interview conducted by author, November 30, 1993.

23

Glossary
of Technical Terms

Willam A. Sugar
Indiana University

Thomas M. Schwen
Indiana University

General Education

accelerated learning: This type of learning is when one progresses at a faster rate than average students.

adult education: It refers to a post-public-school program provided by schools, training centers, and other related agencies. It is usually more adaptable than traditional educational programs. See also **andragogy**; **lifelong learning.**

affective domain: The domain of human learning that involves attitudes, interests, values, or motivations.

andragogy: A teaching model that views the teacher as a facilitator of knowledge and secondarily as a content resource for students. This model is advocated for adult education. It was initially used to mean "the art and science of helping adults learn." See also **adult education.**

artificial intelligence: Sophisticated computers that perform mental processes similar to the way humans do.

behavioral psychology: The branch of psychology that advocates the process of influencing behavior through the systematic adjustment of stimulus-response reinforcements.

closed system: A system that is operating with constrained boundaries with limited interaction with the outside environment. See also **open system; systems thinking.**

cognitive domain: The domain of human learning that involves intellectual skills. See also **intellectual skills.**

cognitive psychology: The branch of psychology that is concerned with the study of individuals' perceptual processes, problem-solving abilities, and reasoning abilities. In contrast to behavioral psychology, the focus is more on internal mental processes.

extrinsic motivation: A need based on obtaining a physical reward that prompts one to strive for and successfully accomplish a particular goal.

individualized learning: A self-directed approach to education and training. Students direct their own experiences by choosing their own sequence, level of performance, and pace.

information technology: The acquisition, processing, storage, and dissemination of data contained on computer and telecommunications technology. Information properly presented is often seen as a substitute for training.

instructional technology: Usually, the systematic use of formal analysis techniques to design solutions to teaching problems. The solutions are tested and revised until they prove to be effective.

intellectual skills: These mental processes require the learner to do some unique cognitive activity such as solving a problem or performing an activity with previously unencountered information or examples. See also **cognitive domain; cognitive psychology.**

intrinsic motivation: A psychological need that prompts one to strive for and successfully accomplishing a particular goal.

learning style: An intellectual or perceptual habit pattern. There are three major learning styles: visual, aural, or physical.

lifelong learning: A belief that adults should acquire formal and informal education throughout their lives and that everyone should continually improve oneself. This is a fundamental value in adult education. See also **adult education.**

literacy training: A training program offered by community colleges and vocational and technical institutes. These programs offer classes for adults who do not have high school diplomas or who do not have basic verbal skills.

open system: A system that is operating with flexible boundaries with a great deal of interaction with the outside environment. See also **closed system; systems thinking.**

pedagogy: A traditional teaching model that views the teacher as the "leader" of the instruction and the student as the "follower." Pedagogy means literally "the art and science of teaching children." See also **andragogy**.

personality: Relatively constant traits of individuals that represent their characteristic ways of behaving.

psychomotor domain: The domain of human learning that involves skill-centered or physical activities. A learner executes muscular actions with or without equipment.

systems thinking: A theory that views an organization of interconnected and interdependent interactions. It considers the interrelationships of the interacting systems. Systems can be viewed as either as "open" or "closed." See also **closed systems; open systems**.

technology transfer: The process of disseminating technical innovations from one culture to another.

vocational education: A type of training for an occupation or for entry into an occupation.

Business

apprenticeship: Work relationship between a novice worker and an expert worker. Novice workers observe and perform tasks in increasing complexity until they are able to perform independently.

audio-based training: Self-instructional materials that contain audio materials.

business-education partnerships: An arrangement between businesses and educational institutions that integrates schools and the workplace. Educational institutions are employed to provide short-term or long-term training for businesses' training needs.

competency-based training: This training approach focuses on the learner's capability for a specific job or task. The process of developing this training includes a job analysis, identification of skill requirements and training needs, and assessment protocols.

continuing training program: An instructional program that regularly teaches its workers. This program renews workers' skills that have been learned previously.

continuous process improvement: A Total Quality Management concept that espouses that small gains in quality will lead to accumulated substantial gains over the long run. See also **Total Quality Management**.

cooperative agreements: Arrangement between two or more organizations to commonly work on a particular job or training program.

cooperative education: Educational programs that provide linkages between businesses and schools. At least half of the educational experience occurs on the job.

core competencies: Identified skills that workers must obtain to perform effectively in their jobs. Also defined as the central or essential skills of a business or corporation.

customer focus: A shift of emphasis from the organization to the customer. Planning decisions are based upon what customers need. See also **Total Quality Management.**

downsized organizations: Businesses and corporations that restructured and reduced their personnel in order to improve effectiveness and/or profit.

driving forces: These are the causal elements that enable or facilitate a particular action or relationship within a work environment.

employee empowerment: Workers who are authorized to participate in their organization's decision making. These individuals have the flexibility and support to pursue their own initiatives as long as these serve the vision of their organization.

employee involvement: See **participative management.**

employer-provided training: Instruction that is provided by the employer. It is the most common form of instruction in the corporate and public sector.

external training: An instructional program that is provided by a vendor or educational institution.

firefighting: A term that refers to reactive response to critical training or performance problems.

high-performance teams: These work units are well aligned to their organization's mission, strategies, objectives, and culture. These units are often cross-functional. Team members, team relationships, team activities, and team culture are important issues to manage in order to achieve success.

Information Mapping: This is the name of a corporate vendor and product. It is also used in a generic sense to describe a process that provides specific guidelines for authoring text that informs, guides, or teaches.

internal training: Training programs that are exclusively for an organization's employees. This is also known as in-house training.

ISO 9000 certification: The International Organization for Standardization's (ISO) 9000 certification, started in Europe and spreading worldwide, establishes guidelines that develop a quality-conscious approach for manufacturers and service providers. To obtain this certification, a company must document related procedures.

mission: This statement should define the organization's fundamental purpose and how it hopes to accomplish it in terms of meeting client needs.

National Standards for Training and Education: Developed by the International Brotherhood of Electrical Workers and a federal committee. It defines and defends the skills of its members.

off-the-shelf instruction: This usually refers to a previously prepared training program that meets a current need.

on-the-job training (OJT): There are two kinds of on-the-job training: unstructured and structured. Unstructured OJT is when a novice employee learns in an informal manner from a more experienced employee. Structured OJT is where the specific skills, methods, and assessment tools are prepared in advance.

participative management: A management approach that allows employee input and employee decision making.

partnering: This is when separate organizations or work teams, with different interests, work together for specific purposes.

performance-based: This focuses on the implementation and evaluation performed by the employee. The instructional focus is on product, accomplishment, or process that the employee must complete on the job.

performance problems: Problems or errors that may have multiple causes. These causes can include lack of motivation, poor work environment, supervision, communication, lack of skills, etc. Solutions can involve changes in any of the problem areas.

performance technology: A systematic process of identifying and solving human achievement problems. Performance technology solutions involve both training and nontraining interventions.

restraining forces: These forces are a set of elements that damage and impede a particular action or relationship within a work environment.

SCANS report: A U.S. Department of Labor Secretary's Commission on Achieving Necessary Skills' report in 1991. It identified five broad competencies that employees must accomplish to achieve "workplace knowhow" in an information-based economy.

self-directed learning: An educational philosophy that adults desire to be self-directing. This is where adults take charge of their lives and are responsible for their own achievement.

self-directed work teams: These work teams are small groups of employees who have day-to-day responsibility for managing their tasks. Each member is held accountable for the finished product.

skilled trades: Jobs that require advanced performance in a particular domain and require the exercise of independent judgment. Skilled trades workers usually apprentice for a long period of time.

skilled trades programs: These programs prepare students for a specific job market. Emphasis is placed on advanced performance through demonstration and practice. Trainers in these programs demonstrate the necessary skills and supervise the students during practice.

stakeholders: Individuals and groups that are significantly affected by an organization or team performance.

strategic planning: An arrangement that facilitates workers and key stakeholders to visualize the organization's future. This plan will help the organization in its decision making. See also **mission; vision.**

systematic approach to training: This approach to the training process identifies needs, objectives, and the instructional training program and evaluates program effectiveness.

technical training: The most common type of skill improvement instruction that seeks to increase the technological capabilities of workers.

technical workers: Employees who use or apply scientific or mathematical knowledge in their workplace.

Total Quality Management (TQM): A business creed that espouses that labor and management must continually improve quality, productivity, and the processes associated with the particular business, service, or government agency. Emphasis is on the improvement of the fundamental organizational processes. It is believed that as quality improves, costs go down and productivity increases.

training consortia: Small companies create a collective that provides instruction for its members. This consortia is often managed by major corporate customers, industry, and trade associations, or educational institutions.

train-the-trainer programs: This refers to developing knowledge and presentation skills among employees. This increase in instruction allows an organization to rapidly develop knowledge or skill among all employees.

vision: A clear understanding of an end-state or future for a particular organization. This vision is usually expressed in a written statement.

workplace expertise: This generally refers to advanced skills available in an organization. Often, a special intervention is needed to make the skill available for training.

workplace literacy: Training programs that teach employees basic skills such as reading, math, and English as a second language. These skills are essential to problem-solving and teamwork skills.

Instruction

affective objectives: A specified instructional intention that deals with attitudes, values, and perceptions. See also **affective domain** under "General Education" terms.

analysis phase: The process in the Instructional Systems Development model that examines the needs of students and necessary tasks involved with knowledge or skill to be learned. See also **Instructional Systems Development.**

case studies: Usually written scenarios that allow students to simulate problem solving or analysis of "real" situations. See also **instructional game; simulation.**

change management: The supervision of the diffusion of new goals, policies, and processes in an organization.

competency-based: A type of instruction based upon mastery levels for skills, knowledge, and, sometimes, attitudes.

content analysis: A step in the analysis phase that identifies the essential content for an instructional module.

cost-benefit analysis: An analytical technique that assesses all of the specific costs and benefits involved with a potential instructional intervention.

course evaluation: A process that assesses the effectiveness and efficiency of instructional modules.

criterion-referenced tests: Evaluation instruments that measure performance based upon stated instructional objectives.

decision table: A diagram that illustrates the critical steps involved with a particular task.

delivery systems: Devices or processes that present instructional content. Self-instructional manuals and interactive video systems are types of delivery systems.

design phase: The process in the Instructional Systems Development model that develops and implements the teaching strategies and testing materials. See also **Instructional Systems Development.**

distance technology: A communication tool used when students are in different geographic locations. A variety of media formats are employed including video, computers, and audio.

drill and practice: An instructional method that consists of repeating the instructional content and related exercises over a period of time until mastery is achieved.

entry behaviors: These are specific competencies or skills that one must have mastered before starting a particular instructional module.

evaluation phase: The phase in the Instructional Systems Design model that evaluates the instructional package. There are two kinds of evaluation: formative and summative. See also **formative evaluation;** Instructional Systems Development; **summative evaluation.**

facilitator: An individual who guides learners in an instructional activity.

fault analysis: This analysis technique is used to find where there are potential causes of failures or performance problems that might exist in a job or task. See also **analysis phase; performance problems** (under "Business" terms).

formative evaluation: The collection of data and information that can be used to validate and/or improve the effectiveness of the instruction.

front-end analysis: See **needs analysis.**

group instruction: A teaching activity that involves groups of learners.

individualized instruction: Learning activities and materials specifically designed to allow students to proceed at their own pace.

instructional design: See **Instructional Systems Design.**

instructional game: A teaching tool that provides a social framework for creative, authentic experiences with complex processes, interactions, and social and technical mechanisms. The game provides access to these complex phenomena that wouldn't normally be available in formal training settings.

instructional goal: Statement of instructional intent that generally expresses what is expected of learners. See also **instructional objective.**

instructional material: Teaching materials that are used in training activities.

instructional objective: A statement of what learners will be expected to do during training. These statements are stated in terms of observable performance. Also known as **performance objective** or behavioral objective.

Instructional Systems Development (ISD): Similar to the systematic approach, this model employs three major phases (analysis, design, and evaluation) to develop instruction. This model is a cyclical and systematic design process.

job aids: Instructional tools that provide assistance for employees during their work.

job analysis: A technique that gives critical information about the work roles within an organization. This analysis aids organizational planning and instructional design.

learner controlled: An instructional method that allows learners to direct the pace and sequence of their activities.

modeling: An instructional method that requires the teacher to perform or demonstrate a job function while students observe this performance or demonstration.

needs analysis: The formal process of identifying discrepancies between current outcomes and desired outcomes. An identification of a gap between what is and what should be especially in respect to employee performance.

peer tutoring: A method whereby learners teach each other, usually with highly structured instructional materials.

performance objective: A detailed description of what learners will be able to do when they complete a unit of instruction. It is sometimes referred to as a behavioral objective. There are three components: the identified behavior, specific conditions, and the evaluative criteria. See also **instructional objective**.

posttest: This instrument should evaluate all of the stated objectives of an instructional program.

prerequisite skills: See **entry behaviors**.

pretest: This instrument has items that measure entry behaviors and knowledge that will be taught in the training program.

programmed instruction: An instructional method composed of frames of instruction. Each frame contains a prompt, a question to be completed, and reinforcement for appropriate responses.

project leader: The individual who facilitates and manages a particular project.

rapid prototyping: An iterative design process that continually evaluates the effectiveness of the particular design. Instructional designers redesign their instruction to address deficiencies that were revealed in the particular evaluation.

role playing: An instructional activity that enables learners to assume a different identity. This activity facilitates students to understand other perspectives than their own. This is usually done in simulations.

satellite-based training: A training program that instructs its learners via satellite technology.

self-instruction module: Instructional programs that enable learners to learn at their own pace. This term is similar to **programmed instruction**.

self-paced instruction: See **individualized instruction**.

simulation: An instructional strategy that teaches its users using an abstraction of some real-life situation. See also **case studies**; **instructional game**.

subject-matter expert: A person knowledgeable about a particular content area or domain.

summative evaluation: This process verifies the overall effectiveness of the instructional design.

systematic approach: A procedure used by instructional designers to create instruction. This approach is divided into three major phases: analysis, design, and evaluation. Each phase is dependent on the other; that is, a prior phase will provide input to the next phase. See also **Instructional Systems Development.**

target audience: The learners that will be served by an instructional design.

task analysis: A step in the analysis phase that focuses on identifying and sequencing the critical steps in a desired performance.

terminal objective: This describes exactly what the student will be able to do when he or she completes a training program.

training: An organized effort to increase the capabilities of individuals.

value-added: A concept that assesses the worth of an instructional or performance intervention in terms of the basic results of an organization. For example, the value that a training program adds to profitability.

video-based training: A training program that instructs its learners with a television format.

Media

analog video: A video format that uses analog signals (electronic signals that resemble the objects they portray) rather than digital. Analog videos are used on VCRs whereas digital videos are used on videodisc players.

authoring system: A system that enables its users to design computer-based instructional programs. Hypercard and Authorware are two examples of authoring systems.

compact disc: A storage format (4.72 in) in which a laser records digital information.

compact disc interactive (CDI): This compact disc format contains graphics, audio, and textual information that its users can manipulate. This is similar to digital video interactive (DVI).

compact disc read-only memory (CD-ROM): A compact disc that contains permanent digital information.

computer-aided design: A computer program that enables its users to design with a variety of computer-enhanced tools. One popular example involves three-dimensional engineering representations of manufacturing parts.

computer-based education: Educational systems or training programs that incorporate computer technology.

computer-managed instruction: A computer system that is used to manage students' performance. The program of studies in this system recommends additional assignments based on student performance.

computer teleconference: An instructional or communications tool using computers to hold meetings between people at different geographic distances.

digital video interactive (DVI): This compact disc format contains graphics, audio, textual information, and also moving images that its users can manipulate. The DVI format can include 72 minutes of digitized audio and video. This is similar to **compact disc interactive (CDI)**.

electronic performance support systems (EPSS): See performance support systems.

expert systems: Computer programs that give advice to their users. These programs serve as "intelligent advisors" that guide their users in the particular subject matter.

help system: Computer tool that assists or explains the function, process, or terminology of computer programs.

hypermedia: Similar to **hypertext**, this computer format is a system of interrelated documents that enables its users to access a large amount of information in an effective manner. The difference between **hypermedia** and **hypertext** is that hypermedia documents contain multimedia data.

hypertext: A term coined two decades ago by Ted Nelson, hypertext is a system of interrelated documents. A hypertext document allows the users to mvoe nonsequentially throughout the document. The system is simple, but very powerful. Two tools, links and nodes, allow any term (node) to be connected (link) to any other term or even to the same term.

interactive media: Instructional tools that enable their users to view various media formats, including text, audio, graphics, and moving images. Interactive media users can alter the sequence of a program.

interactive videodisc: This instructional tool combines both video and computer-assisted instruction. Interactive videodisc users can view instructional content via the videodisc and execute interactive commands via the computer-assisted program.

multimedia: The use of various media formats used either sequentially or simultaneously.

optical disc: See **compact disc**.

performance support systems: An integrated electronic environment that is structured to provide just-in-time information, tools, and advice. These systems are designed to augment job-related tasks throughout the entire workday.

video teleconference: An instructional or communications tool using video technology to hold meetings between people at different geographic distances.

virtual reality: A medium that enables its participant to view a created or "virtual" world. With VR technological tools, participants can observe and interact with an environment that is entirely created by computer-generated representations.

Index

About the Editor in Chief

Leslie Kelly is president of Kelly & Associates, Ltd., a 17-year-old human resource development firm specializing in technical training and small business personnel work. For the past 25 years, Kelly has worked with scientists, engineers, and technicians in a variety of business and industry settings. Coeditor of the *ASTD Sales Training Handbook*, Kelly is also the author of numerous technical training resource books. She resides in Indianapolis, Indiana.

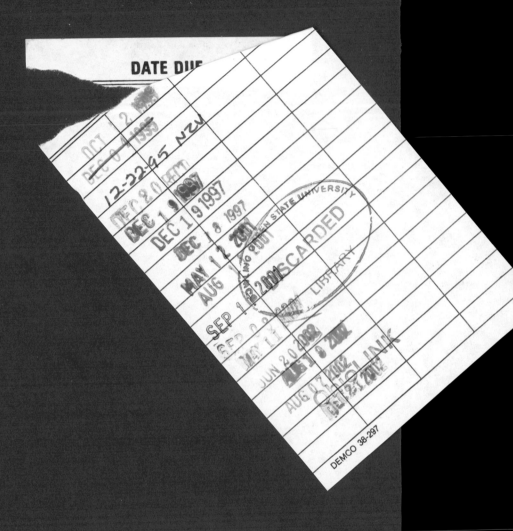